A HISTORY OF IRELAND
IN THE
EIGHTEENTH CENTURY

*Classics of British Historical Literature*

JOHN CLIVE, EDITOR

W. E. H. Lecky

—

# A History of Ireland
# in the Eighteenth Century

ABRIDGED AND WITH AN INTRODUCTION BY

L. P. CURTIS, JR.

The University of Chicago Press

CHICAGO AND LONDON

ISBN: 0–226–46994–8 (clothbound); 0–226–46995–6 (paperbound)
Library of Congress Catalog Card Number: 78–184286
The University of Chicago Press, Chicago 60637
The University of Chicago Press, Ltd., London
© 1972 by the University of Chicago
Published 1972
Printed in the United States of America

# Contents

# Series Editor's Preface

This series of reprints has one major purpose: to put into the hands of students and other interested readers outstanding—and sometimes neglected—works dealing with British history which have either gone out of print or are obtainable only at a forbiddingly high price.

The phrase Classics of British Historical Literature requires some explanation, in view of the fact that the two companion series published by the University of Chicago Press are entitled Classic European Historians and Classic American Historians. Why, then, introduce the word *literature* into the title of this series?

One reason is obvious. History, if it is to live beyond its own generation, must be memorably written. The greatest British historians—Clarendon, Gibbon, Hume, Carlyle, Macaulay—survive today, not merely because they contributed to the cumulative historical knowledge about their subjects, but because they were masters of style and literary artists as well. And even historians of the second rank, if they deserve to survive, are able to do so only because they can still be read with pleasure. To emphasize this truth at the present time, when much eminently solid and worthy academic history suffers from being almost totally unreadable seems worth doing.

The other reason for including the word *literature* in the title of the series has to do with its scope. To read history is to learn about the past. But if, in trying to learn about the British past, one were to restrict oneself to the reading of formal works of history, one would miss a great deal. Often a historical novel, a sociological inquiry, or an account of events and institutions couched in semifictional form teaches us just as much about the past as does the "history" that calls itself by that name. And, not infrequently, these "informal" historical works turn out to be less well known than their merit deserves. By calling this series Classics of British Historical Literature it will be possible to include such books without doing violence to the usual nomenclature.

In the preface to his *History of Ireland in the Eighteenth Century*, Lecky defends the fulness of detail with which he has treated his subject by asserting that he has had to deal with a history which has been very imperfectly written, and usually under the influence of the most furious partisanship. It is for this reason that he has had to bring together a much larger amount of original evidence, drawn from opposite camps, than would be required in dealing with a history of which at least the outlines were well established and generally agreed upon.

It is well to keep this statement of Lecky's in mind when reading the *History*. He himself, after all, was a member of the Anglo-Irish Ascendancy and had his own stake in the subject. The entire project, it seems, had had its origin in his taking umbrage at what he felt had been another historian's errors about modern Irish history. And Ireland was very much a part, and a most controversial part, of English party politics at the time Lecky wrote. As Professor Curtis points out in his introduction, it is the resulting tension between personal involvement and the search for historical truth that lends Lecky's history a good deal of its power.

What is so remarkable is that Lecky managed to produce a work which, though it did not entirely please all sides, was rejected by none; and is still very much worth reading today. This was due in part to the fact that Lecky was a master of his craft; but also to the fact that he possessed wide-ranging historical sympathies. Personal involvement and the controversial nature of a subject do not necessarily diminish the value of a historical work, provided it is handled with the intelligence and discrimination of which Lecky was capable. That is something very much worth remembering in our own day.

JOHN CLIVE

# Editor's Introduction

Almost a century ago William Edward Hartpole Lecky (1838–1903) began work on *The History of England in the Eighteenth Century,* from which this abridgment of the Irish chapters therein has been taken. Although only thirty-two years old at the time, Lecky had already won a glittering reputation for two formidable works, written in his later twenties, the *History of the Rise and Influence of the Spirit of Rationalism in Europe* (1865) and the *History of European Morals from Augustus to Charlemagne* (1869). Among Lecky's admirers today there are a few who consider these two studies his finest products. *The History of England* took Lecky nineteen years and eight volumes to complete, and after seeing the final two volumes through the press in 1890, he produced a separate edition of the Irish sections, which appeared in 1892 under the title *A History of Ireland in the Eighteenth Century* (hereafter abbreviated as *Ireland*).

Measured even by Victorian standards of literary productivity, Lecky's achievement was impressive, but he deserves our attention today not so much for the sheer bulk of his writings as for his ability to illuminate great expanses of the past without forcing his documentation into small, specialized molds. He had that rare capacity, found only in the most distinguished historians, of extracting lasting insights from the sources at his disposal, and he also managed to combine intellectual strength with unusual delicacy of feeling. His erudition and intellectual reach, even as a young man, and his philosophic perceptions contributed to the respect he inspired during his lifetime and for years thereafter. His was not only a sensitive but a deeply ambivalent nature, the result being a mind of both romantic and rationalist leanings which tried hard to understand and even empathize with opposing points of view in the past. In his youth he was drawn to the ideals of Young Ireland without ever committing himself to full repeal of the Act of Union; but there was no more staunch opponent of Home Rule once Parnell had taken command of that movement in the late 1870s. Lecky was also an absentee landlord, however modest his estate, and he was proud of being Irish. But he preferred to live in London and spent most of his holidays on the Continent. His politics were those of an independent Whig whose early ardor for Liberalism began to cool rapidly once Gladstone embarked on his mission to pacify Ireland by sacrificing landlords' rights, as Lecky saw it, in the hopes of appeasing the hydra of Irish nationalism.

Lecky's Anglo-Irish origins explain much about his career and beliefs.[1] He was born into the privileged and still secure circle of a Protestant landowning family in a country where Roman Catholics made up the subordinate, if nominally emancipated, majority. His father, John Hartpole Lecky, belonged to the middle rank of the Irish gentry and had enough private income to be able to afford not to pursue his profession of barrister. Like so many of the declining Ascendancy class in Ireland, the Leckys traced their forebears back to Scotland, whence a Lecky (or Leckie) had emigrated to Ireland in the early seventeenth century. One branch of the family held a small estate in county Carlow, and Edward's grandfather had married into a nearby gentry family, the Hartpoles of Shrule Castle, just north of the town of Carlow. As so often happened in Irish landed society, the Hartpole property in the Queen's county came into the Lecky

---

1. For biographical details of Lecky and his work, see George W. Prothero's article in the *Dictionary of National Biography, Supplement, 1901–1911* (London, 1912), 1:435–40; Elisabeth van Dedem Lecky, *A Memoir of the Right Hon. William Edward Hartpole Lecky by His Wife* (London, 1909), hereafter cited as *Memoir;* H. Montgomery Hyde, ed., *A Victorian Historian: Private Letters of W. E. H. Lecky, 1859–1878* (London, 1947); James Johnston Auchmuty, *Lecky: A Biographical and Critical Essay* (Dublin, 1945); and W. A. Phillips, *Lecky* (Dublin, 1939), a lecture celebrating the centenary of Lecky's birth.

family, once the male line had failed. Lecky's mother was Mary Anne Tallents, the daughter of a successful English solicitor in Newark. She married John in 1837, bore him a son the following year, and died after a short illness in 1839. John was a semi-absentee landlord who lived near Swords, county Dublin, enjoying the leisure made possible from certain investments and the modest rental of his estates.[2] In 1841 he married Isabella, daughter of Lieutenant Colonel Eardley Wilmot, a retired army officer of impeccable gentry stock, who could lay claim to Anglo-Irish cousins, the Wilmot-Chetwodes of Woodbrook House, Portarlington. Isabella proved a most solicitous stepmother to Edward, whom she raised along with her own two children. After John's death in 1852, she waited almost three years before marrying again. Her second husband was a peer, Thomas Dalzell, 7th Earl of Carnwath (1797–1867), whose first wife had been the eldest daughter of Henry Grattan, the great Anglo-Irish statesman. Lecky spent some of his childhood at Bushy Park, near Enniskerry in county Wicklow, not far from Tinnehinch, the estate given to Grattan by a grateful Ascendancy. Nothing could illustrate better the intimacy of so much Irish history than this tenuous but psychologically significant link between the future historian and Anglo-Ireland's most eloquent spokesman.

The death of his father in 1852 and subsequent remarriage of his stepmother aggravated the dislocations of Lecky's boyhood. He was left with no place he could call home, and however kindly they might be, his step-parents were no substitute for what he had lost. His early schooling in Ireland was followed by three relatively lonely years at Cheltenham College. A bout of cramming with a tutor then enabled him to gain admission to Trinity College, Dublin, in February 1856. Lecky's four years at Trinity proved to be a turning point in his life. If he led a rather languorous existence as an undergraduate, eschewing the fierce competition for academic prizes, it was Trinity that stirred his imagination and awakened powerful ambitions. Much of the credit for this awakening belonged to the College Historical

2. In the 1870s, the Lecky estate comprised some 721 acres valued at £649, in county Carlow and some 1,236 acres valued at £668 (close to the annual rental), in the Queen's county. See U. H. De Burgh, *The Landowners of Ireland* (Dublin, 1878), p. 264.

Society, the famous debating society founded by Burke. The "Hist" encouraged Lecky in his desire to become a great orator and it ushered him into an almost adult world wherein wit and sophistication counted as much as intelligence and political awareness. The adolescent who confided to a close friend that he had always been considered "the fool of the family," slowly emerged into manhood, resolved to prove that he could excel at something. At meetings of the "Hist," Lecky treated his fellow members to dazzling displays of eloquence. After he had won the society's coveted Gold Medal in 1859, he found it more difficult to resign himself to the fate of a church living in the depths of county Cork.

During his years at Trinity, Lecky absorbed such prevalent orthodoxies as the Christian rationalism of Bishop Butler (1692–1752), the principles of political economy as collated and interpreted by John Stuart Mill, and the anti-Tractarianism of the venerable Archbishop of Dublin, Richard Whately. Devoted to the cause of moderation in matters of church and state, Lecky cultivated a certain detachment about all systems of belief. A natural dialectician, he used to exasperate friends by arguing for or against any particular doctrine with equal skill and conviction. He enjoyed defending the unpopular side in any argument. His reading of Bacon, Hobbes, Locke, and Hume as well as the philosophes reinforced his belief in a reasoned and reasonable religion. But he never attained Gibbon's profound skepticism about Christianity. Trinity also helped Lecky to develop a carapace or facade characterized by a serene, almost lofty manner, behind which lurked a tense and fretful temperament. Already something of an emotional orphan, he became a "loner," a solitary reaper of the past, more at home with books and ideas than with people. Even after marriage, he spent much of his life in an isolation made splendid by occasional forays to the Athenaeum, meetings of The Club (to which Burke, Grattan, and so many other of his heroes had belonged), and conversations with Carlyle. As he grew older, he turned more and more to intellectual labor as an anodyne for the pain of anxiety. But he had to pay a price for this temporary relief in the form of recurrent illness and minor physical disorders.

When Henry T. Buckle (1821–1862) published the first

volume of his famous *History of Civilization in England* in 1857, Lecky was enthralled. This encyclopedic work held out the promise of a new era in the study of human progress. Lecky was fascinated by Buckle's attempt to discover in the record of the past "certain fixed and universal laws" analogous to the laws of nature. Lecky regarded this self-taught positivist almost as the Newton of English historiography, especially when he claimed to have discovered "the uniformity of sequence" and the interaction of mental and physical phenomena in the advance of mankind from one stage to another. Lecky agreed with Buckle that only in western Europe had the mental faculties of man "succeeded in taming the energies of nature" and prepared the way for untold progress in the intellectual sphere.[3] Both the romantic and rationalist strains in Lecky thrilled to the scientistic audacity and the Comtian certitude of the *Civilization*.

Lecky's infatuation with Buckle's work was intense but brief. Two years later he was reading *On the Origin of Species* with growing awe. Darwin, he realized, was a superb historian, a master of natural history, who made Buckle seem pretentious and even superficial by comparison. After 1859, Lecky could no longer dismiss the role of innate ideas and the mechanisms of heredity in the history of mankind, as Buckle tended to do. It was Darwin who reminded Lecky that man had a will and mental faculties that placed him far above the deadly competition for survival among lower forms of life. Lecky, however, never quite shook off the effects of his first exposure to Buckle. If some of his second thoughts about the *Civilization* approached the uncharitable,[4] he derived from that work a new awareness of the primacy of reason and intellectual forces in the history of man, and he also owed Buckle thanks for having opened his eyes to the possibilities of writing history as a way of life for a gentleman of leisure. Like Buckle, he not only had a comfortable private income, but was attracted to the big themes, the long sweeps, of history. Not for

3. H. T. Buckle, *History of Civilization in England* (New York, 1866), 1:5, 23.

4. Lecky's mature reflections on Buckle may be found in his "Formative Influences," *The Forum* 9 (1890): 387–89. Readers interested in Buckle should consult a companion volume in this series: H. J. Hanham's abridgment of Buckle's *History* under the title, *On Scotland and the Scotch Intellect* (Chicago: University of Chicago Press, 1970).

him the narrow, specialized monograph; he preferred to study nations and civilizations over long periods of time. Lecky lacked Buckle's facility for acquiring foreign languages like so many souvenirs, but he had the advantage of a university education and a loving wife. He also lived some twenty-five years longer than Buckle and was able to complete his *magnum opus.*

After taking his B.A. in 1859, Lecky spent a fourth year in College reading divinity, still intending, presumably, to take up the family living in Cork.[5] In his early twenties he betrayed most of the symptoms of a mid-Victorian romantic with liberal leanings. He basked in the poetry of Shelley and the young Swinburne and wrote a good deal of ardent, if mostly trite, verse himself. He worshipped the Reverend John Kells Ingram, the Junior Fellow at Trinity who had written the famous poem in the heyday of Young Ireland, "Who Fears to Speak of Ninety-eight?" He idealized the Risorgimento, loved solitude, and wandered along mountain trails in Ireland and Switzerland with a heavily annotated copy of Burke's' *Reflections* in his pocket. His enthusiasms also embraced Irish nationality, and he thrilled to the speeches of Grattan and his circle in defense of Irish liberties. Carefully guarded by ambiguities, Lecky's nationalism rested on two assumptions: any nationalist movement worthy of the name had to be led by Ireland's hereditary landowners and had to maintain unswerving loyalty to the (English) Crown. "Nationality with loyalty" represented the essence of his position and revealed his determination to enjoy the best of both worlds. Convinced that Irish Catholics were incapable of governing themselves, he "dreamed a dream of glory"[6] in which he played the role of a new Grattan leading a united as well as deferential Ireland into some vague form of federal self-government. The result of more prosaic labors was an anonymous essay published in 1860, entitled *The Religious Tendencies of the Age,* wherein Lecky insisted on the duty of the historian to "enter into the feelings" of his protagonists. For a young man of twenty-two this

5. Hyde, pp. 32–34.
6. This phrase is taken from one of the poems in Lecky's slender volume, *Friendship and Other Poems* (Dublin, 1859), which he published under the pen name "Hibernicus."

essay was a virtuoso piece, but it attracted far less notice than the author had hoped.

Once his dreams began to center upon a political career, Lecky decided to place his ambition in an appropriate historical setting. So he began work on a book containing the biographical profiles of four eminent men, three of whom were Anglo-Irish: Jonathan Swift, Henry Flood, Henry Grattan, and Daniel O'Connell. *The Leaders of Public Opinion in Ireland* was published anonymously in Dublin in 1861. In this work Lecky traced the steady growth of national self-consciousness or the ideal of "nationality with loyalty" as this was nurtured by these four men. Grattan was the central figure, epitomizing for Lecky all that was sublime and beautiful in the Ascendancy. In a final chapter called "Clerical Influences," Lecky dropped his restraint and warned that Catholic sectarianism threatened to undo all the good work of those leaders who had secularized Irish politics. The *Leaders* ended on a wistful note: Grattan's mantle could not go unclaimed forever; someone was bound to inherit and lead the Irish people out of the wilderness. If Lecky hoped for an immediate summons from Westminster, he was quickly disappointed. The book went almost unnoticed, selling some thirty-four copies in all. A prominent Repealer, W. J. O'Neill Daunt, wrote a kindly review in the *Cork Examiner* (7 February 1862) in which he speculated that the author's refreshing nationalist zeal emanated from Trinity.[7]

With his dream of Grattanite glory dashed, Lecky turned to travel for consolation. For the next few years he led a solitary but active intellectual life, mixing travel on the Continent with hard reading and reflection. Realizing that politics demanded a degree of "pushiness" which he did not possess, he allowed the life of a scholar-gentleman to close in around him, and he became wholly absorbed in the process of self-education. Like Buckle he knew the educational value of travel, and like many privileged Victorians he found in Italy an aesthetic grail to which he kept returning. His other favorite haunt in Europe at this time was more romantic: a small villa, owned by Lord Carnwath, in the Pyrenees

7. All students of Lecky should be indebted to Donal McCartney's article, "Lecky's *Leaders of Public Opinion in Ireland,*" *Irish Historical Studies* 14 (September 1964): 119–41.

(Bagnères de Bigorre), where he often stayed with his step-parents, and where he wrote most of the *Rationalism* in 1863–64.

The *Rationalism* grew out of an essay he had published in 1863, entitled *The Declining Sense of the Miraculous,* and it laid the foundations for almost all his later work. This inquiry into the dominant opinions and ideas held by western Europeans since the Middle Ages tried to place theological creeds and philosophical systems in a broad historical context. However evasive about ultimate causes, Lecky made it clear that ideas moved men and that "the mental habits of society" were shaped not only by the great philosophers (Bacon, Descartes, Locke, et alii) but by advances in science and technology, warfare, commerce, and industrial activity. Writing as a "historian of opinion" rather than a theologian, he set out to explain "the rise and fall of those doctrines . . . found in the general intellectual condition of the age."[8] The *Rationalism* was no simple-minded tale of steady progress in European societies. Lecky recounted in detail the long struggle between the spirits of rationalism and superstition, in which witchcraft and magic had held the upper hand for many generations. He recorded the slow triumph of reason and moderation over irrationalism and fanaticism. Christianity, he argued, had done most to advance "the moral development of Europe." Both volumes were crammed with examples of heroic and virtuous conduct on the part of men who embodied the best qualities of their age.

The *Rationalism* revealed Lecky as an eclectic and moderately Whiggish historian, anxious to reconcile Christianity and science in a Darwinian world. Exhibiting signs of Cobdenite faith in the ability of free trade to usher in an era of international peace, Lecky wrote as an apologist of Christian capitalism. If the future held out hope for continued moral and intellectual improvement, he betrayed a certain nostalgia for the order and self-confidence of the eighteenth century.

Longmans published the *Rationalism* in 1865, and it won immediate acclaim. In maturity of judgment, range of subject matter, moderation, and erudition the work proved that Lecky was not a mere disciple of Buckle. The success of this book opened

8. *Rationalism* (London, 1904), 1: ix, xi.

many London salons to Lecky, and within a short time he received the honor of election to the Athenaeum Club, to which Buckle himself had belonged. Lecky was not one to rest, least of all on a bed of laurels, and he was soon immersed in an equally ambitious project, which was published as the *Morals* four years later. Choosing an earlier time span, he focused on the ideal types of each successive era from Augustus to Charlemagne, surveying the major changes in "the moral standard and in the moral type." The second volume of the *Morals* ended with an eloquent essay entitled "The Position of Women," which ranks with Mill's *The Subjection of Women* in historical, if not political, significance. Although this chapter is best known for its famous pronouncement on the prostitute—"Herself the supreme type of vice, she is ultimately the most efficient guardian of virtue"—it is well worth reading for his exploration of the relations between the sexes before and after the advent of Christian asceticism.[9] No believer in uninterrupted moral progress, he pointed out the peaks and troughs of women's status, revealing his own conviction that women were intellectually inferior but morally superior to men. It pained him to admit that the inequality of the sexes was fully as great in his own day as it had been in Roman times, even though moral standards had much improved. Almost as troubled as Mill by the subordination of women, Lecky prescribed no drastic reforms and was less than enthusiastic about "votes for women." No feminist could have written: "It is the part of a woman to lean, it is the part of a man to stand." Like a number of his fellow Anglicans, he believed that Roman Catholicism was essentially a feminine religion, tending to soften the character and to foster superstition, whereas Protestantism was a masculine creed, capable of making men hard or even fanatic.[10] This was a mixed blessing from Lecky, who believed in strong character as passionately as he deplored fanaticism.

The *Morals* became Lecky's favorite book over the years in spite of the controversy it touched off in the reviews, as Utilitarians attacked its premises. It gave Lecky a chance to observe men and women in and out of love, and he dwelled with Gib-

9. *Morals* (3d ed.; New York, 1895); see chap. 5, "The Position of Women," 2: 275–372.
10. Ibid., pp. 354, 358, 363, 368–69.

bonian relish on the "crimes, follies, and misfortunes" of Europeans. In most quarters the *Morals* was accepted as confirmation of Lecky's ability to handle difficult themes in a perceptive manner and with impartiality. He always regarded the *Rationalism* and the *Morals* as intimately connected, both being concerned with "certain theological opinions": their growth in the *Morals,* their decay in the *Rationalism.*

During the 1860s Lecky paid few visits to Ireland, being fully engaged in intellectual labors and travel on the Continent and in London. In 1865, however, he visited his small estate in county Carlow for the first time, and in an amusing letter to his cousin, Knightley Wilmot-Chetwode, he recalled some of the uncomfortable sensations he experienced as an absentee landlord inspecting his property. Barely able to distinguish between a potato and a turnip, he found conversation with the tenants rather awkward.[11] The gap between landlord and tenant in this and in many other cases was to widen much farther in the next few decades. Lecky's absenteeism, his long residence in London, never lowered the temperature of his feelings about Ireland. He was constantly drawn to the country of his birth, whose past and present inspired some of his finest as well as his most polemical writing. In 1870 he wrote to his fiancée from Killarney: "I wish you knew Ireland. I have so many enthusiasms and associations connected with it, and its history and its politics have so deeply coloured all my ways of thinking."[12] This coloration continued to the end of his life.

11. Hyde, p. 63.
12. *Memoir,* pp. 75–76. Lecky's Irish roots and Anglo-Irish "ethnicity" have not been fully recognized or appreciated. During the 1870s he made it clear that he considered himself "Irish," when that term still had an ecumenical aura. When an Irish writer, Mary Francis Cusack, the "Nun of Kenmare" (who herself had Anglo-Irish roots), referred to him in print as English, Lecky wrote to correct her error. She replied soothingly: "I assure you I would have been only too thankful to claim you as Irish had I known the fact." M. F. Cusack to Lecky, 4 January 1873, Lecky MSS, no. 83, Trinity College Library, Dublin. For permission to publish extracts from Lecky's own letters in the Library of Trinity College, I am most grateful to the Board of Trinity College, Dublin.
  Dr. R. B. McDowell helps to confuse the issue by labeling Lecky (along with Froude, of all people) "British" in *Alice Stopford Green: A Passionate Historian* (Dublin, 1967), p. 83. In his *Edmund Burke and Ireland* (Cambridge, Mass., 1960), p. 240, Professor T. H. D. Mahoney commits the classic mistake of calling Lecky "English." McCartney touches on this sensitive point in his article in *Irish Historical Studies* already cited, p. 127, n. 41.

In 1870–71 Lecky turned briefly from intellectual to matrimonial pursuits. He found his wife in neither the Anglo-Irish Pale nor among the English gentry but in the court of the queen of Holland. Elisabeth van Dedem, the daughter of a Dutch aristocrat, met Lecky while serving as lady-in-waiting to Queen Sophia, who was spending a holiday in London. After visiting the Van Dedems in Holland, Lecky declared his intentions, and with the queen's blessing the couple were married at the Dutch court in June 1871. After a long honeymoon on the Continent, the Leckys returned to London, where they established themselves at 38 Onslow Gardens.[13] They soon entered into a busy social and intellectual life, counting among their friends Leslie Stephen, Browning, Tennyson, Kinglake, Tyndall, Huxley, and Spencer. The Leckys spent most of their holidays in Holland, although Lecky had to go to Ireland from time to time in search of documents. Elisabeth's aristocratic bearing, cosmopolitan outlook, and natural intelligence complemented the reserve and introspection of her husband, and their marriage richly deserved to be called happy.

Scrupulously observing the mid-Victorian precept that work conquers all, Lecky spent much of his honeymoon polishing and proofreading the revised edition of the *Leaders*. This obsession about work was more than a labor of love or a substitute for prayer. Like so many Victorian intellectuals, Lecky relied on advances and royalties to keep genteel poverty from the door. A chronic worrier about money, he knew that the income of his Irish estate would never suffice to maintain his wife in the manner to which she was accustomed. For such reasons his London publisher, Longmans, assumed a vital role in his life. It was Longmans who suggested a new edition of the *Leaders* that would bear the now illustrious name of the author; and Lecky devoted almost a year to the revisions. The second edition appeared in December 1871, when once again the reception fell far short of Lecky's expectations. Like Mill's *Principles of Political Economy*, the *Leaders* reflected the major shifts in Lecky's political commitments during his lifetime. It became an ideological fever chart recording the rise and fall of his enthusiasm for Irish nationalism in the light of changing conditions in Ireland. The first version

13. *Memoir,* pp. 77–82.

had been written in the flush of youthful ardor over the ideals of young Ireland and the Italian Risorgimento. His prime heroes had been the Patriots of Grattanite persuasion, who had combined "nationality with loyalty" to the Crown. But Lecky's nationalism was really a mid-Victorian variation on the aristocratic patriotism of the Volunteers. For Lecky nationality (a term he often preferred to "nationalism") meant the ideals of the Irish constitution of 1782, itself the product of moderate, well-bred Anglo-Irish landowners whose culture Lecky shared. Even in its final edition of 1903, the *Leaders* remained an amalgam of romantic reaction, Liberal Unionism, and patrician patriotism, a muted call to arms addressed to the declining remnants of the old Ascendancy still resident in Ireland.

Lecky revised the *Leaders* in 1870–71 in the aftermath of the abortive Fenian rising of the later 1860s. Gladstone's disestablishment of the Church of Ireland in 1869 and the Irish Land Act of 1870 had not yet undermined his faith in the Liberal party, but he abhorred concessions to physical force or the threat thereof, and like many landowners he suspected Gladstone of having appeased Fenianism with these measures. If his youthful devotion to Irish nationality continued to suffuse the second edition, the rays of light were definitely fainter. He made his intentions clear in the introduction:

> To call into active political life the upper class of Irishmen and to enlarge the sphere of their political power, to give, in a word, to Ireland the greatest amount of self-government that is compatible with the unity and security of the Empire, should be the aim of every statesman.[14]

In the 1871 edition, Lecky refrained from a blanket endorsement of Irish independence. Avoiding specific formulas, he hinted at a political solution along the lines of federal devolution or a transfer of limited powers in domestic affairs to some Irish representative body. He dropped the chapter "Clerical Influences," and he strengthened the passages criticizing Pitt for promoting the Act of Union. The connection in his mind between nationalism and a governing class made Lecky all the more skeptical in the 1870s of Ireland's fitness for self-government, and both his letters and the

14. Quoted, ibid., p. 76.

*Leaders* reflected a mounting concern about the fate of his countrymen in a Fenian climate.[15]

Although the evidence is fragmentary, Lecky seems to have embarked on his *History of England* after deciding not to carry the *Morals* forward to the age of Luther, as he was urged to do. The research and writing of that work, added to the grueling pace he had maintained during the 1860s, had strained his sensitive temperament, and he found a welcome respite in dinner parties and salons. He continued to cast about for a subject less demanding than the *Morals* but still worthy of his mettle. By 1870, he had begun work on a history of England, but he put this aside in order to revise the *Leaders*. He did not return to the "analytic" history of eighteenth-century England and Ireland until he and his wife had settled in London in the autumn of 1872. Lecky then devoted all his energies to the new project. Longmans published the first two volumes in 1878, and these received accolades from reviewers. Two more volumes followed in 1882, taking the story up to 1782. Volumes five and six, dealing with the origins of the French Revolution and the outbreak of war with France in 1793, appeared in 1887. The last two volumes were published in October 1890 and were entirely devoted to Irish politics, the rebellion of 1798, and the passing of the Act of Union.

The *England* was a far cry from Philip Stanhope's Tory history of England from 1701 to 1783, which broke the long reign of Whig interpretations.[16] Lecky paid a generous tribute to Stanhope in his preface but made it clear that he did not intend to pursue a purely narrative line up to 1800. He proposed, instead, to deal with "the permanent forces of the nation," a telling phrase which he defined as follows:

> The growth or decline of the monarchy, the aristocracy, and the democracy, of the Church and of Dissent, of the agricultural, the manufacturing, and the commercial interests; the increasing power of Parliament and of the press; the history of political ideas, of art, of manners, and of belief; the changes that have

15. See ibid., pp. 138–41, and McCartney, pp. 125–27. A thoughtful discussion of Lecky's ambivalent feelings about Irish nationality appears in Helen Mulvey, "The Historian Lecky: Opponent of Irish Home Rule," *Victorian Studies* 1 (June 1958): 337–51.

16. Philip, 5th Earl Stanhope (1805–75) published his *History of England* in seven volumes between 1836 and 1854.

taken place in the social and economical condition of the people; the influences that have modified national character; the relations of the mother country to its dependencies.[17]

All of these features of national life made their appearance in the *England* and established Lecky as the leading historian of modern English and Irish society.

The *England* was by no means confined to England. The volumes took in Europe, the American colonies, India, Scotland, and Ireland, whenever Lecky thought that such excursions would help toward an understanding of "the more enduring features of national life." Ranging far beyond the boundaries of political history, Lecky tried to shed light on "the manners and morals, industrial developments, prevailing opinions, theories, and tendencies" of the English people. In chapters 4 and 23 he echoed Macaulay's famous chapter 3 of *The History of England* by discussing the condition, manners, dress, amusements, occupations, and crimes of all orders in society and added some suggestive thoughts on the political influence of manufactures. Parliamentary politics and cabinet policy may have occupied the limelight, but no orthodox political historian would have looked so deeply into the origins of the French Revolution as Lecky did in chapter 20.[18] The whole work was marked by his concern for the health of the body politic, especially in times when revolution threatened. Lecky revealed himself in the course of this work as an independent Palmerstonian Whig with liberal leanings in matters of faith and morals. Venerating the eighteenth-century constitution, he believed, nevertheless, that the Reform Act of 1832 was a triumph of Whig "firmness and patriotism." Like many later Victorians he regarded the years 1832–67 as "the golden period" of the constitution, when the innate moderation of the English middle classes preserved the balance of social and political forces and kept the peace in domestic affairs. If there was any inherent genius in the English people, Lecky found it in their "reverence for habit, precedent, and tradition; the dislike to pushing principles to their extreme logical consequences, and the[ir] essential moderation."[19] Such were the qualities displayed by the English gov-

17. *England* (London, 1878), 1: i.
18. Ibid. (New York, 1887), 5: 300–342.
19. Ibid., pp. 226–27.

erning class in 1688 and again in 1832, and for Lecky these were the real explanation of the long reign of freedom in England. One of Lecky's devoted admirers, the late J. J. Auchmuty of Trinity College, Dublin, has made a sharp distinction between the moral and the political historian in Lecky.[20] Such a dichotomy, however, is not only more apparent than real but ignores Lecky's deliberate effort to blend morals and politics in the *England*. If he changed his formal subject matter after 1870, Lecky brought the same philosophic assumptions and intellectual concerns to bear on English and Irish history in the eighteenth century. He was constantly on the lookout for clues about the mainsprings of national life, and he continued to search for the connections among and between politics, legislation, institutions, commerce, foreign policy, religion, and morality.

Lecky's efforts to understand all sides of the great issues of the past and his refusal to concede the steady moral and material progress of the English people gave his work a quality not often encountered in Victorian historiography. He became *the* documentary historian of modern Britain, treating his readers to long quotations from the original sources which he tracked down with the assiduity of Sherlock Holmes. The *England* was so steeped in primary sources that the footnotes became an education in themselves. Lecky knew that the *England* was unwieldy and lacked the balance and proportion of Macaulay's masterpiece. But in a Darwinian age he allowed his volumes to evolve and to adapt themselves as much to the documentary environment as to the author's changing moods. The absence of a master plan or design may be seen in the Irish sections, which grew and grew in both length and significance, and also in the way he put together paragraphs, often strewing ideas and events about in no apparent order. Similarly, his chapters defied titles (as distinct from subheadings) because they were packed with many disparate topics and long digressions on minor as well as major points.[21] A keen student of portraiture and physiognomy, Lecky enhanced his work with a series of finely drawn verbal sketches of such eminent men

20. Auchmuty, pp. 49–84.
21. The chapters in the *Ireland* average slightly less than two hundred pages each, with chapter 2 running to a record 335 pages. The Irish sections of the original edition of the *England* took up approximately 43 percent of the whole: 1,951 out of 4,555 pages.

as Walpole, Chatham, Fox, Pitt, Burke, Wesley, Wilkes, Shelburne, and, of course, Grattan, whose features had already loomed large in the *Leaders*. Whenever possible, Lecky studied the portraits of statesmen and leaders in the National Gallery or elsewhere before writing about them. The importance he attached to character may be judged from the pains he took to delineate both the physical and the mental traits of his protagonists.

To all appearances Lecky's *Ireland* was the natural child or foundling of the *England*. But one of his best friends made the plausible suggestion that the *Ireland* was really the clandestine parent of the *England*. Lecky, so this version goes, had set his mind on writing an objective history of Ireland in order to redeem the maligned character of the Irish people, but he sensed that the only way to induce Englishmen to read Irish history was to cover the pill with a heavy coating of English historical matter. Lecky, presumably, wished not only to fulfill his dream of becoming a leader of Irish public opinion but also to expose, if not to ridicule, the error of Froude's ways in *The English in Ireland*. Whatever Lecky's underlying motives in starting this work, there can be no doubt that he appreciated the countless interconnections of English and Irish history, and the surgical operation involved in separating the two in the 1892 "cabinet edition" marred this feature of the original work.

As an exercise in historical demolition, Lecky's onslaught on Froude's interpretation of Irish history may still be read with profit. Too scrupulous and sensitive to relish the art of hostile reviewing, Lecky, nevertheless, felt a solemn responsibility to rescue Irish character from Froude's aspersions and to seek out the true facts of Irish history.[22] In the course of two long reviews

22. From a personal point of view Lecky did not enjoy the task of refuting Froude. In the Lecky MSS at Trinity College there is a draft letter, dated November 1873 (no. 97), in which he wrote to Froude: "You once told me that I would never speak to you again after reading your Irish book. I am afraid that you will never speak to me again after reading my review of it in Macmillan. I am very sorry for this as I hate quarrels & I may say with truth there are very few people with whom it would give me more pain to quarrel than with you. . . . I can assure you it has been no pleasure for me for I have very little of the Donnybrook spirit in my temperament & much less, if you will allow me to say so, than you appear to have had when you wrote your book."

See also the *Memoir,* pp. 95–97, and H. M. Hyde, pp. 20, 85, 88. Arthur Booth speculated about Lecky's motives in embarking on the *England* in "Early Recollections of Mr. Lecky," *National Review* 43 (March 1904): 119.

in *Macmillan's Magazine,* Lecky began the process of refuting his friend Froude which eventually developed into the Irish chapters of the *England.* Had Froude not been so obsessed by his conviction that the Protestant Reformation represented the triumph of reason and light over superstition and barbarism, had he shown more scruples about the use of evidence, and had he not considered the Irish people born to be ruled, Lecky might not have gone into the attack. But then Froude would not have been Froude. Already in his *History of England* Froude had described the Irish in Elizabethan times as a "savage population,"[23] and his study of Irish history seemed to bear out the axiom of his mentor, Carlyle, that any people who allowed themselves to be conquered deserved their fate. Froude's stereotype of the unstable Irish Celt made his history read like a Tory brief on how to solve the Irish question, and his conclusion in *The English in Ireland* that Irishmen and "Asiatics" required equally firm, authoritative government left little to the imagination.[24]

Lecky's sustained attack on *The English in Ireland* in *Macmillan's Magazine* dealt in turn with Froude's "repugnance to modern liberal tendencies," his lack of "the most ordinary humanity," his "over-coloured history," his "partiality, intolerance, intemperance" and "offensiveness of language."' The final charge in the indictment was that Froude had managed "to envenom old wounds and rekindle the embers of old hatreds."[25] In the Irish chapters of the *England* Lecky set out to puncture those prejudices about the Irish which Froude shared with so many of his countrymen. Given his lifelong attraction to Ireland and its problems, and given the revival of the Irish question in English politics in the later 1870s and 1880s, one may reasonably suspect that Lecky also used Froude as an excuse to write the history of the Ascendancy in the age of Grattan which he had long wished to do. For Lecky those Irish chapters were a labor of love and anguish, as he reconstructed the ordeal of Ireland's past and tried to explain why England had failed to solve the Irish question even up to his own day.

23. J. A. Froude, *History of England* (New York, 1881), 10: 486, 563.

24. J. A. Froude, *The English in Ireland in the Eighteenth Century* (London, 1881), 3: 558.

25. See "Mr. Froude's English in Ireland," *Macmillan's Magazine* 27 (January 1873): 246–64, and 30 (June 1874): 166–84.

According to Lecky, Ireland in the eighteenth century was a nation in the throes of a colonial struggle to attain self-government within an imperial framework. The nation he had in mind, however, was neither Catholic nor Celtic but a Protestant landowning elite whose forebears had come from England and Scotland in order to improve their fortunes at the expense of the "natives." The Ascendancy was worthy of study both for its achievements and for the insights it afforded into the "permanent forces" of the Irish nation. Although he sympathized with the sufferings of the Irish people, Lecky's own identification with the Irish aristocracy prevented him from blaming the Ascendancy, as distinct from selfish individuals, for that suffering. The bulk of those Irish sections that later became the *Ireland* dealt with the eventful period from the 1760s to 1800, when the Anglo-Irish won and then lost their legislative independence.

Despite its reputation for completeness, the *Ireland* had its fissures and its flaws. It was undernourished in economic analysis, and little was said about historical geography and demography. Although more conscientious than Froude about the use of evidence and concern for accuracy, Lecky, too, made some errors. He misconstrued the motives of Irish Anglicans in enforcing the penal laws against Protestant dissenters.[26] The Palatine refugees who settled in county Limerick in the early eighteenth century retained their ethnic identity even in Lecky's own day, despite his assertion to the contrary.[27] The use of such terms as "bribery" and "corruption" in connection with certain politicians for whom Lecky had less sympathy was unwarranted, even if one forgives him for not having anticipated Namier's redefinition of the role of corruption in British politics.[28] These and other shortcomings do not disqualify the *Ireland* as a masterpiece. No other historian

26. A "revisionist" work in this respect is J. C. Beckett, *Protestant Dissent in Ireland, 1687–1780* (London, 1948).

27. See H. Blume, "Some Geographical Aspects of the Palatine Settlement in Ireland," *Irish Geography* 2 (1952): 172–79.

28. See the strictures of Maurice R. O'Connell in his *Irish Politics and Social Conflict in the Age of the American Revolution* (Philadelphia, 1965), pp. 255–56. Dr. O'Connell defends the outgoing viceroy, Lord Buckingham, from Lecky's charge that he had indulged in "the most flagrant and overwhelming bribery." See *Ireland* 2: 260–61.

of Ascendancy Ireland has equaled Lecky in the ability to combine narrative with "analytic" history, and intellectual acumen with dignity of expression.

In the preface to volumes seven and eight of the *England,* published in 1890, Lecky explained why he had devoted so much space to Ireland. Because Irish history had been "very imperfectly written and usually under the influence of the most furious partisanship," he had decided to embark on a dispassionate search for the truth in Ireland's troubled past. The extensive quotations from manuscript sources and speeches, he added, were designed to bring the reader into "direct contact with the original materials of Irish history" so that he might draw his own conclusions independently of the historian. Lecky ended this preface with a paragraph which did not reappear in the 1892 edition of the *Ireland,* the last half of which deserves to be quoted for its timeless quality:

> There is a method of dealing with historical facts which has been happily compared to that of a child with his box of letters, who picks out and arranges those letters, and those only, which will spell the words on which he has previously determined, leaving all others untouched. In Irish history this method has been abundantly practised, and among the many crimes and errors that have been committed by all parties, it is not difficult to select on either side the materials of a very effective party narrative. I have endeavoured to write this history in a different spirit. Perhaps another generation may be more capable than the present one, of judging how far I have succeeded.[29]

Lecky confined his assault on *The English in Ireland* to the first volume of the *Ireland,* chipping away relentlessly in the footnotes at Froude's misinterpretations. In the middle of chapter 2 he

29. *England* (London, 1890), 7: viii. It is as likely as it is ironic that Lecky borrowed this comparison or analogy from Froude, who gave a lecture entitled "The Science of History" on 5 February 1864, in which he declared: "It often seems to me as if History was like a child's box of letters, with which we can spell any word we please. We have only to pick out such letters as we want, arrange them as we like, and say nothing about those which do not suit our purpose." This lecture has been reprinted in a new edition of Froude's *Short Studies on Great Subjects* (Ithaca, N.Y., 1967). See also Waldo H. Dunn, *James Anthony Froude: A Biography* (Oxford, 1963), 2: 593–94.

carried his dispute into the text, accusing Froude of grossly misleading readers about the abduction of Irish heiresses.[30] He
lashed out at Froude for contending that sectarian as well as
monetary motives underlay the forced marriages of Protestant
girls with their ardent Catholic abductors. As the *Ireland* pro-
gressed, Lecky's exasperation with Froude waned; but all five
volumes added up to a convincing exposure of the prejudices
which had inspired so many passages in *The English in Ireland*.

Lecky's *Ireland* may deserve its reputation for being free from
partisanship, but it was not conceived in a sterile study, devoid
of all values and beliefs. It is important to remember that Lecky
wrote most of his Irish chapters during a period of social upheaval
and political polarization in Ireland. Parnell's leadership of a
powerful coalition resolved to abolish both the Union and landlordism, the widespread intimidation and suffering arising out of
the land war (1879–82), political assassination, Gladstone's
conversion to Home Rule, and the renewal of agrarian strife after
1886 all impinged on Lecky's historical imagination; and the
*Ireland* became a repository of his growing dismay over the
condition of Ireland. Lecky's correspondence at this time with
W. J. O'Neill Daunt, the veteran of the Repeal movement and a
small landowner in county Cork, reveals the raw materials of his
political creed and deserves comparison with some of the historical passages he was then writing about the age of Grattan. Daunt
was a Catholic and an O'Connellite who believed ardently in
Home Rule, and he tried hard to convince Lecky that the evils of
landlordism had given rise to the evils of the Land League. The
excesses of the agrarian agitation, he contended, did not represent
the true and noble spirit of Irish nationalism. In his replies to
Daunt, Lecky gave vent to his despair about the Irish question.
"Whatever else Parnell and his satellites have done," he wrote on
14 December 1879,

> they have . . . killed Home Rule by demonstrating in the clearest
> manner that the classes who possess political power in Ireland are
> radically and profoundly unfit for self-government. That a set of
> political adventurers who go about the country openly advocating
> robbery and by implication advocating murder ("keep a firm grip

30. *Ireland* (London, 1892), 1: 372–96. For Lecky's footnote treatment, see
ibid., pp. 46, 95, 99–100, 163, 234, 271, 307, 348, and 433.

on your land" without paying rent, in Ireland, means nothing less) should enjoy an unbounded popularity and command a multitude of Irish votes; that a popular press should extoll them as the true leaders and representatives of the Irish race; that great meetings should be held in which cries for murdering landlords elicit loud cheers and not a word of serious rebuke; that such a movement should have attained its present dimensions in Ireland appears to me a most conclusive proof that the very rudiments of political morality have still to be taught. There is no civilised country in Europe where such things would be possible. Whatever else Government has to do, *the protection of life and property is its first duty.* Respect for contracts, *a high sense of the value of human life,* a stern exclusion from public life of all men who in any degree coquet with or palliate crime, and a hatred of disorder and violence and lawlessness are the qualities that are found in all classes which are capable of self-government.[31]

A week later Lecky replied to another equally impassioned letter from Daunt, admitting that he could not believe in "democratic home rule in Ireland." Provoked no doubt by the revolutionary agrarianism of the Land League, Lecky added that the great danger was "this new disease of communism which when it once passes into the constitution of a nation is apt to prove one of the most inveterate and most debilitating."[32] Lecky's reactions— and they were nothing less than reactionary—to the new forces asserting themselves in Ireland, his fears about the security of property in an era of eroding respect for law and increasing class conflict, reflected the anxieties of any elitist, regardless of time and place, who believes that the social order is fragile and that the defenses of civilization against barbarism are paper-thin.

Lecky thus had a mission in writing this history, as befitted a man who regarded himself as the keeper of Ireland's conscience. The *Ireland* was, in fact, shot through with presentist passages which were written from the heart, and if Lecky was too good a historian to confuse deliberately past and present truths, he lost few opportunities to point the moral of his tale. A good example of this presentism may be found toward the end of chapter 5,

31. This letter is quoted in full in *Memoir,* pp. 138–40. For details of Daunt's career, see *A Life Spent for Ireland* (London, 1896), edited by his daughter.
32. Lecky to Daunt, 22 December 1879, Lecky MSS, no. 183.

where he wrote that the old Irish parliament had no "real bearing on modern schemes for reconstructing the government of Ireland on a revolutionary and Jacobin basis." Grattan's Parliament could not be used, in his view, as a precedent for setting up a "democratic assembly" in Ireland, made up "mainly of Fenians and Land Leaguers, of paid agitators and of penniless adventurers." Like most Unionists Lecky believed that English representative institutions could never be worked effectively by Irish Catholics, least of all those without property, and he shared Grattan's pessimism about the consequences of any transfer of power from the Irish landowning class to 'the people.' He was fond of quoting Grattan's "striking prophecy" that Ireland's revenge for the Act of Union would be to send to Westminster some day " 'a hundred of the greatest scoundrels in the kingdom.' " Convinced that civilized societies could only be run by men of his own class and tastes, he dreaded the day when "designing agitators and demagogues" would succeed in detaching "the ignorant and excitable Catholic population . . . from the influence of property and respectability."[33]

Lecky knew only too well that after seven hundred years of English rule, Ireland was "as disaffected as a newly conquered province." And he went so far in the *Ireland* as to describe Irish political sentiment in the 1880s—the heroic age of Parnell and Davitt—as "perhaps the most degraded and the most demoralised in Europe."[34] But his patrician, landowning instincts prevented him from understanding the deeper causes of the rebellion of 1798, just as he failed to appreciate the causes of the land war in the early 1880s. It was beyond Lecky's considerable powers to admit that Ireland's aristocracy sowed the seeds of its own destruction, especially in a country where, as Tocqueville and Beaumont had perceived, the aristocracy represented neither the religion nor the ethnicity of the majority. Steeped in the values of Grattan and Burke, Lecky found it easy to dismiss Irish rebellion as "usually . . . a very rhetorical thing, in which language far outstrips meaning."[35] His devotion to the ideal of a governing class which had been superimposed upon the Irish populace was

33. *Ireland* 3: 150. See also p. 254 of this edition.
34. *Ireland* 3: 546.
35. Ibid. 4: 81–82.

only reinforced rather than shaken by the land war and the militancy of Parnellism. In the last two volumes of the *Ireland,* Lecky betrayed his growing skepticism about the fitness of Irishmen for self-government; and his presentist asides grew in vehemence as he drew nearer to the passing of the Union and its aftermath. At the end of the *Ireland* he outlined the modern alliance between Irish Jacobinism, Fenianism, and democracy. The widening of the franchise, he argued, had virtually disfranchised the "most peaceful, law-abiding, and industrious classes" in every province except Ulster, while enfranchising "the most diseased" elements. "No greater calamity can befall a nation," he declared, "than to be mainly represented and directed by conspirators, adventurers, or professional agitators."[36]

Determined to make it well-nigh impossible for Home Rulers to use the *Ireland* as they had already used the *Leaders* to justify their cause, Lecky made it clear that no changes should take place in Anglo-Irish relations without the full consent of the resident gentry, most of whom, needless to say, were not only Protestant but opposed to Home Rule with all their dwindling power. Lamenting the exclusion of "honourable, loyal and intelligent men" from public life in Ireland, he concluded the *Ireland* with a solemn warning about "the folly of conferring power where it is certain to be misused, and of weakening . . . those great pillars of social order, on which all true liberty and all real progress ultimately depend."[37] These lines were to serve as the text of Lecky's first and last overtly political testament, *Democracy and Liberty,* published in 1896.

Compared with the English chapters of the *England,* Lecky's Irish segments have had a more mixed reception, with most of the mixture involving political or ideological commitments. The Honorable Emily Lawless, daughter of Lord Cloncurry and a gifted writer herself, credited Lecky with having "broken down a barrier of prejudice so solid and of such long standing that it seemed to be invulnerable."[38] A loyal friend and admirer, she relied heavily on Lecky's work for her own *Story of Ireland.* Another admirer of the *Ireland* was the prolific author and

36. Ibid. 5: 481–82.
37. Ibid., p. 494. See also below, p. 494.
38. Emily Lawless, *The Story of Ireland* (New York, 1888), p. 300.

staunch Home Ruler, Stephen Gwynn, M.P.; and Michael Davitt, the sworn enemy of all that Lecky represented, quoted this "eminent historian" on the evils of landlordism and the democratic influence of Irish M.P.'s at Westminster.[39] Seumas MacManus, in his "rough and ready" *Story of the Irish Race* (1921), took a number of quotations from the *Ireland,* but like the good republican he was, MacManus characterized Lecky as "a Protestant of British blood and ardent British sympathy."[40]

More trenchant criticisms of the *Ireland* followed the Easter Rebellion and the Anglo-Irish treaty of 1921. In several cases the most disparaging comments came from men who had fought the British and had been raised in a culture far different from Lecky's. Daniel Corkery's classic study of eighteenth-century Munster poets and Gaelic culture, *The Hidden Ireland,* appeared in 1924, when the wounds of the struggle for independence were still open. Corkery rebuked Lecky for having ignored the Gaelic or Irish culture of the people, and for failing to recognize "the soul of the Gael" as one of the more "enduring features" of Irish national life. Although prepared to admit that the *Ireland* was a "noble work, packaged with knowledge," he also described it as lifeless, devoid of the heart and soul of Irish Ireland. The real Ireland, according to Corkery and most of his readers, lay outside the Anglo-Irish Pale, wherein Grattan's Parliament had disported itself—"that noisy side-show, so bizarre in its lineaments and so tragi-comic in its fate."[41] Because he was "denationalised" Lecky had failed to perceive that the one genuine Irish nation struggling to be free was Catholic and Gaelic with a peasant backbone still unbent in spite of centuries of oppression by the Ascendancy. Corkery's inspiration derived from the work of Douglas Hyde, Arthur Griffith, Padraic Pearse, and other leaders of the Irish cultural revival from which Sinn Fein drew so much strength.

Another veteran of the Irish fight for freedom, P. S. O'Hegarty, lodged a comparable complaint against Lecky in his pon-

39. Michael Davitt, *The Fall of Feudalism in Ireland* (London, 1904), p. 726.

40. Seumas MacManus, *The Story of the Irish Race* (rev. ed.; New York, 1967), p. 454.

41. Daniel Corkery, *The Hidden Ireland* (paperback ed.; Dublin, 1967), pp. 7–9.

derous documentary work, *A History of Ireland under the Union*
(1952). To O'Hegarty, Lecky's book was pure Garrison or Ascendancy history which left out the real Irish people. One could
read that "long and splendid book," he maintained, and never
suspect the existence of any but "the Garrison Nation" in Ireland.
The trouble with Lecky was that he simply denied the existence
of Ireland's "Underground Nation."[42] However presentist or
political their inspiration, the criticisms of Corkery and O'Hegarty carried weight. Lecky was, indeed, more of a prisoner of his
class or caste than he thought, and his values ran directly contrary
to the forces that produced not only Fenianism but Sinn Fein.
Lecky's ignorance of the poets of Munster, however, did not
signify his complete indifference to the harshness of middlemen
and the iniquity of the penal laws.[43] His concentration on the
Anglo-Irish political elite did not blind him to the plight of Irish
Catholics in times of famine, agrarian unrest, and rebellion. Even
absentee Irish landlords could be humanitarians. Lecky was quite
capable of indulging in "telescopic philanthropy" toward the
Irish peasantry, and he did write most of his *Ireland* in the safety
of his London house, far removed from the turmoil of rural Ireland during the land war. But it is equally true that he wrote passages which Home Rulers were fond of quoting in support of
their cause. By his own admission, Lecky knew no Irish, and the
*Ireland* was written from the vantage point of the Big House
rather than the little cottage or cabin. No believer in "the genius
of the Gael," he approached gingerly even the outer fringes of
the Irish cultural revival.[44] For Lecky there was only one brand

42. P. S. O'Hegarty, *A History of Ireland under the Union, 1801–1922*
(London, 1952), pp. 4–5.
43. Lecky was also criticized for having tried to exonerate the Anglo-Irish
gentry from their share of blame in maintaining the penal laws. See Sir James
O'Connor, *History of Ireland, 1798–1924* (London, 1926), 1: 54. Lecky's tendency to exaggerate the effectiveness of the penal code may be seen in Maureen
Wall, *The Penal Laws, 1691–1760* (Dundalk, 1961). See also R. E. Burns,
"The Irish Penal Code and Some of Its Historians," *Review of Politics* 21
(January 1959): 276–99.
44. In the 1890s, Lecky became an honorary member of the Irish Literary
Society, which boasted a number of ardent Home Rulers, and he also gave a
small contribution to the Gaelic League. But he remained skeptical about the
language revival and asked that his name not be used for promotional purposes.
He showed some squeamishness toward the Irish Literary Theatre when it
became politicized. See *Memoir*, pp. 329–30, 367–68, and Stephen Gwynn,
*Experiences of a Literary Man* (London, 1926), p. 216.

of "pure nationalism" in Ireland, and that was represented by men of property and respectability who could afford to be disinterested. Neither Wolfe Tone nor Lord Edward Fitzgerald, not to mention Parnell, met Lecky's criteria of purity or disinterest. In an age of increasing social conflict, Lecky's brand of nationalism had an even more avowed class basis than that of the Patriots of Grattan's day.

Since the 1890s, very few historians of modern Ireland have not used Lecky's work as a foundation or stepping-stone for their own more specialized studies. In spite of new documents and new interpretations, not one of the dozen or so recent monographs on eighteenth-century Ireland has come close to dismantling Lecky's *Ireland*. Most of these books refer readers in footnotes to the *Ireland* as one of the standard authorities for certain aspects of the period.[45] If some modern scholars have found Lecky guilty of overstatement or the occasional error, if others have pursued economic and demographic topics which were not touched on in the *Ireland*, these authors have generally refrained from trying to score points at Lecky's expense. Ironically enough, the most acerbic comments about the *Ireland* in recent years have come not from Irish historians or even Irish patriots but from Froude's latest biographer, Waldo H. Dunn. After defending his protagonist against the familiar charges of bias and inaccuracy, Dunn warned in somewhat menacing tones that "Lecky's turn is just coming."[46] The overall solidity of Lecky's historical foundations, however, makes it highly likely that the Froudophiles have a long wait ahead of them.

From the overtly political conclusion of the *Ireland*, it was a short step to *Democracy and Liberty*, some of which was written during the stormy debates over the second Home Rule bill, defeated in the House of Lords early in September 1893. This two-volume work represented the appeal of an old Whig to the new Liberals, who seemed to him to be bent on sweeping away the

---

45. See, for example, R. B. McDowell, *Irish Public Opinion, 1750–1800* (London, 1944); K. H. Connell, *The Population of Ireland, 1750–1845* (London, 1950); G. C. Bolton, *The Passing of the Irish Act of Union* (London, 1966); L. M. Cullen, *Anglo-Irish Trade 1660–1800* (Manchester, 1968); Hereward Senior, *Orangeism in Ireland and Britain, 1795–1836* (London, 1966); and Thomas Pakenham, *The Year of Liberty* (London, 1969).

46. Waldo H. Dunn, *James Anthony Froude* (Oxford, 1963), 2: 608.

last remnants of the eighteenth-century constitution and with it all of England's traditional liberties. With traces of Tocqueville much in evidence, Lecky explored such subjects as representative government, imperialism, nationalism, socialism, Jesuitism, and sabbatarianism. The fervor of those sections dealing with parliamentary interference in Irish land law verged on the polemical; and the discussion of democratic movements lacked the perspective and calm of his historical writings. In *Democracy and Liberty* Lecky blamed English politicians and Liberal ministers, in particular, for making concessions to Irish agrarian terrorists, the result of which was to drive the most enlightened landlords out of Ireland. The source of his own political discontents was not hard to find:

> The politics of a nation and the character of its public men may deteriorate, not because of the aggregate intelligence or virtue of the nation has diminished, but simply because the governing power has descended to classes who are less intelligent, less scrupulous, or more easily deceived.[47]

Although much of *Democracy and Liberty* echoed Tocqueville's concerns about the dangers to individual liberty from democracy, Lecky avoided the easy road of reaction to all change. With characteristic ambivalence, he discussed the pros and cons of graduated taxation, admitting that the extremes of wealth and property were too pronounced in England, and he had some kind words for the moderate and respectable wing of the suffragette movement. In design, tone, and purpose this series of sermons and admonitions represented Lecky's ambition to write his own "Reflections on the Revolution" in a manner worthy of the master of counter-revolutionary ideology, Edmund Burke. If this was not his happiest work in terms of form and content, and if he taxed the reader's patience with rambling discourses on subjects far and wide, the book became the most significant statement of liberal conservatism since James Fitzjames Stephen's indictment of Mill's liberalism in *Liberty, Equality, Fraternity* (1873).

Shortly before the publication of *Democracy and Liberty*, Lecky was asked to accept the nomination for the parliamentary seat recently vacated by his friend David Plunket, who had been raised

---

47. *Democracy and Liberty* (London, 1896), 1: 204.

to the peerage (as Lord Rathmore). With mixed feelings Lecky agreed to stand for one of the Dublin University seats. In spite of unexpected opposition from another Unionist candidate, backed by a group of Irish Tory lawyers and clergymen who questioned Lecky's devotion to the Union and to God, Lecky won the by-election in December 1895 by a majority of 746.[48] Part, but only part, of Lecky's youthful dream of glory had come true. He turned out to be neither a Gibbon nor a Grattan in the House of Commons.[49] He took his parliamentary duties seriously and defended the Unionist cause whenever possible, but the round of routine chores and advancing old age forced him to retire in 1902. He proved to be more a distinguished representative of Trinity College than a distinguished M.P.

Toward the close of his life Lecky decided to overhaul the *Leaders*. Dismay and even anger at the use Home Rulers had made of the two earlier versions drove him to embark on a second major revision. The committed historian, who had joined the crusade against Home Rule in 1886, wished to make it clear that Grattan's Parliament could not be taken as a precedent or justification for creating a Parnellite parliament and executive in Dublin. Determined to put a halt to the misuse of the *Leaders* by Home Rulers who loved to quote its nationalist sentiments, Lecky denied any change of mind about the integrity and purity of Irish nationalism in the age of Grattan. What had changed, however, were conditions in Ireland since the Union and the complexion of nationalism since the outbreak of Fenianism. The new leaders of Irish public opinion belonged, in his view, to a criminal and disloyal conspiracy whose object was the destruction of both the Anglo-Irish gentry and the Act of Union. There was nothing pure, he believed, about the agrarian terrorism and separatism preached by the Parnellites.

The 1903 edition of the *Leaders* reflected these convictions. Most of the earlier references to "freedom" and "independence" were discarded, the chapter on Swift was dropped, and the section on O'Connell was expanded to fill the whole second volume.

48. *Memoir,* pp. 269–75, and Auchmuty, pp. 85–113.
49. During his election campaign, Lecky had been taunted with the reminder that Gibbon had never spoken in debate during his sojourn in the House of Commons (1774–82). Lecky, in fact, participated in a number of debates.

Lecky's fundamental ambivalence about popular—that is, Catholic and democratic—forms of Irish nationalism, over which the old gentry had little, if any, control, loomed large in his revised portrait of O'Connell, whose career he regarded as both a triumph and a calamity. In form and mood this final edition differed sharply from the first.[50] Even more than the 1871 version, this one was intended to arouse the remaining Irish gentry—Catholic as well as Protestant—from their lethargy and send them to their battle stations in defense of property and intelligence.

Aware that the clock could never be turned back to the 1780s, Lecky hoped nevertheless that his writings would help to galvanize the Irish gentry of his own day into political action in defense of enlightened Unionism. The Act of Union, he realized, had broken the hold of Irish landowners over the people of the country by depriving them of a Parliament which was not only "the centre and organ of a strong and healthy national feeling" but, more important, "an instrument for keeping the government of Ireland in the hands of the Irish gentry." There was no chance of Grattan's Parliament being resurrected in Dublin, least of all in the post-Fenian era; but Lecky never wavered in his conviction that the peculiarities of Irish society and history made it "especially important that property and education should maintain an unbroken control over the currents of national life." Once that control was relaxed, Ireland, he predicted, "would inevitably drift into the worst type of Jacobinism."[51] Such was the message of this late Victorian apostle of Burke. Those Home Rulers who credited Lecky with having converted them to the Parnellite cause were simply deceiving themselves or playing political games, having found in the *Leaders* and the *Ireland* no more than what they wished to find.

Old age descended upon Lecky prematurely. He grew gloomier in mood and more ponderous in judgment, as personal and political cares converged from all directions. Threats to private property and owners of estates in Ireland, in particular, made him despair even more than usual about the future. A close friend wrote that he "became more matter of fact and Teutonic" as the

---

50. See McCartney, pp. 132–35, and *Memoir,* pp. 359–60. Lecky also dropped the definite article from the title.

51. *Leaders* (London, 1903), 1: 281.

combined effects of age and London gradually wore down his "Celtic nature" and sapped "the spontaneity of genius."[52] Burdened by "passing clouds of melancholy," and depleted of resilience by the years of unceasing toil, he began to show impatience with both people and life. A man without either malice or guile, he died in his library on 22 October 1903, at peace with all save the enemies of aristocracy, intelligence, and truth.

Any "final" assessment of Lecky as a historian must await a full-length study of the man and his times, in which Irish, English, and also European history (especially social and intellectual history) will have to be as closely intertwined as they were in the original edition of the *England*. In the absence of such a work one falls back upon impressions and opinions, some of which sooner or later harden into conclusions. To describe Lecky as the last of the great amateur historians of the Victorian era does not do him full justice. To call him the first of the "modern" historians of eighteenth-century England and Ireland will provoke a semantic wrangle about the meaning of the word "modern." And yet Lecky was both these things as well as much more. The "dated" nature of his work, the pre-Namierite interpretation of the structure of English and Irish politics, and the occasionally musty smell of his prose do not add up to obsolescence for either the *England* or the *Ireland*. No two works of history could be more antithetical than the *Ireland* and Edith Johnston's *Great Britain and Ireland, 1760–1800* (1963), but both books are essential for an understanding of Ireland in the age of George III. Sooner or later all works of history must become "dated," but one continues to read Thucydides, Gibbon, Macaulay, or even Lecky for their "dateless" qualities which transcend the latest facts and fashions. Irish historiography has matured considerably since the 1890s, but in terms of intellectual reach, control of materials, and insights, Irish historians still have much to learn from Lecky. The *Ireland* towers over the specialized monographs of recent years, just as a great Irish house such as Castletown or Carton would dominate, if not humiliate, a surrounding suburban housing estate with all its neat cinderblock houses, modern appliances, and deceptive durability.

---

52. Booth, "Early Recollections of Mr. Lecky," p. 122.

There is an overall unity, as distinct from consistency, about Lecky's career which arises out of his social origins, his theological outlook, his conception of history, and his lifelong devotion to the political philosophy of Edmund Burke. Lecky's roots lay deep in the Anglo-Irish Ascendancy, a once flourishing elite which was threatened from many quarters even before his birth. As he matured, he became aware that his own class or caste was steadily disintegrating, and this awareness gave him a perspective into the past which was neither wholly detached nor wholly partisan. What lurked beneath the apparent calm and neutrality of the *Ireland* were powerful emotions which led Lecky to exclaim to his friend Daunt in 1881 that "Irish politics have fallen to a large extent into the hands of swindlers—who may be admirably orthodox on all points relating to the Sacraments and the Creed but whose views about the Decalogue are peculiar and who certainly do not make the protection of either life or property an object of their policy."[53] Still disagreeing with Daunt in 1886 about the possibility of reviving a Grattan-like parliament, Lecky warned: "You have fought the battle of Repeal very long and very steadily, but do not forget what was the fate of the Girondins. I hope we may both keep our heads and something at least of our Irish properties!"[54] Like so many Anglo-Irishmen, Lecky was torn between love of Ireland and loyalty to England, between fear and affection for the Irish Catholic majority. And these often conflicting emotions inspired some of the passion that seethed behind his urbane, disciplined, and slightly shy exterior.

The most obvious sign of unity, even symmetry, in Lecky's life was his affinity for eighteenth-century English culture, along with its Anglo-Irish derivative. Intellectually Lecky was tied all his life to Trinity College as he had known and loved it in his undergraduate years; and eighteenth-century values lingered longer in Trinity than in most other universities in Great Britain and Ireland. Along with his English analogue, Leslie Stephen, Lecky was drawn to the apparent order, self-confidence, elegance, and balance of Georgian society. He admired the ease with which eighteenth-century men of letters absorbed new ideas without agonies of doubt or crises of faith. He idealized the openness of

53. Lecky to Daunt, 8 April 1881, Lecky MSS, no. 224.
54. Lecky to Daunt, 16 January 1886, quoted in *Memoir,* p. 186.

Georgian political life wherein men of talent but modest means could rise under the patronage of enlightened aristocrats such as Rockingham and Charlemont.

Lecky and Stephen were only two of a number of Victorian "philosophes" who had become as critical of Gladstonian rhetoric as they had always been contemptuous of Disraelian guile. Leslie Stephen's brother, James Fitzjames, along with Matthew Arnold, Walter Bagehot, Sir Henry Maine, and Albert Dicey, shared with Lecky a disenchantment with both the quality of politics at Westminster and the new industrial society which surrounded them. Their own political convictions defy simple labels, belonging somewhere between those of lapsed Liberals and pessimistic Peelites looking for a new leader. Like Bagehot, they were "between sizes in politics," wanting to belong to the "Left Center," but finding themselves inexorably pushed—or pulled—to the Right. Committed to cautious reforms designed to remove the most glaring inequities in society, these upper middle-class men worried increasingly about the rise of egalitarian democracy, which threatened their elitist status, and they also resented the upward thrust of middle-class men, especially industrialists and tradesmen, whom they took to be philistines. After the 1860s these intellectuals became outspoken opponents of radicalism and defenders of the rights of property.[55] And after the advent of the land war in Ireland, Lecky's Irish sensibilities and personal interest in the outcome made him the most immoderate of these moderates on the subject of Parnellism and pure democracy. Lecky's moderation was neither Liberal nor Conservative in any conventional sense. It was what Bagehot, in his essay *Physics and Politics,* called "animated," by which he meant the man (of genius) whose writings were neither dull nor exaggerated but combined "instinct with judgment" and "spirit with reasonableness."

Nostalgia for a golden age of natural aristocracy, restricted franchise, and absolute rights of private property does not explain all of Lecky. His own involvement in the vicissitudes of

55. For the migration, if not flight, of some intellectuals from the consequences of industrialism and the logic of Liberalism, see J. P. Roach, "Liberalism and the Victorian Intelligentsia," *Cambridge Historical Journal* 13 (1957): 58–81; and B. E. Lippincott, *Victorian Critics of Democracy* (Minneapolis, 1938).

Irish landlords and his distance from the realities of Irish society and politics made Fenianism and the work of the Land League doubly repugnant to him. Caught up in the perplexity of being an absentee Anglo-Irish landlord without an ancestral Big House to which he could return, Lecky began to treat Ireland as a well-equipped laboratory in which he could study at close quarters the collision of good and evil as well as ideals and interests over the centuries. There is no better proof of the overarching unity of his career and no more convincing example of his confusion of personal and historical concerns than the *Leaders* in its three editions. Even at the very end of his life, he had not given up all hope of leading his countrymen by means of the compelling truth of history back to the "pure'" patriotism of Grattan, which Lecky considered free from such "impurities" as democracy, agrarianism, clericalism, and religious discrimination.

A recurrent theme in Lecky's writing was the "secularization of politics," a phrase he once defined as "conducting politics with an exclusive view to secular interests."[56] In both the *Rationalism* and the *Morals* he discussed the age-old contest between sectarianism and patriotism, dwelling at length on the crimes and villainies of men who acted out of blind faith or unquestioned dogma. Lecky owed much of his concern for the secularizing process to Buckle, who had dealt with this "central principle" in the *Civilization*. The secularization of political life in Ireland absorbed Lecky's attention in the *Leaders* because he saw it as "the chief measure and condition of political progress."[57] Like any good Whig, he believed that moral and intellectual progress was a precondition of political progress, and he devoted a long and important chapter to these themes in the *Rationalism*. Less anxious in the early 1860s about the corrosive effects of democracy, the young Lecky found in the interaction of religion and patriotism the chief elements of "the moral history of mankind." Patriotism was, in his view, "the best cordial of humanity, and all the sterner and more robust virtues were matured to the highest degree by its power."[58] Cherishing an ideal of Christian patriot-

56. See chap. 5, "The Secularisation of Politics," *Rationalism*, pp. 98–228; and Hyde, p. 45.
57. Hyde, p. 42.
58. *Rationalism* 2: 100, 102.

ism such as Grattan embodied, he looked forward to the ultimate union of all civilized nations under God and through representative institutions of which Burke would have approved. The resurgence of clerical influences and the resort to physical force in Ireland as well as the lowering of the franchise in 1867 and the bidding of ambitious politicians for the votes of the new electors deprived Lecky of grounds for hope. He had written in 1864:

> The sympathy between great bodies of men was never so strong, the stream of enthusiasm never flowed in so broad a current as at present; and in the democratic union of nations we find the last and highest expression of the Christian ideal of the brotherhood of mankind.[59]

Thirty years later, he wrote a political manifesto in which he warned that democracy was fundamentally incompatible with and hostile to liberty.[60]

Lecky liked to regard society as an organism susceptible to disease and passing through periods of good, bad, and indifferent health. Irish history was for the "philosophical student of politics" "an invaluable study of morbid anatomy."[61] And in the *Ireland,* he wrote: "In the social system, as in the physical body, the prostration of extreme illness is often followed, with a strange rapidity, by a sudden reflux of exuberant health."[62] With this organic view of society went an organic conception of history and the historian's function. The best historians, he contended, tried to see the past "as an organic whole." Lecky was thus beholden to Burke and guided by Darwin in his study of the way societies evolved through internal conflict and external competition. No believer in linear and absolute progress, he found in European history signs of some improvement in morals and legislation, a decline in standards of political behavior, a more philanthropic spirit among the upper classes, and a growing restlessness and selfishness among the lower orders. Ireland, in short, was not the only country worthy of the attention of a morbid anatomist.

59. Ibid., pp. 227–28.
60. *Democracy and Liberty* 1: 214–15.
61. *Historical and Political Essays* (new ed.; London, 1910), p. 62.
62. *Ireland* 1: 23.

The historian's "first duty," according to Lecky, was to seek out the truth, and "the path of truth is over the corpses of the enthusiasms of our past."[63] Being something of an enthusiast himself, Lecky did not find it easy to practice what he preached. By truth he meant much more than accuracy in using data and objectivity in trying to represent conflicting points of view in the past. Truth in history had to do with ultimate values and the timeless criteria of good character. Inspired by Burke to preserve what was best in the past and to warn his contemporaries against the continued menace of Jacobinism, he searched long and hard for examples of selflessness, courage, and virtue over the centuries. In an increasingly democratic age he conceived it his duty to remind men of the values of an aristocratic society and polity which had made England into both a world power and a haven of civil as well as religious liberty.

Just as Lecky agreed with Burke that government was a matter of experience and not theory, so he shared Bolingbroke's conviction that history had a function to discern and disseminate philosophical truths elicited from the past. Lecky believed that good historians possessed unique insights into public affairs, social systems, and character: only historians knew what had worked well in the past and why, and only they could prescribe the right remedies for the ills of their own age. The prescriptive content of the *Leaders,* the presentist passages in the *England* and the *Ireland,* and the complete presentism of *Democracy and Liberty* all owed something to the idea of "exemplar history" fostered by Polybius, Dionysius, and other humanists of antiquity.[64] But they owed more to Bolingbroke's variations on that classical theme in his *Letters on the Study and Use of History.* If Lecky did see himself as the philosopher and guide of politicians or princes, the history he wrote was no mere procession of heroes by whose conduct his readers were supposed to guide themselves. Although at times the *Ireland* came close to being Grattan teach-

63. *Morals* 2: 275, and *Memoir,* p. 61. Lecky's veneration of Burke only increased with time. See his glowing tribute on the centenary of Burke's death (7 December 1897), which was commemorated in Trinity, ibid., pp. 304–12.

64. For an illuminating discussion of "exemplar history" and its ramifications, see George H. Nadel, "Philosophy of History before Historicism" in Mario Bunge, ed., *The Critical Approach: Essays in Honor of Karl R. Popper* (New York, 1964).

ing by example, Lecky was too philosophic of mind to believe in unrefined exemplary history. He not only partook of the eighteenth-century view of history as "the empirical part of moral philosophy" but followed Taine's path in his search for the permanent values and ultimate truths of a given society or nation. Even more than his "favorite Gibbon," he tried to bore through the outer layers of biography, battles, treaties, and other manifest "events" in order to arrive at the inner core or moral being of civilizations.

In an address given in 1892, entitled significantly "The Political Value of History," Lecky described eighteenth-century historians as primarily concerned with the development of morals, industry, art, intellect, and, of course, the dominant ideas of the past. Such were the subjects taken up and appraised in his *England*. He went on to declare that the hallmark of intelligent history was its ability to delineate "the dominant idea or characteristic" of any given age, and he insisted that only by understanding the past could one understand the present. Admiring the English people for their ability to adapt old institutions to new needs, he argued that a country's institutions preserved "the sense of its organic unity, its essential connection with the past. By their continuous existence they bind together as by a living chain the past with the present, the living with the dead."[65] Thus spoke the philosophic historian teaching Burke by allusion.

In the same address, Lecky reminded his audience of the price paid by France after 1789 for cutting herself off "from all vital connection with her own past." He conceded the existence of a "certain steady and orderly evolution" in the world, but also emphasized the role of "individual action and even mere accident" in bringing about change. Man, he maintained, was "no mere passive weed drifting helplessly upon the sea of life." History could teach man how "to weigh conflicting probabilities, to estimate degrees of evidence, to form a sound judgment of the value of authorities," to exercise the imagination, to expand intellectual horizons, and to enlarge experience.[66] Underlining his own contribution to moral and political history, he declared:

65. *Historical and Political Essays,* pp. 25–26.
66. Ibid., p. 35.

> History is never more valuable than when it enables us, standing
> as on a height, to look beyond the smoke and turmoil of our petty
> quarrels, and to detect in the slow developments of the past the
> great permanent forces that are steadily bearing nations onwards
> to improvement or decay.[67]

It is true that Lecky's search for "the permanent forces of the
nation" kept bringing him back to Burke and the ideal of a hereditary as well as natural aristocracy. But Lecky also tried to diffuse
among his readers a Victorian pastiche of Mill on happiness,
Whately on religion, Palmerston on property, Darwin on evolution, Smiles on character, Tocqueville on democracy, and Fitzjames Stephen on equality. Unable to fulfill his dream of being
a "man of action," he undertook to write history that would teach
men and women to forsake the gratification of immediate desires
for the lasting values of the past. Lecky's humanistic philosophy
thus went beyond the orthodoxies of Oxford and Cambridge
historiography; he served as a bridge between the eighteenth-
century disciples of Tacitus and the twentieth-century admirers of
Elie Halévy.

The fine cartoon by "Spy" of Lecky personifying "The Eighteenth Century" deliberately played down the Victorian ingredi-
ents of his philosophy of history.[68] The *England* and the *Ireland*
were both hung on double hinges: they opened backward onto the
eighteenth century and forward onto the twentieth century. If
the reader knows what to look for, the directional arrows in the
*England* point to Elie Halévy (1870–1937), the acknowledged
master of English history between 1815 and 1914. There may be
few direct references to Lecky's work in Halévy's history of the
English people, but his first Volume, *England in 1815,* shows
signs that he had not only read but inwardly digested the *England*.
When Halévy set out on his long expedition to explain why England, contrary to Marxian dogma, had escaped a revolution, he
soon discarded such explanations as economic and political organization. The real answer, he believed, lay in "another category
of social phenomena," in "beliefs, emotions, and opinions, as

67. Ibid., p. 37.
68. This cartoon by (Sir) Leslie Ward in *Vanity Fair* is reproduced in
Hyde's *A Victorian Historian* as the frontispiece.

well as . . . the institutions and sects in which these beliefs, emotions, and opinions take a form suitable for scientific inquiry."[69] Lecky might have written that passage, except for the word "scientific," for which he would, no doubt, have substituted "philosophic."

Like Lecky, Halévy began his career as a liberal widely read in philosophy and with an insatiable curiosity about the origins of liberty and political stability in England. Like Lecky, he first made his name as a historian of philosophy, construed in its broadest sense, and he too was fascinated by the interaction of ideas, institutions, religious beliefs, and human emotions. Only after finishing his classic study, *The Growth of Philosophic Radicalism,* did Halévy turn to his holistic history of the English people in the century leading up to World War I. In analytic method, philosophical originality, and mastery of many subfields, Halévy surpassed Lecky; but the *England* represents the nearest historical precursor of the *History of the English People in the Nineteenth Century.* However pronounced the differences between these two men in age, social background, culture, and political aspirations, their similarities ought not to be ignored.[70] Both men were outsiders—Halévy far more than Lecky—who looked from an oblique angle into the society they admired so greatly. Both men were thoroughly at home in the world of ideas, beliefs, and morals. Lecky searched for "the permanent forces" of the nation; Halévy sought to divine and analyze "l'esprit anglais," which had made possible England's peace and prosperity—in stark contrast to France's misfortunes. If Halévy produced a more sophisticated thesis to explain how and why England had avoided revolution, Lecky was one of the first historians to appreciate the political as well as religious importance of Wesleyan Methodism. Recent critics have pointed to flaws in this thesis. But it was Lecky, not Halévy, who explained England's escape from "the contagion" of total revolution sweeping across Europe in the eighteenth century as largely due to "the new and

---

69. E. Halévy, *England in 1815* (paperback ed.; New York, 1961), 1: 383.
70. Cogent discussions of Halévy may be found in Charles C. Gillispie, "The Work of Elie Halévy: A Critical Appreciation," *Journal of Modern History* 22 (September 1950): 232–49, and Melvin Richter, "Elie Halévy," *Encyclopedia of Social Sciences* (New York, 1968), 6: 307–10.

vehement religious enthusiasm which was at that very time passing through the middle and lower classes of the people, which
had enlisted in its service a large proportion of the wilder and
more impetuous reformers."[71] More than thirty years later,
Halévy wrote that England avoided "violent revolution" because
"the *élite* of the working class, the hard-working and capable
bourgeois, had been imbued by the evangelical movement with a
spirit from which the established order had nothing to fear."[72]

Both historians tended to idealize the quality and intensity of
English liberty. They found their paragons or supreme exemplars
of statesmanship in the upper rather than the middle or lower
classes: Peel was to Halévy what Grattan was to Lecky. In both
cases, advancing years brought mounting gloom about the future.
Halévy had to endure the horrors of World War I, and socialism
became for him the kind of incubus that Fenianism and pure
democracy had been for Lecky. The similarities may go deeper.
Long an admirer of French intellect, Lecky may well have owed
some of his thoughts on Methodism, not to say history, to
Halévy's own mentor, Hippolyte Taine.

History, for Lecky, was neither an end in itself nor an arcane
dialogue between (German) professors and professional students. As an Anglo-Irish humanist who took his main philosophical inspiration from Bacon and Locke, he held learning in high
esteem but also expected learning to make better citizens or more
virtuous and wise subjects. The complete citizen was one who
despised not only danger but dogma and pedantry. He cultivated
in a pragmatic way those truths buried or partially exposed in the
past. And it was the duty of historians to reveal and refurbish
those truths to which they alone were privy. Lecky, the failed

71. *England* 2: 636. Much of the Lecky-Halévy thesis about the political
significance of Methodism belongs to the shadowy realm of social psychology,
wherein sound methods are almost as scarce as reliable data for the later
eighteenth century. Two important reappraisals of the thesis are: E. J. Hobs-
bawm, "Methodism and the Threat of Revolution in Britain," in *Labouring
Men* (Anchor Books ed.; New York, 1967), pp. 27–39; and E. P. Thompson,
*The Making of the English Working Class* (London, 1964), pp. 37–47, 350–
400.

72. Halévy, p. 425. Bernard Semmel discusses the French origins of the
"Halévy thesis" in his valuable introduction to Elie Halévy, *The Birth of
Methodism in England* (Chicago and London: the University of Chicago Press,
1971,), pp. 1–29.

leader of Irish public opinion, the frustrated "man of action," rationalized that he could accomplish far more from a seat in the British Museum than from one in the House of Commons.

Those who have praised Lecky for his "philosophic detachment" have overlooked the commitment of his philosophy and the mission he had to educate the men and women of his day. His veneration for aristocracy—literally, rule by the best men—was matched by his repugnance for politicians who sought "to gain their ends by setting the poor against the rich" and who planted "in the nation deadly seeds of class animosities and cupidities." No Tory yearning for a preindustrial, semifeudal society, Lecky hoped that his readers would "learn to look with tolerance and with modesty upon the England of the past."[73] A conservative with none of the narrowness of the eighteenth-century squirearchy, Lecky began to show signs toward the end of his life of preferring Burke's to Grattan's mantle.

The moral philosopher and the moralist always hovered near the surface of Lecky's historical writings. As a student of the moral core of nations, he knew that they rose and fell according to the quality or health of their inner being. Because morality was intimately connected with character, he devoted many pages in *The Map of Life* (1899) to the subject of character formation. His prescription for self-fulfillment was eminently Victorian: men had to have a purpose in life, something to do and to strive for. The wise man, as Aristotle perceived, sought to avoid suffering rather than to attain pleasure; and happiness, as Mill knew, came when it was not made the "direct object of pursuit." Only by exercising "prudence, self-restraint, and intelligent regulation" and by forming "active habits, to combat . . . tedium and despondency" could a man fulfill himself. The quality of character vitally affected the "permanent well-being" of individuals, communities, and even nations.[74]

Discerning a constant interaction between morals and politics, Lecky could not help wondering, and worrying, about the fate of England and Ireland when a new morality, based on self-interest and leveling principles, was corroding both politics and character. The values of Burke and Grattan seemed to him the

73. *England* 6: 300.
74. *The Map of Life* (new impression; London, 1901), pp. 19–21.

only effective antidote against the pure democracy that was slowly poisoning the body politic. Convinced that "ideals ultimately rule the world, and each before it loses its ascendancy bequeaths some moral truth as an abiding legacy to the human race,"[75] Lecky used the vehicle of history to accumulate that legacy and promote those moral truths of which his age seemed so much in need. If men of poverty and ignorance, namely, the vast majority, were going to count more than men of property and intelligence in the political scales, then the future belonged to Fenians and new Jacobins who, caring nothing for the past, would squander the present and bankrupt the future. Such was the gravamen of Lecky's case against democracy and the main cause of his growing pessimism.

Lecky, then, was a pivotal figure in nineteenth-century historiography. He practiced philosophic history in a manner that not only evoked Bolingbroke but anticipated Halévy. Instead of inheriting Grattan's mantle, he became a statesman of historical letters and, for a time, a politician teaching philosophy by means of history. He would have disagreed passionately with Carlyle's characteristic dictum: "Happy the people whose annals are blank in history-books." Lecky spent most of his life trying to prove that the happiest people had not only a history but also a philosophic historian who could both discern moral truths and educate the leaders of public opinion.

### A Note about This Edition

This abridgment is based on the five-volume New Edition published by Longmans, Green and Company in London toward the end of 1892. The "cabinet edition" of 1892 also included the *England,* which ran to seven volumes of the same size. The overall reduction of some 76 percent has resulted in placing proportionately more emphasis on Irish society and politics at the expense of English politics and foreign affairs. The design of the

75. *Historical and Political Essays,* p. 18. Lecky's "Thoughts on History" originally appeared in *The Forum,* vol. 14 (1892) under the title "The Art of Writing History."

original *History of Ireland* is illustrated by the number of pages devoted to particular eras:

| Period | Pages |
|---|---|
| c. 1066–1700 | 135 |
| 1700–1760 | 336 |
| 1760–1790 | 517 |
| 1790–1800 | 1,364 |
| 1800–1802 | 128 |
| 1802–1890 | 23 |
| Total | 2,503 |

It took Lecky 2,217 pages, or 89 percent of the original "cabinet edition" to cover the eighteenth century. But within that century he devoted 1,881 pages, 85 percent, to the years 1760–1800 and only 336 pages to the period 1700–1760. The years 1793–1801 received 1,284 pages, or 58 percent of the space devoted to the eighteenth century. Lecky's choice of title thus tends to disguise the fact that his *History of Ireland* really concerned the age of Burke and Grattan.

Any drastic abridgment is bound to violate or distort the integrity of the original work. In some respects the result of the present streamlining process has been to make the *Ireland* more Irish, as distinct from Gaelic, than was Lecky's original. In general, the severest cuts have affected the English political scene, foreign affairs, military campaigns, and long quotations from letters and speeches on the condition of Ireland. Whenever possible, Lecky's own philosophical asides and disquisitions on present discontents have been preserved.

Where space restrictions have permitted, the editor has inserted bridging passages (in italics) in order to maintain a semblance of continuity and to suggest Lecky's intentions or line of thought. However fragmentary, these passages are supposed to link up the more important segments of the narrative. Because the footnotes had to be jettisoned, this edition has lost some priceless gems. It is hoped the result is not "an abridgment of all that was pleasant" in the original.

L. P. Curtis, Jr.

# Bibliographical Note

Readers interested in Lecky's "life and times" should consult:

Auchmuty, James Johnston. *Lecky: A Biographical and Critical Essay*. Dublin, 1945.

Booth, Arthur. "Early Recollections of Mr. Lecky" (by "A College Friend"). *National Review* 43 (March 1904): 108–22.

Hyde, H. Montgomery, ed. *A Victorian Historian: Private Letters of W. E. H. Lecky, 1859–1878*. London, 1947.

Lecky, Elisabeth van Dedem. *A Memoir of the Right Hon. William Hartpole Lecky by His Wife*. London, 1909.

Phillips, W. A. *Lecky: A Lecture in Celebration of the Centenary of Lecky's Birth* . . . Dublin, 1939.

Prothero, George W. Article in the *Dictionary of National Biography, Supplement, 1901–1911*, 1: 435–40. London, 1912.

Discussions of Lecky's politics and philosophy of history may be found in the following:

Lippincott, Benjamin E. *Victorian Critics of Democracy*. Minneapolis, 1938.

McCartney, Donal. "Lecky's *Leaders of Public Opinion in Ireland*." *Irish Historical Studies* 14 (September 1964): 119–41. (Mr. McCartney has completed a Ph.D. thesis at University College, Dublin, on "Lecky and His Circle," based on Lecky's papers in Trinity College, Dublin.)

Mullett, Charles F. Chapter on Lecky in Herman Ausubel, J. B. Brebner, and E. M. Hunt, eds., *Some Historians of Modern Britain.* New York, 1951.

Mulvey, Helen. "The Historian Lecky: Opponent of Irish Home Rule." *Victorian Studies* 1 (June 1958): 337–51.

Students interested in Irish history during the decades covered by Lecky should consult in addition to the works listed in note 45 of the Editor's Introduction, the following:

Beckett, J. C. *Protestant Dissent in Ireland, 1687–1780.* London, 1948.

——. *The Making of Modern Ireland.* London, 1966.

Harlow, Vincent T. *The Founding of the Second British Empire, 1763–93.* Vol. 1. London, 1952.

James, Francis G. *Ireland in the Empire, 1688–1770.* Cambridge, Mass., 1972.

Johnston, Edith M. *Great Britain and Ireland, 1760–1800.* Edinburgh, 1963.

Maxwell, Constantia. *Country and Town in Ireland under the Georges.* Dundalk, 1949.

Murray, Alice E. *A History of the Commercial and Financial Relations between England and Ireland from the Period of the Restoration.* London, 1907.

O'Connell, Maurice R. *Irish Politics and Social Conflict in the Age of the American Revolution.* Philadelphia, 1965.

Wall, Maureen. *The Penal Laws, 1691–1760.* Dundalk, 1961.

An invaluable guide to recent work in modern Irish history is:

Mulvey, Helen. "Modern Irish History since 1940: A Bibliographical Survey (1600–1922)." In E. C. Furber, ed., *Changing Views on British History.* Cambridge, Mass., 1966.

A HISTORY OF IRELAND
IN THE
EIGHTEENTH CENTURY

# I
## The Making of the Protestant Ascendancy

The history of Scotland in the eighteenth century furnishes us with one of the most remarkable instances on record of the efficacy of wise legislation in developing the prosperity and ameliorating the character of nations. In the history of Ireland, on the other hand, we may trace with singular clearness the perverting and degrading influence of great legislative injustices, and the manner in which they affect in turn every element of national well-being. This portion of the history of the Empire has usually been treated by English historians in a very superficial and perfunctory manner, and it has been obscured by many contradictions, by much prejudice and misrepresentation. I propose in the present work to examine it at some length, and in doing so it will be my object, much less to describe individual characters or particular episodes, than to analyse the social and political conditions of the country, to trace historically the formation of the peculiar tendencies, affinities, and repulsions of the national intellect and character.

In order to accomplish this task it will be necessary to throw a brief glance over some of the earlier phases of Irish history. I leave it to professed antiquaries to discuss how far the measure of civilisation, which had undoubtedly been attained in Ireland before the English conquest, extended beyond the walls of the monasteries. That civilisation enabled Ireland to bear a great and noble part in the conversion of Europe to Christianity. It made it, in one of the darkest periods of the dark ages, a refuge of learning and of piety. It produced not a little in architecture, in illumina-

3

tions, in metal-work, and in music, which, considering its early date, exhibits a high degree of originality and of beauty; but it was not sufficient to repress the disintegrating tendencies of the clan system, or to mould the country into one powerful and united whole. England owed a great part of her Christianity to Irish monks who laboured among her people before the arrival of Augustine, and Scotland, according to the best authorities, owed her name, her language, and a large proportion of her inhabitants to the long succession of Irish immigrations and conquests between the close of fifth and ninth centuries, but at home the elements of disunion were powerful, and they were greatly aggravated by the Danish invasions. It was probably a misfortune that Ireland never passed, like the rest of Europe, under the subjection of the Romans, who bequeathed, wherever they ruled, the elements of Latin civilisation, and also those habits of national organisation in which they were pre-eminent. It was certainly a fatal calamity to Ireland that the Norman Conquest, which in England was effected completely and finally by a single battle, was in Ireland protracted over no less than 400 years. Strongbow found no resistance such as that which William had encountered at Hastings, but the native element speedily closed around the new colonists, and regained, in the greater part of the island, a complete ascendency. Feudalism was introduced, but the keystone of the system, a strong resident sovereign, was wanting, and Ireland was soon torn by the wars of the great Anglo-Norman nobles, who were, in fact, independent sovereigns, much like the old Irish kings. The Norman settlers scattered through distant parts of Ireland, intermixed with the natives, adopted their laws and their modes of life, and became in a few years, according to the proverb, more Irish than the Irish themselves. The English rule, as a living reality, was confined and concentrated in the narrow limits of the Pale. The hostile power planted in the heart of the nation destroyed all possibility of central government, while it was itself incapable of fulfilling that function. Like a spear-point embedded in a living body, it inflamed all around it and deranged every vital function. It prevented the gradual reduction of the island by some native Clovis, which would necessarily have taken place if the Anglo-Normans had not arrived, and, instead of that peaceful and almost silent amalgamation of races, customs, laws,

4

and languages which took place in England, and which is the source of many of the best elements in English life and character, the two nations remained in Ireland for centuries in hostility.

Great allowance must be made for atrocities committed under such circumstances. The legal maxim that killing an Irishman is no felony, assumes, as has been truly said, a somewhat different aspect from that which partisan writers have given it, when it is understood that it means merely that the bulk of the Irish remained under their own Brehon jurisdiction, according to which the punishment for murder was not death, but fine. The edicts of more than one Plantagenet king show traces of a wisdom and a humanity beyond their age; and the Irish modes of life long continued to exercise an irresistible attraction over many of the colonists; but it was inevitable, in such a situation and at such a time, that those who resisted that attraction, and who formed the nucleus of the English power, should look upon the Irish as later colonists looked upon the Red Indians—as being, like wild beasts, beyond the pale of the moral law. Intermarriage with them was forbidden by stringent penalties, and many savage laws were made to maintain the distinction. "It was manifest," says Sir John Davies, "that such as had the government of Ireland under the crown of England did intend to make a perpetual separation and enmity between the English and Irish, pretending, no doubt, that the English should, in the end, root out the Irish." A sentiment very common in the Pale was expressed by those martial monks who taught that it was no more sin to kill an Irishman than to kill a dog; and that whenever, as often happened, they killed an Irishman, they would not on that account refrain from celebrating Mass even for a single day.

It was not until the reign of Henry VIII that the royal authority became in any degree a reality over the whole island, but its complete ascendency dates only from the great wars of Elizabeth, which broke the force of the semi-independent chieftains, crushed the native population to the dust, and established the complete ascendency of English law. The suppression of the native race, in the wars against Shane O'Neill, Desmond, and Tyrone, was carried on with a ferocity which surpassed that of Alva in the Netherlands, and has seldom been exceeded in the page of history. Thus a deliberate attempt was made by a servant of the British

Government to assassinate in time of peace the great Irish leader Shane O'Neill, by a present of poisoned wine; and although the attempt failed and the assassin was detected and arrested, he was at once liberated by the Government. Essex accepted the hospitality of Sir Brien O'Neill. After a banquet, when the Irish chief had retired unsuspiciously to rest, the English general surrounded the house with soldiers, captured his host with his wife and brother, sent them all to Dublin for execution, and massacred the whole body of his friends and retainers. An English officer, a friend of the Viceroy, invited seventeen Irish gentlemen to supper, and when they rose from the table had them all stabbed. A Catholic archbishop named Hurley fell into the hands of the English authorities, and before they sent him to the gallows they tortured him to extort confession of treason by one of the most horrible torments human nature can endure—by roasting his feet with fire. But these isolated episodes, by diverting the mind from the broad features of the war, serve rather to diminish than to enhance its atrocity. The war, as conducted by Carew, by Gilbert, by Pelham, by Mountjoy, was literally a war of extermination. The slaughter of Irishmen was looked upon as literally the slaughter of wild beasts. Not only the men, but even the women and children who fell into the hands of the English, were deliberately and systematically butchered. Bands of soldiers traversed great tracts of country, slaying every living thing they met. The sword was not found sufficiently expeditious, but another method proved much more efficacious. Year after year, over a great part of Ireland, all means of human subsistence were destroyed, no quarter was given to prisoners who surrendered, and the whole population was skilfully and steadily starved to death. The pictures of the condition of Ireland at this time are as terrible as anything in human history. Thus Spenser, describing what he had seen in Munster, tells how, "out of every corner of the woods and glens, they came creeping forth upon their hands, for their legs could not bear them. They looked like anatomies of death; they spoke like ghosts crying out of their graves; they did eat the dead carrion, happy when they could find them; yea, and one another soon after, inasmuch as the very carcases they spared not to scrape out of their graves." The people, in the words of Holinshed, "were not only driven to eat horses, dogs, and dead carions, but also did devour the carcases of dead men, whereof there be sundry examples. . . . The land itself, which before these wars was populous, well inhabited, and rich in all the good blessings of God—being plenteous of corn, full of cattle, well stored with fish and other good commodities—is now become . . . so barren, both of man and beast, that whoever did travel from the one end of all Munster, even from Waterford to the head of Smeereweeke, which is about sixscore miles, he would not meet any man, woman, or child saving in towns and cities; nor yet see any beasts, but the very wolves, foxes, and other like ravening beasts, many of them laie dead, being famished, and the residue gone elsewhere." "From Dingle to the Rock of Cashel," said an Irish annalist, "not the lowing of a cow nor the voice of the ploughman was that year to be heard." The troops of Sir Richard Percie "left neither corne, nor horn, nor house unburnt between Kinsale and Ross." The troops of Captain Harvie "did the like between Ross and Bantry." The troops of Sir Charles Wilmot entered without resistance an Irish camp, where "they found nothing but hurt and sick men, whose pains and lives by the soldiers were both determined." The Lord President, he himself assures us, having heard that the Munster fugitives were harboured in certain parts of that Province, diverted his forces thither, "burnt all the houses and corn, taking great preys, . . . and, harassing the country, killed all mankind that were found therein." From thence he went to other parts, where "he did the like, not leaving behind him man or beast, corn or cattle, except such as had been conveyed into castles." Long before the war had terminated, Elizabeth was assured that she had little left to reign over but ashes and carcases. It was boasted that in all the wide territory of Desmond not a town, castle, village, or farmhouse was unburnt; and a high English official writing in 1582, computed in six months, more than 30,000 people had been starved to death in Munster, besides those who were hung or who perished by the sword. Archbishop Ussher afterwards described how women were accustomed to lie in wait for a passing rider, and to rush out like famished wolves to kill and to devour his horse. The slaughter of women as well as of men, of unresisting peasants as well as of armed rebels, was openly avowed by the English commanders. The Irish annalists told, with horrible detail, how the bands of Pelham and Ormond "killed blind and feeble men, women, boys and girls, sick persons, idiots, and old people"; how in Desmond's country, even after all resistance had ceased, soldiers forced men and women into old barns which were set on fire, and if any attempted to escape they were shot or stabbed; how soldiers were seen "to take up infants on the point of their spears, and to whirl them about in their agony"; how women were found "hanging on trees with their children at their breasts, strangled with their mother's hair."

In Ulster the war was conducted in a similar spirit. An English historian, who was an eye-witness of the subjugation of the province, tells us that "Lord Mountjoy never received any to mercy but such as had drawn the blood of some of their fellow rebels." Thus "McMahon and McArtmoyle offered to submit, but neither could be received without the other's head." The country was steadily subdued by starvation. "No spectacle was more frequent in the ditches of towns, and especially in wasted countries, than to see multitudes of these poor people dead, with their mouths all coloured green by eating nettles, docks, and all things they could rend above ground." In the single county of Tyrone 3,000 persons in a few months were starved. On one occasion Sir Arthur Chichester, with some other English officers, saw three small children—the eldest not above ten years old—feeding off the flesh of their starved mother. In the neighbourhood of Newry, famine produced a new and appalling crime. It was discovered that some old women were accustomed, by lighting fires, to attract children, whom they murdered and devoured. At last, hunger and the sword accomplished their work; Tyrone bowed his head before the storm, and the English ascendency was supreme.

It needs, indeed, the widest stretch of historic charity—it needs the fullest realisation of the manner in which, in the sixteenth century, civilised men were accustomed to look upon races they regarded as inferior—to judge this history with equity or moderation. A faint gleam of light falls across the dark and lurid picture in the humanity of Sir John Perrot. There were, no doubt, occasional vacillations and occasional pauses in the massacre. A general pardon was proclaimed in Munster after the suppression of the Desmond rebellion, and through the whole island after that of Tyrone. The cruelties were certainly not all on one side, and it must not be forgotten that a large proportion of the soldiers in the service of England were Irish Catholics. But, on the whole, the direction and the power of England were everywhere in the ascendant, and her policy was a policy of extermination. It is easy to imagine what feelings it must have planted in the minds of the survivors, and what a tone of ferocity it must have given to the intercourse of the races. But, although the circumstances of these wars were recorded by a remarkable concurrence of contemporary annalists, it is probable that their memory would have soon perished had they not coincided with the adoption by the English Government of a new line of policy, vitally affecting the permanent interests of the nation. The devastation of Ireland in the closing years of Elizabeth was probably not at all more savage, and was certainly much less protracted, than that which Scotland underwent in the long succession of English invasions which began in 1296 under Edward I and continued at intervals through the whole of the fourteenth century. But in the first place, in this, as in most other respects, the calamities of Scotland terminated at a much earlier date than those of Ireland; and, in the next place, the English invasions were in the end unsuccessful, and did not permanently affect the internal government of the country. In Ireland the English ascendency brought with it two new and lasting consequences, the proscription of the Irish religion and the confiscation of the Irish soil.

It was a very unfortunate circumstance that the period when the English nation definitively adopted the principles of the Reformation should have nearly coincided with the events I have related; but at the same time religious zeal did not at first contribute at all essentially to the struggle. The Irish chiefs repeatedly showed great indifference to religious distinctions, and the English cared much more for the suppression of the Irish race than for the suppression of its religion. The Bible was not translated into Irish. All persons were ordered, indeed, under penalty of a small fine, to attend the Anglican service; but it was ordered that it should be celebrated only in English, or, if that language was not known, in Latin. The Mass became illegal; the churches and the church revenues were taken from the priests, but the benefices were filled with adventurers without religious zeal and sometimes without common morality. Very naturally, under such circumstances, the Irish continued in their old faith. None of the causes that had produced Protestantism in England existed among them. The new religion, as represented by a Carew or an Essex, was far from prepossessing to their eyes; and the possibility of Catholic alliances against England began to dawn upon some minds. . . .

But, on the whole, theological animosity is scarcely perceptible in this period of Irish history. The chief towns, though almost wholly Catholic, remained faithful to the English all through the Elizabethan wars; large numbers of Catholic Irish served under the English banner. There was little real religious persecution on the one side, and little real religious zeal on the other. At the same time the religious worship of the whole nation was proscribed by law, and although that law was in many districts little more than a dead letter, although it was nowhere rigorously and efficiently enforced, the apprehension of the extirpation of their religion hung as a new terror over the Irish people.

The other cause which was called into action, and which in this stage of Irish history was much more important, was the confiscation of Irish land. The great impulse which the discovery of the New World and the religious changes of the sixteenth century had imparted to the intellect and character of Europe, was shown in England in an exuberance of many-sided activity equalled in no previous portion of her history. It produced among other consequences an extraordinary growth of the spirit of adventure, a distaste for routine, an extreme desire to discover new and rapid paths to wealth. This spirit showed itself in the immense development of maritime enterprise both in the form of discovery and in the form of piracy, and still more strongly in the passion for Irish land. The idea that it was possible to obtain, at a few hours' or days' journey from the English coasts, and at little or no cost, great tracts of fertile territory, and to amass in a few years gigantic fortunes, took hold upon the English mind with a fascination much like that which was exercised by the fables of the exhaustless riches of India in the days of Clive and of Hastings. The Government warmly encouraged it. They believed that the one effectual policy for making Ireland useful to England was, in the words of Sir John Davies, "to root out the Irish" from the soil, to confiscate the property of the septs, and plant the country systematically with English tenants. There were chronic disturbances between the English Government and the Irish chiefs, who were in reality almost independent sovereigns, and these were made the pretexts for gigantic confiscations; and as the hunger for land became more intense, and the number of English adventurers increased, other methods were employed. A race of discoverers were called into existence who fabricated stories of plots, who scrutinised the titles of Irish chiefs with all the severity of English law, and who, before suborned or intimidated juries, and on the ground of technical flaws, obtained confiscations. Many Irish proprietors were executed on the most frivolous pretexts, and these methods of obtaining confiscations were so systematically and skilfully resorted to, that it soon became evident to chiefs and people that it was the settled policy of the English Government to deprive them of their land.

Burke, who had studied Irish history with much care, and whose passing remarks on it always bear to an eminent degree the traces of his great genius, has noticed in a very remarkable passage, how entirely its real clue, during the period between the accession of Elizabeth and the accomplishment of the Revolution, is to be found in this feature of the English policy. The wars of Elizabeth were not wars of nationality. The Irish clans had never been fused into a single nation; the country was much in the condition of Gaul before the conquests of Clovis, and wherever the clan system exists the national spirit is very faint and the devotion of the clansman is almost restricted to his clan. They were not wars of races. Desmond, who was of the purest Norman blood, was supported by his Irish followers with as much passionate devotion as O'Neill; and in the long catalogue of Irish crimes given by the English writers of the time, outrages against old English naturalised landlords find no place. They were not to any considerable extent wars of religion. Tyrone, indeed, made "liberty of conscience" one of his demands; but he was so far from being inspired by the spirit of a crusade against Protestantism that he had assisted the Government against Desmond, and would probably have never drawn the sword had he not perceived clearly that his estate was marked out for confiscation. The real motive that stirred the Irish population through the land was the conviction that they were to be driven from the soil. Under the clan system it may easily be conceived what passionate indignation must have been excited by the attempt to expel the old chiefs from their property, and to replace them by new owners who had no single object except to amass rapid fortunes, who had no single sympathy or interest in common with the natives. But this was not all. The Irish land customs of tanistry and gavelkind, as established by the Brehon laws, were still in full force among the Irish tribes. According to this system, the chief was not, like an English landlord, owner in fee of his land; he was elected, though only out of a single family, and the clan had a vested interest in the soil. The humblest clansman was a co-proprietor with his chief; he was subject, indeed, to many exactions in the form of tribute that were extremely burdensome and oppressive, but he could not be ejected, and he had large rights of inheritance of common land. His position was wholly different from, in some respects it was superior to, that of an English tenant. In the con-fiscations these rights were completely disregarded. It was assumed, in spite of immemorial usage, that the land was the absolute, hereditary property of the chiefs, and that no compensation was due to their tenants; and in this manner the confiscation of territory became a burning grievance to the humblest clansman.

If the object of the Government had been merely to replace the Irish land system by that of English law, such a measure might probably have been effected without exciting much lasting discontent. Great care would have indeed been needed in touching the complicated rights of chief and people, but there were on each side so many disabilities, restrictions, or burdens, that a composition might without any insuperable difficulty have been attained. A very remarkable measure of this kind was actually carried in 1585, by Sir John Perrot, one of the ablest and most honourable men who, in the sixteenth century, presided over Irish affairs. An arrangement was made with "the nobilitie spiritual and temporal, and all the chieftains and Lords," of Connaught, to free them from "all uncertaine cesse, cuttings, and spendings," and at the same time to convert them into English proprietors. They agreed to surrender their titles and to hold their estates by patents of the Crown, paying to the Crown certain stipulated rents, and discharging certain stipulated military duties. In addition to the freedom from capricious and irregular taxation which they thus purchased they obtained an hereditary possession of their estates, and titles which appeared perfect beyond dispute. The common land was to remain common, but was no longer to be divided. The tribes lost their old right of election, but paragraphs were inserted in many of the indentures not only confirming the "mean free-holders and tenants" in their possessions, but also freeing them from all their money and other obligations to their chiefs. They were placed directly under the Crown, and on payment to the Crown of 10*s.* for every quarter of land that bore "corn or horn," they were completely freed from rent and services to their former landlords, but this latter measure was not to come into effect until the death of the chiefs who were then living. The De Burgo's, who were prominent among the Connaught nobles, for a time resisted this arrangement by force, but they were soon compelled to yield; and the creation of a large peasant proprietary was prob-ably one cause of the comparative tranquillity of Connaught dur-ing many years.

But this composition of Connaught stands altogether apart from the ordinary policy of the Government. Their usual object was to obtain Irish land by confiscation and to plant it with En-glish tenants. The system was begun on a large scale in Leinster in the reign of Mary, when the immense territories belonging to the O'Mores, the O'Connors, and the O'Dempseys were confis-cated, planted with English colonies, and converted into two English counties. The names of the Queen's County and of the King's County, with their capitals Maryborough and Philipstown, are among the very few existing memorials of a reign which Englishmen would gladly forget. The confiscation, being carried out without any regard for the rights of the humbler members of the tribes, gave rise, as might have been expected, to a long and bloody guerilla warfare, between the new tenants and the old proprietors, which extended far into the reign of Elizabeth, and is especially famous in Irish memories for the treacherous murder by the new settlers of the Irish chiefs, who are said to have been invited with that object to a peaceful conference at Mullaghamast. In Munster, after Desmond's rebellion, more than 574,000 acres were confiscated and passed into English hands. One of the conditions of the grants was that none of the native Irish should be admitted among the tenantry of the new proprietors. It was intended to sweep those who had survived the war completely from the whole of this enormous territory, or at least to permit

them to remain only in the condition of day-labourers or ploughmen, with the alternative of flying to the mountains or the forests
to die by starvation, or to live as savages or as robbers.

Fortunately it is easier to issue such injunctions than to execute
them, and though the country was in a great degree planted from
England, not a few of the old inhabitants retained their hold upon
the soil. Accustomed to live in wretched poverty, they could pay
larger rents than the English; their local knowledge gave them
great advantages; they were unmolested by the numerous robbers
who had begun to swarm in the woods; and after the lapse of ten
years from the commencement of the Settlement, Spenser complained that the new proprietors, "instead of keeping out the
Irish, doe not only make the Irish their tenants in those lands and
thrust out the English, but also some of them become mere Irish."
The confiscations left behind them many "wood kerns," or, as
they were afterwards called, rapparees, who were active in agrarian outrage, and a vagrant, homeless, half-savage population of
beggars; but the "better sort" of the Irish were by no means entirely uncivilised. . . .

In the north, Tyrone, by a timely submission, succeeded in
saving his land; but soon after the accession of James I a decision
of the King's Bench, which had the force of law, pronounced the
whole system of tanistry and gavelkind, which had grown out of
the Brehon law, and which had hitherto been recognised in a
great part of the island, to be illegal; and thus, without a struggle
and without compensation, the proprietary rights of the natives
were swept away. Then followed the great plantation of Ulster.
Tyrone and Tyrconnel were accused of plots against the Government, whether falsely or truly is still disputed. There was no
rebellion, but the earls, either conscious of guilt, or, quite as probably, distrusting tribunals which were systematically and notoriously partial, took flight, and no less than six counties were confiscated, and planted with English and Scotch. The plantation
scheme was conducted with much ability, partly by the advice of
Bacon. The great depopulation of the country in the last war
rendered it comparatively easy, and Sir John Davies noticed that,
for the first time in the history of the confiscations, some attention
was paid to the interests of the natives, to whom a considerable
proportion of the confiscated land, selected arbitrarily by the

Government, was assigned. The proprietary rights, however, of the clans, in accordance with the recent decision, were entirely disregarded. Great numbers of the old proprietors, or head tenants, were driven from their land, and the large Presbyterian element now introduced into Ulster greatly increased the bitterness of theological animosity. The new colonists also, planted in the old Irish territory, though far surpassing the natives in industrial enterprise, were of a class very little fitted to raise the moral level of the province, to conciliate a people they despised, or to soften the shock of a great calamity. . . .

The aspect of Ireland, however, was at this time more encouraging than it had been for many years. In the social system, as in the physical body, the prostration of extreme illness is often followed, with a strange rapidity, by a sudden reflux of exuberant health. When a nation has been brought to the utmost extremities of anguish; when almost all the old, the sick, the feeble have been hurried to the grave; when the population has been suddenly and enormously reduced; when great masses of property have quickly changed hands; and when few except the most vigorous natures remain, it may reasonably be expected that the cessation of the calamity will be followed by a great outburst of prosperity. Such a rebound followed the Black Death, which in the fourteenth century swept away about a fourth part of the inhabitants of Europe; and a similar recovery, on a smaller scale, and due in part at least to the same cause, took place in Ireland after the Elizabethan and the Cromwellian wars, and after the great famine of the present century. Besides this, a new and energetic element was introduced into Irish life. English law was extended through the island. The Judges went their regular circuits, and it was hoped that the resentment produced by recent events would be compensated or allayed by the destruction of that clan system which had been the source of much disorder, by the abolition of the exactions of the Irish chiefs, and by the introduction of skilful husbandmen, and therefore of material prosperity, into a territory half of which lay absolutely waste, while the other half was only cultivated in the rudest manner. It was inevitable that the English and the Irish should look on the Plantation in very different ways. In the eyes of the latter it was a confiscation of the worst and most irritating description; for, whatever might have been the guilt of the banished earls, the clans, who, according to Irish notions, were the real owners of the soil, had given no provocation; and the measure, by breaking up their oldest and most cherished customs and traditions, by banishing their ancient chiefs, by tearing them from their old homes, and by planting among them new masters of another race, and of a hostile creed, excited an intensity of bitterness which no purely political measure could possibly have produced. In the eyes of the English the measure was essential, if Ulster was to be brought fully under the dominion of English law, and if its resources were to be developed; and the assignment of a large part of the land to native owners distinguished it broadly and favourably from similar acts in previous times. It met with no serious resistance. Even the jury system was at once introduced, and although it was at first found that the clansmen would give no verdicts against one another, jurymen were speedily intimidated into submission by fines or imprisonment. In a few years the progress was so great that Sir John Davies, the able Attorney-General of King James, pronounced the strings of the Irish harp to be all in tune, and he expressed both surprise and admiration at the absence of crime among the natives, and at their complete submission to the law. . . .

But yet it needed little knowledge of human nature to perceive that the country was in imminent danger of drifting steadily to a fearful catastrophe. The unspeakable horrors that accompanied the suppression of the Irish under Elizabeth, the enormous confiscations in three provinces, the abolition of the land customs most cherished by the people, the legal condemnation of their religion, the plantation among them of an alien and hostile population, ever anxious to root them from the soil—all these elements of bitterness, crowded into a few disastrous years of suffering, were now smouldering in deep resentment in the Irish mind. Mere political changes leave the great body of the community untouched, or touch them only feebly, indirectly or superficially; but changes which affect religious belief or the means and conditions of material subsistence are felt in their full intensity in the meanest hovel. Nothing in Irish history is more remarkable than the entire absence of outrage and violence that followed the Ulster Plantation, and for the present at least the people showed themselves eminently submissive, tractable, and amenable to the law.

But the only possible means of securing a permanence of peace was by convincing them that justice would be administered with impartial firmness, and that for the future at least, under the shadow of English rule, their property and their religion, the fruits of their industry, and the worship of their God, would be scrupulously respected. Had such a spirit animated the Government of Ireland, all might yet have been well. But the greed for Irish land which had now become the dominating passion of English adventurers was still unsated, and during the whole of the reign of James a perpetual effort was made to deprive the Irish of the residue which remained to them. The concessions intended in the plantation scheme were most imperfectly carried out. "The commissioners," writes a temperate Protestant historian, "appointed to distribute the lands scandalously abused their trusts, and by fraud or violence deprived the natives of the possessions the king had reserved for them." In the small county of Longford, twenty-five members of one sept were all deprived of their estates, without the least compensation, or any means of subsistence assigned to them. All over Ireland the trade of the Discoverer now rose into prominence. Under pretence of improving the King's revenue, these persons received commissions of inquiry into defective titles, and obtained confiscations, and grants at small rents for themselves. In a country which had but just emerged from barbarism, where English law had but recently become supreme, where most possession rested chiefly on immemorial custom, and where constant civil wars, many forfeitures, and a great and recent change in the tenure of land had all tended to confuse titles, it was totally impossible that the majority of the proprietors could satisfy the conditions that were required of them, and the proceedings in the law courts were soon an infamous mockery of justice. . . .

It is not surprising under these circumstances, that on the accession of Charles I a feverish and ominous restlessness should have pervaded Irish life. The army was increased. Religious animosities became much more apparent than before. The security of property was shaken to the very foundation. The native proprietors began to feel themselves doomed to certain and speedy destruction. Universal distrust of English law had grown up, and the murmurs of discontent, like the first moanings of a coming storm, might be plainly heard. One more effort was made by the Irish gentry to persuade, or rather to bribe, the Government to allow them to remain undisturbed in the possession of their property. They offered to raise by voluntary assessment the large sum of 120,000*l.*, in three annual instalments of 40,000*l.*, on condition of obtaining certain Graces from the King. These Graces, the Irish analogue of the Petition of Rights, were of the most moderate and equitable description. The most important were that undisturbed possession of sixty years should secure a landed proprietor from all older claims on the part of the Crown, that the inhabitants of Connaught should be secured from litigation by the enrolment of their patents, and that Popish recusants should be permitted, without taking the Oath of Supremacy, to sue for livery of their estates in the Court of Arches, and to practise in the courts of law. The terms were accepted. The promise of the King was given. The Graces were transmitted by way of instruction to the Lord Deputy and Council, and the Government also engaged, as a further security to all proprietors, that their estates should be formally confirmed to them and to their heirs by the next Parliament which should be held in Ireland.

The sequel forms one of the most shameful passages in the history of English government of Ireland. In distinct violation of the King's solemn promise, after the subsidies that were made on the faith of that promise had been duly obtained, without provocation or pretext or excuse, Wentworth, who now presided with stern despotism over the government of Ireland, announced the withdrawal of the two principal articles of the Graces, the limitation of Crown claims by a possession of sixty years and the legalisation of the Connaught titles. The object of this great and wicked man was to establish a despotism in Ireland as a step towards a despotism in England. If the King could command without control a powerful army and a large revenue in Ireland, he would have made a great stride towards emancipating himself from the Parliament of England. The Irish Parliament was no serious obstacle. It was too dependent, too intimidated, and a great ruler might safely defy it. "I can now say," wrote Wentworth, "that the King is as absolute here as any prince in the whole world can be." It was necessary, however, to the scheme to increase to the utmost the King's revenue and to neglect no source from which it might be replenished. With this object Wentworth developed with great and commendable energy the material resources of the country, and, though he discouraged the woollen trade in the interests of English manufacturers, he was the real founder of the linen manufacture. With this object the London companies to whom the County of Londonderry had been granted were prosecuted before the Star Chamber for not having strictly fulfilled the terms of their charter, and were condemned to the payment of no less than 70,000*l.* With this object Wentworth induced the King to maintain his ancient claims, and he resolved, at once and on a large scale, to prosecute the plantation of Connaught. The means employed were hardly less infamous than the design. Inquisitions were made in every county in Connaught. In order to preserve the show of justice, juries were summoned, and were peremptorily ordered to bring in verdicts vesting all titles in the King. Every means was taken to insure compliance. Men such "as might give furtherance in finding a title for the King" were carefully selected, and a grant of 4*s.* in the pound was given to the Lord Chief Justice and the Lord Chief Baron out of the first yearly rent raised upon the commissions of defective titles, "which money," the Deputy somewhat cynically adds, "I find to be the best that was ever given. For now they do intend it with a care and diligence such as it were their own private; and most certainly the gaining to themselves every 4*s.* once paid, shall better your revenue ever after at least 5*l.*" The sheriffs and the Judges were the creatures of the Government, and Wentworth was present to overcome all opposition. The juries were assured that the project was for the advantage of the King and of the country, that if they presumed to give unfavourable verdicts those verdicts would be set aside, and that "they might answer the King a round fine in the Castle Chamber in case they should prevaricate." In county after county terrified juries brought in the verdict that was required. In Galway alone the jury refused to do so, and the enraged Deputy at once imposed a fine of 1,000*l.* on the sheriff who had summoned them, and bound the recalcitrant jurors to appear in the Castle Chamber, where they were each sentenced to pay the enormous fine of 4,000*l.* and to lie in prison till it was paid.

The titles of Connaught now lay at the feet of the Deputy, but at the last moment the scheme of plantation was deferred. It was plain that it would produce a rebellion in Ireland; and as the conflict between the King and the English Parliament was now rapidly moving to its crisis, it was thought advisable to postpone the change till a quieter time. From this date, however, the great insurrection had become inevitable. The policy of Wentworth was fully approved by his sovereign; he was made Earl of Strafford, and he soon after passed to England to encounter a dark and a terrible fate; but he left behind him in Ireland rage, and anguish, and despair. It had become clear beyond all doubt to the native population that the old scheme of "rooting them out" from the soil was the settled policy of the Government; that the land which remained to them was marked as a prey by hungry adventurers, by the refuse of the population of England and Scotland, by men who cared not more for their rights or happiness than they did for the rights and happiness of the worms which were severed by their spades. It had become clear to them that no loyalty, no submission, no concession on the part of the people, and no promises or engagements on the part of the Government, would be of any avail to avert the doom which, withdrawn for a time but ever imminent, now hung in perpetual menace over the native race.

There was but one thing which they valued more than their land, and that also was in peril. By the legislation of Elizabeth the Act of Uniformity was established in Ireland; all religious worship except the Anglican was made illegal; all persons who were absent from church without sufficient excuse were liable for each Sunday to a fine of 1s., and all ecclesiastics and other officials were bound under severe penalties to take the Oath of Supremacy. It is clear, however, that this legislation neither was nor could have been enforced. The churches over a great part of the island were in ruins. Protestant ministers were very few. The overwhelming majority of the population within the old Pale, and nearly the whole population beyond its borders, remained attached to the Catholic faith. Law was everywhere very feeble, and the Government was actuated much more by secular than by theological motives. In the towns and the more civilised districts, the churches and their revenues were taken from the Catholics, and in a very few cases the fines stipulated by law were imposed; but even the disqualification for civil offices was by no means generally enforced. In the troubles of this reign five Irish Catholic bishops perished either by execution or by the violence of soldiers, and the Catholic primate died a prisoner in the Tower of London; but in most, if not all, of these cases, political motives were probably at the root of the severity. The Mass, when it was driven from the churches, appears to have been celebrated without molestation in private houses; and it is probable that in a large part of the island the change in the legal religion was hardly perceived.

But on the accession of James I, religious antagonism on both sides became more apparent. Foreign ecclesiastics were fanning the devotion of the people, and their hopes on the accession of the new sovereign speedily rose. In Cork, Waterford, Cashel, Clonmel, and Limerick, the townspeople, with the support or connivance of the magistrates, violently took possession of the churches, ejected the reformed ministers, celebrated the Mass, and erected crosses. It was found necessary to march troops into Munster. At Cork there was some slight opposition; a few lives were lost, and a few executions followed. . . .

Meanwhile, from another quarter, new and terrible dangers were approaching. The Puritan party, inspired by the fiercest fanaticism against Popery, were rising rapidly into power. The Scotch rebellion had the double effect of furnishing the Irish Catholics with an example of a nation taking up arms to establish its religion, and of adding to the growing panic by placing at the head of Scotch affairs those who had sworn the National Covenant against Popery, and from whom the Papists could look for nothing but extirpation. It was rumoured through Ireland that the covenanted army had threatened never to lay down arms till uniformity of religion was established through the whole kingdom; and a letter from Scotland was intercepted, stating that a covenanted army under General Lesly would soon come over to extirpate Catholicism in Ulster. In the English Parliament, one of the first and most vehement objects of the Puritan party was to put an end to all toleration of Popery. By an address from the House of Commons, all Roman Catholic officers were driven from the army. An application was made to the King to enforce the confiscation of two-thirds of the lands of the recusants, as well as the savage law which in England doomed all Catholic priests to the gallows. Some of them were arrested, but reprieved by the King, and this reprieve was made a prominent grievance by the Parliament. Reports of the most alarming character, some of them false or exaggerated, flew rapidly among the Irish Catholics. It was said that Sir John Clotworthy had declared in Parliament that the conversion of the Irish Papists could only be effected with the Bible in one hand and the sword in the other; that Pym had boasted that the Parliament would not leave one priest in Ireland; that Sir William Parsons predicted at a public banquet that within a twelvemonth not a Catholic would be seen in Ireland. Petitions were presented by the Irish Presbyterians to the English Parliament praying for the extirpation of prelacy and Popery in Ireland. It was believed with much reason, that there was a fixed design among the Puritan party, who were now becoming supreme, to suppress absolutely the Catholic worship in Ireland, and to "the publishing of this design" Ormond ascribed the great extension of the rebellion which now broke out.

The rebellion was not, however, due to any single cause, but represented the accumulated wrongs and animosities of two generations. The influence of the ejected proprietors, who were wandering impoverished among the people, or who returned from military service in Spain; the rage of the septs, who had been deprived of their proprietary rights and outraged in their most cherished customs; the animosity which very naturally had grown up between the native population and the alien colonists planted in their old dominions; the new fanaticism which was rising under the preaching of priests and friars; all the long train of agrarian wrongs, from the massacre of Mullaghamast to the latest inquisitions of Wentworth; all the long succession of religious wrongs, from the Act of Uniformity of Elizabeth to the confiscation of the Irish College under Charles—all these things, together with the opportunity caused by the difficulties of England, contributed to the result. Behind the people lay the maddening recollections of the wars of Elizabeth, when their parents had been starved by thousands to death, when unresisting peasants, when women, when children, had been deliberately massacred, and when no quarter had been given to the prisoners. Before them lay the gloomy and almost certain prospect of banishment from the land which remained to them, of the extirpation of the religion which was fast becoming the passion as well as the consolation of their lives, of the sentence of death directed against any priest who dared to pray beside their bed of death. To the most sober and unimpassioned judgment, these fears were reasonable; but the Irish were at this time as far as possible from sober and unimpassioned. The air was hot, feverish, charged with rumours. In this case there was no safety in quiet, and there was no power on which they could rely. The royal authority was manifestly tottering. Sir William Parsons, the most active of the Lords Justices, leaned strongly towards the Parliament; he was one of the most unprincipled and rapacious of the land-jobbers who had, during the last generation, been the curse of Ireland. He had been chief agent in the scandalous proceedings against the O'Byrnes, and if we may believe the account of Carte, who has described this period with far greater means of information than any other historian, Parsons ardently desired and purposely stimulated rebellion in order to reap a new crop of confiscations. Week after week, as the attitude of the English Parliament became more hostile, the panic in Ireland spread and deepened; and as the shadow of approaching calamity fell darkly over the imaginations of the people, strange stories of supernatural portents were readily believed. It was said that a sword bathed in blood had been seen suspended in the air, that a Spirit Form which had appeared before the great troubles of Tyrone was again stalking abroad, brandishing her mighty spear over the devoted land.

I can only give the briefest sketch of the confused and horrible years that followed. The great Irish rebellion broke out in Ulster on the night of October 22, 1641. It had been noticed before, that a large concourse of strangers from distant parts of the kingdom had been thronging to Dublin, and on the evening before the outbreak in the North, the Lords Justices received intelligence, of undoubted weight, of a conspiracy to surprise Dublin Castle. Every precaution was taken to protect it, and for six weeks after the insurrection broke out in Ulster almost the whole of the other three provinces remained passive. On November 12, indeed, a furious popular and agrarian rising broke out in Wicklow in the territory of the O'Byrnes—who had been, as we have seen, so recently and so flagitiously robbed of their property—and all the English were plundered and expelled from the land which had been confiscated; but the Catholic gentry of Munster and Connaught stood firm to their allegiance, and although predatory bands appeared in a few parts of Leinster the general defection of the Pale did not take place till the beginning of December. Although there is no doubt that a few Leinster gentlemen were connected with the plot from the beginning, it is almost certain that the great body were at first completely loyal and were only driven into the rebellion most reluctantly. Carte has strongly maintained, and Leland fully supports his view, that the policy of the Lords Justices was directly responsible for their defection. It is certain that the Lords Justices, representing a powerful party in England, were keenly desirous of obtaining as large forfeitures as possible, and their policy was eminently fitted to drive the Catholic gentry to despair. They began by recalling the arms which they had entrusted to the nobles and inhabitants of the Pale. They then, at a time when the Wicklow rebellion and the multiplication of robbers made the position of unarmed men peculiarly dangerous in the country districts, issued a proclamation ordering all persons who were not ordinary inhabitants of Dublin to leave the city within twenty-four hours, and forbidding them to approach within two miles of it. By this measure the inhabitants of the neighbouring districts were forced into perpetual intercourse with the rebels, compelled to support them by contributions, and thus brought at once into the meshes of the law. The English Parliament recommended the offer of a pardon to such rebels as submitted, but the Lords Justices in their proclamation excluded Ulster, which was the chief seat of the rebellion, confined their offers to Longford, Louth, Meath, and Westmeath, which had been slightly disturbed, and clogged them by such restrictions as made them almost nugatory. Above all, they prorogued the Irish Parliament, contrary to the strong remonstrances both of Ormond and of the Catholic gentry, at a time when its continuance was of vital importance to the country. It contained a large proportion of those who were subsequently leaders of the rebellion, but it showed itself strongly and unequivocally loyal; and at a time when the Puritan party were rising into the ascendant, and when there was a great and manifest disposition to involve as many landed proprietors as possible in the guilt of the rebellion, the Catholic gentry regarded this Parliament as their one means of attesting their loyalty beyond dispute, and protecting in some degree their properties and their religion.

Whether these measures were really taken with the intention that has been alleged, or whether they were merely measures of precaution, has been much contested; and the question is, perhaps, not susceptible of any positive solution. One fact, however, concerning the defection of the Pale is not questionable. It is, that the rebellion only assumed its general character in consequence of the resolution of the English House of Commons which determined, in the beginning of December, that no toleration should be henceforth granted to the Catholic religion in Ireland. It was this policy, announced by the Parliament of England, that drove the Catholic gentry of Ireland very reluctantly into rebellion. In Wicklow, it is true, and in the adjoining county of Wexford, the rebellion, as I have said, assumed an agrarian character; and in many different parts of the country bands of simple robbers were soon called into existence. But in general the rebellion out of Ulster was a defensive religious war entered into for the purpose of securing a toleration, and ultimately an establishment, of the religion of the Irish people. Some of the Catholic gentry, and especially Lord Clanricarde, exhibited in this trying period a loyalty that could not be surpassed; and during all the tangled years of civil war that followed, the Catholic party showed themselves quite ready to be reconciled to the Government if they could only have obtained a security for their religion and their estates. In Ulster, however, the rebellion assumed a wholly distinct character, and was speedily disgraced by crimes which, though they have been grossly, absurdly, and mendaciously exaggerated, were both numerous and horrible. Hardly any page of history has been more misrepresented than that which we are now describing, and it is extremely difficult to distinguish truth from fiction; but without entering into very minute details it will be possible, I think, to establish a few plain facts which enable us to discern clearly the main outline of the events.

It has been asserted by numerous writers, and is still frequently believed, that the Ulster rebellion began with a general and indiscriminate massacre of the Protestants, who were living without suspicion among the Catholics, resembling the massacre of the

Danes by the English, the massacre of the French in the Sicilian Vespers, or the massacre of the Huguenots at St. Bartholomew. Clarendon has asserted that "there were 40,000 or 50,000 of the English Protestants murdered before they suspected themselves to be in any danger, or could provide for their defence;" and other writers have estimated the victims within the first two months of the rebellion at 150,000, at 200,000, and even at 300,000. It may be boldly asserted that this statement of a sudden surprise, immediately followed by a general and organised massacre, is utterly and absolutely untrue. As is almost always the case in a great popular rising, there were, in the first outbreak of the rebellion, some murders, but they were very few; and there was at this time nothing whatever of the nature of a massacre. . . .

*The rebellion broke out in the more recently confiscated counties of Ulster, and the rebels at first attacked only English, rather than the more numerous Scottish, settlers. No general massacre of Protestants took place, but murder, pillage, atrocities, and reprisals were widespread. Estimates of those killed ranged from four to twelve thousand.*

Two things only can be confidently affirmed. The one is that it is absolutely untrue that the rebellion of 1641 broke out with a general massacre. The other is that in the first months of the struggle many, and often unspeakably savage, murders were committed by the Irish, in those portions of the north and centre of Ireland in which the great confiscations had recently taken place.

These facts, as we have seen, are abundantly attested by other evidence. The number of the victims, however, though very great, has been enormously exaggerated; the worst crimes were committed by freebooters or mobs, and it is far from clear upon which side the balance of cruelty rests. "The truth is," as Warner truly says, "the soldiers and common people were very savage on both sides"; and nothing can be more disingenuous than to elaborate in ghastly pictures the crimes that were committed on one side while concealing those that were committed on the other. From the very beginning the English Parliament did the utmost in its power to give the contest the character of a war of extermination. One of its first acts was to vote that no toleration of the Romish religion should be henceforth permitted in Ireland, and it thus at once extended the range of the rebellion and gave it the character of a war of religion. In the following February, when but few men of any considerable estate were engaged in the rebellion, the Parliament enacted that 2,500,000 acres of profitable land in Ireland, besides bogs, woods, and barren mountains, should be assigned to English adventurers in consideration of small sums of money which they raised for the subjugation of Ireland. It thus gave the war a desperate agrarian character, furnished immense numbers of persons in England with the strongest motive to oppose any reconciliation with the Irish, and convinced the whole body of the Irish proprietary that their land was marked out for confiscation. In order that the King's prerogative of pardon might not interfere with the design of a general confiscation, the King was first petitioned not to alienate any of the lands which might be escheated in consequence of the rebellion, and a clause was afterwards introduced into the Act raising the loan by which all grants of rebel lands made by the Crown and all pardons granted to the rebels before attainder and without the assent of both Houses were declared null and void. The Irish Parliament, which was the only organ by which the Irish gentry could express their loyalty to the sovereign in a way that could not be misrepresented or denied, was prorogued. Not content with denouncing vengeance against murderers or even against districts where murders were committed, the Parliaments, both in England and Scotland, passed ordinances in 1644 that no quarter should be given to Irish who came to England to the King's aid. These ordinances were rigidly executed, and great numbers of Irish soldiers being taken prisoners in Scotland were deliberately butchered in the field or in the prisons. Irishmen taken at sea were tied back to back and thrown into the waves. In one day eighty women and children in Scotland were flung over a high bridge into the water, solely because they were the wives and children of Irish soldiers.

If this was the spirit in which the war was conducted in Great Britain, it may easily be conceived how it was conducted in Ireland. In Leinster, where assuredly no massacre had been committed, the orders issued to the soldiers were not only "to kill and destroy rebels and their adherents and relievers, but to burn, waste, consume, and demolish all the places, towns, and houses where they had been relieved and harboured, with all the corn and hay therein; and also to kill and destroy all the men there inhabiting capable to bear arms." But, horrible as were these instructions, they but faintly foreshadowed the manner in which the war was actually conducted. I shall not attempt to go through the long catalogue of horrors that have been too often paraded; it is sufficient to say that the soldiers of Sir Charles Coote, of St. Leger, of Sir Frederick Hamilton, and of others, rivalled the worst crimes that were perpetrated in the days of Carew and of Mountjoy. "The soldiers," says Carte, "in executing the orders of the justices, murdered all persons promiscuously, not sparing (as they themselves tell the Commissioners for Irish Affairs in the letter of June 7, 1642) the women, and sometimes not children." Whole villages as well as the houses of the gentry were remorselessly burnt even when not an enemy was seen. In Wicklow, in the words of Leland, Coote committed "such unprovoked, such ruthless and indiscriminate carnage in the town, as rivalled the utmost extravagance of the Northerns." The saying, "Nits will make lice," which was constantly employed to justify the murder of Irish children, then came into use. "Sir William Parsons," writes Sir Maurice Eustace to Ormond at a later stage of the rebellion, "has, by late letters, advised the Governor to the burning of corn, and to put man, woman, and child to the sword; and Sir Arthur Loftus hath written in the same strain." The Catholic nobles of the Pale, when they at length took arms, solemnly accused the English soldiers of "the inhuman murdering of old decrepit people in their beds, women in the straw, and children of eight days old; burning of houses, and robbing of all kinds of persons without distinction of friend or foe." In order to discover evidence or to extort confessions, many of the leading Catholic gentry were, by order of the Lords Justices, tortured upon the rack. Lord Castlehaven accuses the men in power in Ireland of having "by cruel massacring, hanging, and torturing, been the slaughter of thousands of innocent men, women, and children, better subjects than themselves," and he states that orders were issued "to the parties sent into every quarter to spare neither man, woman, nor child." . . .

*In Ulster the rebellion was triggered by rumors that the Puritan Parliament had resolved to extirpate Catholicism in Ireland.*

*Underlying the fear of religious persecution was a deep resent-*
*ment at the confiscation of Irish land by English and Scottish*
*settlers and speculators. Government forces suppressed the rebel-*
*lion with a severity that left a bitter legacy.*

I have dwelt at some length upon these aspects of the rebellion,
for they have been grossly and malignantly misrepresented, and
they have an important bearing on later Irish history. It is not
necessary to follow with the same minuteness the sequel of the
history. The picture, indeed, is a strangely confused one, the lines
of division of Irish and English, of Catholic and Protestant, of
Royalist and Republican, crossing and intermingling. In the
North the rebellion was chiefly an agrarian war and a war of race.
The confederation of the Catholic rebels in the other provinces
comprised a large proportion of the English families of the Pale,
and they drew the sword for the purpose of defending their
religion from the destruction with which it was threatened and
obtaining for it a full legal recognition. Though actually in arms
against the Government, they disclaimed from the first the title
of rebels, asserted their allegiance to the King, and were quite
ready to be reconciled with him if they could only secure their
religion and their estates. A third party, headed by Ormond and
Clanricarde, remained firm through every temptation in their
allegiance to the King, and before long a new and terrible party
representing the Puritan Parliament rose to the ascendant.

In spite of the vehement efforts of the Lords Justices, of
Temple, and of the other members of the Puritan party, a truce
was signed between the King and the confederate Catholics in
September 1643, but the complete reconciliation of the great body
of the Irish and of the Loyalists was long delayed by the arrogant
pretensions and the most disastrous influence of Rinuccini, the
Papal Envoy, and was only effected by successive stages in 1646,
1648, and 1649. But rebel and royalist sank alike under the sword
of Cromwell. It should always be remembered to his honour that
one of his first acts on going to Ireland was to prohibit the plun-
derings and other outrages the soldiers had been accustomed to
practise, and that he established a severe discipline in his army.
The sieges of Drogheda and Wexford, however, and the massacres that accompanied them, deserve to rank in horror with the
most atrocious exploits of Tilly or Wallenstein, and they made

the name of Cromwell eternally hated in Ireland. At Drogheda there had been no pretence of a massacre, and a large proportion of the garrison were English. According to Carte the officers of Cromwell's army promised quarter to such as would lay down their arms; but when they had done so, and the place was in their power, Cromwell gave orders that no quarter should be given. Ormond wrote that "the cruelties exercised there for five days after the town was taken would make as many several pictures of inhumanity as are to be found in the 'Book of Martyrs,' or in the relation of Amboyna." This description comes from an enemy, and, though it has never been refuted, it may perhaps be exaggerated. In the letters of Cromwell we have a curious picture of the semi-religious spirit which was manifested or at least professed by the victors. It is noticed as a special instance of Divine Providence that the Catholics having on the Previous Sunday celebrated Mass in the great church of St. Peter, "in this very place near 1,000 of them were put to the sword, fleeing thither for safety," and he adds that "all their friars were knocked on the head promiscuously but two," who were taken prisoners and killed. "And now," he continues, "give me leave to say how it comes to pass that this work is wrought. It was set upon some of our hearts that a great thing should be done, not by power or might, but by the Spirit of God. And is it not so clearly? That which caused your men to storm so courageously, it was the Spirit of God, which gave your men courage and took it away again, and therefore it is good that God alone have all the glory." "I wish that all honest hearts may give the glory of this to God alone, to whom indeed the praise of this mercy belongs." Among the English soldiers who were present at this siege was the brother of Anthony Wood, the well-known historian of Oxford, and the vivid and most authentic glimpse of this episode of Puritan warfare which that accurate and painstaking writer has given us in his autobiography, furnishes the best commentary on the language of Cromwell. He relates how his brother "would tell them of the most terrible assaulting and storming of Tredagh, where he himself had been engaged. He told them that 3,000 at least, besides some women and children, were, after the assailants had taken part and afterwards all the town, put to the sword on September 11 and 12, 1649, at which time Sir Arthur Aston, the governor, had his brains beat out and his body hacked to pieces. He told them that when they were to make their way up to the lofts and galleries of the church and up to the tower where the enemy had fled, each of the assailants would take up a child and use it as a buckler of defence when they ascended the steps, to keep themselves from being shot or brained. After they had killed all in the church, they went into the vaults underneath, where all the flower and choicest of the women and ladies had hid themselves. One of these, a most handsome virgin arraid in costly and gorgeous apparel, kneeled down to Thomas Wood with tears and prayers to save her life, and being stricken with a profound pitie, he took her under his arm, went with her out of the church with intentions to put her over the works to shift for herself, but a soldier perceiving his intentions he ran his sword through her . . . whereupon Mr. Wood, seeing her gasping, took away her money, jewels, &c., and flung her down over the works.''

It is possible, as its latest eulogist has argued, that this massacre may have had some effect in accelerating a submission which in the exhausted state of Ireland could in no case have been long delayed, but it left behind it one of those memories that are the most fatal obstacles to the reconciliation of nations and of creeds. The name of Cromwell even now acts as a spell upon the Irish mind, and has a powerful and living influence in sustaining the hatred both of England and Protestantism. The massacre of Drogheda acquired a deeper horror and a special significance from the saintly professions and the religious phraseology of its perpetrators, and the town where it took place is to the present day distinguished in Ireland for the vehemence of its Catholicism.

The war ended at last in 1652. According to the calculation of Sir W. Petty, out of a population of 1,466,000, 616,000 had in eleven years perished by the sword, by plague, or by famine artificially produced. 504,000, according to this estimate, were Irish, 112,000 of English extraction. A third part of the population had been thus blotted out, and Petty tells us that according to some calculations the number of the victims was much greater. Human food had been so successfully destroyed that Ireland, which had been one of the great pasture countries of Europe, was obliged to import cattle from Wales for consumption in Dublin. The stock, which at the beginning of the war was valued at four millions, had sunk to an eighth of that value, while the price of corn had risen from 12*s.* to 50*s.* a bushel. Famine and the sword had so done their work that in some districts the traveller rode twenty or thirty miles without seeing one trace of human life, and fierce wolves—rendered doubly savage by feeding on human flesh—multiplied with startling rapidity through the deserted land, and might be seen prowling in numbers within a few miles of Dublin. Liberty was given to able-bodied men to abandon the country and enlist in foreign service, and from 30,000 to 40,000 availed themselves of the permission. Slave-dealers were let loose upon the land, and many hundreds of boys and of marriageable girls, guilty of no offence whatever, were torn away from their country, shipped to Barbadoes, and sold as slaves to the planters. Merchants from Bristol entered keenly into the traffic. The victims appear to have been for the most part the children or the young widows of those who were killed or starved, but the dealers began at length to decoy even Englishmen to their ships, and the abuses became such that the Puritan Government, which had for some time cordially supported the system, made vain efforts to stop it. How many of the unhappy captives became the prey of the sharks, how many became the victims of the planters' lusts, it is impossible to say. The worship which was that of almost the whole native population was absolutely suppressed. Priests continued, it is true, with an admirable courage, to move disguised among the mud cottages of the poor and to hold up the crucifix before their dying eyes, but a large reward was offered for their apprehension, and those who were taken were usually transported to Barbadoes or confined in one of the Arran Isles. Above all, the great end at which the English adventurers had been steadily aiming since the reign of Elizabeth, was accomplished. All or almost all the land of the Irish in the three largest and richest provinces was confiscated, and divided among those adventurers who had lent money to the Parliament, and among the Puritan soldiers, whose pay was greatly in arrear. The Irish who were considered least guilty were assigned land in Connaught, and that province, which rock and morass have doomed to a perpetual poverty, and which was at this time almost desolated by famine and by massacre, was assigned as the home of the Irish race. The confiscations were arranged under different categories; but they were of such a nature that scarcely any Catholic or even old Protestant landlord could escape. All persons who had taken part in the rebellion before November 10, 1642, all who had before that date assisted the rebels with food or in any other way, and also about one hundred specified persons, including Ormond, Bishop Bramhall, and a great part of the aristocracy of Ireland, were condemned to death and to the absolute forfeiture of their estates. All other landowners who had at any period borne arms against the Parliament, either for the rebels or for the King, were to be deprived of their estates, but were promised land of a third of the value in Connaught. If, however, they had held a higher rank than major, they were to be banished from Ireland. Papists who during the whole of the long war had never borne arms against the Parliament, but who had not manifested a "constant good affection" towards it, were to be deprived of their estates, but were to receive two-thirds of the value in Connaught. Under this head were included all who lived quietly in their houses in quarters occupied by the rebels or by the King's troops, who had paid taxes to the rebels or to the King after his rupture with the Parliament, who had abstained from actively supporting the cause of the Parliament. Such a confiscation was practically universal. The ploughmen and labourers who were necessary for the cultivation of the soil were suffered to remain, but all the old proprietors, all the best and greatest names in Ireland were compelled to abandon their old possessions, to seek a home in Connaught, or in some happier land beyond the sea. A very large proportion of them had committed no crime whatever, and it is probable that not a sword would have been drawn in Ireland in rebellion if those who ruled it had suffered the natives to enjoy their lands and their religion in peace.

The Cromwellian Settlement is the foundation of that deep and lasting division between the proprietary and the tenants which is the chief cause of the political and social evils of Ireland. At the Restoration, it is true, the hearts of the Irish beat fast and high. Many had never rebelled against the sovereign; and of those who had taken arms, when the English Parliament announced its intention of extirpating Catholicism, by far the greater part had submitted to the King in 1648, had received his full pardon, and had supported his cause to the end. Those who had committed murders or other inhuman crimes were to be tried by a commission appointed jointly by the contracting parties, but it had been expressly provided, in the treaty, that all other Roman Catholics who submitted to the articles should be "restored to their respective possessions and hereditaments," and that all treasons and other offences committed since the beginning of the rebellion should be covered by an "Act of Oblivion." The Catholics had thus a clear title to restoration, and Charles II, in a letter from Breda, in the beginning of 1650, emphatically stated his intention to observe the engagement of his father. But the land was for the most part actually in the possession of English settlers, who had obtained it under a parliamentary security, in consequence of the sums they had lent in the beginning of the rebellion, and the Act which raised this money had been sanctioned by the Sovereign. Much of it had also been given to soldiers instead of pay, and their claims could hardly be overlooked. . . .

*Upon his restoration in 1660, King Charles II confirmed the Protestant Adventurers in the lands they held as of 7 May 1659. Government commissioners adjudicated thousands of conflicting claims for Irish land. Divided among themselves, proscribed as Catholics, and suspected as potential or actual rebels, the Irish people had to submit to the expropriation clauses of the Acts of Settlement and Explanation.*

The Irish were accordingly sacrificed with little reluctance. The negotiations that followed were long and tedious, and it will be sufficient here to relate the general result. All attempts to carry out in their integrity the articles of the Peace of 1648, by which the confederate Irish had been reconciled to the King, were completely abandoned, but a Court of English Commissioners was appointed to hear the claims of innocent Papists. 4,000 Irish Catholics demanded restitution as "innocents." About 600 claims were heard, and, to the great indignation of the Protestant party, in the large majority of cases, the Catholics established their claims. The Commissioners, who could have no possible bias in favour of the Irish, appear to have acted with great justice. Those who had the strongest claims were naturally the most eager to be tried. The lapse of time and the confusion of affairs destroyed many proofs of guilt, and it is probable that false testimony was on both sides largely employed. The anger and panic of the English knew no bounds. It was alleged that there would be no sufficient funds to reprise the Protestant adventurers who were removed. Parliament was loud in its complaints. A formidable plot was discovered. There was much fear of a great Protestant insurrection in Ireland, and English public opinion was very hostile to all concessions to Catholics. A new Bill of Settlement, or, as it was termed, of explanation, was accordingly brought in and passed. It provided that the adventurers and soldiers should give up one-third of their grants to be applied to the purpose of increasing the fund for reprisals; that the Connaught purchasers should retain two-thirds of the lands they possessed in September 1663; that in all cases of competition between the Protestants and the Roman Catholics every ambiguity should be interpreted in favour of the former; that twenty more of the Irish should be restored by special favour, but that all the other Catholics whose claims had hitherto, for want of time, not been decided by the Commissioners, should be treated as disqualified. Upwards of 3,000 old proprietors were thus, without a trial, excluded for ever from the inheritance of their fathers. The estimates of the change that was effected are somewhat various. Walsh, with a great and manifest exaggeration, stated that, before the rebellion, nineteen parts in twenty of the lands of the kingdom were still in the possession of Catholics. Colonel Lawrence, a Cromwellian soldier in Ireland, who wrote an account of this time, computed that the Irish had owned ten acres to one that was possessed by the English. According to Petty, of that portion of Ireland which was good ground capable of cultivation, about two-thirds, before 1641, had been possessed by Catholics. After the Act of Settlement, the Protestants possessed, according to the estimate of Lawrence, four-fifths of the whole kingdom; according to that of Petty, rather more than two-thirds of the good land. Of the Protestant landowners in 1689, two-thirds, according to Archbishop King, held their estates under the Act of Settlement.

The downfall of the old race was now all but accomplished. The years that followed the Restoration, however, were years of peace, of mild government, and of great religious toleration, and although the wrong done by the Act of Settlement rankled bitterly in the minds of the Irish, the prosperity of the country gradually revived, and with it some spirit of loyalty to the Government. But the Revolution soon came to cloud the prospect. It was inevitable that in that struggle the Irish should have adopted the cause of their hereditary sovereign, whose too ardent Catholicism was the chief cause of his deposition. It was equally inevitable that they should have availed themselves of the period of their ascendency to endeavour to overthrow the land settlement which had been made. James landed at Kinsale on March 12, 1689. One of his first acts was to issue a proclamation summoning all Irish absentees upon their allegiance to return to assist their sovereign in his struggle, and by another proclamation a Parliament was summoned for May 7. It consisted almost wholly of Catholics. . . .

*The Irish Parliament of 1689 sought to establish religious liberty in the land and also asserted its own independence. Dispossessed Catholic landowners hoped to regain their estates by a repeal of the Act of Settlement. But King William's victory at the Boyne on 1 July 1690 dashed those hopes and confirmed the Protestants in their ascendancy.*

The Parliament was prorogued on the 20th of July, one of its last Acts being to vest in the King the property of those who were still absentees. The heroic defence of Londonderry had already turned the scale in favour of William, and the disaster of the Boyne and the surrender of Limerick destroyed the last hopes of the Catholics. They secured, as they vainly imagined, by the Treaty of Limerick, their religious liberty; but the bulk of the Catholic army passed into the service of France, and the great confiscations that followed the Revolution completed the ruin of the old race. When the eighteenth century dawned, the great majority of the former leaders of the people were either sunk in abject poverty or scattered as exiles over Europe; the last spasm of resistance had ceased, and the long period of unbroken Protestant ascendency had begun.

# II

## *Religion and Society, 1700–1760*

Having now given a brief outline of the events that led to a complete Protestant ascendency in Ireland, I shall proceed to analyse the conditions of Irish society in the period immediately following the Revolution, to trace the effects of legislation and of social and political circumstances on the character of the people, and to investigate the reasons why the later history of Ireland differs in most respects so widely from the contemporaneous history of Scotland. The Revolution had thrown all the resources and government of Ireland into the hands of a small Protestant minority, but it had not given that minority any real security. The ruling class were thinly scattered among a hostile population. Though all active resistance had ceased, the passions and memories of a succession of ferocious civil wars still burnt fiercely beneath the surface of Irish society. The position of the new dynasty was exceedingly precarious, and its downfall would be inevitably followed by a new revolution of property in Ireland. The Irish Protestants from their position were almost wholly dependent for their safety on English support, and they had no power of resisting any conditions that were imposed on them. In England the Revolution had greatly increased the political power of the commercial classes, and a strong spirit of commercial jealousy had begun to prevail in English legislation.

Such were the conditions that produced the penal code against the Irish Catholics, and the commercial restraints against Irish industry, which form the capital facts of Irish history in the generations that immediately followed the Revolution. It will, perhaps, be convenient, instead of following a strictly chronological method, to consider these two systems of legislation as connected wholes, examining the relations between their many parts, and their combined and most fatal influence on Irish life.

In order to judge the penal laws against the Catholics with equity, it is necessary to remember that in the beginning of the eighteenth century restrictive laws against Protestantism in Catholic countries, and against Catholicism in Protestant ones, almost universally prevailed. The laws against Irish Catholics, though much more multifarious and elaborate, were, on the whole, in their leading features, less stringent than those against Catholics in England. They were largely modelled after the French legislation against the Huguenots, but persecution in Ireland never approached in severity that of Lewis XIV, and it was absolutely insignificant compared with that which had extirpated Protestantism and Judaism from Spain. The code, however, was not mainly the product of religious feeling, but of policy, and in this respect, as we shall hereafter see, it has been defended in its broad outlines, though not in all its details, by some of the most eminent Irishmen in the latter part of the eighteenth century. They have argued that at the close of a long period of savage civil war, it was absolutely necessary for the small minority, who found themselves in possession of the government and land of the country, to fortify their position by disqualifying laws; to deprive the conquered and hostile majority of every element of political and military strength. In as far as the code was directed to these objects, it was, it has been said, a measure of self-defence, justified by a plain and urgent necessity, and by the fact that it produced in Ireland for the space of about eighty years the most absolute tranquillity. It has been added that long before these laws were abolished, large portions of them had been allowed to become obsolete, and that some parts which were retained on the statute book were retained only as giving the Government a reserve of power which in times of great public danger might become very valuable.

A candid judge will, I think, acknowledge that these considerations have much weight, and that they may be fairly urged in defence of some portions of the code. He will at the same time acknowledge that the code went far beyond the necessities of self-defence; that it was continued long after all serious danger had past; that if it was not largely due to religious fanaticism, great parts of it bear clear traces of the passions produced by civil war, and of the monopolising, selfish, and oppressive spirit which is the natural result of uncontrolled power; that it produced more pernicious moral, social, and political effects than many sanguinary persecutions, and that a great portion of it constitutes a flagrant breach of public faith.

At a time when the war was going decidedly against the Catholics, but was still by no means terminated, when Limerick was still far from captured, when the approach of winter, the prospect of pestilence arising from the heavy floods, the news of succours on the way from France, and the dangers of another insurrection at home made the situation of the besiegers very grave, the Irish generals had agreed to surrender the city, and thus terminate the war, if by doing so they could secure for their people religious liberty. The consideration they offered was a very valuable one, for the prolongation of the war till another spring would have been full of danger to the unsettled government of William, and the stipulations of the Irish in favour of religious liberty were given the very first place in the treaty that was signed. The period since the Reformation in which the Irish Catholics were most unmolested in their worship was the reign of Charles II; and the first article of the Treaty of Limerick stipulated that "the Roman Catholics of this kingdom shall enjoy such privileges in the exercise of their religion as are consistent with the laws of Ireland, or as they did enjoy in the reign of Charles II; and their Majesties, as soon as their affairs will permit them to summon a Parliament in this kingdom, will endeavour to procure the said Roman Catholics such further security as may preserve them from any disturbance upon the account of their said religion." The ninth article determined that "the oath to be administered to such Roman Catholics as submit to their Majesties' government shall be the oath of allegiance, and no other." These articles were signed by the Lords Justices of Ireland, and ratified by their Majesties under the Great Seal of England.

Such a treaty was very reasonably regarded as a solemn charter guaranteeing the Irish Catholics against any further penalties or molestation on account of their religion. It is true that the laws of

Elizabeth against Catholicism remained unrepealed, but they had become almost wholly obsolete, and as they were not enforced during the reign of Charles II, it was assumed that they could not be enforced after the Treaty of Limerick. It is true also that the sanction of Parliament was required for some parts of the treaty, but that sanction could not, without a grave breach of faith, be withheld from engagements so solemnly entered into by the Government, at a time when Parliament was not sitting, and in order to obtain a great military advantage. The imposition upon the Irish Catholics, without any fresh provocation, of a mass of new and penal legislation intended to restrict or extinguish their worship, to banish their prelates, and to afflict them with every kind of disqualification, disability, and deprivation on account of their religion, was a direct violation of the plain meaning of the treaty. Those who signed it undertook that the Catholics should not be in a worse position, in respect to the exercise of their religion, than they had been in during the reign of Charles II, and they also undertook that the influence of the Government should be promptly exerted to obtain such an amelioration of their condition as would secure them from the possibility of disturbance. Construed in its plain and natural sense, interpreted as every treaty should be by men of honour, the Treaty of Limerick amounted to no less than this. The public faith was pledged to its observance, and the well-known sentiments of William appeared an additional guarantee. William was, indeed, a cold and somewhat selfish man, and the admirable courage and tenacity which he invariably displayed when his own designs and ambition were in question were seldom or never manifested in any disinterested cause, but he was at least eminently tolerant and enlightened, and he had actually before the battle of Aughrim offered the Irish Catholics the free exercise of their religion, half the churches in the kingdom, and the moiety of their ancient possessions. Such an offer is alone sufficient to stamp him as a great statesman, and should have saved his memory from many eulogies which are in truth the worst of calumnies. It must be observed, however, that William, who repeatedly refused his assent to English Acts which he regarded as inimical to his authority, never offered any serious or determined opposition to the anti-Catholic laws which began in his reign.

It must be observed also that the penal code, which began under William, which assumed its worst features under Anne, and which was largely extended under George I and George II, was entirely unprovoked by any active disloyalty on the part of the Catholics. It is surely absurd to describe the Irish Catholics as having manifested an incurably rebellious and ungrateful disposition because, in the contest of the Revolution, they took the part of the hereditary sovereign, to whom all classes had sworn allegiance, whose title when they took up arms had not been disputed by an act of an Irish Parliament, and who, whatever might have been his misdeeds towards other classes of the community, had at least given no provocation to the Catholics of Ireland. And, at all events, after the Treaty of Limerick had been signed, during the long agony of the penal laws, no rebellion took place. About 14,000 Irish soldiers had at once passed into the French service, and a steady stream of emigration soon carried off all the Catholic energy from the country. Deprived of their natural leaders, sunk for the most part in the most brutal ignorance and in the most abject poverty, the Irish Catholics at home remained perfectly passive, while both England and Scotland were convulsed by Jacobitism. It is a memorable fact that the ferocious law of 1703, which first reduced the Irish Catholics to a condition of hopeless servitude, does not allege as the reason for its provisions any political crime. It was called "An Act to prevent the further growth of Popery." It was justified in its preamble on the ground that the Papists still continued in their gross and dangerous errors, that some Protestants had been perverted to Popery, and that some Papists had refused to make provision for their Protestant children. A considerable military force was, indeed, kept in Ireland, but this was chiefly because the ministers desired to keep under arms a more numerous standing army than Parliament would tolerate in England, and also to throw upon the Irish revenue a great part of the burden; and whenever serious danger arose, a large proportion was at once withdrawn. . . .

Almost all the great persecutions of history, those of the early Christians, of Catholics and Protestants on the Continent, and, after the Revolution, of Catholics in England, were directed against minorities. It was the distinguishing characteristic of the Irish penal code that its victims constituted at least three-fourths of the nation, and that it was intended to demoralise as well as degrade. Its enactments may be divided into different groups. One group was intended to deprive the Catholics of all civil life. By an Act of the English Parliament they were forbidden to sit in that of Ireland. They were afterwards deprived of the elective suffrage, excluded from the corporations, from the magistracy, from the bar, from the bench, from the grand juries, and from the vestries. They could not be sheriffs or solicitors, or even game-keepers or constables. They were forbidden to possess any arms; two justices, or a mayor, or a sheriff, might at any time issue a search warrant to break into their houses and ransack them for arms, and if a fowling-piece or a flask of powder was discovered they were liable either to fine or imprisonment or to whipping and the pillory. They were, of course, excluded on the same grounds from the army and navy. They could not even possess a horse of the value of more than 5*l.*, and any Protestant on tender-ing that sum could appropriate the hunter or the carriage horse of his Catholic neighbour. In his own country the Catholic was only recognised by the law, "for repression and punishment." The Lord Chancellor Bowes and the Chief Justice Robinson both dis-tinctly laid down from the bench "that the law does not suppose any such person to exist as an Irish Roman Catholic."

The effect of these measures was to offer the strongest induce-ments to all men of ability and enterprise to conform outwardly to the dominant creed. If they did not, every path of ambition and almost all means of livelihood were closed to them, and they were at the same time exposed to the most constant, galling, and humiliating tyranny. The events of the Revolution had divided the people into opposing sections bitterly hostile to each other. The most numerous section had no rights, while the whole tend-ency of the law was to produce in the dominant minority, already flushed with the pride of conquest and with recent confiscations, all the vices of the most insolent aristocracy. Religious animosity, private quarrels, simple rapacity, or that mere love of the tyranni-cal exercise of despotic power which is so active a principle in human affairs, continually led to acts of the most odious oppres-sion which it was dangerous to resent and impossible to resist. The law gave the Protestant the power of inflicting on the Catholic intolerable annoyance. To avoid it, he readily submitted to illegal tyranny, and even under the most extreme wrong it was hopeless for him to look for legal redress. All the influence of property and office was against him, and every tribunal to which he could appeal was occupied by his enemies. The Parliament and the Government, the corporation which disposed of his city property, the vestry which taxed him, the magistrate before whom he carried his complaint, the solicitor who drew up his case, the barrister who pleaded it, the judge who tried it, the jury who decided it, were all Protestants. Of all tyrannies, a class tyranny has been justly described as the most intolerable, for it is ubiquitous in its operation, and weighs, perhaps, most heavily on those whose obscurity or distance would withdraw them from the notice of a single despot; and of all class tyrannies, perhaps the most odious is that which rests upon religious distinctions and is envenomed by religious animosities. To create such a tyranny in Ireland was the first object of the penal laws, and the effect upon the Catholics was what might have been expected. Great numbers, by dishonest and hypocritical compliances, endeavoured to free themselves from a position that was intolerable. The mass of the people gradually acquired the vices of slaves. They were educated through long generations of oppression into an inveterate hostility to the law, and were taught to look for redress in illegal violence or secret combinations.

A second object of the penal laws was to reduce the Catholics to a condition of the most extreme and brutal ignorance. As Burke has justly said: "To render men patient under such a deprivation of all the rights of human nature, everything which would give them a knowledge or feeling of those rights was rationally forbidden." The legislation on the subject of Catholic education may be briefly described, for it amounted simply to universal, unqualified, and unlimited proscription. The Catholic was excluded from the university. He was not permitted to be the guardian of a child. It was made penal for him to keep a school, to act as usher or private tutor, or to send his children to be educated abroad; and a reward of 10*l.* was offered for the discovery of a Popish schoolmaster. In 1733, it is true, charter schools were established by Primate Boulter, for the benefit of the Catholics; but these schools—which were supported by public funds—were avowedly intended, by bringing up the young as Protestants, to extirpate the religion of their parents. The alternative offered by law to the Catholics was that of absolute and compulsory ignorance or of an education directly subversive of their faith.

The operation of these laws alone might have been safely trusted to reduce the Catholic population to complete degradation; but there were many other provisions, intended to check any rising spirit of enterprise that might appear among them, and to prevent any ray of hope from animating their lot. In the acquisition of personal property, it is true, there is but little in the way of restriction to be added. By the laws I have described, the immense majority of the Irish people were excluded in their own country, from almost every profession, and from every Government office, from the highest to the lowest, and they were placed under conditions that made the growth of industrial virtues and the formation of an enterprising and aspiring character wholly impossible. They were excluded from a great part of the benefit of the taxes they paid. They were at the same time compelled to pay double to the militia, and in case of war with a Catholic Power, to reimburse the damage done by the enemies' privateers. They could not obtain the freedom of any town corporate, and were only suffered to carry on their trades in their native cities, on condition of paying special and vexatious impositions known by the name of quarterage. They were forbidden, after a certain date, to take up their abodes in the important cities of Limerick and Galway, or to purchase property within their walls; and their progress in many industrial careers was effectually trammelled by the law already referred to, preventing them from possessing any horse of the value of more than 5*l.* The chief branches of Irish commerce and industry had, as we shall see, been deliberately crushed by law in the interest of English manufacturers; but the Catholics were not specially disabled from participating in them, and the legislator contented himself with assigning strict limits to their success by providing that, except in the linen trade, no Catholic could have more than two apprentices.

In the case of landed property, however, the laws were more severe, for it was the third great object of the penal code to dissociate the Catholics as much as possible from the soil. Of this policy it may be truly said, that unless it was intended to make the nation permanently incapable of self-government, it was one of

the most infatuated that could be conceived. Land being an irre-
movable property, subject to Government control, has always
proved the best pledge of the loyalty of its possessor, and its acquisition never fails to diffuse through a disaffected class conservative
and orderly habits. One of the first objects of every wise legislator,
and, indeed, of every good man, should be to soften the division
of classes; and no social condition can be more clearly dangerous
or diseased than that in which these divisions coincide with, and
are intensified by, differences of creed. To make the landlord class
almost exclusively Protestant, while the tenant class were almost
exclusively Catholic, was to plant in Ireland the seeds of the most
permanent and menacing divisions. On the other hand, a class of
Catholic landlords connected with one portion of the people by
property and with another portion by religion could not fail to
soften at once the animosities of class and of creed. They would
have become the natural political leaders of their co-religionists,
and it is to the absence of such a class that both the revolutionary
and sacerdotal extravagances of Irish Catholic politics are mainly
to be attributed.

The great confiscations under James I, Cromwell, and William
had done much to make the proprietary of Ireland exclusively
Protestant. It is true that after the Revolution about 300,000
acres were restored to Catholics who were adjudged by the Commissioners to be comprised within the articles of Limerick or
Galway, or who had been freely pardoned by William, but still a
great step had been taken towards placing the soil of Ireland in
Protestant hands. The penal laws continued to work. No Catholic
was suffered to buy land, or inherit or receive it as a gift from
Protestants, or to hold life annuities, or mortgages on land, or
leases for more than thirty-one years, or any lease on such terms
that the profits of the land exceeded one-third of the rent. If a
Catholic leaseholder, by his skill or industry, so increased his
profits that they exceeded this proportion, and did not immediately make a corresponding increase in his rent, his farm passed to
the first Protestant who made the discovery. If a Catholic secretly
purchased either his own forfeited estate, or any other land in the
possession of a Protestant, the first Protestant who informed
against him became the proprietor. The whole country was soon
filled with spies, endeavouring to appropriate the property of

45

Catholics; and Popish discoveries became a main business of the law courts. The few Catholic landlords who remained after the confiscations, were deprived of the liberty of testament, which was possessed by all other subjects of the Crown. Their estates, upon their death, were divided equally among their sons, unless the eldest became a Protestant; in which case the whole was settled upon him. In this manner Catholic landlords were gradually but surely impoverished. Their land passed almost universally into the hands of Protestants, and the few who succeeded in retaining large estates did so only by compliances which destroyed the wholesome moral influence that would naturally have attached to their position. The penal code, as it was actually carried out, was inspired much less by fanaticism than by rapacity, and was directed less against the Catholic religion than against the property and industry of its professors. It was intended to make them poor and to keep them poor, to crush in them every germ of enterprise, to degrade them into a servile caste who could never hope to rise to the level of their oppressors. The division of classes was made as deep as possible, and every precaution was taken to perpetuate and to embitter it. Any Protestant who married a Catholic, or who suffered his children to be educated as Catholics, was exposed to all the disabilities of the code. Any Protestant woman who was a landowner, if she married a Catholic, was at once deprived of her inheritance, which passed to the nearest Protestant heir. A later law provided that every marriage celebrated by a Catholic priest between a Catholic and a Protestant should be null, and that the priest who officiated should be hanged.

The creation by law of a gigantic system of bribery intended to induce the Catholics to abandon or disguise their creed, and of an army of spies and informers intended to prey upon their property, had naturally a profoundly demoralising influence, but hardly so much so as the enactments which were designed to sow discord and insubordination in their homes. These measures, which may be looked upon as the fourth branch of the penal code, appear to have rankled more than any others in the minds of the Catholics, and they produced the bitterest and most pathetic complaints. The law I have cited, by which the eldest son of a Catholic, upon apostatising, became the heir-at-law to the whole estate of his father, reduced his father to the position of a mere life tenant, and prevented him from selling, mortgaging, or otherwise disposing of it, is a typical measure of this class. In like manner a wife who apostatised was immediately freed from her husband's control, and the Chancellor was empowered to assign to her a certain proportion of her husband's property. If any child, however young, professed to be a Protestant, it was at once taken from its father's care. The Chancellor, or the child itself, if an adult, might compel the father to produce the title-deeds of his estate, and declare on oath the value of his property; and such a proportion as the Chancellor determined was given to the child. Children were thus set against their parents, and wives against their husbands, and jealousies, suspicions, and heart-burnings were introduced into the Catholic home. The undutiful wife, the rebellious and unnatural son, had only to add to their other crimes the guilt of a feigned conversion, in order to secure both impunity and reward, and to deprive those whom they had injured of the management and disposal of their property. The influence of the code appeared, indeed, omnipresent. It blasted the prospects of the Catholic in all the struggles of active life. It cast its shadow over the inmost recesses of his home. It darkened the very last hour of his existence. No Catholic, as I have said, could be guardian to a child; so the dying parent knew that his children must pass under the tutelage of Protestants. . . .

It is, however, obviously absurd to speak of the Catholic religion as tolerated in a country where its bishops were proscribed. In Ireland, all Catholic archbishops, bishops, deans, and vicars-general were ordered by a certain day to leave the country. If after that date they were found in it, they were to be first imprisoned and then banished, and if they returned they were pronounced guilty of high treason and were liable to be hanged, disembowelled, and quartered. Nor were these idle words. The law of 1709 offered a reward of 50*l*. to anyone who secured the conviction of any Catholic archbishop, bishop, dean, or vicar-general. In their own dioceses, in the midst of a purely Catholic country, in the performance of religious duties which were absolutely essential to the maintenance of their religion, the Catholic bishops were compelled to live in obscure hovels and under feigned names, moving continually from place to place, meeting their flocks under the shadow of the night, not unfrequently

taking refuge from their pursuers in caverns or among the mountains. The position of all friars and unregistered priests was very
similar. It was evident that if any strong religious feeling was to
be maintained, there must be many of them in Ireland. A Government which avowedly made the repression of the Catholic religion
one of its main ends would never authorise a sufficient number
of priests to maintain any high standard of devotion. The priests
were looked upon as necessary evils, to be reduced to the lowest
possible number. It was not certain that when the existing generation of registered priests died out the Government would suffer
them to be replaced, and no licences were to be granted to those
who refused the abjuration oath, which the Catholic Church pronounced to be unlawful. Very naturally, therefore, numerous
unregistered priests and friars laboured among the people. Like
the bishops, they were liable to banishment if they were discovered, and to death if they returned. It was idle for the prisoner to
allege that no political action of any kind was proved against him,
that he was employed solely in carrying spiritual consolations to a
population who were reduced to a condition of the extremest
spiritual as well as temporal destitution. Strenuous measures were
taken to enforce the law. It was enacted that every mayor or justice
of the peace who neglected to execute its provisions should be
liable to a fine of 100*l.*, half of which was to go to the informer,
and should also on conviction be disabled from serving as justice
of the peace during the remainder of his life. A reward of 20*l.*,
offered for the detection of each friar or unregistered priest,
called a regular race of priest-hunters into existence. To facilitate
their task the law enabled any two justices of the peace at any
time to compel any Catholic of eighteen or upwards to declare
when and where he last heard Mass, who officiated, and who was
present, and if he refused to give evidence he might be imprisoned for twelve months, or until he paid a fine of 20*l.* Anyone
who harboured ecclesiastics from beyond the sea was liable to
fines which amounted, for the third offence, to the confiscation of
all his goods. The Irish House of Commons urged the magistrates
on to greater activity in enforcing the law, and it resolved "that
the saying or hearing of Mass by persons who had not taken the
oath of abjuration tended to advance the interests of the Pre-
tender," and again, "that the prosecuting and informing against

Papists was an honourable service to the Government." But perhaps the most curious illustration of the ferocious spirit of the time was furnished by the Irish Privy Council in 1719. In that year an elaborate Bill against Papists was carried, apparently without opposition, through the Irish House of Commons, and among its clauses was one sentencing all unregistered priests who were found in Ireland to be branded with a red-hot iron upon the cheek. The Irish Privy Council, however, actually changed the penalty of branding into that of castration, and sent the Bill with this atrocious recommendation to England for ratification. The English ministers unanimously restored the penalty of branding. By the constitution of Ireland a Bill which had been returned from England might be finally rejected, but could not be amended by the Irish Parliament; and the Irish House of Lords, objecting to a retrospective clause which invalidated certain leases which Papists had been suffered to make, threw out the bill. It is, however, a memorable fact in the moral history of Europe that as late as 1719 this penalty was seriously proposed by the responsible Government of Ireland. It may be added that a law imposing it upon Jesuits was actually in force in Sweden in the beginning of the century, and that a paper was circulated in 1700 advocating the adoption of a similar atrocity in England. . . .

I have now given a sufficient account of the relation of the Irish law to the religion of the Irish people. It is only necessary to add that the governors of Ireland as the representatives of the Sovereign formally and repeatedly, in times of perfect peace, and in speeches from the throne, described their Catholic subjects as enemies. Lord Pembroke, in 1706, referred to them as "domestic enemies." The Lords Justices, in 1715, urged upon the House of Commons such unanimity in their resolutions "as may once more put an end to all other distinctions in Ireland but that of Protestant and Papist." Lord Carteret, in a similar speech, said, "All the Protestants of the kingdom have but one common interest, and have too often fatally experienced that they have the same common enemy." As late as 1733 the Duke of Dorset called on the Parliament to secure "a firm union amongst all Protestants, who have one common interest and the same common enemy." The phrase "common enemy" was in the early part of the eighteenth century the habitual term by which the Irish Parliament described the great majority of the Irish people. To secure the empire of the law not only over the actions but over the sympathies of the people is the very first end of enlightened statesmanship, and the degree in which it is attained is the very best test of good government. In Ireland nothing of this kind was done, and the strongest of all moral sentiments, the authority of religion, was for about a century in direct opposition to the authority of law.

As regards the system of direct religious repression, the penal code, it is true, became, as we shall hereafter see, gradually inoperative. It was impossible, without producing a state of chronic civil war, to enforce its enactments in the midst of a large Catholic population. Rewards were offered for the apprehension of priests, but it needed no small courage to face the hatred of the people. Savage mobs were ever ready to mark out the known priest-hunter, and unjust laws were met by illegal violence. Under the long discipline of the penal laws, the Irish Catholics learnt the lesson which, beyond all others, rulers should dread to teach. They became consummate adepts in the arts of conspiracy and of disguise. Secrets known to hundreds were preserved inviolable from authority. False intelligence baffled and distracted the pursuer, and the dread of some fierce nocturnal vengeance was often sufficient to quell the cupidity of the prosecutor. Bishops came to Ireland in spite of the atrocious penalties to which they were subject, and ordained new priests. What was to be done with them? The savage sentence of the law, if duly executed, might have produced a conflagration in Ireland that would have endangered every Protestant life, and the scandal would have rung through Europe. Ambassadors of Catholic Powers in alliance with England more than once remonstrated against the severity of English anti-Catholic legislation, and on the other hand the English ministers felt that the execution of priests in Ireland would indefinitely weaken their power of mitigating by their influence the persecution of Protestants on the Continent. The administration of the law was feeble in all its departments, and it was naturally peculiarly so when it was in opposition to the strongest feelings of the great majority of the people. It was difficult to obtain evidence or even juries. It was soon found, too, that the higher Catholic clergy, if left in peace, were able and willing to render inestimable services to the Government in suppressing sedition and crime, and as it was quite evident that the bulk of the Irish Catholics would not become Protestants, they could not, in the mere interests of order, be left wholly without religious ministration. Besides, there was in reality not much religious fanaticism. Statesmen of the stamp of Walpole and Carteret were quite free from such a motive, and were certainly not disposed to push matters to extremities. The spirit of the eighteenth century was eminently adverse to dogma. The sentiment of nationality, and especially the deep resentment produced by the English restrictions on trade, gradually drew different classes of Irishmen together. The multitude of lukewarm Catholics who abandoned their creed through purely interested motives lowered the religious temperature among the Protestants, while, by removing some of the indifferent, it increased it among the Catholics, and the former grew in time very careless about theological doctrines. The system of registration broke down through the imposition of the abjuration oath, and through the extreme practical difficulty of enforcing the penalties. The policy of extinguishing Catholicism by suppressing its services and banishing its bishops was silently abandoned; before the middle of the eighteenth century the laws against Catholic worship were virtually obsolete, and before the close of the eighteenth century the Parliament which in the beginning of the century had been one of the most intolerant had become one of the most tolerant in Europe.

In this respect the penal code was a failure. In others it was more successful. It was intended to degrade and to impoverish, to destroy in its victims the spring and buoyancy of enterprise, to dig a deep chasm between Catholics and Protestants. These ends it fully attained. It formed the social condition, it regulated the disposition of property, it exercised a most enduring and pernicious influence upon the character of the people, and some of the worst features of the latter may be distinctly traced to its influence. It may be possible to find in the statute books both of Protestant and Catholic countries laws corresponding to most parts of the Irish penal code, and in some respects surpassing its most atrocious provisions, but it is not the less true that that code, taken as a whole, has a character entirely distinctive. It was directed not against the few, but against the many. It was not the persecution of a sect, but the degradation of a nation. It was the

instrument employed by a conquering race, supported by a neighbouring Power, to crush to the dust the people among whom they
were planted. And, indeed, when we remember that the greater
part of it was in force for nearly a century, that its victims formed
at least three-fourths of the nation, that its degrading and dividing influence extended to every field of social, political, professional, intellectual, and even domestic life, and that it was enacted
without the provocation of any rebellion, in defiance of a treaty
which distinctly guaranteed the Irish Catholics from any further
oppression on account of their religion, it may be justly regarded
as one of the blackest pages in the history of persecution. In the
words of Burke, "It was a complete system, full of coherence and
consistency, well digested and well composed in all its parts. It
was a machine of wise and elaborate contrivance, and as well
fitted for the oppression, impoverishment, and degradation of a
people, and the debasement in them of human nature itself, as
ever proceeded from the perverted ingenuity of man." The judgment formed of it by one of the noblest representatives of English
Toryism was very similar. "The Irish," said Dr. Johnson, "are in
a most unnatural state, for we there see the minority prevailing
over the majority. There is no instance, even in the Ten Persecutions, of such severity as that which the Protestants of Ireland
have exercised against the Catholics."

The penal laws against the Roman Catholics, both in England
and Ireland, were the immediate consequence of the Revolution,
and were mainly the work of the Whig party. In Ireland some of
them were carried under William, but by far the greater number
of the disabilities were comprised in what Burke has truly described as "the ferocious Acts of Anne." These laws were carried
in 1703–4 and in 1709, and the last of them was brought forward
by the Government of Wharton, one of the most conspicuous
members of the party. It is somewhat remarkable, however, that
the Catholics were not at this time directly deprived of the elective
franchise, except so far as the imposition of the oath of abjuration
operated as a disqualification. Their extreme poverty, the laws
relating to landed property, and their exclusion from the corporations, no doubt reduced the number of Catholic voters to infinitesimal proportions, but the absolute and formal abolition of the
class did not take place till 1727, and appears to have been due to

the influence of Primate Boulter, who was also the author of severe laws against nominal converts.

The penal laws against the Catholics, by depressing the great majority of the Irish people, did much to arrest the material prosperity of Ireland; but, in this respect at least, they were less fatal than the commercial legislation which speedily followed the Revolution. The natural capacities of Ireland for becoming a wealthy country were certainly greater than those of Scotland, though they have often been exceedingly exaggerated. Under no circumstances indeed could Ireland have become a serious rival to England. She is almost wholly destitute of those great coal-fields on which more than on any other single cause the manufacturing supremacy of England depends. Owing to the excessive rainfall produced by proximity to the Atlantic, a large proportion of her soil is irreclaimable marsh; a still larger part can only be reclaimed or kept in proper order by large and constant expenditure in draining, and the evil in the eighteenth century was seriously aggravated by the law forbidding Catholics from lending money in mortgages on land, which considerably diminished the amount of capital expended in agricultural improvement. It is also no small disadvantage to Ireland materially, and a still greater disadvantage to her morally and politically, that she is isolated from Europe, the whole bulk of England being interposed between her and the Continent. In England, too, manufacturing industry dates from the Plantagenets and the Tudors. During many centuries the increase of capital and the formation of industrial habits were uninterrupted, for, with the doubtful exception of the civil war under Charles I, there had been no conflict since the Wars of the Roses sufficiently serious and prolonged to interfere with industrial progress. Ireland had barely emerged into an imperfect civilisation in the time of Elizabeth, and had then speedily passed into a long period of desolating and exterminating war. On the other hand, the greater part of the Irish soil is extremely fertile, in the opinion of the best judges more fertile than that of any other part of the kingdom. Though it is very unsuited for wheat, it is eminently adapted for several other kinds of crops, and it forms some of the richest pasture land in Christendom. Irish cattle have always been famous, and Irish wool in the last century was considered the best in Europe.

No country in the world is more admirably provided with natural harbours. It is not without navigable rivers. It is abundantly supplied with water power, and its position between the Old World and the New points it out as a great centre of commercial intercourse.

A country of which this may be truly said may not have been intended to take a foremost place in the race of industry and wealth, but it was certainly not condemned by nature to abject and enduring poverty. Up to the time of the Restoration no legislative disability rested upon Irish industry, but the people who had but recently acquired the rudiments of civilisation had been plunged by the Cromwellian wars into a condition of wretchedness hardly paralleled in history. At last, however, peace had come, and it was hoped that some faint gleams of prosperity would have dawned. Crowds of Cromwellian soldiers, representing the full average of English energy and intelligence, had been settled on the confiscated lands, and in the utter ruin of the native population the resources of the country were to a great degree in their hands. The land was chiefly pasture, and the main source of Irish wealth was the importation of cattle to England. The English landowners, however, speedily took alarm. They complained that Irish rivalry in the cattle market lowered English rents, and laws were accordingly enacted in 1665 and 1680, absolutely prohibiting the importation into England, from Ireland, of all cattle, sheep, and swine, of beef, pork, bacon, and mutton, and even of butter and cheese.

In this manner the chief source of Irish prosperity was annihilated at a single blow. Crushing, however, as was this prohibition, it was not the only one. The Irish, though far too poor to have any considerable commerce, had at least a few ships afloat, and there were some slight beginnings of a colonial trade. It was feared that under more favourable circumstances this might attain considerable proportions. The two great geographical advantages of Ireland are her proximity to America and her admirable harbours. In the original Navigation Act of 1660 Irish vessels had all the privileges accorded to English ones, but in the amended Act of 1663 Ireland was omitted, and she was thus deprived of the whole colonial trade. With a very few specified exceptions, no European articles could be imported into the English colonies except from England, in ships built in England and chiefly manned by English sailors. With a very few specified exceptions, no articles could be brought from the colonies to Europe without being first unladen in England. In 1670 the exclusion of Ireland was confirmed, and in 1696 it was rendered still more stringent, for it was provided that no goods of any kind could be imported directly from the colonies to Ireland. In this manner the natural course of Irish commerce was utterly checked. Her shipping interest was annihilated, and Swift hardly exaggerated when he said: "The conveniency of ports and harbours which Nature bestowed so liberally on this kingdom, is of no more use to us than a beautiful prospect to a man shut up in a dungeon."

Such measures might easily have proved fatal to the industrial development of such a country as Ireland. In the period, however, that elapsed between the Restoration and the Revolution a very remarkable industrial spirit had arisen, and serious and persevering efforts were made by the Protestant colonists to utilise the great natural advantages of the country. Ireland at last enjoyed a period of profound peace, and the religious liberty which was established effected a rapid improvement in her social condition. It was true that the great mass of the people were impoverished, half-civilised, and divided, but it was also true that taxes were lower than in England, that land, living and labour were extremely cheap, and that the events of the civil war had drawn into the country great numbers of able and energetic Englishmen. Being forbidden to export their cattle to England, the Irish land-owners turned their land into sheep-walks, and began, on a large scale, to manufacture the wool. As early as 1636 Strafford noticed that there were some small beginnings of a clothing trade in Ireland, and he promised to discourage it to the utmost, lest it should interfere with the woollen manufacture in England. "It might be feared," he added, "they might beat us out of the trade itself by underselling us, which they were well able to do." But after this time the manufacture was for some years unmolested and even encouraged by several Acts of Parliament. The export of raw wool from Ireland to foreign countries had been forbidden under Charles II, but as the same restriction was imposed on English wool, Ireland was in this respect at no disadvantage. It was no doubt a grave disadvantage that she was excluded by the Navigation Act from the whole colonial market, but the rest of the world, at least, was open to her manufactures. On the prohibition of the export of Irish cattle, the manufacture began to increase. The quality of the wool, as I have said, was supremely good. A real industrial enthusiasm had arisen in the nation. Great numbers of English, Scotch, and even foreign manufacturers came over. Many thousands of men were employed in the trade, and all the signs of a great rising industry were visible. If it was an object of statesmanship to make Ireland a happy country, to mitigate the abject and heartrending poverty of its people, and to develop among them habits of order, civilisation, and loyalty, the encouragement of this industrial tendency was of the utmost moment. If it was an object beyond all others to make Ireland a Protestant country, the extension of a rich manufacturing population, who would, for some generations at least, be mainly Protestant, would do more to effect this object than any system of penal laws or proselytising schools. Unfortunately there was another object which was nearer the heart of the English Parliament than either of these. After the Revolution, commercial influence became supreme in its councils. There was an important woollen manufacture in England, and the English manufacturers urgently petitioned for the total destruction of the rising industry in Ireland. Their petitions were speedily attended to. The House of Lords represented to the King that "the growing manufacture of cloth in Ireland, both by the cheapness of all sorts of necessaries of life, and goodness of materials for making all manner of cloth, doth invite your subjects of England, with their families and servants, to leave their habitations to settle there, to the increase of the woollen manufacture in Ireland, which makes your loyal subjects in this kingdom very apprehensive that the further growth of it may greatly prejudice the said manufacture here." The House of Commons in very similar terms urged William "to enjoin all those you employ in Ireland to make it their care, and use their utmost diligence to hinder the exportation of wool from Ireland, except to be imported hither, and for the discouraging the woollen manufactures." The King promised to do as he was requested. A parliament was summoned in Dublin, in September 1698, for the express purpose of destroying the Irish industry. The Irish Parliament was then, from the nature of its constitution, completely subservient to English influence, and, had it been otherwise, it would have had no power to resist. The Lords Justices in their opening speech urged the House to encourage the linen and hempen manufacture instead of the woollen manufacture, which England desired to monopolise. The Commons in reply promised their hearty endeavours to establish a linen and hempen manufacture in Ireland, expressed a hope that they might find "such a temperament" in respect to the woollen trade as would prevent it from being injurious to that of England, and proceeded, at the instance of the Government, to impose heavy additional duties on the export of Irish woollen goods. The English, however, were still unsatisfied. The Irish woollen manufactures had already been excluded by the Navigation Act from the whole colonial market; they had been virtually excluded from England itself, by duties amounting to prohibition. A law of crushing severity, enacted by the British Parliament in 1699, completed the work and prohibited the Irish from exporting their manufactured wool to any other country whatever.

So ended the fairest promise Ireland had ever known of becoming a prosperous and a happy country. The ruin was absolute and final. "Ireland," wrote Swift a few years later, "is the only kingdom I ever heard or read of, either in ancient or modern story, which was denied the liberty of exporting their native commodities and manufactures wherever they pleased, except to countries at war with their own prince and state. Yet this privilege, by the superiority of mere power, is refused us in the most momentous parts of commerce; besides an Act of navigation, to which we never assented, pressed down upon us and rigorously executed." The main industry of Ireland had been deliberately destroyed because it had so prospered that English manufacturers had begun to regard it as a competitor with their own. It is true, indeed, that a promise was made that the linen and hempen manufacture should be encouraged as a compensation; but, even if it had been a just principle that a nation should be restricted by force of law to one or two forms of industry, there was no proportion between that which was destroyed and that which was to be favoured, and no real reciprocity established between the two countries. The linen manufacture may, indeed, be dimly traced far back into Irish history. It is noticed in an English poem in the early part of the fifteenth century. A century later Guicciardini, in his description of the Low Countries, mentions coarse linen as among the products imported from Ireland to Antwerp. Strafford had done much to encourage it, and after the calamities of the Cromwellian period, the Duke of Ormond had laboured with some success to revive it. But it had never attained any great extension; it was almost annihilated by the war of the Revolution, and in 1700 the value of the whole export of Irish linen amounted to little more than 14,000*l.* The English utterly suppressed the existing woollen manufacture in Ireland in order to reserve that industry entirely to themselves; but the English and Scotch continued as usual their manufacture of linen. The Irish trade was ruined in 1699, but no legislative encouragement was given to the Irish linen manufacture till 1705, when, at the urgent petition of the Irish Parliament, the Irish were allowed to export their white and brown linens, but these only, to the British colonies, and they were not permitted to bring any colonial goods in return. The Irish linen manufacture was undoubtedly encouraged by bounties, but not until 1743, when the country had sunk into a condition of appalling wretchedness. In spite of the compact of 1698, the hempen manufacture was so discouraged that it positively ceased. Disabling duties were imposed on Irish sailcloth imported into England. Irish checked, striped, and dyed linens were absolutely excluded from the colonies. They were virtually excluded from England by the imposition of a duty of 30 per cent., and Ireland was not allowed to participate in the bounties granted for the exportation of these descriptions of linen from Great Britain to foreign countries. We have a curious illustration of the state of feeling prevailing in England in the fact that two petitions were presented in 1698 from Folkestone and Aldborough complaining of the injury done to the fishermen of these towns "by the Irish catching herrings at Waterford and Wexford and sending them to the Straits, and thereby forestalling and ruining petitioners' markets"; and there was even a party in England who desired to prohibit all fisheries on the Irish shore except by boats built and manned by Englishmen.

The effect of the policy I have described was ruinous in the extreme. It had become abundantly evident to all reasonable men that England possessed both the power and the will to crush every form of Irish industry. . . .

*The bulk of the Irish people lived in the midst of squalor, deprivation, and disease. Death rates remained abnormally high for many years. A severe famine in 1740–41 caused widespread distress and untold thousands died from starvation.*

It will be observed that the conduct of England in destroying the trade and the most important manufacture of Ireland was a much less exceptional proceeding than Irish writers are disposed to maintain. England did to Ireland little more than she had done to America and to Scotland, and she acted in accordance with commercial principles that then governed all colonial policy. It was a fundamental maxim that the commercial interests of a dependency should be wholly subordinated to those of the mother country, and to an English mind there was no reason why this maxim should not be rigidly applied to Ireland. Davenant, who in the early years of the eighteenth century was the most influential writer on commercial questions, strenuously maintained that the greater cheapness of living and labour in Ireland rendered her a dangerous rival, and that therefore every form of industry which could compete with English manufacture should be discouraged or suppressed. All encouragement, he says, that can possibly consist with the welfare of England should be given to Irish planters, and he suggests that the admission of Irish cattle into England would be, on the whole, advantageous to England and the best means of diverting the Irish from manufactures, but he strongly supports the absolute prohibition of the Irish wool manufacture and objects to all encouragement of the linen manufacture. The Catholics, who formed the bulk of the Irish people, were looked upon in England with unmingled hatred. The Irish Protestants owed their ascendency to England, and she had but lately re-established it by an expensive war. The real peculiarity of the case lay much less in the commercial legislation of England than in the situation of Ireland. Scotland possessed an independent parliament, supported by the entire nation, and she was therefore able to make herself so troublesome that England purchased the Union by ample commercial privileges. The American colonies contained within themselves almost unlimited resources. No legislation could counteract their great natural advantages. They were inhabited by a people who, from the circumstances of the case, possessed much more than average energy, and they were so large and so distant from the mother country that it was practically impossible very seriously to injure their trade. The position of Ireland was totally different. Her parliament was wholly dependent on that of England. Her ruling caste were planted in the midst of a hostile and subjugated population. She lay within a few hours of the English coast. The bulk of her people were crushed to the very dust by penal laws, and most of the men of energy and ambition were driven from her shore. She was thus completely within the grasp of England, and that grasp was tightened till almost every element of her prosperity was destroyed.

According to the maxims then prevailing, the policy was a very natural, but, as far as the true interests of England were concerned, it was a very short-sighted one. If the Protestants were to be treated as an English garrison in Ireland, it was the obvious interest of the mother country that they should be as numerous, as powerful, and as united as possible. England, on the contrary, by her commercial laws, deliberately crushed their prosperity, drove them by thousands into exile, arrested the influx of a considerable Protestant population from Great Britain, prevented the formation of those industrial habits and feelings which are the most powerful support of a Government, and inspired the Presbyterians of the North with a bitter hatred of her rule. Not content with this, she proceeded to divide her friends. The English Toleration Act was not extended to Ireland, and the Nonconformists in the first years of the eighteenth century only celebrated their worship by connivance. The sacramental test was inserted by the English ministers in the Anti-Poverty Bill of 1704, and the Dissenters were thus excluded from all municipal offices. Their marriages, unless celebrated by an Episcopal clergyman, were irregular, and subjected them to vexatious prosecutions in the ecclesiastical courts; and in 1713 the English Parliament extended the provisions of the Schism Act to Ireland. The Catholics were, no doubt, for a time paralysed, but in this quarter also the seeds of future retribution were abundantly sown. By a long course of hostile legislation, directed expressly against their religion, they were educated into hatred of the law. The landlords of their own persuasion, who would have been their natural and their most moderate leaders, were, as a class, gradually abolished. Education, industrial pursuits, ambition, and wealth, all of which mitigate the intensity of religious bigotry, were steadily denied them. Every tendency to amalgamate with the Protestants was arrested, and the whole Catholic population were reduced to a degree of ignorance and poverty in which the normal checks on population wholly ceased to operate. Starvation may check the multiplication of population, but the fear of starvation never does. In a peaceful community, in which infanticide is almost unknown and gross vice very rare, the real check to excessive multiplication is a high standard of comfort. The shame and dread of falling below it, the desire of attaining a higher round in the social ladder, lead to self-denial, providence, and tardy marriages. But when men have no such standard, when they are accustomed to live without any of the decencies, ornaments, or luxuries of life; when potatoes and milk and a mud hovel are all they require and all they can hope for; when, in a word, they are so wretched that they can hardly, by any imprudence, make their condition permanently worse than it is, they will impose no restraint upon themselves, and, except in periods of pestilence, famine, or exterminating war, will inevitably increase with excessive rapidity. In Ireland early marriages were still further encouraged by the priests, partly, no doubt, as conducive to morality, and partly because fees at weddings and baptisms were of great importance to an impoverished clergy, excluded from every kind of State provision. In this manner, by a curious nemesis, one of the results of the laws that were intended to crush Catholicism in Ireland was, that after a few years the Catholics increased in a greater ratio than any other portion of the population.

The same complete subordination of Irish to English interests extended through the political system. Of the revenue of the country the larger part was entirely beyond the control of Parliament. The hereditary revenue, as it existed after the Revolution, still rested substantially on the legislation of Charles II, and it grew in a great measure out of the confiscations after the Rebellion. The lands which had been then forfeited by the Irish, and which were not restored by the Act of Settlement, had been bestowed during the Commonwealth on English soldiers. If the Crown at the Restoration had exercised its legal right of appropriating them, it would have obtained a vast revenue; but as such a course would have been extremely difficult and dangerous, it was arranged by the Act of Settlement that the Crown should resign its right to these forfeitures, receiving in compensation a new hereditary revenue. The older forms of Crown property were at the same time either incorporated into this revenue or abolished with compensation, and the new hereditary revenue, as settled by Parliament, was vested for ever in the King and his successors. It was derived from many sources, the most important being the Crown rents, which arose chiefly from the religious confiscations of Henry VIII and from the six counties that were forfeited after the rebellion of Tyrone; the quit rents, which had their origin in the confiscations that followed the rebellion of 1641; the hearth-money, which was first imposed upon Ireland under Charles II; licences for selling ale, beer, and strong waters, and many excise and Custom House duties. For many years this revenue was sufficient for all the civil and military purposes of the Government, and no Parliament, with the exception of that which was convoked by James after his expulsion from England, sat in Ireland in the twenty-six years that elapsed between the Restoration and the Parliament which was summoned by Lord Sydney in 1692. The increase of the army, the erection of barracks, and other expenses resulting from the Revolution had made the hereditary revenue insufficient, and it became necessary to ask for fresh supplies. This insufficiency of the hereditary revenue laid the foundation of the power of Parliament, and that power was increased when the Government found it necessary in 1715 to borrow 50,000*l.* for the purpose of taking military measures to secure the new dynasty. The national debt, which had before this time been only 16,000*l.*, became now a considerable element in the national finances. It grew in the next fifteen years to rather more than 330,000*l.*, and a series of new duties were imposed by Parliament for the purpose of paying the interest and principal.

These circumstances led to the summoning of Parliament every second year, and to the gradual enlargement of its power, but its legitimate prerogative was a matter of constant and vehement dispute, and its actual position was of most humiliating dependence. It exercised a partial and imperfect control over the finances of the country, and claimed unsuccessfully the sole right of originating Money Bills; but the English Parliament, though it refrained from taxing Ireland, assumed and repeatedly exercised the right of binding it by its legislation without any concurrence of the national legislature. By a declaratory English Act of George I this right was emphatically asserted, and even in its own legislation the Irish Parliament was completely subordinate to the English Privy Council. Its dependence rested upon Poynings' Act, which was passed under Henry VII, and amended under Philip and Mary. At one time the Irish Parliament could not be summoned till the Bills it was called upon to pass were approved under the Great Seal of England; and, although it afterwards obtained the power of originating heads of Bills, it was necessary before they became law that they should be submitted to the English Privy Council, which had the right either of rejecting or of altering them, and the Irish Parliament, though it might reject, could not alter a Bill returned in an amended form from England. The appellate jurisdiction of the Irish House of Lords was withdrawn from it by a mere act of power in the Annesley case in 1719. The constitution of the House of Commons was such that it lay almost wholly beyond the control of public opinion. By an English law passed at a time when the Irish Parliament was not sitting, the Catholics were precluded from sitting among its members, and as they were afterwards deprived of the suffrage, the national legislature was thus absolutely cut off from the bulk of the Irish people. The Nonconformists were not formally excluded, but the test clause, which was also of English origin, shut them out from the corporations by which a large proportion of the members were elected. At the same time the royal prerogative of creating boroughs was exerted to an extent unparalleled in England. No less than forty boroughs had been created by James I, thirty-six by the other sovereigns of his house, and eleven more boroughs were for the first time represented in the Parliament which met in 1692. The county representation appears to have been tolerably sound; but out of the 300 members of the Irish House of Commons,

216 were elected by boroughs and manors, and of these members 176, according to the lowest estimate, were elected by individual patrons, while very few of the remainder had really popular constituencies. It was stated in 1784 that fifty Members of Parliament were then elected by ten individuals. . . .

*Just as the Irish revenue enabled men of influence and con-nection to enjoy lucrative sinecures, so the payment of tithes to the Irish Established Church perpetuated an elaborate system of Church patronage. The Irish Church was distinguished by leth-argy, intellectual paralysis, and jobbery. But the Irish Parliament was far too unrepresentative and far too involved in jobbery to alter the situation.*

Serious, however, as was this drain upon the revenues of a country so miserably poor, it was trivial compared with that pro-duced by the absenteeism of the Irish landlords. Swift asserted that at least one-third of the rent of the country was spent in England, and nearly all the Irish writers of the last century dilate upon the evil, though they differ somewhat as to its magnitude. Prior, in 1730, calculated the rental spent by absentees in En-gland at about 620,000*l.* Another list, drawn up in 1769, put the value at no less than 1,200,000*l.* Hutchinson, in his "Com-mercial Restraints," which was published in 1779, stated that "the sums remitted from Ireland to Great Britain for rents, inter-est of money, pensions, salaries, and profits of offices amounted, on the lowest computation, from 1668 to 1773 to 1,110,000*l.* yearly." Arthur Young, in 1779, estimated the rents alone of the absentees at about 732,000*l.* The causes of the evil are not difficult to discover. A very large part of the confiscated land was given to Englishmen who had property and duties in En-gland, and habitually lived there. Much of it also came into the market, and as there was very little capital in Ireland, and as Catholics were forbidden to purchase land, this also passed largely into the hands of English speculators. Besides, the level of civilisation was much higher in England than in Ireland. The position of a Protestant landlord, living in the midst of a degraded population, differing from him in religion and race, had but little attraction; the political situation of the country closed to an Irish gentleman nearly every avenue of honourable ambition, and owing to a long series of very evident causes, the sentiment of public duty was deplorably low. The economical evil was not checked by any considerable movement in the opposite direction, for after the suppression of the Irish manufactures but few Englishmen, except those who obtained Irish offices, came to Ireland.

The moral effects of absenteeism, and especially its influence on the land question, can hardly be exaggerated. One of its first results was the system of middlemen, which continued till within the memory of living men almost universal in Ireland. The landlord disliking the trouble and difficulty of collecting his rents from numerous small tenants, and looking solely at his property as a source of a moderate but secure income, abdicated all his active functions, and let his land at a long lease to a large tenant, who raised the rent of the landlord as well as a profit for himself by sub-letting, and who undertook the whole practical management of the estate. The tenants were therefore under the immediate control of men of a wholly inferior stamp, who were necessarily Protestant, but who had none of the culture and position that soften the asperities of religious differences, and who at the same time, having no permanent interest in the soil, were usually the most grasping of tyrants. As the demand for land increased, or the profits of land rose, the head tenant followed the example of his landlord. He often became an absentee. He abandoned all serious industry. He in his turn sublet his tenancy at an increased rent, and the process continued till there were three, four, or even five persons between the landlord and the cultivator of the soil.

The poor, in the meantime, sank into the condition of cottiers —a condition which has been truly described as "a specific and almost unique product of Irish industrial life." Unlike the peasant proprietor, and also unlike the mediaeval serf, the cottier had no permanent interest in the soil, and no security for his future position. Unlike the English farmer, he was not a capitalist, who selects land as one of the many forms of profitable investment that are open to him. He was a man destitute of all knowledge and of all capital, who found the land the only thing that remained between himself and starvation. Rents in the lower grades of tenancies were regulated by competition, but it was competition between a half-starving population, who had no other resource except the soil, and were therefore prepared to promise anything rather than be deprived of it. The landlord did nothing for them. They built their own mud hovels, planted their hedges, dug their ditches. They were half naked, half starved, utterly destitute of all providence and of all education, liable at any time to be turned adrift from their holdings, ground to the dust by three great burdens—rack-rents, paid not to the landlord, but to the middleman; tithes, paid to the clergy—often the absentee clergy—of the Church to which they did not belong; and dues, paid to their own priests. Swift declared that Irish tenants "live worse than English beggars." The few travellers who visited the country uniformly described their condition as the most deplorable in Europe. "I never met," writes a very intelligent tourist who visited Ireland about 1764, "with such scenes of misery and oppression as this country, in too many parts of it, really exhibits. What with the severe exactions of rent, even before the corn is housed—a practice that too much prevails here among the petty and despicable landlords, third, fourth, and fifth from the first proprietor . . . of the parish priest—who, not content with the tithe of grain, exacts even the very tenth of half a dozen or half a score perches of potatoes, upon which a whole family perhaps subsists for the year—and of the Catholic priest, . . . who comes armed with the terrors of damnation, and demands his full quota of unremitted offerings, . . . the poor reduced wretches have hardly the skin of a potatoe left them to subsist on. . . . The high roads throughout the southern and western parts are lined with beggars, who live in cabins of such shocking materials and construction that through hundreds of them you see the smoke ascending from every inch of the roof, for scarce one in twenty of them have any chimney, and the rain drips from every inch of the roof on the half-naked, shivering, and almost half-starving inhabitants within. . . . The case of the lower class of farmers, indeed, is little better than a state of slavery. . . . The land, though often rich and fertile, almost universally wears the face of poverty, from want of good cultivation, which the miserable occupiers really are not able to give it, and very few of them know how if they were, and this indeed must be the case while the lands are canted (set to the highest bidder, not openly, but by private proposals, which throw every advantage into the hands of the landlord) in small parcels of 20 *l.* or 30*l.* a year, at third, fourth, and fifth hand from the first proprietor. From the most attentive and minute inquiries at many places, I am confident that the produce of this kingdom, either of corn or cattle, is not above two-thirds, at most, of what by good cultivation it might yield. Yet the gentlemen, I believe, make as much or more of their estates than any in the three kingdoms, while the lands, for equal goodness, produce the least. . . . The landlords first and subordinate get all that is made of the land, and the tenants, for their labour, get poverty and potatoes." "Ireland," continues the same writer, "would be indeed a rich country, if made the most of, if its trade were not reduced by unnatural restrictions and an Egyptian kind of politics from without, and its agriculture depressed by hard masters from within itself."

This description is amply borne out by other authorities, and it is easy to explain it. The mass of the people became cottiers because in most parts of Ireland it was impossible to gain a livelihood as agricultural labourers or in mechanical pursuits. This impossibility was due to the extreme paucity of circulating capital, and may be chiefly traced to the destruction of Irish manufactures, and to the absence of a considerable class of resident landlords, who would naturally give employment to the poor. The popular remedy in Ireland for the latter evil was an absentee tax, but as most of the absentees lived in England, it was felt by men of sense that such a measure could never obtain the assent of the authorities in that country.

The economical evil at the same time was aggravated at every stage by the laws against religion. The facility of selling land, and its value in the market, were unnaturally diminished by the exclusion of all Catholics from competition. Its agricultural condition was enormously impaired by the difficulty of borrowing money on landed security in a poor country, where this form of investment was legally closed against the great majority of the people. All real enterprise and industry among the Catholic tenants was destroyed by the laws which consigned them to utter ignorance, and still more by the law which placed strict bounds to their progress by providing that if their profits ever exceeded a third of their rent, the first Protestant who could prove the fact might take their farm. For reasons which have been often explained, Catholicism is on the whole less favourable to the industrial virtues than Protestantism, but yet the cases of France, of Flanders, and of the northern States of Italy, show that a very high standard of industry may under favourable circumstances be attained in a Catholic country. But in Ireland the debilitating influence of numerous Church holidays, and of a religious encouragement of mendicancy, was felt in a society in which employment was rare, intermittent, and miserably underpaid, and in which Catholic industry was legally deprived of its appropriate rewards. Very naturally, therefore, habits of gross and careless idleness prevailed, which greatly aggravated the poverty of the nation. At the same time the class of middlemen or large leaseholders was unnaturally encouraged, for while they escaped some of the most serious evils of the landlord, they were guarded by law from all Catholic competition, and accordingly possessed the advantage of monopoly. It was soon discovered that one of the easiest ways for a Protestant to make money was by taking a large tract of country from an absentee landlord at a long lease, and by letting it at rack-rents to Catholic cottiers. The Irish tenant, said a high authority on this subject, speaking of the middleman class, "will not be satisfied unless he has a long lease of lives of forty, fifty, or sixty years, that he may sell it, and 'tis rare to find a tenant in Ireland contented with a farm of moderate size. He pretends he cannot maintain his family with less than 200 acres—nay, if at any distance from town, 200 or 300 acres."

Another influence which aggravated the sufferings of the people was the tendency to turn great tracts of land into pasture, which produced numerous evictions, and greatly restricted the scanty resources of the poor. This tendency is, indeed, not one which can be regarded with unqualified condemnation. It is certain that pasture is the form of agricultural industry which the conditions of soil and climate make most suitable to Ireland. . . .

Over a great part of Ireland the cottiers were driven for the most part to the mountains, where they obtained little plots of potato ground, too small, however, to support them during the year. They eked out their subsistence by migrating from place to place during the summer and autumn in search of work. The rate of wages was usually sixpence in summer and fourpence in winter, but even at this rate continuous work could seldom for any long period be counted on. Saving was therefore impossible, and the people depended for their very existence on the produce of the year. Their houses and dress were so miserable that food was almost their only expense, and it was computed that 10*l.* was more than sufficient for the whole annual expense of an Irish family. But the first bad year brought them face to face with starvation. The practice of houghing cattle in Connaught, which was the most prominent form of agrarian crime in Ireland during the first half of the eighteenth century, was probably largely due to this rapid conversion of arable land into pasture, which drove the people to the verge of starvation, and to the same cause Boulter mainly attributed the great stream of recruits who passed from Ireland into the armies of the Continent. The tendency to throw land into pasture became very general about 1715, when the peace opened the ports of the Continent to Irish beef. The average export of corn of all sorts during that and the two preceding years was 189,672 barrels, but from this time it steadily declined. Boulter, Swift, Berkeley, Dobbs, Madden, Prior, and Skelton all agreed in representing the excessive amount of pasture as a leading cause both of the misery and the idleness of the people. In 1728 and 1729 the paucity of tillage greatly aggravated the severity of the famine. The distress was so poignant that the Parliament tried to remedy it by an artificial encouragement of tillage, but its measures were feeble and vacillating, and it was hampered by the jealousy of England, which feared lest Irish corn should enter into competition with her own. Swift had strongly censured a system, which had sprung up in his time, of landlords forbidding their tenants to break up or plough their land; and the House of Commons in 1716 passed a resolution against such covenants. . . .

The moral and economical conditions of nations are closely connected, and it is not surprising that under such circumstances as I have described, industrial habits should have been almost entirely wanting among the Irish poor. In the emphatic words of Berkeley, they grew up "in a cynical content in dirt and beggary to a degree beyond any other people in Christendom." Their "habitations and furniture" were "more sordid than those of the savage Americans," and the good bishop asked "whether there be upon earth any Christian or civilized people so beggarly wretched and destitute as the common Irish." An inevitable consequence, too, of the pressure of pasture upon population was an enormous increase of that nomadic pauperism which is one of the chief sources of national idleness and crime. I have shown in a former volume, from the testimony of Fletcher of Saltoun, the gigantic proportions this evil had attained in Scotland, and Defoe describes it as serious even in England. Arthur Dobbs, in a work published in 1731, gives us a corresponding picture of its magnitude in Ireland. Numerous ejections and the absolute necessity of going from place to place in search of work contributed largely to maintain it, and great multitudes who began their wanderings under the pressure of want soon acquired a taste for an idle, vagrant, and adventurous life. Work was scanty and intermittent. Its rewards were so miserably small that providence was almost useless and saving almost impossible. A spirit of humble charity was very widely diffused, and the poorer classes had been reduced to such a condition of squalor that food was almost their only want. Under these circumstances extreme idleness and wretched habits of mendicancy naturally spread. There were, Dobbs assures us, 2,295 parishes, and an average of at least ten vagrants begging in each the whole year round, and above thirty for three or four months in the summer. For the whole year he computes the number of strolling beggars at 34,000. The vast increase during the summer he ascribes to the fact that in the mountainous parts of the country, great numbers who have houses and farms sufficient to maintain them, as soon as they have sown their corn, planted their potatoes, and cut their turf, were accustomed either to hire out their cows, or to send them to the mountains, to shut their houses, and with their whole families to go begging till harvest time. Farmers as a speculation gave fixed sums to labourers for their chance of a summer's begging. Servants often quitted their service, and day labourers their work, giving as their reason that they could gain more by begging. Petty thieving, and the other forms of crime that always accompany this mode of life, inevitably increased, and there was one graver evil which we should hardly have expected. The strong domestic attachment which binds together the members of the poorest family has been for above a century a conspicuous feature of the Irish character; but Dobbs assures us that in his time beggars often mutilated or even blinded their children, in order, by making them objects of compassion, to increase their earnings; and that children who were quite able to support their parents often sent them abroad as vagrants when they became old, without giving them any more relief than they would give to common beggars. The prevailing idleness extended through both sexes. The custom of making the women do the severe field-work, while the men looked on in idleness, which scandalised every English traveller in Scotland, appears to have been unknown in Ireland. Women were, on the contrary, singularly exempt from those labours to which in a low state of civilisation they are usually condemned; but there were loud complaints that, except in the North, where they were largely employed in the linen trade, they lived for the most part in perfect idleness. . . .

*The Irish Government tried to repress mendicancy and vagrancy but met with little success. Charter Schools were created in order to provide Catholic children from six to ten years of age with a general education. To qualify for these schools, however, the pupils had to convert to Protestantism. This insistence on conversion and the harsh conditions in Charter Schools became a source of lasting resentment for the Catholic majority.*

It is probable that under the circumstances that have been enumerated in the preceding pages, the population of Ireland during the first half of the eighteenth century remained almost stationary. For many years after the great rebellion of 1641 the country had been extremely under-populated, and the prevailing habit of early and prolific marriages would naturally have led to very rapid multiplication, but famine, disease, and emigration were as yet sufficient to counteract it. Unfortunately, our sources of information on this subject are very imperfect. No census was taken; our chief means of calculating are derived from the returns of the hearth-money collectors; and the number of cabins that were exempted from the tax, as well as the great difference in different parts of the country in the average occupants of a house, introduce a large element of uncertainty into our estimates. It appears, however, according to the best means of information we possess, that the population in the beginning of the century was not far from two millions, and that it increased in fifty years to about 2,370,000. The proportion of Roman Catholics to Protestants is also a question of much difficulty. In the reign of Charles II, Petty had estimated it at eight to three. In a return based on the hearth-money collection, which was made to the Irish House of Lords in 1731, it was estimated at not quite two to one. It is probable, however, that the inequality was considerably understated. The great poverty of many of the Catholics, and the remote mountains and valleys in which they lived, withdrew them from the cognisance of the tax-gatherer; and Primate Boulter, in 1727, expressed his belief that there were in Ireland at least five Papists to one Protestant. He adds a statement which, if it be unexaggerated, furnishes an extraordinary example of the superiority of Catholic zeal in the midst of the penal laws, and at a time when Protestantism enjoyed all the advantages of an almost universal monopoly. He says: "We have incumbents and curates to the number of about 800, whilst there are more than 3,000 Popish priests of all sorts here."

Of the many depressing influences I have noticed in the foregoing pages, there is, perhaps, no one that may not be paralleled or exceeded in the annals of other countries; but it would be difficult, in the whole compass of history, to find another instance in which such various and such powerful agencies concurred to degrade the character and to blast the prosperity of a nation. That the greater part of them sprang directly from the corrupt and selfish government of England is incontestable. No country ever exercised a more complete control over the destinies of another than did England over those of Ireland for three-quarters of a century after the Revolution. No serious resistance of any kind was attempted. The nation was as passive as clay in the hands of the potter, and it is a circumstance of peculiar aggravation that a large part of the legislation I have recounted was a distinct violation of a solemn treaty. The commercial legislation which ruined Irish industry, the confiscation of Irish land, which disorganised the whole social condition of the country, the scandalous misapplication of patronage, which at once demoralised and impoverished the nation, were all directly due to the English

Government or to the English Parliament. The blame of the penal laws rests, it is true, primarily and principally on the Parliament of Ireland; but, as I have already shown, this Parliament, by its constitution and composition, was almost wholly subservient to English influence or control.

All this must be fully acknowledged, but there are other circumstances to be taken into account, which will considerably relieve the picture. Whoever desires to judge the policy of England without passion or prejudice will remember that Ireland was a conquered country, and that the war of the Revolution was only the last episode of a struggle which had continued for centuries, had been disgraced on both sides by revolting atrocities, and had engendered the most ferocious antipathies. He will remember that the bulk of the Irish people were Catholics, and that over the greater part of Europe the relations of Protestantism and Catholicism were still those of deadly hostility. He will remember that from a much earlier period than the Revolution it had become a settled maxim in England that Ireland was the most convenient outlet for English adventurers, and that Irish land might be confiscated without much more scruple than the land over which the Red Indian roves. The precedents were set by Mary, Elizabeth, and James I. The confiscations after the Revolution appeared to most English minds the normal result of conquest, and when this one step was taken, most of the other results inevitably followed. Above all, it must be remembered that the policy of a nation can only be equitably judged by a constant reference to the moral standard of the age, and that it is equally absurd and unjust to measure the actions of statesmen in one stage of civilisation by the rules of conduct prevailing in another. The more the history of bygone centuries is examined, the more evident it will appear that in the scheme and theory of government which under many external forms was almost universally accepted, the interests of the subordinate parts of an empire were habitually sacrificed to those of the centre. This was not peculiarly English: it was equally true of every considerable Power on the Continent.

These considerations will somewhat mitigate the judgment which a candid reader will pass upon the history of Ireland. They do not, however, affect the fact that a long train of causes of irresistible power were crushing both the moral and material energies of the country. One of the most obvious consequences was that for the space of about a century she underwent a steady process of depletion, most men of energy, ambition, talent, and character being driven from her shores. The movement, it is true, was by no means new, for long before the English power had crossed the Channel, Irish talent and Irish energy had shown a remarkable tendency to seek a sphere for action on the Continent. From about the middle of the sixth till near the close of the eighth century, Irishmen had borne a part second to that of no other European nation in the great work of evangelising Europe. . . .

It would be difficult indeed to conceive a national condition less favourable than that of Ireland to a man of energy and ambition. If he were a Catholic, he found himself excluded by his creed from every position of trust and power, and from almost every means of acquiring wealth, degraded by a social stigma, deprived of every vestige of political weight. If he were a Presbyterian, he was subject to the disabilities of the Test Act. If he were a member of the Established Church, he was even then compelled to see all the highest posts in Church and State monopolised by Englishmen. If he were a landlord, he found himself in a country where the law had produced such a social state that his position as a resident was nearly intolerable. If his ambition lay in the paths of manufacture or commerce, he was almost compelled to emigrate, for industrial and commercial enterprise had been deliberately crushed.

The result was that a steady tide of emigration set in, carrying away all those classes who were most essential to the development of the nation. The landlords found the attractions of London and Bath irresistible. The manufacturers and the large class of energetic labourers who lived upon manufacturing industry were scattered far and wide. Some of them passed to England and Scotland. Great numbers found a home in Virginia and Pennsylvania, and they were the founders of the linen manufacture in New England. Others, again, went to strengthen the enemies of England. Lewis XIV was in general bitterly intolerant to Protestants, but he warmly welcomed, encouraged, and protected in their worship, Protestant manufacturers from Ireland who brought their industry to Rouen and other cities of France. Many others took refuge in the Protestant States of Germany, while Catholic manufacturers settled in the northern provinces of Spain and laid the foundation of an industry which was believed to be very detrimental to England.

The Protestant emigration, which began with the destruction of the woollen manufacture, continued during many years with unabated and even accelerating rapidity. At the time of the Revolution, when great portions of the country lay waste, and when the whole framework of society was shattered, much Irish land had been let on lease at very low rents to English, and especially to Scotch Protestants. About 1717 and 1718 these leases began to fall in. Rents were usually doubled, and often trebled. The smaller farms were generally put up to competition, and the Catholics, who were accustomed to live in the most squalid misery, and to forego all the comforts of life, very naturally outbid the Protestants. This fact, added to the total destruction of the main industries on which the Protestant population subsisted, to the disabilities to which the Nonconformists were subject on account of their religion, and to the growing tendency to throw land into pasture, produced a great social revolution, the effects of which have never been repaired. For nearly three-quarters of a century the drain of the energetic Protestant population continued, and their places, when occupied at all, were occupied by a Catholic cottier population, sunk in the lowest depths of ignorance and poverty. All the miserable scenes of wholesale ejections, of the disruption of family ties, of the forced exile of men who were passionately attached to their country, were enacted. Carteret, in 1728, vainly deplored the great evil that was thus inflicted on the English interest in Ireland, and urged the Presbyterian ministers to employ their influence to abate it. Madden ten years later echoed the same complaint, and declared that at least one-third of those who went to the West Indies perished either on the journey or by diseases caught in the first weeks of landing. The famine of 1740 and 1741 gave an immense impulse to the movement, and it is said that for several years the Protestant emigrants from Ulster annually amounted to about 12,000. More than thirty years later, Arthur Young found the stream still flowing, and he mentioned that in 1773, 4,000 emigrants had sailed from Belfast alone. Many, ignorant and credulous, passed into the hands of designing agents, were inveigled into servitude or shipped by false pretences, or even with violence, to the most pestilential climates. . . .

*Irish emigrants to the American colonies played a prominent part in the War of Independence. In the seventeenth and eighteenth centuries thousands of Irish Catholics enlisted in Continental armies, contributing both courage and skill to the cause of England's enemies. During the wars of the mid-eighteenth century a number of Irish émigrés rose to positions of command in the Russian, French, Austrian, and Spanish armies.*

If, as there appears much reason to believe, there is such a thing as an hereditary transmission of moral and intellectual qualities, the removal from a nation of tens of thousands of the ablest and most energetic of its citizens must inevitably, by a mere physical law, result in the degradation of the race. Nor is it necessary to fall back upon any speculations of disputed science. In every community there exists a small minority of men whose abilities, high purpose, and energy of will, mark them out as in some degree leaders of men. These take the first steps in every public enterprise, counteract by their example the vicious elements of the population, set the current and form the standard of public opinion, and infuse a healthy moral vigour into their nation. In Ireland for three or four generations such men were steadily weeded out. Can we wonder that the standard of public morals and of public spirit should have declined?

But not only were the healthiest elements driven away: corrupting influences of the most powerful kind infected those who remained. It is extremely difficult in our day to realise the moral conditions of a society in which it was the very first object of the law to subvert the belief of the great majority of the people, to break down among them the sentiment of religious reverence, and in every possible way to repress, injure, and insult all that they regarded as sacred. I have already described the principal provisions of the penal code.¹ I have given examples of the language employed on the most solemn occasions and in their official capacities, by viceroys and by judges; but it is only by a minute and detailed examination that we can adequately realise the operation of the system. In all the walks and circumstances of life the illegal character of the faith of the people was obtruded. If a Catholic committed a crime, no matter how unconnected with his creed, the fact that he was of the Popish religion was usually recorded ostentatiously in the proclamation against him. If a petitioner could possibly allege it, his Protestantism was seldom omitted in the enumeration of his merits. A Catholic, or even the husband of a Catholic, was degraded in his own country by exclusion from every position of trust from the highest to the lowest, while Frenchmen and Germans were largely pensioned, avowedly in order to strengthen the Protestant interest. The form of recantation drawn up for those who consented to join the Established Church was studiously offensive, for it compelled the convert to brand his former faith as "the way of damnation." In the eyes of the law the prelates and friars, whom the Catholic regarded with the deepest reverence; the priest, who without having taken the abjuration oath celebrated the worship which he believed to be essential to his salvation; the schoolmaster, who, discharging a duty of the first utility, taught his children the rudiments of knowledge, were all felons, for whose apprehension a reward was offered, and who only remained in the country by connivance or concealment. . . .

*The penal laws were enforced in an inconsistent and often arbitrary manner. Most priests managed to elude the snares of professional priest-hunters, and they refused to take the oath of abjuration as required by an act of 1709.*

Towards the first quarter of the eighteenth century the spirit of persecution, as shown by the resolutions and other acts of the House of Commons, seems to have been very intense, but it soon after began to subside. Persecution can hardly be really stringent when met by the passive resistance of the great majority of a nation. The priests, with great courage, continued to defy the law. Many Mass-houses were built when the system of registration began; they continued to be employed though the officiating clergymen had never taken the oath of abjuration, and new ones, though usually of a very humble and unobtrusive description, were rising. Much depended on the character of the landlords, on the disposition of the neighbouring magistrates, and on the proportion the Catholics bore to the Protestants. Priests were nearly everywhere numerous, but in many districts the Mass was still celebrated in some old barn or secluded hovel. Sometimes it was celebrated in the fields or on the mountains. A movable altar was placed under the shadow of a great tree, and there the priest gathered the worshippers about him, and distributed to them the sacred food. At the instigation of Primate Boulter, who was a bitter enemy of the Catholics, the House of Lords, in 1732, appointed a committee to inquire into the state of Popery in Ireland; and a report, based upon evidence sent in by the Protestant clergy in each district, was drawn up. It stated that there existed in Ireland 892 regular Mass-houses and 54 private chapels, served by 1,445 priests, that there were 51 friaries containing in all 254 friars, that there were 9 nunneries, and not less than 549 Popish schools. Of the Mass-houses 229 had been built since the death of George I. The Papists, it was added, attended their Mass-houses as openly as the Protestants their churches, but the regulars lived in more concealment. It is probable that this report, being derived exclusively from a hostile clergy, rests largely on conjecture, but there is no doubt that a great organisation existed in defiance of law. . . .

*Toleration of Catholics increased noticeably during and after the 1740s. The priesthood continued to show courage in defying the penal code. But Catholic tradesmen and merchants in the towns generally fared better under the penal laws than did their co-religionists in rural areas.*

These examples may be sufficient to illustrate the position of the Catholic worship and clergy in Ireland during the first half of the eighteenth century. It is easy to understand how pernicious must have been the effect of this opposition between law and religion on the national character. In England many particular legislators or laws have been unpopular, but if we except a few years that followed the Reformation, and also the brief period of Puritan ascendency, law, as a whole, has always been looked upon as a beneficent agency representing the sentiments, securing the rights, and commanding the respect of the great body of the community. Generation after generation grew up with this sentiment, and reverence for law became in consequence a kind of

hereditary instinct lying at the very root of the national character. The circumstances of Scotland were much less favourable,
and in the first half of the eighteenth century it was certainly
more lawless than Ireland. Until after the abolition of the hereditary jurisdictions English law was practically inoperative in the
Highlands, but it was disliked chiefly as a form of restraint, without any peculiar inveteracy of hatred, and certainly without any
moral reprobation. In Ireland, except in a few remote districts in
the south and west, law was recognised by the Catholic community as a real, powerful, omnipresent agent, immoral, ir-
religious, and maleficent. All their higher and nobler life lay
beyond its pale. Illegal combination was consecrated when it
was essential to the performance of religious duty. Illegal violence
was the natural protection against immoral laws. Eternal salvation, in the eyes of the great majority of the Irish, could only be
obtained by a course of conduct condemned by the law.

It would, no doubt, be possible to exaggerate this aspect of
the penal code. Irish history did not begin with the eighteenth
century, and a long train of causes had before this time made the
people but little amenable to law. Irish crime has very rarely been
directly connected with religion, and its great ebullitions may
usually be traced either to the pressure of extreme poverty, or
to disputes about the possession or the occupancy of land. But the
penal code had an influence which, if indirect, was at least
enormously great. It rendered absolutely impossible in Ireland
the formation of that habit of instinctive and unreasoning reverence for law which is one of the most essential conditions of
English civilisation, and at the same time, by alienating the people
from their Government, it made the ecclesiastical organisation to
which they belonged the real centre of their affections and their
enthusiasm. It made the Irish people the most fervent Catholics
in Europe, but yet it was not without an injurious influence on
the moral side of their religion. No class among them had such
moral influence as the priests, but few classes have ever subsisted
under more demoralising conditions. Springing for the most part
from the peasant ranks, sharing their prejudices and their passions, and depending absolutely on their contributions, miserably
ignorant, and miserably poor, they were an illegal class compelled to associate with smugglers, robbers, and privateers, to

whose assistance they were often obliged to resort in order to escape the ministers of justice. Their bishops were at the same time in a position of such peculiar danger that the exercise of ecclesiastical discipline was often almost impossible. It could hardly be expected that a class so situated should be either able or disposed to set themselves in bold opposition to disloyalty or popular crime. From the Government they could expect nothing beyond a contemptuous toleration, while every motive of self-interest and of ambition urged them to identify themselves thoroughly with the passions of their people. Their conduct, indeed, in many respects was very noble. The zeal with which they maintained the religious life of their flocks during the long period of persecution is beyond all praise. . . .

The strength of their principles was sufficiently shown by their almost unanimous refusal of the abjuration oath, and by the extreme paucity of conversions among them at a time when a large reward was offered for the apostasy of a priest. But their influence, though sometimes exerted to save life and to repress disorder, has not on the whole been favourable to law. Inheriting the traditions, they have exhibited many of the tendencies, of an illegal class, and have sometimes looked, if not with connivance, at least with a very insufficient abhorrence upon crimes which as religious teachers it was their first duty unsparingly to denounce.

The moral influence of the penal laws was not less baneful in that part which related to property. The scandalous, unscrupulous misrepresentation of those writers who have described the code as a mere dead letter can hardly be more strikingly evinced than by glancing at the place which property cases under the code occupy in the proceedings of the Irish law courts. Even in trade the Catholics were, as we have seen, by no means free from disabilities, and the law gave their Protestant rivals such means of annoying them that they were compelled to acquiesce in the most illegal exactions. . . .

A Protestant gentry grew up, generation after generation, regarding ascendency as their inalienable birthright; ostentatiously and arrogantly indifferent to the interests of the great masses of their nation, resenting every attempt at equality as a kind of infringement of the laws of nature. The social distinction was carefully preserved. A Catholic could not carry the arms that were still the indispensable sign of the position of a gentleman, without a licence, which it was often very difficult to obtain; and he only kept his hunter or his carriage-horses by the forbearance of his Protestant neighbours. A story is told of a Catholic gentleman who once drove into Mullingar at the time of the assizes in a carriage drawn by two beautiful horses. A man stopped the carriage, and tendering ten guineas, in accordance with the Act of William, claimed the horses for his own. The gentleman, drawing a brace of pistols from his pocket, shot the horses dead upon the spot. The class feeling, indeed, produced by the code was much stronger than the purely theological oppugnancy. Archbishop Synge truly wrote, "There are too many amongst us who had rather keep the Papists as they are, in an almost slavish subjection, than have them made Protestants, and thereby entitled to the same liberties and privileges with the rest of their fellow-subjects."

And behind all this lay the great fact that most of the land of the country was held by the title of recent confiscation, and that the old possessors or their children were still living, still remembered, still honoured by the people. It was the dread of a change of property springing from this fact that was the real cause of most of the enactments of the penal code. It was this that paralysed every political movement by making it almost impossible for it to assume national dimensions. It was this which gave the landlord class most of their arrogance, their recklessness, and their extravagance. It was this above all that made them, in the early years of the century, implacably hostile to every project for ameliorating the condition of the Catholics. In 1709 the House of Commons presented an address to the Queen, urging strongly the fatal consequences of reversing the outlawries of any persons who had been attainted for the rebellions either of 1641 or of 1688, on the ground that any measure of clemency would shake the security of property. "The titles of more than half the estates," they said, "now belonging to the Protestants depend on the forfeitures in the two last rebellions, wherein the generality of the Irish were engaged."

This fact lies at the very root of the social and political history of Ireland. In Scotland the greater part of the soil is even now in the possession of the descendants of chiefs whose origin is lost in the twilight of fable. In England, notwithstanding the fluctuations which great industrial fortunes naturally produce, much of the land of the country is still owned by families which rose to power under the Tudors, or even under the Plantagenets. In both countries centuries of co-operation, of sympathy, of mutual good services, have united the landlord and tenant classes by the closest ties. But in Ireland, where the deplorable absence of industrial life marks out the landlords as pre-eminently the natural leaders of the people, this sympathy has been almost wholly wanting. Only an infinitesimal portion of the soil belongs to the descendants of those who possessed it before Cromwell, and the division of classes which was begun by confiscation has been perpetuated by religion, and was for many generations studiously aggravated by law. Its full moral significance was only felt at a much later period, when political life began to stir among the great masses of the people. It was then found that the tendons of society were cut, and no fact has contributed more to debilitate the national character. In an army, if once the confidence of the soldiers in their officers is destroyed, the whole organisation is relaxed, discipline gives way, military courage rapidly sinks, and troops who under other circumstances would have been full of fire, enthusiasm, and steady valour, degenerate into a dispirited and vacillating mob. With nations it is not very different. Few things contribute so much to the strength and steadiness of a national character as the consciousness among the people that in every great struggle or difficulty they will find their natural leaders at their head— men in whom they have perfect confidence, whose interests are thoroughly identified with their own, who are placed by their position above most sordid temptations, to whom they are already attached by ties of property, tradition, and association. A nation must have attained no mean political development before it can choose with intelligence its own leaders, and it is happy if in the earlier stages of its career the structure of society saves it from the necessity, by placing honest and efficient men naturally at its head. The close sympathy between the Scotch people and the Scotch gentry in most of the national struggles has been one great cause of that admirable firmness of national character which learnt at last to dispense with leadership. In Ireland, in spite of adverse circumstances, this attachment between landlord and tenant in many particular instances was undoubtedly formed, but in general there could be no real confidence between the classes. When the people awoke to political life, they found their natural leaders their antagonists; they were compelled to look for other chiefs, and they often found them in men who were inferior in culture, in position, and in character, who sought their suffrages for private ends, and who won them by fulsome flattery, false rhetoric, and exaggerated opinions.

And the same evil is only too apparent in literature. That proportion of the national talent and scholarship which ought in every country to be devoted to elucidating the national history, has in Ireland not been so employed. Something, as we shall hereafter see, of real value was done in this direction in the latter half of the eighteenth century, and not a little has been accomplished within the last thirty years, but still Irish history is shamefully chaotic, undigested, and unelaborated, and it presents in this respect a most humiliating contrast to the history of Scotland. The explanation is very obvious. For a long period the classes who possessed almost a monopoly of education and wealth, regarded themselves as a garrison in a foreign and a conquered country. Their religion, their traditions, and the tenure by which they held their properties, cut them off from real sympathy with the people. The highest literary talent was accordingly diverted to other channels, and Irish history has passed to a lamentable extent into the hands of religious polemics, of dishonest partisans, and of half-educated and uncritical enthusiasts.

The effect of all this upon the character, the politics, and the literature of the Irish Catholics is very obvious. Its effect on the ruling caste was not less pernicious. In England one of the most eminently successful parts of the prevailing system of government has been its action upon the higher classes. It has succeeded to so great a degree in associating dignity with public service, and in forming a point of honour in favour of labour, that it has induced a larger proportion of men of rank and fortune to utilise for the public good the great opportunities of their position than can be found in any other nation. In Ireland a long train of complicated, connected, and irresistible causes operated in the opposite direction. The upper classes were exposed to all the characteristic vices of slaveholders, for they formed a dominant caste, ruling over a population who were deprived of all civil rights and reduced to a condition of virtual slavery. They were separated from their tenants by privilege, by race, by religion, by the memory of inexpiable wrongs, and it was one of the worst moral features of their situation that a chief element of their power lay in their complete control of the administration of justice. At the same time, the penal laws secured a perpetual influx into their ranks of men of lax principles or tarnished honour. The poor remained steadfast and devoted to their religion, but many of the more educated Catholics conformed, in order to secure their estates, to enter professions, or to free themselves from social and political disabilities. Apostasy was the first step in the path of ambition. . . .

The vices of Irish society have been often described, and they lay at the surface. The worst was the oppression of the tenantry by their landlords. The culprits in this respect were not the head landlords, who usually let their land at low rents and on long leases to middlemen, and whose faults were rather those of neglect than of oppression. They were commonly the small gentry, a harsh, rapacious, and dissipated class, living with an extravagance that could only be met by the most grinding exactions, and full of the pride of race and of the pride of creed. Swift and Dobbs bitterly lament this evil, and nearly every traveller echoed their complaint. Chesterfield, who as Lord Lieutenant studied the conditions of Irish life with more than ordinary care, left it as his opinion that "the poor people in Ireland are used worse than negroes by their lords and masters, and their deputies of deputies of deputies." We are assured on good authority that it was "not unusual in Ireland for great landed proprietors to have regular prisons in their houses for the summary punishment of the lower orders," that "indictments against gentlemen for similar exercise of power beyond law are always thrown out by the grand jurors," that "to horsewhip or beat a servant or labourer is a frequent mode of correction." What the relations of landlord and tenant were in the first half of the eighteenth century may be easily inferred from the description which Arthur Young gives of its state in 1776, when the memory of the confiscations had in a great degree faded, and when religious animosity was almost extinct.

He tells us that "the age has improved so much in humanity that even the poor Irish have experienced its influence, and are every day treated better and better." Yet, even at this time, he assures us, "the landlord of an Irish estate inhabited by Roman Catholics is a sort of despot, who yields obedience, in whatever concerns the poor, to no law but that of his will. . . . A long series of oppressions, aided by many very ill-judged laws, have brought landlords into a habit of exerting a very lofty superiority, and their vassals into that of an almost unlimited submission. Speaking a language that is despised, professing a religion that is abhorred, and being disarmed, the poor find themselves in many cases slaves even in the bosom of written liberty. . . . A landlord in Ireland can scarcely invent an order which a servant, labourer, or cotter dares to refuse to execute. Nothing satisfies him but an unlimited submission. Disrespect, or anything tending towards sauciness, he may punish with his cane or his horsewhip with the most perfect security. A poor man would have his bones broken if he offered to lift his hand in his own defence. Knocking down is spoken of in the country in a way that makes an Englishman stare. Landlords of consequence have assured me that many of their cotters would think themselves honoured by having their wives and daughters sent for to the bed of their master. . . . It must strike the most careless traveller to see whole strings of cars whipped into a ditch by a gentleman's footman, to make way for his carriage. If they are overturned or broken in pieces, it is taken in patience. Were they to complain, they would perhaps be horsewhipped. The execution of the law lies very much in the hands of the justices of the peace, many of whom are drawn from the most illiberal class in the kingdom. If a poor man lodges his complaint against a gentleman, or any animal that chooses to call itself a gentleman, and the justice issues a summons for his appearance, it is a fixed affront, and he will infallibly be called out."

Duelling in the eighteenth century was very frequent in England, but the fire-eater and the bravo never attained the position in English life which was conceded him in Ireland. The most eminent statesman, the most successful lawyers, even the fellows of the university, whose business was the training of the young, were sometimes experienced duellists. An insolent, reckless, and unprincipled type of character was naturally formed.

Drunkenness and extravagance went hand in hand among the gentry, and especially among the lesser gentry, and the immense consumption of French wine was deplored as a national calamity. . . .

There is no class who have improved more conspicuously or more incontestably during the last hundred and fifty years than the country gentry both in England and Ireland, and the Squire Westerns of the one country were hardly of a higher type than the Lord Eyres of the other. Irish magistrates, scattered thinly over wild, hostile, Catholic districts, and stimulated to vigilance by the constant fear of rebellion or outrage, were placed under circumstances likely to elicit in a really superior man some high qualities of administration and command; and their correspondence with the Government, which is still preserved, exhibits a very respectable level of culture and intelligence. School and university education among the Irish Protestants in the first half of the eighteenth century appears to have been fully equal to what then existed in England; and the great prevalence of social habits did something to soften the tone both of manners and of feeling. But on the whole, and in the most important respects, the country gentry in Ireland were greatly inferior to the corresponding class in England. They inherited traditions of violence, extravagance, and bigotry. Their relations to their tenants were peculiarly demoralising. Their circumstances were eminently fitted to foster among them the vices of tyranny; and an oligarchy, disposing almost absolutely of county revenues and of political power in a country where nearly all political and professional promotion was given by favour, and where all government was tainted by monopoly, soon learnt to sacrifice habitually public to private interest. Spendthrift and drunken country gentlemen, corrupt politicians, and jobbing officials were, indeed, abundantly common in England in the first half of the eighteenth century, but in Ireland the tone of dissipation was more exaggerated, and the level of public spirit was more depressed. There was little genuine patriotism, and political profligacy was sometimes strangely audacious. The shameful jest of the politician who thanked God that he had a country to sell is said to be of Irish origin, and it reflected only too faithfully the prevailing spirit of a large section of the gentry.

These vices were more or less diffused through the whole class, but they attained their extreme development in the small land-lords, and especially in the middlemen. At a time when in England economical causes were steadily weeding out the poorer and less cultivated members of the squirearchy, and replacing them by large landlords, the tendency in Ireland was precisely opposite. Absenteeism drew away a great part of the richer land-lords, while the middlemen rapidly multiplied. A hybrid and ambiguous class, without any of the solid qualities of the English yeomen, they combined the education and manners of farmers with the pretensions of gentlemen, and they endeavoured to support those pretensions by idleness, extravagance, and ostentatious arrogance. Men who in England would have been modest and laborious farmers, in Ireland sublet their land at rack-rents, kept miserable packs of half-starved hounds, wandered about from fair to fair and from race to race in laced coats, gambling, fighting, drinking, swearing, ravishing, and sporting, parading everywhere their contempt for honest labour, giving a tone of recklessness to every society in which they moved. An industrial middle class, which is the most essential of all the elements of English life, was almost wholly wanting; and the class of middlemen and squireens, who most nearly corresponded to it, were utterly destitute of industrial virtues, and concentrated in themselves most of the distinctive vices of the Irish character. They were the chief agents in agrarian tyranny, and their pernicious influence on manners, in a country where the prohibition of manufactures had expatriated the most industrious classes and artificially checked the formation of industrial habits, can hardly be overrated. They probably did more than any other class to sustain that race of extravagance which ran through all ranks above the level of the cottier, and that illiberal and semi-barbarous contempt for industrial pursuits, which was one of the greatest obstacles to national progress. False ideals, false standards of excellence, grew up among the people, and they came to look upon idleness and extravagance as noble things, upon parsimony, order, and industry as degrading to a gentleman.

These are signs of a society that was profoundly diseased, and it is not difficult to trace the causes of the malady. It must, however, be added that there was another and a very different side of Irish life. Its contrasts have always been stronger than those of

England, and though the elements of corruption extended very far, it would be a grave error to suppose that in the first half of the eighteenth century everything in Ireland was frivolous and corrupt, that there was no genuine intellectual life, no real public spirit moving in the country. Considering how unfavourable were the circumstances of the nation, the number of its eminent men, in the period of which I am writing, was very respectable. During a considerable portion of that period Swift was illuminating Dublin by the rays of his transcendent genius, while Berkeley, who was scarcely inferior to Swift in ability, and incomparably his superior in moral qualities, who was, indeed, one of the finest and most versatile intellects, and one of the purest characters of the eighteenth century, filled the See of Cloyne. . . .

The most important, however, of the signs of public spirit in Ireland was the Dublin Society, which was founded in 1731, chiefly by the exertions of Thomas Prior, and of Samuel Madden, a very benevolent and very able clergyman of the Established Church, for the purpose of improving husbandry, manufactures, and other useful arts. The part which this society plays in the history of Irish industry during the eighteenth century is a very eminent one. It attracted to itself a considerable number of able and public-spirited members, and it was resolved that each member, on his admission, should select some particular branch, either of natural history, husbandry, agriculture, gardening, or manufacture, should endeavour as far as possible to make himself a complete master of all that was known concerning it, and should draw up a report on the subject. The chief object of the society was as far as possible to correct the extreme ignorance of what was going on in these departments in other countries which, owing to poverty, to want of education or enterprise, and to the isolated geographical position of the country, was very general. The society published a weekly account of its proceedings, collected statistics, popularised new inventions, encouraged by premiums agricultural improvement and different forms of Irish industry, brought over from England a skilful farmer to give lessons in his art, set up a model farm and even model manufactories, and endeavoured as far as possible to diffuse industrial knowledge through the kingdom. The press cordially assisted it, and for some years there was scarcely a number of a Dublin newspaper that did not contain addresses from the society with useful receipts or directions for farmers, or explanations of different branches of industry, and at the same time offers of small prizes for those who most successfully followed the instructions that were given. Thus—to give but a few out of very many instances —we find prizes offered for the best imitation of several different kinds of foreign lace; for the best pieces of flowered silk, of damask, of tapestry, of wrought velvet; for the farmers who could show the largest amount of land sown with several specified kinds of seed, or manured with particular kinds of manure; for draining; for reclaiming unprofitable bogs, for the manufacture of cider, of gooseberry wine, and of beer brewed from Irish hops; for the best beaver hats made in the country; for the baker who baked bread or the fisherman who cured fish according to receipts published by the society; for every cod crimped in the method that was in use in England and Holland, which was brought on a certáin day to the market on Ormond Quay.

Such methods of encouragement would be little suited to a high stage of commercial or agricultural activity, but they were eminently useful in a country where, owing to many depressing circumstances, industrial life was extremely low. For many years the society was supported entirely by the voluntary subscriptions of the Irish gentry, and Chesterfield said with truth that "it did more good to Ireland with regard to arts and industry than all the laws that could have been formed." In 1746, however, it obtained a small annual bounty of 500*l.* from the Civil List. In 1750 it received a Royal Charter, and it was afterwards assisted by considerable grants from the Irish Parliament. About 1758, when there was still no public institution for the encouragement of art in England, the Dublin Society began to undertake this function in Ireland, and it discharged it during many years with great zeal. . . .

*George Berkeley, the enlightened Bishop of Cloyne, and a few other liberal-minded Church leaders preached the need for toleration of Catholics. In 1725 Edward Synge, son of the Archbishop, preached a sermon before the Irish House of Commons in which he rejected the use of coercive measures against the Catholic populace.*

The spirit of tolerance, however, steadily grew, and it was accompanied by a strong desire, based upon economical motives, to permit Catholics to invest money in land. Being almost restricted to trade, they had gradually acquired a preeminence in this field, and at a time when the dearth of money was extremely great, and when agriculture was suffering bitterly in consequence, it was found that a very large, if not the greater part of the ready money of the country was in their hands. The more ardent Protestants added that the law dividing equally the landed property of the Catholic among his children, unless the eldest consented to conform, had produced more converts than any other agency, and they predicted that if the Catholics were permitted to take beneficial leases with the restriction that these should descend by preference to the children who embraced Protestantism, the movement of proselytism would be greatly stimulated.

The laws were at the same time suffered to fall in a great degree, over large districts and for long periods of time, into comparative desuetude. The decline of religious fanaticism among the Protestants, their indignation at the commercial disabilities, and at English patronage and pensions, as well as the natural feelings produced by neighbourhood and private friendships, all conspired to this result. Besides this, over a large part of Ireland there were fifteen or twenty Catholics for one Protestant, and it was impossible to carry out such a system as the penal code without a perpetual employment of military force. Society cannot permanently exist in a condition of extreme tension, and it was necessary for the members of both religions to find some way of living together in tolerable security. The very features of the Irish character that make it slow to remedy abuses—its careless, easy good-nature, its good-humoured acquiescence in the conditions in which it finds itself—were here of great service, and a lax and tolerant administration gradually mitigated the severity of intolerant laws. The aspect of the country was not altogether what might be inferred from a mere perusal of the statute book. The division of classes was very profound, but it may be doubted whether class hatred in Ireland was ever as intense as that which existed between the French peasants and the French nobles at the time of the Revolution, or as that which at a still later period divided the middle and working classes in great

French cities. The Catholic worship for many years, and in many parts of Ireland, was celebrated with little less publicity than the Protestant worship. Galway and Limerick were intended to be exclusively Protestant, but early in the eighteenth century they were almost exclusively Catholic, and in spite of the laws and of many isolated acts of persecution the country was full of friars, Catholic schoolmasters, and unregistered priests.

The code was in most respects extremely demoralising, yet some fine qualities of friendship, confidence, and honour were fostered under its influence. Though the law expressly condemned such evasions, a few Catholic families preserved their land undivided, and even purchased fresh land by the assistance of Protestants, in whom the nominal ownership was vested, and the confidence was scarcely ever abused. Protestant friends enabled the Catholic parent to evade the savage law which doomed his young children, if left orphans, to a Protestant education. . . .

The Government, too, though very bad, was not without its redeeming features. A Parliament, representing almost exclusively a single class in a country where religious disqualifications and recent confiscations made class divisions very profound, was naturally on many questions exceedingly selfish and arbitrary. But an assembly of resident landlords can hardly fail to take a real interest in the material welfare of their country, or to bring a large amount of valuable experience to legislation. Many measures of practical, unobtrusive utility were passed, and a real check was put upon the extravagance of the executive. Had there been no Parliament—had the whole revenues of the country remained under the control of such statesmen as Newcastle or Walpole, there can be no reasonable doubt that the condition of Ireland would have been much worse. Some tens of thousands of pounds were annually squandered in scandalous pensions or sinecures; but still taxation was moderate, and it had little tendency to increase. A very able statesman who was Chief Secretary under Lord Townshend has observed that since the first year of George II, for the space of fifty years, the only additional taxes imposed in Ireland were some inconsiderable duties, appropriated to the payment of the interest and principal of the debt, and some small duties, the produce of which was specifically assigned to the encouragement of tillage or of some particular branch of Irish trade or manufacture. As in England, there were some constituencies which were really open, and in the first half of the eighteenth century the expenses at elections appear to have been extremely moderate. Some interesting letters are preserved describing a severely contested election which took place in 1713 in the great county of Londonderry, in which Joshua Dawson, the active Secretary at the Castle, was defeated. The writer speaks of the cost of this election as very great, yet he estimates the expenses of the victorious party at only 400*l.* The viceroys lived for most of their term of office in London; but the great mass of Government correspondence which is still extant shows that the Government officials discharged the ordinary duties of administration with considerable industry and fidelity.

The character of the poorer classes was forming under circumstances that were on the whole exceedingly unfavourable. It was impossible, as we have seen, that the habits of respect for law which had been already created in England, and which were gradually forming in Scotland, should have grown up under the shadow of the penal laws, and the conditions of the nation were equally unfavourable to the political and to the industrial virtues. But other qualities, which are, perhaps, not less valuable, were developed under the discipline of sorrow. In the earlier periods of Irish history, English writers constantly speak of the licentiousness of the people, and of their extreme laxity in marriage. Spenser, Campion, and Davies dwelt upon it with equal emphasis. But in the eighteenth century such complaints had wholly ceased. Under the influence of the religious spirit which was now pervading the nation, a great moral revolution was silently effected. A standard of domestic virtue, a delicacy of female honour, was gradually formed among the Irish poor higher than in any other part of the Empire, and unsurpassed, if not unequalled, in Europe. The very extension of poverty and mendicancy had produced among them a rare and touching spirit of charity, a readiness to share with one another the last crust and the last potato. Domestic affections were more than commonly warm. The memorable fact that in the present century not less than twenty millions of pounds have been sent back in the space of twenty years by those who went for the most part penniless emigrants to America, to their relatives in Ireland, illustrates a side of the

Irish character which was already noticed by many observers; and in modern times, concerning which alone we can speak with confidence, infanticide, desertion, wife-murder, and other crimes indicating a low state of domestic morality have been much rarer among the Irish poor than among the corresponding classes in England. The division of classes in the middle of the eighteenth century was still very deep, but very often where the landlord lived among his people, and treated them with kindness, the old clan spirit was displayed in an attachment as fervid, as uncompromising, and as enduring as was ever shown by the Highlander to his chief.

Religious convictions acquired a rare depth and earnestness. A strangely chequered character was forming, tainted with some serious vices, very deficient in truthfulness, industry, and energy, in self-reliance, self-respect, and self-control, but capable of rising, under good leadership, to a lofty height of excellence, and with its full share both of the qualities that attract and fascinate the stranger, and of the qualities that brighten and soften the daily intercourse of life. It was at once eminently passionate and eminently tenacious in its gratitude and its revenge. It often rewarded kindness by a complete and life-long devotion. It bowed before the arrogance and transient violence of authority with a tame submission and absence of resentment scarcely conceivable to the Englishman, but when touched to the quick by serious wrong, or by the violation of some cherished custom, it was capable of the most savage, secret, and deliberate vengeance. A traditional religion strengthened its retrospective tendencies. No people brooded more upon old wrongs, clung more closely to old habits, were more governed by imagination, association, and custom. There was a strange and subtle mixture of rare stability of tendency and instinct, and of a vein of deep poetic, religious melancholy, with a temperament in many respects singularly buoyant, lighthearted and improvident, with great quickness, vividness, and versatility both of conception and expression. Catholicism, compelled to take refuge in mud hovels, associated with sordid poverty and degradation, and obliged to avoid every form of ostentation, never became in Ireland the instrument of aesthetic culture which it has proved in other lands; but every traveller was struck with the natural courtesy, the instinctive tact, the gay, hospitable, and cheerful manners of the Irish peasant, and with the contrast they presented to the deplorable poverty of his lot. The country was naturally very fertile, and the cheapness of provisions in some districts was probably exceeded in no part of Europe. This cheapness was, no doubt, on the whole, an evil, and arose from the wretched condition of the country, which made it impossible for the farmer to find sufficient markets for his produce; but it, at least, secured in good years an abundance of the first necessaries of life, and stimulated the spirit of hospitality in the poorest cabin. Owing, probably, to the dense, smoky atmosphere of the hovels, in which a hole in the roof was often the only chimney, blindness was unusually common, and innumerable blind fiddlers traversed the land, and found a welcome at every fireside. Dancing was universal, and the poor dancing-master was one of the most characteristic figures of Irish life. Hurling was practised with a passionate enthusiasm. The love of music was very widely spread. Carolan, the last, and it is said the greatest, of the old race of Irish bards, died in 1737. When only eighteen, he became blind through the smallpox, and he spent most of his life wandering through Connaught. His fame now rests chiefly upon tradition, but all who came in contact with him appear to have recognised in him a great genius; and Goldsmith, who was fascinated by his music in early youth, retained his admiration for it to the end of his life.

The gradual extension of roads was at the same time steadily reclaiming the west and south from Highland anarchy; the traditions and habits of civil war were slowly subsiding both among the conquerors and the conquered, and religious bigotry more rapidly diminished. It is, of course, impossible to mark out with accuracy the stages of this progress, but the fact is altogether incontestable. Few legislative bodies ever exhibited a more savage intolerance than the Irish Parliament in the first quarter of the eighteenth century. In the last quarter of the same century the Irish Parliament showed itself far more liberal in its dealings with Catholics than the Parliament of England, and measures which would have been utterly impossible in England were carried with scarcely perceptible difficulty in Ireland. Duelling and drinking, though both scandalously prevalent, were steadily diminishing, and, before the century had closed, the Irish gentry appear to have been little more addicted to the latter vice than the corresponding class in England.

What I have written may be sufficient to show that Irish life in the first half of the eighteenth century was not altogether the corrupt, frivolous, grotesque, and barbarous thing that it has been represented; that among many and glaring vices some real public spirit and intellectual energy may be discerned. It may be added that great improvements were at this time made in the material aspect of Dublin.

In the middle of the eighteenth century it was in dimensions and population the second city in the Empire, containing, according to the most trustworthy accounts, between 100,000 and 120,000 inhabitants. Like most things in Ireland, it presented vivid contrasts, and strangers were equally struck with the crowds of beggars, the inferiority of the inns, the squalid wretchedness of the streets of the old town, and with the noble proportions of the new quarter, and the brilliant and hospitable society that inhabited it. The Liffey was spanned by four bridges, and another on a grander scale was undertaken in 1753. St. Stephen's Green was considered the largest square in Europe. . . .

*Dublin in the age of William Molyneux and Dean Swift was a thriving capital, rich in the arts and architecture as well as in science and commerce. Among the enduring monuments of this neoclassical era was the Irish Parliament House, built in the 1730s and designed by Sir Edward Pearce.*

The civilisation of the nation was concentrated to a somewhat disproportionate extent in the capital, yet provincial life had already in its leading features more of its modern aspect than has sometimes been imagined. Resident country gentlemen, and especially improving country gentlemen, were much rarer than in England, but there were few counties in which some did not exist, and there were some parts of Ireland where they were numerous. Considerable attention was paid to the improvement of the roads. After about the first quarter of the eighteenth century the journals of the House of Commons are crowded with notices of works of this kind in almost every part of the country. When Whitefield visited Ireland for the first time, in 1738, he was especially struck with the cheapness of the provisions and the goodness of the roads. An English traveller in 1764, who traversed the three provinces of Ulster, Leinster, and Munster, states that he found no serious difficulty during his journey, that the roads were in general tolerably good for riding, but by no means equal to those in England for carriages, and that there were turnpikes on all the principal highways. In 1776 Arthur Young found their condition greatly improved, and described them as, on the whole, superior to those in England. Inland navigation was also considerably extended, especially in the counties of Armagh and Down.

There were the usual meetings of country gentlemen at the assizes; there were county races and county fairs, and long before the middle of the eighteenth century Dublin actors were accustomed to make their rounds by Mullingar, Clonmel, Carlow, and other county towns. A taste for private theatricals was very general about the middle of the century, and they were a favourite amusement in country houses. In the vicinity of Dublin highwaymen were numerous, but in the rest of the country they appear to have been at least as rare as in England, and in the worst periods of political disturbance and of Whiteboy outrages travellers were usually unmolested. The strong belief in the value of mineral waters which was then at its height in England extended to Ireland, and appears to have given some stimulus to travelling. The deer which once wandered in numbers over the mountains were growing rare. The last wolf was shot in Kerry in 1710. With the increased facilities of locomotion, and in part perhaps through the operation of the charter schools, the Irish tongue over large districts was rapidly disappearing. A very competent authority in 1738 states that not more than one person in twenty was ignorant of English; and another writer, who described the county of Down a few years later, declared that Irish was there only prevalent among the poorer Catholics, and that they showed a strong desire that their children should learn English. . . .

The state of agriculture was miserably low. A law of Charles I, which is strikingly indicative of the barbarous condition of the nation, mentions and condemns the common practices of attaching ploughs and harrows to the tails of horses and of pulling off the wool from living sheep instead of shearing them. Both of these practices might be also detected in the Highlands of Scotland, and in Ireland the former custom long survived the law which condemned it. Sir W. Temple, in an essay published in 1678, speaks of it as very general. Madden, in 1738, noticed that it still lingered in some districts. Arthur Young, as late as 1777, found it common in the counties of Mayo and Cavan, and traces of it in some remote quarters may be found even in the present century. Over a great part of Ireland toward the middle of the eighteenth century only a single kind of plough, and that of the most primitive description, was employed. A slow but steady improvement, however, had begun under the auspices of the Dublin Society. A gentleman named Edwards brought over some English farmers to teach the Irish tillage, and Bolton, Archbishop of Cashel, who died in 1744, and Hoadly, Archbishop of Armagh, who died in 1746, are said to have both done good service to the country by draining bogs and improving husbandry. The extreme precariousness, however, of tenures, and the extreme ignorance and abject poverty of the cottiers, made great progress impossible. The detailed examination of Arthur Young showed that Irish husbandry continued still far inferior to that of England, though hardly, I think, to that of France; and a writer who visited Ireland about the same time, notices that at Limerick the farmers habitually flung the manure into the Shannon, on the supposition that their land was already sufficiently rich. The great development of pasture was unfavourable to agriculture, but the cattle trade brought a considerable amount of wealth into the country. It was not until the dearth of 1758 that the Irish were allowed to send salted beef, pork, and butter to England, but the continental market was so great that the prohibition was probably but little felt, and most of the energy of the farmers was turned in this direction. A great advance, however, was made in gardening in the first half of the eighteenth century, and many new plants, fruits, and flowers were introduced. . . .

*The revival of the linen industry in the North spurred urbanization in Belfast, but the fishing industry underwent a serious decline during the middle decades of the eighteenth century.*

Of county towns, Cork, in the middle of the eighteenth century, was by far the most important. Its population at this time was probably not less than 60,000. In the middle of the seventeenth century it was still only fourth of the Irish towns, but, owing to its admirable harbour, and to the great trade which had sprung up in beef, it had considerably oustripped both Waterford and Limerick. The exports of beef and butter from Cork in the middle of the eighteenth century are said to have been greater than those of any other city in the King's dominions. "From Michaelmas to Christmas," wrote a traveller, "a stranger would imagine it was the slaughter-house of Ireland." Except the great natural beauty of its situation, it exhibited little or nothing to attract the eye of the artist, but it had all the animation of a gay, prosperous, and improving town. . . .

Of the other county towns the most important were Limerick, Waterford, and Kilkenny. The first, in the middle of the eighteenth century, is said to have contained 3,959 houses. It was divided, like many Irish cities, into an English and an Irish town. It retained a stronger Milesian character than any other considerable centre out of Connaught, and travellers found much in the customs of its inhabitants that reminded them of Spain. The provision of the penal code which forbade Catholics from residing in Limerick without special permission, speedily became a dead letter. After 1724 the formality of registration was no longer exacted, and long before that date the population had become chiefly Catholic, though no special building for the Catholic worship was erected within the walls till 1744. Much of the surrounding country was extremely wild and lawless, but the town itself seems to have seldom given serious trouble to the Government, and in 1760 it was declared no longer a fortress, and was dismantled. About 1736 we find a society, probably connected with that of Dublin, and comprising many of the leading gentry, instituted "for the improvement of tillage, arts, and manufacture," in the county, and occupied in distributing prizes for different branches of industry. The inhabitants of Limerick were accustomed to export serges to Spain and Portugal; they had a small glove manufactory, and a considerable trade in cattle, but for the most part they lived in great idleness. Like most Irish towns, Limerick had more than one place of amusement, and it was remarkable for the cheapness of its living. Arthur Young, writing in 1776, mentions the case of a gentleman with 500*l.* a year who kept "a carriage, four horses, three men, three maids, a good table, a wife, three children, and a nurse." The city was so poor that between 1740 and 1750 there were only four gentle-men's carriages in or about it, one of which belonged to the bishop, another to the dean, and a third to another Protestant clergyman. After the middle of the century, however, the beef trade, and with it the prosperity of the town, very greatly increased; and before the century had closed a local writer was able to dilate upon the many graceful country seats that already fringed the Shannon between Limerick and the sea, and upon the crowds of all ranks who resorted every summer to the superb cliff scenery on the coast of Clare.

Waterford, though somewhat smaller than Limerick, was more actively commercial. It had a large fishery, and considerable dealings with Newfoundland, while Kilkenny, which derived some wealth from the neighbouring coal mines, was noted for a school which was the most important in Ireland, for its manufactures of frieze, flannel, and druggets, for the purity of its air and water, and for its four annual fairs. Owing, perhaps, to the influence of the great though decaying family of Ormond, it possessed a more agreeable society than any other provincial town; it was the scene of numerous private theatricals, and it was early connected with Dublin by a turnpike road, with good inns at intervals of ten or twelve miles.

There was one other provincial town which is deserving of a brief notice, for though less populous and wealthy than those I have mentioned, it had a great military and geographical importance, and its history presents features of considerable interest. Like Limerick, Galway had been subject to special provisions of the penal code, intended to make it an essentially Protestant town, and, like Limerick, it was suffered to become almost exclusively Catholic. It had been provided that, after March 1703, no person of the Popish religion except seamen, fishermen, and day labourers, who did not pay upwards of 40s. a year rent, should come to live within its walls; that no Papist should purchase any house or tenement in the city or in its suburbs, and that those who were living there at the date of the enactment should be compelled to find Protestant sureties for their good behaviour. The town, however, at this date was almost entirely Catholic. It was the capital of the wildest, the most untravelled, the most purely Catholic part of Ireland. It was far removed from the beaten track of commerce and civilisation, and in spite of the penal code it continued intensely Catholic, Celtic, and anti-English; the centre of a great smuggling trade, the favourite landing-place of Popish ecclesiastics from the Continent, and of recruiting agents for the Irish brigade. The penal laws were, indeed, frequently enforced, but their intermittent action was more injurious to the prosperity than to the Catholicism of the town. . . .

*The decline of Galway as a port and commercial center became more marked after 1750. The number of ships owned by Galway merchants had fallen from fourteen or fifteen in the 1730s to three or four in 1762, when the population of the town was estimated at 14,000, including about 350 Protestants. The arrival of several thousand French Huguenots and, later, German Palatines, fleeing from religious persecution, brought both "useful elements" and enterprise into Irish society. Most of the Palatine families settled in counties Kerry and Limerick, where they became successful farmers.*

It is not surprising that the amount of crime and disorder in the country should have been very considerable. Extreme poverty, nomadic habits, the antagonism of law and religion, recent civil war, and the prevalence of smuggling were obvious causes, and there was another influence peculiar to Irish life. While the more enterprising members of the innumerable families that were driven from their ancestral properties found honourable careers upon the Continent, most of the feebler and the baser elements remained. Ejected proprietors whose names might be traced in the annals of the Four Masters, or around the sculptured crosses of Clonmacnoise, might be found in abject poverty hanging around the land which had lately been their own, shrinking from servile labour as from an intolerable pollution, and still receiving a secret homage from their old tenants. In a country where the clan spirit was intensely strong, and where the new landlords were separated from their tenants by race, by religion, and by custom, these fallen and impoverished chiefs naturally found themselves at the head of the discontented classes; and for many years after the Commonwealth, and again after the Revolution, they and their followers, under the names of tories and rapparees, waged a kind of guerilla war of depredations upon their successors. After the first years of the eighteenth century, however, this form of crime appears to have almost ceased; and although we find the names of tories and rapparees on every page of the judicial records, the old meaning was no longer attached to them, and they had become the designations of ordinary felons, at large in the country. The tradition of the original tories, however, had a very mischievous effect in removing the stigma from agrarian crime, while, on the other hand, the laws against them bore clear traces of the convulsions of civil war. Felons at large were proclaimed by the grand juries "tories in arms and on their keeping." By a law of 1697, any tory who killed two other proclaimed tories, was entitled to his pardon. By a law which was enacted in 1717, and which did not finally expire till 1776, the same indulgence was conceded to any tory who brought in the head of one of his fellows. When Bishop Nicholson first visited his diocese in the North, he found the heads of numerous rapparees placed in all the northern counties over the gaols, and their quarters (for they were executed as for treason) gibbeted through the country. Small bands of armed men might be found in many districts attacking houses and levying blackmail. Thus, in 1705, a band under a noted tory named Callihan—numbering at one time five or six, at another as many as fourteen men—infested the counties of Kerry and Cork. In the same year a magistrate of Dungannon speaks of about fifty tories who were then out in the country. In 1725 a band of this kind hovered about the mountains where the Queen's County, the county of Kilkenny, and the county of Carlow touch. In 1739 and 1740 a large band struck terror through the county of Carlow. In 1743 the horrors of famine produced a great increase of highway robbery, and in 1760 a formidable party of agrarian criminals, under a leader known as Captain Dwyer, committed numerous outrages in Tipperary.

In these facts, however, there is little that was distinctive or peculiar to Ireland. If a bishop had occasionally to be escorted through the mountain passes by guards as he travelled to his diocese, if in advertisements of county fairs we sometimes find notices that the roads on these occasions would be specially protected, such incidents might easily have happened in England. The neighbourhood of London swarmed with highwaymen, and many parts of England were constantly infested by bands which hardly differed from the Irish rapparees. The Whiteboy movement had not yet arisen; the magistrates were on the whole active and efficient, and over about five-sixths of Ireland, life and property during the first half of the eighteenth century appear to have been little less secure than in England.

The condition of the remaining part was, however, very different. In the greater part of the county of Kerry, in the more remote districts of the counties of Cork and Limerick, and in a very large section of Connaught, a state of society subsisted to which we find no parallel in England, but which bore a striking resemblance to that which was then existing in the Highlands of Scotland. These districts—consisting almost exclusively of wild mountains and bogs, doomed by the nature of the soil to great poverty, traversed by few or no regular roads, far removed from all considerable centres of civilised life, and inhabited chiefly by a wild and wretched population of Catholics—lay virtually beyond the empire of the law. Smuggling was the one lucrative trade, and it was practised equally by landlord, middleman, and tenant, by Catholic and Protestant. The officers of the revenue were baffled by a conspiracy of all classes, and informers were in such danger from popular outrage that they soon abandoned their trade. In the deep natural harbours among the mountains, privateers found their shelter, priests and friars from the Continent landed in safety, recruits were shipped by hundreds for the service of France, and the finest native wool was exchanged for the wines and brandies of the South. Here and there barracks were built, but regular soldiers employed to discharge police functions were in such a country very inefficient. From time to time some half-starved robber appeared with the bloody head of his comrade, claiming pardon and asking for reward or at least for food. From time to time tory hunts were undertaken in the mountains, but in the face of a sullen or hostile population they had little result. . . .

*Agrarian crime was endemic in rural Ireland, and the wave of cattle houghing which spread across the western counties in*

*1711–13 was only one of its crueler manifestations. Magistrates often had to call on the military to capture the more notorious bands of outlaws. The refusal of witnesses to testify made conviction of cattle houghers and horse thieves more than difficult. The violence and disorder in Irish society permeated both the army and the prisons. Although much exaggerated in extent, the forcible abduction and marriage of heiresses by fortune hunters was a common crime. The historian Froude perpetuated a grave error by asserting that many Protestant girls were abducted by Catholic males who sought to return them to the old faith by marrying them. The penal code forbade mixed marriages, but the authorities could not stamp out clandestine marriages between Protestant settlers and the more alluring Catholics in the country.*

My own object has been to represent as far as possible both the good and the evil of Irish life, and to explain in some degree its characteristic faults. Irish history is unfortunately, to a great extent, a study of morbid anatomy, and much of its interest lies in the evidence it furnishes of the moral effects of bad laws and of a vicious social condition. It will appear clear, I think, from the foregoing narrative, how largely the circumstances under which the national character was formed explain its tendencies, and how superficial are those theories which attribute them wholly to race or to religion. Without denying that there are some innate distinctions of character between the subdivisions of the great Aryan race, there is, I think, abundant evidence that they have been enormously exaggerated. Ethnologically the distribution and even the distinction of Celts and Teutons are questions which are far from settled, and the qualities that are supposed to belong to each have very seldom the consistency that might be expected. Nations change profoundly in the very respects in which their characters might be thought most indelible, and the theory of race is met at every turn by perplexing exceptions. . . .

Writers who are accustomed to attribute the differences between Scotland and Ireland solely to the difference of their religion, forget some of the most salient facts in the national history. They forget that during seventy memorable years that followed the Scotch union, while Scotland enjoyed perfect free trade, and was advancing with gigantic strides in industrial prosperity, Ireland still lay under the weight of the commercial disabilities, and the most energetic classes were driven to the Continent. They forget that for nearly a century after the establishment of the Scotch Kirk the great majority of the Irish people were crushed and degraded by the Penal Code. They forget that Scotland had never known to any considerable extent that confiscation of lands which in Ireland has produced not only a division, but an antagonism of classes, and has thrown the mass of the people for political guidance into the hands of demagogues or priests.

Religious convictions during the long oppression of the eighteenth century sank deeply into the minds of the people. In the upper classes the tendencies of the time, the profligacy of public life, and the great numbers who went through a nominal conversion in order to secure an estate, or to enter a profession, gradually lowered the theological temperature; but it was otherwise with the poor. They clung to their old faith with a constancy that has never been surpassed, during generations of the most galling persecution, at a time when every earthly motive urged them to abandon it, when all the attraction and influence of property and rank and professional eminence and education were arrayed against it. They voluntarily supported their priesthood with an unwearying zeal, when they were themselves sunk in the most abject poverty, when the agonies of starvation were continually before them. They had their reward. The legislator, abandoning the hopeless task of crushing a religion that was so cherished, contented himself with providing that those who held it should never rise to influence or wealth, and the penal laws were at last applied almost exclusively to this end. Conversion to Catholicism was a criminal offence, and was sometimes punished as such, but in the darkest period of the penal laws not a few of the scattered Protestant poor lapsed into Catholicism. . . .

*The great majority of Irish Catholics not only tolerated such Protestant dissenters as the Quakers and Methodists but also remained loyal to the Crown. The British Government kept some 12,000 soldiers stationed in the country at Irish expense, but when at war, they had to draw on this garrison for reserves. The laws prohibiting Catholics from enlisting in the army deprived the British of countless Irish recruits, many of whom acquitted themselves well in Continental armies.*

For some years after the Revolution a steady stream of Scotch Presbyterians had poured into the country, attracted by the cheapness of the farms or by the new openings for trade, and in the reign of Anne the Nonconformists boasted that they at least equalled the Episcopalian Protestants in Ireland, while in the province of Ulster they immensely outnumbered them. In 1715, Archbishop Synge estimated at not less than 50,000 the number of Scotch families who had settled in Ulster since the Revolution. Three years later Bishop Nicholson, writing from Londonderry, states that this parish—which extended far beyond the walls— though one of the most Episcopalian in the province, contained 800 families of Protestant Nonconformists, and only 400 of Conformists, while in some of the parishes in his diocese there were forty Presbyterians to one member of the Established Church. But the political power of the Dissenters even before the imposition of the test, was by no means commensurate with their number, for they were chiefly traders and farmers, and very rarely owners of the soil. In the House of Lords they were almost unrepresented. In the House of Commons they appear to have seldom if ever had more than twelve members. When the Test Act expelled them from the magistracy only twelve or thirteen were deprived. In the province of Ulster, Archbishop Synge assures us that there were not in his time more than forty Protestant Dissenters of the rank of gentlemen, not more than four who were considerable landowners, and according to Bishop Nicholson they had not one share in fifty of the landed interest in that province.

At the same time they were rapidly becoming a great and formidable body, and their position was extremely anomalous. The Toleration Act, which established the position of the English Dissenters after the Revolution, had not been enacted in Ireland. William, it is true, had endeavoured with his usual liberality to promote such an Act, but Sir Richard Cox and the bishops, who formed about half the active members of the House of Lords, strenuously maintained that it would be fatal to the Irish Church unless it were accompanied by a Test Act like that of England, and they succeeded in defeating the attempts of Lord Sydney and Lord Capel in the direction of a legal toleration. The Dissenters themselves appear to have preferred a simple indulgence to an assured position encumbered by a test clause, and though lying beyond the strict letter of the law, their worship was not only openly celebrated, but was even to a small extent endowed. The Regium Donum bestowed upon the ministers, which was first given by Charles II and afterwards revived and increased by William III, amounted only to an annual sum of 1,200*l*, but it involved the whole principle of legal recognition, and it continued to be paid in spite of the protest of Convocation, and of resolutions of both Houses of Parliament. The attitude of the Presbyterians was at the same time as far as possible from conciliatory, and it formed a curious contrast to that of the Catholics. The latter, conquered, dispirited, deprived of their natural leaders, and reduced to a miserable poverty, continued with quiet and tenacious courage to celebrate their rites in mud cabins or in secluded valleys; but they cowered outwardly before the Protestants, shrank from every kind of collision, and abstained for the most part from every act that could irritate or alarm. But the Presbyterians, who were conscious of their unswerving attachment to the existing Government, who boasted that the great majority of the heroic defenders of Londonderry had sprung from their ranks, and who were indignant, and justly indignant, at the ingratitude with which they were treated, stooped to no evasion. They were chiefly of Scotch birth or extraction, and they were endowed with a full share of Scotch stubbornness, jealousy, and self-assertion. Not content with building their meeting-houses and celebrating their worship, they planted under the eyes of the indignant bishops an elaborate system of Church government not less imperious, and far more efficient, than that of the Established Church, and imported into Ireland the whole machinery of Church judicatories which had made the Kirk almost omnipotent in Scotland. In the words of Archbishop Synge, "their ministers marry people, they hold synods, they exercise ecclesiastical jurisdiction, as is done in Scotland, excepting only that they have no assistance from the civil magistrate, the want of which makes the minister and his elders in each district stick the closer together, by which means they have almost an absolute government over their congregations, and at their communions they often meet from several districts to the number of 4,000 or 5,000, and think themselves so formidable as that no government dares molest them."

The irritation on both sides was soon as strong as possible. The sin of schism became a favourite topic in the pulpits of the Established Church, while catechisms, describing Episcopacy as idolatrous and anti-Christian, were circulated broadcast over Ulster. Some landlords, and all bishops, in letting their lands inserted clauses prohibiting the erection of meeting-houses. Presbyterians were prosecuted and fined by the ecclesiastical courts for celebrating their marriages. Some, who refused to take the abjuration oath, were obliged to abandon their ministry. There were disputes at the graves about the service for the dead. There were disputes about the payment of church dues. . . .

The Presbyterians, however, rapidly threw out their branches; they sent missionaries among the Roman Catholics, and occupied many parishes which Episcopalian neglect had left almost deserted. Their attitude grew more and more defiant. A story was often repeated of how one of their most distinguished advocates in Parliament shook the Bishop of Killaloe by the lawn sleeves, telling him in a threatening tone "that he hoped to see the day when there should not be one of his order in the kingdom." They were accused of continually insulting the clergy, of forming a separate interest in the North, of engaging no apprentices except of their own sect, of planting their farms exclusively with Presbyterians, of favouring them systematically when serving as jurymen. The landlords saw, with no small apprehension, the rise of a new organised power which threatened to subvert their ascendency. "The true point," wrote Archbishop King, some years after the test clause had been imposed, "between them and the gentlemen is whether the Presbyterians and lay elders in every parish shall have the greatest influence over the people, to lead them as they please, or the landlords over their tenants. This may help your Grace in some degree to see the reason why the Parliament is so unanimous against taking off the test."

It is not surprising, under these circumstances, that when the English Government, in 1704, apparently without the solicitation of anyone in Ireland, thought fit to tack the test clause to a Bill for the repression of Popery, it should have been accepted by the Irish Parliament. It is still less surprising that when the test had in this manner become law, the Irish House of Lords, in which the bishops commanded a majority of votes, and the Irish House of Commons, in which ecclesiastical influence was very strong, should have maintained it on the statute book for more than seventy years. The Presbyterians were thus expelled from all civil and military offices under the Crown. Their political importance was lowered, and another deep line of disqualification was introduced into Irish life. Most of the great evils of Irish politics during the last two centuries have arisen from the fact that its different classes and creeds have never been really blended into one nation, that the repulsion of race or of religion has been stronger than the attraction of a common nationality, and that the full energies and intellect of the country have in consequence seldom or never been enlisted in a common cause. We have already seen how fatally the division between Protestants and Catholics was aggravated by its coincidence with the division of classes, and how by a strange and singular infelicity the same train of causes that greatly diminished among the lower classes the capacity of self-government made the higher class peculiarly unfit to be the guardians and the representatives of their interests. The Test Act was another great step in the path of division, and did much to make Protestant co-operation impossible. . . .

*The Irish Toleration act of 1719 began to bring the Irish Church Establishment into conformity with its English counterpart. The rise of a Latitudinarian spirit gradually eased doctrinal tensions within the Irish Church and reduced antipathies toward Nonconformists. The appointment of numerous English divines to Irish bishoprics continued to anger Irish Churchmen.*

*Constitutional conflicts between England and Ireland reached a peak in 1722–24 when the Crown granted the patent to mint an Irish halfpenny to an English iron-merchant named William Wood. Highly resentful over the absence of an Irish mint and fearing a debased coinage with the profits therefrom going to English speculators, the Irish Ascendancy raised such a clamor that the patent had to be withdrawn. Swift's powerful pen helped to defeat the project known ever since as "Wood's halfpence."*

The patriotism of Swift himself was of a very mingled order. Though Irish by birth and education, he always looked upon his country as a place of exile, and upon the great mass of its people with undisguised contempt. He had seen without a word of disapprobation the enactment of the most atrocious of the penal laws, which crushed the Catholics to the dust, and though declaring himself that there was no serious disloyalty among them, he looked forward with approval to the legal extirpation of their religion by the refusal of the Government to permit any priest to celebrate its rites. If there was any hope of the Irish people maintaining their position in the face of English jealousy, it could only be by their union; but not content with cutting himself off from the Catholics by his approval of the penal laws, he allowed his passions as a Churchman to impel him to the bitterest animosity towards the Protestant Nonconformists. The Irish party in the Church during the first half of the eighteenth century being usually in opposition to the Government, which was Whig, and therefore supported by the Dissenters, threw itself into the opposite scale, and became in general supporters of the Test Act. From a national and patriotic point of view, no blunder could have been more egregious; but Swift lent it all the weight of his genius and of his influence. Much of his indignation was, no doubt, due to personal disappointment acting on a nature singularly fierce, gloomy, and diseased, and to bitter animosity against the Whig party, which had crushed his hopes and scattered his friends. Nor should it be forgotten that, though in the Drapier controversy he spoke with much severity of the contempt which Wood had shown for the Irish Parliament, no sooner had that Parliament, by its resolutions concerning the tithe of agistment, touched the interests of his order, than he did everything in his power to discredit it, by an invective which is perhaps the most savage in English literature.

Yet, in spite of all this, Ireland owes much to Swift. No one can study with impartiality his writings or his life without perceiving that, except in questions where ecclesiastical interests distorted his judgment, he was animated by a fierce and generous hatred of injustice, and by a very deep and real compassion for material suffering. Endowed by nature not only with literary talents of the highest order, but also with the commanding intellect of a statesman, accustomed to live in close intimacy with the governing classes of the Empire, he found himself in a country where all popular government was reduced to a system of jobbery, where the most momentous material and moral interests were deliberately crushed by a tyranny at once blind, brutal, and mean, where the people had lost all spirit of self-reliance and liberty, and where public opinion was almost unknown. He succeeded— no doubt by very questionable means—in uniting that people for great practical ends. He braced their energies; he breathed into them something of his own lofty and defiant spirit; he made them sensible at once of the wrongs they endured, of the rights they might claim, and of the forces they possessed; and he proved to them, for the first time, that it was possible to struggle with suc- cess within the lines of the Constitution. The independent and at the same time practical tone of his writings, and the many admirable principles and maxims they contain, made them an invaluable tonic for the Irish mind, and the seed that he had sown sank deeply and germinated hereafter. . . .

The Viceroyalty of Chesterfield, though it unfortunately only lasted for eight months, was eminently successful. He came over in the beginning of the rebellion of 1745, and the care with which he watched over the material prosperity of the country, the happy ridicule with which he discouraged the rumours of Popish risings, the firmness with which he refused to follow the precedent of 1715, when all Catholic chapels were closed during the rebellion, the unusual public spirit with which he administered his patron- age, and the tact he invariably exhibited during the very critical circumstances of the time, made his government one of the most remarkable in Irish history, and probably contributed largely to the tranquillity of Ireland at a time when England and Scotland were torn by civil war. It was followed by that of Lord Harring- ton, during which the dead calm that had long prevailed in Irish politics was slightly ruffled. Outside the House a political agita- tion was organised and directed by Charles Lucas, a Dublin apothecary of very moderate means and position, who now rose to a prominent place in Irish politics. He was a cripple, wholly destitute of oratorical power, and bitterly intolerant of his Cath- olic fellow-countrymen; and there is nothing in his remains to show that he possessed any real superiority either of intellect or knowledge, or even any remarkable brilliancy of expression. He was, however, courageous, pertinacious, industrious, and vitu- perative. He detected and exposed some serious encroachments that had been made on the electoral rights of the Dublin citizens. He became the most popular writer in the Dublin press, advocat-

ing the principles of Molyneux and Swift, and urging especially
the necessity of shortening the duration of Parliament; and he
made himself so obnoxious to the ruling powers that the Parliament, in 1749, at the instigation of the Government, voted him
an enemy to the country, issued a proclamation for the seizure of
his person, and thus compelled him to go for some years into
exile. . . .

*Irish politics in the 1730s and 1740s was dominated by com-
petition for place and preferment. Jobbery and bribery were the
accepted means of advancement for all ambitious men. In the
important money-bill dispute of 1751–55, the Speaker of the
Irish House of Commons, Henry Boyle, made a bid to assert the
powers of that House by assigning the budget surplus of 1753 to
the reduction of the national debt without any reference to the
customary prior consent of the Crown. When the money-bill
returned from Westminster with the royal assent clause duly inserted, Boyle and his supporters defeated the measure amidst
much popular rejoicing. The impasse was resolved only by Boyle's
willingness to sacrifice office for the Earldom of Shannon. The age
of genuine Irish patriotism had not yet arrived for the Protestant
Ascendancy.*

As long as Parliament lasted for a whole reign, as long as it
represented only a fraction of a fraction of the nation, as long, in
a word, as there was virtually no external restraint upon the corruption of its members, it was inevitable that this should be the
case. As political parties became more balanced, the system of
corruption was enlarged, the pension list rose with startling
rapidity, and one of the first signs of the growing importance of
Parliament was the great increase in the price of boroughs. In
1754 an Irish borough sold for three times as much as in 1750.
The extraordinary interest now taken in the proceedings of Parliament was shown in Dublin by considerable and sometimes very
riotous popular demonstrations, in the country, and especially in
the North, by the formation of patriotic societies, and by innumerable petitions, addresses, and resolutions supporting the
Speaker. In 1755, however, a comparative calm ensued. The Duke
of Dorset was replaced as Viceroy by Lord Hartington, who soon
after became Duke of Devonshire. The influence of the Primate

was almost destroyed. Boyle was made Earl of Shannon, and received a pension of 2,000*l.* a year; and several other members of the Opposition obtained places or pensions. The effect of these measures was clearly shown when a Bill for securing the freedom of Parliament, by vacating the seats of such members of the House of Commons as should accept pensions or places from the Crown, was defeated, in 1756, by 85 against 59, many members of the former Opposition voting against it. Some strong resolutions were carried in the following year condemning improper pensions, and especially pensions to persons not resident in Ireland; but they seem to have produced no effect, for only a few months later, and in spite of the depressed condition of the finances, a pension of 5,000*l.* a year on the Irish establishment was granted to the Princess of Hesse-Cassel, and 2,000*l.* a year to Prince Ferdinand of Brunswick. The Viceroy, as usual, spent only one winter in every two years in the country, and the chief management of affairs rested with the Lords Justices. The predominant power among them now rested with great Irish borough-owners, who were known as "undertakers," and who, in consideration of a large share of the patronage of the Crown, "undertook" to carry the King's business through Parliament.

The transient prosperity which had produced the surpluses in 1751 and 1753 soon passed. In 1755 war broke out between Great Britain and France, and in the three following years the Irish revenue steadily decreased. In 1756 and 1757 the potato crop failed, and great numbers throughout the country are said to have perished by famine. The Duke of Bedford came over as Viceroy in 1757, and one of the first acts of his administration was to provide a sum of 20,000*l.* for the relief of the poor. Rumours of invasion seriously affected credit; three Dublin banks failed in 1759. A new national debt was created, and, in order to encourage tillage, a law was passed granting bounties on the land carriage of corn and flour to the metropolis. The Primate Stone had by this time returned to power, though he never regained his former ascendency; and a remarkable letter by him is extant, dated August 1758, in which he speaks very despondingly of the material condition of the country. "Its substance and manners," he said, "are not to be estimated by the efforts towards luxury and splendour made by a few in the metropolis. The bulk of the people are not regularly either lodged, clothed, or fed; and those things which in England are called necessaries of life are to us only accidents, and we can and in many places do subsist without them. The estates have risen within these thirty years to more than double the value, but the condition of the occupiers of the land is not better than it was before that increase." In 1759 there were rumours that a legislative union was contemplated, and a riot broke out among the Protestants in Dublin, which was perhaps the most furious ever known in the metropolis. The mob burst into the Parliament house, placed an old woman in the chair, searched for the journals which they desired to burn, stopped the carriages and killed the horses of the members, insulted the Chancellor and some of the bishops, erected a gallows, on which they intended to hang an obnoxious politician, and compelled all who fell into their hands to swear that they would oppose the measure. The Catholics, on the other hand, received the rumour with indifference, and were at this time forward in their professions of loyalty; and on the news of approaching invasion, a deputation of Catholic gentry tendered an expression of their loyalty to the Government, and received a very gracious reply.

The Duke of Bedford was the first Lord Lieutenant who showed himself unequivocally in favour of a relaxation of the penal code. The Catholic gentry began to organise and take measures for obtaining a removal of their disabilities, and three men of considerable ability—Curry, O'Conor, and Wyse—appeared in their ranks. The laws were now directed almost exclusively against property, but there were occasional menacing symptoms of reviving persecution. The Bill already mentioned for restoring the now obsolete system of registering priests had been carried through the House of Lords in 1757, in spite of the opposition of Primate Stone and the bishops, but had been thrown out by the Privy Council. In a law case, in 1759, a Catholic was reminded from the bench that "the laws did not presume a Papist to exist in the kingdom, nor could they breathe without the connivance of the Government." An order had been issued to deface all ensigns of honour borne by persons who had no legal title thereto, and the armorial bearings of Lord Kenmare were erased from his carriage in the very yard of the Castle.

On the whole, however, the position of the Catholics in the last years of the reign of George II was evidently improving. Religious fanaticism had greatly subsided; a new line of party division was forming. The nearer balance of parties rendered it certain that one side would at length seek support from the Catholics, and a spirit of nationality had arisen, which, though as yet very feeble and deeply impregnated with baser motives, could not fail sooner or later to be advantageous to the great majority of the people. The perfect absence of disturbance among them, when the country was very seriously menaced with invasion, strengthened their cause. The threatened danger was indeed in a great degree averted by the defeat of the fleet of Conflans at Quiberon by Hawke; but on the 21st of February, 1760, Thurot, one of the most enterprising commanders in the service of France, succeeded in escaping from Dunkirk, and, with three frigates, surprised Carrickfergus. His success, however, ended there. There was no rising whatever in his favour. A large body of volunteers from Belfast marched to attack him, and, after holding the town for five days, he was compelled to re-embark, was overtaken by the English fleet, and lost his life in the combat.

This was the last event of any importance in Irish history during the reign of George II. On the 25th of October the old King died. A new and eventful reign began, and in a few years all the conditions of Irish politics were profoundly changed.

# III

# The Growth of Political Consciousness,
## 1760–1778

The first years of the reign of George III are memorable in the economical and moral history of Ireland, as having witnessed the rise of that Whiteboy movement which may be justly regarded as at once the precursor and the parent of all subsequent outbursts of Irish agrarian crime. Its chief causes are to be found in the rapid conversion of arable into pasture land which has been already described. In addition to the more permanent causes which were then enumerated, the movement had been greatly accelerated by a murrain which had broken out in 1739 among the horned cattle of Holstein, had spread rapidly to other parts of Germany, and had at length extended to Holland and England. The price of cattle was enormously raised. In 1758 their free importation into Great Britain for the space of five years was permitted. Whole baronies were turned into pasture land. Common lands, which alone enabled the overburdened cottier to subsist, and which had long been tacitly, if not expressly, open to him, were everywhere invaded, and the country was full of a starving peasantry turned out of their wretched cottages to make room for a more lucrative industry. Their misery can scarcely be exaggerated, and it was mixed with a strong sense of injustice. In the almost complete absence of manufacturing industry the great majority of the people were wholly dependent on the soil. In a country where poverty was perhaps as extreme as in any part of Europe there was no poor-law. The greater landlords were commonly absentees. The keen competition for the soil, and the

constant practice of subletting, had reduced the immediate cultivators to such abject poverty that the most transient calamity
brought them face to face with starvation. As Catholics and as
tenants they were completely unrepresented in the great council
of the nation. The law of 1727, which provided that, out of every
100 acres, not less than five should be under cultivation, was, in
the words of a very competent witness, "as dead as the letters of
it, for all the rich were delinquents, and none but the impotent
poor were left to enforce the performance of it." The local magistracy planted in the midst of a Catholic tenantry were in quiet
times almost omnipotent, and they consisted exclusively of Protestant landlords.

It is not surprising that such a condition should have at length
produced an insurrection of despair. The country, it is true, was,
on the whole, improving. It was stated by Arthur Young that in
the twenty-five years preceding 1778 the rent of land had at least
doubled. The growth of the chief towns, the muliplication of
roads, plantations, country seats, and public buildings attested the
accumulation of considerable wealth; the influence of a middle
class may for the first time be detected in Irish politics, and the
larger tenants and shopkeepers, and especially those who were
connected with the victualling trade, were rising rapidly in prosperity. But there was a large section of the population by whom
that prosperity was never felt, whose condition was little, if at all,
better than in the time of Swift, whose means of subsistence were
with the growth of pasture steadily contracting, and to whose
almost hopeless wretchedness the most competent witnesses are
agreed in ascribing the Whiteboy organisation. Chesterfield, who
knew Ireland well, said that they "were used worse than negroes
by their lords and masters, and their deputies of deputies of deputies," and he ascribed Whiteboyism to "the sentiment in every
human breast that asserts man's natural right to liberty and good
usage, and that will and ought to rebel when oppressed and provoked to a certain degree. . . ."

It is essential, indeed, in considering the economical condition
of Ireland in the last century to bear steadily in mind the distinction between the landowner and the middleman, and to remember
that the latter, with whom alone the cottier came in much contact,
was constantly spoken of as the landlord. The "little country

gentlemen," whom Arthur Young described as the pest of the country, and the great graziers, who were the immediate causes of the depopulation of large districts, were not landowners but tenants. I have endeavoured in the preceding chapter to trace the history of their rise, and it is only necessary to say a few more words on the subject. In spite of a great deal of conflicting evidence and of many emphatic denunciations, I do not think that the charge of exacting exorbitant or oppressive rents can be sustained against the Irish landowners of the eighteenth century considered as a class. The middleman, as Grattan once said, is in this respect their best defence, and the fact that the greater part of the country was sublet two, three, and sometimes four deep, appears to me to establish to demonstration that the real landlord did not exact an excessive or a competitive price. The faults of Irish landowners have, indeed, at most periods of Irish history been much more faults of negligence than of oppression. In the beginning of the century, when absenteeism was especially common, and when the conditions of residence were often not only disagreeable but dangerous, it was their main object to obtain from their land a secure revenue without trouble and without expense, and, in order to attain this end, they were prepared to grant fixity of tenure at extremely low rents. Leases, sometimes for ever, more often for lives extending over forty, fifty, sixty, or even seventy years, were general. Arthur Young, who describes this system, significantly observes that "if long leases, at low rents, and profit incomes given, would have improved it, Ireland had long ago been a garden." When the long leases fell in, rents were, no doubt, greatly raised; but probably not more than in proportion to the general rise of prices and increase of prosperity; and it is very doubtful whether, when every due allowance has been made for the immense difference between the two countries, the Irish landlords compare in this respect at all unfavourably with the English ones.

The occupancy of land was still regulated strictly by contract, and leases were almost always given by the landowners to their immediate tenants, though towards the close of the century it became common to restrict them to twenty-one years. The first tenants also usually sublet their tenancies on leases, though for shorter periods and on much more severe terms, and they were accustomed to turn out their sub-tenants and to resume the occupation before their own leases expired in order to treat with the landowner as occupying tenants for a renewal of them. A detestable custom was very common when leases fell in, of publishing the fact in the chapels or market towns, inviting private proposals and accepting the highest bidder without any regard to the previous occupant. In the arable counties, where husbandry was best, and where some degree of prosperity had been attained, Arthur Young found that the head tenants usually had leases for three lives if they were Protestants, for thirty-one years if they were Catholics. The latter period was the longest for which a Catholic was yet allowed to hold a lease, and it was burdened by a most mischievous provision that two-thirds of the profits must go in rent. Young describes in detail a great number of resident landlords who were devoting themselves with much earnestness and intelligence to the improvement of agriculture, and many of these were steadily labouring, as far as local customs and old contracts would permit, to root out the system of middlemen, which was the master curse of Irish agrarian life. Clauses against subletting were not popular or easy to enforce in a country where the opposite system had long prevailed, but some progress in this direction was gradually effected, and a very able Irish writer in 1793 noticed that the middlemen were then "wearing out in the more rich and best cultivated counties," though they were still "almost universal" in the poorer districts.

In nearly every part of Ireland agriculture was still extremely rude. Absenteeism, great ignorance, want of capital and want of enterprise, all contributed to depress it, and in the more backward parts it was as barbarous as can well be conceived. The head tenant invariably became a middleman and land-jobber, and beneath him lay a multitude of wretched cultivators or labourers who were ground to the very dust by extortionate and oppressive exactions. In some parts of the kingdom it was a rare thing to find an occupying tenant who was the possessor of a plough. There were, perhaps, half a dozen ploughs—and these of the most primitive description—in a parish, which were let out by their owners at a high rate, but often the whole cultivation was by spade. Frequently large tenancies were held by co-operation, "knots" of poor men combining to bid for them, and managing them in common, and frequently, too, labour was exacted in addition to a money rent. The purely labouring class were generally cottiers —paid for their labour not by money, but by small potato plots, and by the grazing of one or two cows, and they worked out these things for their employers usually at the rate of 6½d. a day. Their homes and clothing were to the last degree degraded; they had no security of tenure and no possibility of saving, and they depended for their very subsistence on the annual produce of their potato plots; but in the better parts of Ireland, and under favourable circumstances, Arthur Young did not consider that their condition compared altogether unfavourably with that of English labourers. Their food was much more abundant. Their children, unlike those of the Englishmen, were seldom without milk, and the absence of money in their dealings with their employers made it impossible for them to drink, as was common in England, a week's wages in a single night. But the cottier population, who multiplied recklessly by early marriages over the barren lands of Kerry or the West, were perhaps as miserable as any class of men in Europe. To escape starvation was almost their highest aim, and even for this it was often necessary for them to spend a part of every summer in vagrant mendicancy. The months of July and August, when the old potatoes were exhausted, were generally months of absolute famine. Cabbages, boiled in water and mixed with some milk, were then the sole sustenance of the poor, who died in multitudes from diarrhoea; and a still remembered saying, that "Kerry cows know Sunday," recalls the time when the cattle being fattened by the summer grass underwent a weekly bleeding to make a holiday-meal for their half-starving owners. . . .

The Whiteboy movement was first directed against the system of inclosing commons, which had lately been carried to a great extent. According to the contemporary and concurrent statements of Crawford, the Protestant, and of Curry, the Catholic historian of the time, landlords had often been guilty not only of harshness, but of positive breach of contract, by withdrawing from the tenants a right of commonage which had been given them as part of their bargain, when they received their small tenancies, and without which it was impossible that they could pay the rents which were demanded. It was at the close of 1761 that the first signs of resistance appeared. Wesley, who six months later was travelling through Ireland, took great pains to obtain an accurate account of their origin, and he was given the following description of it. "About the beginning of December last," he says, "a few men met by night near Nenagh, in the county of Limerick, and threw down the fences of some commons which had been lately inclosed. Near the same time, others met in the counties of Tipperary, Waterford, and Cork. As no one offered to suppress or hinder them, they increased in numbers continually, calling themselves Whiteboys, wearing white cockades and white linen frocks. In February there were five or six parties of them, 200 to 300 men in each, who moved up and down chiefly in the night, . . . levelled a few fences, dug up some grounds, and hamstrung some cattle, perhaps fifty or sixty in all. One body of them came into Clogheen, of about 500 foot, and 200 horse. They moved as exactly as regular troops, and appeared to be thoroughly disciplined." They sent threatening letters, compelled every one they met to swear allegiance to their leader, "Queen Sive," and to obey her commands, and threatened savage penalties against those who refused to do so. . . .

The outburst spread rapidly through many counties of Munster, and while in some districts it was specially directed against inclosures, in others it was more peculiarly turned against certain kinds of tithes. The great tithes or tithes of corn were, indeed, readily paid; but several other tithes were much disputed, and had long attained a foremost place among the popular grievances.

The Irish tithe system was, indeed, one of the most absurd that can be conceived. Tithes in their original theory are not absolute property, but property assigned in trust for the discharge of certain public duties. In Ireland, when they were not appropriated by laymen, they were paid by an impoverished Catholic peasantry to a clergy who were opposed to their religion, and usually not even resident among them, and they were paid in such a manner that the heaviest burden lay on the very class who were least able to bear it. It was a common thing for a parish to consist of some 4,000 or 5,000 acres of rich pasture-land held by a prosperous grazier who had been rapidly amassing a large fortune through the increased price of cattle, and of 300 or 400 acres of inferior land occupied by a crowd of miserable cottiers. In accordance with the vote of the House of Commons in 1735, the former was exempted from the burden which was thrown on the latter. In Limerick, Tipperary, Clare, Meath, and Waterford, there were to be found, in the words of Arthur Young, "the greatest graziers and cowkeepers perhaps in the world, some who rent and occupy from 3,000*l.* to 10,000*l.* a year, . . . the only occupiers in the kingdom who have any considerable substance". These men were free from the tithes which were extorted from the wretched potato plot which was the sole subsistence of the cottier. The poor man was probably too ignorant to know that the exemption of pasture-land, being due to the vote of one House of Parliament, had no legal validity, and was sustained only by the terrorism which the landlords and larger tenants exercised over the clergy, but he could hardly fail to feel the gross injustice of his lot, or to perceive that those who had acquired a monopoly of political power had used it to throw their share of the common burdens on the unrepresented poor.

If the clergy had been a resident clergy, discharging duties that were useful to the whole or the great majority of the people, the amount received by them in tithes would probably not have been thought excessive. Their advocates maintained with truth that the full legal tenth was rarely or never exacted. In many, perhaps most, cases a fixed sum called a *modus* was paid by the parishioners instead of the legal tithe of kind, and these customary rates had by long prescription obtained the force of law. There were instances, no doubt, of extortionate and tyrannical clergymen, but they were not common, and in general it was the tithe-farmer and not the clergyman, as it was the middleman and not the landlord, who oppressed the people. The tithe-proctor who collected tithes for the clergyman, and the tithe-farmer who bought them from him at a fixed rate, were among the worst figures in Irish life, and they were at the same time an inevitable product of the Irish ecclesiastical system. . . .

Under such circumstances, and encouraged by the supineness which was at first generally shown by the local magistrates, the Whiteboy organisation struck deep root and spread silently but rapidly through many counties; and although before 1770 it had nearly ceased, it burst into a new vigour in Kildare, Kilkenny, and the Queen's County in 1775, and continued there with partial interruptions till 1785, when it again spread widely through

Munster. Every season of distress intensified it, and although it has undergone many transformations, assumed many names, and aimed at many different objects, it cannot be said to be extinct at the present hour. The names of those who constructed it will never be known, but they were evidently men of some education and of no small organising ability, and they created a system of intimidation which in many districts became the true representation of the Catholic peasantry, and which often made it much safer to violate than to obey the law.

In some cases the Whiteboys acted with all the audacity of open insurgents. Great bodies of men traversed the country, often in the open daylight, wearing white cockades and blowing horns. In several cases they awaited an encounter with soldiers. They broke open the gaol of Tralee and released the prisoners. They threatened to burn the town of Newmarket, in the diocese of Cloyne, unless a Whiteboy confined there was released. They burnt several houses which soldiers had occupied, and alarms were spread, though apparently without real foundation, that they were seeking by intercepting provisions to threaten Limerick, Cork, and Ennis with famine. On one occasion in the beginning of the outbreak they assembled at Lismore, and affixed a placard at the post-office door requiring the inhabitants on the following night to illuminate their houses and provide a certain number of horses bridled and saddled, and the injunction was punctually obeyed. On another, they marched into the large village of Cappoquin, drew up in front of a horse barrack, fired several shots, and marched by the sentry who was on guard while their piper played "The Lad with the White Cockade." On a third, a large party well mounted and clad in white rode into the little town of Kilworth, in the county of Cork, at three in the morning, firing many shots, and compelled the inhabitants at once "to illuminate their windows, which was done speedily and in great order, more from fear than respect." The terrified inhabitant who wrote to inform the Government, had heard that 7,000 men were assembled in the mountains near Dungarvan, and that 20,000 would "assemble next week near this town to go on some grand project." More commonly, however, the tactics of the Whiteboys were less ostentatious, but much more formidable, and their small parties moving silently in the dead of night committed depredations which threatened to reduce a great part of Ireland to absolute anarchy.

They announced from the beginning, that their object was "to do justice to the poor by restoring the ancient commons and redressing other grievances," and they soon undertook to regulate the whole relation between landlord and tenant, and to enforce a new system of law wholly different from the law of the land. They waged especially a desperate war against tithe-proctors and tithe-farmers, against the system of Kerry bonds, against a class of men called canters, who were accustomed to bid for the tithe of their neighbours' land, and who by Whiteboy terrorism were almost extirpated from Munster. They issued proclamations forbidding any man under terrible penalties to pay higher rates of tithe than they specified. They seized arms wherever they could obtain them, compelled all whom they suspected of connivance with the Government to abandon their farms under pain of having their houses burnt over their heads, and avenged by fearful crimes every infringement of their code. . . .

The exportation of corn and flour was sometimes obstructed by force, masters were compelled to release their apprentices, daughters of rich farmers were carried away and forced into marriage, sums of money were levied from farmers to defend the Whiteboys on their trial. In some districts large bodies of men appeared on market day on the roads round some country town, or on Sundays near the chapel doors, compelling all who passed to swear that they would obey the laws and future commands of Captain Right. Many fictitious names were attached to the Whiteboy proclamations, but that of Captain Right soon predominated, and it became more powerful in Munster, and in many counties of Leinster, than King or Viceroy or Parliament.

A few murders were committed; but they were much more rare in the early Whiteboy movement than in the later periods of Irish agrarian crime, and the writers who showed the strongest disposition to aggravate the character of the disturbances are almost silent about them. Sometimes those who had violated some article of the Whiteboy code were merely seized and compelled to swear that they would never repeat the offence; but more commonly they were punished with great atrocity. One of the mildest punishments was to drag a man at midnight from his bed, often in mid-winter, beat him, and leave him bound and naked in a ditch by the roadside. In one case, which is related in detail, the captors bound their prisoner to the post of a turnpike gate and compelled the keeper to swear that he would not relieve him till a certain number of hours had passed. In another, they carried a man who had threatened to inform against some illicit distillers about a mile on a bier, and left him bound in the very streets of Cahir, where he remained unrescued the whole night. Not unfrequently they carried their victim to a newly dug grave and left him, sometimes with his ears cut off, buried up to the chin in earth, or in thorns or furze. Men were placed naked on horseback on saddles covered with thorns, or with a hedgehog's skin. Many cottages were burnt and their inmates forced to abandon the country. A man once appropriated two pounds of powder which had been concealed for the Whiteboys. They discovered him, and having obliged him to pour the powder into his hat, they placed it beneath him, ignited it, and blew him to pieces. Their threatening notices were filled with the most savage menaces, and their outrages in some districts were so frequent and so severe that scarcely anyone dared to resist them. The description given, by a conspicuous magistrate, of the agrarian crime in 1831 may be applied without qualification to the period of the first Whiteboy rising: "The combination is directly opposed to the law, and it is stronger than it, because it punishes the violation of its mandates with more severity and infinitely more certainty. If a peasant resists the combination it is scarcely possible he can escape punishment; if he violates the law his chance of escape is at least fifty to one."

The insurrection sprang in the first instance from intolerable misery not a little aggravated by injustice; but it speedily drew into its vortex all the restless, criminal, and turbulent elements of the community, and its demoralising influence can hardly be exaggerated. For a time it almost paralysed the law. Over large districts no tithes were paid, and scarcely anyone dared to distrain for rent, or even to impound trespassing cattle. Unlike ordinary crime, the Whiteboy outrages were systematically, skilfully, and often very successfully directed to the enforcement of certain rules of conduct. Strangers were wholly unmolested, and in this, as in later periods of agrarian crime, extreme social disturbance led to no highway robbery. It must be added, however, that although the crimes of the Whiteboys were undoubtedly many and grievous, they were greatly and often systematically exaggerated. The panic they inspired, the mystery hanging over obscure, nocturnal, ill-reported outrages in remote districts, the natural desire of the classes who were chiefly menaced to magnify the disturbances in order to compel Government to send troops for their protection, the animosities of class and creed which coloured most Irish narratives, all contributed to the exaggeration. Every crime that took place in a country which had at all times been exceedingly lawless was attributed to the Whiteboy organisation, and later writers have a very natural tendency to relate acts of extreme and exceptional atrocity as if they were fair samples of the ordinary crimes. Among the many curious Whiteboy proclamations which fell into the hands of the Government there are some disclaiming all connection with some particular outrages, and complaining that unauthorised men were going about the country pretending for their own purposes to be Whiteboys. There was no general attack either on landlords or on the clergy of the Established Church, and particular proprietors are sometimes spoken of with marked respect. In a very remarkable and touching proclamation, which was issued in the county of Cork in the beginning of 1787, Captain Right disclaims any wish to break the law or to rob the landlord, but denounces the unjust, and, as he believed, illegal confiscation of the improvements of tenants as the chief grievance to be redressed.

In some districts and periods the outbreaks were chiefly agrarian; in others they were more especially directed against tithes. At first the Protestant clergymen appear to have been rarely or never molested, and the tithe-farmer was the special object of the popular antipathy. There were, however, some instances of clergymen who received savage threatening letters, and were obliged to fly from their parishes through fear of Whiteboys, and in a few cases their houses were attacked, their property was injured, and they themselves underwent atrocious personal outrages. Lord Luttrell related to the Irish House of Commons how one of his friends riding one morning near the town of Urlingford, in the county of Kilkenny, found a pair of ears and a cheek nailed to a post, and soon after he overtook a muffled figure riding on in great and evident pain, which proved to be the clergyman to whom they belonged. . . .

*Local grievances arising out of the agrarian system, rather than
sectarian feeling and disloyalty, inspired Whiteboyism. In some
counties the Catholic landlords and tenantry were the first to take
steps to eradicate Whiteboy disturbances.*

The truth is, that the real causes of the Whiteboy outbreak
are to be found on the surface. Extreme poverty, extreme ignorance, and extreme lawlessness made the people of a great part of
the South of Ireland wholly indifferent to politics; but their
condition was such that the slightest aggravation made it intolerable, and it had become so miserable that they were ready to resort
to any violence to improve it. Perhaps the best picture of the
condition of affairs is to be found in one of the reports of Robert
Fitzgerald, the Knight of Kerry, a very active, and apparently a
very able and upright magistrate of that county. "The better sort
of the Roman Catholics," he says, "seem extremely well affected
to Government: the Popish bishop and clergy have exerted themselves in promoting this; the lower orders are in a state of distress
beyond anything known in the memory of man. The great rents
of this county belong to persons resident out of Ireland, whose
agents are severe in collecting them; the lower class, upon whom
the burthen falls, cannot dispose of their goods, for there are
literally no buyers, the little money the country affords is carried
off for absentees, and there is scarcely a guinea left. The miserable
tenantry, when pressed by their landlords, bring them all their
cattle, and having no grass for them, offer them at half-price, and
the common people are actually in a state of despair, ready for
any enterprise that might relieve their present suffering. In the
three baronies, which are maritime, remote, and exceedingly
mountainous, there are a great number who are indicted for
various offences, and secure themselves from justice in their inac-
cessible mountains." He suggests that if the skeleton of a regiment under command of officers of the county were formed,
the people would gladly flock in multitudes to the standard of the
King, and there would not be the smallest difficulty in filling
the ranks. "It seems," he adds "to me equally certain that if the
enemy should effect a landing anywhere within one hundred
miles of these people they will most assuredly join them."

The supineness with which the movement was at first regarded by the magistrates soon terminated, and the Irish Parliament passed a series of very severe enactments against the Whiteboys. By an Act of 1765, all persons who went by night in parties of five or more men wounding, beating, tying up, or otherwise assaulting human beings, destroying property, or digging up ground—all who were engaged in breaking open gaols or rescuing felons, and also all who imposed unlawful oaths by violence, were made liable to death, and stern measures were adopted to meet the connivance of the district. Unless the offenders were given up, or at least unless some evidence was given against them, the grand juries were empowered to levy on the barony in which a crime was committed a sum to compensate the injured person; and another clause, copying one of the enactments of the penal code against Papists, enabled any magistrate to summon before him any persons whom he suspected of having taken an illegal oath, examine them upon the subject, and imprison them for six months if they refused to answer. The Act was only for two years, but it was afterwards prolonged on the ground that it had "greatly contributed to the peace and quiet of the kingdom." But ten years later it was found necessary to make an additional law which, besides creating some new misdemeanours, immensely added to the list of capital offences. Among these were now reckoned maiming or disfiguring human beings, sending threatening letters, compelling men to quit their farms, habitations, or employments, or to join in Whiteboy offences, entering houses by force or menace between sunset and 6 A.M., in order to take horses, weapons, or money, and, finally, assisting or concealing Whiteboys who had committed any capital offence. The magistrates were given full powers of searching for arms, of obliging those who could give evidence to enter into recognisances to prosecute, and of compelling all suspected persons to answer their questions on oath. Nothing said on examination was to be used as evidence against these persons unless they were indicted for perjury; but, on the other hand, if they refused to answer or to prosecute when required, they were liable to an unlimited imprisonment.

By the stringent enforcement of these Acts, and by the enrolment of large parties of volunteers under the command of the local magistrates, the Whiteboy organisation was, for a time at least, successfully stamped out over large districts. As might have been expected from the provocation, the repression was often very violent, and it is to be feared that acts of cruel, arbitrary, or unjust violence were not unfrequently committed. . . .

*A notorious case of injustice took the life of Father Nicholas Sheehy, a Tipperary priest held in high esteem by his parishioners. In 1766 Sheehy was arrested, tried, and convicted by Protestant magistrates at Clonmel for allegedly "inciting to riot and rebellion." Although his suspected ties to local Whiteboys were never established beyond doubt, Father Sheehy was summarily hanged and quartered. The Irish people thus acquired another martyr.*

While the Whiteboy disturbances were spreading widely among the Catholic peasantry of Munster and part of Leinster, other disorders, which seemed at first scarcely less serious, broke out among the Protestants of the North. The Oakboys appear to have first risen against the Road Act, which ordered that all highways should be repaired by the personal labour of the housekeepers. It was stated that the landed proprietors, who constituted the grand juries, had many roads made which were of little or no use to the community at large, and were intended for the exclusive benefit of their own estates, and that they threw the chief burden of making and repairing these roads on the poorer ratepayers. In addition to this grievance, the question of tithes had recently acquired in the North, as well as in the South, a new prominence. It was acknowledged that tithes were much lighter in the North of Ireland than in the South, and that the customary rate was considerably below the strict legal rate, but some clergymen had recently endeavoured to break down the custom of the country. Dr. Clarke, the Rector of Armagh, appears to have been the first to try the experiment, and he discovered that it was possible by a stricter exaction of tithes to raise his ecclesiastical revenue from 900*l.* to 1,300*l.* a year. The example was followed by others, and it was justified on the ground that the price of living had so largely increased that a curate with 40*l.* a year in the beginning of the reign of George II was at least as well off as a curate with 80*l.* a year in the beginning of the reign of George III. Tithes had long been paid with much reluctance in Ulster, and the clergy had often, without any actual violence, been grossly defrauded of their rights. Thus it frequently happened that the farmers of a large and scattered parish, though they cut their corn at different times, agreed to give notice to the clergyman that they would all draw it on the same day; and as they refused to furnish him with any horses to secure his share he was obliged either to leave it on the field, where it was sure to be wasted, spoiled, or stolen, or to compound for his tithes at perhaps a fourth part of the value.

It was in the summer of 1763 that bodies of men, sometimes 400 or 500 strong, assembled to the sound of a horn, wearing oak boughs in their hats. They erected gallows, attacked houses, compelled clergymen to swear that they would not levy more than a specified proportion of tithe, and laymen that they would not assess the county at more than a stipulated rate, entered into an engagement to make no more high roads, and assaulted all whom they found working on the roads. Dr. Clarke was seized and carried in derision through various parts of the country, and many of the clergy were compelled to take refuge within the walls of Derry. The flame spread rapidly through Armagh, Tyrone, Derry, and Fermanagh; but no very serious crimes were committed, and the Protestant rising of the North was wholly free from the atrocious cruelty which disgraced the Catholic insurgents of the South. It arose among a people who were much less wretched and much less ignorant. Their tithes, even at the worst, were more moderate than in Munster, and the Protestants were not, like the Catholics, deprived of all legitimate means of expressing their will. The Government appear to have acted with great wisdom and moderation, and a letter of Primate Stone is preserved which is exceedingly honourable to that much-abused prelate, and shows his great desire to limit as much as possible the severities that were necessary. Charlemont, as Governor of Armagh, took an active and successful part in restoring tranquillity in his county. The whole movement was suppressed with very little bloodshed, and a new and more equitable Road Act restored in a few months peace to the North.

Another and more formidable, though less extensive, outbreak, occurred about eight years later in the counties of Antrim and Down, and was mainly attributed to the oppression of a single man. The Marquis of Donegall was one of the largest proprietors in the North of Ireland. He was an absentee, and when his leases fell in, instead of adopting the usual plan of renewing them at a moderate increase of rent, he determined to raise a sum which was stated at no less than 100,000*l.* in fines upon his tenants, and as they were utterly unable to pay them, two or three rich merchants of Belfast were preferred to them. The improvements were confiscated, the land was turned into pasture, and the whole population of a vast district were driven from their homes. . . .

The conduct of Lord Donegall brought the misery of the Ulster peasantry to a climax, and in a short time many thousands of ejected tenants, banded together under the name of Steelboys, were in arms. They were mainly, at first almost exclusively, Presbyterians. Their distress was much greater than that of the Oakboys, who preceded them, and, as is usually the case, their violence was proportioned to their distress. They destroyed or maimed great numbers of cattle. They attacked many houses, and were guilty of many kinds of violence, and they soon administered illegal oaths, and undertook the part of general reformers. One of their number being confined at Belfast, a large body of Steelboys, accompanied by many thousands of peasants, who neither before nor after took any part in the insurrection, marched upon that town and succeeded in obtaining his surrender. Large bodies of soldiers were soon sent to the disturbed districts, and several Steelboys were tried at Carrickfergus, but by the supposed partiality of the juries they were acquitted. The Parliament then passed an Act authorising the removal of the trials from the disturbed counties to the city or county of Dublin, and some rioters were accordingly tried at Dublin, but the feeling against the new law was so strong that they were acquitted. In December 1773, Parliament retraced its steps and repealed the obnoxious Act. From this time the insurrection speedily subsided, and after some fierce conflicts with the soldiers many insurgents were taken, tried, and executed.

The complete subsidence of this formidable insurrection in the North forms a remarkable contrast to the persistence with which the Whiteboy disturbances in the South continued to smoulder during many generations. It is to be largely attributed to the great Protestant emigration which had long been taking place in Ulster. The way had been opened, and the ejected tenantry who formed the Steelboy bands and who escaped the sword and the gallows, fled by thousands to America. They were soon heard of again. In a few years the cloud of civil war which was already gathering over the colonies burst, and the ejected tenants of Lord Donegall formed a large part of the revolutionary armies which severed the New World from the British Crown.

While these events were occurring in some of the counties most remote from the capital, a strong political life was arising in the chief centres of population, and beginning to show itself clearly in the debates of Parliament. The growth of a middle class, the evanescence of the old passions of civil war, the great decline of religious intolerance, and the sudden rise of a free press, conspired to stimulate it. The political passions roused by the struggle of 1753 had not wholly subsided, and the dissolution which followed the accession of George III introduced a new element into Irish politics.

It was scarcely possible, indeed, that the contagion of English liberty should not have spread to Ireland, and that its political condition should not have appeared intolerable to those Irishmen who derived their notions of freedom from the English Constitution. The Parliament, as we have seen, lasted an entire reign, and that of George II had sat for thirty-three years. About two-thirds of the revenue of the country, including the quit-rents, the hearth-money, and the greater part of the customs and excise, was included in the Hereditary Revenue which had been settled in perpetuity and was therefore beyond the control of Parliament. Parliament only sat every second year, and could only legislate in combination with two other bodies, deliberating in secret, and appointed by the Crown. Heads of Bills arising in either House first passed to the Irish Privy Council, which might either suppress them altogether, or alter them as it pleased. If this body thought fit to throw them into the form of a Bill, it at once transmitted that Bill to England, where it was submitted to the examination of a committee of the English Privy Council, assisted by the English Attorney-General, and this body, like the Irish Privy Council, had an unlimited power of suppressing or altering it. If the Bill passed through this second ordeal it was returned with such changes, additions and diminutions as the two Privy Councils had made, to the House of Parliament in which it took its rise, and it then passed for the first time to the other House. Neither House, however, had now the power of altering it, and each House was therefore reduced to the alternative of rejecting it altogether, or accepting it in the exact form in which it had been returned from England. The British Legislature claimed the right of binding Ireland by its acts. The judges only held their seats during pleasure. The right of supreme and final judicature in Irish cases had been taken from the Irish House of Lords and transferred to that of England. There was no Habeas Corpus Act, no national militia, no Irish Mutiny Act, no Act obliging members of Parliament who accepted places or pensions under the Crown to vacate their seats.

Such a state of things could hardly fail in settled times to rouse a spirit of resistance among the Irish Protestants. It appeared tolerable only while the country was still heaving in the convulsions of civil war, while property was utterly insecure, and while the religious conflict was at its height. The grievance was by no means a merely speculative one. The suppression by law of the most important manufactures of Ireland, the ruinous restrictions imposed on Irish commerce, the systematic appointment of Englishmen to nearly all the highest and most lucrative posts in the ecclesiastical, legal, and political establishments, the employment of the Irish Pension List to reward persons who had done no kind of service to Ireland, were all largely, if not entirely, due to the small power which the Irish gentry had in the government of their country. An active Press had lately arisen, and there were already several able men, both in Parliament and beyond its pale, who, following the steps of Molyneux, aspired to make the Irish Parliament in Irish affairs what the English Parliament was in English ones, and to secure for the Irish Protestants all those constitutional rights which the Revolution of 1688 had established in England, and of which the English people were so justly proud. . . .

The system of government by Undertakers, or, in other words, by a few great personages who possessed an extraordinary parliamentary influence, and who "undertook" to carry the King's business through Parliament on condition of obtaining a large share of the disposal of patronage, still continued. Lord Shannon and Primate Stone were now cordially united, and being steadily supported by Ponsonby, the Speaker of the House of Commons, and usually by Lord Kildare, they had acquired a complete, ascendency in the Irish Parliament and Privy Council. The influence of Lord Shannon had been greatly increased by the conflict of 1753, for, though he had been driven from power by the Duke of Dorset, he regained in the succeeding Viceroyalty all that he had lost, and the Government purchased his assistance by an earldom and a large pension. There was a general conviction that, though he might be for a time disgraced, every Administration would be eventually obliged to resort to his assistance, and the fidelity to his friends, which was the best point in his character, secured him a large and steady following. In conjunction with Stone and Ponsonby, he was Lord Justice at the accession of George III.

The power of the Undertakers was largely, though not exclusively, due to the fact that the Lord Lieutenant only resided in the country for six months in two years, while Parliament was sitting, and that the chief efficient power had passed in consequence to the Lords Justices, who governed in his absence. In England the royal influence was supposed to be most strong at the time when Parliament was in vacation. In Ireland it was noticed that it was precisely at this period that aristocratic influence attained its height, for in the absence of the Lord Lieutenant the administration of affairs was wholly in the hands of a few great men who were virtually the leaders of the House of Commons. At the same time the power of the Undertakers was less absolute than has been imagined, and it is, I think, a complete misconception to regard them as a peculiar product of Irish politics. The great Irish families only reproduced on a smaller scale the political ascendency which the Pelhams and a few other families had obtained in England during the comparative eclipse of the royal authority which followed the accession of the House of Hanover. Even the term "Undertakers" was sometimes employed in England to designate the great Whig families, and the position of Lord Shannon in the one country was not very unlike that of Newcastle in the other. In each country family relationships and connections, the acquisition of much borough influence, and a considerable dexterity in party management, had enabled a few men to make themselves the necessary channel of the favours of the Crown. In each case this oligarchical connection was unpopular with the people on account of its narrowness and corruption, while it became a great object of the Crown to dissolve it as one of the chief limitations of royal power. In each case the oligarchical leaders were thrown into temporary alliance with the people, and in each case more corruption was employed to overturn their ascendency than had ever been required to maintain it.

It is of course true that the distinctive evils of the Undertakers were greater in Ireland than they had ever been in England. In a Parliament in which at least two-thirds of the seats consisted of small boroughs at the disposal of a very few individuals; in a country in which the great majority of the population were absolutely excluded from political privileges, there was necessarily a concentration of political power, and an absence of political control that had never, in the worst times, been equalled in England. Yet at the same time the government by Undertakers was by no means without its advantages, and the period in which it flourished is very far from being the worst in Irish history. . . .

*In 1760, a new constitutional conflict flared up over the right of the Irish Parliament to initiate legislation. The Irish Lords Justices and Privy Councillors disputed with the English Privy Council the necessity of sending a money-bill to Westminster for prior approval by the Crown in order to summon a new Parliament in Dublin. Under Poynings's Law of 1495, only those bills submitted to London for the King's consent could be introduced into the Irish Parliament. The English Privy Council insisted that the money-bill be sent over for the usual approval, and Government placemen in Dublin effectively stifled this attempt of the Irish Privy Council to originate bills. For his help in defeating the Irish Opposition on this issue the Earl of Kildare was raised to the rank of Marquess, and in 1765 he became the Duke of Leinster.*

The Parliament was, of course, mainly a Parliament of landlords, and the immense multiplication of nomination boroughs had placed the controlling power in a few hands. Property was largely, perhaps extravagantly, represented; but the debating power of the Irish House of Commons was chiefly due to the very unusual number of lawyers who sat in it. Anthony Malone, who had long been the foremost man in the profession, was now in the decline of life, and although his quarrel with the Government was soon terminated, he does not appear to have taken a very conspicuous part under George III. The foremost place in the Government ranks was conceded to Hely Hutchinson, the Prime Sergeant, an inveterate place-hunter, but a man of brilliant and versatile ability, and at the same time of great political tact and moderation. In spite of his general support of the Government he voted for many of the popular measures, such as free trade, the claim of right, the abrogation of a large part of the penal laws, and the reform of Parliament, and his influence on other questions appears to have been usually employed to moderate and assuage. He is one of the very earliest politicians in the three kingdoms who show clear traces of the influence of Adam Smith, and he wrote a work on the commercial disabilities of Ireland, which is one of the best specimens of political literature produced in Ireland in the latter half of the eighteenth century. He is said to have greatly raised the standard of debate, and to have been a master of polished sarcasm; but he was not a consistent and certainly not a disinterested politician. In general, however, the lawyers were exceedingly independent of the Government. The profession was at this time unusually flourishing in Ireland. The incomes made at the bar were, perhaps absolutely, certainly relatively to the cost of living, much greater than at present. The most conspicuous barristers nearly always found their way into Parliament, and their presence was particularly valuable on account of the great prominence which questions of constitutional law speedily attained. With the exception of the Chief Justiceship of the King's Bench, which was so inadequately remunerated that it was scarcely an object to a great lawyer, the highest posts in the law were monopolised by Englishmen, and this fact was not without its influence upon the politics of the Irish Bar. Henry Flood, the son of a Chief Justice of the King's Bench, and a gentleman of large fortune and considerable political connection, was the most popular and powerful speaker of the small party known as patriots, and he was very ably seconded by

Sir William Osborne, a country gentleman, whose excellent conduct towards his tenants has been commemorated by Arthur Young. Lucas had returned to Ireland after his long exile on a *noli prosequi,* and sat for Dublin; but he had no parliamentary ability or success. Gerard Hamilton, so well known in England as Single-Speech Hamilton, was Secretary to Lord Halifax and to Lord Northumberland, the first two Viceroys of George III, and his eloquence, which on one memorable occasion had electrified the English House of Commons, was more than once heard with extraordinary effect in the Irish Parliament.

The first seven years, however, of the reign of George III were singularly uneventful in Ireland. The Undertakers still co-operated cordially with the Castle, and public affairs under Halifax, Northumberland, Hertford, and Bristol moved on very, smoothly. During the Viceroyalty of Halifax the Spanish declaration of war placed England in enmity with the two branches of the House of Bourbon, and her resources seemed strained to the utmost limits of endurance. . . .

There were, however, certain questions brought forward at this time in the Parliament which had a more purely Irish interest. The objects of the National party were simply to obtain for the Irish Protestants the laws which were regarded by Englishmen as the most essential guarantees of their liberty. The immovability of the judges and a Habeas Corpus Bill were frequently brought in; but the two measures on which their efforts were now mainly concentrated, were the restriction of pensions and the limitation of the duration of Parliament.

The grievance of the Pension List had been rapidly becoming insupportable; for, though none of the pensions granted under George III were as scandalous as several which had been granted in former reigns, the aggregate amount was steadily and rapidly increasing. During the greater part of the reign of George II it had been nearly stationary, and on the succession of the Duke of Devonshire to the Viceroyalty in April 1755, the pension list, exclusive of the French pensions and the military pensions, amounted to 38,003*l.*, but from this time it rapidly rose. On the accession of Bedford, in January 1757, it was 51,583*l.*; on the accession of Halifax, in April 1761, it was 64,127*l.* In the two years of this administration it rose to 70,752*l.*, and when Lord

Townshend assumed the reins of power in August 1767, it had increased to 86,741*l.* In 1753 the law imposing a tax of 4*s.* in the pound upon places and pensions held by absentees had been suffered to drop, for it was found that the clause enabling the Sovereign to grant exemptions rendered it wholly nugatory. The tax produced scarcely anything, and the exemption was always granted in the worst cases. The war had left Ireland with a debt of more than half a million, and her resources were so scanty that she staggered under the weight. With no foreign trade, with a people sunk in extreme poverty, with a permanent military establishment far larger in proportion to her population than that of England, at a time when her finances were greatly disordered, and when it might be supposed that her exertions might have entitled her to some consideration, Ireland found herself burdened with this vast increase of pensions, the greater part of them intended either to reward services which were not Irish or to increase the influence of the Crown. In 1757, when the pension list was comparatively moderate, the House of Commons passed resolutions denouncing the increase of pensions as alarming; and it compelled the Duke of Bedford, by a threat of witholding supplies, to transmit its resolutions to the King. In 1763, shortly after Lord Northumberland had come over, and at a time when the pension list had risen to 72,000*l.*, which was 42,000*l.* more than the whole Civil List, the subject was taken up with great ability by John Fitzgibbon, the father of the well-known Lord Clare. The House agreed that the pensions charged on the Civil List were an intolerable grievance, and it resolved itself into a committee to investigate the subject, but the Government succeeded in defeating the project of an address to the King. In the course of the debates of this year Mr. Pery revealed to the House the remarkable fact that under a false name an Irish pension of 1,000*l.* a year had been granted to Count de Viri, the Sardinian ambassador, who took a prominent part in negotiating the Peace of Paris. In 1765, as the pension list was still increasing, a new but abortive attempt was made to procure an address to the King. . . .

The National party was at this time unable to put any effectual stop to this great evil; but, in 1763, the Government of Lord Northumberland gave a distinct assurance that the King would not grant any more pensions for lives or years upon the establishment "except on extraordinary occasions." The King appears to have had a real wish to restrict the pension list, but under the system of government which was established it was not easy to do so, and in spite of all pledges it continued to increase.

The other subject which occupied a foremost place in popular politics was the limitation of the duration of Parliament. This question, with which Lucas had especially identified himself, and which was powerfully supported by the eloquence of Flood, was one of the very few that profoundly agitated the whole Protestant community of Ireland, and a large proportion of the members of the first Parliament of George III were bound by the most stringent pledges to do their utmost to carry it. It was brought forward on the very first day on which the new Parliament sat, and heads of a Bill for septennial Parliaments were repeatedly carried through the Commons. There were, however, many different motives and influences at work, and a very large amount of insincerity was displayed. It was noticed with indignation in the country that, though the House of Commons in 1761 voted the heads of the Bill, it refused to present it in a body to the Lord Lieutenant and to request him to recommend it to his Majesty. The majority of the members in their hearts detested a measure which would increase their dependence on their constitutents and expose them to the risk and expense of frequent elections. Some, who were less purely selfish, dreaded the effects of such elections in promoting idleness and disorder. The Undertakers feared that an increase of the popular element in Parliament would be fatal to their power; and the Government, both in England and Ireland, were afraid that it would eventually lead to a complete revision of the Constitution. On the other hand, it was impossible to mistake the earnestness of the constituencies, and the pressure they placed upon their representatives was such as had never before been known in Ireland, and had not often been known in England. In all parts of the country resolutions, addresses, and petitions in favour of septennial Parliaments were adopted at county meetings. Instructions of the most peremptory kind were sent up to the members. They were continually reminded of their election pledges, and every sign of languor was jealously watched.

The Undertakers, in spite of their boasted strength, could

neither oppose nor divert the stream. Members of Parliament were not prepared to meet the storm of obloquy which assailed those who voted against the Bill, and they were extremely glad to transfer the unpopularity of rejecting it to the Irish Privy Council or to England. The Irish Privy Council detested the Bill, but it passed it, trusting that the English Council would take upon itself the odium of the rejection. . . .

*To the relief of those politicians who feared costlier elections, the English Privy Council rejected the Irish Septennial Bill. Lord Halifax's viceroyalty lasted from 1760 to 1762, when he was replaced by the Earl of Northumberland.*

Northumberland was recalled in March 1765, and at this time the determination seems to have been taken in England to make the Lord Lieutenant for the future constantly resident in Ireland, in order by this means to break down the Government by Under-takers. It was not, however, then easy to find politicians who would accept the post. Lord Weymouth, who was in very em-barrassed circumstances, was first nominated; but though he re-ceived the usual grant of 3,000l. given to a new Lord Lieutenant for his equipage and voyage, he resigned before going over. Lord Hertford, who followed, was succeeded in October 1766 by Lord Bristol, and on the appointment of the latter the King wrote with his own hand to Chatham that he expected "his constant residence while he held his office." Bristol, however, threw up his office without coming to Ireland, though he also received from the Irish exchequer 3,000l. for his voyage and equipage; and in October 1767, Lord Townshend came over as Viceroy to establish the new system of government.

He was brother of Charles Townshend, and his appointment was nearly the last act of that brilliant but erratic statesman. His antecedents were wholly military. He had served at Dettingen, Fontenoy, Culloden, and Laffeldt, and at the siege of Quebec had become commander-in-chief upon the death of Wolfe and the disablement of Monckton; but his conduct on this last occasion had not raised his fame, for he was accused of having persistently thwarted Wolfe during his lifetime, and of having endeavoured after his death to rob him, by a very invidious silence, of the honour of the capture of Quebec. Townshend, however, was by no means an unamiable man. He was brave, honest, and frank; popular in his manners, witty, convivial, and with a great turn for caricature, but violent and capricious in his temper, and exceedingly destitute of tact, dignity, and decorum. He certainly drank hard, and he was accused of low vices, and a great love of low companions. His military knowledge was of much use in some parts of his Irish government, but he was totally inexperienced in civil administration. . . .

It seemed at first as if Townshend could not fail to be popular in Ireland. His constant residence, however displeasing it might be to a few great families, was likely to be generally acceptable, and he was authorised, not only to reiterate the declaration of Northumberland that, except on very important occasions, no new pensions should be granted, but also to inform the chief persons in Ireland that the English Government had resolved to grant the capital points of the limitation of the duration of Parliament, and of the security of the judges' tenure of office, and to consider with a favourable disposition the demand for a Habeas Corpus Act, and for the creation of a national militia. His secretary, Sir George Macartney, was an Irishman, and the Irish Chancellor Bowes having died in July 1767, it was thought not impossible that an Irishman might be appointed to succeed him.

No Irish administration had opened under more favourable circumstances. Although the residence of the Lord Lieutenant was ultimately intended to subvert the power of the Undertakers, Townshend at first showed no hostility to them, and was quite prepared to co-operate with them. He was instructed to employ all his power and all his popularity in carrying a measure on which the personal wishes of the King were intensely set. This measure was the augmentation of the Irish army to a little more than 15,000 men.

In his very first speech from the throne, however, he committed the grave indiscretion of announcing formally and publicly that he had it in charge from the King that provision should be made for securing the judges in their seats during good behaviour, though, in fact, the ministers at home had only authorised him privately and in general terms to offer this, as well as other concessions, to the chief people whose support he desired. The measure was a favourite one of the National party in Ireland, and on the first day of the Session heads of a Bill to carry it into effect were unexpectedly brought forward by an independent member and carried without difficulty. It soon, however, appeared that the views of the English ministers and those of the popular party in Ireland were irreconcilable. The Irish wished a law exactly like that which had been enacted in England after the Revolution, and, as in England a judge could be removed by an address of both Houses of Parliament, they proposed to give a similar power in Ireland to their own Parliament. The English ministers were determined that the Irish Privy Council should be recognised as an essential part of the Irish Constitution, and that the dependence of Ireland on the English Parliament should be emphatically asserted. Shelburne wrote to Townshend that the Irish judges must be removable only upon a representation of the two Irish Houses of Parliament and the Irish Privy Council conjointly, or upon an address of the two Houses of the British Parliament. Townshend at once summoned the confidential servants of the Crown, and directed them to have clauses to this effect inserted in committee, but they all answered that such clauses would be rejected with indignation, and they entreated him to keep it a secret that they had ever been thought of. The Bill was therefore suffered to proceed in England in a form corresponding with the English Act, but it was returned with clauses making it necessary for addresses of the two Irish Houses for the removal of a judge to be certified by the Privy Council, and making the Irish judges removable by the British Parliament. The Irish House of Commons at once rejected the Bill, and the promise in the speech from the throne was branded with some reason as not much better than a deception. . . .

*During 1767 Townshend worked hard to overcome Parliament's resistance to the Government's plan to augment the imperial forces at Irish expense. Before this controversial bill could be passed, the English executive had to break the power of the Irish Undertakers. In an attempt at conciliation the Octennial Act of 1768 was approved by the Crown, thus limiting the duration of Irish Parliaments to eight years.*

Parliament was dissolved on May 28, 1768, and Townshend at once threw himself with characteristic vehemence into the task of breaking down the power of the Undertakers. "The constant plan of these men of power," he wrote, speaking of Shannon and Ponsonby, "is to possess the government of this country, and to lower the authority of English government, which must in the end destroy that dependence which this kingdom has upon Great Britain." He complained that they had almost reduced the Lord Lieutenant to "a mere pageant of State," and he warned the Government that the crisis had arrived, and that upon the determination now shown in resisting the Undertakers depended the future strength of English government in Ireland. A complete change of persons, though for a time delayed, must eventually be effected; the aristocratic party must be thoroughly broken; in order to restore vigour to the government of the Crown, Ireland must remain under the constant attention of a resident Viceroy; every place, office, and honour must depend exclusively upon his favour, and in this manner an overwhelmingly political influence must be gradually concentrated in the Crown. Immediately after the Session of 1768, as an earnest of the favours to be expected by those who supported the Viceroy, four peers were raised a step in the peerage, four new peers, three baronets, and four Privy Councillors were made, and Townshend urged the propriety of creating an Irish Order like that of the Thistle or the Bath in order to reward those members of the nobility who were foremost in supporting the Government.

The system was not yet fully matured, but it was at least fully conceived. The overwhelming preponderance of nomination boroughs in the Irish Parliament had given three or four men an extraordinary power, which the Viceroy was resolved to destroy, and for this purpose he designed to attach as many as possible of the minor borough-owners to himself by a lavish creation of peerages. Apart from the pension list, direct pecuniary bribes to members of Parliament did not exist. There was no fund from which they could be drawn, but places were extravagantly multiplied, and pensions, in spite of royal promises, were soon granted anew for the purpose of securing parliamentary support. At the same time, Townshend had no wish to rely solely on corrupt means, and he hoped to secure the assistance of the independent country gentlemen, and even of the leaders of the most advanced party. "The Octennial Bill," he wrote, "gave the first blow to the dominion of aristocracy in this kingdom, and it rests with Government to second the good effects of it," and he strongly urged the ministers to call Flood and Sir W. Osborne to office.

It is not easy to realise the conditions of Irish parliamentary politics at this time, for all analogies drawn from the Irish contingent in the Imperial Parliament are wholly misleading. In the Parliament of the early years of George III all the members were Protestants and elected by Protestants, and the most liberal regarded the propriety of Protestant ascendency as an axiom. The party which now calls itself distinctively national was absolutely unrepresented. The Catholic priesthood, who are now perhaps the strongest element in Irish political life, had not a vestige of power; and although corrupt and factious motives may be often detected, the great tribe of knaves and fanatics who now win political power by stimulating disloyalty, or class hatred, or agrarian crime, had as yet no existence. There was a great and justifiable discontent at the constitutional and commercial restrictions; but there was at bottom no real disloyalty, and in times of danger Parliament was ever ready to bear its full share, and something more than its full share, in the defence of the Empire. In the counties the ascendency of the landlords was undisputed. In the large towns there was an active political life and a strong democratic spirit aspiring towards constitutional privileges, but Irish democracy had as yet no leaning towards the Catholics. Some of the numerous small boroughs were held by men who had purchased their seats. Some were attached to the properties of country gentlemen of moderate fortune. Some were under the direct influence of the Government, or were connected with ecclesiastical preferments and filled by the nominees of bishops. Very many belonged to a few rich members of the House of Lords, who had made it an object to accumulate political power. It appears to have been considered a point of honour that a borough member should not on an important question vote against the policy of his patron.

The body which was thus formed was not divided like a modern Parliament into clearly marked party divisions. Lord Shannon, the Duke of Leinster, Lord Ely, Lord Tyrone, Lord Drogheda, and Mr. Ponsonby had each of them a considerable group of personal adherents, but the lines of Whig and Tory,

Government and Opposition, were not drawn with any clearness or constancy. Usually the Government in ordinary business carried with it an enormous majority, but there were questions on which the strongest Government nearly always became suddenly powerless. Money Bills that took their rise or were materially modified in England were almost always rejected, and on several constitutional questions Parliament had a very decided will of its own. It was a common thing for paid servants of the Crown, while in general supporting the Government, to go on particular questions into violent opposition, and for men, who had on particular questions been the most active opponents of Government, to pass suddenly into its ranks; and there was a rapid fluctuation of politicians between Government and Opposition which is very perplexing to a modern reader. Many corrupt motives no doubt mingled with these changes, but the root of the matter lay in the fact that settled parties had not yet been formed, that all questions were considered mainly in isolation, and that there was little or nothing of that systematic and disciplined concurrence of opinion based upon party lines which prevails in a modern Parliament.

The absence of parties was partly due to the rudimentary character of Irish parliamentary life and to the nature of the constituencies, which gave a predominating influence to a few personal interests, and traces of a somewhat similar state of things may be detected in English parliamentary life between the Revolution and the close of the reign of George II. There was, however, another cause which was peculiar to Ireland, and the importance of which has not, I think, been sufficiently noticed. The position which the Privy Council held in the Irish constitution enabled the Government to withdraw from serious parliamentary conflict the capital questions around which party divisions would have been naturally formed. Short Parliaments, a secure tenure for judges' seats, and a Habeas Corpus Act were during many years among the chief objects of the popular party; but year after year they were carried without opposition and without division through Parliament, and Government ostensibly acquiesced in them, reserving it for the Privy Council in Ireland or England to reject them. One of the effects of this system was to check the normal growth of Parliament and confuse the lines of party division. . . .

*Renewing the conflict with England over the legislative initiative, the Irish Commons in 1769 rejected a money-bill which had originated in the English Privy Council. The Irish Opposition then declared that the bill owed its defeat to its English origins. Townshend managed to induce the Commons to vote supplies, and the Augmentation scheme also passed by a large majority. Having secured these measures, Townshend promptly prorogued Parliament on 26 December 1769. This move infuriated the Opposition and led to noisy protests as well as petitions for the recall of Parliament. When Parliament reassembled on 26 February 1771, the Address of thanks to the King was carried by 132 to 107. Only by means of "the most constant and lavish corruption" was Townshend able to maintain a Government majority. By 1772 the personal and political animosity against the Viceroy had reached a breaking point.*

In September 1772 Townshend was recalled and made Master of the Ordnance in England; and the Earl of Harcourt, who had been for some time the representative of Great Britain at the Court of Versailles, was appointed to succeed him.

No previous administration had done so much to corrupt and lower the tone of political life in Ireland, and Lord Townshend is one of the very small number of Irish Viceroys who have been personally disliked. "The people of this kingdom," said Sir John Davies, "both English and Irish, did ever love and desire to be governed by great persons"; and one of the best arguments in favour of the Viceroyalty is the historical fact that under this system of government, in spite of party fluctuations and of intestine discord and disaffection, the supreme representative of English law and authority has usually been the most popular man in Ireland. The Irish character, indeed, naturally attaches itself much more strongly to individuals than to systems, and is peculiarly susceptible to personal influences. Chesterfield, like Townshend, detested the system of Undertakers, and took a large share of the government into his own hands, but he was as much beloved and respected as his successor was despised. Townshend certainly desired sincerely the welfare of the country, and his abilities were superior to those of many of his predecessors and successors; but he was entirely destitute of tact and judgment, and he committed a fault which is peculiarly fatal in an Irish ruler. He sought for popularity by sacrificing the dignity and the decorum of his position, and he brought both his person and his office into contempt.

Under Lord Harcourt, Irish politics suddenly calmed. The new Viceroy was an elderly nobleman of immense fortune, undistinguished in public life, and with no conspicuous ability, but painstaking, dignified, decorous, and conciliatory; and his secretary, Sir John Blaquiere, had some debating power and great skill and adroitness in managing men. As Parliament did not meet till October 1773, the Lord Lieutenant had ample time to frame his measures and obtain a personal acquaintance with the leading politicians. He found all parties prepared to welcome him; and Shannon, Leinster, Ponsonby, and Flood were all present at his early levees. He received secret instructions from Lord Rochford to aim specially at two ends. He was to discourage to the utmost of his power all applications for new peerages and promotions, additional pensions and salaries, new offices, employments for life, and all grants of revenue, as well as the sale of offices, places, and employments. He was also to do his utmost to regain for the King the full control of the hereditary revenue by inducing the Parliament to make good by new taxation the many charges which had been thrown upon it in the form of premiums and bounties, and especially the large bounty voted in perpetuity on the inland carriage of corn. . . .

*Under increasing financial pressure, the Irish administration, headed by Lord Harcourt, tried in vain to raise more funds by imposing a 10 percent tax on the rentals of absentee landlords. Opposition spokesmen denounced this proposal, and the absentee tax was finally defeated in November 1773 with the aid of five prominent Whig peers in England who owned land in both countries.*

The relations of Lord Harcourt with the Irish Parliament at the close of 1774 were as friendly as possible, and the two most conspicuous debaters in the House of Commons soon after received favours from his hand. Hely Hutchinson had for a long time disliked the profession of the law, and had desired to turn to a wholly different sphere. The great position of Provost of Trinity College having fallen vacant, he asked for and obtained it, the statute which required that the Provost should be in holy orders being dispensed with in his favour. Hutchinson, on accepting this post, resigned the office of Prime Serjeant, and the sinecure of Alnager, as well as his professional practice; but in spite of these sacrifices, the new appointment did not escape severe and merited blame. There was a manifest impropriety in making the headship of a great University a prize to be given for mere parliamentary services, and in passing over the claims of the resident fellows in favour of a man who had no experience in academic pursuits, and only a faint tincture of academic learning. Hutchinson continued to retain his seat in Parliament, and his name for some years longer occurs frequently in Irish politics.

A more important and a more contested appointment was that of Henry Flood, who, after a long period of negotiation, accepted in October 1775 the position of Vice-Treasurer. This very remarkable man had for some years been rising rapidly as a debater to the foremost place in the House of Commons. His eloquence does not, indeed, appear to have been of the very highest kind. It was slow, formal, austere, and somewhat heavy. When he passed, late in life, into the English Parliament, he failed, and Wraxall gave a reason for his failure which is so curious as indicating a great change that has taken place in national tastes that the reader must pardon me if I make it the text of a short digression. "The slow, measured, and sententious style of enunciation which characterised his eloquence," says Wraxall, "however calculated to excite admiration it might be in the senate of the sister kingdom, appeared to English ears cold, stiff, and deficient in some of the best recommendations of attention." In truth, the standard of taste prevailing in Ireland, or at least in Dublin, during the first three-quarters of the eighteenth century, appears to have been as far as possible removed from the exaggerated, over-heated, and over-ornamented rhetoric which is so commonly associated with the term Irish eloquence. The style of Swift, the style of Berkeley, and the style of Goldsmith are in their different ways among the most perfect in English literature, but they are simple sometimes to the verge of baldness, and they manifest a much greater distaste for ornamentation and rhetorical effect than the best contemporary writings in England. Burke had by nature one of the most exuberant of human imaginations, and his literary taste was by no means pure; but it is very remarkable that it was not until a long residence in England had made him indifferent to the canons of Irish taste that the true character of his intellect was fully disclosed. His treatise on "The Sublime and Beautiful," though written on a subject which lends itself eminently to ornamentation, is severe and simple to frigidity, and his historical articles in the "Annual Register," though full of weighty and impressive passages, do not show a trace of the gorgeous rhetoric which adorns the "Reflections on the French Revolution," and the "Letters on a Regicide Peace." With very different degrees of literary merit, the same quality of eminent simplicity and sobriety marks the writings of Hely Hutchinson, of Hutcheson the philosopher, of Henry Brooke, of Leland, Curry, Gordon, and Warner, and, as I have already noticed, of the more important pamphlets of the time. It represented, no doubt, in a great measure, the reaction of the cultivated taste of the nation against popular and prevalent faults, just as it is common to find among the illustrious writers and critics who have in the present century arisen in America a severity of taste and of literary judgment, and a fastidious purity of expression rarely equalled among good English writers. . . .

Inquiries into the secret motives that governed politicians are usually among the most worthless and untrustworthy portions of history. Except in the case of a very few of the most conspicuous figures, our materials for deciding are utterly inadequate, and the best contemporary judgments are largely based upon indications of character which are much too subtle and evanescent to pass into the page of history. Looking, however, at the facts as they have been stated, it is not easy to see why the conduct of Flood, in accepting office, should have been stigmatised as dishonourable. At no period of his life had he entered into an engagement not to do so. The violent and systematic opposition in which he was engaged during the latter part of the administration of Townshend grew out of the distinctive policy of that Viceroy, and naturally terminated with his recall. It was, no doubt, true that

Poynings' law could not be discussed by a statesman in office, but in the state of parties in 1774 there did not seem the smallest probability of discussing it with effect. The limitation of Parliament had been secured. A militia was hardly needed, since the establishment had been augmented, and although Charlemont strongly maintained that a permanent and well-organised opposition was essential to the healthy growth of the Irish Constitution, the fact remained that after the recall of Townshend such an opposition did not exist. It was surely open to an honest politician to contend that, under these circumstances, he could gain more for the country by co-operating with the Government than by opposing it. The Government of Harcourt was certainly not deserving of unqualified reprobation. The reunion of the divided revenue board, the Absentee Tax, and the bounty on the exportation of corn were three measures in which Flood took a keen interest. They were all of them ostensibly supported, and two of them were actually carried by the Government. By accepting the office of Vice-Treasurer, Flood broke the custom which reserved that post for Englishmen. He obtained a seat in the Privy Council where questions of vital interest to Ireland were decided, and he might very reasonably expect a great extension of his influence. To his own friends he justified his conduct by the utter impossibility of inducing any considerable body of men to remain in steady opposition after the recall of Townshend. "The only way," he said, "anything could be effected for the country, was by going along with Government, and making their measures diverge towards public utility." He spoke also of the advantage of restoring to the kingdom a great office which had been alienated from it, and his public language, when he was called upon, some years later, to defend his conduct, is perfectly consistent with these views. Charlemont, whose own character was of the highest kind, and who had hitherto been one of the most intimate friends and one of the warmest admirers of Flood, never forgave him for having accepted office; but he acknowledged that his "chief" reason was the incessant falling off of his party after the recall of Townshend, and "the belief that by accepting a great and apparently ministerial office he would be more able to serve his country." It is difficult to see why reasons so plausible, and indeed so cogent, should not have been deemed sufficient.

The truth is, that there was much in the public character and in the subsequent career of Flood which led men to judge him with severity. By the lowest form of political temptation he does not seem to have been seriously influenced. It was, no doubt, sometimes said that his object was to repair the waste which a recent election had made in his estate; but those who knew him best appear to have agreed that money was no consideration to him, and in this respect, indeed, a childless man, with a fortune of about 5,000*l.* a year, in Ireland, and in the eighteenth century, was not much tempted. Nor was he ever accused of seeking or desiring a peerage, which was the usual bribe held out to rich country gentlemen. His prevailing fault was an excessive love of power and reputation, which led him extravagantly to overrate his own political importance, to exaggerate his services, to look with great jealousy on any competitor for fame, and to aspire on all occasions to exercise an absolute influence on those about him. In private life, his hospitable and convivial manners, his love of field sports, his excellent classical scholarship, his great patience under contradiction and his very considerable conversational powers made him generally popular; and Burke, Charlemont, and Grattan were at one time among his friends. But in public life a strong personal element seems to have always mixed with his politics. He was jealous, domineering, irritable, easily imagining slights, prone to take sudden turns of conduct through motives of personal ambition or personal resentment, more feared than trusted by those with whom he acted. . . .

*Ambitious for high office, Flood bargained with Lord Harcourt for the post of Vice-Treasurer in the Irish establishment. After some tactical shuffling, Flood agreed to accept the post, hoping eventually to sit in the English House of Commons. His seat in the Irish Commons was taken by Henry Grattan, his most formidable rival.*

Events which were destined to exercise an extraordinary influence over Irish politics were now rapidly hastening on. The American dissensions had all but reached their climax, and there were great numbers in Ireland who regarded the American cause as their own. Already the many disastrous circumstances of Irish history had driven great bodies of Irishmen to seek a home in the more distant dominions of the Crown. The island of Monserrat is said to have been entirely occupied by planters of Irish origin; at least a third of the planters of Jamaica were either Irish or of Irish origin; and great districts of the American colonies were almost wholly planted by settlers from Ulster. But this was by no means the only interest which Ireland had in the colonial struggle. Never before had the question of the relations of the mother-country to its dependencies been brought before the world with such a distinctness of emphasis and of definition. The Irish party which followed the traditions of Swift and Molyneux had always contended that, by the ancient constitution of their country, Ireland was inseparably connected with the English Crown, but was not dependent upon, or subject to, the English Parliament. By Poynings' Law a great part of the independence of the Irish Parliament had indeed been surrendered; but even the servile Parliament which passed it, though extending by its own authority to Ireland laws previously enacted in England, never admitted the right of the English Parliament to make laws for Ireland. English lawyers had sometimes asserted and sometimes denied the existence of such a right, but the first explicit text in its favour was the Declaratory Act of George I by which the English Parliament asserted its own right of legislating for Ireland. It was precisely parallel to the Declaratory Act relating to America which was passed when the Stamp Act was repealed. In both cases the right was denied, but in both cases the great majority of politicians were practically ready to acquiesce, provided certain restrictions and limitations were secured to them. The Americans did not dispute the power of the English Legislature to bind their commerce and regulate their affairs as members of an extended empire, as long as they were untrammelled in their local concerns and were not taxed except by their own representatives. The position of most Irish politicians was very similar. The Irish Parliament legislated for the local concerns of Ireland, and it still retained with great jealousy a certain control over the purse, which it justly looked upon as incomparably the most important of its prerogatives.

This control was, it is true, much less complete than that which was possessed in England by the English Parliament. The great changes affecting the revenue which had been made in England at the Revolution of 1688 had not extended to Ireland. The hereditary revenue was beyond the control of Parliament, but the other portions of the Irish revenue could not be levied without a parliamentary vote, and the hereditary revenue was not sufficient for the government of the country. . . .

*The insistence of the British Parliament on the right to tax the American colonies without their consent had ominous implications for Ireland, where legislative subordination to Westminster already rankled the more independent politicians. If the American colonists were defeated, Ireland might well lose what political liberties it possessed. Blackstone's* Commentaries, *published in 1765, had upheld Parliament's right "to bind Ireland by its laws," and even Lord Rockingham believed that the Declaratory Act of George I enabled England to tax Ireland. The crisis in America stimulated the Irish "patriot party," which was determined to assert the rights of the Irish Parliament against British imperial controls. In 1775, however, the Irish Government commanded a safe majority in Parliament, and Lord Harcourt had no trouble in persuading the Irish Commons, when it met in October, to condemn the American rebels in the course of the Address. This pious declaration did not reflect the sympathy of many Irish Protestants for the American cause. Although Ireland was formally committed to support Britain's imperial war, the "patriots" grew increasingly defiant. To bolster his parliamentary majority, Lord Harcourt had to resort to the creation of seventeen new peerages and the promotion of twelve Irish nobles one step in rank.*

This was one of the last events in the administration of Lord Harcourt. His relations with the English ministers had for some time been growing tense, and he now resigned office and was replaced in November 1776 by the Earl of Buckinghamshire. The administration of Harcourt in its opening had enjoyed great popularity, but it carried the system of corruption which Townshend had established to a still greater excess. Though large economies in the establishments had been promised, though the deficiency in most branches of the revenue was already threatening bankruptcy, yet no less than 80,000*l.* had been added in this administration to the public expenditure of Ireland. Several thousands of pounds were spent in creating new offices or annexing new salaries to old ones, and in the words of Grattan, "there was scarcely a sinecure whose salary Government had not increased." In the space of twenty years the Civil List had nearly doubled, the Pension List had nearly doubled, and a national debt of a million had been accumulated. Between March 1773 and September 1777 the Pension List had risen from 79,099*l.* to 89,095*l.* Loans were raised in 1769, in 1771, in 1773, in 1775, and in 1777. In 1773 and 1775 new taxes were imposed which were estimated to produce 140,000*l.* a year, yet these measures and the withdrawal of a large body of troops from the establishment had failed to restore the equilibrium. It was no longer possible to urge that the public revenue was largely wasted in private grants for stimulating private enterprises. Most of the new expenses emanated from the Government itself. Nearly half the debt had been accumulated in time of perfect peace, and candid men were obliged to confess that the old system of Undertakers was much more economical, and was certainly not more corrupt, than that which had succeeded it.

It seemed, indeed, scarcely possible that the country could escape bankruptcy, for, while the establishments were steadily mounting, the few sources of wealth which the commercial restrictions had left were now cut off. The rupture with the colonies closed one of the chief markets of Irish linens, while the provision trade, on which the landed interest mainly depended, was annihilated by an embargo which was laid by proclamation, and without consultation with the Irish Parliament, on the export of provisions from Ireland, and which was continued during three years. It was ostensibly to prevent Irish provisions passing to the colonists or to the French, but it was very positively stated that it was imposed by an unconstitutional stretch of the prerogative at the instigation of private individuals, in order to favour a few private contractors in England. The rupture with France was in no part of the Empire felt so severely as in Ireland; for one of the effects of the laws restraining Irish commerce with England and her colonies had been to establish a close commercial connection between Ireland and France. It was said by a very able writer on the economical condition of Ireland, that "two of her provinces may at this very day be called provinces of France as much as of

Great Britain." All this commercial intercourse was now cut off. French and American privateers swarmed around the coast, and universal distress set in. The price of black cattle, and of wool; rents, credit, private business and public revenue in all their branches rapidly sank, and thousands of manufacturers lived on charity or abandoned the country. In Dublin, half-starving crowds, carrying a black fleece in token of their distress, paraded the streets. The pressure was so severe that in 1778 Ireland was obliged to borrow from England 50,000*l.* for the payment of her troops, and the value of the imports from England was 634,444*l.* below the average of the four preceding years. The want of employment, complained one of the best economical writers in Ireland, was at this time such that two-thirds of the country was uninhabited. At least 15,000 Irishmen were seeking their living in foreign armies; and, perhaps, a still greater number in other capacities on the Continent. At every opportunity great numbers were flying across the sea, and as the same extension of pasture which diminished the demand for labour raised the price of bread, over a great part of Ireland, "the wretches that remained had scarcely the appearance of human creatures." "In England," he concluded, "there is no such thing as poverty in comparison of what is to be found in every part of Ireland except the cities and principal towns."

The necessity under these circumstances of abandoning the system of commercial restrictions began to force itself upon many minds. It was plain that without some alteration in her economical condition Ireland could not much longer contribute her share to the military expenditure of the Empire. It was plain that a large part of the discontent which was rapidly severing the American colonies from the Empire had been due to the commercial policy of the mother country, and it was only too probable that in Ireland similar causes would ultimately produce similar effects. The disaster of Saratoga, in 1777, had revealed the full gravity of the situation, and, now that the sword of France was thrown into the hostile scale, the issue of the contest was at least very doubtful. Besides this, the wisdom of the code was becoming widely questioned. From a very early time a few weighty voices had broken the unanimity in its favour. . . .

*During the American War of Independence Irish political economists and mercantile interests actively lobbied for free trade between Ireland and the rest of the empire. But in 1778 English industrial interests showed how afraid they were of competition by once again defeating a measure that sought to abolish restrictions against the Irish export trade.*

The almost absolute silence about the Catholic population of Ireland in the present chapter will perhaps have already struck the reader. The truth is that the period of tension and acute conflict between the two religions had passed, and the very name of Papist rarely occurs in Irish politics. Of purely religious intolerance there was now very little, though we may still find a few signs that Catholicism as a religion was looked upon as an evil. The Charter Schools, which were distinctly proselytising, were steadily encouraged by the Irish Parliament. Under Lord Townshend, 10*l*. was added to the annual sum granted to any priest who became a convert. The merchants and traders of Dublin, in petitioning for a limitation of the duration of Parliament, urged among other reasons that it "would render the generality of landlords assiduous in procuring Protestant tenants, and by such visible advantages to Protestants induce Catholics to conform." The Irish Privy Council, in 1772, recommending a Bill for enabling Catholics to borrow on landed security, gave as one argument, that it may "induce them to become Protestants in order to acquire landed property."

But in general there was little spirit of proselytism and still less religious enthusiasm among the Irish Protestants, and questions relating to Catholics were nearly always argued rather on economical and political than on religious grounds. There were politicians of no mean order who sincerely believed that the admission of Catholics to any degree of political power would be fatal to the stability of the country, and there was still an ignoble spirit of ascendency which looked down upon Catholics as upon a servile and subjugated caste, and resented, both on grounds of sentiment and on grounds of interest, any attempt to raise them. The penal laws made the Protestant landlord in a Catholic district little less than a despot. The lawyer found that they diminished the competition while they increased the business of his profession. Corporations had become under their influence small monopolising bodies which were able to levy oppressive quarterage on Catholic traders. In almost every walk of life when a Protestant and a Catholic were in competition, the former found the ascendency of his religion an advantage. Many who would never have sought ascendency if it had not been established, wished to preserve the privileges they had inherited, and the most worthless Protestant, if he had nothing else to boast of, at least found it pleasing to think that he was a member of a dominant race.

Traditional antipathies and distinctions, though they had lost their old vitality, passed languidly and passively into the mind, but they were only slightly and remotely connected with religion, and, as Arthur Young truly said, the penal laws were now directed much more against the property than against the creed of the Catholic. Though the whole Catholic system in Ireland existed only by connivance, it appears to have been practically unmolested. Even in Ulster, where the spirit of intolerance was much stronger than in other provinces, sumptuous mass-houses were everywhere arising, and bishops and monks, as well as ordinary priests and schoolmasters, lived in the country without concealment or difficulty. Of the Catholic laity at least nineteen-twentieths were too poor and too ignorant to be affected by any disabling laws or to take any interest in political questions. The landlords of the persuasion had dwindled, under many disabilities and many temptations to apostasy, into a small and insignificant body, who seldom appeared before the world except in times of great national danger, when, under the guidance of a few conspicuous Catholic peers, they came forward to express in hyperbolical terms their loyalty to the Crown. A great part of the more energetic Catholics passed steadily to the Continent. Shut out from the University, from the magistracy, from the legal profession in all its grades, from all forms of administration and political ambition, scarcely anything remained for them at home except industrial life, and a considerable body of wealthy Catholic merchants had grown up, especially at Cork, Limerick, and Waterford. Time, however, had gradually done its work. The habits and pursuits of all classes had been accommodated to their conditions, and a state of society which was in truth very anomalous had grown into a kind of second nature, and was acquiesced in without much conflict or irritation.

The Catholic Association, which was founded in 1759 by a physician named Curry, by the antiquary Charles O'Conor, and by a Waterford gentleman named Wyse, was the first important effort to create an independent Catholic opinion. The object was to establish a committee in Dublin comprising representatives of every Catholic diocese, to watch over the interests of the whole body....

*The exigencies of England's imperial wars forced the British army to end its restrictions against recruiting among Catholics in Ireland. Although the Government showed greater leniency toward Irish Catholics in the hope of keeping the country quiet, the penal code still had a demoralizing effect on the populace.*

More than eighty years had now passed by since any act of rebellion or conspiracy or political turbulence had been proved against Catholics in Ireland. They had maintained an absolute, unbroken tranquillity during the Scotch rebellion of 1715, during the expedition organised against the House of Hanover by Alberoni in 1719, during the great rebellion of 1745, during the long and desperate war that terminated in 1763, and amid all the complications that had since arisen. Standing completely apart from the factions and violence of Protestant politics, they had rarely appeared in public life except to proffer their services to the Crown; and officials in high position had repeatedly acknowledged that the severest scrutiny had discovered no trace of treasonable conduct among them, and had consented that, in times of great danger to the Empire, Ireland should be left almost destitute of troops. Those who might have been leaders or agents in sedition had long since been scattered over the Continent. The ascendency of the landlords over their tenants was as yet undisputed, and the Catholic landlords were ardent in their loyalty to the Crown. No independent Catholic press had yet arisen. The mass of the population remained torpid, degraded, and ignorant; but, although crimes of violence and turbulence were common among them, those crimes were wholly unconnected with politics. Protestants were beginning to ask themselves

157

how long, under such circumstances, the system of proscription was to continue—whether laws which paralysed the industry of the great majority of the Irish people, which kept them in enforced ignorance and poverty, which directly discouraged those manly and energetic qualities that are most essential to national well-being, could be or ought to be maintained for ever.

The general aspect of Catholicism, both in Europe and America, greatly strengthened the case. Probably at no period since the days of Constantine was Catholicism so free from domineering and aggressive tendencies as during the Pontificates of Benedict XIV and his three successors. The spirit of Ultramontanism seemed to have almost evaporated even in Italian counsels, and in Western Europe the prevailing type of theology was studiously moderate. In 1757, the Catholic Association issued a declaration of principles drawn up by O'Keefe, the Bishop of Kildare, in which they abjured in the strongest terms the doctrine that any ecclesiastical power in the Church had the right of deposing sovereigns, absolving subjects from their oaths, making war upon heretics as such, exercising any temporal power or jurisdiction in Ireland, or committing any act which is in its own nature immoral. They denied with much truth that the infallibility of the Pope was an article of the Catholic creed, and they solemnly pledged themselves to do nothing to disturb or weaken the existing establishments either of property, government, or religion. All over Europe the influence of the Catholic clergy was employed on the side of authority, and Catholic populations were nearly everywhere almost wholly destitute of that spirit of political self-assertion, and of that systematic jealousy of authority which leads to civil liberty, but which also makes nations difficult to govern. Nearly all the political insurrections of modern times had been among Protestants. Political liberty since the Reformation had nearly everywhere followed its banner, and the countries where even the worst rulers found themselves most uncontrolled were nearly everywhere Catholic. . . .

These considerations were beginning to have their weight upon Irish politicians, and in truth, if the question had been merely one of religion, if it had not been aggravated by a confiscation of property and by profound historical antipathies and antagonisms, it would probably have presented little difficulty. It was, however, quite certain that the great mass of the Catholic population in Ireland were as yet utterly unfit for the exercise of political power except under the guidance and training of the more enlightened classes. In a well-constituted society, property, tradition, and social eminence would have marked out for them natural leaders of their own creed. In Ireland such leaders did not, as a rule, exist, and it was the misfortune of the country that the most powerful influences dissociated the upper classes from the lower. Was it possible for a gentry who were almost all Protestant, and who were burdened by so many unhappy historical antecedents, to fulfill the indispensable task of leading, controlling, and educating the masses of their countrymen? On the answer to this question the political future of Ireland mainly depended.

It was only by slow degrees that Irish Protestant opinion became actively favourable to the Catholics. Whig traditions in Ireland, as in England, were extremely anti-Catholic, and many of the earlier defenders of Irish liberty desired that liberty only for a small minority of their fellow-countrymen. Anthony Malone, it is true, seems to have early seen the evil of the penal laws, and Langrishe and Dennis Daly were steady friends of the Catholics, but Lucas, who was long so prominent in the Irish national party, was virulently and aggressively anti-Catholic. No one wrote more ably against the commercial restrictions than Sir James Caldwell, but when the Bill enabling Catholics to lend money on landed security was introduced, this measure, which was politically so moderate and economically so beneficial, was opposed by Caldwell not only in the Parliament but in the Press. He dilated upon the contrast between the indifference of the Protestant clergy and the indefatigable earnestness of the Catholic priests, and upon the peculiar intensity which a long period of persecution had given to the Catholicity of the Irish people. He said that there was scarcely a Popish family in Ireland which had not some relative who was either a priest, or enlisted in a foreign army, or engaged in trade in France or Spain; that their children were all taught Latin in the hedge schools which were scattered through the southern parts of the kingdom in order to qualify for foreign service; that the few Popish landlords had none but Papists on their estates; that one Justin McCarthy, merely by the number of his debtors, kept the Protestants of a large district in awe of him, and had prevented during many years the execution of the penal code; and he concluded that any measure which increased the power of Catholics would be dangerous to Ireland. Flood was prepared to give the Catholics complete religious toleration and some economical advantages, among others the right of taking long leases and even of purchasing land; but through the whole of his career he was inflexibly opposed to giving them any measure of political power.

Charlemont, one of the purest as well as one of the most prominent of Irish patriots, took the same course. While frequently supporting measures for mitigating the economical condition of the Irish Catholics, he steadily maintained that neither arms nor votes could be safely given to them. In a private letter to one of his most intimate friends, he predicted that at least a century must pass before the Catholics could be safely entrusted with the rights of citizens, and in an autobiographical fragment which he bequeathed to his children he expressed his full approbation of the penal code. It was absolutely necessary, he said, that the armed minority should take away from their numerous antagonists every element of power. "Their inferiority in numbers could only be compensated by such a superiority in arms and discipline as might make one man equal to ten." An exclusive legislative power was necessary, and therefore the penal laws relating to land were necessary, and it was good policy to hold out every inducement to conformity. "From the natural operation of the laws, and from many other concomitant causes, the Protestants increased in strength, and the Catholics, though still retaining a great superiority in numbers, grew weaker. The greater part of the old Catholic gentry had, either from conviction or convenience, conformed to the established and ruling religion, and the quiet behaviour of the oppressed people had, or ought to have, well nigh obliterated the memory of their former excesses."

While himself firmly holding these views, Charlemont acknowledged that towards 1778 a great and rapid change had passed over the sentiments of the Irish Protestants, and he has taken much pains to analyse its causes. He attributes it partly to a prevailing spirit of toleration, springing in his opinion "rather from fashionable Deism than from Christianity, which was now unfortunately much out of fashion," and partly to the growth of a considerable Catholic interest which, directly or indirectly, exercised some political power. Catholics who had conformed in order to keep their lands, or to enter the law, were still united by blood and friendship and sympathy to the recusant body. In the southern counties, at the time when the provision trade was flourishing, many Catholic merchants had acquired large fortunes and great local influence, and they exercised some indirect patronage over Protestants, and were the chief money-lenders in the island. In some counties, land was let in very large portions to Catholic tenants, and it was the obvious interest of the landlords that those tenants should not be prevented by law from improving their farms. But in addition to these reasons there were others of a more purely political character. The desire for national independence was growing stronger and stronger in Ireland. The wretched condition of the finances, the corrupt disposal of patronage, the refusal of the English Parliament to grant that commercial liberty which was essential to Irish prosperity, and, above all, the example of America, had strengthened incalculably the old spirit of Swift and of Molyneux. In the words of Flood, "a voice from America had shouted to liberty," and, although the loyalty of the Irish Protestants to the English Crown was unshaken, there had arisen among them a strong aspiration towards legislative independence, and a conviction that it could only be attained if the Catholics were at least conciliated.

A great personal influence had also arisen in the Irish Parliament. A young man had lately entered its walls whose eloquence —surcharged, indeed, with epigram, and disfigured by a strong, though perfectly unaffected mannerism, but in the highest degree original, vivid, nervous, thoughtful, and picturesque—placed him, for the space of forty years and in two Legislatures, in the first rank of contemporary orators, while his transparent simplicity and purity of character, and his ardent and self-sacrificing patriotism, gave him a rare power of influencing those about him. It was the first principle of Henry Grattan that "the Irish Protestant could never be free till the Irish Catholic had ceased to be a slave"; and as early as 1778 Charlemont attributed to the extraordinary eloquence and influence of Grattan a great part of the change which on the Catholic question had passed over the minds of the Irish Protestants. . . .

It appears, then, that the measure of relief originated not with the Government, but with the independent members of Parliament, but it is also certain that the Government readily accepted and warmly supported it. Lord North, in the debate on Irish commerce, had taken occasion to say a few sympathising words in favour of the Catholics, and when Mr. Gardiner introduced his Bill in 1778, members attached to the Government were ready to assist him. No detailed report of the debates exist, but we know that Yelverton, who was one of the ablest of the party which on national questions supported the views of Grattan, took a leading part in preparing the Bill and that Grattan himself spoke in its favour. Lord Buckingham's secretary writes that "a general inclination to give relief to the Roman Catholics" was expressed in Parliament, "but there was a variety of opinion both as to the mode and as to the extent." The great question of division was whether Catholics should be permitted to purchase land in freehold or should only be allowed to take land at leases of 999 years. The latter was carried by 111 to 108, and, although it was now one in the morning, those who desired to restrict the Catholic concessions were so encouraged by the division that they desired still to continue the debate; but the Government, in the interest of the Catholics, carried an adjournment by a majority of three.

A new and very serious difficulty, however, was produced by a clause for relieving the Presbyterians from the test, which was introduced by Sir Edward Newenham, a member who afterwards showed a strong desire to strengthen the democratic element in the constitution. As the sacramental test had originally been introduced into Ireland in a Popery Bill, there was a manifest propriety in relieving the Dissenters in this manner as well as at this time; but the Government, who looked upon the Presbyterians as preeminently the American party, were extremely opposed to it. "It was intended," the secretary wrote, "to oppose giving liberty to receive this clause, but it being urged, even by the servants of the Crown, that the refusing to hear what might be said in favour of that considerable body of his Majesty's subjects would be an aggravation of what they deemed a grievance, the motion was suffered to pass." "It appears that this question respecting the test will occasion very great difficulties, as many people seem inclined to the measure."

The debates appear to have been very animated. They were prolonged for several nights, and lasted till two or three in the morning. It was agreed that the Catholics in taking a 999 years' lease, should pay a money rent; but as its amount was not specified, it might be merely nominal. The Test Clause was supported partly by the genuine friends of the Presbyterians, and partly by a small body of whom Lord Shannon and Lord Ely were the leaders, who were hostile to the whole Bill, and who imagined that the new clause would introduce such an element of dissension that it would be wrecked; but the House of Commons passed the Bill with the additional clause. . . . The English Privy Council sent back the Bill, shorn of its concession to the Presbyterians, and the enemies of the Catholics hoped that the Irish House of Commons would be so exasperated at the mutilation that they would reject the whole measure. They acted, however, more wisely, and the first great relief Bill for the Irish Catholics was carried through the Commons by 127 to 89, through the Lords by 44 to 28. . . .

# IV

## *The Irish Volunteers*
## *and the Constitution of 1782*

The modification of the Commercial Code and of the Popery
Code is sufficient to make the year 1778 very memorable in Irish
history. Another movement, however, which was even more important in its immediate consequences, may be dated from the
same year. I mean, of course, the creation of the Irish Volunteers.

We have seen that in every war which had taken place since the
Revolution, Ireland had been an assistance and not an embarrassment to England, and that, whatever may have been the faults of
the Irish Parliament—and they were many and great—the English Government, at least, had no reason to complain of any
want of alacrity, or earnestness, or liberality in supporting the
military establishments. This, however, was partly due to the disturbed, half-civilised, and half-organised condition of the country, which had given its ascendant class a peculiar aptitude and
taste for military life, and which at the same time made the
presence of a considerable armed force necessary for its security.
Outrages like those of the Whiteboys, the Oakboys, and the
Steelboys could not be otherwise repressed, and in the wilder parts
of the country soldiers were often required to discharge ordinary
police functions. It was an old complaint that in time of war
Ireland had often been left almost unprotected, and it was an old
desire of the country gentlemen that a permanent militia should
be organised which would be less expensive than regular troops,
and equally efficient in maintaining internal tranquillity.

Bills to this effect more than once passed the Irish House of

Commons. Lord Townshend, though seeing some difficulties in the way of the scheme, was disposed to recommend it, but nothing in his time was done. When the war with France appeared inevitable, the question of a militia revived, and a Bill creating such a force was carried, and returned from England; but it was not put in force. Financial difficulties, the lateness of the season, hopes that the French danger might pass away, fears lest the militia might interfere with recruiting for the army, and, perhaps, jealousy of a purely national force, appear to have been the principal motives of the delay, and when the war actually broke out, Ireland found herself almost absolutely without the means of maintaining tranquillity at home, or of repelling a foreign invasion. The English fleet was occupied elsewhere, and the Irish coast was unprotected. It was said that little more than a third part of the 12,000 men who were considered necessary for the defence of the country were actually there, and they were concentrated chiefly in one or two encampments. The treasury was empty, and Government was, therefore, utterly unable to form a militia. In April 1778, Lord Buckingham wrote with great urgency that it was the general sense of the House of Commons, of the Lords of the Council, and of all degrees of people in Ireland, that in case of invasion, or apprehended invasion, either a militia, or independent companies of volunteers, were absolutely necessary for the protection of the country.

But the Government, with the best intentions, was utterly unable to discharge the primary duty of securing the country. Its poverty was such that it was found necessary to borrow 20,000*l.* from La Touche's Bank, and all salaries and pensions, all civil and military grants, were suspended. A militia was impossible, for there were no means of supporting it, but "several gentlemen of considerable property declared in the House of Commons that they would, if authorised, raise, without loss of time, independent companies, formed out of their respective tenantries, of men upon whom they could depend."

Buckingham recommended that such companies should be raised under royal sign manual, the Government providing the arms, accoutrements, and pay; but it was soon found that even this, though much less expensive than a militia, was financially impossible. Meanwhile privateers were beginning to swarm around the coast. The communications even with England were greatly obstructed, and rumours of invasion increased. Parliament was in recess, and Government feared to assemble it. All through the country, but especially in the maritime towns, there was terror and insecurity, and it became evident that as Government was completely paralysed, as the Executive could do nothing for the defence of the country, the greatest disasters were to be feared unless the gentry took the matter into their own hands and acted very much as if Government had been dissolved.

They were fortunately peculiarly well fitted to do so, and the strong feudal attachment which in spite of many faults on both sides, and many causes of discord and antagonism, still subsisted over the greater part of Ireland between the landlords and the tenants, enabled them with very little difficulty to summon a large force. The number of Irishmen who had served in the last war was extremely great, and there was no want of old soldiers who were quite capable of marshalling the recruits. It had been a common custom, when soldiers were wanted in Ireland to commission great proprietors to raise them; and Lord Aldborough, Lord Bellamont, Lord Drogheda, Sir James Caldwell, and several other large proprietors, had raised considerable forces for the Crown. In 1760, when Thurot had effected a landing on the Irish coast, the rapidity with which the northern peasantry could organise themselves for self-defence was strikingly displayed. Lord Charlemont, as governor of the county, hastened to the scene of the invasion, and he found that more than 2,000 men, armed for the most part with the weapon called in Scotland the Lochaber axe —a scythe fixed longitudinally to the end of a long pole—had already assembled around Belfast, formed themselves into regular bodies, chosen their own officers, and, without the smallest tumult or riot or drunkenness, organised the defence of the town. The impression the scene made on his mind was not forgotten amid the dangers of 1778, and it was remembered that the Duke of Bedford in his speech from the throne had eulogised in warm terms the spirit shown on this occasion by the people, and had attributed it solely to their firm attitude that the French had not advanced beyond the walls of Carrickfergus. In the Whiteboy agitation a similar spirit had been shown, and large bodies of volunteers organised by the country gentry had done much to pacify the disturbed districts and hunt down the marauders. Now, again, in the face of a still more pressing danger, associations for defence were everywhere formed among the Irish gentry. Official news having come about this time that a French invasion of Belfast was imminent, the mayor asked for troops for its protection; but it was answered that only half a troop of dismounted horsemen and half a company of invalids could be spared to defend the capital of Ulster.

The people at once flew to arms. A sudden enthusiasm, such as occurs two or three times in the history of a nation, seems to have passed through all classes. All along the coast associations for self-defence were formed under the direction of the leading gentry. They elected their officers, purchased their arms and accoutrements, assembled regularly under the direction of old soldiers to acquire military discipline, and without any legal obligation submitted themselves to the rules of a strict discipline. The chief persons in Ireland nearly everywhere placed themselves at the head of the movement. The Duke of Leinster commanded the Dublin corps; Lord Altamont that of the county Mayo; Lord Charlemont that of the county Armagh; and in most counties the principal landlords appeared at the head of bodies of their tenants. Large private subscriptions were raised to purchase accoutrements, and great sacrifices were made. The Catholics were not yet enrolled, but they subscribed liberally towards the expense. Those of the county of Limerick alone, raised 800*l.,* and those of Drogheda, Dingle, and other parts, exhibited a similar spirit.

Lord Buckingham watched the rising movement with mingled sentiments, of which the most prominent was an impotent dismay. He could not deny that the volunteer movement was indispensably necessary to the security of the State; that the men who formed and guided it were the most considerable and upright in the country; that they were fulfilling with great energy and great ability a task which belonged properly to the Government, but which the Government was entirely unable to accomplish. On the other hand, he could not but look with alarm on a great body of armed men, rising up altogether independently of the Government at a time when so many causes and elements of discontent were circulating through the nation. . . .

From that memorable year when the English barons availed

themselves of the destruction of an English army by the French near the bridge of Bouvines, to rise against their sovereign and to extort from him the great charter of English liberty, there had been many instances of the pressure of foreign affairs being employed to obtain concessions of civil liberty. Something of this kind was, no doubt, occurring in Ireland. The Irish Protestants, who were rapidly rising everywhere to arms, were determined, while defending their country as a member of the British Empire, to insist upon the abolition of the trade restrictions which had destroyed its prosperity, and another and still higher object was rapidly strengthening among them. The doctrine that self-government is the characteristic feature of English liberty, that Ireland, though subject to the King of England, was not subject to the English Parliament, that no laws were valid in Ireland which had not been made exclusively by the King, Lords, and Commons of Ireland—this doctrine was now rapidly becoming the dominant creed of the country. The American discussions had done much to convince all classes of Protestants that it was essential to their liberty, essential if they were to be permanently secured from taxation by a body in which they were wholly unrepresented, essential if they were to maintain any commercial liberty in the face of the great commercial jealousy of English industries. It had been, as we have seen, the doctrine of a long series of Irish antiquaries that the English settlers in Ireland had originally possessed a constitution in all respects similar to that of England, and that Poynings' law was the first of a series of encroachments which had been ratified and consummated by the Declaratory Act of George I. The right of Ireland to parliamentary independence had been unanimously asserted by the Irish Parliament of 1641; it had been a leading topic in the Remonstrance presented by the Irish Catholics to the Commissioners of Charles I in 1642, and in the negotiation of the Catholic Confederates for peace in 1645, and it was reiterated in emphatic terms by the Parliament of James II, convened at Dublin in 1689. On the ruin of the Catholics, the banner which dropped from their hands was caught up by Protestants. The doctrine of the legitimate independence of the Irish Parliament passed from Molyneux to Swift, from Swift to Lucas, from Lucas to Flood. It was strongly asserted in the writings of Henry Brooke. It was clearly though less strongly intimated by Sir James Caldwell. It was the first principle of the policy of Charlemont; and the eloquence of Grattan, assisted by the example of America, and by the spirit of independence which the sense of power naturally gives, was rapidly preparing its triumph. It had become a leading topic in the press, and made daily converts among all classes.

At the same time the volunteer body was essentially and ardently loyal, and Buckingham fully admitted that there was not the smallest disposition among them to detach themselves from the English Crown, that there was no question that they would exert themselves to the utmost in repelling invasion, and that they were in truth rendering a great service to the Empire. They alone, in a time when the danger of invasion was extremely great, made Ireland defensible. They had liberated for the defence of the Empire large bodies of troops who must otherwise have been scattered over the country. They had greatly relieved the public treasury, and they were discharging with admirable ability and success the difficult task of maintaining public order. A great part of Ireland was so uncivilised that criminals could only be arrested and carried to execution by soldiers. There were whole districts where the law was almost inoperative, and it was a common thing for prisoners to be rescued as they were carried to prison, by men who were perfect strangers to them and who knew nothing more of them than that they were in duress. It was the just boast of the Irish patriots that at no period of Irish history was internal tranquillity so fully preserved or the law so strictly obeyed as between the rise of the volunteers and the close of the American war, and the volunteers themselves maintained an admirable discipline. Men of all political opinions were enrolled in their ranks, and they appear at this time to have been guilty of absolutely no acts of violence or disorder. Some overtures to bring them under the direct control of the Government were rejected without hesitation, but they asked one thing from Government which could hardly be refused. A large number of militia arms had recently been provided by the Irish Parliament, and as Government were unable to call out the militia at the time when it was most needed, and as the volunteers at their own expense were discharging the duties of a militia, the Administration could hardly refuse to put these arms at their disposal. . . .

The condition of foreign politics, however, was such that it was not possible for the Government to treat the volunteers as a wholly alien body. The fears of invasion became stronger and stronger. In June, Buckingham wrote that "some of the most respectable noblemen of this kingdom, who are governors of counties," represented that in case of invasion it would not be in the power of gentlemen of the country without additional arms to defend themselves, and they urgently requested that the arms prepared for the militia should be granted. Soon the hostile squadron of Paul Jones, which in 1778 had already hovered around the Irish coast, and had even captured a ship of war in Belfast Lough, was again seen, while a combined fleet of sixty-five French and Spanish ships entered the British Channel, insulted unopposed the British coast, and might easily have destroyed Plymouth. Ireland was in daily, almost hourly, expectation of invasion. The Government thought it necessary to issue directions about the course to be pursued if the French landed; but it could give no efficient protection by land or sea. The country was left almost destitute of English troops. The volunteers, and the volunteers alone, were there. Their numbers under the pressure of imminent danger had risen to about 42,000, and they were rapidly acquiring the discipline of regular soldiers. It was felt under such circumstances that the responsibility of withholding the arms that were lying idle was overwhelming, and, upon the urgent advice of the Irish Privy Council, 16,000 stand of militia arms were distributed among the volunteers.

The year was one of the most agitated Ireland had ever known. Internally, indeed, there was no real disloyalty, though there was much discontent; but all classes were looking forward to the necessity of defending their country from invasion. France and Spain were now united against England, while a great part of the British army was imprisoned in America. The Catholics exhibited on this occasion a spirit of warm gratitude for the favour that had last year been shown them, and seem to have done all in their power to assist the Government. Addresses poured in from them, expressive of the most unbounded loyalty and the most lively gratitude for the Relief Bill of 1778. In May, Lord Tyrone wrote to the Government that they were forming independent companies to defend the coast against invasion; but that, though he was convinced that the measure was well intended, it was one which would be sure "to raise such a noise at this and the other side of the water as must distress Government;" and he accordingly persuaded their leaders to desist from their intention, and to offer, in an address to the Government, to co-operate in case of invasion with the Protestant inhabitants, in any way the Government should point out. The Catholics of Waterford and of Limerick subscribed largely to the volunteers, and also for additional bounties to those who would enlist in the King's troops; while O'Leary, the most brilliant writer of the sect, published a not very skilful address to the common people exhorting them to loyalty, and intimating his hope that they might be allowed to share with Protestants in the defence of their country.

The Volunteer movement was spreading rapidly over all parts of the country. Nearly the whole resident landed gentry took part in it, and a large proportion of the foremost names in Ireland may be found among its leaders. Volunteer rank became an object of ambition; ladies gave it precedence in society, and to be at the head of a well-appointed corps was now the highest distinction of an Irish gentleman. Great efforts of self-sacrifice were made to obtain the funds necessary to keep the force together, to maintain without any assistance from the civil power a high standard of discipline, to preserve this great body of armed men from all crime and violence and disorder. Never before in Ireland had public opinion shown itself so strong, so earnest, and so self-reliant. A sincere loyalty to the Crown, and a firm resolution to defend the country from invasion, were blended with a resolute determination to maintain a distinctively Irish policy; and it was soon noticed that even among the poorer farmers there was a marked improvement in dress, cleanliness, and self-respect. Agreements to use only domestic manufactures, and to abstain from purchasing English goods till the commercial restrictions were removed, were now entered into by the grand juries of many counties, and by numerous county meetings, and were signed in most of the great towns. Ladies of high social position set the example. The scarlet, green, blue, and orange uniforms of the volunteers were all manufactured at home. It was proposed, in imitation of the Americans, to publish in the newspapers the names of those traders who had infringed the agreement, but this proposal, which would probably have led to much crime, was generally reprobated, and soon abandoned. Many of the counties sent up urgent instructions to their representatives, enjoining them not to vote any Money Bill for more than six months till the commercial grievances were redressed.

The position of the Lord Lieutenant was both painful and embarrassing. The expense of the establishments exceeded the net produce of the revenue for the year, by more than 240,000*l.,* and yet Ireland did not obtain from those establishments the most ordinary security. Irish ships were taken within sight of her ports. But for the presence of the volunteers a hostile invasion might at any time be expected. . . .

*The Irish Parliament met in October 1779 amid widespread discontent over restrictions imposed on Irish trade, and the drain of Irish revenue to the English Treasury also aroused indignation. Grattan made an eloquent plea for free trade, and the Commons approved an address to the King to that effect.*

The answer of the King to the address was studiously colourless and ambiguous, and it greatly increased the popular discontent. In Dublin, especially, a very dangerous spirit was abroad. On the anniversary of the birthday of William III, the Dublin volunteers paraded round his monument, which was hung on all sides with very significant inscriptions, and two cannon bore the labels, "Free Trade—or this." A few days later a violent riot broke out in the Liberties, and a crowd of weavers, dyers, tanners, and other workmen attacked the house of the Attorney-General, and obliged some of the members of Parliament to swear that they would vote "for the good of Ireland, free trade, and a short Money Bill." The Government, at the request of the House of Commons, offered a reward for the apprehension of the rioters; but the Lord Lieutenant complained that the Lord Mayor had been very remiss in repressing the disturbance. In the House of Commons the feeling against the legislative authority of the British Parliament in Ireland was so strong that even the Attorney-General found it necessary to disclaim any acknowledgment of that authority. Grattan, alarmed at the violence that had been displayed, urged moderation, implored the people to abstain from any act of tumult and violence, and thus gradually to win all classes to the popular cause; but his own policy showed no signs of flinching or timidity. In the teeth of the opposition of the Government, he carried by 170 to 47 a resolution, "that at this time it would be inexpedient to grant new taxes;" and next day, when the House resolved itself into a Committee of Supply, it was moved and carried by 138 to 100, that the appropriated duties should be granted for six months only. It was on this occasion that Burgh finally broke from the Government by a speech of such surpassing eloquence that the spectators who thronged the gallery burst into uncontrollable applause. Describing the condition of the country, he exclaimed, "Talk not to me of peace—it is not peace, but smothered war. England has sown her laws in dragon's teeth, and they have sprung up in armed men." A few days later, Burgh sent in his resignation. "The gates of promotion," said Grattan, "were shut as the gates of glory opened."

Another measure of great significance was taken. The clause relieving the Dissenters from the sacramental test had in 1778 been added by a large majority to the measure for the relief of Catholics, and had been strongly opposed by the Government, and extinguished in England. It was now brought forward again as a distinct measure. The Presbyterians of the North had been the earliest and the most numerous of the volunteers, and there was a keen and general desire that they should participate in the benefits which had of late been so largely extended to the Catholics. The abolition of the test, the Lord Lieutenant confessed, "met with a general concurrence, great numbers of those members who had opposed it last session having pledged themselves for its support in the present session." While refusing to impose new permanent taxes, Parliament at the same time granted 340,000*l.*, chiefly by a lottery, for discharging arrears.

Buckingham, thoroughly alarmed at the condition of the country, strongly counselled the ministers to yield. The evils of free trade to Great Britain must indeed be great, he significantly said, if they overbalanced those which she might incur from the present resentment of Ireland against the commercial restrictions. Lord North, as we have seen, had been already disposed to grant a very liberal measure of commercial relief to Ireland, though he proposed to except the capital article of the wool trade; but he had been intimidated by the clamour of the manufacturers in Enland. Now, however, the danger was too extreme for further delay. The fear of bankruptcy in Ireland, the non-importation agreements which were beginning to tell upon English industries, the threatening aspect of an armed body which already counted more than 40,000 men, the determined and unanimous attitude of the Irish Parliament, the prediction of the Lord Lieutenant that all future military grants by Ireland depended upon the course that was now adopted, the danger that England, in the midst of a great and disastrous war, should be left absolutely without a friend, all weighed upon the English Minister; and, at the close of 1779, and in the beginning of 1780, measures were carried in England which exceeded the utmost that a few years before the most sanguine Irishman could have either expected or demanded. The Acts which prohibited the Irish from exporting their woollen manufactures and their glass were wholly repealed, and the great trade of the colonies was freely thrown open to them. It was enacted that all goods that might be legally imported from the British settlements in America and Africa to Great Britain might be in like manner imported directly from those settlements into Ireland, and that all goods which might be legally exported from Great Britain into those settlements, might in like manner be exported from Ireland, on the sole condition that duties equal to those paid in British ports were imposed by the Irish Parliament on the imports and exports of Ireland. The Acts which prohibited carrying gold and silver coin into Ireland were repealed. The Irish were allowed to import foreign hops, and to receive a drawback on the duty on British hops. They were allowed to become members of the Turkey Company, and to carry on a direct trade between Ireland and the Levant Sea.

Thus fell to the ground that great system of commercial restriction which began under Charles II, which under William III acquired a crushing severity, and which had received several additional clauses in the succeeding reigns. The measures of Lord North, though obviously due in a great measure to intimidation and extreme necessity, were at least largely, wisely, and generously conceived, and they were the main sources of whatever material prosperity Ireland enjoyed during the next twenty years. The English Parliament had been accustomed to grant a small bounty—rising in the best years to 13,000*l.*—on the importation into England of the plainer kinds of Irish linen. After the immense concessions made to Irish trade, no one could have complained if this bounty had been withdrawn; but North determined to continue it. He showed that it had been of real use to the Irish linen manufacture, and he strongly maintained that the prosperity of Ireland must ultimately prove a blessing to England.

After a long period of hesitation and delay, the other capital demand of the Irish Parliament was conceded. In March 1780, the Bill relieving the Irish Dissenters from the sacramental test was returned from England, and a very curious page in Irish ecclesiastical history was thus terminated. The first imposition of the sacramental test was, as we have seen, wholly due to the English Ministers, who forced it on the Irish Parliament by adding a clause to that effect to the Anti-Popery Bill of 1704. A generation later the parts were inverted. The English Whig ministers of George II wished to abolish the Irish test, but they found insuperable obstacles in the anti-Presbyterian feeling of the Irish House of Commons, and in the preponderance of bishops in the Irish House of Lords. Now, at last, under a Tory King and a Tory ministry, at a time when the Church was in the height of its power in England, and when the Presbyterians were looked upon with more than common disfavour, the sacramental test was abolished at the request of the Irish Parliament, and by the influence of the volunteers. The Irish Dissenters were thus placed politically on a level with their fellow-countrymen, and they obtained this boon forty-eight years before a similar favour was granted to their coreligionists in England.

The aspect of affairs in Ireland still appeared very alarming to the Government. Buckingham seems to have been severely blamed for having allowed the volunteer movement to attain its present formidable height, and his letters are full of exculpations of his conduct. He maintained, with much truth, that, in the financial condition of Ireland, it was impossible to avoid it; that the alternative was to leave the country a prey to complete internal anarchy and to the first invader who chose to land on its unprotected shore, or to suffer it to defend itself; that the volunteer movement in its beginning was intended solely to protect the country from invasion; and that it was in a great degree in consequence of encouragement from England that it was afterwards turned to home politics. At the same time, he had no illusion about the gravity of the situation. . . .

*The rapid growth of the Irish Volunteers in both numbers and influence, and the mounting demand for Irish legislative independence, prompted some officials in Dublin to consider the possibility of a union of the two countries. But the idea was dropped as inexpedient. The Irish administration counted on its power of patronage, including peerages and pensions, to preserve the necessary majority in both Houses of Parliament.*

"The epidemic madness," as Lord Buckingham called it, "so assiduously circulated by Lord Charlemont, Mr. Grattan, Sir W. Osborne, and Lord Carysfort," rapidly spread, and on April 19, 1780, Grattan introduced a declaration of independence into the Irish House of Commons. It consisted of a series of resolutions asserting that while the crown of Ireland was inseparably annexed to that of Great Britain, while the nations, united under one sovereign, were indissolubly connected by ties of interest, loyalty, and freedom, no power on earth but the King, Lords, and Commons of Ireland was competent to make laws for Ireland. The speech introducing these resolutions was long remembered as the most splendid that had ever been heard in the Irish Parliament, and no one who reads it, can fail to feel the wonderful fire and energy both of thought and language which it displayed. One passage the Lord Lieutenant especially remarked as having made an extraordinary impression. It was that in which, having read the offers of reconciliation lately made to the revolted colonies, in which, not only the power of taxation was given up and freedom of internal legislation established, but all power of the Parliament of Great Britain over America was renounced, Grattan asked whether it could be suspected that Great Britain would refuse to the most loyal of subjects what she had offered to those who had been declared in rebellion.

It was plain, however, that the majority were on the side of the ministers, though scarcely a voice was heard opposing the declaration on any other ground than that it was premature or inexpedient; and at last, after fifteen hours of debate, the question was indefinitely adjourned, leaving no entry of it in the Journals. . . .

*In 1780, Irish Opposition leaders challenged the validity of the English Mutiny Act as it operated in Ireland. To overcome this new impasse, English ministers countered the demand for a separate Irish mutiny bill by making the measure into a perpetual one, thereby depriving the Irish Parliament of a chance to revise its provisions on an annual basis. The Irish Opposition greatly resented this calculated move.*

The session ended on September 2, and nearly the last act of the House of Commons was to censure the volunteer resolutions as seditious and libellous, and to call upon the Lord Lieutenant to institute prosecutions against the printers and publishers.

So ended one of the longest and one of the most eventful sessions hitherto known in Ireland, and it was speedily followed by the recall of Buckingham. For a long time the nerves of the Viceroy had been strained almost beyond the limits of endurance. He spoke of himself as "a man whose mind has been ulcerated with a variety of embarrassments for thirty weary months." The utterly defenceless state of the country in the beginning of a great war, the weekly and almost daily fears of invasion, the rise of a great army of volunteers wholly beyond the control and influence of Government; the rapid increase of the popular demand for a fundamental change in the constitution of the country, the doubts that hung upon the constitution of the Irish army, the determination of the Government, even at the last moment and in spite of his remonstrance, to drain the country of almost every available soldier, all these things had reduced the Lord Lieutenant to a state of deplorable anxiety. The Home Government, profoundly ignorant of Irish affairs, saw a great movement rising which was completely beyond their control, and they blamed the Viceroy; they compelled him on several occasions to pursue a policy opposed to his judgment, and they slighted several of his recommendations. Scott, the Attorney-General, and Beresford, who was soon after First Commissioner of the Revenue, had long been intriguing against him, and had been endeavouring by repeated letters to Robinson, the English Secretary of the Treasury, to procure his recall. In the last months of his administration Buckingham had been reduced to the necessity of opposing the overwhelming preponderance of national sentiment and nearly all the honest men in Parliament, by the most flagrant and overwhelming bribery. Nothing now remained but the distribution of the rewards; and the despatches, which have fortunately been printed, written at the close of his administration, reveal the true character of the contest. . . .

The English ministers were startled by the multitude of requests, and refused to grant them all. The King consented, however, besides many minor favours in the shape of places and pensions, to make five new peers, and to raise eleven peers one or more steps in the peerage. This was the price at which the perpetual Mutiny Act and a few other slight triumphs were purchased, and the Lord Lieutenant considered it exceedingly insufficient. . . .

It would be difficult to have a clearer illustration of the manner in which, through the extreme concentration of political power, it was possible in the Irish Parliament to override the real sentiments of the country, and these transactions should be remembered by those who would form a just estimate of the later conduct of the volunteers on the question of parliamentary reform. It is manifest, too, how serious must have been the effect upon the Irish peerage of creations so lavish and so corrupt as those under Lord Townshend, Lord Harcourt, and Lord Buckingham. The sale of peerages had become the ordinary resource of Government; and Grattan, in a speech made some years later, predicted with great force its inevitable tendency "to taint the nobility," to "undermine the moral props of opinion and authority," and to produce in Ireland a levelling, democratic, and revolutionary spirit of the most dangerous kind. In truth, the respect for rank, however much it may be decried by philosophers as a mere figment of the imagination, is, politically, a very real thing, for it is a great power of guidance and influence in the affairs of men. In a country like Ireland, which is torn by historical antagonisms and religious differences, where the mass of the population are poor, ignorant, credulous, and excitable, and at the same time passionately loyal to their leaders, none of the natural forms of healthy influence can be safely neglected, for nothing is more needed than wise guidance and well-directed respect. That the Irish gentry were not incapable of political leadership is sufficiently shown by the volunteer movement, and by many honourable episodes in the history of the Irish Parliament; and even in the disgraceful contest about the Perpetual Mutiny Act, Grattan was able to assert that, although the great borough owners had gone over to the Government, "the weight of property, beyond comparison," was on the popular side. A dishonest historian, who selects or conceals his facts according to the impression he wishes to convey, may, no doubt, discover without difficulty authentic materials for an unqualified diatribe against the Irish Protestants and their Parliament; but a true picture will contain many lights as well as many shades, and a faithful narrator will make large allowance for unfavourable circumstances and antecedents. He will be struck with the smallness of the military force with which Ireland in many troubled periods was kept in perfect peace. He will recognise the large amount of ability, loyalty, and public spirit which undoubtedly existed in the Irish Parliament during the last thirty years of its existence, the many steps of constitutional and material progress that were taken under its auspices, the noble efforts that it made to break down the system of religious proscription, and to bridge the chasm which yawned between the two great sections of the Irish people. But the taint of corruption had sunk deeply into the great borough owners. The peerage, which was the natural representative of the landed classes, was systematically degraded; and the majority of Irish titles are historically connected with memories, not of honour, but of shame.

Lord Buckingham was succeeded as Viceroy by Lord Carlisle, who took Sir W. Eden—afterwards the first Lord Auckland—as his chief secretary, and arrived in Ireland towards the close of December 1780. The new Lord Lieutenant was a young man of considerable promise and accomplishments, but exceedingly inexperienced in official life. He had been educated at Eton with Charles Fox, and with the Duke of Leinster; had published a few short poems, among others a translation of the story of Ugolino from Dante; had thrown himself ardently into the fashionable dissipations of his time, but, like his close friend, Charles Fox, had never lost his interest in politics, and had been selected in 1778 as one of the Commissioners who were sent out to negotiate with the Americans. Eden had on this occasion been one of his colleagues. He was bound to his future chief by a very warm friendship, and in 1779 he had addressed to him some rather valuable letters on the trade restrictions of Ireland.

As more than nine months elapsed before it was necessary to summon Parliament, Carlisle had ample time to master the circumstances of the country, and his general impression was decidedly favourable. Great caution, indeed, was required, and he especially urged that Ireland should not be included in the English Mutiny Act; but he found among the chief people in Ireland a widespread sentiment, strengthened, no doubt, by the recent resolutions in favour of parliamentary reform, "that the aristocratic part of the Government had lost its balance, that there was an evident necessity of regaining from the people that power which, if suffered to continue in their hands, must end in the general ruin of the whole; and that, for their own security and happiness, English Government must be supported." "The wild notions of republicanism," he thought, "were every day more the objects of contempt and derision," and "the national fever was subsiding. . . .

In the summer months provincial reviews of the volunteers were held with much success. The movement showed no signs of flagging, and the volunteers had greatly increased in number and improved in discipline and in their equipments. At the Belfast review, which was the most considerable, 5,383 volunteers were on the field, with no less than thirteen field-pieces. The number of volunteers in this review was nearly double that in the review of 1780; and it was alleged, though probably with some exaggeration, that the volunteers throughout Ireland towards the close of 1781 amounted to not less than 80,000 men. The dangers of foreign invasion were still sufficient to stimulate all the energies of the country, and in June it was found necessary to provide convoys for vessels trading between England and Ireland. In September a combined French and Spanish fleet of thirty-four sail appeared in the Channel, and some ships approached the southern coast of Ireland. Charlemont, who had recently been elected head of the Leinster and Ulster volunteers, at once waited upon the Lord Lieutenant, who informed him that there was every reason to believe that an immediate invasion was meditated, that an express had just been received furnishing many particulars, and that the city of Cork was probably the intended point of attack. The moment of danger was well fitted to show whether the political agitation in Ireland had yet taken the form of disaffection, but no traces of such a spirit were shown. The Ulster volunteers under the command of Charlemont, the Dublin volunteers under the command of the Duke of Leinster, volunteered in great numbers to march at once into Munster, to act under the King's Commander-in-Chief and to assist the very small force of regular troops. The offer was accepted in grateful though guarded terms, and it was computed that 15,000 men could be spared from Ulster for the defence of Munster without leaving the former province undefended. In Newry it was resolved to send all the younger volunteers southwards, and a corps called the Ladies' Fencibles was organised for the defence of the town and neighbourhood, in which no man was to be enrolled who was under fifty or was without a wife and children. . . .

*While Government officials were becoming alarmed at the strength of the resistance movement against English political controls, the Viceroy had to walk warily with the Volunteers, who were ostensibly protecting Ireland against England's enemies. The aggrieved Flood turned against his administration friends, and Lord Carlisle dismissed him from office. Anxious to conciliate Irish public opinion, the Government approved an Irish habeas corpus act and raised the salaries of judges. The news of English defeats at Saratoga and Yorktown spurred the Opposition, with Flood and Yelverton in the forefront, to demand legislative independence. Popular feeling in Dublin and elsewhere also ran strongly against the content of Poynings's Law.*

It was on February 15, 1782, that the delegates of 143 corps of Ulster volunteers assembled in obedience to this invitation, in full uniform, in the great church of Dungannon. They were some of them men of high rank, and most of them men of large property and of excellent character, and they conducted their debates with a gravity, decorum, and moderation which no assembly could have surpassed. Elected by a popular constituency of 25,000 armed men, free from the borough influence and from the corruption which tainted the Parliament in Dublin, animated with a consciousness of great services performed and with a sincere and ardent patriotism, they were undoubtedly the most faithful representatives then sitting of the opinions and wishes of the Irish Protestants. Colonel William Irvine was called to the chair, and a series of resolutions, drawn up by Charlemont, Flood, Grattan, Stewart the member for Tyrone, and Francis Dobbs, were submitted to the assembly.

They first unanimously asserted their right of deliberation by resolving that "a citizen by learning the use of arms does not abandon any of his civil rights." They then resolved with equal unanimity that "a claim of any body of men, other than the King, Lords, and Commons of Ireland, to make laws to bind this kingdom is unconstitutional, illegal, and a grievance"; that "the ports of this country are by right open to all foreign countries not at war with the King"; "that any burden thereupon or obstruction thereto, save only by the Parliament of Ireland, is unconstitutional, illegal, and a grievance"; and that "the independence of judges is equally essential to the impartial administration of justice in Ireland as in England." With a single dissenting voice they resolved "that the power exercised by the Privy Council of both kingdoms under, or under colour or pretence of, the law of Poyning, was unconstitutional and a grievance"; that "a Mutiny Bill not limited in point of duration from session to session is unconstitutional and a grievance"; and that "the minority of Parliament were entitled to their most grateful thanks." With eleven dissenting voices they pledged themselves "as freeholders, fellow-citizens, and men of honour," at every coming election to support only those candidates who would seek a redress of these grievances, and to use all constitutional means to make the pursuit of redress speedy and effectual. They then unanimously determined that four members from each county in Ulster should be formed into a committee to act for the volunteers till the next general meeting, and to call general meetings of the province when required; that another general meeting should be summoned in twelve months from the present, or within fourteen days of the dissolution of Parliament, should such an event take place sooner; that the committee should appoint nine of their number to be a committee in Dublin, in order to enter into communication with such volunteer associations in other provinces as may enter into similar resolutions, and to deliberate with them on the most constitutional means of carrying them into effect.

Then, after pledging themselves to consume no Portuguese wine till the restrictions had been taken off Irish exports to Portugal, they passed two memorable resolutions which had been drawn up by Grattan. They resolved, "that we hold the right of private judgment in matters of religion to be equally sacred in others as in ourselves; that as men and as Irishmen, as Christians and as Protestants, we rejoice in the relaxation of the penal laws against our Roman Catholic fellow-subjects, and that we conceive the measure to be fraught with the happiest consequences to the union and the prosperity of the inhabitants of Ireland." These resolutions, which marked the close of the long political schism between the Protestants and Catholics, were carried through the great representative body of the most Protestant province of Ireland with only two dissentient voices. Three clergymen, one of them an Anglican and the other two Presbyterians, were among the delegates, and they were also among the prominent supporters of the resolutions, not only on grounds of policy, but on grounds of Christianity. "The place we met in," wrote Dobbs, who took a conspicuous part in these transactions, "was the church, and I trust our proceedings did not pollute it." The assembly before breaking up issued an address to the minority in Parliament. "We thank you," they said, "for your noble and spirited though hitherto ineffectual efforts in defence of the great constitutional rights of your country. . . . The almost unanimous voice of the people is with you, and in a free country the voice of the people must prevail. We know our duty to our sovereign, and are loyal. We know our duty to ourselves, and are resolved to be free. We seek for our rights, and no more than our rights, and in so just a pursuit we should doubt the being of a Providence if we doubted of success."

The assembly at Dungannon had an immediate influence of the most decisive kind. Ulster was the heart of the volunteer movement as it was the heart of the Protestantism of Ireland; and it became evident that no reliance could be henceforth placed on the continuance of those divisions and religious animosities which had hitherto paralysed the political energies of the nation. In all parts of the country the volunteer corps, guided by the leading gentry, and including all that was most respectable and most energetic among the Protestants, hastened to give their adhesion to the resolutions of Dungannon. The grand juries in almost every county passed resolutions asserting the right of Ireland to legislative independence, and it was evident that on this question all classes were substantially united. A few days after the Dungannon resolutions, Grattan, in a speech two hours long, moved in the House of Commons an address to the King containing a declaration of the independence of the Irish Legislature. His speech comprised a full review of the authorities in favour of the doctrine of the sole competency of the King, Lords, and Commons of Ireland to make laws binding Ireland; he maintained that the doctrine of Ireland being bound by British Acts of Parliament was subsequent to the Restoration, and rested not on any basis of right but solely on precedents such as might be adduced in England for the violation of the great charter, for forced loans, for ship-money, or for royal proclamation having the authority of law, and he concluded that the present moment was an eminently favourable one for securing the liberties of Ireland. It was impossible that England could safely refuse to the loyalty of Ireland the privilege she had offered to the arms of America, and he predicted, in a passage to which a hundred years have only given an additional significance, that American influence would long be felt in Irish politics. "Do you see nothing," he said, "in that America but the grave and prison of your armies? And do you not see in her range of territory, cheapness of living, variety of climate and simplicity of life, the drain of Europe? Whatever is bold and disconsolate . . . to that point will precipitate, and what you trample on in Europe will sting you in America." . . .

*Lord Carlisle realized the futility of trying to carry on the Irish administration in the face of growing popular resistance. By 1782, the Patriot party was led by Lord Charlemont and his brilliant protégé, Grattan. The Patriots sought to combine loyalty to the Crown with the kind of constitutional freedom enjoyed by the English Parliament since the Glorious Revolution.*

The establishment of legislative independence had become inevitable from the simple impossibility of governing Ireland on any other condition. The overwhelming majority of the classes in whose hands the administration of the country practically lay, were determined to obtain it, and no Government could have long delayed it; but the merit or the humiliation of conceding it was not reserved for the Administration of Lord Carlisle. Before the Irish Parliament met after the Easter recess the Government of Lord North had fallen. The disasters in America had struck a death-blow to its popularity; in division after division its supporters steadily diminished, and on the 20th of March Lord North announced that the ministry only held office till their successors were appointed. Rockingham became First Lord of the Treasury, Fox and Shelburne were Secretaries of State. Lord Carlisle was removed with circumstances of great abruptness and discourtesy from the government of Ireland; the Duke of Portland was appointed in his place, and Mr. Fitzpatrick accompanied him as Chief Secretary.

The men who now rose to power had long advocated the claims of America on those Whig principles which were the basis of the claims of Ireland to self-legislation. Rockingham and Fox, as well as Burke, were intimate friends of Charlemont, the leader of the volunteers. On April 8 the English Parliament met, and on that very day an attempt was made from an unexpected quarter to force the hand of the Government on the question of Ireland. Lord Carmarthen had been removed by the late Administration from the Lieutenancy of the East Riding of Yorkshire, and Lord Carlisle had been appointed in his place. One of the first acts of the new Government was to remove Carlisle and replace Carmarthen. Eden had just come to England with the resignation of the Viceroy, and he resented bitterly, and resolved to revenge, the manner in which his chief was treated. He refused positively to hold any communication with the new Government, and availing himself of the seat which he still held in the English House of Commons, he appeared there on the first day of its assembly, and after a vehement speech in which he described the overwhelming power of the volunteers, the unanimity of Irish opinion, and the impossibility of withholding independence, he gave notice of his intention to move a repeal of the Declaratory Act of George I. Such a notice, emanating at such a time from a late Chief Secretary who had been officially employed in resisting the motions for independence, was extremely embarrassing to the Government, and Fox in a very powerful speech rebuked the attempt to hurry the ministry into a premature disclosure of their designs. Next day a Royal message was sent to both Houses deploring the discontent prevailing in Ireland, and calling on Parliament to take it into consideration, "in order to such a final adjustment as may give mutual satisfaction to both kingdoms."

In Ireland a special summons in a very unusual form had been already issued by the Speaker at the direction of the House, ordering the members to attend on April 16, the day following the Easter recess, "as they tender the rights of the Irish Parliament." As the Duke of Portland and Mr. Fitzpatrick only arrived in Ireland on the 14th, great efforts were made to procure an adjournment for a fortnight or three weeks, in order to enable them to master the situation of the country before Parliament had taken any decisive line, and both Fox and Rockingham wrote strongly to Charlemont in this sense. Grattan was still very ill, having lately undergone a painful surgical operation, but he refused to allow any adjournment, declaring that the expectations of the country had been raised to the highest point by the very unusual call of the House, that the proposed measures were now public property, and that whatever course Government chose to take, Parliament owed it to itself and to the country to lose no time in asserting the claims of Ireland. Both Charlemont and Grattan agreed in this course, and they both refused the offers of the Government to take office.

Their course was probably a prudent one, for it is quite evident from the confidential letters of the Duke of Portland that he was anxious to yield as little as possible, and it is probable that a delay would have created widespread suspicion, and have led to much manoeuvring hostile to the popular party. Dublin was full of volunteers who had come up for an approaching review, and on the 16th they paraded the streets and lined the path through which Grattan passed to move the legislative independence of Ireland. The nation was wound up to the highest pitch of excitement. Many thousands of spectators filled the streets, but there was no tumult or disorder. The spacious galleries of the House were crowded with all that was most brilliant and weighty in Dublin society, and in the body of the House scarcely a seat was vacant. Portland had refused to adopt the declaration of independence, or to commit himself to any definite line of policy, but a message from him was read to the House by Hely Hutchinson, now Secretary of State, to the effect that "His Majesty, being concerned to find that discontents and jealousies were prevailing among his loyal subjects in Ireland upon matters of great weight and importance, recommended to the House to take the same into their most serious consideration, in order to effect such a final adjustment as might give mutual satisfaction to his kingdoms of Great Britain and Ireland." Hutchinson accompanied the message with a few words in which, while disclaiming all authority from the Lord Lieutenant, he expressed his personal sympathy with the popular cause. A formal reply, thanking the King for his goodness and condescension, and assuring him that the Commons would act on his recommendation, was moved by George Ponsonby, and it was then that, after a short pause, Grattan rose to move as an amendment a declaration of rights and grievances.

He was still pale and weak from recent illness, and his appearance denoted the evident anxiety of his mind, but as he proceeded his voice gathered strength, and the fire of a great orator acting on a highly excited and sympathetic audience, soon produced even more than its wonted effects. The strange swaying gestures, which were habitual to him, were compared by one observer to the action of the mower as his scythe sweeps through the long grass, and by another to the rolling of a ship in a heavy swell; but he possessed beyond all other orators the peculiar gift of illuminating a subject with an almost lightning-like intensity, and his speeches, with much that is exaggerated and overstrained, contain some of the finest examples in the English language of great energy and vividness, and condensed felicity of expression. On the present occasion he knew that the Parliament was with him, and he treated the victory as already won. He described in a few picturesque words the progress of the nation "from injuries to arms, and from arms to liberty," till "the whole faculty of the nation was braced up to the act of her own deliverance," and the spirit of Swift and of Molyneux had prevailed; and then, after a very exaggerated but perhaps not impolitic eulogy of the Parliament and public of Ireland, he touched with much discrimination on the services of the volunteers to the cause he was defending. "It was not the sword of the volunteer, nor his muster, nor his spirit, nor his promptitude to put down accidental disturbance or public disorder, nor his own unblamed and distinguished deportment. This was much, but there was more than this. The upper orders, the property, and the abilities of the country formed with the volunteer, and the volunteer had sense enough to obey them. This united the Protestant with the Catholic, and the landed proprietor with the people. There was still more than this. There was a continence which confined the corps to limited and legitimate objects. . . . No vulgar rant against England, no mysterious admiration of France. . . . They were what they professed to be, nothing less than the society, asserting her liberty according to the frame of the British Constitution, her inheritance to be enjoyed in perpetual connection with the British Empire. . . . And now having given a Parliament to the people, the volunteers will, I doubt not, leave the people to Parliament, and thus close specifically and majestically a great work. . . . Their associations, like other institutions, will perish; they will perish with the occasion that gave them being, and the gratitude of their country will write their epitaph. . . . Connected by freedom as well as by allegiance, the two nations, Great Britain and Ireland, form a constitutional confederacy as well as one empire. The Crown is one link, the Constitution another, and in my mind the latter link is the most powerful. You can get a king anywhere, but England is the only country with whom you can participate a free constitution."

He concluded by moving an address to the King, asserting that while the crown of Ireland was inseparably united to that of England, Ireland was by right a distinct kingdom, that her King, Lords, and Commons, and these alone, had a right to bind her, and that the discontents and jealousies of the nation were chiefly due to three great infringements of her freedom. These were the claims advanced by the British Parliament in the Act of George I to legislate for Ireland and exercise a right of final judicature; the power exercised under Poynings' law by the Privy Council to suppress or alter Irish Bills, and the perpetual Mutiny Act, which placed the Irish army beyond the control of the Irish Parliament. The address concluded with reminding his Majesty that "the people of this kingdom have never expressed a desire to share the freedom of England without declaring a determination to share her fate likewise, standing or falling with the British nation."

The address was seconded by Brownlow, and it passed unanimously. . . .

*Under severe pressure from the Irish Volunteers and their Whig allies in London, the Rockingham administration entered into negotiations and agreed to concede the Patriots' chief demands.*

It was plain that whatever negotiations were made they must be subsequent to a surrender by England of the chief points at issue. We have committed ourselves, Grattan wrote to Fox, only to measures which are indispensable to our freedom, and which you have thought indispensable to yours. "The powers, legislative and jurisdictive," claimed by England, "are become impracticable. We have rendered them so ourselves, and all we ask of England is that she will withdraw a barren claim, that we may shake hands with her." "If you delay, or refuse to be liberal," wrote the Duke of Portland, "Government cannot exist here in its present form, and the sooner you recall your Lieutenant and renounce all claim to this country the better. But, on the contrary, if you can bring your minds to concede largely and handsomely, I am persuaded that you may make any use of this people, and of everything that they are worth, that you can wish."

In accordance with this opinion resolutions were brought forward on May 17, in the British House of Lords by Shelburne, and in the British House of Commons by Fox, for the purpose of giving satisfaction to Ireland. The first resolution announced the opinion of the House that the Declaratory Act of George I should be repealed. The second stated that "it was indispensable to the interest and happiness of both kingdoms that the connection between them should be established by mutual consent upon a solid and permanent footing, and that an humble address should be presented to his Majesty that his Majesty will be graciously pleased to take such measures as his Majesty in his royal wisdom should think most conducive to that important end." Lord Carlisle was one of the first to express his warm approval of these resolutions, and he bore ample testimony to the zeal and loyalty of the Irish, and to the services of the volunteers during his administration. In the Commons, Fox enumerated the different demands of the Irish, and announced the resolution of the Government to concede them absolutely and unconditionally. They were determined to repeal the Declaratory Act of George I, to abandon the appellate jurisdiction of the English House of Lords, to consent to such a modification of Poynings' law as would annihilate the exceptional powers of the two Privy Councils, and to limit the Mutiny Act. He would "meet Ireland on her own terms and give her everything she wanted in the way she herself seemed to wish for it." At the same time he intimated that a formal treaty should be made between England and Ireland "establishing on a firm and solid basis the future connection of the two kingdoms." At present, however, he proposed no such treaty, and contented himself with suggesting that commissioners might at some future time be appointed to negotiate it. Of the volunteers he spoke with warm eulogy. "They had acted with temper and moderation notwithstanding their steadiness, and . . . had not done a single act for which they had not his veneration and respect." "The intestine divisions of Ireland," he added, "are no more; the religious prejudices of the age are forgotten, and the Roman Catholics, being restored to the rights of men and citizens, would become an accession of strength and wealth to the Empire at large, instead of being a burthen to the land that bore them."

It is a striking proof both of the necessity of these concessions and of the grace and dignity with which that necessity was accepted, that the two resolutions I have cited passed unanimously through the House of Commons, and with the single negative of Lord Loughborough, through the House of Lords.

The promises of Fox were fully kept; a Bill repealing the 6 Geo. I was at once introduced, and in due course carried through the English Parliament, and when the Irish Parliament met on May 27, 1782, the Duke of Portland was instructed to announce to it that the King was prepared to give his unconditional assent "to Acts to prevent the suppression of Bills in the Privy Council of this kingdom, and the alteration of them anywhere," and to limit the duration of the Mutiny Act to two years. Grattan, immediately after the Speech from the Throne was read, rose to move an address of thanks and to express in the strongest terms his full satisfaction with what was done. . . .

It was greatly to be wished that England could avail herself of some of the regular forces now in Ireland if means could be discovered "for getting over any difficulty arising from the engagements formerely entered into, which, however unadvisable and unwarrantable at the time, require to be attended to."

The Irish Parliament at once acceded to the wishes of the minister, and authorised the King at any time before December 25, 1783, to withdraw from Ireland an additional force of 5,000 men. The measure was far from pleasing to Portland, for it threw the country almost wholly into the hands of the volunteers, and Portland, though he was carrying out a popular policy, looked upon that force with much more jealousy and dislike than his predecessor. He represented to the Government that if 5,000 troops were withdrawn there would not be sufficient in Ireland for the country guards; that "although the volunteers had uniformly and very much to their credit been ready to co-operate with the civil magistrate in enforcing obedience to the laws," he "had great reason to doubt of the same disposition being shown in support of the revenue officers"; that they had so little camp equipage that few in case of invasion could be employed at distances from their neighbourhood; that they were not likely to take commissions under the crown, or to place themselves under the Articles of War; that they were chiefly concentrated in Ulster, and that Munster was the province most liable to invasion. Ultimately, however, 3,245 troops out of the 5,000 were sent to England.

Another class of measures which were now brought to a completion dealt with the disabilities that divided different sections of Irishmen. The penal laws against the Catholics had been a great subject of discussion during the Administration of Carlisle, but it was only in the succeeding Administration that the contemplated measures were finally carried. There was a general agreement in Parliament that the policy of reconciliation which had inspired the Relief Bill of 1778 should be extended, but there was much difference as to the degree, and there was a strong, and at this time successful opposition, supported by Flood in the Commons and by the bishops in the Lords, to giving Catholics any measure of political power. The penal laws formed so large and complicated a system that Gardiner thought it advisable to divide his propositions into three Bills. The first, which was called "An

Act for the further relief of his Majesty's subjects professing the Popish religion," applied to all Catholics who had taken the oath of allegiance and the declaration enacted under Lord Harcourt. It enabled them to purchase and bequeath land like Protestants, provided it was not in a parliamentary borough. It abolished a number of obsolete laws making it penal for Catholic bishops or regulars to subsist in the country, subjecting priests to the necessity of registration, enabling any two justices of the peace to oblige Catholics to declare on oath where they last heard mass, and forbidding Catholics to live in Limerick or Galway. These concessions, however, were encumbered with some slight restrictions, and the Act expressly reaffirmed the provisions against proselytism, against perversion to Catholicism, against Catholics assuming ecclesiastical titles or rank, or wearing vestments outside the precincts of their chapels, against chapels having steeples or bells, and against priests officiating anywhere except in their accustomed places of worship. Some grossly oppressive enactments which were still in force were at the same time repealed. A Protestant could no longer appropriate the horse of his Catholic neighbour if he tendered him 5*l*. Horses of Catholics could no longer be seized at every alarm of invasion. Catholics were no longer obliged to provide Protestant watchmen at their own expense, or to reimburse the damage done by the privateers of an enemy. By a second Bill they were allowed to become schoolmasters, ushers, and private tutors, provided they took the oath of allegiance, subscribed the declaration, received a licence from the ordinary, and took no Protestant pupils. A Popish university or college, or endowed school, was still forbidden in Ireland, but Catholic laymen were now permitted to be guardians to Catholic children. . . .

In the same session the last serious grievance of the Protestant Dissenters was removed. They had already been freed from the vexatious prosecutions and penalties to which they had been liable on account of the marriages celebrated in their meeting-houses by their ministers, but the legal validity of those marriages was very doubtful. A short Act was now passed to set those doubts at rest, and to give Protestant dissenting ministers, as far as their co-religionists were concerned, the same right of celebrating valid marriages as Anglican clergymen. It is worthy of notice that it was only in 1836 that the Imperial Parliament, under the influence of Lord John Russell, granted a similar boon to the Dissenters in England.

Acts were at the same time passed repealing the greater part of Poynings' law, confirming a large number of British statutes relating to Ireland, limiting the Mutiny Act, and establishing the right of final judicature in Ireland, and the independence of the Irish judges. One other measure also was taken of a different kind. The man who during the last anxious years had stood forth from his countrymen beyond all rivalry and all comparison was Henry Grattan. His splendid eloquence, the perfect confidence which was felt in his honour and in his disinterestedness, the signal skill, energy, and moderation with which he had at once animated and controlled the patriotic party, were universally acknowledged, and at this time, almost universally admired. He had shown that it was possible to combine very ardent attachment to Irish interests with a not less loyal devotion to the connection, and to conduct a great popular movement without any of the violence, the dishonesty, or the untruthfulness of a demagogue or an agitator. One of the most incontestable signs of the profound degradation of modern political opinion in Ireland is the class of men who have risen to be popular idols. One of the best signs of the Ireland of 1782 was the ardour with which popular gratitude still centred upon Grattan. The son of the Recorder of Dublin, he was a man of good family, but of very modest patrimonial estate, and as he had refused the offers of the Government, and had announced his intention to accept no office carrying emoluments, he was quite prepared to resume his profession as a barrister; but Parliament, expressing in this respect most faithfully the general sentiment of the country, determined to bestow on him such a gift as would at once mark the gratitude of the nation for his services and enable him to devote his undivided energies to political life. Without the consent or knowledge of the intimate personal friends of Grattan, Bagenal, one of the members for the county of Carlow, moved that a grant of 100,000*l.* should be made to Grattan, and the proposition was unanimously accepted; but Grattan's particular friends at his instance interposed, and declared that nothing would induce him to accept such a grant. At last, however, after some discussion, and acting on the advice of his friends, and upon the urgent wish of the Parliament, he agreed to accept 50,000*l.*, and from this time he gave up all thought of practising at the bar, and devoted himself exclusively to the service of his country. Government would gladly have attached him to themselves by rewarding him from the pension list, and Portland even offered to confer upon him the new Viceregal Lodge in Phoenix Park, but he soon found that these offers were wholly unacceptable.

In this manner, without the effusion of one drop of blood, and with singularly little of violence and disorder, the whole Constitution of Ireland was changed, and a great revolution was accomplished, which Burke described without exaggeration as the Irish analogue of the English Revolution of 1688. Abuses, perplexities, and dangers no doubt lay thickly around the infant Constitution. The extreme difficulty of making it work in harmony with the Parliament of England; the excessive concentration of political power in a very few hands; religious and historical antipathies, great ignorance and great poverty, the exclusion of more than three-fourths of the population from all political rights, scandalous abuses of patronage, and many forms both of corruption and of anarchy, still continued. Yet when all this is admitted, a noble work had been nobly achieved. Ireland from the slave of England had now risen to the dignity of independence. She participated at last in all that was best in the English Constitution. Her religious animosities were rapidly fading beneath the strong national sentiment which had arisen, assisted by the intellectual tendencies of an eminently tolerant age. She had regained her freedom both of commerce and manufacture, and might reasonably hope with returning peace to attain some measure of material prosperity. After a long winter of oppression and misery, the sunlight of hope shone brightly upon her, and a new spirit of patriotism and self-reliance had begun to animate her people. Nor had her loyalty to England ever shown itself more earnest or more efficacious. The intellect, the property, the respectability of the country still led the popular movement, and as long as this continued no serious disloyalty was to be apprehended. . . .

# V

## *Grattan's Parliament, 1782–1789*

The victory which had been achieved by the Irish popular party in 1782 was a great one, but many elements of disquietude were abroad. An agitation so violent, so prolonged, and so successful, could hardly be expected suddenly to subside, and it is a law of human nature, that a great transport of triumph and of gratitude must be followed by some measure of reaction. Disappointed ambitions, chimerical hopes, turbulent agitators thrust into an unhealthy prominence, the dangerous precedent of an armed body controlling or overawing the deliberations of Parliament, the appetite for political excitement to which Irishmen have always been so prone, and which ever grows by indulgence, the very novelty and strangeness of the situation, all contributed to impart a certain feverish restlessness to the public mind. Unfortunately, too, one of the foremost of Irish politicians was profoundly discontented. Flood, who had been the earliest, and, for a long period, by far the most conspicuous advocate of the independence of the Irish Parliament, found himself completely eclipsed by a younger rival. He had lost his seat in the Privy Council, his dignity of Vice-Treasurer, and his salary of 3,500*l.* a year, but he had not regained his parliamentary ascendency. All the more important constitutional questions were occupied by other, and usually by younger, men. He was disliked by the Government and distrusted by the Parliament. Even his eloquence had lost something of its old power, and by too frequent speaking in opposition to the sense of the House, he had often alienated or irritated his hearers. . . .

*Not satisfied with the repeal of the Declaratory Act of 1719, some of the Patriots pressed for a formal renunciation by the British Parliament of any right to legislate for Ireland. The re-opening of the sensitive constitutional issue so soon after the concessions of 1782 stirred resentment on both sides of the Irish Sea.*

It was known that the Constitution of 1782 had been reluctantly conceded, that it had been conceded mainly in consequence of the desperate condition of public affairs, that it was detested by the Tory party on grounds of prerogative and by a large section of the Whig party as putting an end to the system of commercial monopoly. Lord Rockingham, whose character was universally respected, had just died. The dispute for his succession had thrown English politics into great confusion and uncertainty, and brought other men to the helm, and Portland was now replaced by Lord Temple as Lord Lieutenant of Ireland. It was widely believed that there was a disposition on the part of men in authority to undo in time of peace what had been granted in time of war, and a revulsion of feeling speedily set in. The judges, indeed, in Ireland, and several of the leading lawyers, asserted the sufficiency of what had been done, but the lawyers' corps of volunteers, which comprised a very large part of the legal profession, drew up a declaration that in their opinion no real security had been obtained, until the British Legislature had in express terms acknowledged its capacity to legislate for Ireland. The popularity of Grattan suddenly sank, and that of Flood rose with a corresponding rapidity. It was said that the nation was deceived, that nothing had been really gained, that England was already showing a manifest disposition to withdraw what she had granted. . . .

*The English Government acted with restraint and moderation on the constitutional issue, and with Lord Temple using his viceregal influence to reconcile opposing interests in Ireland, the Renunciation Act of 1783 passed through both Houses of Parliament.*

The Renunciation Act forms the coping-stone of the Constitution of 1782, and before we proceed with our narrative it may be advisable to pause for a moment in order to form a clear conception of the nature of that Constitution—its merits, its defects, and its dangers. Much had indeed been gained—the independence of the judges, the control of the army, the appellate jurisdiction of the Irish House of Lords, the extinction of the power of the Privy Council to originate, suppress, or alter Irish legislation, the renunciation of the power of the British Parliament to legislate for Ireland, the full and repeated acknowledgment of the doctrine that the King, Lords and Commons of Ireland had alone the right to make her laws. An Irish Act of Henry VIII and the Irish Act of recognition of William and Mary, had established that the crowns of England and Ireland were inseparable, so that whoever was King of England was *ipso facto* King of Ireland; but the two Legislatures were now regarded as independent, co-ordinate, and in their respective spheres co-equal.

It is sufficiently plain, however, that this was not, and could not be, the case. English Ministers were necessarily dependent on the support of the British Parliament and of that Parliament alone, and even apart from corrupt agencies, English Ministers exercised an enormous influence on Irish legislation. The King's veto was obsolete in England, but it was not likely to be obsolete in Ireland, and it could only be exercised on the advice of his ministers in England. The British Parliament claimed and enjoyed a right of watching over and controlling the conduct of the Executive Government, even in the exercise of what are justly considered undoubted prerogatives of the Crown, and this right, or at least this power, was wholly, or almost wholly, wanting in Ireland. Even the English Privy Council, though it had lost all recognised and formal control over Irish legislation, still retained a not inconsiderable influence. When Bills were sent over from Ireland to receive the royal sanction, it was the custom to submit them in the first place to a committee of the Privy Council, who were instructed to examine them and report on them to the King's law officers in England. This wheel of the machine of administration, indeed, was not public, and it appears to have escaped the notice of historians, but there is reason to believe that it was not inoperative. Occasionally mistakes were detected by the Committee of the Privy Council in Bills which came over from Ireland, and the Secretary of State then directed the Lord Lieutenant to introduce into the Irish Parliament supplemental Bills for the purpose of correcting them, and sometimes, where this was not possible, Irish Bills were not returned.

Much more important was the fact that there was, properly speaking, no ministry in Ireland responsible to the Irish Parliament. The position of Irish Ministers was essentially different from the position of their colleagues in England. Ministerial power was mainly in the hands of the Lord Lieutenant and of his Chief Secretary, and this latter functionary led the House of Commons, introduced for the most part Government business, and filled in Ireland a position at least as important as that of a Prime Minister in England. But the Lord Lieutenant and the Chief Secretary were not politicians who had risen to prominence and leadership in the Irish Parliament. They were Englishmen, strangers to Ireland, appointed and instructed by English Ministers, and changed with each succeeding Administration. The Irish Government was thus completely subordinated to the play of party government in England. An Irish Administration which commanded the full confidence of the Irish Parliament might at any moment be overthrown by a vote in the English Parliament on some purely English question.

This appears to me to have been a fatal fault in the Constitution of 1782. It explains why the duty of "supporting English Government," as distinguished from party allegiance, was represented by very honest politicians, as a maxim essential to the safe working of the Irish Constitution. . . .

*Under the Irish Constitution of 1782, the House of Commons differed from its British counterpart in both structure and powers. Ministerial changes in London continued to affect Irish political life, and the determination of foreign policy, including the decision to make war or peace, remained in the hands of English ministers. The Renunciation Act, in short, had not solved all of Ireland's political problems.*

Flood strenuously maintained that one more great battle must be fought before the Irish Constitution could be secure. The volunteers must induce or coerce Parliament to pass such a reform bill as would make it a true representative of the Protestant section of the nation.

The question was not altogether a new one, nor was it exclusively of home growth. In England, as we have seen, parliamentary reform had acquired a foremost place among political topics, and there was scarcely any other which stirred so strongly the popular sentiment. Chatham had strenuously advocated it, and he had predicted that, "before the end of the century, either the Parliament will reform itself from within, or be reformed with a vengeance from without." The question was brought before the British Parliament with great elaboration by Wilkes in 1776, by the Duke of Richmond in 1780, by the younger Pitt in 1782 and in 1783. Propositions for disfranchising the rotten boroughs, for enfranchising the great manufacturing towns, for adding to the electors and to the members of the counties, for annual parliaments, for universal suffrage, and for equal electoral districts, had been eagerly discussed both in Parliament and beyond its walls. Powerful democratic societies had been formed in the great cities, and they were already in close correspondence with the Irish volunteers, and extremely anxious to induce them to make the attainment of parliamentary reform a capital object of their policy.

It was obvious that a victory in one country would accelerate a victory in the other, and the arguments in favour of reform were much stronger in Ireland than in England. Among the English reformers who corresponded with the Irish volunteers were the Duke of Richmond, Price, Cartwright, and Lord Effingham. In June 1782 Portland, when forwarding to the Government an address from the volunteer delegates of Ulster, thanking the British Parliament for the concessions that had been made, mentions the appearance in their resolutions of "some new matter respecting the state of the representation in this country, which . . . has been endeavoured of late to be brought into discussion by a very active emissary, who has come from England expressly for that purpose"; but it was not until the simple repeal question was raised, that the subject of reform acquired real importance. In March 1783 a provincial meeting of volunteers at Cork passed resolutions in favour of parliamentary reform, and on July 1 following, delegates of forty-five companies of Ulster volunteers assembled at Lisburn, resolved to convoke for the ensuing September a great meeting of volunteers at Dungannon, to consider the best way of obtaining a more equal representation in Parliament.

In truth, even putting aside the great anomaly that the Roman Catholics were wholly unrepresented, it was a mockery to describe the Irish House of Commons as mainly a representative body. Of its 300 members, 64 only represented counties, while 100 small boroughs, containing ostensibly only an infinitesimal number of electors, and in reality in the great majority of cases at the absolute disposal of single patrons, returned no less than 200. Borough seats were commonly sold for 2,000*l.* a parliament, and the permanent patronage of a borough for from 8,000*l.* to 10,000*l.* The Lower House was to a great extent a creation of the Upper one. It was at this time computed that 124 members of the House of Commons were absolutely nominated by fifty-three peers, while ninety-one others were chosen by fifty-two commoners.

It needs no comment to show the absurdity and the danger of such a condition of representation. In Ireland, it is true, as in England, borough influence was not always badly used, and the sale of seats, and the system of nomination, neither of which carried with them any real reproach, introduced into Parliament many honourable, able and independent men, who were thoroughly acquainted with the condition of the country. But the state of the Irish representation was much worse than that of the English, and incomparably more dangerous to the Constitution of the country. England was at least her own mistress. The strongest minister only kept his power by a careful attention to the gusts of popular feeling, and no external power desired to tamper with her Constitution. But the relation of Ireland to England was such that it was quite conceivable that an Irish parliament might act in violent opposition to the wishes of the community which it represented, and quite possible that an English minister might wish it to do so. As long as the volunteers continued, public opinion possessed such a formidable and organised power that it could act forcibly on Parliament. But once that organisation was dissolved, the reign of a corrupt oligarchy must revive. However independent the Irish Parliament might be in the eyes of the law and in the theory of the Constitution, it could not fail to be a dependent and subordinate body holding a precarious existence, as long as a full third of its members were placemen or pensioners, and as long as the English Minister could control the election of the majority of its members. Some borough seats were at the disposal of bishops appointed by Government. Some were in the hands of great English noblemen. It was only necessary to secure a small number of great native borough owners, to obtain a compact majority independent of all fluctuations of popular feeling. The lavish distribution of peerages had proved the cheapest and most efficacious means of governing Parliament, and a pamphleteer in 1783 reminded his countrymen that since 1762 inclusive, the Irish peerage had been enriched or degraded by the addition of thirty-three barons, sixteen viscounts, and twenty-four earls.

During the short Administration of Lord Temple, which lasted only from September 1782 till the following spring, and corresponded with the Shelburne Ministry in England, the Reform agitation scarcely appeared. . . .

*Lord Northington succeeded Lord Temple as Viceroy once the Fox-North coalition had been formed. Although England achieved peace in 1783, the Irish Volunteers showed no signs of disbanding. The growing rift between Grattan and Flood began to affect the quality of Irish political life.*

In October 1783, in one of the debates on the proposed reduction of the forces, a violent altercation broke out between Flood and Grattan, and two invectives, both of them disgracefully virulent, and one of them of extraordinary oratorical power, made all cordial co-operation, for the future, extremely difficult. The interposition of the House prevented a duel. Flood afterwards very magnanimously occupied the chair at a volunteer meeting, when a vote of thanks to Grattan was passed, and Grattan long afterwards, in his pamphlet on the Union, and on many occasions in private conversation, bore a high testimony to the greatness of Flood; but the old friendship of the two leaders was at an end, and words had been spoken which could never be forgiven.

The essentially political attitude which the volunteers were now assuming created much alarm. In July 1783, "a committee of correspondence," appointed by the delegates assembled at

Lisburn for the purpose of arranging the forthcoming meeting at Dungannon, wrote to Charlemont asking his support and advice. They begged him to indicate "such specific mode of reform" as appeared to him most suitable for the condition of Ireland, and at the same time to inform them, whether in his opinion the volunteer assembly should bring within the range of their discussions at Dungannon, such subjects as the propriety of shortening the duration of parliaments, exclusion of pensions, a limitation of the numbers of placemen, and a tax on absentees. Charlemont perceived with much alarm the disposition of the force to attempt to regulate and perhaps control the whole field of legislation, and he urged the committee to confine themselves to the single question of reform, and on this question to content themselves with asserting the necessity of the measure, leaving the mode of carrying it out exclusively to the mature deliberation of Parliament.

The volunteers could hardly have had a safer counsellor, and Charlemont, though by no means a man of genius, exercised at this time a very great influence in Irish politics. He was now in his fifty-fifth year. He had inherited his title when still a child, and having never gone through the discipline of a public school, had spent more than nine years in travelling on the Continent. For some years he plunged deeply into the dissipations of the lax society in Italy, but he never lost a sense of higher things, and he brought back a great taste and passion for art, a wide range of ornamental scholarship, and a very real earnestness and honesty of character. At Turin he had formed a close intimacy with Hume, but it had not impaired either his religious principles or his strong Whig convictions. In Paris he had discussed Irish politics very fully with Montesquieu, and was struck with the earnestness with which that great philosopher recommended a legislative union with England as the best safeguard of Irish liberty. He afterwards became an intimate friend of Burke, an early member of that brilliant club which Johnson and Reynolds had formed, a careful and discriminating student of the debates in the English Parliament, and then an almost constant resident in Ireland and a leading figure in Irish politics. A nervousness which he was never able to overcome, and which was aggravated by much ill health, kept him completely silent in the House of Lords, and in his inti-

mate circle he often showed himself somewhat vain and irreso-
lute and easily offended; but in addition to his great social position, he had personal qualities of a kind which often go further
in politics than great brilliancy of intellect, and he was one of
the very few prominent Irish politicians who had never stooped
to any corrupt traffic with the Government.

Like his contemporary Rockingham he possessed a transparent
purity and delicacy of honour, which won the confidence of all
with whom he came in contact, a judgment singularly clear, temperate and unbiassed, a natural affability of manner which made
him peculiarly fitted to conciliate conflicting interests and characters. He wrote well, though often with a vein of weak sentimentalism which was the prevailing affectation of his time, and he
threw himself into many useful national enterprises with great
industry, and with invariable singleness of purpose. He was a
Whig of Whigs—with all that love of compromise; that cautious
though genuine liberality; that combination of aristocratic tastes
and popular principles; that dislike to violence, exaggeration, and
vulgarity; that profound veneration for the British Constitution,
and that firm conviction that every desirable change could be
effected within its limits, which characterised the best Whig
thought of the time. His property lay in the province which
was the centre of the volunteer movement. He was one of the
earliest and most active of its organisers, and the unbounded
confidence of the more liberal section of the Irish gentry in his
penetration and his judgment, had raised him speedily to its
head.

His position was, however, now becoming very difficult. Flood
and Grattan, with whom he had hitherto most cordially co-
operated, were alienated from each other, and both of them were
in some degree alienated from him. Though he ultimately admitted the expediency of passing the Act of Renunciation, and
though he cordially maintained the necessity of parliamentary
reform, he strongly disapproved of the conduct of Flood in
raising the first question, and in bringing the second question
under the deliberations of an armed body. Grattan had been
first brought into Parliament by Charlemont, and a deep attachment subsisted between them; but a coldness had lately grown
up which soon culminated in a breach. Grattan was now wholly

alienated from the volunteers; he would evidently have gladly seen their dissolution at the peace, and he cordially supported Lord Northington's Administration. Charlemont, on the other hand, was strongly in favour of the maintenance in arms of the volunteer force. He had more and more gravitated to opposition, and he was in consequence rarely consulted by the Administration with which Grattan was in close alliance. Grattan appears to have done everything in his power to soothe the irritation of his friend, and his letters to him are extremely honourable to the writer; but he had to deal with a somewhat fretful and morbid temperament, and he was not able to succeed. . . .

*The Irish Volunteers were soon at odds with each other over the question of parliamentary reform. One group favored the Charlemont-Grattan policy of consolidating the gains of 1782, while others followed the flamboyant Earl of Bristol, who was also Bishop of Derry, in the direction of substantial reform of the legislature. A large convention of Volunteers in Dublin produced a reform bill which was thrown out by Parliament late in November 1783 and again in March 1784.*

The question is not susceptible of any positive solution, and the difficulties on all sides seemed nearly insuperable. The experience of all countries shows that a monopoly of power, as complete as that which was possessed by a small group of borough owners in Ireland, is never, or scarcely ever, broken down except by measures bordering on revolution. The Reform Bill of 1832 would never have been carried, but for an agitation which convinced the most enlightened statesmen that the country could not be peacefully governed on any other condition. Yet the English monopoly before 1832 was but a faint shadow of that Irish Parliament, in which more than two-thirds of the representatives were nominated by individual patrons, and a majority were dependent on a few great families. Corruption ever follows monopoly as the shadow the substance, and where political power was concentrated in so few hands, party management necessarily resolved itself into personal influence. The Protestant yeomanry of the North, and the great bulk of the Protestant gentry, found themselves either unrepresented or most inadequately represented; and these classes, who comprised most of the intelligence, and a great preponderance of the property, of the country, mainly constituted at this time both the volunteers and the reformers of Ireland.

To create popular, but at the same time purely Protestant, institutions was the aim of Charlemont and Flood, and the whole history of the volunteer organisation appears to me to show that the ascendant caste had attained a level of political intelligence and capacity which fully fitted it for increased political power. Beyond this Flood and Charlemont refused to go. To place political power in the hands of the vast, ignorant, and turbulent Catholic peasantry would, they maintained, be an act of madness which would imperil every institution in the country, shake property to its very basis, and probably condemn Ireland to a long period of anarchy. I have already quoted the remarkable letter, in which as late as 1791 Charlemont predicted that a full century was likely to elapse before the mass of the Irish Catholics could be safely entrusted with political power; and in his comments on the proceedings of the Convention of 1783, he expressed his views on the subject with great clearness. "Every immunity," he wrote, "every privilege of citizenship should be given to the Catholics excepting only arms and legislation, either of which being granted them would, I conceive, shortly render Ireland a Catholic country, totally break its connection with England," and force it to resort to the protection of France or Spain. Flood, as we have seen, held very similar opinions, and it appears to have been partly in order to divert the volunteers from taking up the Catholic question that he pushed on so strenuously the question of reform. A democracy planted in an aristocracy, popular institutions growing out of an intelligent and ascendant class, formed their ideal, and the memory of ancient Athens with its democracy of 30,000 free citizens rising above a vast population of unrepresented slaves was probably present to many minds.

Such a reform, they maintained, would have at least placed the Irish Parliament on a secure basis, made it a real representative of the intelligence and property of Ireland, put an end to the inveterate system of corruption, and called the action of party government into full and healthy play. The result may appear to show that it would have been wise at almost any hazard, and without any delay, if possible, to have at this time forced a large infusion of the popular element into Parliament, but the result is a less decisive test than is often thought of the wisdom of statesmen. Politics are little more than a calculation of probabilities, and the train of events which appears reasonably the most probable does not always occur. If the course of the world for fifty years after 1782 had been as peaceful as it had been during the first three quarters of the century, reforms might probably have been introduced by slow steps, and no great catastrophe would have occurred. Mere political difficulties and ordinary wars had never seriously affected the loyalty and the peace of the country. The American Revolution with its direct and evident bearing on the relations of dependencies to the mother country was the first contest which acted powerfully upon opinion, and even its influence was of a very sober, measured, and rational kind. Unfortunately for the peace of Ireland, before the close of the century an event occurred which in its immediate moral and political effects was wholly unequalled since the great religious convulsions of the sixteenth century. The fierce spirit of democracy, which the French Revolution had engendered, swept like a hurricane over Europe, lashed into sudden fury popular passions which had slumbered for centuries, and strained to the utmost every beam in the Constitution. Six or seven quiet years were granted to Ireland after her legislative emancipation to prepare for the storm, but when the first blast was felt, nothing had as yet been done, and the Parliament was as far as ever from a real representative of the nation. . . .

*Several months after Pitt's return to power in December 1783, the Duke of Rutland replaced Lord Northington as Irish Viceroy. The economic depression and resultant distress of 1784 added weight to Irish demands for preferential terms in Anglo-Irish trade relations. The Irish Parliament approved an address to the King on 13 May 1784 requesting freer trade between the two countries. The passage of Foster's Corn Law in 1784 placed large bounties on Irish exports as well as duties on imports of corn. This protective measure induced many of the more substantial farmers to convert their land from pasturage to tillage. The premiums thus placed on corn production altered Ireland's rural economy and also raised the rental of land. Many farmers profited from the rising demand for foodstuffs from industrializing Brit-ain. Toward the end of 1784, Whiteboyism again flared up in several midland counties.*

The change, indeed, which was now taking place in the char-acter of the volunteer body, was especially alarming. The original volunteers had consisted of the flower of the Protestant yeomanry, commanded by the gentry of Ireland, and in addition to their services in securing the country from invasion in a time of great national peril, they had undertaken to preserve its internal peace, and had discharged with admirable efficiency the functions of a great police force. But after the signature of peace, and, again, after the dissolution of the Volunteer Convention, a great portion of the more respectable men connected with the movement con-sidered their work done and retired from the ranks, and they were being replaced by another and wholly different class. The taste for combining, arming, and drilling had spread, and had descended to the lower strata of society. Demagogues had arisen who sought by arming and organising volunteers to win political power, and who gathered around them men who desired for very doubtful purposes to obtain arms. Grattan, who at all times dreaded and detested anything that withdrew political move-ments in Ireland from the control and guidance of the gentry, was one of the first to denounce the change. "I would now draw the attention of the House," he said, "to the alarming measure of drilling the lowest classes of the populace. . . . The old, the orig-inal, volunteers had become respectable because they represented the property of the nation, but attempts had been made to arm the poverty of the kingdom. They had originally been the armed property of Ireland. Were they to become the armed beggary?" "The populace," he added, "differ much and should be clearly distinguished from the people," and he spoke of the capital that has been drained, the manufacturers who have been deterred, the character of the nation that has been sunk by indiscriminate arming, and by the establishment of representative bodies uncon-nected with Parliament. . . .

By far the greater part of the disturbances of 1784 and 1785 were probably due to no deeper cause than commercial depression acting upon a very riotous population, and with the return of

prosperity they gradually ceased; but there was a real and dangerous element of political agitation mixing with the social disquietude. The decisive rejection of Flood's Reform Bill, in spite
of many petitions in its favour, and the refusal of the House of
Commons to impose protective duties, stimulated political agitation, and the question of the Catholic franchise now began to rise
into prominence. Several of the opponents of Flood's Reform
Bill had made the omission of the Roman Catholics an argument
against it; and some of the supporters of that Bill accused the
Government of raising the Catholic question in order to divide
and weaken the reformers. On the other hand a democratic party
had arisen, who, following the advice of the Bishop of Derry,
contended that the best way of breaking the power of the aristocracy and carrying parliamentary reform was to offer the franchise
to the Catholics, and thus enlist the great body of the nation in
the agitation. Dr. Richard Price, the eminent Nonconformist
minister who was so prominent among the reformers in England,
wrote to the volunteers: "I cannot help wishing that the right of
voting could be extended to Papists of property in common with
Protestants"; and Todd Jones, one of the members for Lisburn,
published a letter to his constituents strongly advocating the measure. In July 1784 an address in this sense was presented to
Lord Charlemont by the Ulster volunteers who were reviewed at
Belfast; but Charlemont in his reply, while reiterating his adhesion to parliamentary reform, pronounced himself strongly
against Catholic suffrage.

In Dublin a small knot of violent and revolutionary reformers,
chiefly of the shopkeeper class, had arisen, and some of them
were members of the Corporation. Napper Tandy, the son of an
ironmonger in the city, was the most conspicuous, and he afterwards rose to great notoriety. By the exertions of his party, meetings in favour of reform were held in Dublin. A permanent
committee was created, and in June 1784 this committee invited
the sheriffs of the different counties to call meetings for the purpose of electing delegates to meet in Dublin in the ensuing
October. This was an attempt to revive in another form the convention of the previous year, with this great distinction, that it
was to have no connection with any armed force but was to be
a true representative of the Irish Protestants. . . .

The feeling in favour of reform continued to be very strong throughout the country, and it was accompanied with great irritation against the majority in Parliament. The prediction of Flood that without a reform of Parliament there was no security for the stability of the present Constitution, and that a corrupt majority might one day overturn it, had sunk deeply in the popular mind, and petitions to the King poured in from many quarters, describing the House of Commons as having wholly lost the confidence of the nation and fallen completely into the hands of a corrupt oligarchy. . . .

*The agitation for parliamentary and economical reform gave an additional stimulus to the more democratic elements in Irish society, especially in the North. The bulk of the Catholic population, however, remained relatively indifferent to the niceties of parliamentary reform. Government suspicions that French agents were at work fomenting disturbances in Ireland had no foundation in fact.*

The tension, however, soon passed, and several years elapsed before French ministers were seriously occupied with Ireland. The next few years of Irish history were quiet and uneventful, and although no great reform was effected, the growing prosperity of the country was very perceptible. The House of Commons gave the Government little or no trouble, and whatever agitations or extreme views may have been advocated beyond its walls, the most cautious conservative could hardly accuse it of any tendency to insubordination or violence. It consisted almost entirely of landlords, lawyers, and placemen. Its more important discussions show a great deal of oratorical and debating talent, much knowledge of the country and considerable administrative power; it was ardently and unanimously attached to the Crown and the connection, and the accumulation of borough interests at the disposal of the Treasury, and the habitual custom of "supporting the King's Government," gave the Government on nearly all questions an overwhelming strength. The majority had certainly no desire to carry any measure of reform which would alter their own very secure and agreeable position, or expose them to the vicissitudes of popular contests, but the influence of the Government was so overwhelming that even in this direction much might have been done by Government initiative, and it is remarkable that in all the letters of the Irish Government opposing parliamentary reform, nothing is said of the impracticability of carrying it. On the whole, it would be difficult to find a legislative body which was less troublesome to the Executive. There was one subject and only one upon which it was recalcitrant. It was jealous to the very highest degree of its own position as an independent Legislature, and any measure which appeared even remotely designed to restrict its powers and to make it subordinate to the British Parliament, produced a sudden and immediate revolt.

The prosperity of the country was advancing, and the revenue was rising, but the expenses of the Government still outstripped its income, and there were loud complaints of growing extravagance. Many things had indeed recently conspired to increase the national expenditure. Free trade opening out vast markets for Irish products, had induced Parliament to give larger bounties for the purpose of stimulating native manufactures. The erection of a magnificent custom-house; great works of inland navigation; an augmentation of the salaries of the judges in 1781; additional revenue officers required by an expanding trade; additional officials needed for the New National Bank, fell heavily on the finances....

The Irish Administration, on the other hand, was strongly opposed to any measure of reform. They had got their majority by the small borough system, and they wished to keep it, and opposed a strong passive resistance to every attempt from England to impel them in the direction of reform. The chief governor was naturally surrounded by great borough owners, whose personal interests were bound up with the existing political system, and the spirit both of resistance and of anti-Catholicism was very greatly strengthened when, on the promotion of Yelverton to the Bench in 1783, Fitzgibbon became Attorney-General. This remarkable man, who for the last sixteen years of the century exercised a dominant influence in the Irish Government, and who, as Lord Clare, was the ablest, and at the same time the most detested, advocate of the Union, had in 1780 opposed the Declaration of Right moved by Grattan in the House of Commons, but had supported the policy of Grattan in 1782, and had used strong language in censuring some parts of the legislative authority which Great Britain exercised over Ireland. It is very questionable whether he ever really approved of the repeal of Poynings' Law, and his evident leaning towards authority made him distrusted by several leaders of the popular party, but Grattan does not appear to have shared the feeling, and when he was consulted on the subject by Lord Northington, he gave his full sanction to the promotion of Fitzgibbon. For some time there was no breach between them, and in one of his speeches in 1785 Fitzgibbon spoke in high terms of the character and services of Grattan, but the dispute on the commercial propositions appears to have separated them, and Fitzgibbon soon followed the true instincts of his character and his intellect, in opposing an iron will to every kind of reform. In private life he appears to have been an estimable and even amiable man; several acts of generosity are related of him, and the determination with which in spite of a large inherited fortune he pursued his career at the bar, shows the energy and the seriousness of his character. He is said not to have been a great orator, but he was undoubtedly a very ready and skilful debater, a great master of constitutional law, a man who in council had a peculiar gift of bending other wills to his own, a man who in many trying periods of popular violence displayed a courage which no danger and no obloquy could disturb. He was, however, in public life arrogant, petulant, and overbearing in the highest degree, delighting in trampling on those whom he disliked, in harsh acts and irritating words, prone on all occasions to strain prerogative and authority to their utmost limits, bitterly hostile to the great majority of his countrymen, and, without being corrupt himself, a most cynical corrupter of others. Curran, both in Parliament and at the bar, had been one of his bitterest opponents, and a duel having on one occasion ensued, a great scandal was created by the slow and deliberate manner in which, contrary to the ordinary rules of duels, Fitzgibbon aimed at his opponent, and when he became Lord Chancellor he was accused of having, by systematic hostility and partiality on the bench, compelled his former adversary to abandon his practice in the court.

As a politician, Fitzgibbon, though his father had been one of the many Catholics who abandoned their faith in order to pursue a legal career, represented in its harshest and most arrogant form the old spirit of Protestant ascendency as it existed when the smoke of the civil wars had scarcely cleared away, and he laughed to scorn all who taught that there could be any peace between the different sections of Irishmen, or that the century which had elapsed since the Revolution had made any real change in the situation of the country. A passage in his great speech in favour of the Union is the keynote of his whole policy. "What, then," he asked, "was the situation of Ireland at the Revolution, and what is it at this day? The whole power and property of the country has been conferred by successive monarchs of England upon an English colony composed of three sets of English adventurers, who poured into this country at the termination of three successive rebellions. Confiscation is their common title, and from their first settlement they have been hemmed in on every side by the old inhabitants of the island, brooding over their discontents in sullen indignation."

In accordance with these views his uniform object was to represent the Protestant community as an English garrison planted in a hostile country, to govern steadily, sternly, and exclusively, with a view to their interests, to resist to the utmost every attempt to relax monopoly, elevate and conciliate the Catholics, or draw together the divided sections of Irish life. Even in the days when he professed Liberalism, he had endeavoured to impede the Catholic Relief Bill of 1778 by raising difficulties about its effect on the Act of Settlement; and after he arrived at power, he was a steady and bitter opponent of every measure of concession. He was sometimes obliged to yield. He was sometimes opposed to his colleagues in Ireland, and more often to the Government in England, but the main lines of his policy were on the whole maintained, and it is difficult to exaggerate the evil they caused. To him, more perhaps than to any other man, it is due that nothing was done during the quiet years that preceded the French Revolution to diminish the corruption of the Irish Parliament, or the extreme anomalies of the Irish ecclesiastical establishment. He was the soul of that small group of politicians, who, by procuring the recall of Lord Fitzwilliam and the refusal of Catholic emancipation in 1795, flung the Catholics into the rebellion of 1798, and his influence was one of the chief obstacles to the

determination of Pitt to carry Catholic Emancipation concurrently
with the Union. . . .

*Grattan's politics and ideals stood in "sharp contrast" to those
of Fitzgibbon, who hoped to deny the Catholic majority any form
of political power. Having helped to win legislative independence, Grattan wished to "pacify the public mind, to lead it back
to the path of gradual administrative reform . . . and to discourage all feeling of disloyalty to England."*

No politician had ever less sympathy than Grattan with disorder and anarchy; and his whole theory of Irish politics was very
far from democratic. From first to last it was a foremost article
of his policy that it was essential to the safe working of representative institutions in Ireland that they should be under the full
guidance and control of the property of the country, and that the
greatest of all calamities would be that this guidance should pass
into the hands of adventurers and demagogues. He desired the
House of Commons to be a body consisting mainly of the independent landed gentry and leading lawyers, and resting mainly
on a freehold suffrage; and he would have gladly included in it
the leading members of that Catholic gentry who had long been
among the most loyal and most respectable subjects of the Crown.
He believed that a body so constituted was most likely to draw
together the severed elements of Irish life; to watch over Irish
interests; to guide the people upwards to a higher level of civilisation and order; to correct the many and glaring evils of Irish
life. But in order that it should perform this task, it was indispensable that it should be a true organ of national feeling; a faithful
representative of educated opinion and of independent property;
able and willing to pursue energetically the course of administrative reform which was imperatively needed. It was necessary
above all that the system of governing exclusively by corruption
and family interest should be terminated. Such a system was absolutely inevitable in a Parliament constituted like that of Ireland,
and without any one of the more important legislative guarantees
of parliamentary purity that existed in England. . . .

*While Grattan pleaded the cause of moderation, Irish com-
mercial interests demanded preferential terms from England.*

*Pitt's plans for a completely free trade between the two countries were embodied in a series of commercial propositions which received the assent of the Irish Parliament early in 1785. When these resolutions were introduced into the English Parliament on February 22, both the Opposition and manufacturing interests outside Parliament objected vehemently. Pitt exerted all his influence in order to secure the passage of these resolutions, albeit in amended form. The Irish Parliament, however, rejected the amended version because it appeared weighted in favor of English industries. Pitt's high hopes for Anglo-Irish reconciliation were thus dashed. The Irish Parliament did not hesitate to pass a stringent Crimes Act in 1787 in order to cope with Whiteboy outrages.*

The Whiteboy Act of 1787 is another of the many examples of the prompt and energetic manner in which the Irish Parliament never hesitated to deal with epidemics of outrage. Fitzgibbon complained, however, that much of the evil was due to the supineness and sometimes even to the connivance of magistrates, and he alleged that they were prone on the slightest occasion to call for military assistance. An important Act "for the better execution of the law" was carried in this year, for reforming the magistracy and establishing throughout the country a constabulary appointed by the grand juries but under the direction of peace officers appointed by the Crown.

But while Grattan warmly supported the Government in measures for the suppression of disorder and crime, he maintained that it was equally imperative for the Parliament to deal with those great evils from which Irish crime principally sprang. The enormous absurdity, injustice, and inequality of the Irish tithe system has been explained in a former chapter, and tithes and the tithe proctor were the chief cause of the Whiteboy disturbances which were spreading every kind of evil and disaster over a great part of Ireland. Pitt with the instinct of a true statesman had expressed his wish, as early as 1786, that tithes in Ireland should be commuted into a money rate, levied on the tenants of the parish, regulated by the price of corn and calculated on an average of several years. But although many of the poorer clergy would have gladly accepted such a plan, and although in the opinion of

Rutland the majority of the laity "were opposed to tithes, and strong advocates for some settlement," the bishops "considered any settlement as a direct attack on their most ancient rights and as a commencement of the ruin of the Establishment"; and the Irish Government, discarding the advice of Pitt, obstinately resisted every attempt to modify the offensive system. Grattan had mastered the subject in its minutest details, and in 1787, in 1788, and in 1789 he brought it forward in speeches which were among the greatest he ever delivered, suggesting as alternative and slightly varying plans to pay the clergy a sum calculated on the average of several years and raised by applotment like other county charges; to institute a general modus in lieu of tithes; to make a commutation by a general survey of every county, allowing a specified sum for every acre in tillage, and making the whole county security for the clergymen. These plans were in principle very similar to the suggestion of Pitt, and in addition to their other advantages they might have made the collection of tithes by the resident clergy so simple and easy that the whole race of tithe farmers and proctors would have gradually disappeared. Grattan also proposed that lands which had been barren should for a certain time after their reclamation be exempt from tithes; that the partial or complete exemption of potatoes and linen, which existed in some parts of the kingdom, should be extended to the whole; and that a moderate tax should be imposed on the non-residence of the clergy. The exemption of barren lands from tithes was approved of by Fitzgibbon, and although it was for some years rejected on account of the opposition of the clergy, it was ultimately carried. But the other proposals of Grattan were met by an obstinate resistance. Fitzgibbon, and the majority which he led, refused even to grant a committee to investigate the subject, and the Irish tithe system continued to be the chief source of Irish crime till the Commutation Act of Lord John Russell in 1838.

The persistant refusal of the Irish Parliament to rectify or mitigate this class of abuses, appears to me the gravest of all the many reproaches that may be brought against it. Although about seven-eighths of the nation dissented from the established religion, the general principle of a Protestant establishment had as yet very few enemies; but the existing tithe system was detested both by the Catholics and the Protestant Dissenters, and it was exceedingly unpopular among the smaller landed gentry. Its inequalities and injustices were too glaring for any plausible defense, and the language of Pitt seems to show that England would have placed no obstacle in the way of redress. How possible it was to cure the evil without destroying the Establishment was abundantly shown by the Act of 1838. That Act, which commuted tithes into a land tax paid by the landlord with a deduction of twenty-five per cent. for the cost of collection, is probably the most successful remedial measure in all Irish history. It proved a great benefit to the Protestant clergy, and it at the same time completely staunched an old source of disorder and crime, and effected a profound and immediate change in the feelings of men. Very few political measures have ever effected so much good without producing any countervailing evil. The Irish Church when it was supported by tithes was the most unpopular ecclesiastical establishment in Europe, and it kept the country in a condition verging on civil war. After the commutation of tithes nearly all active hostility to it disappeared. The Church question speedily became indifferent to the great mass of the people; the Protestant clergy were a beneficent and usually a popular element in Irish society, and the measure which finally disendowed them was much more due to the exigencies of English party politics than to any genuine pressure of Irish opinion. But no such measure as that of 1838 could be carried in the Irish Parliament, and in the last ten years of its existence even Grattan desisted from efforts which were manifestly hopeless. Yet at no time had the question been more important. Resistance to the exaction of tithes was year by year strengthening habits of outrage and lawless combination, and in the hope of abolishing the tithes the Irish Jacobins found the best means of acting upon the passions of the nation.

But whatever social or agrarian disturbances may have existed in the remoter counties, the political condition of Ireland in the closing period of the administration of Rutland presented an aspect of almost absolute calm. Prosperity was advancing with rapid strides. The credit of the nation was re-established. Both the young Viceroy and his beautiful Duchess were extremely popular. A gay, brilliant, and dissipated court drew men of many opinions within its circle or its influence, and political tension had almost wholly ceased. . . .

*The Duke of Rutland died of fever on 24 October 1787, and he was succeeded as Viceroy by the unpopular Lord Temple, who had since become the Marquess of Buckingham. The Regency crisis of 1788, caused by the King's temporary insanity, opened up deep rifts in the Irish political nation between the supporters of Pitt and Fox. To the embarrassment of the Irish administration an address asking the Prince of Wales to become Regent of Ireland passed through Parliament. Upon the King's recovery in 1789, several placemen who had supported the Irish Regency Bill were removed from office. For his services to the Government John Fitzgibbon was made Lord Chancellor of Ireland and raised to the peerage. Irish prosperity increased in the 1790s, as new trades and industries found a footing.*

.The true history of the Irish Parliament is not to be found in the fantastic pages of Barrington, and still less in the dishonest pictures of modern partisans. It is to be found in the excellent reports of its debates; in the Irish statute book, which contains the nett results of its work; in the volumes of those contemporary writers who have most fully examined the industrial and economical conditions of Ireland under its rule. The character of this body I have tried to draw with a steady and an impartial hand, both in its lights and in its shades, and I am conscious that the task is both a difficult and a thankless one, at a time when the whole subject is generally looked upon under the distorting influences of modern politics.

To an historian of the eighteenth century, however, few things can be more grotesquely absurd than to suppose that the merits or demerits, the failure or the success, of the old Irish Parliament has any real bearing on modern schemes for reconstructing the government of Ireland on a revolutionary and Jacobin basis; entrusting the protection of property and the maintenance of law to some democratic assembly consisting mainly of Fenians and Land-leaguers, of paid agitators and of penniless adventurers. The parliamentary system of the eighteenth century might be represented in very different lights by its enemies and by its friends.

Its enemies would describe it as essentially government carried on through the instrumentality of a corrupt oligarchy, of a large, compact body of members holding places and pensions at the pleasure of the Government, and removed by the system of rotten boroughs from all effectual popular control. Its friends would describe it as essentially the government of Ireland by the gentlemen of Ireland, and especially by its landlord class.

Neither representation would be altogether true, but each contains a large measure of truth. The nature of the Irish constituencies and the presence in the House of Commons of a body of pensioners and placemen forming considerably more than a third of the whole assembly, and nearly half of its active members, gave the Government a power which, except under very rare and extraordinary circumstances, must, if fully exerted, have been overwhelming. The system of corruption was largely extended after the Regency controversy, and it produced evils that it is difficult to overrate. It enabled a small oligarchy to resist the most legitimate demands of Irish opinion, and as Grattan vainly predicted it taught the people to look elsewhere for their representatives, and exposed them to the fatal contagion of the revolutionary spirit that was then circulating through Europe. On the other hand, the Irish Parliament was a body consisting very largely of independent country gentlemen, who on nearly all questions affecting the economical and industrial development of the country, had a powerful if not a decisive influence. The lines of party were but faintly drawn. Most questions were settled by mutual compromise or general concurrence, and it was in reality only in a small class of political questions that the corrupt power of Government seems to have been strained. The Irish House of Commons consisted mainly of the class of men who now form the Irish grand juries. It comprised the flower of the landlord class. It was essentially and pre-eminently the representative of the property of the country. It had all the instincts and the prejudices, but also all the qualities and the capacities, of an educated propertied class, and it brought great local knowledge and experience to its task. Most of its work was of that practical and unobstrusive character which leaves no trace in history. Several useful laws were made to rectify the scandalous abuses of Irish prisons; to improve the condition of insolvent debtors; to prevent burials in churches; to establish hospitals and infirmaries; to check different kinds of disorder as they arose; to make harbours and canals; to encourage local institutions and industries; and except during the conflict on the Regency question, the parliamentary machine had hitherto moved on with very little friction or disturbance.

Of the large amount of ability which it comprised there can be no reasonable question, and this ability was by no means confined to the independent section. Several very able men accepted the general system of government, as, on the whole, the best suited for the circumstances of the country. Ireland has seldom or never produced, in the province of politics, men of wider knowledge and more solid ability than John Foster and Hely Hutchinson, while Fitzgibbon, Langrishe, and Parnell were all men of much more than ordinary talents. All of these were during the greater part of their lives connected with the Government.

The system of government indeed, though corrupt, anomalous, and exposed to many dangers, was not one of those which are incompatible with a large measure of national prosperity. There were unfair monopolies of patronage; there was a pension list of rather more than 100,000*l.* a year, a great part of which was grossly corrupt; there was a scandalous multiplication and a scandalous employment of sinecures; but these are not the kind of evils that seriously affect the material well-being of the great mass of the community. In spite of much corrupt expenditure the Government was a cheap one; Ireland was among the most lightly taxed nations in Europe. . . .

The elements of turbulence in the country were very numerous, and little provocation was needed to fan them into a flame. The contests between the Peep of Day Boys and the Defenders in Ulster are said to have originated in a private quarrel unconnected with religion, but they speedily assumed the character of a religious war. The former, who were exclusively Protestants and mainly Presbyterians, professed a determination to enforce the law disarming Papists, and they were accustomed to enter their cottages in early morning to search for and to seize arms. The Defenders were exclusively Catholics, and were professedly, as their name imports, a purely defensive body. In truth, however, both sides were animated by a furious hatred, and both sides committed many acts of violence and aggression. The disturbances appear to have begun in 1785, but they continued for several years, and the Peep of Days ultimately merged into Orangemen, and the Defenders into United Irishmen. Bodies of several hundreds of men of the lowest class on more than one occasion came into collision: several lives were lost; a reign of terror prevailed in large districts of Ulster, and it led to a new enrolment of Protestant volunteers to maintain the peace. In Munster the Whiteboy outrages were certainly not of a religious origin, but they were directed mainly, though not exclusively, against the payment of tithes, and they appear to have been not unfrequently organised in Catholic chapels. . . .

The country was awakening to a keen consciousness of it's political existence; and it was inevitable, if the peace of Ireland was to be maintained, that something should be done to make the Irish Parliament a really representative body, and to put an end to the system of monopoly and corruption which ran through every pore of the Irish Administration. Sooner or later this problem must inevitably have been faced; and the sudden impulse which the French Revolution had given to the democratic spirit in Europe forced it on, at a time when the system of corruption was at its height, and when the Irish Administration was in the hands of bitter enemies of reform. On the capital question of granting the suffrage to the Catholics, the ministers in England, as we shall hereafter see, were in favour of concession, while the Administration in Ireland was bitterly opposed to it; and the result was a vacillation and division of policy in a critical and dangerous period, which led to consequences most fatal to the prosperity of Ireland.

The problem before the Irish Parliament would, under the most favourable circumstances, have been an extremely difficult one, and most analogies drawn from purely English experience, and especially from later English experience, only tend to mislead. The goodness of laws and political institutions is essentially relative, depending upon their adaptation to the character, circumstances, wants and traditions of the people for whom they are intended; and in all these respects, England and Ireland were wholly different. There is no greater delusion than to suppose that the same degree of popular government can be wisely accorded to nations in all stages of development, and that a country in a backward stage is really benefited by a servile imitation of the institutions of its more advanced neighbours. A country where the traditions of many peaceful centuries have knitted the various elements of national being into a happy unity, where there is no disaffection to the Crown or the Government, where the relations of classes are normal and healthy, where the influence of property is unbroken, and where those who are incapable of judging for themselves find natural leaders of character and intelligence everywhere at their head, can easily bear an amount of democracy which must bring utter ruin upon a country torn by sedition, religious animosities, and agrarian war, in which all the natural ligatures of society have been weakened or disjointed. An amount of democracy which in one country leaves the main direction of affairs in the hands of property and intelligence, in another country virtually disfranchises both, and transfers all controlling authority to an ignorant and excitable peasantry, guided and duped by demagogues, place-hunters, and knaves. A system of criminal law and of criminal procedure which is admirably adapted for a country where crime is nothing more than the outbreak of isolated bad passions, and where every man's hand is against the criminal, must fail to fulfil the first purposes of justice, if it is applied without modification to a country where large classes of crime are commonly looked upon as acts of war, where jurymen will acquit in the face of the clearest evidence, and where known criminals may live in security under the shelter of popular connivance or popular intimidation. In a rich country, in which many generations of uninterrupted prosperity have raised the industrial spirit to the highest point, in which energy and self-reliance are almost redundantly displayed, and in which the middle class is the strongest power in the State, nearly all industrial enterprises may be safely left to the unassisted action of private individuals. It is not so in a very poor country, where the middle class is small and feeble, and where a long train of depressing circumstances have reduced the industrial spirit to the lowest ebb. Perhaps, the worst consequence of the legislative union has been the tendency it produces to measure Irish legislation by English wants and experience, and to force Ireland into a plane of democracy for which it is wholly unfitted. Very different conditions require very different types of administration, and, in Ireland, the elements of self-government lie, and always have lain, within a higher plane and a more restricted circle than in England, and the relations of classes and the conditions of opinion are incomparably less favourable to popular institutions. A stronger and firmer executive, a more restricted suffrage, a greater concentration of power, a more constant intervention of Government both in the way of assistance and initiative, and in the way of restriction and control, is imperatively required.

These essential conditions of Irish politics do not appear to me to have been unrecognised by the statesmen of the Irish Parliament, but they had two great and difficult tasks to fulfil, and the permanence of the Irish Constitution depended mainly upon the question whether in the next few years these tasks could be successfully accomplished. It was necessary to withdraw the direction of affairs from a corrupt but intelligent aristocracy without throwing it into the hands of demagogues and rebels, and it was no less necessary to take some serious step to put an end to the vicious system of religious ascendency without destroying the healthy and indispensable ascendency of property and intelligence.

# VI

## Political Ferment and Catholic Relief, 1790–1793

It was hoped by the English Government that with the recall of the Marquis of Buckingham most of the unpopularity which attached to the system he had pursued would disappear, and the Earl of Westmorland came over with the object of carrying out that system without change. Contrary to the usual custom, Major Hobart, who had been Chief Secretary during the last six months of the Viceroyalty of Buckingham, continued to hold the same office under his successor, and there was no important change in the Administration. Parliament was summoned on January 21, 1790, and a short but very stormy session ensued. An Opposition, numbering about ninety members and led with great ability by Grattan and by George Ponsonby, vehemently arraigned the proceedings of the present ministers under the late Viceroyalty. They complained of the great recent increase in the Pension List, in the number of places and salaries held by members of Parliament, and in the expense of collecting the revenue. They introduced without success a Place Bill, a Pension Bill, a Responsibility Bill, a Bill for disfranchising revenue officers modelled after the English legislation, and they raised a new and very serious question by accusing the late ministers of a systematic sale of peerages. Grattan, in the most explicit terms, charged them with having "not in one or two, but in many instances" made corrupt agreements to recommend politicians for peerages, for money, which was to be employed in the purchase of seats in the House of Commons. Such an act, Grattan truly said, was an impeachable

223

offence, and both he and Ponsonby pledged themselves in the most positive manner to adduce evidence before a committee which would lead to conviction.

The House of Commons, however, at the invitation of the Government refused by 144 votes to 88 to grant a committee of inquiry, and Hobart refused to give any answer when challenged by Grattan, if the charge was unfounded, to declare on his honour that he did not believe such corrupt agreements to have taken place. Defeated in these efforts, the Opposition, shortly before the close of the session, placed some of the chief facts of their case on the journals of the House, in the form of an address to the King. It stated, among other things, that although civil pensions amounting to 14,000*l.* a year had lapsed since the Lady Day of 1784, yet the Pension List was now 16,000*l.* a year higher than at that date; that in the same space of time the expense of collecting the revenue had risen by 105,000*l.;* that no less than forty places or salaries held by members of Parliament had been created or revived within the last twenty years; that, exclusive of pensions, fourteen places and salaries had been created or revived, and distributed among members of Parliament during the last Viceroyalty in a single year, and that out of the 300 members who composed the Irish House of Commons, there were now 108 who were in receipt of salaries or pensions from the Crown.

Though the Opposition failed in shaking the majority of the Government, their speeches had much influence in the country, and as signs of discontent were rapidly approaching, Government thought it wise to hasten the election, and the Parliament was dissolved on April 8. The calculation was a just one, for on the whole the ministry appear to have slightly increased their majority, though for the first time since the death of Lucas they were defeated in the City of Dublin, where Lord Henry Fitzgerald and Grattan triumphed over the Court candidates. Among the new members were Arthur O'Connor the United Irishman, and Barrington the historian of the Irish Parliament; and two young men who were born in the same year, and who were destined for a long period to co-operate in the foremost rank of English politics, now for the first time appeared in public life. Robert Stewart, after a severe contest against the Hillsborough interest, was elected in the popular interest; pledged to vote for a Place

Bill, a Pension Bill, a disfranchisement of revenue officers, and a reform of that Parliament which a few years later, as Lord Castlereagh, he succeeded by the most lavish corruption in over-throwing. Arthur Wellesley, or, as the name was then spelt, Wesley, was already an aide-de-camp at the Castle, and he now took his seat as a supporter of the Government, and appears to have spoken for the first time in seconding an address to the King in January 1793. The new Parliament sat for a fortnight in July in order to pass a vote of credit for 200,000*l.* for the apprehended war with Spain. The vote was carried unanimously, and with the warm approval of Grattan, who only urged that it should be strictly devoted to the military purposes for which it was intended. Parliament was then adjourned and did not sit till the following January.

The signs of combination, agitation, and discontent outside the walls of Parliament were becoming very formidable, and there was a growing conviction that nothing could be done without a real reform of Parliament, and that such a reform could only be achieved by a strong pressure of external opinion. In June 1789 a large number of the principal gentlemen in Ireland, including Charlemont, Grattan, and Ponsonby, formed themselves into a Whig Club for the purpose of maintaining in its integrity the Constitution of 1782; preserving to Ireland "in all time to come a Parliament of her own, residing within the realm and exclusively invested with all parliamentary privileges and powers," and endeavouring by all legal and constitutional means to check the extravagance of Government and its corrupt influence in the Legislature. Their object, as Grattan afterwards said, was "to obtain an internal reform in Parliament, in which they partly succeeded, and to prevent the Union, in which they failed." The new society was as far as possible from being revolutionary or democratic. Among its original members were an archbishop, a bishop, and twelve peers, and among them were the Duke of Leinster, and Lord Shannon, the greatest borough owner of the kingdom. Whatever might be the opinion of its individual members, the club did not as a body demand either a reduction of the franchise, or the abolition of nomination boroughs, or the en-franchisement of the Catholics. The measures it stated to be essential were a Place Bill, a Pension Bill, a Bill to repeal or modify the

Dublin police, a disqualification of revenue officers, and a curtailment of the unnecessary offices which had recently been created, and distributed among members of Parliament.

The Whig Club was warmly eulogised by Burke; and it would have been happy if the conduct of the reform question had rested in hands that were at once so responsible and so moderate. The formation of a powerful and connected party of moderate reformers, pledged to seek by all constitutional means the ends which have been stated, was of no small importance; but it was scarcely possible that in a country situated like Ireland, the democratic and levelling principles with which the French Revolution was now intoxicating the most ardent spirits throughout Europe should not have had an extraordinary power. . . .

The elements of revolution were indeed abundantly provided, and two aspects of the French Revolution had a very special significance for Ireland. It proclaimed as its first principle the abolition of every kind of religious disqualification, and it swept away the whole system of tithes. The triumph of the volunteers in 1782, though it had been used with great moderation, formed a very dangerous precedent of a Legislature overawed or influenced by military force; and the volunteers, though they had dwindled in numbers, and were now generally discountenanced by the better classes, were still a formidable body. In 1790, Charlemont found that the Derry army alone was at least 3,400 strong; and two years later Lord Westmorland ascertained that the volunteer force possessed no less than forty-four cannon. The Presbyterianism of the North, and especially of Belfast, had long been inclined to republicanism. The population of Belfast, according to a paper drawn up by the Government, had increased between 1779 and 1791 from 8,549 to 18,320. A Northern Whig Club was speedily established there, in imitation of that at Dublin, but its timid or moderating counsels were not suited for the political temperature. Towards the close of 1790 the Irish Government sent information to England that a dangerous movement had begun among the volunteers at Belfast. Resolutions had been passed, and papers circulated, advocating the abolition of all tithes, or at least of all tithes paid by Protestant Dissenters and Catholics, as well as a searching reform of Parliament and of Administration; eulogising the "glorious spirit" shown by the French in "adopting the wise system of Republican Government, and abrogating the enormous power and abused influence" of the clergy; inviting the Protestant Dissenters to support the enfranchisement of the Catholics, and to co-operate with the Catholics in advocating parliamentary reform and the abolition of tithes. The volunteers were reminded that whatever constitutional progress Ireland had obtained had been due to them, and they were urged to make every effort at once to fill their ranks.

In July 1791 the anniversary of the French Revolution was celebrated at Belfast with great enthusiasm. All the volunteers of the neighbourhood attended. An address drawn up in a strain of the most fulsome admiration was sent to France. Democratic toasts were drunk, and speeches made eulogising Paine, Washington, and the French Revolution, and demanding an equal representation in Parliament, and the abolition of the remaining Popery laws. A resolution was shortly after drawn up by the first volunteer company, in favour of the abolition of religious disqualifications, and it was responded to by an address of thanks from some Catholic bodies. This was said to have been the first considerable sign of that union of the Presbyterians and Catholics which led to the formation of the United Irish Society. Paine's "Rights of Man" was about the same time widely distributed in the North, and it made many converts. His controversy with Burke "and the gigantic event which gave rise to it changed in an instant the politics of Ireland. . . . In a little time the French Revolution became the text of every man's political creed." "The language and bent of the conduct of these Dissenters," wrote Westmorland in July, "is to unite with the Catholics, and their union would be very formidable. That union is not yet made, and I believe and hope it never could be."

In the September of the same year an extremely able pamphlet appeared under the signature of "A Northern Whig," urging the necessity of a reform of Parliament, and, as a means of attaining it, a close alliance between the Catholics and the Presbyterians. It was written by Theobald Wolfe Tone, a young Protestant lawyer of no small ability, but much more fitted by his daring, adventurous, and enthusiastic character, for military enterprise and for political conspiracy than for the disputes of the law courts. He had for a short time been connected with the Whig Club, but soon broke away from it, and was passionately imbued with the principles of French democracy.

His pamphlet is especially remarkable for the clearness with which it sounded a note which now became common in Irish popular politics—unqualified hatred of the Irish Parliament, and profound contempt for the revolution of 1782. He described that revolution as "the most bungling, imperfect business that ever threw ridicule on a lofty epithet by assuming it unworthily." It doubled the value of the property of every borough owner in the kingdom, but it confessedly left three-fourths of the Irish people without even the semblance of political rights, and the remaining fourth completely helpless in the hands of an alien Government. As all the counties and considerable towns of Ireland combined only returned eighty-two members, the parliamentary direction rested wholly with the purchased borough members. All that had really been effected in 1782 was to increase the corrupt price by which the Government of Ireland was carried on. "Before 1782 England bound us by her edict. It was an odious and not very safe exertion of power, but it cost us nothing. Since 1782 we are bound by English influence acting through our own Parliament," and paid for out of our own resources. In England "the people suffer in theory by the unequal distribution of the elective franchise; but practically it is perhaps visionary to expect a Government that shall more carefully or steadily follow their real interests. No man can there be a minister on any other terms." In Ireland, alone among European countries, the Government is not only unnational but anti-national, conducted by men whose first duty is to represent another nation, and by every method in their power to repress every Irish interest which could in the most distant way interfere with the commerce or policy or patronage of England. This is esteemed the measure of their skill and of their success, and it is always their chief recommendation to the favours of the Crown. How successfully they accomplished their task was sufficiently shown by the fact that the Irish Parliament, by its own law, excluded itself from a commerce with half the known world, in the interest of a monopolising English company, and had just voted a military expenditure of 200,000*l.* to secure the very commerce from which Ireland was for ever excluded. Without a searching parliamentary reform the overwhelming stress of English influence in the Irish Legislature can never be resisted, and it is a wild dream to suppose that such a reform could be attained without the efforts of the whole nation. This was the error which ignominiously wrecked the Convention of 1783 in spite of the genius of Flood, and has left Ireland struck with political paralysis at a time when the spirit of reform has descended on all other nations and when the most inveterate abuses are withering beneath its touch. As long as the Irish sects are at enmity with each other, it will be always easy for the Administration by playing on the fears of the Protestants and the hopes of the Catholics to defy them both. But if the whole body of the people demand a reform of Parliament, which will include the concession of the elective franchise to the Catholics, Ireland will then at last obtain an honest and an independent representation.

It was the main object of this pamphlet to prove that no serious danger would attend the enfranchisement of the Catholics, and that members of the two religions might sit side by side in an Irish Legislature as they did in the French National Assembly and in the American Congress. The last remnants of Jacobitism, he argued, had vanished with the extinction of the Stuarts. "The wealthy and moderate party of the Catholic persuasion with the whole Protestant interest would form a barrier against invasion of property" if any party among the Catholics were mad and wicked enough to attempt it. A national provision for the education of the Catholic priests would remove "that which daily experience shows to be one of the heavy misfortunes of Ireland, that the consciences, the morals, and the religion of the bulk of the nation are in the hands of men of low birth, low feelings, low habits, and no education." The clouds of religious bigotry and intolerance were vanishing rapidly before the great light that had arisen in France. The Catholic gentry were fully fitted for the exercise of power, and considering the great disproportion of property and therefore of power in the hands of Protestants, even a reformed Parliament would consist mainly of Protestants. At the same time Tone added one passage which is not a little remarkable as coming from a writer who in the general type of his politics was an unqualified democrat. "If," he wrote, "there be serious grounds for dreading a majority of Catholics, they may be removed by a very obvious mode. Extend the elective franchise to such Catholics only as have a freehold of ten pounds by the year, and on the other hand strike off the disgrace to our Constitution and our country, the wretched tribe of forty-shilling freeholders whom we see driven to their octennial market by their landlords, as much their property as the sheep or the bullocks which they brand with their names."

It is said that not less than ten thousand copies of this pamphlet were sold, and its teaching was rapidly diffused. The letters of Lord Westmorland show the activity with which papers of the same tenor were disseminated during the summer of 1791; and in October, Wolfe Tone founded at Belfast the first Society of United Irishmen. It consisted of thirty-six original members, and was intended to aim at "an equal representation of all the people of Ireland." It adopted as its first principles three resolutions asserting "that the weight of English influence in the government of this country is so great as to require a cordial union among all the people of Ireland to maintain that balance which is essential to the preservation of our liberties and the extension of our commerce; that the sole constitutional mode by which this influence can be opposed is by a complete and radical reform of the representation of the people in Parliament, and that no reform is just which does not include Irishmen of every religious persuasion." Very soon a branch of the Society was established at Dublin. Napper Tandy, who had long been working as a demagogue in the more obscure forms of Irish agitation, was the Secretary of the Dublin Society. A lawyer named Simon Butler, brother of Lord Mountgarret, was the chairman. A test was adopted which each member of the Society subscribed, pledging him "in the presence of God" to devote all his abilities and influence to the attainment of an impartial and adequate representation of the Irish nation in Parliament, and as a means to this end, to forward a union and co-operation of Irishmen of all religious persuasions. In December, the Society issued a circular letter expounding its principles, and inviting the people of Ireland of all creeds to establish similar societies in every district; and in the beginning of the following year, a newspaper called "The Northern Star," which soon attained a great circulation and influence, was established at Belfast to advocate their views. Its editor was a woollen draper named

Samuel Neilson, a son of a Presbyterian minister, and one of the most active original members of the United Society of Belfast.

The Society of United Irishmen was at first constituted for the simple purpose of forming a political union of Protestants and Catholics, and thus obtaining a liberal measure of parliamentary reform. In the remarkable memoir drawn up after the rebellion, by Thomas Emmet, McNevin, and Arthur O'Connor, which is the clearest and most succinct statement of the views of some of its leading members, it is positively asserted that although from the beginning they clearly perceived "that the chief support of the borough interest in Ireland, was the weight of English influence," the question of separation was not at first so much as agitated among them; that a considerable period elapsed before the conviction that parliamentary reform could not be attained without a revolution, led them, timidly and reluctantly, to republicanism; and that even after a large proportion of the members had become republicans, the whole body would have stopped short at reform.

It is probable that this statement represents truly the opinions of the majority of the first leaders of the Society, but it is certain that there were some among them, who from the beginning were more than mere speculative republicans, and who clearly saw that revolution was the natural issue of their movement. Among these must be reckoned both Wolfe Tone and Napper Tandy. The former has frankly acknowledged in his autobiography, that a desire to break the connection with England was one of his first objects, and that hatred of England was so deeply rooted in his nature that "it was rather an instinct than a principle." The journal which he wrote at Belfast, at the time when he was engaged in founding the Society, shows that he was at that time speculating much on the possibility of Ireland subsisting independently of Great Britain, and on the prosperity she might in that case attain, and in a letter written by him some months earlier, he expressed this opinion most explicitly. "My unalterable opinion," he wrote, "is that the bane of Irish prosperity is in the influence of England. I believe that influence will ever be extended while the connection between the countries continues. Nevertheless, as I know that opinion is for the present too hardy, though a very little time may establish it universally, I have not made it a part of the resolutions; I have only proposed to set up a reformed Parliament as a barrier against that mischief, which every honest man that will open his eyes must see in every instance overbears the interest of Ireland. I have not said one word that looks like a wish for separation, though I give it to you and your friends as my most decided opinion that such an event would be a regeneration to this country."

From the beginning of the French Revolution, Tandy is said to have carried on a correspondence with French agents or politicians, and the Belfast members of the Society appear to have been especially intoxicated by the French Revolution. In general, however, the Society differed from its predecessors rather in tendency than in principle. One of the points most prominent in the confidential correspondence of Tone is his great dislike to the Whig Club, and to the whole type of Whig politics: "They are not sincere friends to the popular cause, they dread the people as much as the Castle does." He described them as peddling with insufficient measures, and he desired above all things that the respect for the names of Charlemont and Grattan should be dismissed, and the conduct of the national movement placed in other and more energetic hands.

The opposition so strongly stated between the two types of policy was a very real one. Grattan was quite as earnest as Tone in advocating the enfranchisement of the Catholics and the reform of Parliament. He was quite as fully convinced that it should be the supreme end of every Irish patriot gradually to blend into a single body the descendants of the conquerors and of the conquered. But in every period of his career he maintained the necessity of the connection with England, and in times of danger and of war there was scarcely any sacrifice he was not prepared to make to support Imperial interests. He had nothing of the French and cosmopolitan sympathies of the English Whigs, and he always made it a vital principle of his Irish policy to discourage all hostility towards England. The spirit of the United Irishmen was from the beginning wholly different. They believed, in opposition to Grattan, that it was possible for Ireland to subsist and flourish as a separate State, and their attitude towards Great

Britain, when it was not one of disaffection and hostility, was at least one of alienation and indifference.

Grattan's theory of parliamentary reform, again, was essentially a Whig one. He looked with undisguised abhorrence on the subversive and levelling theory of government which the French Revolution had introduced into the world; that "Gallic plant," as he picturesquely described it, "whose fruit is death, though it is not the tree of knowledge." He always believed that a country with social and religious divisions, and antecedents of property such as exist in Ireland, is totally unfit for democracy, and he clearly saw that to govern Ireland on democratic principles would lead to political ruin. Although he strenuously maintained that religious belief should not form the line of political division or exclusion, he was in one sense a strong advocate for Protestant ascendency. At every period of his life he contended that Ireland could only be well governed when its political system was so organised that the direction and control of the country was in the hands of Irish property and Irish intelligence. . . .

And a very similar train of thought continually appears in his opposition to the Union. One of his strongest arguments against that measure was that it would do what in Ireland was peculiarly dangerous, take the government of the country out of the hands of the resident gentry, shatter or seriously weaken the authority of property and education, and thus throw the political guidance of the nation into the hands of demagogues and charlatans. I have elsewhere quoted his striking prophecy that Ireland would one day avenge herself for the loss of her Parliament and Constitution by sending into the English Parliament "a hundred of the greatest scoundrels in the kingdom."

This type of policy is not popular in the present day, but it is necessary clearly to understand it, in order to estimate truly the position of Grattan in Irish history. With two or three exceptions the reforming party which followed his banner in Parliament was wholly alien to the spirit of the French Revolution; and even in advocating parliamentary reform, the language of the most prominent members of the party was much more akin to that of Burke than to that of Paine. "The right of universal suffrage," said one of them, "is utterly incompatible with the preservation of property in this country or any other. I know well that the means by which the hands of the many are held off from the possessions of the few are a nice and artificial contrivance of civilised society. The physical strength is theirs already. If we add to that the strength of convention and compact, all is at their mercy." And the same speaker added that the opposition between the French party and the Whig Club in Ireland was so strong that the former would prefer the present system with all its anomalies to Ponsonby's Reform Bill. Among all the considerable politicians in the Irish Parliament, Parsons was the one who in general approached most nearly to the United Irishmen. But on the question of the true principle of representation the language of Parsons was emphatically Whig. "The distemper of the times," he said, "is that most men consider how they shall get political power, not how they shall get good government. . . . Speculators may talk of the right of the many, but the true consideration is the good of the many, and that is to dispose the franchise so that it will produce the best representatives."

The distinction between these views and those of the United Irishmen was very manifest. The Whig Club, as we have seen, originally confined itself to supporting measures of secondary reform, which had been carried in England, such as Pension Bills, Place Bills, and a disqualification of revenue officials; and when at last in 1794 Ponsonby and Grattan introduced a Reform Bill, it was much less ambitious even than the Reform Bills of Flood. It left the suffrage and the duration of Parliament entirely unchanged, but it proposed to give an additional member to each county and to the cities of Dublin and Cork, and to enlarge the constituencies of the boroughs by throwing into them considerable sections of the adjoining country. All these measures proceeded on the assumption that the Constitution of Ireland was essentially a good one, and might be amended without subverting any of its fundamental principles. In the eyes of the United Irishmen the boasted Constitution of Ireland was a mere caricature of representation, and they proposed a complete reconstruction on the most approved principles of French democracy. . . .

While this democratic spirit was rising up among the reformers, a similar spirit was appearing in that body which was especially devoted to the interests of the Catholics. Since the quarrel of 1783 the Catholic Committee had led a very dormant existence, and it was a common feeling that the initiative in matters relating to the Catholics should be left to the Government. This appears to have been the decided opinion of Grattan, who knew that the Opposition were by no means unanimous on the question, and who keenly felt that it would be very unfavourable to the Catholic cause if it were made a party question. The direction of the Catholic body had hitherto been almost altogether in the hands of their prelates, and of a few noblemen—among whom Lord Kenmare was the most conspicuous—closely connected with the Government. But another type of Catholic leader, springing out of the rich trading class, was now appearing, and it found a leader of some ability in John Keogh, a Dublin tradesman, who for many years exercised much influence over Irish politics.

Several circumstances were conspiring to make this party ascendant in the Catholic Committee. Towards the close of 1790 the Catholic Committee waited upon Major Hobart, requesting him to support a petition to Parliament which asked for nothing specific, but simply prayed that the case of the Catholics should be taken into consideration; but their request was refused, and they could not find a single member to present their petition to Parliament. In the course of the same year an address of loyalty, intended to be presented to Lord Westmorland by the Catholics, on the occasion of a visit of the Lord Lieutenant to Cork, was returned to them, because it concluded with a hope that their loyalty would lead to a further relaxation of the penal code. In the beginning of 1791 a deputation from the Catholic Committee went to the Castle with a list of the penal laws which they were anxious to have modified or repealed, but they were dismissed without even the courtesy of an answer.

Lord Kenmare and the leading gentry on the Committee would have gladly desisted from all further agitation; they regarded with extreme aversion the projects of union for the purpose of achieving parliamentary reform held out by the Dissenters, and a quarrel broke out on these points between the two sections of the Committee, which continued during a great part of 1791. At last the party of Lord Kenmare, which included most of the country gentry, proposed a resolution leaving the measure and extent of future relaxations of the disabilities wholly to the Legislature; but the more democratic members of the Committee successfully resisted it. Lord Kenmare and more than sixty of the principal gentry of the party then formally seceded from the Committee, and presented, in December 1791, a separate address to the Lord Lieutenant, asking for a further repeal of the laws affecting the Catholics, but leaving the extent wholly to the Legislature. The original Committee thus passed completely under the influence of the more democratic party, and it was noticed as a symptom of the new spirit appearing in the Catholic body, that resolutions were passed in almost all the counties and large towns of the kingdom approving of its conduct, and censuring the sixty-eight seceders.

The great and rapid growth of the Catholic commercial interest is one of the facts most constantly adverted to in the early years of George III, and it had given a new independence to the Catholic body. Their political importance had been greatly increased by the tendency to unite the Catholic question with the question of parliamentary reform which had appeared among the reformers of the North, and a considerable amount of new and energetic life was infused into the Catholic Committee by an election which took place in the spring of 1790. The position of the Catholics was, it is true, very different from what it had been twenty years before, but it may be questioned whether their sense of their grievances had proportionately abated. They were no longer a crushed, torpid, impoverished body with scarcely any interest in political affairs. The relaxations that enabled them to live in peace, and the industrial prosperity that enabled them to acquire wealth, education, and local importance, had retained in the country enterprising and ambitious men who in a former generation would have sought a career in France, or Austria, or Spain. Every great movement which had taken place since the accession of George III had contributed to deepen their sense of the anomaly of their position. The Octennial Act had created a strong political life in Ireland, but the Catholics alone were excluded from its benefits. The American struggle had made it a commonplace of politics that representation and taxation were inseparably connected, but the denomination which included some four-fifths of the Irish people did not possess the smallest control over the national revenue. The Revolution of 1782 had placed Ireland, ostensibly at least, in the rank of free and self-governed kingdoms, but it left the Catholics with no more political rights than the serfs of Russia or of Poland. The very law that enabled them to acquire land, made them more sensible of the disqualification, which in their case alone, deprived land of the franchise which the Constitution had annexed to it. The French Revolution had persuaded multitudes that government is the inalienable right of the majority, and even among those who repudiated the principles of Rousseau and Paine, it had greatly raised the standard of political requirements, and increased the hostility to political inequalities and disqualifications.

It was impossible, indeed, that in such a state of society, intelligent Catholics could contemplate their own position in Ireland without feelings of the keenest humiliation and resentment. Though they represented the immense majority of the people, they were wholly excluded from the executive, from the legislative, from the judicial powers of the State; from all right of voting in parliamentary and municipal elections; from all control over the national expenditure; from all share in the patronage of the Crown. They were marked out by the law as a distinct nation, to be maintained in separation from the Protestants, and in permanent subjection to them. Judged by the measure of its age, the Irish Parliament had shown great liberality during the last twenty years, but the injury and the insult of disqualification still met the Catholic at every turn. From the whole of the great and lucrative profession of the law he was still absolutely excluded, and by the letter of the law the mere fact of a lawyer marrying a Catholic wife and educating his children as Catholics incapacitated him from pursuing his profession. Land and trade had been thrown open to Catholics almost without restrictions, but the Catholic tenant still found himself at a frequent disadvantage, because he had no vote and no influence with those who administered local justice, and the Catholic trader because he had no voice in the corporations of the towns. Catholics had begun to take a considerable place among the moneyed men of Ireland; but when the Bank of Ireland was founded in 1782, it was specially provided that no Catholic might be enrolled among its directors. Medicine was one of the few professions from which they had never been excluded, and some of them had risen to large practice in it, but even here they were subject to galling distinctions. They were incapacitated from holding any of the three medical professorships on the University establishment, or any of the four professorships at the School of Physic, or the more recently created clinical professorship; and the law, while excluding native Catholics from these professorships, actually ordered that, for three months previous to the nomination to a vacancy in them, invitations should be circulated through Europe inviting Protestants of all nations to compete for them. Catholic physicians were excluded from all situations on the army establishment, from the offices of State physician or surgeon, and from a crowd of places held under charter, patent, or incorporation; and as they could not take the rank of Fellow in the College of Physicians, they were unable to hold any office in that body.

The social effects of the code continued with little abatement, though mere theological animosity had almost died away. The political helplessness of the lower orders in their relation with the upper classes had injuriously affected the whole tone of manners, and the few Catholic gentry could not but feel that they were members of an inferior class, living under the stigma and the disqualifications of the law. Most Catholics who had risen to wealth had done so as merchants or cattle dealers, and the mercantile classes in Ireland had very little social position. The old Catholic gentry lived much apart, and had but small intercourse with the Protestants. The exclusion of Catholics from the bar was in this respect peculiarly mischievous, for of all professions the bar is that which does most to bring men of various religions into close and frequent contact. There were convivial clubs in Ireland in which it was a by-law that no Papist should be admitted, and Burke, probably, scarcely exaggerated when he asserted that there were thousands of persons of the upper orders in Ireland, who had never in their lives conversed with a Catholic, unless they happened to talk to their gardener's workmen, or to ask their way, when they had lost it, in their sports.

It was quite evident that such a state of society was thoroughly unnatural and demoralising, and it was equally evident that it could not possibly be permanent. One great work of the Irish Parliament during the past generation had been the gradual removal of religious disqualifications and monopolies, but the most serious part of the task was still to be accomplished, and the French Revolution had forced on the question, to an immediate issue. The process of slow enfranchisements, which had once been gratefully received, was scarcely possible in the changed condition of the public mind. A declaration issued by the Catholic Committee in October 1791, demanding in strong terms a complete abolition of all parts of the penal code, was a significant sign of the new spirit which had arisen, and it was evident that the principles of the North had found some lodgment in the minds of the new Catholic leaders. The Catholic Committee was reorganised, and placed more completely under the influence of the democratic party; and despairing of help from the Administration of Ireland, it resolved to send a deputation to England. The resolution was accomplished, and in January 1792 Keogh and four other delegates laid the petition of the Catholics before the King.

The task which now lay before the ministers was one which demanded the highest statesmanship, and the whole future history of Ireland depended mainly on the manner in which it was accomplished. If the enfranchisement of the Catholics could be successfully carried out, if the chasm that yawned between the two great sections of the Irish people could be finally bridged, if an identity of interests and sympathies could be established between the members of the two creeds, Ireland would indeed become a nation, and she might reasonably look forward to a continuous growth of power and prosperity. If on the other hand the task was tardily or unskilfully accomplished, there were dangers of the most terrible and the most permanent character to be feared. Religious animosities and class antipathies which had long been slumbering might be revived in all their fierceness. The elements of anarchy and agitation which lay only too abundantly in a population poor, ignorant, turbulent, and superstitious beyond almost any in Europe, might be let loose and turned into politics. The Catholics of Ireland, who had hitherto scarcely awakened to political life, and whose leaders had been uniformly loyal, and much more inclined to lean toward the English Government than towards the Irish Parliament, might be permanently alienated from the connection. In the clash of discordant elements, Ireland might be once more cursed with the calamities of civil war; and confiscations and penal laws had placed landed property so exclusively in the hands of the ascendant class, that a danger still graver than rebellion might be feared. It was that which Burke truly called "the most irreconcilable quarrel that can divide a nation—a struggle for the landed property of the whole kingdom."

While the sentiments I have described were rapidly extending among the more intelligent Catholics and among the Presbyterians of the North, the governing classes in Ireland experienced a full measure of that dread of reform and innovation which the French Revolution had made predominant among men in authority. The Catholic question now presented itself to them, not as in 1778 and 1782 as a question of religious toleration, and of the removal of penal inflictions, but as a question of the transfer of political power and of the destruction of an old monopoly of representation. It was also avowedly and ostentatiously associated with the demand for a searching parliamentary reform which would break down the system of nomination boroughs, and establish the representation on a broad popular basis. No prospect could be more alarming to the small group of men who controlled the Government and almost monopolised the patronage of Ireland. The Chancellor, Fitzgibbon, was steadily opposed to all concessions to the Catholics, and he devoted his great ability and his arrogant but indomitable will to rallying the party of the Opposition. The Beresfords, the Elys, and several other of the great borough owners, and in general the officials who were most closely connected with the Castle, were equally violent in their opposition. . . .

*The question of enfranchising Irish Catholics deeply divided politicians in both Dublin and London. Edmund Burke's Catholic sympathies moved him to support political emancipation for qualified Catholics. In 1790 his only son, Richard, became secretary of the influential Catholic Committee. Pitt and his colleagues in the Cabinet feared the consequences of a coalition of aggrieved Catholics and radical Presbyterians in Ulster. To prevent such a popular front, he tried to ease certain restrictions against Catholics. The Irish administration reluctantly accepted most of his recommendations but balked at the enfranchisement of respectable Catholics. Lord Westmorland persuaded Pitt not to jeopardize*

*the Protestant Ascendancy by granting Catholics a measure of*
*political power at that time, and the franchise scheme was dropped*
*by the wayside.*

The chief members of the Irish Government made it their
deliberate object to revive the religious animosities which had so
greatly subsided, to raise the standard of Protestant ascendency,
and to organise through the country an opposition to concession.
How little religious bigotry there had of late been in the great
body of the Irish Protestants was clearly shown by the facility with
which the Relief Acts of 1778 and 1782 were carried; by the
resolutions in favour of the Catholics passed by the volunteers,
who more than any other body represented the uninfluenced
sentiments of the Protestants of Ireland; by the recent attitude of
the Presbyterians and especially of Belfast, which was the centre
of the most decided Protestantism. That these sentiments, in spite
of the exertions of the Castle, were not yet very materially
changed appears to me conclusively proved by the fact that the
concession of Catholic franchise, which was pronounced utterly
impossible in 1792, was carried without the smallest difficulty in
1793, and by the fact that nothing but the recall of Lord Fitzwilliam prevented the admission of Catholics into the Irish
Parliament in 1795. There were, no doubt, some independent
opponents of great weight. The Speaker was strongly opposed to
the Catholic claims, and so was Sir Edward Newenham, who had
been prominent among the followers of Flood; but the strength of
the Opposition consisted mainly of placemen under the leadership
of Fitzgibbon.

Fitzgibbon was the first Irishman to whom Westmorland
hinted the intentions of the Government, and Fitzgibbon was
opposed to all further concessions to Catholics. The chief borough
owners connected with Government agreed with him, and although they could not prevent the introduction of a Relief Bill in
1792, they succeeded in greatly limiting its provisions, and in
depriving it of the grace and authority of a Government measure.
It was seconded, indeed, by Hobart, but it was introduced by Sir
Hercules Langrishe, a private member, though a steady supporter
of the Government, and one of the oldest and steadiest friends
of the Catholics. It enabled the Catholics to be attorneys, solicitors,

notaries, and attorneys' clerks, and to practise at the bar, though they could not rise to the position of King's counsel or judge. It repealed the laws prohibiting barristers from marrying Catholics, and solicitors from educating their children as Catholics; the laws of William and Anne directed against the intermarriage of Catholics and Protestants; the obsolete Act against foreign education; and the equally obsolete clause of the Act of 1782, which made the licence of the ordinary necessary for Catholic schools; and finally it removed all restrictions on the number of apprentices permitted to Catholic trade.

The concessions fell far short of the Catholic expectations, but the ascendency spirit which had been evoked, stimulated, and supported by the Administration, now ran very high. . . .

*Unappeased by token concessions, the Catholic Committee stepped up its campaign to enfranchise Catholics. Their demands alarmed the Ascendancy which already felt threatened by the turn of events in France.*

In the course of the discussion of the Catholic question, the words Legislative Union were more than once pronounced. There were rumours that if the Catholic suffrage was granted, the Protestants in alarm would endeavour to obtain one. Burke mentions the persistence of the report, and while pronouncing his own opinion that a Legislative Union would not be for the mutual advantage of the two kingdoms, he thought that Pitt himself would have no desire to see a large body of Irish members introduced into Westminster. Grattan spoke of the possibility of a legislative union being effected by giving the Catholics the prospect of enfranchisement, and at the same time acting on the fears of the Protestants. He regarded such a measure with the most unqualified hostility, and maintained that it would be fraught with the worst consequences not only to Ireland, but to the Empire. "It would be fatal to England, beginning with a false compromise which they might call a union to end in eternal separation, through the progress of two civil wars." Curran spoke of a possible union with equal apprehension, predicting that it would mean the emigration of every man of consequence from Ireland, a participation of British taxes without British trade, and the extinction of the Irish name as a people.

It is a curious subject of inquiry whether the idea of a legislative union had at this time taken any hold of the mind of Pitt, and this inquiry I am fortunately able to answer. Replying to a question in a despatch of Westmorland, which has been already quoted, he wrote: "The idea of the present fermentation gradually bringing both parties to think of an union with this country has long been in my mind. I hardly dare flatter myself with the hope of its taking place, but I believe it, though itself not easy to be accomplished, to be the only solution for other and greater difficulties. The admission of Catholics to a share of suffrage could not then be dangerous. The Protestant interest in point of power, property, and Church Establishment would be secure, because the decided majority of the supreme Legislature would necessarily be Protestant, and the great ground of argument on the part of the Catholics would be done away; as compared with the rest of the Empire they would become a minority. You will judge when and to whom this idea can be confided. It must certainly require great delicacy and management, but I am heartily glad that it is at least in your thoughts."

In spite of the fears and predictions of the Lord Lieutenant, Langrishe's Bill passed through Parliament with scarcely any opposition, and although the Catholic petition for the franchise was rejected by 208 to 23, no pledge against the future extension was given by or required from the Government. . . .

The form of government, indeed, which had for a long time existed in Ireland only bore a faint and distant resemblance to a representative system. Between 1585 and 1692 there had been intervals amounting altogether to nearly eighty-five years during which no Irish Parliament sat. During nearly two-thirds of the eighteenth century the members of the House of Commons held their seats for the entire reign. The House of Lords was so constituted that it did not possess even a semblance of independence. At one time the bishops, who were appointed directly by the Crown, formed a majority of its active members. At other times the constant stream of ministerial partisans that was poured into it had made all real opposition an impossibility. It was chiefly important in Irish parliamentary history as an assembly of borough owners, and its moral authority was so low, that the restitution of its right of final judicature in 1782 was regarded by some good judges as a most dubious benefit. The anomalies of the borough system were not, as in England, chiefly the result of decay or time, but of innumerable creations under the Stuarts, made for the express purpose of rendering the Legislature completely subservient to the Crown. The same system in a different form had since then been steadily pursued whenever any symptoms of independence appeared. It had been the admission or rather the boast of the man who was now Lord Chancellor of Ireland, that in the contest under Lord Townshend, half a million of money had been expended in purchasing a majority. The declaration of 1782 made the Irish Parliament in theory independent, but it was the first object of the ministers to regain in influence everything which had been lost in prerogative, and it seemed idle to expect that a Reform Bill could be carried through the two Houses without their concurrence. Flood, as the representative and inspirer of the Volunteer Convention of 1783, had endeavoured by the display of military force to overawe the Government and the Parliament, and through fear of a rebellion to force through a measure of reform. It was a step, dangerous, unconstitutional, and exceedingly likely to produce a civil war, but it might have been successful. It failed mainly because Grattan and the more moderate reformers refused to support it. The volunteers were induced to dissolve their convention, to lay aside their arms, and to trust to the Government to carry out a measure which was plainly demanded by public opinion, and necessary if the Constitution of 1782 was to become a reality. The result of their forbearance was that the system of corruption was steadily aggravated, and the influence of the Government was steadily exerted in opposition to reform. On the Regency question, it is true, Parliament broke away from ministerial control, but no one seriously believed that it would have done so had it not been supposed that the King was hopelessly incapacitated, and that there was likely to be in consequence a permanent transfer of patronage and power. And no sooner had the Government triumphed than they resolved to render the Parliament even more corrupt and subservient than before, and no less than fourteen parliamentary places were created in a single year. Under the forms of constitutional Government the spirit was thus almost wholly lost, and the property, the intelligence, the opinions of the country had not much more than a casual or precarious influence over legislation. . . .

From an English point of view the divisions and ferment in Ireland appeared not altogether an evil. It had always been a leading English object to induce the Irish Parliament to support as large an army as possible, and the present time seemed well fitted for carrying out this object. "The augmentation of the army is a point that I believe, if the agitation continues, would meet with the universal approbation of the Protestants . . . and I am convinced they would be equally ready to incur any expense that may be rendered necessary." Another remark, which is certainly not less significant, occurs in a later letter: "The Protestants frequently declare they will have a union rather than give the franchise to the Catholics; the Catholics that they will have a union rather than submit to their present state of degradation. It is worth turning in your mind how the violence of both parties might be turned on this occasion to the advantage of England."

On the whole, up to the close of November the situation, though anxious, did not appear to the Lord Lieutenant seriously alarming. "If some pains are not taken to prevent it," he wrote, "there will be a very general spirit of volunteering with the Protestants . . . owing to the opinion I have so often told you, that the British Government means to desert them. Every intelligence that reaches me respecting the Catholics bears the most pacific appearance. . . . The mind of the people is certainly very much heated by political discussions, and therefore one cannot foretell what may occur out of fortuitous circumstances, but no one fact has yet reached me, that manifested any plan for insurrection from the Catholics. The regular formation of a government, and correspondence with one another, seems to be more alarming and more difficult to counteract." Reports were persistently sent from England to the effect that arms had been largely imported into Ireland, but these reports after very careful investigation appeared either greatly exaggerated or wholly false. The real disaffection was confined to a few, though there was agitation and alarm over a great area. . . .

*The two momentous issues of Catholic suffrage and parliamentary reform gave Irish politics an even more partisan flavor.*

*Outside Parliament only a few food riots disturbed the country
during 1792. Westmorland continued to oppose major concessions to Catholics, while Pitt contemplated the possibility of a
union joining the legislatures of the two countries.*

French affairs were now beginning to influence Irish politics
as powerfully as American affairs had done ten years before. The
passionate enthusiasm which the principles of the Revolution had
produced among large classes, rose higher and higher when it
became evident that almost all Europe was likely to be involved
in the struggle. The insulting manifesto of the Duke of Brunswick, the invasion of French territory and the capture of Verdun,
were speedily followed by the check of the Prussians at Valmy,
and by the ignominious retreat of the allied army across the Rhine.
French soldiers entered Worms, Mentz, and Frankfort: Savoy
and Nice were annexed. Royalty in France was abolished, and
the triumphant Republic held out the promise of support and
brotherhood to every suffering nationality in Europe. In November, the great victory of Jemmapes placed Austrian Flanders at its
feet; and before the year had closed, the French power extended
to the frontier of Holland. England was now rapidly arming, and
it was becoming more and more evident that she would soon be
drawn into the war.

The effects of these events in Ireland were soon felt. The new
spirit of volunteering which the Lord Lieutenant had deplored,
and which he still ascribed chiefly to the Protestant dread of the
Catholics, continued to increase, and it was evident that it was
assuming a republican form. In July, a great meeting of the volunteers and inhabitants of Belfast, numbering about six thousand,
voted unanimously an address to the French nation congratulating
them on the capture of the Bastille, and also an address in favour
of the Catholic claims, and it was observed that some of the most
popular Dissenting ministers of the district spoke strongly in
their favour. In Dublin a new military association was formed,
modelled after the French National Guards and openly avowing
republican principles. Napper Tandy, Hamilton, Oliver Bond,
and Henry Jackson, appear to have been the chief organisers.
They adopted as their emblem the harp without a crown, surmounted with the cap of liberty. It was intended to form three

battalions, and it was reported that they were to bind themselves not to lay down their arms till they had obtained the privileges desired by the Catholics and a reform of Parliament, and that similar battalions were to be formed at Belfast and Derry. . . . Grattan, like the other leaders of the old reform party in Parliament, was extremely anxious that the questions of reform and Catholic emancipation should be dissociated from disloyal and republican principles. He strongly censured the conduct of the new national guard in adopting republican emblems, declaring that though he wished the ministers of the Crown changed, the Crown itself was very essential to the prosperity of Ireland. He was decidedly in favour of the Catholic Convention, but his advice to the Catholics was beyond all things to avoid "republican principles and French politics," and he warned them that men connected with the Irish Government were representing them as in a state of rebellion probably in order to induce the English to assist in crushing them. He refused to join the United Irishmen, but as the Whig Club had declined to commit itself to the two measures which he now deemed imperatively necessary, a new association called the "Friends of the Constitution" was formed in December 1792, under the presidency of the Duke of Leinster. It was probably imitated from the society of "The Friends of the People," which had been established a few months earlier in England by Sheridan and Grey, and it was intended to promote in every way Catholic emancipation and parliamentary reform, while resisting all republican innovations. Grattan saw clearly that the ties of influence that bound the Catholics to their gentry were severely strained, and he feared greatly that the Government policy would give a confirmed ascendency to new and dangerous influences, which might one day precipitate the Catholic body into a career of rebellion.

The danger was indeed obvious. On the one side the Catholics found the Irish Government surrounded and supported by the men who were the most vehement and the most powerful opponents of their enfranchisement. Fitzgibbon, the Beresfords, the Elys, the great body of the large borough owners who were the pillars of the oligarchical system in Ireland, contended that the Catholics should be absolutely excluded from all share of political power. They had steadily exerted their influence against them both in the Parliament, in the Privy Council, and in the country. Men connected with or trusted by the Government had originated or stimulated the recent movement of the grand juries and county meetings, which had done so much to revive the smouldering embers of religious animosity. Nor did it appear probable that their sentiments would change, for they believed, and justly believed, that the continued subjection of the Catholics was essential to the maintenance of their political monopoly. On the other hand a party supported by a great part of the Dissenters of the North were labouring in the first place to abolish that oligarchical monopoly, and to replace it by a democratic representation entirely irrespective of religious distinctions, and in the next place to abolish the system of tithes, which was the greatest practical grievance, both of the poorer Catholics and of the Presbyterians. And this party was now offering its alliance to the Catholics.

Some steps of approximation soon took place. Simon Butler, the chairman of the United Irishmen, drew up and published by the direction of the society a digest of the Popery laws in Ireland, which exercised a powerful influence on opinion by its clear statement of the number and magnitude of the disabilities under which, at least by the letter of the law, the Catholics still laboured. The United Irishmen gladly admitted Catholics among their members, and they issued many addresses advocating complete emancipation. Keogh, who was the ablest of the new Catholic leaders, was a regular attendant at the meetings of the United Irishmen, and in the spring of 1792 Wolfe Tone, the founder of the United Irishmen, and one of the most active republicans in Ireland, became paid secretary of the Catholic Committee in the place of Richard Burke. He owed his appointment to the brilliant pamphlet which he had published in the previous September, and he has recorded the interesting fact that when that pamphlet was published he did not reckon a single Catholic among his acquaintances.

On the Presbyterian side the tendency towards Catholic alliance was very marked. It was shown not only by the growing power of the United Irishmen and by many successive demonstrations at Belfast, but also by the significant fact that a large number of the most popular Presbyterian ministers were active members of the new party. At the same time it is no doubt true, that the primary object of the Presbyterians was not Catholic emancipation but parliamentary reform; that they had in general very little natural sympathy with Catholics; that their true and governing motive was the conviction that the existing system of oligarchical and English ascendency could only be destroyed by a cordial union of the whole Irish people. Though written with directly opposite aims and wishes, the confidential letters of Lord Westmorland agree curiously with the writings of Wolfe Tone and the other leading United Irishmen in their judgment of the situation. They both contended that a real union between the different religious sects in Ireland, and the introduction of Catholics into political life, would inevitably lead to a reform of Parliament, which would destroy at once the oligarchical ascendency and the controlling influence of the English Executive over the Irish Parliament, and would induce Irish statesmen to regulate their policy mainly by the public opinion of their own country. It was the Belfast doctrine that the English Government desired to keep the people divided in order to govern them, and that to put an end to this division should be the first object of every Irish patriot. . . .

*There was no noticeable disaffection or disloyalty among the Catholic populace in the countryside. The Convention summoned by the Catholic Committee met in Dublin on 3 December 1792 and promptly adopted a moderate platform. But the Convention did insist upon petitioning the King directly on behalf of Catholic relief. Apprehensive of radicals who sympathized with the French Revolution, the Government took steps to ban all popular demonstrations.*

Ulster had caught the passion for reform, but though much speculative republicanism may have existed among the Presbyterians, and though most of the United Irishmen may have convinced themselves that reform could only be extorted by revolution, there were probably very few who would not have been contented with reform. The same assertion may be made still more confidently of the Catholic democracy of the towns, while the great body of the Catholics were as yet almost untouched by politics and completely subservient to landlords and prelates who were devoted to the connection, and extremely hostile to republican ideas. The Catholic prelates were now cordially in favour of the Convention, and the reconciliation of the seceding party to the old Committee had effectually moderated its proceedings. It was plain, however, that large measures of reform were required, and would the Protestants of the Established Church who had the ascendency in Ireland consent to carry them? The Catholic question, as we have seen, had been excluded from the objects of the Whig Club, and when an attempt was made in November to take it into consideration, the resolution was negatived by a majority of thirteen. The Association of the "Friends of the Constitution," however, which was a purely Protestant body presided over by the Duke of Leinster, and supported by Grattan, made "an effectual reform in the representation of the people in Parliament, including persons of all religious persuasions," its first object.

A clear distinction must here be drawn between the main body of the country gentlemen, lawyers, and yeomen, and the small group of great borough owners who chiefly controlled the Parliament. There is reason to believe that Grattan truly represented the former, and that a majority at least were quite prepared for Catholic enfranchisement. It is true that the cry of danger to property held under the Act of Settlement had been raised by Fitzgibbon, and had influenced some considerable minds, but there is I think no evidence that it had spread very far. The fact that in our own day popular Irish politics have taken the form of an organised attack upon landed property, will probably mislead those who do not consider how widely the events which we have witnessed, differ from those which were feared in 1792. In our generation a small body of Irish landlords, divested through legislation and social changes of their former political power, and at the same time firmly attached to the connection and the Union, have found themselves confronted by an organisation which was hostile to both, and which accordingly made the expatriation and ruin of the class who were the chief supporters of the English connection one of its main objects. Having signally failed in obtaining the support of the great mass of the Irish tenantry by appeals to national or anti-English sentiment, it skilfully resorted to the policy of appealing to their cupidity; it gave the movement an essentially agrarian character by making it a war against rents, and it thus succeeded for a time in combining them in a dishonest compact to refuse the payment of their debts. The movement was favoured by a period of genuine distress; by some undoubted acts of landlord harshness, committed chiefly by men who had purchased land at the invitation of the Government under the Encumbered Estates Act, and who treated it as an ordinary form of investment; by the system of party government which gives a wholly disproportionate power to isolated groups of members, who are indifferent to the interests of the Empire; and especially by the passing of a land law which was popularly attributed to the agitation, and which had the undoubted effect of confusing the ownership of land, and of transferring without compensation to one class of the community, a portion of the legal property of another.

But the question in 1792 was not one between landlords and tenants. It was whether existing titles could be seriously disputed by the descendants of those who had been deprived of their properties by the Act of Settlement. The great majority of the descendants of the old families had long since been scattered over the Continent. Nearly one hundred and thirty years had elapsed since the Act that was complained of. Innumerable purchasers, leaseholders, mortgagees, and other encumbrancers had grafted new interests on the existing titles. The security of a great part of the property of the Catholics of Ireland was inextricably blended with them, and the tenantry and the labourers would have gained nothing by their overthrow. Under such circumstances an attempt to impugn them might well be deemed in the highest degree improbable, and the success of such an attempt almost impossible.

But apart from this, the Protestant gentry had little to lose and much to gain by Catholic enfranchisement. The hierarchy of middle men which rose between the cottier and the owner of the soil was a great economical evil, but it at least saved the landowning class from the invidious isolation which is now the great source of their weakness and their unpopularity. Their political ascendency over their tenants was indisputable, and an Act which multiplied the voters on their estates tended directly to their political importance. On grounds of interest they had no reason to regret the destruction of the corrupt oligarchical monopoly which had so greatly dwarfed their consequence. On public grounds they had every reason to desire it. They had always murmured against the system of tithes, and their theological feelings were extremely languid.

That the great borough owners were, as a rule, strongly opposed to Catholic enfranchisement is unquestionable, and this fact was the chief difficulty of the situation. It was, however, contended by the supporters of the Catholics that the influence of the Government on this class was overwhelming; that the opposition to Catholic enfranchisement drew its real force from the countenance which was given to it by the leading members of the Irish Government, and that if the Government pronounced decidedly in favour of the measure, all serious opposition to it would melt away. . . .

*By November 1792, Pitt had decided to go ahead with his original plan for enfranchising Catholics who met the property qualifications. With some trepidation the Government forced the Irish Parliament to take up the question of Catholic suffrage. A stormy debate ensued in the Commons after the Speech from the Throne on 10 January 1793, and it soon became clear that Parliament would not consider Catholic emancipation unless accompanied by a measure of parliamentary reform.*

On February 4 Hobart moved for leave to bring in his Catholic Relief Bill, and stated the nature of its provisions. It was of a kind which only a year before would have appeared utterly impossible, and which was in the most glaring opposition to all the doctrines which the Government and its partisans had of late been urging. He proposed to give Catholics the franchise both in towns and in country on exactly the same terms as Protestants; to repeal the laws which still excluded them from grand juries except when there was not a sufficient number of Protestant freeholders, and from petty juries in causes between Protestants and Papists; to authorise them to endow colleges, universities, and schools, and to obtain degrees in Dublin University, and to remove any provisions of the law which might still impose disabilities upon them respecting personal property. He proposed to enable them to become magistrates, to vote for magistrates in corporations, and to carry arms, subject, however, to a property qualification. They were also, with the concurrence of the English Government, to be admitted to bear commissions in the army and navy, and with a few specified exceptions all civil offices were to be thrown open to them.

This great measure was before Parliament, with several intermissions, for rather more than five weeks. The chief arguments on both sides have been already given, but the true state and division of opinions is a question of much interest and of some difficulty. If we judged only by the letters from the Castle, we should infer that the majority of the House would gladly have conceded nothing, and there is strong reason to believe that the Irish Government, during the greater part of the time when the question was pending, made it a main object to alarm as much as possible the ministers in England, and to induce them to recede from the position they had taken. On the other hand it is a simple fact that this great and complicated measure, which revolutionised the whole system of government in Ireland, and presented so many openings for attack, passed through Parliament almost entirely unmodified, and without even any serious opposition. The vital clause giving the unlimited franchise to Catholics was the most contested, and it was carried by 144 to 72. . . .

In truth, the long agitation of O'Connell has given the admission of Catholics to Parliament an altogether factitious magnitude in the public mind. It was the culmination of a long struggle for political equality, but in real importance it was immeasurably inferior to the Irish Act of 1793, which gave the great bulk of the Irish Catholics the franchise. Catholic constituencies have never found any difficulty in obtaining Protestants to act as their instruments, and with the leverage which was now obtained they were certain to obtain the rest. One member predicted, with admirable accuracy, the event which took place in Clare in 1828. "Suppose," said Ormsby, "the electors should choose a Roman Catholic and persist in returning him, as in the case of Mr. Wilkes in England, the House would then be committed with the people, a situation which he was sure they did not desire." Few greater mistakes of policy could be made than to give political equality to the great mass of ignorant Catholics, who were for the most part far below political interests, and at the same time to refuse it to the Catholic gentry. The continued disability was certain to produce renewed agitation, and it was equally certain that this agitation would be ultimately successful. The disability fell on the very class which would feel it most keenly and which deserved it least. Whatever controversy there might be about the sentiments of the mass of the Catholic peasantry or of the Catholic priesthood, there was at least no question that the few Catholic gentry of Ireland had shown themselves for generations uniformly and almost effusively loyal. The presence of ten or twenty members of this class in Parliament would have had a conciliatory effect out of all proportion to its real importance, and it could have had no effect but for good. "By giving the Catholics equality of suffrage," said Hamilton, "with the Protestants, Parliament would invest the lower, the more numerous, and of course the less enlightened part of the Catholic community with that privilege which must in fact include every other; and yet if it went no farther it would establish an exclusion which, even if it were desirable, must be but temporary and ineffectual, against the higher and more enlightened order, against those men who had the deepest stake in the country, and who from every motive of interest and ambition must be pledged, as much as they were themselves, for its prosperity and advantage." "I should be sorry," added the same speaker, "if the disseminators of sedition should have it in their power to tell the people that Parliament had not followed the example of their constituents, who had generously offered the participation of their rights to their fellow-subjects of every description, while their representatives persisted in retaining an exclusive monopoly. . . . Every motive of expediency and wisdom suggested to the House that this was the moment when every distinction should be done away."

These appear to me to have been words of wisdom, and there was another argument which was not less weighty. As I have already shown, Grattan had always foreseen that by far the greatest danger which the peculiar circumstances of Ireland foreshadowed, was that the ignorant and excitable Catholic population might be one day detached from the influence of property and respectability, and might become a prey to designing agitators and demagogues. By giving full political power to the Catholic democracy, and at the same time withholding political power and influence from the Catholic gentry, the legislation of 1793 materially hastened this calamity, and it was in the long popular agitation for Catholic emancipation that the foundation was laid for the political anarchy of our own day. . . .

*A motion to allow Catholics to sit in Parliament was defeated by 163 to 69 early in 1793. Sir Lawrence Parsons, one of the more enlightened landowners of King's County, made a memorable speech on the need for a rational approach to both emancipation and reform of the representative system in Ireland.*

The question of Catholic franchise was a very difficult one, owing to the fact that the Protestants already possessed the forty-shilling freehold franchise. At a time when all political power was in the hands of a small section of the Irish people, and when Ireland was especially suffering from the evils of extreme monopoly, a democratic Protestant suffrage in the counties was not altogether incapable of defence. It corresponded in some measure to the democratic scot and lot franchise, which existed in some of the English towns before the Reform Bill of 1832. But on the whole it was quite clear that the great mass of the forty-shilling freeholders out of Ulster were utterly unfit for political power; and in a country where the difficulties of government were unusually great, it would be a grave calamity if this class of men became the source or foundation of all political power. In several speeches made during the debates this danger was clearly recognised, and by no one more clearly than by Forbes, who was one of the ablest and most consistent of the reformers. Forbes maintained, however, that the evil of withholding the franchise from the Catholic forty-shilling freeholder, while it was conceded to his Protestant neighbour, would be still greater; that it would prevent the political union and amalgamation of creeds, which was the first object of the measure; that it would embody the excluded Catholics for the purpose of destroying the limitation, and that "nothing was so dangerous in a State as an unequal distribution of constitutional privileges."

There was, it is true, another alternative, which was suggested by Hely Hutchinson, who said that, "to prevent the influx of small freeholders and any disparity between Protestants and Catholics, he would wish that ten-pound freeholds were made indispensable to voters of all persuasions." A clause to this effect was actually proposed by Graydon, but withdrawn at the joint request of Hobart and Grattan. It was indeed plainly impracticable. A period in which the democratic and levelling spirit ran so high was not one in which a great measure of disfranchisement could be safely carried. The policy of uniting the Protestants and Catholics would certainly not succeed, if the admission of Catholics to the Constitution was purchased by the disfranchisement of the majority of Protestant voters, and a large part of the Protestant forty-shilling freeholders in the North were not mainly employed in agriculture, and were eminently fitted for the franchise. "Gentlemen talk of prohibiting forty-shilling freeholders from voting," said Foster; "they will not attempt so wild a project when they consider it. What! to disfranchise nearly two-thirds of all the Protestants! to disfranchise those persons who sent them into this House! The law in their favour had existed since Henry VI, and now forms a principle of the Constitution. Did the gentlemen who lived in the North recollect that this would disfranchise all their manufacturers? . . . Did they wish to force manufacturers to look for ten-pound freeholds? They would be spoiled as manufacturers, and would be miserable farmers. The weaver, with his little piece of land and his garden, is generally a forty-shilling freeholder; he is a useful member, a good voter, and a good subject, and on such men as him may the safety of the Constitution often depend."

These arguments were very powerful, and the Government scheme of extending the franchise to Catholic forty-shilling freeholders, and at the same time excluding Catholics from Parliament, was carried in its integrity. In one of his last speeches on the question, Hobart said that "the principle of the Bill was not to admit Roman Catholics to the State," but many who supported the Government must have agreed with Grattan that "he must be a visionary politician who could imagine that, after what the Bill granted to the Catholics, they could long be kept out of the State," and at least one prominent member looked still further. "I do not deprecate the day," said Bushe, "when we may grant the Catholics a full participation of power; but if we should do so, that measure should be accompanied by another—a satisfactory ecclesiastical establishment, paid out of the Treasury, and no such measure is now proposed. For it is idle to say we should have nothing left to contend for if we gave them seats in Parliament."

Few things in Irish parliamentary history are more remarkable than the facility with which this great measure was carried, though it was in all its aspects thoroughly debated. It passed its second reading in the House of Commons with only a single negative. It was committed with only three negatives, and in the critical divisions on its clauses the majorities were at least two to one. The qualification required to authorise a Catholic to bear arms was raised in committee on the motion of the Chancellor, and in addition to the oath of allegiance of 1774, a new oath was incorporated in the Bill, copied from one of the declarations of the Catholics, and abjuring certain tenets which had been ascribed to them, among others the assertion that the infallibility of the Pope was an article of their faith. For the rest the Bill became law almost exactly in the form in which it was originally designed. It swept away the few remaining disabilities relating to property which grew out of the penal code. It enabled Catholics to vote like Protestants for members of Parliament and magistrates in cities or boroughs; to become elected members of all corporations except Trinity College; to keep arms subject to some specified conditions; to hold all civil and military offices in the kingdom from which they were not specifically excluded; to hold the medical professorships on the foundation of Sir Patrick Dun; to take degrees and hold offices in any mixed college connected with the University of Dublin that might hereafter be founded. It also threw open to them the degrees of the University, enabling the King to alter its statutes to that effect. A long clause enumerated the prizes which were still withheld. Catholics might not sit in either House of Parliament; they were excluded from almost all Government and judicial positions; they could not be Privy Councillors, King's Counsel, Fellows of Trinity College, sheriffs or subsheriffs, or generals of the staff. Nearly every post of ambition was still reserved for Protestants, and the restrictions weighed most heavily on the Catholics who were most educated and most able. . . .

*The Catholic Relief Bill passed through the Irish House of Lords despite the objections of Lord Charlemont and other peers.*

*Anxious to retain office, Lord Fitzgibbon, who was an outspoken critic of emancipation, resolved to vote for the Bill while vigorously attacking its provisions. Fitzgibbon's baneful influence wrecked any chance of reconciling the Catholic populace to the Government.*

The Relief Bill, with all its drawbacks, was a measure of the very highest importance, and it was impossible to mistake the satisfaction which it gave in the country. Just before it had passed its first stage in the committee, Hobart wrote to England that the prospect was already brightening. "The declarations of the Catholics which we receive from all quarters of their gratitude to Government for the Bill now in its progress had so far operated as to raise bank stock 10 per cent. in the course of last week." The North was, however, still full of sedition, and before the Catholic Bill had passed, the great French war had begun. An Alien Bill guarding against the danger of foreign emissaries, a severe Bill preventing the importation, removal, or possession of arms or ammunition without licence, an augmentation of the military establishment from 15,000 to 20,000 men, and a Bill directing the enrolment for the space of four years of a militia force of 16,000 men, raised, according to the English model, by conscription, passed speedily, and with little discussion. The movement for forming volunteer corps modelled after those of France, and pervaded by a strong republican spirit, was successfully met. The proclamation against the National Guard in Dublin was extended to all volunteer meetings in Dublin, and afterwards in other parts of the kingdom, and the nightly drills, the collection of arms, the adoption of seditious emblems, which for a time seriously disquieted the Government, gradually ceased. The success of these measures Westmorland attributed largely to the cordial support of Parliament and the unanimity with which all parties in it reprobated "levelling and French principles." From the Militia Act great things were expected. "I look upon the militia," wrote the Chief Secretary, "as the most useful measure both to England and Ireland that ever has been adopted, and if I am not extremely mistaken, it will operate effectually to the suppression of volunteering, to the civilisation of the people, and to the extinction of the means which the agitators of the country have repeatedly availed themselves of to disturb the peace. . . . I am happy to add that there is every appearance of the restoration of peace in Ireland."

The Catholic Relief Bill received the royal assent in April 1793, and in the same month the Catholic Convention dissolved itself. Before doing so it passed a resolution recommending the Catholics "to co-operate in all loyal and constitutional means" to obtain parliamentary reform. It at the same time voted 2,000*l.* for a statue of the King, 1,500*l.* and a gold medal to Wolfe Tone, 500*l.* to Simon Butler for his "Digest of the Popery Laws," and a plate of the value of 100 guineas to each of the five gentlemen who had gone to England to present the Catholic petition to the King. . . .

*During 1793 the commercial depression in England had injurious effects on the Irish economy. The Irish Parliament passed several measures of economical reform which sought to reduce corruption and the number of placemen in the Irish administration. Rising political and social unrest moved Parliament to prohibit popular conventions or assemblies until further notice.*

The session of 1793 extended to the middle of August, and was one of the longest as well as one of the most important ever known in Ireland. Whatever divisions there may have been on the great questions of internal policy, the Government at least could complain of no slackness or division in the support of Imperial policy, and the French party, which undoubtedly existed in the country, found no countenance or representative among the leaders of the Opposition.

Only a single discordant note on foreign politics was this session heard in Parliament, and it proceeded from a young man of thirty who had no political weight or ability, though the charm of his character and the deep tragedy of his early death have given him an enduring place in the hearts of his countrymen. Lord Edward Fitzgerald, the younger brother of the Duke of Leinster, had, through the influence of his brother, been elected for the county of Kildare during his absence, and contrary to his wish, in 1790. His life had hitherto been purely military. When a very young man, he had served with distinction at the close of the American war, under Lord Rawdon, and was afterwards for some time quartered in British America. His artless and touching correspondence with his mother has been preserved, and it enables us to trace very clearly the outlines of his character. Warmhearted, tender, pure-minded, and social to an unusual degree, he endeared himself to a wide circle, and his keen devotion to his profession gave promise of a distinguished military career, but he was not a man of serious or well-reasoned convictions, and he had all the temperament of a sentimentalist and an enthusiast. To such men the new lights which had arisen in France were as fatally attractive as the candle to the moth. Already in Canada the philosophy of Rousseau had obtained an empire over his mind, and on his return to Europe he plunged wildly into revolutionary politics.

In the autumn of 1792 he was staying at Paris with Paine, and he took part in a banquet to celebrate the victory of the Republic over the invaders, at which toasts were drunk to the universal triumph of the principles of the Revolution and the abolition of all hereditary titles and feudal distinctions. Such a proceeding on the part of an English officer could hardly be passed over, and Lord Edward was summarily dismissed from the army. In Parliament he appears to have been a silent member till an address to the Lord Lieutenant was moved, thanking him for having suppressed the National Guard which had been enrolled in imitation of the French, and pledging the House to concur in all measures that were necessary for the suppression of sedition and disaffection. Fitzgerald starting from his seat vehemently expressed his disapprobation of the address, and pronounced the Lord Lieutenant and the majority of the House the worst subjects the King had. The House was cleared, and a scene of confusion followed which has not been reported. Lord Edward's explanation of his words was of such a nature that it was unanimously voted by the House "unsatisfactory and insufficient." On the following day some kind of apology was at last extorted, but it was so imperfect that a large minority voted against receiving it. The incident would be hardly worth recording but for the subsequent career of Lord Edward, and it is also remarkable because he alone in the Irish Parliament represented sentiments which were spreading widely through the country.

Burke in his "Letter to Sir Hercules Langrishe," which was

published in 1792, has expressed his deliberate opinion that notwithstanding the grave difficulties of the time, the Irish Revolution of 1782 had hitherto produced no inconvenience either to England or Ireland; and he attributed this fact to the admirable temper with which it had in both kingdoms been conducted. The real meaning of the Irish Parliament of the eighteenth century was that the government of the country was essentially in the hands of its Protestant landlords, qualified by the fact that the Executive possessed a sufficient number of nomination boroughs to exercise a constant controlling influence over their proceedings. It was a type of government that grew out of political ideas and out of a condition of society that have irrevocably passed, and these pages will furnish abundant evidence of the many forms of corruption and abuse that attended it. The belief, however, that the owners of landed property are the natural rulers of a country, the class by whom its government is likely to be most safely, most efficiently, and most justly carried on, was in the eighteenth century scarcely less prevalent in England than in Ireland, and even in America it was countenanced by no less acute and independent a writer than Franklin. Nor can it, I think, be reasonably disputed that the Irish Parliament in the latter years of the century, though it had great defects, had also conspicuous merits. Though animated by a strong national spirit, it was thoroughly loyal to the English connection, prepared to make great sacrifices in defence of the Empire, and extremely anxious to work in harmony with the Legislature in England. With two exceptions, of which the importance has been enormously exaggerated, it had hitherto done so. The prosperity of the country had undoubtedly increased under its rule. It contained many men who would have done honour to any Legislature. Its more important debates exhibited a singularly high level of knowledge and ability. Its later legislation, and especially the system of taxation it established, will certainly not appear illiberal, intolerant, or oppressive, when compared with the contemporary legislation of Europe; and the session of 1793 abundantly shows that it was ready, with the assent of the Government, to carry great measures of reform.

It is a remarkable, but an incontestable fact, that at the opening of the great French war there was far more unanimity in supporting the Government against the foreign enemy in the Parliament at Dublin than in the Parliament in London. But outside the Protestant Parliament the state of feeling was very different, and the condition of the country was very alarming. . . .

The elements of anarchy and sedition, however, were manifestly multiplying, and from many different quarters dark clouds were gathering on the horizon. The French Revolution, and the rapidly growing political agitation which had arisen, had profoundly altered the conditions of Irish politics, and a great war had immensely added both to their difficulty and to their danger.

# VII

## *The Failure of Reform, 1793–1795*

We have seen in the last chapter the remarkable contrast which was presented between the attitude of the Irish Parliament in the spring and summer of 1793 and the general condition of the country. In Parliament the Government, at the outbreak of the great French war, was supported with an almost absolute unanimity. Grattan had declared in the strongest terms that it was both the duty and the interest of Ireland to give England an unequivocal support, and all the important measures of this memorable session for the purpose of maintaining the war, of repressing sedition and insurrection, and of relieving the Catholics from their disabilities, were either carried without a division or by overwhelming majorities. But in the meantime, throughout the country, sedition and anarchy were rapidly spreading. Demonstrations in favour of France and in opposition to the war were constantly multiplying. An extremely seditious press had arisen, and Paine's writings were profusely distributed. Clubs of United Irishmen were formed in numerous counties, and were actively engaged in democratic and revolutionary propagandism. The Defender movement was assuming a new character and a new importance, and efforts were made in the towns to enroll national guards modelled after those of France. . . .

The great majority of the more conspicuous United Irishmen at this period, as well as in the subsequent periods of the movement, were nominally either Presbyterians or members of the Established Church, though a large proportion of them were indifferent to theological doctrines. Tone, Butler, Emmet, Hamilton Rowan, Napper Tandy, Arthur O'Connor, Lord Edward Fitzgerald, Bond, Russell, Drennan, Neilson, and the two Sheares were all Protestants, and Belfast and other parts of Presbyterian Ulster were the special centres of Irish republicanism. On this point the Government despatches and the writings of the United Irishmen were perfectly agreed. The Test Act and the disabilities relating to marriage which especially affected the Presbyterians, and the commercial restrictions which were peculiarly felt by a section of the population that was essentially commercial, had, it is true, of late years been abolished, but the resentments they had produced had not passed away. The republican religion of the northern Presbyterians gave them some bias towards republican government, and their sympathy with the New England Puritans in their contest against England had been passionate and avowed. They had scarcely any part among the landed gentry of Ireland, and were therefore less sensible than other Protestants of the necessity of connection with England for the security of their property, while they were more keenly sensible than any other class to the evils of the existing system of government. They claimed to outnumber the members of the Established Church, but under the existing system of monopoly they had scarcely any political power, and scarcely any share in the patronage of the Crown. An intelligent, educated, energetic middle-class community naturally resented such a system of exclusion and monopoly far more keenly than a poor, dependent, and perfectly ignorant Catholic peasantry, and they especially detested the legal obligation of paying tithes to an Episcopalian Church. The growth of religious scepticism or indifference in the intelligent town populations had at the same time prepared the way for the reception of the doctrines of the French Revolution, and for that alliance with the Catholics which the United Irishmen preached as the first condition of obtaining a democratic reform. We have seen the powerful assistance which the northern Protestants had given to the Catholic cause in the latter stages of its struggle, and their strenuous support of the democratic party in the Catholic body, and it is an undoubted and most remarkable fact that almost the whole guiding influence of the seditious movement in 1793 was Protestant or Deistical, while the Catholic gentry, the Catholic prelates, and, as far as can now be judged, the bulk of the Catholic priesthood were strongly opposed to it.

The power of the priesthood, however, in Ireland, as in all other countries, had been diminished by the influences that led to the French Revolution. The Catholic gentry were too small a body to exercise much authority, and their weight had been in the last months steadily declining, partly through the growth of a great Catholic trading interest in the towns, and partly through the secession of Lord Kenmare and his followers from the committee, and the triumph of the democratic party in that body. It is probable, too, that the prediction of Parsons was verified, and that the Relief Act of 1793 still further weakened them. As they could be neither members of Parliament, sheriffs, nor sub-sheriffs, they could not assume their natural place as the leaders of the great political power which the new Act had suddenly called into existence. It is incontestable that a party had arisen among the Catholics which was in full sympathy with the United Irishmen, not only in their desire for Catholic emancipation and parliamentary reform, but also in the spirit that animated them, and in the ulterior objects which were gradually dawning on their minds. We have seen that the aims and wishes of Wolfe Tone had been from the beginning directed to a complete separation of Ireland from England, and he tells us that he had privately communicated his genuine political sentiments without any reserve to John Keogh and Richard McCormick, the two men who, after the secession of Lord Kenmare and of his party, were most powerful in the Catholic Committee. It was observed by a Government informer in 1793 that Keogh was a regular attendant at the meetings of the committee of the United Irishmen in Dublin. Tone notices that almost from the first formation of the United Irish Society "the Catholics flocked in, in crowds," and he had no more doubts than Duigenan or Clare about the future sedition of the Catholic democracy. "I well knew," he wrote, "that however it might be disguised or suppressed, there existed in the breast of every Irish Catholic an inextinguishable abhorrence of the English name and power." ...

The United Irish movement in the North was chiefly directed by a secret committee which sat at Belfast, and which had established a small sub-committee of correspondence for the purpose of entering into communications with sympathisers in other parts of Ireland. In Dublin there was another committee, which met at fortnightly and sometimes weekly intervals. The Government had secured one of its members, whose subscription to the society was paid, and who received from time to time remittances in money from the Castle, and in return forwarded anonymous reports of the proceedings of every meeting. The society as yet differed very little from the democratic clubs that had long existed in Great Britain. Several of its members were undoubtedly speculative republicans. All of them were advocates of a measure of very democratic reform, warm admirers of the French Revolution, and strong opponents of the war, and they were bound together by a resolution which stated that the weight of English influence was the master evil in the Government of Ireland, and that it could only be resisted by a cordial union of Irishmen of all religious persuasions. But their real and final object at this time was parliamentary reform on a democratic and unsectarian basis, though some of them were from the first convinced that this could only be obtained by separation, while others believed that it would be attained, like the Constitution of 1782, by a menace of force. This had been the object of the attempted organisation of the National Guards, and two sentences of Flood were often quoted among the United Irishmen: "When have you negotiated," he had once said, "that you have not been deceived? When have you demanded, that you have not succeeded?"

About forty or fifty members were usually present at the meetings of the Dublin Committee. The chief business was electing new members, corresponding with societies in England and Scotland, drawing up addresses which were chiefly written by Dr. Drennan, elaborating a plan of parliamentary reform which Irishmen of all classes were exhorted to hang up in their houses or cabins. The quarrel of Napper Tandy with the House of Commons had made "undefined parliamentary privilege" a leading grievance, and when the House of Lords in the spring of 1793 established a Committee of Secrecy for investigating the disturbances in some counties, and when this committee assumed the power of compelling attendance and enforcing answers upon oath to interrogatories tending to criminate the person examined, the United Irishmen issued a paper contending that it had exceeded its legal power. The House of Lords promptly took up the matter, and by their order Simon Butler, the chairman, and Oliver Bond, the secretary of the society, who signed the paper, were imprisoned for six months and fined 500*l.* each. The fines were paid by the society.

Two other important members of the society about this time passed for a short period from the scene. Napper Tandy, the most indefatigable of the agitators in Ireland, being threatened with prosecutions for libel and for having taken the Defender oath, sought safety on the Continent, and soon after Hamilton Rowan was prosecuted for seditious libel on account of an address to the volunteers. He was defended by Curran in one of the most eloquent speeches ever delivered at the bar, but was found guilty and sentenced to two years' imprisonment and to a fine of 500*l.* . . . .

As we have already seen, the quarrel between the Defenders and the Peep of Day Boys appears to have been at first of the nature of a faction fight, originating in 1784 to 1785 in the hatred which had long subsisted between the poorer Catholics and the poorer Presbyterians in the county of Armagh, and it principally took the form of the plunder of arms, and the wrecking of Catholic chapels and houses. The name taken by the Catholics implies that the Protestants were the aggressors, and the stress of evidence favours the conclusion that in the northern counties this was the case, but many atrocious crimes were perpetrated on each side, and many lives were lost. The disturbances rose and fell during several years. For a time they appear to have been suppressed by the volunteers, but in 1791 and 1792 they broke out again on a much larger scale in the counties of Tyrone, Down, Louth, Meath, Cavan, and Monaghan. There were frequent combats of large bodies of armed men, numerous outrages, rumours of intended massacres of Catholics by Presbyterians and of Presbyterians by Catholics, threatening letters which showed by clear internal evidence that they were the work of very ignorant men. In the county of Louth the Catholics appear to have been the chief offenders, for it is stated that in the spring assizes of 1793 at Dundalk twenty-one Defenders were sentenced to death and thirty-seven to transportation and imprisonment, while thirteen trials for murder were postponed. In the county of Meath, also, which was during several months in a condition of utter social anarchy, it is admitted by the best Catholic authority that the Catholics were the aggressors. The disturbances broke out near the end of 1792, in a part of the county adjoining the county of Cavan, where there were large settlements of Presbyterians, between whom and the Catholics there had long subsisted a traditional animosity. At first the Catholics plundered the Protestants of their arms with impunity, but soon a large body of well-armed Presbyterians, or, as they were still commonly called, "Scotch," came from the county of Cavan, accompanied by some resident gentry, and turned the scale. There were pitched battles in broad daylight; soldiers were called out, and many persons were shot. The Presbyterians were accused of having "overrun the country, pillaged, plundered, and burned without requiring any mark of guilt but religion." Magistrates were alternately charged with apathy, connivance, timidity, and violent oppression. There was great difficulty in obtaining legal evidence, and two or three informers were murdered.

For six or eight months Defender outrages continued in this county almost uncontrolled, and it was noticed that every kind of crime was perpetrated under the name. It was found that the most efficient means of suppressing the Defenders was the formation of a secret committee of gentlemen—one of whom was a Catholic—who bound themselves not to disclose the names of informers. At last the gang was broken up and several members turned approvers. . . .

Lord Bellamont at this time showed great activity both in Cavan and Meath, but in general the great proprietors were absentees, and the difficult and dangerous duty of suppressing the disturbances was thrown chiefly on the smaller Protestant gentry. The motives that were at work in convulsing the country were evidently of many kinds. There was an extreme chronic lawlessness which a spark could at any moment ignite. There was some religious animosity and a great deal of race hatred, for the Scotch Presbyterians and the Irish Catholics were still like separate nations. The late measure of enfranchisement had aroused wild hopes and expectations on one side, exaggerated fears and resentments on the other, and the new position acquired by Catholic forty-shilling freeholders was likely to affect to a considerable degree the competition for land. There was also much keen and real distress, for the year 1793 was eminently a "hard year," and great numbers of labourers were out of employment. Defenderism soon ceased to be either a league for mutual protection or a mere system of religious riot. It assumed the usual Irish form of a secret and permanent organisation, held together by oaths, moving under a hidden direction, attracting to itself all kinds of criminals, and making itself the organ of all kinds of discontent. It became to a great extent a new Whiteboy movement, aiming specially at the reduction and abolition of tithes and the redress of agrarian grievances, and in this form it passed rapidly into counties where the poorer population were exclusively Catholic, and where there was little or no religious animosity. It was also early noticed that it was accompanied by nightly meetings for the purposes of drill, and by a profuse distribution of incendiary papers.

Another element of disturbance of a different nature broke out about the same time. The creation of a militia was intended by the Government to be a great measure of pacification; but the new system of compulsory enlistment, which was wholly unnecessary in a country where voluntary recruits were always most easily obtained, was fiercely resented and resisted. Truly or falsely it was generally believed that in the American war the Irish Government had shamefully broken faith with a regiment nicknamed the Green Linnets, which had been enlisted on the understanding that it was not to serve out of Ireland, and which had notwithstanding been transported to America. A report was now spread, and readily believed, that they meant to act with still greater perfidy towards the new militia. It was said that they wished to expatriate or banish those who had signed the declarations originated by the Catholic Committee, and that they were accordingly forcing them into the militia in order to send them to Botany Bay. The officers of the new force were all Protestants, while the privates were Catholics, and there was a growing belief that the ministers were hostile to the Catholics and had not forgiven their recent agitation. The attitude of the grand juries, and the speeches of Foster, and still more of Fitzgibbon, had created suspicions which were industriously fanned, and which passed swiftly and silently from cabin to cabin. In nearly every county there was resistance, and in some it was very formidable. At Athboy, in the county of Meath, 1,000 men took arms. They searched the country houses for guns, and resisted the soldiers so effectually that the result was a drawn battle in which several men were killed. An attack was made on the town of Wexford in order to rescue some prisoners. The expense of soldiers billeted among the people, the fines exacted when the Act was not obeyed, the severe punishment of rioters, many of whom besides long periods of imprisonment were publicly and severely whipped, and the acts of violence and injustice which were tolerably certain to be occasionally perpetrated by soldiers and perhaps by magistrates in a society so convulsed and disorganised, all added to the discontent. In three or four months, it is true, the military riots were allayed by a measure encouraging voluntary enlistments and making some provision for the families of those who were drawn by lot, but they contributed largely to the growing disaffection and to swell the ranks of the Defenders. . . .

The Defender movement is extremely important in Irish history, for it appears to have been mainly through this channel that the great mass of the poorer Roman Catholics passed into the ranks of disaffection. It was ultimately connected with and absorbed in the United Irish movement, and it formed one of the chief Catholic elements in the rebellion of 1798. The parallel between what was then taking place in Ireland and what we have ourselves witnessed is very striking. There were two movements which were at first completely distinct. One was purely political, and was directed by educated men, influenced by political theories and aiming at political ends. The other was a popular movement which speedily became agrarian, and was to a great extent directed against the owners of property. These two movements at last combined, and the result was the most bloody rebellion in modern Irish history.

They were, however, in their origin not only distinct but violently antagonistic. It was the main object of the United Irishmen to put an end to the dissension between Catholics and Protestants, and especially to unite the Presbyterians and the Catholics in the closest alliance, for the purpose of breaking the influence of England in Irish politics, and obtaining a democratic and unsectarian measure of parliamentary reform. This was the very purpose for which their society had been constituted, and they had met with great success in the large towns of the North, and especially among the Dissenting ministers. Nothing could be more disconcerting to their plans than a new and violent outburst of religious animosity in the country districts. Wolfe Tone declared that it was "certainly fomented by the aristocrats of this country," and he himself, in conjunction with Neilson, Keogh, and Leonard McNally, went on a mission to the county of Down for the purpose of putting an end to the quarrel, and enlisting both parties in the cause of the United Irishmen. He found the soil to a considerable extent prepared for his seed. In one place there had been a meeting of eighteen Dissenting ministers from different parts of Ulster, who were all of them well disposed towards Catholic liberty. At Ballinahinch a United Irishman named McClokey had laboured so effectually, that a corps of volunteers which had been originally raised on Peep of Day principles had chosen him as their lieutenant, and the Catholics now lent the Protestants arms for their exercises and came to see them on their parade. At Newry the delegates induced a large party of Catholics, who had been bickering, to meet them at the inn, where Keogh preached peace and union, and advised them to direct their animosities against the common enemy, the monopolists of the country, and the whole company rose with enthusiasm and shook hands, promising to bury all past feuds in oblivion. At Rostrevor a number of Catholics and Protestants were brought together at a public dinner, and a Dissenting minister pronounced the benediction, and the toasts of the United Irishmen were received with enthusiasm. Napper Tandy made similar efforts to turn the Defender movement into the United Irish channel, and he appears to have actually taken the Defender oath in order to penetrate into the secrets of the organisation. The Government discovered the fact, and this, as we have seen, was one cause of his flight to the Continent.

As far as can now be ascertained, however, there was as yet scarcely any political element in the religious riots of the North, or in the outrages that were perpetrated in other parts of Ireland. The rioters belonged almost exclusively to classes sunk in the deepest ignorance and poverty, and a village schoolmaster of Naas, who was hanged in 1796, is said to have been the only educated person who is known to have been identified with them. At the same time it was not difficult to predict that illegal organisations at war with the Government, in the existing condition of Ireland and of Europe, would ultimately become political. The contagion of the great centres of agitation established at Dublin and Belfast; the influence of the "Northern Star"; the writings of Paine, which were disseminated at an extremely low price, and the proclamations of the "United Irishmen" inviting the co-operation of the Catholics, were sure to affect an anarchical population suffering under some grievances and much poverty. Besides this, rumours of French invasion were already spreading, and the connection between France and Ireland was so close that any agitation in the greater country produced a responsive pulse in the smaller one. Among educated men, and especially among those of the middle class, the French Revolution had been from the beginning a subject of the keenest interest and discussion, but the interest was not restricted to them. The ideas of an English peasant seldom extended beyond his county town, and the continental world was to him almost as unknown as the world beyond the grave. But tens of thousands of young Irishmen had passed from the wretched cabins of the South and West to the great armies of the Continent. From almost every village, from almost every family of Catholic Ireland, one or more members had gone forth, and visions of sunny lands beyond the sea, where the Catholic was not looked upon as a slave, and where Irish talent and ambition found a welcome and a home, continually floated before the imaginations of the people. The letters of the Irish exiles, the active smuggling trade which was carried on around the Irish coast, the foreign education of the innumerable priests and monks who moved among the poor, kept up the connection, and it was strengthened by the strong natural affinity of character between the Irish and the French. Names of great battles where Irish soldiers had borne an honoured part under a foreign flag were remembered with pride, and vague, distorted images of the events that were happening in France—of the abolition of tithes, of the revolution in landed property, of the offer of French assistance to all suffering nations—soon began to penetrate to the cottier's cabin, and to mingle with the cottier's dreams. . . .

*By the second half of 1793, the anti-militia riots had ceased and Defender outrages were on the wane. With a few exceptions the country remained tranquil during 1794. The ideals of the French Revolution, however, appealed to more and more Irishmen, and the United Irishmen grew more aggressive. Parliament was in no mood for constructive measures and rejected both Grattan's motion for a commercial treaty with England and Ponsonby's bill for parliamentary reform.*

A more marked tone of disloyalty was now manifestly spreading through the country. A large proportion of the Belfast party had long been theoretical republicans, but they always declared that they would have been content with a democratic parliamentary reform. The attitude of the Government and of the Parliament during the last session convinced them that it would be easier to obtain a republic than a reform under the existing Government; that without foreign aid they could never effectually resist the coalition between the English Government and the Irish aristocracy, and that their chance of obtaining such aid was now very considerable. They had at the same time begun to argue, as Adams and his colleagues had argued in the beginning of the American troubles, that the French would only assist them in a struggle for independence. The reform of the Irish Parliament could be no object to France. The establishment of an independent Irish republic would be a great triumph of French policy. With the vast dissemination of seditious or republican literature the area of discontent was enlarging, and it was spreading more and more among the Catholics. The signs, indeed, were not yet clear and unequivocal, and some months were still to elapse before they became so; but it was impossible that the new doctrines of political equality, of the indefeasible right of majorities to govern, of the iniquity of tithes and other religious endowments, should not have their influence upon men who would gain so greatly by their triumph. The gentry and the higher clergy reflected very faithfully the Catholic conservatism of Europe; but the tradesmen and merchants, who were so active in the towns, were of a different type. Some of the most important members of the Catholic Committee were unquestionably seditious, and, in spite of the very earnest remonstrance of Grattan, the committee retained Wolfe Tone as its secretary. Colonel Blaquiere in the session of 1794 startled and scandalised the House of Commons by declaring his belief that "there was not a man among them who, in case of commotion, could find fifty followers on his estate perfectly attached to the Constitution." "What," he continued, "had the poor to defend? Was it because their landlord now and then gave them a dinner or treated them civilly when he met them, that they should be attached to him?" He believed that half the nation, or more than half, were attached to the French.

His words were drowned in indignant denials. In no country, it was said, were the landlords less oppressive than in Ireland; but an uneasy feeling was abroad, and although outrages and riots appear to have somewhat diminished, those who knew the country best, believed that the Defender system was advancing with a rapid though stealthy progress. Our best evidence seems to show that it was not yet connected with the United Irish movement, and that it aimed chiefly at Whiteboy objects, but a political element was beginning very perceptibly to mingle with it. The idea was spreading that the redress of all grievances would be effected by a French invasion, and that in the event of such an invasion it was the duty of the defenders to assist it. Oaths pledging them to do so were in some districts largely taken, and in others the project was well understood. That it had not taken as much hold upon the people as was sometimes thought, is proved by the most decisive of all arguments, by their actual conduct when an invasion took place; but there were at least signs that what was to be feared among the poorest Catholic population was not merely turbulence and lawlessness, but also a positive hostility to the connection.

The influence of Grattan also had been fatally weakened. His position was at this time one of the most difficult that can fall to the lot of any statesman, and he was maintaining it with admirable courage and skill. At a time when the enthusiasm for the French Revolution was at its height, when French ideas and theories of reform were making numerous proselytes among the adventurous and enthusiastic, he was steadily opposing the stream, preaching at once the duty of a close connection with England and the Whig theory of the Constitution. But unlike those who occupied a corresponding position in England, Grattan continued to be a zealous and consistent reformer, contending that without the abolition of political distinctions on account of religion and a temperate reform of Parliament there could be no security in Ireland. In one aspect of his policy he resembled Burke; in the other he resembled Fox. It was inevitable under these circumstances that his position should have been somewhat isolated. The coalesced interests opposed to all reform detested him as the most formidable enemy to their monopolies, and much of the enthusiasm which had in old days supported him was passing into new channels. His loyalty to the connection, his support of the war, his inflexible opposition to the United Ireland scheme of radical and democratic reform, had alienated the class of mind which naturally bends with the dominant enthusiasm of the time. With the better class of Catholics he had, it is true, still great authority, and his influence was perhaps even greater with his own class—with the great body of Protestant gentlemen of moderate fortune who were unconnected with the chief borough owners, and who, though they were very inadequately represented in Parliament, comprised perhaps the largest part of the patriotism, the intelligence, and the energy of Ireland.

It seemed, however, for a time as if his policy and his power were about to rise higher than ever. In July 1794 the long-pending secession from the Whig party in England took place, and the Duke of Portland, Lord Fitzwilliam, Lord Spencer, and Windham joined the Government. By this change, at a time when the aspect of affairs on the Continent was peculiarly menacing, parties in England were virtually united in support of the war, and opposition sank into complete insignificance; but if the adhesion of the Whig leaders gave Pitt a great accession of strength, it also brought with it some embarrassments. The section of the Whig party which joined him was so important that it was entitled to claim a large share both of patronage and power, but Pitt was scarcely less autocratic in his cabinet than his father and Walpole, and Dundas appears to have been the only minister to whose judgment he greatly deferred. . . .

*Lord Fitzwilliam's reluctant acceptance of the Viceroyship in the autumn of 1794 raised Catholic hopes of full emancipation. Grattan declined his friend's offer of a place in the viceregal administration. Lord Fitzwilliam cherished an ambition to transform Irish political life in spite of the confusion surrounding the precise nature of his commission from the English Cabinet. Pitt*

*was informed on good authority that rebellion was inevitable if
the Irish political system underwent no reform.*

The quarrel between Pitt and his new allies lasted for some
weeks, but it was finally composed by an imperfect and unsatisfactory compromise. The recall of Lord Westmorland was hastened; he was transferred to the position of Mastership of the
Horse, and Lord Fitzwilliam was appointed to succeed him.
Thomas Grenville declined the office of Chief Secretary, and it
was conferred upon Lord Milton. It was agreed that Fitzgibbon
should remain Chancellor, and that no general change should be
made in the Irish Administration. It is extraordinary and most
inexcusable that, after the experience he had just had, Lord
Fitzwilliam did not insist on the exact terms of his powers being
clearly defined, and defined in writing, but so it was. He, at least,
fully believed that he was authorised to remove some men in
whom he could not place confidence, though probably not without compensation. We shall see that this power was afterwards
disputed.

Apart from questions of patronage, the great pressing question
was that of the admission of Catholics to Parliament, and on this
question the line indicated to Lord Fitzwilliam was tolerably clear.
He was instructed not to bring it forward as a Government measure, and if possible to prevent its agitation, and to obtain its
postponement till the peace. At the same time, Pitt announced
himself in principle favourable to the measure, and if, contrary
to the wishes of the Government, Lord Fitzwilliam found it so
pressed that it could not be evaded, he was authorised to accept
and to support it.

It may be advisable to give the exact words of some of the chief
persons concerned in the question, as a controversy subsequently
arose upon it. "I was decidedly of opinion," Lord Fitzwilliam
afterwards wrote, "that not only sound policy, but justice, required, on the part of Great Britain, that the work which was left
imperfect in 1793 ought to be completed, and the Catholics relieved from every remaining disqualification. In this opinion the
Duke of Portland uniformly concurred with me; and when this
question came under discussion previous to my departure for
Ireland, I found the Cabinet, with Mr. Pitt at their head, strongly

impressed with the same conviction. Had I found it otherwise, I never would have undertaken the government. I at first proposed that if the additional indulgences should be offered from the Throne, the very best effects would be secured; . . . but to this proposal objections were stated, that appeared of sufficient weight to induce the adoption of another plan. I consented not to bring the question forward on the part of Government, but rather to endeavour to keep back until a period of more general tranquillity, when so many material objects might not press upon the Government; but as the principle we agreed on, and the necessity of its being brought into full effect, was universally allowed, it was at the same time resolved, that if the Catholics should appear determined to stir the business, and to bring it before Parliament, I was to give it a handsome support on the part of Government."

This statement of fact has never been disputed, though after the quarrel, which is to be described, the Government accentuated somewhat more strongly than Lord Fitzwilliam had done, the undoubted fact that they had desired that the question should, if possible, be adjourned. "As to the Catholic question,'" wrote Portland, "it was understood that Lord Fitzwilliam was to exert his endeavours to prevent its being agitated at all."

Lord Fitzwilliam arrived in Ireland on January 4, 1795; but before his arrival, the agitation for Catholic emancipation had fully begun. The knowledge that statesmen who were avowedly favourable to it were in power, and the belief, that was rapidly spread, that they had full authority to carry the measure, had very naturally an instantaneous effect. The Catholic Committee, which had fallen into a somewhat dormant state, at once became active, and in December 1794 it was resolved that in the ensuing session an application should be made to Parliament, praying for a total repeal of the penal and restrictive laws affecting the Catholics of Ireland, that this address should be entrusted for presentation to Grattan, that the Catholics all over Ireland should be recommended to petition for the measure, and that an address should be presented to Lord Fitzwilliam on his arrival. "I was no sooner landed," he afterwards wrote, "and informed of the real state of things here, than I found that this question would force itself upon my *immediate* consideration."

There was an interval of not quite three weeks before the

meeting of Parliament, and Fitzwilliam employed it in endeavouring to obtain full information on the subject, and in reporting the result of his inquiries to the Duke of Portland. On January 8 he wrote: "I tremble about the Roman Catholics. I mean, about keeping them quiet for the session, because I find the question already in agitation, and a committee appointed to bring forward a petition for the repeal of the penal and restrictive laws. I will immediately use what efforts I can to stop the progress of it, and bring them back to a confidence in the good intentions of Government, and, relying on that, to defer for the present agitating the question." Lord Shannon agreed in thinking it ought to be postponed, and if it is brought on, "I think," said Fitzwilliam, "he will be against it, more, I see, for the sake of consistency, than from any fear of mischief arising from its being granted; and, indeed, he expressed very explicitly an opinion, that if its stop could not be negotiated on grounds of temporary expediency, it ought not to be resisted by Government." ...

*A sharp increase in public disorder and disloyalty forced Fitzwilliam to approve repressive measures. In his view the administration of law left much to be desired. Seeking ways of conciliating Catholics, he proposed several changes in Government personnel, among them the appointment of William Ponsonby as Secretary of State and George Ponsonby as Attorney General.*

The change, however, which was really important from its consequences, was the removal of John Beresford, who held the not very prominent office of Commissioner of the Revenue. Beresford was one of the most distinguished examples of a class of politicians who were a peculiar and characteristic product of the Irish political system. He belonged to a family which, though entirely undistinguished in Parliament and in responsible statesmanship, had secured so large a proportion of the minor offices in Administration, had employed its patronage so exclusively for the purpose of building up a family influence, and had formed in this manner so extensive a system of political connections and alliances, that it had become one of the most powerful controlling and directing influences in the Government of Ireland. In a curious and valuable paper drawn up for or by Lord Abercorn in

1791, called an "Analysis of the Irish Parliament," in that year, the party which was called the Beresford party is reckoned at only eight members, but it is added that the Chancellor, the Attorney-General, and Cooke were allied with it. John Beresford, the writer says, was the First Commissioner, with an official house and a salary of 2,000*l.* a year, and he had obtained the office of Taster of Wines, with a salary of 1,000*l.* a year, for his own life and that of his eldest son. His son Marcus—an active and useful member of the House—was first counsel to the commissioner, with a salary of 2,000*l.* His second son, John Claudius, had a very lucrative office in the revenue. His son-in-law would probably be provided for in the first law arrangement. William Beresford was Bishop of Ossory, he looked for the highest Church preferment, and he was married to the Chancellor's sister. The son of the Bishop was member for the episcopal borough. The Chancellor had a large following, and the Attorney-General sat in the House of Commons with his son and his nephew. Lord Waterford had the patronage of the counties of Waterford and Derry. "This party," it was added, "undoubtedly govern the kingdom." "Lord Waterford is said to stand remarkably well with the King, and to have had a constant connection with England, with the persons who had the ear of the minister, such as Mr. Robinson, Mr. Rose, &c."

The influence was steadily growing. A few years after the vice-royalty of Lord Fitzwilliam, it was said that at least a fourth of all the places in the island were filled with dependants or connections of the Beresfords, and during Fitzwilliam's time the influence of John Beresford was, or was believed to be, so overwhelming, that he was called the King of Ireland. He was politically closely allied with the Chancellor, who was bitterly and notoriously hostile to Fitzwilliam and his policy, and among his correspondents and supporters in England were Auckland, and the last two viceroys, Buckingham and Westmorland. From the first announcement of Lord Fitzwilliam's appointment, Beresford had written of it to England with undisguised hostility and apprehension, and he and his family were strenuously opposed to the Catholic policy of the Viceroy. It was not in the character of Fitzwilliam to brook this rivalry. He said that his confidential servants must be men in whom he could confide; that it was essential to the consequence and dignity of the English Government, that family cabals for monopolising the power of the State should be broken up; and that the Government, and Government patronage, in all its branches, should be in the hands of the representative of the Sovereign. One of his first acts after his arrival in Ireland was the dismissal of Beresford. He acted in this matter hastily, curtly, and probably injudiciously, and without waiting for any act of overt opposition; but Beresford was granted for life his entire official salary, and he received an assurance that none of the other members of his family would be removed. "They were still left," wrote Fitzwilliam, "in the full enjoyment of more emoluments than ever were accumulated in any country upon any one family." . . .

*While Fitzwilliam rapidly antagonized the more reactionary elements within the Ascendancy, French military successes on the Continent were causing concern in London. Grattan's eloquence helped to rally the Irish Commons in support of the British war effort against France.*

The condition of the country was at this time very remarkable. The Catholics all over Ireland were evidently thoroughly aroused, and their hopes were raised almost to the point of certainty. For some days a perpetual stream of petitions for relief had been pouring in from every quarter, and, although they were perfectly loyal and respectful in their tone, they clearly showed that a complete removal of religious disabilities must be carried if Catholic loyalty was to be retained. Above half a million of signatures are said to have been appended to the petitions for complete emancipation of the Catholics, which lay upon the table of the House of Commons.

All classes of Catholics—the committee and the seceders, the Tories and the democrats—were on this question united, and never since 1782 had an expression of national will so genuine, so strong, and so unequivocal, been brought to the threshold of Parliament. On the other hand, the Protestants of Ireland as a body were perfectly ready to concede what was asked. An aristocratic faction, very powerful from its borough influence, disliked the measure as threatening their monopoly, but it was plain that they would not resist the determination of the Government. A furious sectarian spirit raged among the farmers and labourers in some counties of the North, but it found scarcely any echo in political life. The great mass of the Protestants were plainly convinced that the time had come for completing the Act of 1793. The Act had given the Catholic body the substance of power, but had left the badge of degradation and inferiority unremoved. It had granted power to the most ignorant, most turbulent, and most easily disaffected, and it had confirmed the incapacities of a loyal and conservative gentry, whose influence over the lower classes of the community it was vitally important to maintain. The Protestant gentry of Ireland had many faults, but they were at this time remarkably free from religious bigotry, and, unlike the English Ministers, they at least knew Ireland. They saw that the United Irishmen were successfully using the Catholic question as a lever for uprooting the masses from their old allegiance; that, under the influence of the democratic spirit, which the French Revolution had engendered, the ascendency of property, rank, and intelligence, was strained and weakened; that multitudes of ignorant and turbulent men were drifting away from their old moorings, and were beginning to follow new and dangerous leaders; that classes which had hitherto at worst been only lawless and riotous, were rapidly becoming steadily and systematically disaffected. The evil could only be met by at once depriving the agitator of his most formidable weapon, by conferring political power on men who were tolerably certain not to misuse it, by uniting the upper ranks of all denominations in support of the Constitution. There were doubtless many who wished that the Catholic question had never been raised, but such regrets were now very idle. A revolution of power had been made in 1793. A revolution of opinion, which was much more formidable, had followed or accompanied it. The Catholics had become keenly sensible of their rights, their degradation, and their power. It remained for the Government to decide between a policy of concession, and a policy of resistance, which, in the excited state of Ireland, was almost certain to lead to bloodshed.

The former policy would have encountered no serious difficulty in Ireland. As we have already seen, the Chancellor, who was the ablest of all its opponents, admitted that it could easily be carried. When Grattan moved for leave to introduce the Bill into Parliament, Duigenan and Ogle were the sole opponents, and there was, as yet, not a single petition to Parliament, not a single address to the Lord Lieutenant, on the part of any Protestant body, against it. There may be endless controversy about the effects that would have followed Catholic emancipation in 1795, and about the propriety of the conduct of Lord Fitzwilliam. One fact, however, is as certain as anything in Irish history—that if the Catholic question was not settled in 1795, rather than in 1829, it is the English Government, and the English Government alone, that was responsible for the delay. . . .

*Fitzwilliam moved gradually toward full Catholic emancipation, unaware that English ministers opposed any such concession. In February 1795, the Duke of Portland firmly ruled out the possibility of emancipation in a letter to the Viceroy. Fitzwilliam then made a closely reasoned appeal to the Cabinet but failed to convince them of the necessity of making a timely and generous concession.*

After the best consideration, however, I can give, I can see no other course which Fitzwilliam could have adopted. The agitation had acquired formidable dimensions before he arrived in Ireland. He lost no time in informing the Government most fully of its pressing character, and as early as January 15 he clearly told them that he would exercise the discretion which he had received when he was appointed, and would accede to the Catholic demands, unless he received peremptory instructions to the contrary. The Government sent him no such instructions, though the Catholic movement was acquiring almost hourly additional strength: they pronounced no hostile opinion, when they had been emphatically told that, in the judgment of those who were responsible for the government of Ireland, the rejection or postponement of the measure would probably throw the country into a flame of rebellion; they never proposed that the meeting of Parliament, which was appointed for January 22, should be deferred, and they suffered Fitzwilliam to meet that Parliament under the full impression that his representations of the state of the country had been accepted by the Cabinet. When Parliament met, it was totally impossible that the introduction of the Catholic question could have been prevented. The country was thrilling with the most passionate excitement on the subject. Even if Grattan had consented to relinquish it for the session, there were many members who were desirous of introducing it, and in that case, as Lord Fitzwilliam truly said, "the measure might come into hands with which neither he nor the King's Ministers had any connection, which would leave the Government only the disagreeable part of altering or modifying, if any alteration or modification had been thought necessary by the British Government, depriving his Majesty thereby of the whole grace and effect of what was done." The only possible way in which Fitzwilliam could have prevented the Bill coming before the House of Commons, would have been by openly opposing the leave to introduce it, and in that case he would have thrown himself into violent opposition to the whole current of excited Catholic feeling, would have precipitated the very evils of which he had warned the Government, and would have acted in direct contradiction, not only to his own sentiments, but to the instructions which he had received when he was appointed.

Under these circumstances, he had adopted the most judicious course in putting himself in connection with Grattan, who was not in office, who had been entrusted with the petition of the Catholic Committee, but who at the same time was in the close confidence of his Administration, and anxious to do all that was in his power to smooth its path. As we have seen, Grattan consented to postpone introducing the measure till its leading provisions had been sent to England. As early as February 10, the Cabinet had been fully apprised of them, as well as of the opinion of the Irish Parliament upon them, in order that the English Government should be able to limit and modify the Bill if it appeared to them too unrestricted. When leave was given to introduce it, its terms were kept back from Parliament and from the Catholics until the opinion of the Cabinet had been received upon it, and they had not yet been communicated when the censure of the Cabinet arrived. If the measure was not sufficiently discussed, this was entirely the fault of the English Ministers, who had so strangely neglected it during the whole interval before Parliament met, and during the first fortnight of its session. If, with the usual ignorance of their class, they understood Ireland so little as to imagine that the question was one which might safely be indefinitely postponed, they had only themselves to blame, for nothing could be clearer or more emphatic than the warning they had received. The censure, therefore, which they sent to Fitzwilliam on February 18, appears to me perfectly unmerited. The next day the Cabinet agreed to recall Fitzwilliam, and on the 23rd he was directed to appoint lords justices to conduct the government till the arrival of his successor.

After all that has been written on the subject, a considerable obscurity still hangs over the real motives that induced the English Government to take a step which, they were repeatedly assured, must bring down upon Ireland a train of calamities of the most appalling description. The final opinion of Fitzwilliam, which was strongly shared by the Ponsonbys and by Grattan, was that the Catholic question had in reality nothing to say to their decision. The question they considered was merely one of family influence. The great social and political weight of the Beresfords, supported by Westmorland, Buckingham, and Auckland in England, and by Fitzgibbon in Ireland, was strained to the utmost against the Ponsonbys, and the influence they brought to bear was such that, although Pitt was believed by Fitzwilliam to have acquiesced in the removal of Beresford when it was first proposed, he now determined at all hazards to resist it. . . .

Pitt, on the other hand, understood that no important change of men or measures was to be effected without previous communication with the English Cabinet, and that no old servants of the Crown were to be removed contrary to their wish, unless they had entered into a course of insubordination or opposition to the Government. But Fitzwilliam had not been more than two days in Ireland when he removed Beresford, peremptorily and curtly, and it seemed probable that the changes which were proposed or effected would amount to a most serious displacement of power in the permanent administration of Ireland. Appeals were made to Pitt, by men who had great weight with his party, "to hold up a shield for the shelter of persons who had merited the favour of the last Lord Lieutenant by their services, and on whose conduct no blame or censure had been attached"; and they were accompanied by the most alarming pictures of the dangerous fermentation which the measures of Lord Fitzwilliam were producing in Ireland.

Other political motives, which I have already indicated, very probably blended in his mind with these considerations. He was told that if the Ponsonbys, who were usually connected with the Whigs, obtained a real ascendency in Ireland, the whole department of Irish influence and patronage would pass into Whig hands. He may have believed that the easiest and safest way of governing Ireland was through that system of family monopoly which enabled the Government to count at all times, and amid all political changes, upon a subservient majority in the House of Commons. He shared the prevailing sentiment in England, that in the agonies of a revolutionary war, all great political changes should be as far as possible avoided or postponed, and he may have foreseen that if Grattan and Ponsonby carried the promised reforms, and gave a comparatively popular character to the Parliament of Ireland, the whole system of its past government would be infallibly destroyed, and the chances of obtaining a legislative union indefinitely diminished.

These were probably leading motives in producing the recall, but I do not think that the Catholic question was as completely foreign to it as the viceroy supposed. As far as "the Irish clique" were concerned, it is probable that Burke did not greatly misjudge them when he wrote that their one object was "to derive security to their own jobbish power. This is the first and the last in the piece. The Catholic question is a mere pretence." They employed it most skilfully for their purpose, and Fitzgibbon deserves to be remembered in history as probably the first very considerable man who maintained the doctrine that the King would violate the coronation oath, the Act of Settlement, and the Act of Union with Scotland, if he consented to a measure allowing the Catholic electors to send Catholic representatives into Parliament. Even the English Chancellor, he wrote, would "stake his head" if he affixed the Great Seal of England to such a measure. No more extravagant doctrine has ever been maintained by a responsible statesman, but it fell upon a soil which was prepared for its reception, and it has had a great and most fatal influence on English history.

Even before Fitzgibbon had written to this effect, the King had declared his emphatic hostility to Catholic emancipation, and drawn up an elaborate memorandum in opposition to it. It was dated on February 6, and in it the King mentioned that it was only on the preceding day that he heard, to his great astonishment, that Fitzwilliam had proposed a total and immediate change of the system of government which had been followed in Ireland since the Revolution. The admission of Catholics to sit in Parliament, and the formation in Ireland of a yeomanry which would be essentially Catholic, were measures which, in the opinion of the King, could not fail, sooner or later, to separate the two kingdoms, or lead England into a line of conduct which it was the very object of the English Revolution and of the Act of Settlement to prevent. Such a measure, the King continued, was beyond the decision of a cabinet of ministers; even if they favoured it, "it would be highly dangerous, without previous concert with the leading men of every order in the State, to send any encouragement to the Lord Lieutenant on this subject; and if received with the same suspicion I do (*sic*), I am certain it would be safer even to change the new administration in Ireland, if its continuance depends on the success of this proposal, than to prolong its existence on grounds that must sooner or later ruin one, if not both kingdoms."

It is obvious what a formidable obstacle the attitude of the King threw in the way of Fitzwilliam; and while the King was in this state of mind, Fitzgibbon's views about the coronation oath were communicated to him by Lord Westmorland. He readily embraced them, and he ever after employed them as the best reason or pretext for resistance. . . .

When the news arrived that the English Government had determined to recall Lord Fitzwilliam, and to dash to the ground the hopes which the Catholics had been given every reason to entertain, those who knew Ireland best foresaw nothing but ruin. Fitzwilliam himself predicted that the English Ministers must face "almost the certainty of driving this kingdom into rebellion." Forbes, who was one of the most acute members of the Irish Parliament, wrote to a private friend: "It is reported that Pitt intends to overturn the Irish Cabinet by rejecting Catholic claims. Should he pursue that line, . . . it will end in the total alienation of Ireland." The ablest English-speaking Catholic bishop of the time was Dr. Hussey, who was largely employed by the Government in negotiations with the Irish Catholics, and who was a constant correspondent of Burke. At the end of January, when the Catholic question seemed certain to triumph under the auspices of the English Government, he wrote to Burke, that he found the loyal spirit of the Irish Catholics so strongly roused, that he believed that there were not five of them in the kingdom worth 10*l.* who would not spill their blood to resist a French invasion. Three weeks later, when doubts about the policy of the Government had begun to circulate, he wrote very solemnly that the question of this Emancipation Bill involved another very awful one—whether the Cabinet "mean to retain Ireland, or to abdicate it to a French Government, or to a revolutionary system of its own invention." When the decision was taken, he wrote in absolute consternation: "The disastrous news of Earl Fitzwilliam's recall is come, and Ireland is now on the brink of civil war." From a wholly different point on the political compass, Charlemont, who had been so firm and steady an opponent of the concession of political power to the Catholics, pronounced that in the existing state of Ireland the recall of Lord Fitzwilliam was "utterly ruinous," and he predicted that by next Christmas the mass of the people would probably be in the hands of the United Irishmen. . . .

*The second Earl of Camden replaced Fitzwilliam at the end of March. Thomas Pelham was reappointed Chief Secretary at the same time. Both the Catholic Committee and a number of prominent Protestants in Dublin and other urban areas held meetings and drafted resolutions protesting the recall of Fitzwilliam and the failure of emancipation.*

The signs of disaffection were so menacing, that Fitzwilliam, who desired immediately to leave Ireland, was obliged, at the urgent request of the leading members of the Irish Government, to postpone his departure for a fortnight, as it was represented to him that the country would not be safe in the weak hands of the lords justices, till his successor arrived. He at first peremptorily refused to adjourn the Parliament; but Fitzgibbon declared that unless such an adjournment took place, he would not be responsible for twenty-four hours, for the government of Ireland. The twenty-fifth of March, when he sailed for England, was one of the saddest days ever known in Ireland. The shops of Dublin were shut. All business was suspended. Signs of mourning were exhibited on every side. The coach of the Lord Lieutenant was drawn by some of the most respectable citizens to the waterside, and the shadow of coming calamity cast its gloom upon every countenance. It was indeed but too well justified. From that time the spirit of sullen and virulent disloyalty overspread the land, "creeping," in the words of Grattan, "like the mist at the heels of the countryman."

It has been strongly maintained by some modern English writers, that the importance of the recall of Lord Fitzwilliam in Irish history has been greatly overrated. That some exaggeration mingled with the first excited judgments on the subject, is no doubt true, and something of it may have passed into later history. Long before the arrival of Lord Fitzwilliam, some of the most active members of the Catholic Committee were in full sympathy with Wolfe Tone, and in large districts of Ireland the Defender movement had drawn great bodies of the Catholic peasantry into an armed organisation, aiming at Whiteboy objects, but already looking forward to French assistance and invasion as the means of attaining them. No one can read the letters of Westmorland, and especially of Fitzwilliam, without perceiving that the condition of Ireland was very serious, and that the danger would have been extreme if a French army had succeeded in establishing itself firmly on the soil, and had promised the abolition of tithes and the subversion of the existing system of landed property. Lawlessness, ignorance, extreme poverty, and a complete separation in character and sentiment of the Catholic tenantry in a great part of Ireland from the owners of the soil, were evils on which Catholic emancipation could have had little direct influence, though national education, and, still more, a commutation of tithes, might have done much to mitigate them. Under any circumstances, the condition of Ireland in the last years of the eighteenth century must have been exceedingly dangerous. Nothing disorganises and demoralises a country in which there are great internal elements of disorder, so certainly as a constant menace of invasion, prolonged through many years; and the situation was enormously aggravated by the fact, that the probable invaders were the soldiers of a great and contagious Revolution, whose first object was to set the poor against the rich, to sweep away established churches, and to destroy the whole existing distribution of property and power. Ireland was full of sympathisers with this

Revolution, and no moderate reform would have contented them. Whether the introduction of a few Catholic gentry into the Legislature, and the moral effect of the abolition of religious disabilities, would have enabled Ireland successfully to meet the storm, is a question which may be easily asked, but which no wise man will confidently answer.

It appears to me, however, undoubtedly true, that the chances were immensely diminished by the recall of Lord Fitzwilliam. Great classes who were as yet very slightly disaffected, now passed rapidly into republicanism, and Catholic opinion, which had been raised to the highest point of excited hope, experienced a complete, a sudden, and a most dangerous revulsion. The recall of Fitzwilliam may be justly regarded as a fatal turning point in Irish history. For at least fifteen years before it occurred, the country, in spite of many abuses and disturbances, had been steadily and incontestably improving. Religious animosities appeared to have almost died away. Material prosperity was advancing with an unprecedented rapidity. The Constitution in many important respects had been ameliorated, and the lines of religious disabilities were fast disappearing from the statute book. The contagion of the French Revolution had produced dangerous organisations in the North, and a vague restlessness through the other provinces, but up to this time it does not appear to have seriously affected the great body of Catholics, and Burke was probably warranted when, in estimating the advantages which England possessed in her struggle with France, he gave a prominent place to the loyalty, the power, and the opulence of Ireland. With the removal of the few remaining religious disabilities, a settlement of tithes, and a moderate reform of Parliament, it seemed still probable that Ireland, under the guidance of her resident gentry, might have contributed at least as much as Scotland to the prosperity of the Empire. But from the day when Pitt recalled Lord Fitzwilliam, the course of her history was changed. Intense and growing hatred of England, revived religious and class animosities, a savage rebellion savagely repressed, a legislative union prematurely and corruptly carried, mark the closing years of the eighteenth century, and after ninety years of direct British government, the condition of Ireland is universally recognised as the chief scandal and the chief weakness of the Empire.

# VIII

## Irish Reactions to the French Revolution, 1795–1797

Lord Camden arrived in Ireland on March 31, 1795. His Chief Secretary, Pelham, had been already there for some days, and the state of the country was so evidently dangerous, that there were great fears for the safety of the viceroy on his entry into Dublin. In consequence, it is said, of secret information furnished by Francis Higgins, the proprietor of the "Freeman's Journal," the arrangements for the entry were at the last moment changed, and it was deemed a matter of no small congratulation that the procession passed almost unmolested through the streets. When Lord Fitzgibbon and the Primate were returning from the Castle, their carriages were attacked by a furious mob, and the Chancellor, who was especially obnoxious to the popular party, was wounded by a stone, which struck him upon the forehead. The riot rapidly spread. The mob attacked the custom-house, and the houses of the Chancellor, the Primate, the Speaker, and Beresford. It was found necessary to call out the soldiers, and two men were killed.

It was an ill-omened beginning of a disastrous viceroyalty. On the day when Grattan, who was regarded as the mouthpiece of the Government of Lord Fitzwilliam, obtained leave to bring in a Bill for Catholic emancipation, the loyalty of the Catholic population seemed to rise higher than it had ever risen since the Revolution, and it was believed that the policy of religious disqualification was for ever at an end. On the day when the English Government disavowed the acts of its Irish representatives, recalled Lord Fitzwilliam, and again brought to the helm the most violent opponents of the Catholics, a cloud seemed to fall on the spirit of the nation which has never been removed. Just before the arrival of Camden, Pelham wrote to England that he had received very alarming accounts of the proceedings of the Catholic Committee. A select and secret committee, consisting of a very few, and entrusted with a larger power, was forming, and they were to be bound by an oath of secrecy and perseverance. "It is said," he continued, "that upon a closer investigation of their strength and influence, upon the recall of Lord Fitzwilliam, they [the Catholic Committee] are led to despair of anything effectual without the assistance of the French, and it is seriously in their contemplation to send an embassy to Paris, if the Catholic question should be lost in the Irish Parliament."

The replies of Grattan to the numerous addresses presented to him were eagerly scanned. They were marked by a great deal of that strained and exaggerated mannerism of expression which was habitual to him, and they speak in no doubtful tones of his indignation at what had occurred; but they were, at the same time, in substance eminently moderate, and evidently intended to maintain the Catholics in their allegiance. Their true policy, he told them, was to maintain strictly their union with Protestants, and to press on their claims steadily within the lines of the Constitution. "Your emancipation will pass," he said, "rely on it, your emancipation must pass; it may be death to one viceroy; it will be the peace-offering of another, and the laurel may be torn from the dead brow of one governor to be craftily converted into the olive for his successor." If, however, the old "taskmasters" and the old system of government were restored, he predicted that they would "extinguish this country." He asserted that the public measures of the late Administration, and especially that which was now disputed, had been stipulated and agreed to, and he pledged himself to bring in the Emancipation Bill of which he had given notice. Language was employed, which excited much alarm among the English Ministers, about the independence of the Irish Cabinet as a body responsible directly to the King, and not a mere subordinate department of the English Ministry.

It had been one of the great misfortunes of the English Government that, during a considerable period of its history, it had been either compelled or persuaded to adopt as its method of managing Ireland, the worst of all expedients, that of endeavouring to inflame the animosities and deepen the divisions between the Protestants and Catholics. This was the policy of Cromwell, and it was the policy which was systematically pursued for a long period after the Revolution. The exclusion of Catholics by an English Act from the Irish Parliament; the lament of Bishop Burnet that the division of Whig and Tory was beginning to appear in a country where the sole divisions had hitherto been those between Protestants and Papists; the habitual employment by the governors of Ireland, in the early years of the eighteenth century, of the terms "common enemy" and "domestic enemies" when speaking of the Roman Catholics, clearly indicate a policy which was steadily carried out. For a long time, as we have already seen, this spirit had almost wholly passed away. The relations of the English Government to the Irish Catholics had become very friendly. The penal laws had for the most part fallen into desuetude before they had been formally abolished, and the influence of English Ministers had been usually exerted in favour of the Catholics. The declarations of the grand juries in 1792 against the admission of the Catholics to political power had, no doubt, been chiefly inspired by men who were high in office in Ireland, but this was at a time when the Irish Administration on this very question was endeavouring to defeat the tolerant views of the English Cabinet. On the accession of Lord Camden, however, a great and most pernicious change took place. The English Cabinet had determined to resist the emancipation of the Catholics, contrary to the dominant sentiments of the Irish Protestants, and it therefore directed its Irish representatives to endeavour to kindle an anti-Catholic feeling in Ireland, and exert its enormous influence to organise an Irish party of resistance. . . .

*Although Lord Camden had no time for Catholic emancipation, he tried to appease the Catholics by granting subsidies to seminaries and the parochial clergy. Parliament met on April 13, and after a heated debate on Fitzwilliam's recall, Grattan spoke in favor of allowing Catholics to sit in the House of Commons. The emancipation question came to a head on May 4–5, when the House considered the second reading of Grattan's Catholic*

*Relief Bill. The arguments of the Grattanite reformers, however, "dashed uselessly and impotently against a great purchased majority," and the bill was decisively defeated.*

No one, I think, can read this debate without acknowledging that the immense preponderance of argument and ability was on the side of emancipation. Duigenan and some of the other genuine opponents of the Catholics restated their old arguments, but the Government case was entrusted to Toler, the Solicitor-General. He was one of those officials whom Fitzwilliam had desired to replace; and having been long known as a selfish, violent, and unprincipled advocate, he was made Chief Justice of the Common Pleas, was created Lord Norbury, and has left a most scandalous judicial reputation behind him. He placed the Government opposition to the admission of Catholics to Parliament on the highest possible grounds. It would violate the fundamental principles of the Constitution as established by the Revolution. It would be contrary to the coronation oath by which the King held his throne, to the Bill of Rights, to the compact on which the connection of the two countries depended. The Roman Catholic was asking that the Constitution should be changed. "He has no right to demand it, nor have the Crown and Parliament, who are but trustees for its preservation, a right to alienate what has been confided to them as a trust." In other words, the Catholics, at a time when the most cautious and conciliatory policy was imperatively required, were told on high Government authority that their disqualifications were permanent and indelible, essential to the connection of their country with England, essential to the maintenance of the monarchical constitution under which they lived. The independent voices in Parliament, and the voices of the Protestants beyond its walls, had spoken in no dubious terms; but the majority in the House of Commons, who a few months before had been perfectly ready to carry the Bill, were now equally ready to reject it, and it was thrown out by 155 votes to 84.

From this time the Catholic question lost most of its prominence in the Irish Parliament, and from this time there is scarcely a page of Irish history on which a good man can look with pleasure. Anarchy and bloodshed, religious and class warfare, great measures almost wholly failing to produce their expected results, disaffection widening and deepening as grievances were removed, public opinion more and more degraded and demoralised, political life turned more and more into a trade in which the vilest men are exalted—these are the chief elements in the miserable story which the historian of modern Ireland is called upon to relate. It is impossible to say, with just confidence, whether this train of calamities could have been averted if all religious disqualifications had been removed in 1793 or 1795. The Protestants then undoubtedly desired it. Political agitation was almost unknown. The indispensable ascendency of property and loyalty was still unbroken; the relations of classes and creeds, which were hopelessly convulsed by the rebellion of 1798, and by the long agitation that followed it, were not yet essentially unsound, and more than a century had passed since Ireland had witnessed the clash of arms. In my own judgment, little permanent good could have been effected unless a moderate parliamentary reform and a commutation of tithes had been added to the abolition of religious distinctions; but with these measures, Ireland would probably have weathered the revolutionary storm. But though the chapter of what might have been lies beyond human sagacity, the actual train of cause and effect is sufficiently evident, and it is not too much to say, that the undecided and contradictory policy of these critical years was a leading cause of the rebellion of 1798, and of the fatal consequences that flowed from it. . . .

*Lord Fitzgibbon was promoted to the Earldom of Clare both as a reward for his anti-Catholic activities and a sign of the Government's intention to uphold the Protestant Ascendancy. The Catholics received a consolation prize in the form of a seminary at Maynooth for the training of Irish priests, who had hitherto received their education on the Continent. Maynooth seminary was established in spite of the objections of Grattan, Burke, and other opponents of an avowedly sectarian institution. Reports of the revolutionary plans of the United Irishmen reached the administration through an enterprising Dublin lawyer named Leonard McNally.*

The United Irishmen, whose meetings had been forcibly suppressed in 1794, reconstructed their society, in 1795, on a new basis, and it now became distinctly republican and treasonable.

An oath of secrecy and fidelity was substituted for the old test, and great precautions were taken to extend and perfect its organisation. The inferior societies, which had at first consisted of thirty-six, were now composed of only twelve members each, and an elaborate hierarchy of superior directing committees was created. There were lower baronial committees, upper baronial committees, district and county committees, and provincial directories, each being formed of delegates from the inferior bodies; and at the head of the whole there was a general executive directory of five members, elected by ballot from the provincial directories, sitting in Dublin, and entrusted with the government of the whole conspiracy. The oath bound the members to form a bond of affection between Irishmen of every opinion, and to endeavour to obtain a "full representation of all the people." This phrase was substituted for "an equal representation of the people in Parliament," which was used in the original test, and the suppression of all mention of Parliament was not without its significance. In order to preserve secrecy, the names of the members of the supreme directory were only communicated to a single member of each provincial directory, and orders were transmitted from committee to committee by a secretary appointed in each. Emissaries were sent out, and much seditious literature disseminated, to propagate the system. A subscription of one shilling a month was paid by every member. Nightly drilling took place in many districts; arms were collected, and the prospect of a French invasion was kept continually in view. According to the Government information, there were sixteen societies in Belfast, a vast number in the counties of Antrim, Down, Derry, Armagh, and Dublin, and between two and three thousand in all Ireland. At Cork, the Government was informed, there were, in 1795, about 600 United Irishmen—"shopkeepers, merchants' clerks, one or two physicians, farmers residing in all parts of the county, and very young men who attend for the pleasure of debate. . . . They are mostly Protestant. The mayor and sheriffs are suspected of being friendly to them." . . .

Much more serious than the United Irish movement, was the rapid spread of Defenderism among the Catholic peasantry. It radiated in the first instance from the county of Armagh, and grew out of the local quarrel between Protestants and Catholics, but, as we have already seen, it almost immediately lost in most places its first character, and became a revived Whiteboy system, with the very serious difference, that a strong political element now mingled with it, through the belief that a French invasion was the most probable method by which its different objects might be attained. Numerous letters in the Government correspondence, show the terrible rapidity and simultaneity with which it broke out in many counties, the various forms of outrage that were perpetrated, the manner in which all agrarian and ecclesiastical grievances were drawn into the system, and the utter demoralisation that it produced. "One of the first acts of violence," said Lord Camden, "and of system, was to put all the smiths into requisition, compelling them to make pikes and spears, some new, and others out of old scythes." Parties went about plundering gentlemen's houses of arms, and their information was so good, that it was evident that they were in correspondence with the servants. There were instances of servants quitting their master with tears, saying that they would be murdered if they remained. In many parts of Leitrim, Sligo, Galway, Longford, and Mayo, depredations were taking place in the early summer of 1795. In Roscommon, the great graziers were "so afraid of their cattle being houghed and killed, that they yielded to the demands of the people, by agreeing to raise their wages and lower the rent of the potato ground." "Both these measures," writes Camden, "were very just and necessary in themselves, but very improper and impolitic, forced, as they were, by intimidation," and the concession naturally gave an immense encouragement to the rioters. "In Galway," it was noticed, "there was not an equal pretence for discontent, the rent of the potato ground being lower, though the wages were higher," and the disturbances there were, for a time at least, quelled when the adjournment of Parliament enabled the principal gentlemen of the county to return to their estates. The usual Irish type of an agrarian code contrary to the law of the land, and enforced by outrages, was very apparent. The rioters "summoned people to appear before Captain Stout, the nickname for their leaders, and settled differences about wages and rent by a jury, and imposed fines." "I fear," wrote the Lord Lieutenant, "there is too general an expectation among the common people, of some good that they are to derive from fraternity, and they have lately assumed the name of brothers, and they are encouraged with the hope of being what they call up, or getting uppermost, which is totally unconnected with any religious sentiment, except so far as it serves as a pretext for influencing them at particular times."

The circle of disorder in a few weeks spread over Meath, West Meath, and Kildare. Emissaries, it was said, "swear the lower Roman Catholics to secrecy, and to the French when they land," and there were nightly meetings, and constant robberies of firearms. In most of the counties in Ireland the better sort of people showed but little energy, and there were many large districts without a single important resident gentleman. Very much, therefore, was thrown on the Central Government, who were obliged, as far as they could, to create "an artificial, if they cannot establish a natural, civilisation." "The greatest pains appear to be taken to infuse a spirit of discontent through all the lower orders of people"; and although the disturbances were not likely to be seriously dangerous unless an invasion took place, they made it impossible to withdraw the troops. From the North it was reported, that Defender lodges were everywhere multiplying, the principal one being at Armagh. There was an active correspondence kept up, but never through the post office. Everywhere the Defenders were administering unlawful oaths and seizing arms. They were accustomed to burn the turf and root up the potatoes of those who refused to be sworn, cut down plantations for pike handles, dig up meadows, level banks, hough cattle, rob or set fire to houses, ravish or murder. In eight months there were 147 acts of murder, robbery, or rape, in the single county of Longford. All the Protestants for forty miles round Carrick-on-Shannon were disarmed. Bodies of Defenders numbering 2,000 or 3,000 appeared in arms, and no less than thirteen counties in the course of this year were infected. There were notices put up threatening all who paid tithes or taxes, or let potato grounds for more than four guineas an acre. There were attempts to regulate the price of land and lower priests' dues. According to one proclamation, labour was to be paid one shilling a day for half the year, and tenpence a day for the other half, and though tithes might be paid to the clergymen, they might not, under pain of death and destruction of goods, be paid to tithe proctors or tithe farmers.

The Government were very anxious to ascertain whether there was any connection between the United Irishmen and the Defenders; but after several hesitations of opinion, Camden at this time acknowledged himself unable to discover any clear proof of such connection. A careful digest was made of the evidence relating to both societies, and a comparison was sent over to England of their plans and objects. Personal representation, Camden said, was an aim peculiar to the United Irishmen. Using signs and catechisms was peculiar to the Defenders; and abolishing taxes and Church cess, lowering the priests' fees, lowering the prices of land, of potatoes, and of meal, raising the price of labour, equalising property, and restoring Popery, were Defender objects, of which there was no trace among the United Irishmen. The characteristics or objects common to both were fraternising, numbering their committees, naming delegates, providing by all means pikes and guns, seducing the military, abolishing tithes and royalties, separating the two kingdoms, expecting assistance from France, looking forward to a general rising.

The outrages came and went, and sometimes almost disappeared in some of the infected counties, but then again broke out in neighbouring districts. On the whole, in the latter part of the year they appear to have perceptibly diminished, but they were still very serious, and wherever they had appeared, they left behind them sedition and demoralisation. . . .

*Defenderism spread havoc through many counties, as the economic condition of the tenantry further deteriorated. Too many landlords lived extravagantly, and, whether or not they were absentees, they cared more about maximizing their rents than improving their estates. Rising rents and uneconomic subdivision of holdings depressed the occupiers and reinforced their subsistence economy.*

This mass of extreme and chronic poverty was now beginning to surge with wild and indefinite hopes, and busy missionaries were actively fanning the flame. As outrages multiplied, the landlord had every inducement to leave his estate, and the system of tenure existing in Ireland made his absence peculiarly easy. Since the world began, no large class of men have ever discharged efficiently, dangerous, distasteful, and laborious functions, if they had no inducement to do so except the highest sense of duty, and this was rapidly coming to be the position of the landlord, whose lot was cast in the midst of the anarchy of Defenderism. It was not a natural thing that a landlord should have great power, when his land was placed beyond his control by the system of long leases, and the authority which Irish landlords had for so many years exercised under this system, was to a great degree artificial. Among the many contradictions and anomalies of Irish life, nothing is more curious than the strong feudal attachment and reverence that frequently grew up between the resident Protestant landlord and his Catholic tenantry, in spite of all differences of race and creed and traditions. It is a fact which is attested by everything we know of Irish life in the eighteenth century, and it subsisted side by side with the Whiteboy outrages, with vivid memories of the old confiscations, and with many other indications of war against property. The country gentleman had many qualities, not all of them very estimable that were eminently popular among the people—a lavish hospitality, keen sporting tastes, great courage in duels, a careless, thriftless, good-natured ostentation, a tone of absolute authority and command, mixing curiously with extreme familiarity, in dealing with inferiors; a great knowledge of their character, and a great consideration for their customs and prejudices. In the management of his property there was a combination of negligence and indulgence, which has always been peculiarly popular in Ireland. His kitchen was open to all comers from his estate; he seldom or never interfered when his tenants wished to settle their children on a portion of his land, or insisted on much punctuality of payment, and he laid great stress on hereditary attachment to his family. The pride of family and of county influence was nowhere stronger than in Ireland, and it was fully shared by the humblest dependant.

The feudal spirit was clearly reflected in the customs and contracts of land. Clauses were constantly inserted in leases, obliging tenants to furnish their landlords with horses or labour for several days in the year, or with tributes of poultry, turkeys, or geese; there were sometimes clauses, which fully coincided with the political ethics of the Irish tenant, obliging the leaseholder to vote always with his landlord; there was the curious custom of "sealing money"—a perquisite given to the squire's wife by the tenant on the sealing of their leases. The penal code concentrated immense magisterial and administrative powers in the hands of the landlord class, and formed a tradition which long survived the laws, while the middlemen diverted from them much of the unpopularity which in times of distress might have attached to them. The landlord was the arbiter of innumerable disputes; he often exercised his influence as magistrate to protect his tenants who were in difficulties through faction fights or illicit distilling, and they in their turn were always ready to keep the bailiff from his door. There was on neither side much regard for law, but the landlord usually maintained both his authority and his popularity.

A governing type was developed in the class, which was very remote from modern English ideas, but which was well adapted to the conditions under which they lived. The admirable picture which Miss Edgeworth has drawn in "Ormond," of the relations between King Corney and his people, will enable the reader to understand it. The Irish landlords were able, without the assistance of any armed constabulary, to keep the country quiet during the greater part of the eighteenth century, even in times of war, when it was almost denuded of troops. They again and again suppressed Whiteboy disturbances, by parties raised among their own tenantry; and when they placed themselves at the head of the volunteer movement, the nation followed them with enthusiasm. A class who were capable of these things may have had many faults, but they can have been neither impotent nor unpopular. . . .

In the meantime, another and most formidable and persistent element of disturbance was growing up in the North. The year 1795 is very memorable in Irish history, as the year of the formation of the Orange Society, and the beginning of the most serious disturbances in the county of Armagh.

It is with a feeling of unfeigned diffidence that I enter upon this branch of my narrative. Our authentic materials are so scanty, and so steeped in party and sectarian animosity, that a writer who has done his utmost to clear his mind from prejudice, and bring together with impartiality the conflicting statements of partisans, will still, if he is a wise man, always doubt whether he has succeeded in painting with perfect fidelity the delicate gradations of provocation, palliation, and guilt. The old popular feud between the lower ranks of Papists and Presbyterians in the northern counties is easy to understand, and it is not less easy to see how the recent course of Irish politics had increased it. A class which had enjoyed and gloried in uncontested ascendency, found this ascendency passing from its hands. A class which had formerly been in subjection, was elated by new privileges, and looked forward to a complete abolition of political disabilities. Catholic and Protestant tenants came into a new competition, and the demeanour of Catholics towards Protestants was sensibly changed. There were boasts in taverns and at fairs, that the Protestants would speedily be swept away from the land and the descendants of the old proprietors restored, and it was soon known that Catholics all over the country were forming themselves into committees or societies, and were electing representatives for a great Catholic convention at Dublin. The riots and outrages of the Peep of Day Boys and Defenders had embittered the feeling on both sides. In spite of the strenuous efforts of some of the principal gentry of the county, and especially of Lord Charlemont and Mr. Richardson, and in spite, too, of the hanging or public flogging of several culprits of both creeds, these riots had continued at short intervals for ten years before the Orange Society was established. . . .

Outrages, however, were by no means confined to one side, and the violent alternation of hope and despondency that followed the appointment and the recall of Lord Fitzwilliam, the constant rumours of rebellion and invasion, and the great extension of the Defender movement through Ireland, contributed to aggravate the situation. In the county of Armagh the Protestants were decidedly in the ascendant, but there was a considerable minority of Catholics, who were generally Defenders, and there were numerous collisions between the two parties.

In September 1795 riots broke out in this county, which continued for some days, but at length the parish priest on the one side, and a gentleman named Atkinson on the other, succeeded in so far appeasing the quarrel that the combatants formally agreed to a truce, and were about to retire to their homes, when a new party of Defenders, who had marched from the adjoining counties to the assistance of their brethren, appeared upon the scene, and on September 21 they attacked the Protestants at a place called the Diamond. The Catholics on this occasion were certainly the aggressors, and they appear to have considerably outnumbered their antagonists, but the Protestants were better posted, better armed, and better organised. A serious conflict ensued, and the Catholics were completely defeated, leaving a large number—probably twenty or thirty—dead upon the field.

It was on the evening of the day on which the battle of the Diamond was fought, that the Orange Society was formed. It was at first a league of mutual defence, binding its members to maintain the laws and the peace of the country, and also the Protestant Constitution. No Catholic was to be admitted into the society, and the members were bound by oath not to reveal its secrets. The doctrine of Fitzgibbon, that the King, by assenting to Catholic emancipation, would invalidate his title to the throne, was remarkably reflected in the oath of the Orangemen, which bound them to defend the King and his heirs "so long as he or they support the Protestant ascendency." The society took its name from William of Orange, the conqueror of the Catholics, and it agreed to celebrate annually the battle of the Boyne.

In this respect there was nothing in it particularly novel. Protestant associations, for the purpose of commemorating the events and maintaining the principles of the Revolution, had long been known. Such a society had been founded at Exeter immediately after the Revolution. Such a society, under the name of "The Old Revolution Club," had long existed in Scotland. In Ireland, too, the Revolution of 1688 was so closely connected with the disposition of property and power, that it naturally assumed a transcendent importance, and the commemorations which are commonly associated with the Orange Society were in truth of a much earlier date. The twelfth of July—which by a confusion between the old and new styles was regarded as the anniversary of both the battle of the Boyne and the battle of Aughrim—and the relief of Londonderry were annually commemorated in Ireland long before the Orange Society existed. From the time of the Revolution till the beginning of the nineteenth century, November 4, which was the birthday of William III, was celebrated in Dublin with the greatest pomp. The Lord Lieutenant held a court, and followed by the Chancellor, the judges, the Lord Mayor, and a long train of the nobility and gentry, he paraded in state round the statue of William III in College Green. At the drawing-room the ladies appeared decorated with orange ribbons, and orange cockades were worn by the soldiers. These commemorations were universally recognised as mere manifestations of loyalty to the Constitution and the dynasty, and were fully countenanced by men who were very friendly to the Catholics. The volunteers, who did so much to bridge the chasm between the two sects, held some of their chief assemblies around the statue of William III. Every year, during the great period of the volunteer movement, they met there on the birthday of William; decorated with orange lilies and orange cockades; and the "Boyne Water" was played, and a *feu de joie* was fired in honour of the occasion. Wolfe Tone has noticed, as a most significant fact, that in 1792, for the first time since the institution of the volunteers, this ceremony was objected to, and omitted. It was on the occasion of the commemoration of July 12, that the Ulster volunteers assembled at Belfast, presented their famous address to Lord Charlemont in favour of the admission of Catholics to the suffrage.

A very different spirit, however, animated the early Orangemen. The upper classes at first generally held aloof from the society. For a considerable time it appears to have been almost confined to the Protestant peasantry of Ulster, and the title of Orangeman was probably assumed by numbers who had never joined the organisation, who were simply Peep of Day Boys taking a new name, and whose conduct was certainly not such as those who instituted the society had intended.

A terrible persecution of the Catholics immediately followed. The animosities between the lower orders of the two religions, which had long been little bridled, burst out afresh, and after the battle of the Diamond, the Protestant rabble of the county of Armagh, and of part of the adjoining counties, determined by continuous outrages to drive the Catholics from the country. Their cabins were placarded, or, as it was termed, "papered," with the words, "To hell or Connaught," and if the occupants did not at once abandon them, they were attacked at night by an armed mob. The webs and looms of the poor Catholic weavers were cut and destroyed. Every article of furniture was shattered or burnt. The houses were often set on fire, and the inmates were driven homeless into the world. The rioters met with scarcely any resistance or disturbance. Twelve or fourteen houses were sometimes wrecked in a single night. Several Catholic chapels were burnt, and the persecution, which began in the county of Armagh, soon extended over a wide area in the counties of Tyrone, Down, Antrim, and Derry. . . .

*The Protestant terrorists known as Peep of Day Boys forced between 700 and 1,400 Catholic families to flee from their homes in county Armagh, as the fighting between Defenders and Protestant farmers' defense groups increased in intensity. Many of the Catholic refugees from Armagh wandered west and settled in Connaught. Fierce sectarian clashes continued along the borders of Ulster and Leinster during 1796.*

In addition to the Indemnity Act, the Insurrection Act, and the suspension of the Habeas Corpus Act, a few measures were carried in 1796, which deserve a brief notice. There was an Act which, in my opinion, ought never to have been altered, making conspiracy to murder, a felony of the same nature as murder itself. It might indeed be reasonably contended that this offence, whether measured by its effects upon society, or by the moral guilt it implies, is the more heinous of the two, and in a country like Ireland, where a very large proportion of the worst crimes are prepared in secret societies and committed by a deputy, it is especially dangerous. A new Act was passed, preventing the importation, and regulating the sale, of arms and ammunition; the salaries of the judges were again raised; the punishment of hanging was substituted in Ireland, as it had a few years before been in England, in the execution of women, for the much more horrible punishment of burning; and the greater part of the Dublin Police Act, which was still exceedingly unpopular, was repealed, thus restoring to the Corporation the chief control over the maintenance of order.

Whatever may be thought of the coercive legislation of 1796, no one who reads the correspondence of the time can doubt, that remedies of a most exceptional and drastic character were imperatively needed. At the same time, during the whole of this year, the disease appears to have been mainly, though certainly not exclusively, in the North. In August, when a project of raising a yeomanry force was entertained, Toler, the Solicitor-General, wrote: "I think I can venture to say, from what I know of the South and West of Ireland, the Government may, with safety and effect, appeal to the gentry and farmers in those parts to act under commissions from the Crown, prudently issued. . . . It is evident to demonstration, that the opinion of the multitude, and of all descriptions in the provinces of Munster, Leinster, and Connaught, has grown infinitely more loyal during the war, which evidently saved Ireland, by the exclusion of Jacobins, and by bringing the idle and dangerous under the control of military discipline." But the state of the North was extremely alarming, and insurrection was constantly expected. Frequent efforts were made to tamper with the loyalty of the soldiers and the militia; several militiamen were found to have taken the United Irishman's oath, and the dispute between Protestant and Catholic, which originated at Armagh, soon extended to the forces, and showed itself in a violent quarrel between the Mayo and Kilkenny Militia, on the one hand, and the Tyrone Militia on the other.

In August, Camden described the state of the country as growing rapidly worse. Trees of liberty had been planted in Antrim, and bonfires lit in consequence of French victories. Officers of the County Limerick Militia declared that they could place very little dependence on their men. There were great fears about the Queen's County and the West Meath Militia, which were both Catholic, and two men of the latter regiment had been punished for attempting to plant a tree of liberty in the camp. Many of the artillery soldiers quartered at Belfast, were believed to be infected, and four informers had been recently murdered. . . .

*Public disturbances and reports of widespread disloyalty, especially in Ulster, caused the authorities much anxiety. During 1796 the Protestant gentry organized a paramilitary force known as the Yeomanry to deal with internal disorder and subversion. Disaffected tenants in Ulster held large meetings to air their grievances. Some of these orderly meetings took place in the fields where the tenant farmers gathered on the pretext of digging potatoes. In the meantime the United Irishmen intensified their search for arms and drilled openly, to the growing discomfort of local landowners and officials in Dublin Castle.*

One of the most remarkable facts in this period of Irish history is the tranquillity of the greater part of Catholic Ireland, at the time when both Protestants and Catholics in Ulster were in a condition so nearly approaching anarchy. How far it was loyalty, apathy, or calculation, may be disputed, but the fact cannot be denied. "I do really believe," wrote a clergyman, who was accustomed to correspond greatly with the Government, "that the Catholic priests have more influence than they are willing to acknowledge, and I am fully persuaded, notwithstanding the apparent calm in the southern provinces, that the Papists there, many families of whom have lately emigrated from the North, are fully acquainted with the designs of the same party, who have remained behind." Seditious violence, however, was at this time confined to Ulster, to a very few points in Leinster, and to a somewhat larger area of Connaught. A gentleman from Ballinrobe, in the county of Mayo, wrote that he had been trying to get up a district corps of yeomen, and had summoned his tenants, and asked them to take the oath of allegiance, but they all positively refused, and he did not venture to place Government arms in their hands. The hills about were said to be full of arms. Contraband cargoes from France were constantly run into the Killeries, and numerous deserters found a shelter among the mountains. "The vast numbers of people from the county of Armagh, who have resided for some time among them, may have instilled into the minds of these people some of their own principles." Sir Edward Newenham stated, in the early part of this year, that a magistrate near Ballintubber, in the county of Roscommon, was accused of having given the Defenders a grove of ash trees, to make pike handles, and that many men in comfortable circumstances had joined them openly. A day or two before the Defenders appear in any district, he said, a man of decent appearance goes through the country, telling the people that the French will soon come to their assistance, that ships have already arrived in the North, that Napper Tandy and Hamilton Rowan will lead them, and that Grattan will defend them in Parliament. When the way is thus prepared, the Defenders appear in small detached bodies, first disarming, and then swearing in the people. . . .

In 1796 the United Irishmen very generally succeeded in their efforts to incorporate the Defenders into their own body. For some time, the United Irish emissaries had been going among them, endeavouring to learn their views and intentions. They reported that Defenderism was not so much an association, as a mass of associations, with little or no uniformity of views and actions, differing in different counties in its tests and signs, and for the most part wasting its strength in partial and ill-directed insurrections against local grievances. As the Defender organisation owed its origin to religious animosities, and consisted exclusively of the most ignorant Catholics, it was very likely to be turned into a mere engine of bigotry, and very unfit for political enterprise. The United Irishmen now made it their business to impress upon the Defenders the great superiority of the United Irish organisation, the necessity of an alliance with the Protestants, the expediency of pursuing only one thing, "an equal, full, and adequate representation of the people," which would put an end to religious distinction and to most of the grievances of which they complained. They at last succeeded, and the Defenders in great bodies took the oath, and were incorporated into the Union. The most turbulent Catholic element in Ireland thus passed into it, and its introduction into the Catholic militia regiments was greatly facilitated.

It was in the autumn and winter of 1796 that Arthur O'Connor, Thomas Addis Emmet, and Dr. McNevin first formally joined the society, which from this time was to a large extent under their guidance. Tone, Napper Tandy, and Rowan, the most prominent of the original members, had been driven from Ireland, and Rowan appears to have given up all politics. About the same time, the United Irishmen began to give a military organisation to their society. This military organisation was grafted on the civil one, and it was fully elaborated at the close of 1796 and in the beginning of 1797. The secretary of each ordinary committee of twelve was appointed a non-commissioned officer; the delegate of five societies to a lower baronial committee was commonly made a captain, with sixty men under him. The delegate of ten lower baronials to the upper and district committee became a colonel, commanding a battalion of 600 men; the colonels in each county sent in the names of three persons, one of whom was appointed, by the executive Directory, adjutant-general for the county, and it was the duty of these adjutant-generals to communicate directly with the executive. Orders were given that every member of the society should endeavour to procure a gun, bayonet, and ammunition, or, if this was not possible, a pair of pistols, or at least a pike. . . .

*The Irish administration received many ominous reports from informers and other sources about the revolutionary activities of the United Irishmen and their allies the Defenders. United Irish leaders reckoned that a popular rising would easily overwhelm the 20,000 troops stationed in the country. French military victories on the Continent made the prospect of a rebellion in Ireland all the more likely as well as lethal in Government eyes. Wolfe Tone left America on 1 January 1796 and made his way to Paris where he helped the French Directory to plan an expedition to Ireland. Of the United Irish leaders in Paris, including Lord Edward Fitzgerald and Arthur O'Connor, Tone most impressed the French officials with his ability and revolutionary zeal.*

All this time, however, he never for a moment forgot the mission that he had undertaken, and in the perfect candour of his journals we can trace most clearly the various motives that actuated him. There was much of the spirit of an ambitious adventurer, who hoped to carve his way, amid the stormy scenes that were opening, to wealth and power and fame. There was much of the spirit of the revolutionist, to whom the democratic ideal of Rousseau had become almost what religion is to a devotee. There was also a true strain of self-sacrificing patriotism; a real sense of the degradation of his country, the corruption of her Government and the poverty of her people, but, like much Irish patriotism, that of Tone was mixed with great levity, and was largely compounded of hatreds. He hated and despised the Parliament of Ireland. He hated the Irish country gentry. He hated the Whig Club, and always remembered with bitterness how Grattan had warned the Catholic Committee against him; but above all things he hated England as the main cause of the evils of Ireland, and looked forward with passionate eagerness to her downfall.

Yet not many years had passed since Tone had sent to Pitt and Grenville memorials of a project for establishing a military colony in the South Sea, for the purpose of assisting England in war with Spain, and if these memorials had been acted on, and Pitt had thrown the young adventurer into a career of enterprise under the English flag, he has himself acknowledged that it is extremely improbable that he would have ever been heard of as an Irish rebel. Even after he had been deeply immersed in the conspiracy, even at the time when he was obliged to leave Ireland, he appears to have been perfectly prepared to abandon Irish politics if the Government he deemed so odious would provide for him in the East Indies. He was not a bloodthirsty man, and he was sincerely anxious that rebellion in Ireland should be as little sanguinary as possible, but he distinctly contemplated a massacre of the gentry as a possible consequence of what he was doing, and he became more and more callous about the means that were to be employed. A proclamation was stated in France to have been issued by the United Irishmen enjoining that all Irishmen in the British service who were captured with arms in their hands should be instantly shot. Tone expressed his warm approval of the measure, and even claimed to have been its first proposer. He opposed a French project for landing a devastating force in Ireland to prey upon the property of the country, but he supported, though not without evident qualms of conscience, an atrocious scheme for landing some thousand criminals in England, and commissioning them to burn Bristol, and commit every kind of depredation in their power. "My heart," he wrote very candidly, "is hardening hourly, and I satisfy myself now at once on points which would have staggered me twelve months ago." "I do not think my morality or feeling is much improved by my promotion to the rank of adjutant-general. The truth is, I hate the very name of England. I hated her before my exile, and I will hate her always." . . .

*Tone's detailed reports on conditions in Ireland convinced the Directory that the country was ripe for revolution and that 20,000 French soldiers would suffice to conquer the British forces there. General Hoche was put in command of the expeditionary force, comprising some 43 ships and 15,000 troops. The invasion fleet sailed from Brest on December 15 with Tone wearing the uniform of a French Adjutant-General. Dense fog, inept navigation, crossed signals, and adverse winds scattered the fleet. Only*

*15 ships ever reached Bantry Bay, the original destination, and then no concerted landing was attempted owing to gale force winds. The combination of bad weather and disputes among the commanders turned the expedition into a fiasco, and the fleet returned to France in fragments.*

It was a strange and startling thing, that a great French fleet should have been able to sail unmolested to the coast of Ireland, to remain in an Irish bay for five whole days, and then to return to France without encountering an English fleet. In one respect, however, the expedition was very reassuring. It furnished a most valuable, if not decisive, test of the disposition of the Catholics in the South of Ireland, and some test of the disposition of those in the other parts of the kingdom, and their conduct appears to me to show clearly that, although treason had of late years been zealously propagated among them, its influence was as yet very superficial. An invasion had long been expected. Rumours of a coming French army, which was to emancipate the people from tithes and rents, and English rule, had been industriously spread through the Catholic population, and as soon as the fleet appeared in Bantry Bay, the gravity of the crisis was fully understood. If disloyalty had really reached the point which the United Irish leaders imagined, and which some subsequent historians have supposed, it could scarcely have failed under such circumstances to have risen to the surface, and an immediate explosion might have been expected. But all the evidence we possess concurs in showing, that the great body of the Catholics did not at this time show the smallest wish to throw off the English rule, and that their spontaneous and unforced sympathies were with the British flag. . . .

It is a memorable fact that Cork, Galway, and Limerick, the great centres of Irish Catholicism, the cities where at the present time the spirit of sedition is probably most formidable, vied with one another in 1796 in proofs of loyalty to the English Government when a French fleet was on the coast. It is a not less memorable fact, that the town which then showed the worst spirit was undoubtedly Belfast, the capital of the most advanced Irish Protestantism, and in the present day one of the most loyal cities of Ireland. Camden described it as the only town where bad dispositions had been shown. A meeting of the principal inhabitants was convened for the purpose of raising a corps for defence against the French, but the only result was the appointment of a committee, which, by a majority of seven to two, passed strong resolutions in favour of parliamentary reform; and Brown, the Sovereign of Belfast, wrote, "that in this moment of danger there was extreme difficulty in enlisting any yeomen, and that the disaffection was grave and general." ...

The main problem of Irish history is the fact that Ireland, after a connection with England of no less than 700 years, is as disaffected as a newly conquered province, and that, in spite of a long period of national education, of the labours of many able and upright statesmen, of a vast amount of remedial legislation, and of close contact with the free, healthy, and energetic civilisation of Great Britain, Irish popular sentiment on political subjects is at the present hour perhaps the most degraded and the most demoralised in Europe. The year 1796 contributed largely to this demoralisation. Anarchy and organised crime had greatly extended, and they were steadily taking a more political form, while Grattan and the other really able, honest, moderate, and constitutional reformers, had lost almost all their influence. The discredit which was thrown on the Constitution of 1782, and the utter failure of Grattan to procure either parliamentary reform or Catholic emancipation, had combined with the influences that sprang from the French Revolution to turn many into new and dangerous paths, and to give popularity and power to politicians of another and a baser type.

Still the mass of people seem as yet to have been but little touched, and the problem of making Ireland a loyal and constitutional country was certainly not an impossible one. But the men in whose hands the direction of affairs was placed, were determined to resist the most moderate and legitimate reforms, and they made the perpetual disqualification of the Catholics, and the unqualified maintenance of all the scandalous and enormous abuses of the representative system, the avowed and foremost objects of their policy. Their parliamentary majority was overwhelming, and with the existing constituencies there seemed no prospect of overthrowing it. Very naturally, then, the reforming energy of the country ebbed more and more away from the constitutional leaders, and began to look to rebellion and foreign assistance for the attainment of its objects. ...

# IX
## *Disaffection and Polarization,*
## *1797–1798*

The loyalty displayed by the militia and the Catholic peasantry when the French lay in Bantry Bay, made a great impression on all classes of politicians. The United Irishmen, indeed, urged that the French had attempted to land in one of the parts of Ireland where the organisation was least extended; that they had sent no intimation to the leaders of the conspiracy which could render it possible to prepare for their reception, and that if a French fleet had appeared in the North or North-west the result would have been very different. In these statements there was no doubt much truth, but still the attitude of positive and even enthusiastic loyalty exhibited in so many parts of Ireland seemed to show that the seditious spirit was less formidable than might have been imagined, and that a large element of unreality mingled with it. It by no means followed from the fact that the bulk of the peasantry in any district had been sworn in as United Irishmen or as Defenders, that they were prepared to appear in arms for the French, or even seriously desired an invasion. The intimidation exercised by small bands of conspirators induced multitudes to take an oath which they had very little intention of keeping, and even where intimidation did not come into operation, disloyalty was often a fashion, a sentiment, and almost an amusement, which abundantly coloured the popular imagination, but was much too feeble and unsubstantial a thing to induce men to make any genuine sacrifice in its cause. Everyone who has any real knowledge of Irish life, character, and history knows how widely a sentiment of this kind has been diffused, and knows also that districts and classes where it has been most prevalent have again and again remained perfectly passive in times when the prospects of rebellion seemed most favourable, and have furnished thousands of the best and most faithful soldiers to the British army. Genuine enthusiasts, like those who, at the close of the eighteenth century, were sending skilful memoirs to the French Government, representing all Ireland as panting for revolution, or like a few brave men who in later times have sacrificed to their political convictions all that makes life dear, have usually miscalculated its force, and have learnt at last, by bitter experience, that, except when it has been allied with religious or agrarian passions, it usually evaporates in words.

There is indeed, perhaps, only one condition in which its un-assisted action can be a serious danger to the State. It is when legislation breaks down the influence of the educated and proper-tied classes of the community, and then by a democratic suffrage, under the shelter of the ballot, throws the preponderating voting power of the country into the hands of the most ignorant and the most disaffected. A majority of votes represents very imper-fectly deliberate opinion. It represents still more imperfectly the course which men desire with real earnestness, for which they will make real sacrifices; but a languid preference or an idle sentiment may be quite sufficient to place desperate and un-scrupulous men in power, and to give them the means of dis-locating the whole fabric of the State. It has been reserved for the sagacity of modern English statesmanship to create this dan-ger in Ireland.

But after all that can be said, it is impossible to read this narra-tive without being impressed with the extremely precarious tenure upon which British dominion in Ireland at this time rested. With a little better weather, and a little better seamanship on the part of the French, the chances were all against it. If an army of 14,000 good French soldiers, under such a commander as Hoche, had succeeded in landing without delay, and if a rebellion had then broken out in any part of the country, Ireland would most prob-ably have been, for a time at least, separated from the British Empire. . . .

*Ireland's close brush with a French invasion prompted the administration to strengthen the country's security forces. After Parliament met on 16 January 1797, Grattan criticized the English conduct of the war and their failure to make peace with France. A motion to tax absentee landlords was defeated by 122 to 49. On March 2, the Bank of Ireland followed the Bank of England by temporarily suspending cash payments.*

Much more serious, however, than the shock to public credit was the anarchy which was now rapidly spreading through the North, and which in a few weeks rose to the point of virtual rebellion. In order to estimate the coercive measures that were taken by the Government, it is necessary to endeavour to obtain a clear notion of the extent, and the kind of the evil. The subject is one which lends itself easily to opposing exaggerations, and it has been chiefly dealt with by historians who are violent partisans. There exists, however, in the confidential letters of magistrates, which are now in Dublin Castle, a large amount of authentic and entirely unused material, and by pursuing the sure, though I fear very tedious, process of bringing together a multitude of detailed contemporary testimonies, it will, I think, be possible to arrive at some just conclusions.

The disturbances were clearly organised, and their centres were innumerable small societies of United Irishmen, which acted very independently of one another, and which were multiplied by incessant propagandism. They consisted of men who, either through French principles, or through disgust at the corrupt and subservient condition of the Government and Parliament in Dublin, now aimed distinctly at a separate republic, and hoped to attain it by armed rebellion. This rebellion was not to take place till a French army had landed. In the mean time, their business was to prepare for the French by nightly drilling, by the manufacture of pikes, by the plunder of arms, by preventing the farmers from enlisting in the yeomanry, by seducing the soldiers and the militia, by systematically paralysing the law. But with the political movement, there was now combined the whole system of Whiteboyism and Defenderism—all the old grievances about tithes, and taxes, and rent, which had so often stirred the people to outrage—and on the outskirts of the whole movement hung a vast assisting mass of aimless anarchy; of ordinary crime; of the restlessness which is the natural consequence of great poverty. . . .

*During the spring of 1797, a wave of outrages, often inspired by United Irishmen and Defenders, spread through counties Donegal, Roscommon, Londonderry, Tyrone, Down, and Armagh. Armed gangs roamed the countryside with impunity plundering and intimidating. The lawlessness in Ulster forced General Lake, on the urging of Chief Secretary Pelham, to declare martial law. Lake's proclamation was debated in both the English and Irish Parliaments. Although Grattan and other moderates denounced this measure, Lord Camden's administration secured the special powers necessary for the repression of disorder. In the next few months there were numerous sharp skirmishes between soldiers and United Irishmen, and both sides made preparations for a showdown.*

The belief of Camden that no policy of conciliation could now be efficacious, was strengthened by the reports from Ulster. General Lake, who held the chief command in the province, wrote from Belfast at the time of the proclamation, to the effect that all the information he received tended to convince him that matters were rapidly coming to a crisis; that a speedy rising was fully determined on; that, although it would probably not take place till the landing of the French, there could be no certainty, and that every precaution must be taken. Scarcely an hour, he said, passed without accounts of the success of the United Irishmen in swearing in men of the militia. "The lower order of the people," he continued, "and most of the middle class are determined Republicans, have imbibed the French principles, and will not be contented with anything short of a Revolution. My ideas are not taken up hastily, but from conversation with men of all descriptions, many of whom, though strong for Parliamentary Reform, are now frightened, and say we have been the cause of this measure originally, and have now no power over our tenants and labourers." "Nothing," adds Lake, "but coercive measures in the strongest degree can have any weight in this country."

The great Irish Rebellion of the eighteenth century is always called the Rebellion of 1798; but the letters from Ulster in the spring and summer of 1797, habitually speak of the province as in a state of real, though smothered rebellion, and the measures superseding civil by military law were justified on that ground.

The first military raid for the purpose of seizing unregistered arms, appears to have come upon the people as a surprise. Between March 10 and 25, more than 5,400 guns, more than 600 bayonets, and about 350 pistols, besides other arms and military accoutrements, were seized; but very soon there was a general concealment of arms which baffled the soldiers, while the condition of the province became continually worse. It is extremely difficult within a short compass to give a vivid and unexaggerated description of it. It varied in different districts, and it is only by the perusal and comparison of great numbers of confidential letters, written by magistrates and military authorities to the Government in Dublin, that a clear picture is gradually formed. . . .

The military forces in Ireland were at this time very considerable. In February 1797 there was an effective force of about 15,000 regular soldiers, 18,000 militia, and 30,000 yeomanry, of whom 18,000 were cavalry. But an invasion was continually expected, and the country was exposed on all sides. There were scarcely any fortresses in which troops could be concentrated. Soldiers were habitually employed, to a far greater extent than in England, to discharge police functions, such as suppressing riots, and enforcing revenue laws, and they were now called on to put down innumerable concerted outrages, carried on by night over an immense area of wild country, and to disarm a scattered and disloyal population. Lake wrote in the strongest terms about the inadequacy of his force. "I believe," he wrote, "this district requires more than half the troops in Ireland to manage it, as there is no part of it that does not require double the number we have." A meeting of magistrates and yeomanry officers in the counties of Down and Armagh drew up a remarkable memorial, stating that the late vigorous measure of disarming the people—"which, however," they added, "has in many parts disarmed only the well affected, the others hiding their arms"—would be useless without a very large standing force to follow it up by constant piquets and patrols, both of horse and foot, "and this force," they said, "should be the greater, as the yeomanry even in towns are assembled with much difficulty and delay, require so long notice that the design is often foreseen and frustrated, and being scattered in their private houses they may (as is now openly threatened) be either disarmed or murdered in their houses, or on their way to parade ground." They added, "that the daily threats (actually executed in many late instances here) of personal and other injury to those continuing yeomen or supporters of them; and the loss of all trade or employment from the numerous body United, or affecting to be so through fear or interest," had weakened the yeomanry, and that the protection of the country in a time of extreme danger, and when measures of desperate vigour might be required, could not be safely entrusted to mere volunteers, liable to no coercion except honour and regard to character.

It will be sufficiently evident to anyone who considers the subject with common candour, that under such circumstances numerous military outrages were certain to occur. The only method by which the disarming could be carried out and the men who were engaged in nightly outrages detected, was by nightly raids, in rebellious districts. The Chief Secretary strongly pressed upon the commander in the North, that the soldiers searching for arms should always be accompanied by a superior officer; but Lake answered that, though he would do what he could to prevent abuses, this, at least, was absolutely impossible. Success could only be attained by surprise, by the simultaneous search of innumerable widely scattered cabins. If it was known that a search was proceeding in one place, arms were at once concealed in fifty others. It was impossible that an officer could be present in every cabin which was being searched, and the task had to be largely entrusted to little groups of private soldiers. No one who knows what an army is, and how it is recruited, could expect that this should go on without producing instances of gross violence and outrage, and without seriously imperilling discipline.

This, however, was by no means the worst. The danger of invasion and armed rebellion was so great, and the regular troops in Ireland were so few, that it was necessary to collect those troops in points of military importance, and to entrust services which did not require a serious display of force to militiamen and yeomen, newly enrolled and most imperfectly disciplined. The yeomen, from their knowledge of the country and its people, were peculiarly efficient in searching for arms, and they were the force which was naturally and primarily intended for the preservation of internal security, as the regular troops were for the defence of the country against a foreign invasion. The creation of a large yeomanry force for the former purpose had been, as we have seen, one of the projects of Fitzwilliam. It had been strongly and repeatedly urged by Grattan and by Parsons, and, as we shall presently see, the most liberal and enlightened English commander entirely agreed with the most liberal members of the Irish Parliament, that the suppression of outrage which did not rise to the height of actual armed rebellion, ought to be the special province of the yeomanry. But such a force was at this time perfectly certain to be guilty of gross violence. It was recruited chiefly in districts which had been for years the scene of savage faction fights between the Defenders and the Peep of Day Boys; between the United Irishmen and the Orangemen; and it was recruited in the face of the most formidable obstacles. The United Irishmen made it one of their main objects to prevent the formation of this new and powerful force, and they pursued this object with every kind of outrage, intimidation, abuse, and seduction. There had been not a few murders. There were countless instances of attacks on the houses of the yeomen. Their families were exposed to constant insult, and to constant peril. The system had already begun in some disaffected districts of treating the yeomen as if they were lepers, and refusing all dealings with them; while in other districts every art was employed to seduce them from their allegiance.

That a powerful yeomanry force should have been created in spite of all these obstacles, and at a time when Irishmen were pouring into the regular army, the militia, and the navy, appears to me to be a striking proof both of the military spirit and of the sturdy independence and self-reliance which then characterised the loyalists of Ireland. The estimate first laid before Parliament was for 20,000 men, but in six months above 37,000 men were arrayed, and during the rebellion the force exceeded 50,000, and could, if necessary, have been increased. But although the United Irishmen failed in preventing the formation of this great force, they at least succeeded in profoundly affecting its character. In great districts which were torn by furious factions it consisted exclusively of the partisans of one faction, recruited under circumstances well fitted to raise party animosity to fever heat. Such men, with uniforms on their backs and guns in their hands, and clothed with the authority of the Government, but with scarcely a tinge of discipline and under no strict martial law, were now let loose by night on innumerable cabins.

These circumstances do not excuse, but they explain and largely palliate, their misdeeds, and they do much to divide the blame. Disarming had plainly become a matter of the first necessity at a time when a great portion of the population were organising, at the command of a seditious conspiracy, for the purpose of co-operating with an expected French invasion, and it could hardly be carried out in Ireland without excessive violence. Martial law is always an extreme remedy of the State, but when it is administered by competent officers and supported by an overwhelming and well-disciplined force, its swift stern justice is not always an evil. But few things are more terrible than martial law when the troops are undisciplined, inadequate in numbers, and involved in the factions of the country they are intended to subdue. . . .

*The Government's efforts to disarm the United Irishmen before any rebellion could take place provoked a campaign of terror. The "Ancient Britons," a Welsh regiment of fencible cavalry, killed young and old alike and burned many houses in the Newry area. In Dublin, Valentine Lawless, Grattan, and other moderates denounced these military excesses but to no avail.*

All these things naturally tended to stir up fierce and enduring animosities, and the condition of Ulster at this period was almost as horrible and as critical as can be conceived, except in the case of open war or rebellion. The gaols and guard-houses were thronged with untried prisoners, who were often detained for many months. Many were sent to the fleet, but it was soon found that grave dangers attended this course. The signs of mutiny which this year appeared in the British fleet, and which at last culminated in the mutiny of the Nore, were believed to be not unconnected with the number of seditious Irishmen who had been sent to it. There is even some evidence of a secret correspondence between the Ulster rebels and the mutineers. In more than one letter, Lake complained that he was overburdened with prisoners, whom he could not prosecute with any hope of conviction, but who were notorious villains, quite unfit to be let loose or, through physical defects, to serve in the fleet, and who, if they were sent there, would probably do their utmost to corrupt the sailors. "These villains," he wrote, "pretend to rejoice at going to sea, as they say by that means they will be able to corrupt the sailors, and completely settle the business. . . . I believe the whole country, at least the lower orders of it, are the same in every particular."

Another fact, which added greatly to the anarchy of the North, and had ultimately a most serious influence on the remainder of Ireland, was the growing importance of the Orange movement, and the alliance which was gradually forming between it and the Government. At first, as we have seen, Orangism was simply a form of outrage—the Protestant side of a faction fight which had long been raging in certain counties of the North among the tenants and labourers of the two religions—and the Protestants in Armagh being considerably stronger than the Catholics, Orangism in that county had assumed the character of a most formidable persecution. Magistrates were frequently accused of being shamefully passive during these outrages; but the movement, in its earlier stages, appears to have been wholly unprompted by and unconnected with the gentry of the country. It was a popular and democratic movement, springing up among the lowest classes of Protestants, and essentially lawless. As, however, it was the main object of the United Irishmen to form an alliance between the Presbyterians and the Catholics; as in pursuance of this policy they constituted themselves the champions of Catholics who had been persecuted by Orangemen; and as the Defenders steadily gravitated to the ranks of the United Irishmen, the Orangemen, by a natural and inevitable process, became a great counterpoise to the United Irishmen, and the civil war which raged between the two sects a great advantage to the Government. The successful efforts of the United Irishmen to prevent their party from enlisting in the yeomanry, resulted in that force being largely composed of men with Orange sympathies; and when the outrages of the Defenders and United Irishmen multiplied, and when the probability of invasion became very great, several considerable country gentlemen in Ulster changed their policy, placed themselves at the head of their Orange tenantry, and began to organise them into societies. The name of Orange was not, even at this time, associated in Ulster, only with the outrages in Armagh. Its primary meaning was simply loyalty to the Revolution settlement, and before the battle of the Diamond it appears to have been sometimes assumed by loyal societies which had no connection whatever with the disputes between the Peep of Day Boys and the Defenders. The country gentlemen who now took the name of Orangemen were mainly, or exclusively, strong opponents of the admission of Catholics to Parliament, though some of them were of the school of Flood, and desired a parliamentary reform upon a Protestant basis. The society as organised by them, emphatically disclaimed all sympathy with outrage and all desire to persecute. It was intended to be a loyal society for the defence of Ulster and the kingdom against the United Irishmen and against the French, and also for maintaining the Constitution on an exclusively Protestant basis, but it included in its ranks all the most intolerant and fanatical Protestantism in the province, and it inherited from its earlier stage, traditions and habits of violence and outrage which its new leaders could not wholly repress, and which the anarchy of the time was well fitted to encourage. . . .

*Brigadier-General Knox, the commanding officer at Dungannon, wrote to Pelham suggesting that Orangemen should be armed and used to help disarm the United Irishmen. According to Knox, Orange bigotry mattered less than Orange loyalty. Several Orange lodges were eventually incorporated into the yeomanry, but there was no general arming of the Orange order.*

In the correspondence of this time, the magistrates and gentry in the North of Ireland are constantly spoken of with great severity. They are represented as flying from their estates to the towns, or as remaining passive in the midst of the popular outrages, and Dean Warburton in more than one letter compares their conduct to that of the French gentry in the earlier stages of the Revolution. There were, indeed, a few conspicuous exceptions. Lord Downshire and Lord Cavan were specially noted for their zeal and courage; Charlemont, though his health was now much broken, hastened, in a manner which the Chief Secretary recognised as extremely honourable to him, to use his influence in the cause of order, even under a Government from which he was wholly separated; and other men in less prominent positions took the same course. But in general, Lake pronounced that "the system of terror practised by the United Irishmen" had "completely destroyed all ideas of exertion in most of the magistrates and gentry throughout the country."

The fact is especially remarkable when it is remembered what a prominent part the Ulster gentlemen had taken twenty years before in organising the volunteers, and how admirably they had then secured the province not only from invasion, but also from internal disorder. It is possible that some considerable moral and political decadence may have set in among them, but it is at least certain that the spread of republican ideas had enormously aggravated the situation. A country gentleman, in a wild district, who could no longer count upon the support of his tenantry, was almost helpless in the midst of the armed anarchy that was surging around him, and he had the strongest motives to avoid as much as possible a conflict with his people. Every active magistrate was in constant, immediate danger of murder, and in the forecast of events the separation of Ireland from England seemed now extremely probable. The landing of any considerable French force in Ulster would almost certainly have effected it, and it was not, perhaps, astonishing that many men of influence and property should have hesitated under these circumstances to hazard everything they possessed in the defence of a Government which had taken the administration of affairs out of their hands, and which was pursuing a policy that they regarded as absolutely ruinous. . . .

*Martial law and military atrocities alienated many of the Irish gentry who looked to Catholic relief and parliamentary reform as more effective measures to pacify the country. On 15 May 1797 William Ponsonby moved a series of resolutions calling for removal of all religious disabilities and reform of the representative system. Grattan defended these resolutions, ending his impassioned speech as follows:*

"I cannot, however, banish from my memory the lesson of the American war. . . . If that lesson has no effect on ministers, surely I can suggest nothing that will. We have offered you our measure. You will reject it. We deprecate yours; you will persevere. Having no hopes left to persuade or dissuade, and having discharged our duty, we shall trouble you no more, and after this day shall not attend the House of Commons."

The House was deaf to this appeal; the adjournment was carried by 117 to 30, and Grattan fulfilled his promise. Accompanied by Ponsonby, Curran, and a few others, and following the example of Fox and his immediate followers in England, he seceded from parliamentary life, and did not again appear upon the scene till the stirring debates upon the Union. This secession, among other effects, had that of taking away almost all public interest from the proceedings of the Irish House of Commons. From 1781 to the close of the session of 1797 there are excellent reports of its debates, which were evidently revised by the speakers, and which are of the greatest possible value to every serious student of this period of Irish history. They are a source from which I have drawn largely in this work, and there are even now few books on Irish politics which are either so interesting or so instructive. From this period to the period of the Union debates, our knowledge of what passed in the House of Commons is of the vaguest or most fragmentary character, derived chiefly from short newspaper reports, and we almost wholly lose the invaluable check which parliamentary criticism imposes on the extravagances of partisan statements.

Of the conduct of Grattan himself at this time, there is little more to be said. I have stated that since the recall of Fitzwilliam his speeches had assumed a more violent and more distinctly party character, and that all his hopes were placed in a change of ministry. Peace he believed to be vitally necessary, and he shared the belief which was then very prevalent, though the publication of confidential documents has now shown it to be unfounded, that Pitt did not sincerely desire it. Like Fox, with whom he was in close correspondence, he feared the imminent ruin both of the Empire and of Ireland. No one could doubt that if the war continued, a French invasion of Ireland was in the highest degree probable, and Grattan well knew that it was scarcely possible to exaggerate or to measure the calamities it might produce. But even apart from this, there was the danger of national bankruptcy, the growing probability of a great rebellion, the certainty of a complete and rapid demoralisation of public opinion. The new

revolutionary spirit was sweeping over the country like an epidemic, destroying the social and moral conditions on which all
sound self-government must rest. In the judgment of Grattan,
there was but one policy by which it could be effectually stayed. It
was, in his own words, "to combat the wild spirit of democratic
liberty by the regulated spirit of organised liberty"—to carry as
speedily as possible through the Irish Parliament measures of
parliamentary reform, Catholic emancipation, and a commutation
of tithes. It was now evident that existing Government was inexorably opposed to these measures, and it was dimly seen that if
they were ever to be conceded, it was likely to be in connection
with or subsequent to a legislative Union. Such an Union, Grattan
had foreseen as early as 1785, and he regarded it with implacable
hostility. But his own ideal was visibly fading, and it was becoming evident that the policy of 1782 was not destined to succeed. In
spite of the Place Bill, the Pension Bill, and the Catholic Bill of
1793, the Parliament was sinking in character, influence, and
popularity, and the independent minority had greatly diminished.
This may be attributed, partly to the more determined attitude of
hostility to reform which the Government had assumed, but in
part also to a genuine feeling of panic and reaction which the
French Revolution had produced in all privileged classes, and
which had reduced to insignificant proportions the reform party
in the English Legislature.

Outside the House, also, the position of Grattan was no longer
what it had been. He was still followed by a large body of the
country gentry, and of the more intelligent farmers and tradesmen
of the North, but he was no longer sustained by a strong force of
national enthusiasm. Another policy, other leaders and other principles, were in the ascendant, and they were hurrying the nation
onward to other destinies. In all the utterances of Grattan at this
time, private as well as public, a profound discouragement and a
deep sense of coming calamities may be traced. . . .

One of the most alarming signs of the dangerous condition of
Ireland was the disaffection which now constantly appeared in the
militia, and was not infrequently discovered or suspected among
the yeomanry and the regular troops. The seduction of soldiers
was a main object of the United Irishmen, and Lake and Knox
urged in many letters that it had proceeded so far that little or no

reliance could be placed upon the militia, and that the introduction of a large additional force from England was imperatively needed. "It answers no end," wrote an active magistrate, "to station small parties of the military in different cantonments, for they are regularly corrupted." This evil was by no means confined to the North. Infinite pains were taken in Dublin to secure the presence of at least one United Irishman in every company, and sedition spread so fast that one regiment was actually removed, and the Lord Lieutenant doubted whether it would not be necessary to move a second from the capital, for the express purpose of checking the contamination. There were, in May, courts-martial sitting at the same time on disaffected soldiers, in Cork, Limerick, and Belfast. Several militiamen were condemned and shot; no less than seventy men in the Monaghan Militia confessed that they had been seduced into taking the oath of the United Irishmen, and, as might have been expected, the air was charged with vague rumours and suspicions, magnifying and multiplying the real dangers. Lake believed that many United Irishmen had enlisted in the yeomanry for the purpose of obtaining arms. Even the Orangemen were at one time suspected, and apparently not quite without reason, of having been tampered with. . . .

*A number of prominent United Irishmen were arrested early in 1797, among them Arthur O'Connor and the proprietors of the Northern Star. The Society of United Irishmen, especially in Belfast, contained many passionate disciples of the French Revolution along with Whiteboy elements advocating the familiar methods of agrarian outrage. On May 17, the Lord Lieutenant and Council imposed more drastic martial laws on the country, forcing the United Irishmen on to the defensive. In the next few months more United Irish leaders were rounded up and arms seized by the authorities.*

The military powers which were entrusted to the Commander-in-Chief were at this time very terrible, and it was felt by the Government that they ought to be placed in stronger and more skilful hands than those of Lord Carhampton and Lake. An offer of the command in Ireland was accordingly made, in the May of 1797, to Lord Cornwallis, and Lord Camden very warmly supported it. Camden, indeed, desired to resign into the hands of

Cornwallis the Viceroyalty itself, believing that, in the very critical condition of Ireland, all power should, as much as possible, be concentrated in the hands of a competent soldier. If, however, Cornwallis refused to accept the Viceroyalty, Camden implored him to accept the military command, and promised to relinquish into his hands all the military control and power which the Lord Lieutenant possessed. It was extremely unfortunate for Ireland that this negotiation failed. Cornwallis differed radically from the political conduct pursued there, and he believed that it was not possible to dissociate the defence of the country from political measures. As Portland wrote to Camden, he refused to undertake the command in Ireland, "unless means were taken to separate the Catholics from the Dissenters, and it was evident that the bias of his opinion strongly inclined him to suppose that very great concessions, little, if at all, short of what is termed Catholic emancipation, were necessary for that purpose, and ought not to be withheld." Cornwallis declared that, in the event of actual or imminent invasion, he was prepared, if necessary, to cross the Channel, but that nothing, in his opinion, could put Ireland in a state of obedience and security, unless strong measures were taken "to prevent the union between the Catholics and Dissenters, and that he should not act honestly in countenancing a contrary opinion, by undertaking a task which, he believed in his conscience, could never be accomplished." Portland communicated this answer to Pitt and Dundas, and the proposed appointment was abandoned.

A similar offer was made to Cornwallis on the eve of the outbreak of the rebellion, and was again declined. It is not probable that if it had been accepted on either occasion, the rebellion could have been averted; but if a general of real and commanding ability had at this time presided over the defence of Ireland, the military excesses that took place might at least have been diminished. The almost unlimited discretion that was actually left to subordinate military authorities inevitably led to gross abuses, and it was in the summer of 1797 that the practice of burning houses, as a measure of punishment or police, came into use. Sometimes they were burnt because arms were not surrendered; sometimes because arms had been discovered; sometimes because a great crime had been committed in the district; sometimes because they were found empty at night in proclaimed districts, where the inhabitants were forbidden to leave them after sunset, and because their owners were believed to be absent on marauding expeditions. At the same time, in many quarters, the Orange movement burst out afresh in its old form of outrage and persecution, while the United Irishmen made a skilful use of the partial alliance of the Government with the more respectable Orangemen, to lash the Catholics into madness and rebellion. The state of Ulster can only be truly realised by collecting much fragmentary information; but if the reader has the patience to follow with me the casual lights furnished by officers and magistrates, it will, I think, gradually dawn upon him, and he will certainly have no difficulty in understanding the dangers and the animosities that were arising. . . .

*In the summer of 1797, Orangemen and their friends in the yeomanry committed many outrages against Catholics suspected of being United Irishmen or their sympathizers. Hundreds of new refugees fled from this paramilitary persecution in Ulster and headed for Connaught. With the tacit approval of the Government this repression soon spread into the midland counties where fierce religious antagonism was revived by the attacks of armed Orangemen on Defenders and United Irishmen. Both Protestants and Catholics believed the many rumors that the other side was bent on exterminating them. Sectarian riots broke out in county Tyrone during Orange celebrations of the Battle of the Boyne.*

At the same time, during the summer and autumn of 1797, real steps had been made towards the pacification of the North. The process of disarming was steadily carried on, and it met with some considerable success. It appears, from a confidential Government report, that in the first twenty days of July, there were surrendered in the northern district and in Westmeath 8,300 guns, and about 1,100 pikes, besides a large number of swords, pistols, and bayonets, while about 2,500 other guns, and about 550 pikes, were seized by force. Several quarters which, in the spring, had been great centres of disaffection, had become at least passively loyal. From Belfast, Lake wrote: "The town is more humbled than it has ever been, and many of the villains have quitted it." Newry, which was only second to Belfast as a centre of disturbance, seems to have been effectually pacified. Dundalk and its surrounding country were pronounced perfectly quiet. The courage and moderation with which Dean Warburton laboured to pacify his district of the county of Armagh received its reward, when he was able to announce to his parishioners in July, that the proclamation was revoked which placed that county under the Insurrection Act. Dungannon also, but not its neighbourhood, had been pacified by General Knox. "We are under no apprehensions," wrote a clergyman from that town, "but to the north of us it is quite lost. Dungannon is frontiered by Stewartstown, an advanced post in the enemies' country, with many royalists in it. Thence, to the northern sea, scarce a friend. . . . Be assured Orange is now loyal." "In consequence of threats and some rigour," wrote General Nugent, from Hillsborough, "the country people are bringing in their arms very fast, and taking the oath of allegiance. . . . Accounts from all parts of the country are very favourable, and agree that the lower orders of people are dropping off rapidly from the cause of the United Irishmen, and we have every reason to think that, with the assistance and continuance of the system which has been lately adopted against them, we shall have nothing to apprehend from their machinations." . . .

*Although the courts were beginning to function with more efficiency in bringing offenders to justice, the law could not be called impartial. The conviction on dubious legal grounds of a Presbyterian yeoman farmer named William Orr for being a United Irish recruiter, and his execution under the provisions of the Insurrection Act, provoked United Irishmen all over the country.*

The general judgment which will be formed of the policy and proceedings of the Irish Government at this time, and of the share of responsibility that belongs to them in hastening on the rebellion which was manifestly impending, will vary much according to the character of the reader, and perhaps still more according to the political predisposition with which he reviews the facts that have been related. It is manifestly absurd to describe the severities in Ulster as if they were unprovoked by a savage outburst of anarchy and crime, or to deny that in the midst of a great war, and with the extreme probability of a French invasion of Ireland, the disarming of a disaffected province had become urgently necessary. The rigour and violence of the measures that were adopted were chiefly due to the complete inadequacy of normal means for repressing widespread and organised revolt; to the want of any such body as the modern constabulary; to the military exigency which made it necessary in time of war to entrust semipolice functions to an undisciplined yeomanry. Those measures were judged as might have been expected in a country which, for more than a hundred years, had known nothing of martial law. In countries which were, in this respect at least, less happily situated, they would have excited less astonishment, and they will appear pale and insignificant when compared with the proceedings of those French revolutionists who were extolled by the United Irishmen as ideal champions of Liberty and Progress. The Insurrection Act was an extreme remedy for a desperate disease, limited to a brief period and to the proclaimed districts. Even the burning of houses, though unauthorised by law and eminently fitted to infuriate the people, can hardly be regarded as indefensible as a military measure, if it was found to be the necessary condition of carrying out a necessary disarming.

But although all this may, I think, be truly said, the faults of the Irish government during the few years before the rebellion of 1798 appear to me to have been enormously great, and a weight of tremendous responsibility rests upon those who conducted it. By habitual corruption and the steady employment of the system of nomination boroughs, they had reduced the Irish Legislature to a condition of such despicable and almost ludicrous subserviency, that a policy which was probably supported by the great majority of educated Irishmen, could not command more than twenty or thirty votes in the House of Commons. They had done this at a time when the French Revolution had made the public mind in the highest degree sensitive to questions of representation; at a time when the burden of the war was imposing extraordinary hardships on the people. They had resisted the very moderate Reform Bills of Ponsonby and Grattan, which would have left the overwhelming preponderance of political power in the hands of property, loyalty, and intelligence, as strenuously as the wild democratic schemes of the United Irishmen, and they had thus thrown into the path of treason a crowd of able and energetic men, who might have been contented by reform. No one who follows the history of the long succession of dangerous conventions which had existed in Ireland since 1782, can doubt that the Convention Act, making illegal, delegated and representative assemblies other than Parliament, was required; but it could be justified and acquiesced in, only on the condition that the popular branch of the Legislature was in some real sense a representative body; and to this condition the Irish Government was inexorably opposed.

The management of the Catholic question had been still more disastrous—disastrous not only in what was denied, but also in much that was granted. The Relief Act of 1793 had deluged the county constituencies with an overwhelming multitude of illiterate Catholic 40s. freehold voters, who were totally unfit for the exercise of political power; who were certain at some future time to become a great political danger, and whose enfranchisement added enormously to the difficulty and danger of reforming the Parliament, while it still left the Catholics under the brand of inferiority, excluded the Catholic gentry from Parliament, and thus deprived them of political influence at the very period when their services were most needed. At the same time, by the fatal error of not connecting—as might then most easily have been done—the college for the education of the priesthood with the University of the country, they prepared the way for an evil of the most serious kind.

The recall of Lord Fitzwilliam, under circumstances that were calculated to inflame to the utmost, popular passions; the deliberate appeal by the Government to the sectarian spirit among the Protestants, and Pelham's language of eternal proscription against the Catholics, soon completed the work. The loyal and respectable, though unfortunately small and timid, body of Catholic gentry lost all power and influence, and the guidance of the Catholics passed into the hands of seditious demagogues in the towns, who were in close alliance with the United Irishmen. At the same time the transportation by Lord Carhampton of multitudes of suspected persons to the fleet, without a shadow of legal justification; the Act of Indemnity, by which the Irish Parliament closed the doors of the law courts against those who sought for redress, and the shameful apathy shown towards the earliest outrages of the Orange banditti in the North, convinced great masses of the poor, that they were out of the protection of the law. It is not true that the Government inspired or approved of those outrages; but when it was found that a proclamation which specifically condemned the crimes of the Defenders, was silent about those of the Orangemen; that a parliamentary inquiry into these outrages, though repeatedly asked for, was always refused; and that hundreds, and possibly thousands, of Catholics, were obliged by terror to fly from their homes, at a time when Ulster was full of English troops, it cannot be wondered at that the Catholics should have come to look on themselves as completely unprotected, and should have been well prepared to receive the seditious teaching which was so abundantly diffused. In the summer and autumn of 1797 Ulster had grown more quiet, but evidence was almost daily pouring in, that all Catholic Ireland was passing rapidly into active sedition.

It is not surprising that it should have been so. Anarchy is like a cancer, which, once it has effected a lodgment in one portion of the body politic, will inevitably spread. Already, the Catholics of Ulster, as well as of one or two adjoining counties, and the Catholic leaders in Dublin, were thoroughly disaffected, while in many other counties the great mass of the Catholic peasantry were organised as Defenders; and Defenderism, as we have seen, though essentially a Whiteboy movement, and aiming at Whiteboy objects, was now in connection or alliance with the United Irishmen, and hoped to attain its objects by a French invasion and a consequent revolution.

It is important, however, to form a clear idea of the true motives that agitated the great Catholic masses. Catholic emancipation and parliamentary reform, which were the original and ostensible objects of the United Irishmen, had probably no place among them. The refusal of emancipation had been important in decisively turning a number of active Catholics in the towns to rebellion. It had a negative influence in withholding from loyal leaders influence and power, and in maintaining the broad political distinction between the two creeds; but both Lord Clare and the most intelligent leaders of the United Irishmen fully agreed with General Knox, that to the overwhelming majority of the Catholic people of Ireland, it was a matter of utter indifference. At a much later period, the combined influence of O'Connell and the priests made it a really popular question, but this time had not yet come.

A very similar remark may be made about parliamentary reform. To the illiterate Catholic cottiers and small farmers, who covered three out of the four provinces of Ireland, questions of this kind could have but little significance. For itself, they cared nothing, but the United Irishmen, who clearly saw this, tried to persuade them that a reform of Parliament must be followed by the abolition of tithes.

The tithe question, on the other hand, was one of real and passionate popular interest, and it had borne a prominent part in almost every agrarian disturbance of the century. The object of the leaders of the United Irishmen was a complete abolition of religious establishments, as in France; they continually, and, no doubt, sincerely, denied that they had the smallest wish to set up a Catholic establishment, or that they believed such an idea to be entertained by the Catholics; and they added, that any such attempt would encounter their strenuous resistance. With the mass of the Catholic peasantry, the question was not, I believe, one of privilege or establishment. It was a desire to be relieved from a heavy and unequal burden, which pressed most severely on the poorest cottiers; which was greatly aggravated by the system of tithe proctors, and by the constant disputes about new and old tithes; which was levied directly on the produce of the soil, and which was levied for the benefit of the clergy of another creed. To abolish this impost was one of their most earnest and unwavering desires, and it is probable that if this had been done they would have cared very little for the existence of the Establishment. We have seen how earnestly, in three successive years, Grattan had pressed upon the Irish Government and Parliament the vital necessity of dealing with this question; how he had proposed schemes for commutation, which would probably have completely allayed the discontent; how Pitt, at a still earlier period, had suggested the same policy; and how the Irish Government had steadily resisted it. The tithe grievance was now the chief political bond between the Presbyterians of the North and the Catholics of the South; and the fact that the French had begun their Revolution by abolishing tithes, was one of the chief motives put forward for welcoming a French invasion.

After the question of tithes, but after it at a considerable distance, came the question of rent. I have described the great and sudden increase of rents which corn bounties and war prices had produced, and the way in which it acted on different classes of the community. The many instances of hardship and distress which followed, had an undoubted part in producing Catholic disaffection; and hopes of a lowering of rents, and, still more, of a great agrarian revolution, or confiscation of lands, to be carried out by French assistance, were abroad. At the same time, while the question of tithes appeared habitually, the question of rents only appeared occasionally, in the popular appeals, and it was not, in the main, a question between the owner and the occupier of land. The frequent conduct of landlords in setting up leases to auction, had, no doubt, contributed to the evil, but the great majority of extortionate rents were exacted not by landlords, but by tenants—by the race of middlemen and landjobbers, who held tracts of land upon lease, subdivided them into small plots, and sublet them at an enormous profit.

There was another influence, which was not the less serious because it was somewhat more indefinite in its character. It was a vague feeling of separate nationality, which was thrilling powerfully through the Catholic masses. The events of history had divided the inhabitants of Ireland into two distinct and separate nations, divided broadly in creed, and, in some measure, in character and in race, and one of these was an ascendant and governing nation, which had displaced, by conquest, the old rulers and possessors of the soil. A keen sense of the danger of this situation was the keynote of the whole policy of Grattan. In all that he accomplished, and in all that he aimed at, it was his main object to make the Irish one people, instead of two, to soften and efface the old lines of distinction, by blending in the Government and in the Legislature, the representatives of the rival creeds. For some years, this policy seemed destined to succeed. Time had dimmed the memory of old conflicts and confiscations. Religious animosities had subsided. Nearly all the penal code had been abolished. A large share of political power had been conceded to the Catholics. Although the ownership of land was still, almost exclusively, in Protestant hands, there was no longer any law to prevent Catholics from acquiring it, and a great amount of Catholic property, in mortgages and other forms, was now identified with the established disposition of property. Increasing material prosperity was raising up a wealthy class among them, and their most energetic and ambitious members no longer sought a career in France, or Austria, or Spain. It was the dream of Grattan that a loyal Irish gentry of both denominations could form a governing body who would complete the work, and that, although a Protestant ascendency would continue, it would be the modified and mitigated ascendency which naturally belongs to the most educated section of the community and to the chief owners of property, and not an ascendency defined by creeds, and based on disqualifying laws. But, from the time when the principles of the French Revolution took root in Ireland, and, still more, after the recall of Lord Fitzwilliam, events had taken another turn. The new democratic leaders were chiefly Protestants, and they aimed, like Grattan, though by very different methods, and on a very different basis, at union between Catholics and Protestants, and the abolition of religious disqualifications; but the result of their movement was a furious revival of religious animosities, and a panic among the possessors of property, which greatly deepened the division of classes. At the same time, the extreme probability of a French conquest of Ireland, and the tremendous events on the Continent, which foreshadowed nothing less than a total destruction of the whole political and social order in Europe, and the downfall of the British Empire, aroused hopes in the Catholic population which had slumbered for more than a century. Prophecies, attributed to St. Columkill, pointing to the reinstatement of the old race, and the expulsion of the stranger, had circulated in Ireland during the great troubles of 1641. They were now, once more, passing from lip to lip, and vague, wild hopes, of a great coming change were rapidly spreading.

Another point in which the situation resembled that of 1641, was the belief which was fast growing among the Catholics, that they were marked out for massacre. In the seventeenth century the Catholic population had been driven to madness, by the belief that the English Puritans were about to exterminate their creed. At the end of the eighteenth century a similar fear prevailed, but the object of terror was the Orangeman. It was asserted by the newspapers of the United Irishmen, and it was taught and believed in every quarter of Ireland, that the secret oath sworn by every Orangeman was, "I will be true to the King and Government, and I will exterminate, as far as I am able, the Catholics of Ireland."

Whether such a statement was a pure calumny, or whether any such oath may have been in use among the banditti, who were wrecking by night the homes of Catholic farmers in Armagh and in some adjoining counties, it is impossible to say. The charge was like that which was afterwards brought against the Catholic insurgents, of designing nothing less than a massacre of the whole Protestant population. In both cases it was essentially false, but in both cases it may have derived some colour of plausibility from the frantic utterances and the ferocious actions of excited fanatics. In the Orange Society, as organised by the Ulster gentry, there was no oath even distantly resembling what was alleged, and the masters of all the Orange lodges in Ulster had, as we have seen, most emphatically disclaimed any wish to persecute the Catholics. But the seed had been already scattered among an ignorant, credulous, and suspicious peasantry. The United Irishmen persistently represented the Orange Society as a society created for the extermination of the Catholics, by men high in rank and office, and under the direct patronage of the Government, and they were accustomed to contrast its pretended oath with that of the United Irishman, which bound him only to endeavour to form a brotherhood of affection among Irishmen of every religious persuasion; to labour for the attainment of an equal, full, and adequate representation of all the people of Ireland in Parliament; and never, either directly or indirectly, to inform or give evidence against any member of the society. This was probably their most successful mode of propagandism, and the panic which it created had, as we shall see, a great part in producing the horrors that followed. It is, however, a curious fact, that the fear of the Orangemen appears to have been most operative upon populations who came in no direct contact with them. The worst scenes of the insurrection were in Wexford, where the Society had never penetrated; while in Ulster, and in Connaught, which was full of fugitives from Ulster, the rebellion assumed a far milder form. . . .

*Serious disorder spread through the midland counties as Government forces clashed repeatedly with Defenders and United Irishmen seeking arms and supplies. Disaffection and seditious speeches flourished in a climate of fear and bigotry. In Munster, Whiteboyism was on the increase, judging by the number of agrarian outrages and murders. Although the most tranquil of all the provinces, even Connaught had its United Irishmen, and there was much disaffection among the Catholic refugees who had fled from Orange oppression in Ulster.*

It would be difficult to conceive a more dreary or a more ignoble picture than Ireland at this time presented. The Parliament had lost almost every quality of a representative body; the Government was at once bigoted and corrupt, and steadily opposed to the most moderate and most legitimate reforms; and in three provinces almost every county was filled with knots of conspirators and incendiaries, who were trying to bring down on their country a foreign invasion, and were stirring up the people to rebellion and to crime. A few of them were men of genuine enthusiasm, and real, though certainly not extraordinary, talent; but the great majority were mere demagogues, adventurers, and criminals—such men as in days of anarchy and revolution ever rise to the surface—and scarcely one of them had the smallest right or title to speak as the representative of the nation. In the mean time, the country as a whole presented the most melancholy of all spectacles, that of general, rapid, and profound demoralisation. Religious animosities were steadily increasing. The old ties of reverence and affection, which, in spite of many unhappy circumstances, had bound the poor to the rich, were giving way. Crimes were multiplying, and they were constantly assuming a character of savage ferocity, while organised outrage was encountered by a military repression which often exceeded the limits of the law, led to horrible abuses, and was fast demoralising the forces that were employed in it. It was evident that there was no sentiment in the great mass of the poorer Catholics that was sufficiently powerful to be turned into a serious political movement, or to bring armed forces into the field, though there was a vague dislike to the English race and name, which was now being steadily fanned. But in 1797, as in later periods, political agitators found it necessary for their purposes to appeal to other than political motives—to agrarian grievances and agrarian cupidity; to religious passions; to the discontent produced by the pressure of poverty in a population which was very poor; to the panic which skilful falsehood could easily create in a population which was very ignorant. All these engines were systematically, unscrupulously, and successfully employed, and what in one sphere was politics, in another soon turned into ordinary crime. Camden noticed in June, that the first leaders of the conspiracy seemed to have in some degree lost their ascendancy, and that "a set of lower mechanics" had "the greatest sway." . . .

*The leaders of the United Irishmen finally agreed in the summer of 1797 to postpone any rising until a French invasion force had landed. The failure of the Anglo-French peace talks at Lille in September 1797 improved the prospects of another French expeditionary force for the conquest of Ireland.*

It was in the midst of the conferences of Lille, that the greatest Irishman of the eighteenth century—one of the greatest and best men who have ever appeared in English politics—vanished from the scene. The last days of Edmund Burke, though soothed by that deep, passionate, and devoted friendship, which he had pre-eminently the gift of inspiring, were very sad. The death of his only son had broken his heart; and in the triumph of the Revolution, he saw the eclipse of all that he valued the most in public life. "If I shall live much longer," he wrote shortly before his death, "I shall see an end of all that is worth living for in this world." Among the subjects that occupied his thoughts during the last months of his life, Irish affairs took a prominent place, and he watched them with the gloomiest forebodings. "The Government," he wrote, "is losing the hearts of the people, if it has not quite lost them. . . . The Opposition in that country, as well as in this, is running the whole course of Jacobinism, and losing credit amongst the sober people, as the other loses credit with the people at large." The United Ireland movement he regarded as one of the greatest calamities that could have befallen the country, and he predicted utter ruin if it succeeded. "Great Britain," he wrote, "would be ruined by the separation of Ireland; but as there are degrees even in ruin, it would fall the most heavily on Ireland. By such a separation, Ireland would be the most completely undone country in the world; the most wretched, the most distracted, and in the end, the most desolate part of the inhabitable globe. Little do many people in Ireland consider how much of its prosperity has been owing to, and still depends upon, its intimate connection with this kingdom." Burke died on July 9, and at his own urgent request he was buried, without pageantry or ostentation, in the quiet churchyard of Beaconsfield, and in the same grave as his son and brother. "There is but one event," wrote Canning to Malmesbury, "but that is an event for the world. Burke is dead. . . . He had among all his great qualities, that for which the world did not give him sufficient credit, of creating in those about him, very strong attachments and affection, as well as the unbounded admiration, which I every day am more and more convinced was his due. . . . He is the man that will mark this age, marked as it is itself by events, to all time."

The intrigues of the French Revolutionists with the United Irishmen, which had been in some degree suspended by the probability of peace, received a new stimulus from the rupture of the negotiations, but only a small part of them escaped the notice of the English Ministers. Their channels of information were numerous and very good. . . .

*Through its spies and informers the Government learned of the efforts of United Irishmen in Hamburg and Paris to bring about another French invasion of Ireland. In April and May 1797 the mutinies in the Royal Navy threatened to spread through the entire fleet, but the hopes of the United Irishmen were disappointed, when the mutineers of the Nore surrendered on June 14. Wolfe Tone arrived at the Texel on July 8 to take part in a Dutch expedition to Ireland, but strong head winds prevented the Dutch ships from sailing for six weeks. The expedition was eventually abandoned after the defeat of the main Dutch fleet at Camperdown on October 11. General Hoche died of consumption on September 19, and because Napoleon had given up hope of an Irish revolution, no new invasion plan was formulated.*

*In the last parliamentary election before the Act of Union, the advent of Catholic voters barely altered the composition of the Irish House of Commons. Refusing to stand for election, the dis-*

*illusioned Grattan wrote a pamphlet warning against the internal
and external threats to the independence of Parliament.*

Except perhaps in Ulster, where matters had been for some
time subsiding, the last months of 1797 produced no alleviation
in the state of Ireland, and Grattan and the Government differed
little about its gravity, though they differed much about its causes
and its remedies. Pelham, in a desponding private letter to Portland, complained that the language of the Opposition tended to
alienate the people from England, and that absenteeism had a
similar effect, but he laid special stress upon "the religious distinctions, which will always make the lower class of the people more
open to seduction than the same class of men in other countries,
and will make it impossible to expect any permanent security,
either in peace or war, without a great military force." Nothing,
he thought, short of an establishment of the Catholic religion,
would satisfy them; and he added with more truth, "As long as
the poor and the rich are of different persuasions in religious matters, there will always be a jealousy between the democratic and
aristocratic parts of the Constitution."

Clare, who knew the country much better, expressed the Government view with force and candour. "Emancipation and reform," he said, "were far short of the designs of the disaffected;
the separation of the country from her Imperial connection with
Great Britain, and a fraternal alliance with the French Republic,
were the obvious purposes of the insurgents." . . .

*Rumors of an impending rebellion led by Lord Edward Fitz-
gerald alarmed officials in Dublin Castle. The new Commander-
in-Chief, Sir Ralph Abercromby, who arrived in Ireland in
November, found both the army and the militia poorly trained
and disorganized. Abercromby tried to tighten discipline and
curb military brutality against civilians. His general orders of 26
February 1798 sought to improve the conduct of the troops under
his command but they succeeded only in antagonizing many
officers as well as influential politicians in Dublin and London.
An Irish cabal worked to remove him from his post, and Pelham's illness deprived him of an important ally. In March, Abercromby resigned in exasperation at the obstacles placed in his
way by men of influence. General Lake succeeded him, and the*

*army returned to its brutal ways, as though resolved to drive the Irish people into rebellion.*

The discontent produced by the refusal of the Irish Parliament to grant any measure of redress or of reform, was seriously increased by the renewed rejection of the absentee tax. The arguments, both of principle and policy, which Burke had urged against this tax, were very powerful, and in ordinary times they might have been accepted as conclusive, but Ireland was now struggling with no ordinary difficulties. It was scarcely possible that any small and poor country could bear, for many successive years, the financial strain of such a war as that which was now raging. England herself staggered under the burden, and seemed to many good judges on the verge of bankruptcy; and in Ireland the situation was aggravated by the necessity of immense military preparations to maintain the Government at home, and by the collapse of credit and paralysis of industry that always follow extreme anarchy and imminent danger of invasion and rebellion. I have described the excellent financial condition of Ireland when the war began, and the very moderate and equitable taxation imposed by the Irish Parliament. But in 1797, the fifth year of the war, the condition of affairs had become very serious.

The Government deemed it necessary to raise nearly four millions by loan, and they found the operation exceedingly difficult. They were obliged to issue five per cent. 100*l.* debentures at 63, and they obtained with some difficulty a loan of a million and a half from England. It was no longer possible to exempt the poor from taxation, and the salt tax and the leather tax fell upon them with great severity. Some of the principal articles of Irish manufacture, it is true, still showed a surprising vitality, and high prices gave prosperity to agriculture, but those prices greatly aggravated the distress of large classes, and it was stated that in 1797 there were no less than 37,000 persons in Dublin alone, in a state of extreme destitution.

Under these circumstances, and at a time when the poor were suffering so severely, the exemption of the great absentee proprietors from all taxation for Irish purposes seemed peculiarly unjust. Another year of war was now opening; there was no prospect of returning peace, and it was certain that new sacrifices would be required. The tax was proposed by La Touche, the principal banker, and one of the most respected characters in Dublin, but he desisted, when he found the Government inflexibly opposed to it. It was then taken up again by Vandeleur, and it was defeated by 104 to 40. In this case, the real opposition came not from Ireland, but from England, and Portland gave the Lord Lieutenant peremptory orders that the tax must be rejected. "It is impossible," writes Camden, "to describe the ill humour which pervades all descriptions of persons, from finding Government determined to oppose this measure. It will, however, I trust, be defeated by a larger majority than your grace might have supposed; but I must repeat the great disgust with which most of the friends of Government support it upon the present occasion."

This session of Parliament did nothing to quiet the country, and nothing to regain the affections of the people, and the shadow of great coming calamity fell darkly on the land. In Ulster, it is true, there was a sudden, mysterious, perplexing calm. Cooke wrote to England in March, that, although the leading agitators were still busy there, the lower classes were at work, and peaceable and industrious, and he added, "I believe no part of the King's dominions more apparently quiet, or more evidently flourishing, than the North of Ireland." Clare, as we have seen, boasted of it in the House of Lords, as a clear proof of the success of martial law. Lake wrote from Belfast: "The natives continue quiet, waiting with anxious expectation for the arrival of the French, which, they are taught to believe, will happen very shortly; their dispositions remain precisely the same. The flame is smothered, but not extinguished." Others believed that the very calm of Ulster was an evil sign, for it only showed how perfectly the people were organised, how fully they obeyed the order to remain passive till the French invasion, which was confidently expected in the early spring. But over a great part of Leinster and Munster, horrible murders were of almost daily occurrence, and an extreme terror prevailed. Lord Longueville, writing from the county Cork, to report the murder of Sir Henry Merrick, said that Abercromby's order forbidding the military to act without the presence of a magistrate, would be fatal, as the magistrates would not dare to expose themselves to the lasting vengeance that would pursue them, and he mentioned that, in a single week, three men had been shot in clear daylight, within eight miles of his own house. Even the sentinels on guard in Dublin were frequently fired at. Dr. Lanigan, the Catholic Bishop of Ossory, wrote in March to Archbishop Troy, describing the condition of the Queen's County, and some charges that had been brought against the priests, and his letter contains this very significant sentence: "The priests told me, and I believe them, that the fear of assassination prevents them from speaking as much as they wished against United Irishmen."

In the towns, the United Irish ranks were rapidly recruiting. McNally writes that men in respectable and independent positions, and even "of considerable property," were "daily Uniting;" that the conspiracy was making rapid progress in the public offices, and among the yeomen; that nearly all the clerks in banks and great merchant and trading houses were involved in it; that there was hardly a house with three men servants which had not a domiciliary committee; that the United Irishmen had already their agents and their spies in the most confidential departments of the Castle and the law courts, and that they were actively introducing them into the post offices." . . .

*The United Irishmen gained many recruits in urban areas as discontent increased and the administration of the law fell into ever greater disrepute. The Irish gentry were divided between moderate reformers of the Grattan persuasion, those who sympathized with the United Irishmen, and a growing number who advocated harsh repression of all dissidents.*

Amid the blinding mists of passion, prejudice, and exaggeration that sweep over this dismal period of Irish history, one great change may be distinctly discerned. The movement which owed its origin in a great measure to the decline of theological fanaticism, which was chiefly originated by Protestants and freethinkers, and which aimed at the political union of Irishmen of all religious denominations, was gradually turning into a religious war; reviving fierce religious passions which had been for generations subsiding, and which had at last become almost dormant. Beresford spoke of Ireland as suffering from a Presbyterian plot, and also from a Popish plot, but it was not possible that two such plots could co-exist in alliance, though it was quite possible that members of the two denominations might be blended in one political conspiracy. I have traced the beginning of the change which was taking place—the rise and rapid extension of the Orange movement; the attempts of some conspicuous loyalists to organise it for the defence of the country; the partial alliance between it and the Government; the persistent efforts of the United Irishmen to goad the Catholic masses into rebellion, by representing the Orange society as a conspiracy to massacre them, and by representing the English Government as supporting it. The United Irish conspiracy when it passed into a perfectly ignorant Catholic population at once changed its character, and its original political objects almost disappeared. "The Popish spirit," wrote Cooke, "has been set up against the Protestants, by reporting every Protestant to be an Orangeman, and by inculcating that every Orangeman has sworn to exterminate the Papists; to these fictions are added the real pressure of high rents from the undertakers of land, and high tithes from tithe proctors." Fanaticism was rapidly rising, and it was rising on both sides. "The most alarming feature of the movement," Camden wrote in April, is "the appearance of the present contest becoming a religious one." Loyalty in Ireland was beginning more and more to rally round the Orange standard, and to derive a new energy and courage from religious passion. At the same time, the essentially Popish character which the revolution was assuming in Leinster and Munster, had begun to shake the confidence of the conspirators in Ulster. . . .

I will conclude this chapter by a few remarks illustrating the designs and the secret dispositions of the English Government towards Ireland at the eve of the rebellion. There is, I believe, no evidence that they at this time contemplated a legislative Union as likely to be introduced in the immediate future, or even that they had formed any fixed determination that the existing Parliament was to be the last in Ireland. It is indeed abundantly evident, that they looked forward to an Union as the ultimate solution of the Irish question; that with this view they were determined, in accordance with the Irish Government, to maintain unaltered the borough system, which made the Irish Legislature completely subservient to the Executive; and that they wished Catholic emancipation, as well as parliamentary reform, to be adjourned till an

Union had been carried. But in none of the confidential correspondence which took place at the time of the election for the Parliament which met at the beginning of 1798, is there, as far as I am aware, any mention of a legislative Union; no opinion appears to have been as yet formed about the time or circumstances of introducing it, and beyond the lines that I have indicated, it is not, I think, true, that English Ministers were directing Irish policy with that object. In general, they allowed the administration of Ireland to be almost wholly shaped by the Irish Government; and even when they interfered with advice, they did so with little energy or persistence. When Fox and Lord Moira introduced into the British Parliament a discussion upon the military outrages, the ministers replied that those matters were within the sole competence of the Irish Parliament and Government. If they resented Sir Ralph Abercromby's order, it was because it was certain to furnish a formidable weapon to the English Opposition; if they opposed an absentee tax, it was chiefly because it would affect men who had great political influence in England. They assisted the Irish Government, by intercepting the correspondence of suspected rebels, and by collecting evidence through confidential agents on the Continent, and they more than once assisted it by loans in the great financial crisis of the war. On the other hand, they insisted that a considerable though much diminished number of lucrative Irish posts should be bestowed on Englishmen, and they wished to make the Irish peerage in some measure a reward for English services. For the rest, they only asked that Ireland should not be an embarrassment; that England should derive trade advantages from her connection with her, and that Ireland should contribute larger forces to carry on the war, than were needed for keeping her in her allegiance.

The advice of the English Government was usually in the direction of moderation, and especially in the sense of conciliating the Catholics. To separate as much as possible the Catholics from the Dissenters, and the Catholic question from the question of reform, was for some considerable time the keynote of the Irish policy of Portland. He was much struck with the fact that Protestant Ulster was the most disaffected of the four provinces; that at least five-sixths of the leaders of the United Irishmen were Protestants; that Munster, though now profoundly disturbed, had shown itself perfectly loyal during the French expedition at the end of 1796; that Connaught, the most purely Catholic province in Ireland, was the one province which was still almost untainted. He believed with good reason that the genius of the Catholic Church was essentially opposed to the revolutionary spirit, and that the higher clergy, at least, were sincere in their hostility to it, and he probably hoped that the influence of the Papacy might contribute something to the peace of Ireland. . . .

I must now draw this long and melancholy chapter to a close. Like that which preceded it, it is a record of steadily growing disorganisation; of many distinct forms of anarchy and discontent, combined and directed by one seditious conspiracy. Much of the evil had long existed in Ireland, though it had for some generations been steadily diminishing. It was quickened into a new vitality by the French Revolution, and by the near prospect of invasion, but it also owed a great part of its energy to enormous political faults, and to many acts of illegal and oppressive violence. We have now arrived at the brink of the catastrophe. A scene of blood was about to open, which not only left an indelible stain on the page of history, but also gave a fatal and enduring bias to the future of the nation.

# X

## *The Rebellion of 1798*

The United Irish Society had, as we have seen, passed through several distinct phases since its foundation at Belfast in October 1791. It was originally a perfectly legal society consisting of men who pledged themselves "in the presence of God" to use all their influence to obtain "an impartial and adequate representation of the Irish nation in Parliament," and, as a means to this end, to endeavour to secure the co-operation of Irishmen of all religious persuasions; and although some of its leaders undoubtedly aimed from the first at separation, the real objects of many, and the ostensible objects of all, were merely Catholic emancipation and parliamentary reform. After the suppression of the society in 1794 it had been reconstructed on a new basis, and became distinctly treasonable. An oath was substituted for the original test, and it comprised an obligation to secrecy and fidelity. The mention of Parliament in the declaration of aims was suppressed; a very elaborate organisation was created consisting of a hierarchy of committees, each committee except the lowest being formed by election from the subordinate sections; and the whole was directed by a General Executive Directory of five members, elected by ballot from the Provincial Directories, and sitting in Dublin. In 1795 the society appears to have been almost confined to Ulster and to Dublin. In 1796 it spread more widely through Leinster. In 1797 it extended over the greater part of that province, had become very powerful in Munster, and had gained some slight footing in Connaught. At the close of 1796 and in the beginning of 1797 a military organisation was grafted on it, and it became a main object to create, arm, and discipline regiments for a rebellion.

The organization on paper appeared very perfect, but its real was very different from its apparent strength, and it was enormously weakened by want of subordination, earnestness, discipline, arms, and military skill. The executive and higher committees had not, in fact, the absolute power assigned to them in the constitution of the body, and it is probable that each committee acted with great independence. Of the multitude who had joined the society, only a few were genuine political fanatics. Many had taken the oath, coerced by the intimidation, or persuaded by the example of their neighbours; many others had done so through the belief that the United Irish body were likely to govern Ireland, through hopes that they would gain something in a confiscation of land, or through simple fear of the Orangemen, against whom the great rival organisation was supposed to be the chief protection. Such men were hardly likely to make serious sacrifices for political ends. But still the fact remains that the bulk of the peasantry in three provinces in Ireland, were in the beginning of 1798 enlisted in a conspiracy which was daily extending, and were looking forward to an immediate rebellion in conjunction with a French invasion. The manufacture, plunder, and concealment of arms, the constant attempts to seduce the soldiers and yeomen, the nightly drills, the great organised assemblies under the pretext of potato diggings, the frequent murder of magistrates, soldiers, and informers, abundantly showed the seriousness of the situation.

In February 1798—before the declaration of martial law, before the establishment of free quarters—the executive body computed that half a million of persons had been sworn into the society, and that more than 280,000 of them could be counted on to appear in the field. In a paper drawn up by Lord Edward Fitzgerald shortly before his arrest, it was calculated that the number of armed men enlisted was 279,896. Of these men, 110,990 were in Ulster, 100,634 in Munster, and 68,272 in Leinster. From Connaught no returns appear to have come in.

A few words may be said about the members of the Supreme Executive. At the beginning of 1798 they appear to have been

Thomas Addis Emmet, Arthur O'Connor, William James Mc-Nevin, Oliver Bond, and Richard McCormick. The last had been formerly Secretary of the Catholic Committee, and with McNevin he represented the Catholic element in the Directory. He was a warm friend of Tone, and he both knew and sanctioned Tone's first application for French assistance. He belonged, however, to the section of the Directory who were opposed to a rebellion before the arrival of the French, and he appears to have been much alarmed by the crimes and violence into which the movement had degenerated. In February 1798 he told Reynolds that he had ventured, at a provincial meeting in that month, to recommend less violent measures, and that he had been attacked in such a manner that he believed his life to be in danger, and had resolved to realise his property and escape from Ireland. He fulfilled his intention, fled from Ireland in March, and did not return till long after the rebellion. McNevin, as we have seen, had gone on a mission to France, but he had returned in October 1797, and had reported to the Irish Directory that they might fully rely on French succour, and, like McCormick, he desired that all rebellion should be prevented till that succour arrived. Oliver Bond was a rich woollen draper, the son of a Dissenting minister in Donegal. He had been imprisoned for his political conduct as early as 1793, and had borne a prominent part in the conspiracy from its commencement. He asserted on his examination by the Committee of the House of Lords, that though he had been elected to the Supreme Executive body, he had "declined to act officially," but he was in the closest confidence of the leaders of the movement, and he is said to have filled the important post of treasurer.

Emmet and Arthur O'Connor were perhaps abler, they were certainly more conspicuous men than their colleagues, and the first is one of the few really interesting figures connected with the rebellion. He was a respectable lawyer, an excellent writer, a very honest and disinterested man, and he had certainly not embarked in treason either through motives of selfish ambition or through any mere love of adventure and excitement. He became a United Irishman in order to obtain a radical parliamentary reform and Catholic emancipation; he found that these things were never likely to be attained except by force, and he at last succeeded in persuading himself that if Ireland were only detached from England she would soar to an unprecedented height of prosperity. Nature had intended him much more for the life of a man of letters than for the scenes in which he was now engaged, and his type is one which is often found in the earlier stages of a rebellion, but is usually discarded, or eclipsed in blood, long before the struggle has run its course. His writings and his examination before the Privy Council are singularly interesting and instructive as showing the process by which a humane, honourable, and scrupulous man could become the supporter of a movement which was the parent of so many crimes. Grattan knew Emmet slightly and admitted his integrity, but he had a profound contempt for his political understanding. He described him, somewhat unceremoniously, as a quack in politics who despised experience, set up his own crude notions as settled rules, and looked upon elections and representation as if they were operations of nature rather than the work of art. Anyone, Grattan maintained, who could bring himself to believe that a country like Ireland, in which the people were so destitute that one-third of them were exempted from the payment of hearth money on account of their poverty, could be safely or tolerably governed with annual parliaments elected by universal suffrage, must be politically mad, and had forfeited all right to be considered in Irish politics. Emmet afterwards rose to considerable distinction in America and became Attorney-General of New York. Grattan— perhaps unjustly—thought his success much beyond his talents, and such as he would never have attained if he had remained at home.

Arthur O'Connor was of a very different type. He was a man of wealth and high social position; a nephew of Lord Longueville; a member of a family remarkable for its violence, its eccentricities, and its domestic quarrels. He had some parliamentary standing, some shining talents, boundless courage and enterprise, and he risked and sacrificed for his opinions more than most of his colleagues. He was, however, rash, obstinate and arrogant, very incapable of waiving his personal pretensions for a public end, and very destitute of most of the higher qualities of a real leader of men. In one of his latest writings he mentions that early in life he had been deeply impressed by reading in Leland's

349

"History of Ireland" a description of the Irish policy advocated by some of the counsellors of Elizabeth. "Should we exert ourselves," they had said, "in reducing this country to order and civility, it must acquire power, consequence, and riches. The inhabitants will be thus alienated from England; they will cast themselves into the arms of some foreign Power, or perhaps erect themselves into an independent and separate state. Let us rather connive at their disorder; for a weak and disordered people never can attempt to detach themselves from the Crown of England." This passage, O'Connor said, appeared to him to furnish the keynote explaining the English policy of his own day, and he declared that it was this conviction that chiefly shaped the political conduct of his life. He lived to extreme old age; he became a general in the French service, and has left some writings which throw much curious light on his character and on his times. Like several of the early advocates of Catholic emancipation, he was utterly without sympathy for the Catholic creed. Few men, indeed, can have had a greater contempt for priests and for what they teach, and in his last work he expressed his unmingled detestation of O'Connell, and of the movement which had placed the guidance of popular politics in Ireland under the direction of an ignorant and low-born priesthood. In spite of his admiration for the French Revolution, he was in his tastes and temper essentially aristocratic, though he believed that the Irish gentry by appealing to the Irish people could break the ascendency which English influence had hitherto exercised on the counsels of the nation, and put an end to the religious and class divisions by which that ascendency had been chiefly maintained.

Several other men were at this time active in guiding the conspiracy, most of them being in the Provincial Directory of Leinster. The most important was Lord Edward Fitzgerald, who was chiefly entrusted with the military organisation and who was intended to be commander-in-chief, though it is doubtful whether he was ever formally elected to the Supreme Executive. The cooperation of a member of the first family of the Protestant aristocracy was of no small advantage to the conspiracy in a country where the genuine popular feeling, amid all its aberrations, has always shown itself curiously aristocratic, and where the first instinct of the people when embarking in democratic and revolutionary movements has usually been to find some one of good family and position to place at their head. Lord Edward's very transparent character has been already described. No one could doubt his courage, his energy, his intense enthusiasm, or his perfect disinterestedness, and, as he had been a captain in the army and had seen active service, he had some military knowledge, but no competent judge appears to have discovered in him any real superiority of intellect.

The question of an immediate rising independently of the French, had been much discussed in Ulster after the proclamation of General Lake in May 1797, and it was again agitated in the first weeks of 1798. Arthur O'Connor, as we have seen, had formerly maintained that a French landing ought to precede any rising in Ireland, but he now believed the organisation to have become sufficiently powerful for independent action, and in conjunction with Fitzgerald he strongly advocated it. The dispute ran very high, and it made O'Connor a bitter enemy of Emmet, whom he accused, very unjustly, of cowardice. The party of Emmet, however, which desired to postpone the explosion till the arrival of the French, again prevailed, but it prevailed only through the belief that a French invasion was imminent. Lewins and McNevin in 1797 had been instructed to ask only for 10,000 French troops, but for a very large quantity of arms. It was calculated that such assistance would be amply sufficient to overthrow the English power in Ireland without bringing any danger of a French domination. Promises of support had more than once come from France, and although the battle of Camperdown had thrown a great damp on the hopes of the conspirators, they were revived by new assurances, and especially by a message which was received at the beginning of 1798 promising that French assistance would arrive in Ireland in April, or at the latest in the beginning of May. The English Government on their side received secret intelligence in February and March of extensive preparations that were making at Dunkirk, Havre, Honfleur, and Calais.

The invasion was eagerly looked forward to. A new military committee was appointed at Dublin in February for the express purpose of preparing a plan of co-operation with the French, and instructions were furnished to the adjutant-generals of the conspiracy to collect full information about the state of the United Irish regiments within their districts; about the roads, rivers, and bridges; the capacities of the towns and villages to receive troops, and the strength and movements of the enemy. Arthur O'Connor determined to go to France to arrange a combined movement, but he was arrested at Margate on February 28, in company with a priest named O'Coigly or Quigley, an English agitator named Binns, and two other men who appear to have been his servants. McNally, in commenting upon this arrest, significantly observed that it would have very little effect upon the conspiracy, and that McCormick, McNevin, Drennan, and other leading Irishmen considered O'Connor so impetuous that they were not sorry to have him out of the way.

It has often been asked why the Irish Government, with all the information at its disposal, and at a time when the Habeas Corpus Act was suspended, did not arrest the leading members of the conspiracy before it attained its height. In truth, however, the information they possessed was less full than has been supposed. Most of the schemes of the United Irishmen were communicated to them, and they had a general knowledge of the leading members of the conspiracy, but they appear to have known little about the Supreme Executive, and they were conscious that they could produce no evidence against the leaders which was the least likely to secure a conviction. From the June of 1797 they had received from an informer at Saintfield, in the county of Down, regular reports of county and provincial meetings of the United Irishmen in Ulster. In the same month McNally had informed them that there was a secret directory of about six members at the head of the United Irishmen. In September and October he told them that Bond was the treasurer of the conspiracy; that the chief management was now transferred from Belfast to Dublin and confined to a very few; that Keogh, McCormick, Lord Edward Fitzgerald, Arthur O'Connor, Sweetman, Dixon, Chambers, Emmet, Bond, and Jackson were in the secret, but that he was convinced that even their part in the conspiracy was only a secondary one. Some full and very valuable additional information was soon after sent by Turner from Hamburg. But there was never any question of McNally appearing as a witness, and neither Turner nor the Saintfield informer would consent to do so.

From the beginning of 1798, however, it was the urgent desire of the Irish Government to arrest the conspirators. . . .

*Informers enabled the authorities to capture fifteen members of the Leinster Provincial Committee of the United Irishmen on 12 March 1798. Amid reports of an imminent rising, the Government pressed its search for the elusive Lord Edward Fitzgerald. On March 30, martial law was proclaimed in disturbed districts, and the army redoubled its efforts to disarm the United Irishmen before an insurrection could take place.*

The expectation of revolution was universal, but the rising was not to take place till the arrival of the French. There was now, therefore, a short respite—an ominous and imperfect calm, broken by constant accounts of the murder of magistrates and informers, of attacks upon sentries, of nightly raids for arms, of which that on the town of Cahir was the most conspicuous and the most audacious. Upon the use that was made of this short interval the result of the contest might depend.

No one who will honestly face this situation can doubt that it demanded extreme vigour—a vigour which would inevitably transcend the limits of ordinary law. One of the ablest of the rebels afterwards acknowledged, that up to the proclamation of March 30 the process of arming the people for rebellion went smoothly on, and that it was this proclamation and the measures that followed, that alone arrested it. On the other hand, no one who knew the state of Ireland could doubt that such measures, when adopted, must lead to horrible abuses. Ireland was now wholly unlike what it had been at the outbreak of the French Revolution. The crimes and panics of the last few years, the fierce passions that had been aroused, and the tension of long-continued danger and suspense, had filled it with savage and inveterate hatreds, broken down all discipline in the army, set class against class, and creed against creed. When a half-disciplined yeomanry and militia, demoralised by a long course of licence and irritated by many outrages, came to live at free quarters upon a hostile peasantry, who regarded them as Orangemen, and who were taught that every Orangeman had sworn to exterminate the Catholics, it was not difficult to anticipate the result.

The burnings of houses which had been well known in the

North were now carried on upon a yet larger scale in Leinster, and the free quarters formed a new and terrible feature in the system of military coercion. There is reason to believe that this system was adopted contrary to the general wishes of the Irish gentry, and one of the principal of those in the Queen's County wrote a letter to Cooke clearly pointing out its evils. "I have my fears," he wrote, "this plan will not answer the end. It will unavoidably involve in punishment the innocent with the guilty. The soldiers will find miserable means of living among those who are the robbers and defenders. Of course they will not, cannot be restrained from laying hold of the substance and property of farmers who are innocent and loyal. Indiscriminate punishment and much mischief must ensue. Surely, my dear Cooke, this is a more violent and coercive system than burning the houses of those who were known to be delinquents."

If Abercromby had continued in command, it is possible that the abuses resulting from this system might have been restrained, though they could not have been wholly prevented, but neither Lake nor the Irish Government appear to have made the smallest effort to check them. District after district was now proclaimed, and after the stated interval the soldiers descended like a flight of locusts upon them. They were quartered in the best of the houses of the suspected persons in proportion to the supposed means of the owners, and they lived as in an enemy's country. Many men were ruined by their exactions and their depredations. All the neighbouring houses were searched, and any house in which any weapon was found was immediately burnt. Many others were burnt because the owners, terror-stricken perhaps by the violence around them, had abandoned them, or because some of the innumerable seditious papers were found in them. One of the rebel leaders afterwards described how in one small corner of Wicklow in a single morning no less than fourteen houses were burnt by a single man. Sometimes, after a period of coercion had failed to produce a surrender of arms, a proclamation was issued stating that the nightly patrols would for a time be withdrawn in order that the people might be able without fear to collect the arms and to bring them to an appointed place, and that if this was not done before a given date the whole district would be burnt. Great piles of arms came in this way into the possession of the Government, though the people sometimes showed their feelings by breaking them to pieces before they deposited them in the place that was assigned.

This method of disarming appears to have been adopted in all the towns of the county of Kildare, and a few particular instances which are preserved will enable the reader to understand the manner in which it was worked. Thus the inhabitants of the town of Kildare had refused to give up the arms which the commanding officer was convinced they possessed, and they alleged that there were none in the town. General Walford at once called the inhabitants together, and announced to them on his honour that if they did not bring in their arms in twenty-four hours he would burn every house in the town, and he at the same time assured them that if they complied with his order they should have complete protection, and that not a single soldier would appear out of his barracks on that evening in order that the people should have the opportunity of collecting and depositing their arms without fear. The measure proved successful, and great quantities of arms were brought in. From Athy in the same county Colonel Campbell wrote: "In consequence of burning a few houses in this town and the neighbourhood, together with a little military discipline, we have got a number of pikes." In other cases the resistance was more obstinate. "This last week," wrote Lady Louisa Conolly to Mr. Ogilvie on May 21, "was a most painful one to us. Maynooth, Kilcock, Leixlip, and Celbridge have had part of a Scotch regiment quartered at each place, living upon free quarters and every day threatening to burn the towns. I have spent days in entreaties and threats to give up the horrid pikes. Some houses burnt at Kilcock yesterday produced the effect. Maynooth held out yesterday, though some houses were burnt and some people punished. This morning the people of Leixlip are bringing in their arms. Celbridge as yet holds out, though five houses are now burning. Whether obstinacy or that they have them not I cannot say; . . . we have fortunately two most humane officers, that do not do more than is absolutely necessary from their orders." "I expect," wrote Colonel Napier on the same day, "on my return to find Celbridge and Maynooth in ashes, as that was the 'order of the day.' "

Horrible abuses and horrible sufferings inevitably accompanied these things. Many who resisted, and not a few it is said who did not resist, were shot dead on their thresholds, while countless families were deprived of all they possessed and were driven homeless into the world. Farm horses were seized and carried away. Stores of provisions were broken into and shamefully wasted or destroyed, and acts of simple robbery and purely wanton violence were of daily occurrence.

Torture was at the same time systematically employed to discover arms. Great multitudes were flogged till they almost fainted; picketed and half strangled to extort confessions. Blacksmiths were the special objects of suspicion and vengeance, and many of them were scourged almost to death in the streets of the villages in order to compel them to state what pikes they had made, and to reveal the persons to whom they had consigned them.

It had been the habit of the republican party in Ireland, as in France, to cut short their hair as a distinctive sign, and the "croppies," as they were termed, were an obvious mark for military violence. The torture of these men soon became a popular amusement among the soldiers. Some soldiers of the North Cork Militia are said to have invented the pitched cap of linen or thick brown paper, which was fastened with burning pitch to the victim's head and could not be torn off without tearing out the hair or lacerating the skin. One soldier obtained a special reputation by varying the torture. He was accustomed to cut the hair of the victims still shorter, to rub into it moistened gunpowder and then to set it on fire. Sometimes also an ear or a portion of an ear was cut off.

All this went on in the proclaimed districts without interference and without restraint. In the great majority of cases no doubt the sufferers were justly suspected of being enrolled in a treasonable conspiracy and of possessing concealed arms. But it was constantly asserted, and it is in the highest degree probable, that in the complete military licence that prevailed, many of the victims were perfectly innocent. Men were acting under the blinding influence of panic and widespread suspicions, and often under influences that were still more pernicious. In a country where every informer was at once marked out for assassination, secret information naturally and necessarily played a great part, and it gave terrible opportunities for the gratification of private cupidities and private malice. Every Irish country district is sure to be full of quarrels about leases and boundaries and trespasses, quarrels between landlords and tenants, between competing tenants, between debtors and creditors, between farmers and labourers. The burning of houses and the flogging of individuals were very often not the result of any judicial or quasi-judicial investigation, or even of the decision of an experienced and superior officer. Young subalterns, sergeants of militia, common soldiers ordered and perpetrated these things, and it is but too probable that they often acted on the whispered suggestion of a private enemy. If some men cut their hair short to attest their republican sentiments, others did so for simple convenience, while the hair of others was cut short by the United Irishmen for the express purpose of exposing them to the vengeance of the soldiers. Quakers, who had scruples about applying for military protection, often fell under suspicion, though they were among the most orderly and peaceful inhabitants of the country.

Outrages on women were very common. Peasant girls had often thrown themselves enthusiastically into the United Irish movement, and attested their sentiments by their green ribbons, while many others who knew or cared nothing about politics wore something green in their dress. Every person who did so was tolerably sure to be exposed to insults which planted far and wide, among a peasantry peculiarly susceptible on such matters, the seeds of deadly, enduring hatred. . . .

*Military outrages continued throughout the spring, leaving indelible memories in the minds of those victims who escaped death. A notorious offender in this respect was Thomas Judkin Fitzgerald, High Sheriff of Tipperary, who used sadistic methods to disarm United Irishmen in his county.*

The hatred and distrust of law and government, the inveterate proneness to seek redress by secret combination and by barbarous crimes, the savage animosities of class and creed and party, that make Irish government so difficult, were not created, but they were all immensely strengthened, by the events which I am relating. It must be added, too, that if martial law forced the rebellion into a premature explosion, and thus made it comparatively easy to deal with it, it also undoubtedly turned into desperate rebels multitudes who, if they had been left unmolested, would have been, if not loyal subjects, at least either neutral spectators or lukewarm and half-hearted rebels. When Emmet was asked what caused the late insurrection, he answered, "The free quarters, the house burnings, the tortures, and the military executions in the counties of Kildare, Carlow, and Wicklow." The answer was not a candid one, for long before these things had begun a great part of Ireland had been organised for rebellion, and was only waiting for the appearance of the French. The true causes, as we have seen, were partly political, and for these the Government was very largely responsible. The rebellion, however, among the ignorant Catholic peasantry was not mainly political. They had been in the first place allured into the conspiracy by promises of the abolition of tithes, the reduction or abolition of rents, and the redress of all real or imaginary grievances. They had then been persuaded by the United Irishmen that the Orangemen, with the connivance of the Government, intended to massacre them, and that they could only find safety in the protection of a great armed Catholic organisation. Once that organisation was planted among them, it spread rapidly by example, intimidation, or persuasion. The worst and most dangerous men came inevitably to the front. Many crimes were committed. There was no regular and well-disciplined force like the modern constabulary sufficiently powerful to maintain the peace. Martial law was declared, and the tortures, the house burnings, and other manifold abuses that followed it soon completed the work, and drove the people in large districts to desperation and madness.

One of the most energetic of the leaders in Wicklow has left an account of his own experiences which is well worthy of attention. "Self-preservation," he says, "was the motive which drove me into rebellion. . . . As to effecting a change of Government, it gave me little trouble or thought. Reform was much more necessary among the people of all ranks than the Government, which was good enough for me. If the laws were fairly and honestly administered, the people would have little reason to complain. It was private wrongs and individual oppression, quite unconnected with the Government, which gave the bloody and inveterate character to the rebellion in the county of Wicklow. The ambition of a few interested individuals to be at the head of affairs first lighted up the flame everywhere. . . . The poor people engaged in the Irish rebellion of 1798 had very little idea of political government. Their minds were more occupied with their own sufferings or enjoyments; and many, I might say most, were compelled to join in the rebellion on pain of death."

The capture at Bond's house on March 12 of the principal leaders of the organisation, and the general disarming under martial law which speedily followed, had given an almost fatal blow to the conspiracy; but efforts, which for a short time seem to have escaped the knowledge of the Government, were made to reconstruct it under a new Directory, in which the most prominent members were two brothers of the name of Sheares. They were lawyers, sons of a very estimable and generous Cork banker, who had sat for many years in the House of Commons, and they had ever since 1793 borne an active, though not a very considerable, part in the conspiracy. Henry Sheares, the elder, was a weak, vain, amiable, insignificant man, utterly unsuited for the position he assumed, and chiefly governed by the stronger will of his brother. Of John Sheares I have already spoken. He impressed most of those with whom he came in contact as a man of ability and great energy, a genuine and dangerous fanatic of the type which rose to the ascendant in France during the Reign of Terror. Fitzgerald also, the destined commander, was still at large. . . .

*Slowly and remorselessly the authorities closed in on Lord Edward Fitzgerald, as "the shadow of impending revolution hung visibly over the land."*

The place pointed out was on the road from Thomas Street, where Lord Edward was now concealed, to Usher's Island, where Magan lived, and there is some reason to believe that the intention was to arrest him when he was going to the house and on the invitation of his betrayer. Major Sirr at the head of a party was present at the appointed hour, and the two parties encountered. A confused scuffle took place in the dark, narrow, tortuous streets. Sirr was knocked down. Lord Edward escaped and made his way to the house of Murphy in Thomas Street, where he had been formerly concealed, and where he intended to remain through the 19th [of May].

The extreme fatuity with which the conspiracy was conducted is curiously shown by the fact that on this very day, on which the most careful concealment was so imperatively required, the brilliant uniform which Fitzgerald was to wear at the rising, was sent to the house of Murphy. Neilson, who had been sixteen months in prison, and was therefore well known to the authorities, called there in the course of the morning. The street was swarming with soldiers, who were well aware that Lord Edward must be in the neighbourhood, and a public-house belonging to Moore was searched. In spite of all this Neilson came a second time to the house in the broad daylight of the afternoon, stopped with Fitzgerald to dinner, then left the house, it is said, very abruptly, and did not even shut the hall-door behind him.

A few minutes after his departure, Major Sirr, accompanied by Major Swan, Captain Ryan, and eight or nine private soldiers, arrived. As the door had been left open they entered without noise, resistance, or delay, but Sirr remained with the soldiers below to prevent a rescue or an escape, while Swan and Ryan mounted the staircase. Swan first entered the room where Fitzgerald and Murphy were. The latter remained completely passive, but Fitzgerald sprang from the bed on which he was lying, and brandishing a very formidable dagger, attacked and wounded Swan. The details of the conflict that ensued have been somewhat variously related. The wounded man fired a pocket pistol at Fitzgerald, but missed his aim, and, according to the account of Murphy, he then rushed out of the room to summon the soldiers to his aid. Whether he left it or not, it is certain that Ryan, armed only with a sword-cane, now grappled most courageously with Fitzgerald, and although he speedily received a mortal wound in his stomach, and was again and again stabbed, he clung to his prisoner till the soldiers arrived. They found Ryan bathed in blood and rapidly sinking, and Fitzgerald stood so fiercely at bay that Sirr fired in self-defence. The ball lodged in Fitzgerald's right arm near the shoulder; he staggered for a moment, and then struggling desperately was seized and captured.

The capture of Lord Edward Fitzgerald was undoubtedly due to the information which was furnished by Magan through Higgins. It was owing to them that he had been obliged to take refuge in Murphy's house on the night of the 18th, and they had clearly pointed out the quarter of Dublin in which he was concealed. I do not, however, think that it was they who indicated the particular house. There is no trace of any communication having been received from them on the 19th, and Major Sirr afterwards stated that he only obtained the information of the hiding place of Lord Edward a few minutes before he went there. It is probable that the fact of Neilson, who was well known to be a constant companion of Fitzgerald, having been seen to leave Murphy's house, furnished the clue, and it is tolerably certain that many of the neighbours must have known that this house had been for a considerable time the hiding place of the rebel chief. It is not surprising that grave suspicions of treachery should have attached to Neilson, but they are, I believe, unfounded. Neilson, though he is one of the heroes of a class of popular writers in Ireland, is not a man deserving of any respect. He had been released from prison in the preceding February on condition that "he should not belong to any treasonable committee," but immediately after the arrest at Bond's house he broke his promise and became one of the most active organisers of the conspiracy. He was a drunkard, and therefore peculiarly likely to have betrayed a secret, and the letters I have quoted appear to me to establish a strong probability that he either had, or intended to have, some secret communication with the Government. Two facts, however, are quite sufficient to acquit him of the charge of having deliberately betrayed Fitzgerald. Major Sirr discovered that he was one of the chief organisers of a desperate plot to rescue the prisoner, and the promised 1,000*l.* was duly, though tardily, paid through Higgins to Magan.

The capture was a matter of transcendent importance, for the insurrection was planned for the 23rd, and Fitzgerald was to be its commander. There is not, indeed, the smallest reason to believe that Fitzgerald had any of the qualities of a great man, or was in the least likely to have led his country to any high, or honourable destiny. But he was a well-known public man. He was a Protestant. He was a member of a great aristocratic family, and if he had appeared at the head of the rebellion, it is extremely probable that the northern rebels would have risen at his call, though they remained almost passive when they found the rebellion in Leinster headed by fanatical priests and by obscure country gentlemen of whom they had never heard. In that case the sea of blood which in the next months deluged a few counties would have probably overspread the whole island. From this great calamity Ireland was saved by the arrest of May 19. . . .

Lord Edward Fitzgerald was removed to Newgate, and confined in a cell which had lately been occupied by Lord Aldborough. The vicissitudes of that sick-bed have been followed by several generations of Irish readers and writers with an intensity of interest hardly bestowed on any other page of Irish history. On the first day he suffered greatly from the inflammation of his wound, but it was soon relieved by suppuration; it was then believed for several days that he would recover, but fever, brought on and aggravated by anxiety of mind, set in. The death of Ryan, which took place on Thursday, the 31st, made an ignominious death the almost certain result of a trial, and it probably had a great part in hastening the catastrophe. The Government determined that in the very dangerous condition of affairs no friends or relations should be admitted to persons confined for treason, and they refused till the last moments to relax their rule. They offered, however, to permit Lord Edward to see the family chaplain, which he declined, but he saw and prayed with the chaplain of the gaol. On Friday he became much worse. On Saturday there was an execution in the gaol that agitated him greatly. He prayed fervently that God would pardon and receive all who fell in the cause. On Sunday morning he seemed a little better, but the improvement was slight and transient, and on that day his aunt, Lady Louisa Conolly, received a message from the doctor that he was dying.

This lady, whose rare gifts of mind and character made a deep impression on her contemporaries, was sister of the Duke of Richmond, and wife of one of the most important members of the Irish Parliament. She was deeply attached to Lord Edward, and she at once came from Castletown to Dublin in hope of seeing him for the last time. She was accompanied by her niece, Miss Emily Napier, who has written a singularly interesting account of what occurred. They drove first to the Viceregal Lodge in the Phoenix Park, to ask permission from Lord Camden. Lady Louisa entered alone, but soon returned in a state of extreme agitation, saying that although she had even knelt at the feet of the Lord

Lieutenant he had refused her, declaring that neither the Speaker nor the Chancellor would approve of any relaxation of the rule. Orders had been given to the coachman to return to the country, when Miss Napier suggested that her aunt should apply to the Chancellor, who had always been her warm admirer. The suggestion was adopted. Lord Clare happened to be dining at home, and he at once received Lady Louisa with great kindness, told her that although the Lord Lieutenant had refused her, and although the orders were peremptory, he would take the responsibility of admitting her, and would himself accompany her to the gaol. With a thoughtful kindness he suggested that they should first drive to Leinster House and take up Lord Henry, the favourite brother of Lord Edward, who had hitherto been denied access to the prisoner. Lord Clare and Lord Henry Fitzgerald drove first in Lord Clare's carriage, followed by Lady Louisa Conolly and her niece. At the door of the prison Lord Clare said that he must restrict his permission to the aunt and brother, and Miss Napier was driven back to Leinster House to await their return. They were but just in time. Lord Edward at first knew them, but soon after became delirious. He died early on the morning of June 4. . . .

*Other directors of the United Irishmen were soon rounded up, among them the Sheares brothers. A few leaders made good their escape to France. In an important trial at Maidstone, Kent, Arthur O'Connor and three other United Irishmen were acquitted of high treason, to the dismay of the Government. One other defendant, Father O'Coigly, was found guilty and hanged on June 7.*

The 23rd of May, which was the day appointed for the insurrection, had arrived. The signal was to be the stopping of the mail coaches from Dublin; and although the programme was not fully carried out, those which were going to Belfast, to Athlone, to Limerick, and to Cork, were that night seized. Long before daybreak on the 24th, numerous rebel parties were in arms in the counties of Dublin, Kildare, and Meath. In Kildare, in spite of the stringent measures for disarming the people, the rising was especially formidable, and about 2.30 on the morning of the 24th a party of rebels vaguely estimated at 1,000 men, and commanded by a farmer named Michael Reynolds, whose house had lately been burnt by the soldiers, attempted to surprise and capture the important town of Naas. Lord Gosford, however, who commanded there, had been made aware of their intention, and a party of Armagh Militia with a detachment of dragoon guards were ready to meet them. Three times the rebels dashed themselves desperately against the troops, who were stationed near the gaol, and three times they were repulsed. They then changed their tactics, took possession of almost every avenue into the town, fought the troops with great intrepidity for nearly three-quarters of an hour, but at last gave way, broke and fled, closely pursued by the cavalry. Hundreds of guns and pikes were brought in, either taken from the dead or cast away by the fugitives in their flight. Four prisoners only were taken, of whom three were hanged in the streets of Naas, while the fourth saved his life by giving valuable information. The loss on the King's side was variously estimated at from fourteen to thirty. Of the rebels, about thirty were believed to have been killed in the streets, and more than one hundred in the flight.

Nearly at the same time, and at a distance of but a few miles from Naas, 300 rebels attacked a small garrison of yeomen and militia at Clane. But though the loyalists were surprised and immensely outnumbered, their captain, Richard Griffith, speedily rallied them, dispersed the rebels by a well-directed fire and pursued them for some distance, killing many, and burning every house in which they took refuge. Six prisoners were taken; one was condemned at the drumhead and shot at Clane; "the other five were hanged the same day with less ceremony by the soldiers in Naas."

About five in the morning, Griffith brought back his little body of soldiers, and he then learnt a terrible tragedy that had been enacted three miles from Clane. The small town of Prosperous, which was the centre of the cotton industry of Ireland, had been garrisoned by forty or fifty of the North Cork Militia under Captain Swayne, and by twenty of the Ancient Britons. In the deadest hour of the early morning the sentinels on guard were surprised and killed. Some soldiers were slaughtered in their beds in the houses in which they were billeted, while the barracks were surrounded and set on fire. Many of the men who were in them perished by the flames or by suffocation. Some sprang from the windows and were caught upon the pikes of the assailants. The remainder tried to cut their way through the enemy, but nearly all perished. A gentleman named Stamer, who was the principal proprietor of Prosperous, and an English gentleman named Brewer, who was a prominent manufacturer, were murdered in cold blood. Several of the party, it is said, were recognised as men who on the very day before the tragedy, had come forward to profess their loyalty, to express contrition for past offences, and to receive protections from Captain Swayne.

Griffith foresaw that the party from Prosperous would soon attack him, and he at once drew out his small and gallant force in Clane. He had scarcely done so when a great disorderly body of insurgents poured in, their ragged clothes strangely variegated by the scarlet uniforms and glittering helmets taken from soldiers who had perished. The loyalists were vastly outnumbered, but Griffith drew up his force in an advantageous post in the corner of a field where they could not be outflanked, and awaited the attack. The rebels opened a heavy fire, but they were evidently totally unacquainted with the use of firearms, and every ball flew high above its mark. A deadly volley from the militia and the yeomen, and a fierce charge, soon put them to flight. Many were killed. "The roads and fields," writes Griffith, "were instantly covered with pikes, pitchforks, sabres and some muskets. Five of the Ancient Britons, whose lives the insurgents had spared and put in the front of the battle on foot, armed only with pikes, deserted to us and gave us the horrid detail of the massacre at Prosperous. We pursued the rebels to near that town, but did not think it prudent to enter it lest we should be fired at from the houses. We therefore returned to Clane, got our men reported, and having put our wounded men on cars proceeded to Naas, whither we had received orders to march." . . .

*The first phase of the rebellion was marked by skirmishes between small groups of yeomen or militia and United Irishmen. In county Kildare the rebels occupied a few small towns and plundered houses. After several costly ambushes, the army showed no mercy toward those whom they caught with arms. The number of Catholics in the militia and the number of Protestant United Irishmen meant that the rebellion was not sectarian in inspiration. Although deprived of their leaders, most of whom were in jail, and infiltrated by informers, the rebels showed great tenacity and resourcefulness. Dublin was placed under martial law, and the army carried out a rigorous search for arms.*

Countless rumours of impending acts of murder or treachery were circulated, and for some days there was a complete ignorance about the extent of the rebellion. Camden wrote on the 25th that all communications with the South were cut off, and that the judges who were going to the assizes at Clonmel were compelled to turn back. Reinforcements, he said, were urgently needed, but there was as yet no news of insurrection in the North.

There is much reason to believe that the outbreak was witnessed with gratification by many of the members and supporters of Government, who believed that the disease which had been during the last years poisoning all the springs of Irish life would be now by a short sharp crisis effectually expelled. I have quoted the imprudent language to this effect used by Beresford in the House of Commons in 1797. Just a month before the rebels appeared in the field, the Knight of Kerry made a remarkable speech in which he declared that the country was incontestably in a state of rebellion; that it was the lurking and mysterious character of the conspiracy that constituted its real danger, and that once the rebels appeared in the field, that danger would soon be over. At the very beginning of the rebellion Lord Clare predicted that the country "would be more safe and peaceable than for many years back." "I consider," wrote Cooke in a very confidential letter, "this insurrection, however distressing, as really the salvation of the country. If you look at the accounts that 200,000 men are sworn in a conspiracy, how could that conspiracy be cleared without a burst? *Besides, it will prove many things necessary for the future settlement of the country when peace arises.*"

The Queen's County, as we have seen, had long been in a state of extreme disturbance. It had been proclaimed towards the end of January, and under the influence of martial law great numbers of suspected rebels had been imprisoned, and great quantities of arms discovered and surrendered. On the 25th an open rebellion broke out in it, but only in the feeblest, the most unorganised, and inefficient form. There was much robbery. There were also, it is said, some isolated murders of Protestants, and at four in the morning a party variously estimated at 1,000 or 2,000 attacked the little town of Monasterevan, which was garrisoned by eighty-four yeomen. There was some serious fighting, and the issue for one or two hours seemed very doubtful, but the yeomanry then drove back their assailants, who set fire to some houses and retired under the shelter of the smoke, leaving sixty or seventy of their number dead on the field. Only four or five of the yeomen appear to have fallen. It was noticed that of the gallant little band that defended Monasterevan, fourteen were Catholics, and that ten others were Methodists, who had been deprived of their arms for refusing to exercise on Sundays, but who now offered their services and bore a distinguished part in the fight.

With this exception, no event of any real importance took place during the rebellion in this county. Some of the rebels who had attacked Monasterevan proceeded towards Portarlington, but they had now dwindled to a disorderly mob of about 200 poor, unguided men, and they were met and easily dispersed by a small body of cavalry at Clonanna, some four miles from Portarlington. Twenty of them were killed at that place, and in or near the wood of Kilbracken. It has been stated that the escape of the remainder was largely due to a yeomanry officer whom they had taken prisoner and whose life they had spared. They at first entreated him to command them, and on his refusal they piteously implored him to advise them. He recommended them to fling away their pikes and to fly across the quaking bog, where the cavalry could not pursue them.

On the same morning on which Monasterevan was attacked, 1,000 or 1,500 rebels attempted to surprise the town of Carlow. They assembled in the middle of the night on the lawn of Sir Edward Crosbie, who lived a mile and a half from the town, and at two in the morning they proceeded to the attack. But either from secret information, or through their total neglect of the most ordinary precautions, their design was known, and the garrison of 450 men, some of them being regular soldiers, were prepared to receive them. The rebels entered Carlow by Tullow Street, unopposed, and proceeded to the open place at the end, where they set up a sudden yell. It was at once answered by a deadly fire from the soldiers, who had been posted at many different points. The panic-stricken rebels endeavoured to fly, but found their retreat cut off; the houses in which they sought a refuge were set on fire, and the soldiers shot or bayoneted all who attempted to escape from the flames. Not less than eighty houses were burnt, and that evening nineteen carts were constantly employed in carrying charred or mangled corpses to a gravel pit near the town. During several days, it is said, roasted remains of rebels fell from the chimneys in which they had concealed themselves. It was believed that more than 600 perished in the fight, or in the flames, or by martial law, without the loss of a single life on the other side. . . .

*By the end of May, the rebellion had almost run its course in counties Carlow, Meath, Kildare, and the Queen's County, although pockets of United Irishmen lingered on. In several cases soldiers shot down rebels who were in the act of surrendering.*

If a French force of disciplined soldiers had arrived in Ireland at the beginning of the outbreak, or even if without that arrival the rebel plot for seizing Dublin and the Irish Executive had succeeded, the rebellion would very probably for a time at least have triumphed, and Ireland might have passed out of English rule. Neither of these things had happened, and the one remaining chance of the rebels lay in a simultaneous rising, extending over all parts of the island. Such a rising was part of the scheme of the original leaders, and if their plans had not been dislocated by their arrest, it might have taken place. As yet, however, the rebellion had only appeared in a small part of Leinster. Connaught was perfectly peaceful. In Munster, though some pikes were captured, and some slight disorders appeared near Cork and Limerick, there was no semblance of regular rebellion. Above all, Ulster, where the conspiracy had begun, where its organisation was most perfect, and where its outbreak was most dreaded, was absolutely passive, and remained so for a full fortnight after the rebellion began. The plan of the rebellion had been wholly frustrated. The expected capture of Dublin had failed. The desertion of the Catholic militia, which had been fully counted on, had not taken place, and the forces on the side of the Government had displayed an unexpected energy. The Irish yeomanry have been much and justly blamed by historians for their want of discipline, for their extreme recklessness in destroying both life and property, and for the violent religious passions they too frequently displayed. But if their faults were great, their merits were equally conspicuous. To their patriotic energy, to their ceaseless vigilance, to the courage with which they were always ready to encounter armed bodies, five or even ten times as numerous as themselves, the suppression of the rebellion was mainly due. But the flame had no sooner begun to burn low in the central counties, than it burst out with redoubled fierceness in Wicklow and Wexford, and soon acquired dimensions which taxed all the energies of the Government.

In neither county was it fully expected. Wicklow was one of the most peaceful and most prosperous counties in Ireland. It possessed a large and very respectable resident gentry. The condition of its farmers and labourers was above the average, and it had always been singularly free from disturbance and outrage. Its proximity to Dublin, however, made it peculiarly open to the seductions of the United Irishmen, and it is said that, from an early period of the movement, a party among the Wicklow priests had favoured the conspiracy. The organisation spread so seriously, that some districts were proclaimed in November 1797. There was no branch of the Orange Society in the county of Wicklow, but the yeomanry force in this county is said to have taken a peculiarly sectarian character, for the strenuous and successful efforts of the United Irishmen to prevent the Catholics from enlisting in it, made it necessary to fill the ranks with Protestants of the lowest order. Having thus succeeded in making the armed force mainly Protestant, the conspirators industriously spread reports that the Orangemen were about to massacre the Catholics, and were supported and instigated by the Government. I have already noticed the maddening terror which such rumours produced, and a Catholic historian states, that in this county not once only, but on several occasions, the whole Catholic population for the extent of thirty miles deserted their homes, and slept in the open air, through the belief that the armed Protestants were about to sweep down upon them to massacre them, or at least to expel them from the county.

By these means a population with very little interest in political questions were scared into rebellion; the conspiracy took root and spread, and the methods of repression that were adopted soon completed the work. The burning of houses, often on the most frivolous grounds, the floggings of suspected individuals, the insults to women, and all the many acts of violence, plunder, brutality, and oppression, that inevitably follow when undisciplined forces, drawn mainly from the lowest classes of society, are suffered to live at free quarters upon a hostile population, lashed the people to madness. I have quoted from the autobiography of Holt the remarkable passage, in which that Wicklow rebel declared how foreign were political and legislative grievances from the motives that turned him into a rebel, and the persecution of those who fell under suspicion was by no means confined to the poor. We have seen a striking example of this in the treatment of Reynolds in the county of Kildare. Grattan himself lived in the county of Wicklow, but fortunately he was detained in England, during the worst period of martial law, by the postponement of the trial of O'Connor; his family, however, found themselves exposed to so many insults, and even dangers, that they took refuge in Wales. A great part of the Ancient Britons were quartered in the county of Wicklow, and these Welsh soldiers appear to have everywhere aroused a deeper hatred than any others who were employed in Ireland.

Some time before the rebellion began, those who knew the people well perceived that a dangerous movement was on foot. A general indisposition to pay debts of any kind, or fulfil any engagements; a marked change in the manner of the people; mysterious meetings by night; vague but persistent rumours, pointing to some great coming change; signal fires appearing frequently upon the hills; busy strangers moving from cottage to cottage, all foreshadowed the storm. There was also a sudden cessation of drinking; a rapid and unnatural abatement of the usual turbulence at fairs or wakes, which, to those who knew Ireland well, was very ominous.

The adjoining county of Wexford was also one of the most prosperous in Ireland. Land sold there at an unusually high price. It had a considerable and intelligent resident gentry, and in general the peasantry were comfortably situated, though there were some districts in which there was extreme poverty. The

people were Catholic, but mainly descended from English settlers, and this county boasted that it was the parent of the volunteer movement, the first corps having been raised by Wexford
gentlemen, under the command of Sir Vesey Colclough, for the
purpose of repressing Whiteboy outrages.

Unlike Wicklow, however, Wexford had been an important
centre of Defenderism. A great part of the county had been
sworn in to resist the payment of tithes, and in 1793 bodies,
numbering, it is said, more than 1,000 men, and very bravely
commanded by a young farmer named Moore, had appeared in
arms around Enniscorthy. A distinguished officer named Vallot-
ton, who had been first aide-de-camp to General Elliot during the
famous siege of Gibraltar, lost his life in suppressing these obscure disturbances, and more than eighty of the Defenders were
killed. After this period, however, Wexford appears to have
been remarkably free from crime and from illegal organisations,
though it took a considerable part in the agitation for Catholic
emancipation. It has been asserted by its local historians, that the
United Irish movement had made little way in it before the
rebellion, and that it was one of the latest and least organised
counties in Leinster; but this statement is hardly consistent with
the progress which had been made in arming the population, and
Miles Byrne, who took an active part in the Wexford rebellion,
assures us that before a shot was fired, the great mass of the
people of Wexford had become United Irishmen. How far there
was any real political or anti-English feeling smouldering
among them is very difficult to determine. My own opinion,
for which I have collected much evidence in this book, is, that
there was little positive political disloyalty, though there was
much turbulence and anarchy, among the Irish Catholic peasantry,
till shortly before the rebellion of 1798, and their attitude at the
time of the French expedition to Bantry Bay can hardly be mistaken. Byrne, however, stated in his old age, that he could well
remember the sorrow and consternation expressed in the Wexford chapels when the news arrived that the French had failed
to land, and he mentions that his own father had told him, that he
would sooner see his son dead than wearing the red uniform of
the King, and had more than once shown him the country around

371

their farm, bidding him remember that all this had belonged to their ancestors, and that all this had been plundered from them by the English invaders.

In the latter part of 1797, the magistrates became aware that the conspiracy was spreading in the county. It was found that secret meetings were held in many districts, and the usual rumours of plots of the Orangemen to murder their Catholic neighbours were being industriously circulated by seditious agents, although, "in fact," as an historian who lived in the county observes, "there was no such thing as an Orange association formed in the county of Wexford until a few months after the suppression of the rebellion, nor were there any Orangemen in the county at its breaking out, except a few in the towns, where detachments of the North Cork Regiment of Militia were stationed." The yeomanry officers discovered that numbers of the Catholics in their corps had been seduced, and they tried to combat the evil by imposing a new test, obliging every man to declare that he was not, and would not be, either an Orangeman or a United Irishman. Many refused to take it, and the Government did not approve of it; but the evil was found to be so serious, that a great part of the yeomanry were disbanded and disarmed. These precautions, as the rebellion shows, were certainly far from needless; but the result was, that the yeomanry became almost exclusively Protestant. It was discovered about the same time, by means of an informer, that several blacksmiths were busily employed in the manufacture of pikes, and one of them, when arrested, confessed that he had been making them for upwards of a year without being suspected. At the end of November there was a meeting of magistrates at Gorey, and by the votes of the majority, 16 out of the 142 parishes in the county were proclaimed. Lord Mountnorris adopted a course which was at that time frequent in Ireland, and went, accompanied by some other magistrates, from chapel to chapel during mass time, exhorting the people to come forward and take the oath of allegiance, promising them "protections" if they did so, but threatening free quarters if they refused. Great numbers, headed by their priests, took the oath, received protections, and succeeded in disarming suspicion. Many of these were soon after prominent in the rebellion. . . .

It was evident that the county was in a very dangerous state, and it was equally evident that if the conspiracy exploded, it would take the form of a religious war. On April 27, the whole county was proclaimed and put under martial law, and it was martial law carried out not by the passionless and resistless force of a well-disciplined army, but mainly by small parties of yeomen and militia, who had been hastily armed for the defence of their homes and families, who were so few that if a rebellion broke out before the population had been disarmed, they would almost certainly have been massacred, and who were entirely unaccustomed to military discipline. As might have been expected, such circumstances at once led to outrages which, although they may have been exaggerated and multiplied by partisan historians, were undoubtedly numerous and horrible. Great numbers of suspected persons were flogged, or otherwise tortured. Some were strung up in their homes to be hanged, and then let down half strangled to elicit confession, and this process is said to have been repeated on the same victim as much as three times. Numbers of cabins were burnt to the ground because pikes or other weapons had been found in them, or because the inhabitants, contrary to the proclamation, were absent from them during the night, or even because they belonged to suspected persons. The torture of the pitched cap, which never before appears to have been known in Ireland, was now introduced by the North Cork Militia, and excited fierce terror and resentment. . . .

*Aided and abetted by the local Protestant magistrates, the North Cork Militia terrorized much of county Wexford. Arson, torture, and imprisonment were used against those suspected of having weapons or United Irish convictions. These ruthless methods drove the bulk of the Catholics into panic.*

It was on the evening of Saturday, May 26, that the standard of insurrection was raised at a place called Boulavogue, between Wexford and Gorey, by Father John Murphy, the curate of the parish, a priest who had been educated at Seville, and whose character is very variously, though not quite incompatibly, represented by the opposing parties. He is described by one set of writers as an ignorant, narrow-minded, sanguinary fanatic, and by another set of writers as an honest and simple-minded man, who had been driven to desperation by the burning of his house and chapel, and of the houses of some of his parishioners. A small party of eighteen or twenty yeomanry cavalry, on hearing of the assembly, hastened to disperse it, but they were unexpectedly attacked, and scattered, and Lieutenant Bookey, who commanded them, was killed. Next day the circle of devastation rapidly spread. Two very inoffensive clergymen, and five or, according to another account, seven other persons, were murdered, and the houses of the Protestant farmers in the neighbourhood were soon in a blaze. A considerable number of Catholic yeomen deserted to the rebels, who now concentrated themselves on two hills called Oulart and Killthomas, the former ten miles to the north of Wexford, the latter nine miles to the west of Gorey. Two hundred and fifty yeomen attacked and easily dispersed the rebels on Killthomas Hill, though they were about ten times as numerous as their assailants. The retribution was terrible. About one hundred and fifty rebels were killed; the yeomen pursued the remainder for some seven miles, burning on their way two Catholic chapels and, it is said, not less than one hundred cabins and farmhouses, and they are accused of having shot many unarmed and inoffensive persons. Two or three Catholic priests were among the rebels of Killthomas.

A more formidable body of rebels, estimated at about 4,000, under the command of Father John, had assembled on the hill of Oulart. With the complete contempt for disorderly and half-armed rebel mobs which characterised the Irish loyalists, a picked body of only 110 of the North Cork Militia, under the command of Colonel Foote, proceeded at once to attack them, while a few cavalry were collected below to cut off their retreat. The confidence of the loyalist militia seemed at first justified, for the rebels fled at the first onset, hotly pursued up the hill by the militia, when Father John succeeded in rallying his pikemen. He told them that they were surrounded, and must either conquer or perish, and placing himself at their head, he charged the troops. These were scattered in the pursuit, and breathless from the ascent, and they had never before experienced the formidable character of the Irish pike. In a few moments almost the whole body were stretched lifeless on the ground; five only of the force that mounted the hill succeeded in reaching the cavalry below and escaping to Wexford.

This encounter took place on the morning of Whitsunday, May 27. Its effects were very great. The whole country was at once in arms, while the loyalists fled from every village and farmhouse in the neighbourhood. Father John lost no time in following up his success. He encamped that night on Carrigrew Hill, and early on the following day he occupied the little town of Camolin, about six miles from Oulart, where he found 700 or 800 guns. Some of them belonged to the yeomen, but most of them had been collected from the surrounding country when it was disarmed. He then proceeded two miles farther, to Ferns, whence all the loyalists had fled, and after a short pause, and on the same day, resolved to attack Enniscorthy, one of the most important towns in the county, and a chief military centre.

The great majority of his followers consisted of a rabble of half-starved peasantry, drawn from a country which was sunk in abject squalor and misery—men who were assuredly perfectly indifferent to the political objects of the United Irishmen, but who were driven into rebellion by fear of Orange massacres, or by exasperation at military severities. Most of them had no better arms than pitchforks, and great numbers of women were among them. They had no tents, no commissariat, no cavalry, hardly a vestige of discipline or organisation; and although the capture of Camolin had given them many guns, they were in general quite incapable of using them. There were, however, some exceptions to the general inefficiency. There were among them men from the barony of Shilmalier, who had been trained from boyhood to shoot the sea birds and other wild fowl for the Dublin market, and who were in consequence excellent marksmen; there were deserters from the yeomanry, who were acquainted with the use of arms and with the rules of discipline; and after the success at Oulart Hill, a few sons of substantial farmers gradually came in with their guns and horses, while even the most unpractised found the pike a weapon of terrible effect. No other weapon, indeed, employed by the rebels, was so dreaded by the soldiers, especially by the cavalry; no other weapon inflicted such terrible wounds, or proved at close quarters so formidable.

Enniscorthy was attacked shortly after midday on the 28th, and captured after more than three hours of very severe fighting. The garrison appears to have consisted of about 300 infantry and cavalry yeomen, and militia, and they were supported by some hastily raised volunteers. The rebel force had now swollen to 6,000 or 7,000 men. The little garrison sallied forth to attack the assailants, and a severe and obstinate fight ensued. Adopting a rude but not ineffectual strategy, which they more than once repeated in the course of the rebellion, and which is said to have been practised in Ireland as far back as the days of Strongbow, the rebels broke the ranks of the soldiers by driving into them a number of horses and cattle, which were goaded on by the pikemen. The yeomen, at last, finding themselves in danger of being surrounded, were driven backwards into the town, and made a stand in the market-place and on the bridge across the Slaney. For some time a disorderly fight continued, with so fluctuating a fortune, that orange and green ribbons are said to have been alternately displayed by many in the town. Soon, however, a number of houses were set on fire, and a scene of wild confusion began. The ammunition of the yeomanry ran short. The rebels forded the river; and a general flight took place. The loyalists in wild confusion fled through the burning streets, and made their way to Wexford, which was eleven Irish miles distant. The rebels, fatigued with their labours of the day, attempted no pursuit, and after searching the town for ammunition, they retired, and formed their camp around the summit of Vinegar Hill, a small rocky eminence which rises immediately behind the town. Three officers and rather more than eighty soldiers had fallen, and between four and five hundred houses and cabins had been burnt. The loss of the insurgents is vaguely estimated at from one hundred to five hundred men.

When the news of the capture of Enniscorthy arrived at Wexford, the wildest terror prevailed. The wives of soldiers who had been killed ran screaming through the streets, while streams of fugitives poured in, covered with dust and blood, half fainting with terror and fatigue, and thrown destitute upon the world. The few ships that lay in the harbour were soon thronged with women and children, and most of the adult men who possessed or could procure weapons, prepared to defend the town from the anticipated attack. Fears of massacre, however, from without, and of treachery from within, hung heavy on every mind, and an attempt was made to avert the calamity by negotiation. . . .

*Indecision lost the rebels valuable time in exploiting their victory at Enniscorthy. Father John Murphy had great difficulty in keeping his forces together and maintaining discipline. They camped that night at Three Rocks, only a few miles from Wexford town, and on the morning of May 30 they routed a small detachment of soldiers, capturing two cannon. The Wexford garrison now had no hope of repulsing a force of almost 16,000 men.*

The alarm in Wexford was now extreme. Early on the morning of the 30th, the toll house and part of the bridge were found to be in flames, and there were great fears of an extensive conflagration. The town was not made for defence. Two-thirds of its inhabitants were Catholics, and could not be counted on; several yeomen deserted to the rebels, and among the remainder there was scarcely any discipline or subordination. Some desired to kill the prisoners in the gaol, and Bagenal Harvey was so much alarmed, that he climbed up a chimney, where he remained for some time concealed. If the insurgents had at once advanced and blocked the roads of retreat, especially that to Duncannon Fort, the whole garrison must have surrendered. Hay, who surveyed the situation with the eye of a practised soldier, implored them to do so, but his advice was neglected, and it is, perhaps, scarcely to be wondered at, that a disorderly and inexperienced force like that of the rebels, having on this very day crushed one detachment and repulsed another, should have relaxed its efforts, and failed to act with the promptitude of a regular army under a skilful general. At Wexford a council of war was now hastily summoned, and it was decided that the town must be surrendered. Bagenal Harvey was prevailed on to write a letter to the rebels, stating that he and the other prisoners had been treated with all possible humanity, and were now at liberty, and imploring the insurgents to commit no massacre, to abstain from burning houses, and to spare their prisoners' lives. Two brothers of the name of Richards, who were known to be popular in the county, were sent to the rebels to negotiate a surrender. They tied white handkerchiefs round their hats as a sign of truce, brought some country people with them, and reached the rebel camp in safety. After some discussion and division, the rebels agreed to spare

lives and property, but insisted that all cannon, arms, and ammunition should be surrendered. They detained one of the brothers
as a hostage, and sent back the other with Edward Fitzgerald to
Wexford to arrange the capitulation.

But long before they had arrived there, almost the whole garrison had fled from the town by the still open road to Duncannon
Fort, leaving the inhabitants absolutely unprotected, but carrying
with them their arms and ammunition. The yeomen, commanded
by Colonel Colville, are said to have kept some order in the flight,
but the other troops scattered themselves over the country, shooting peasants whom they met, burning cottages, and also, it is said,
several Roman Catholic chapels. In the town the quays, and every
avenue leading to the water-side, were thronged with women and
children, begging in piteous tones to be taken in the ships. One
young lady, in her terror, actually threw herself into the sea, in
order to reach a boat. The shipowners, who were chiefly Wexford
men, or men from the neighbouring country, had promised to
convey the fugitives to Wales, and received exorbitant fares; but
when the town was occupied by the rebels, most of them betrayed
their trust, and brought them back to the town.

It was, indeed, a terrible fate to be at the mercy of the vast,
disorderly, fanatical rabble who now poured into Wexford. It
was not surprising, too, that the rebels should have contended
that faith had been broken with them; that Fitzgerald and Colclough had been sent on a sham embassy, merely in order to
secure a period of delay, during which the garrison might escape
with their arms. The inhabitants, however, either through sympathy or through a very pardonable policy, did all they could to
conciliate their conquerors. Green handkerchiefs, flags, or
branches of trees, were hung from every window, and most of the
townsmen speedily assumed the green cockade, flung open their
houses, and offered refreshment to the rebels. It was observed that
many refused it till the person who offered it had partaken of it
himself, for there was a widespread rumour that the drink had
been poisoned. The rebels, who had been sleeping for many
nights without cover on the heather, presented a wild, savage,
grotesque appearance. They were, most of them, in the tattered
dress of the Irish labourer, distinguished only by white bands
around their hats and by green cockades, but many were fan-

tastically decorated with ladies' hats, bonnets, feathers, and tip-
pets, taken from plundered country houses, while others wore
portions of the uniform of the soldiers who had been slain. Their
arms consisted chiefly of pikes, with handles from twelve to
fourteen feet long, and sometimes, it is said, even longer. A few
men carried guns. Many others had pitchforks, scrapers, currying
knives, or old rusty bayonets fixed on poles. A crowd of women
accompanied them on their march, shouting and dancing in the
wildest triumph.

On the whole, they committed far less outrage than might
reasonably have been expected. Two or three persons, against
whom they had special grudges, were murdered, and one of
these lay dying all night on the bridge. Many houses were plundered, chiefly those which had been deserted by their owners, but
no houses were burned, and there was at this time no general
disposition to massacre, though much to plunder. In Wexford
also, as at Enniscorthy, and elsewhere, the rebels abstained most
remarkably from those outrages on women which in most countries are the usual accompaniment of popular and military anarchy. This form of crime has, indeed, never been an Irish vice,
and the presence of many women in the camp contributed to
prevent it. The rebels also were very tired, and, in spite of some
intoxication, the streets of Wexford on the night of May 30
were hardly more disturbed than in time of peace. . . .

*Bagenal Harvey, a Protestant landlord and barrister, was re-
leased from jail by the rebels and made their commander. Hundreds of Protestants in and around Wexford, who were suspected
of Orange sympathies, were seized and imprisoned. The rebel
commander of Wexford, Captain Matthew Keogh, did his best
to prevent any massacre in the town. Although the rebels dominated most of the southern half of the county, a force of 350
yeomanry and militia defeated some 4,000 rebels at Newtown-
Barry on June 1. This encounter marked the first serious reverse
for the United Irishmen in county Wexford.*

The Wexford rebellion, however, from its magnitude, and
also from its sanguinary character, speedily became the centre of
the scene, attracting to itself the rebel elements in the surrounding
counties, and reducing all the other disturbances in Ireland almost

to insignificance. Though the larger body of the rebel force that had captured Enniscorthy had proceeded to Wexford, and had chosen Bagenal Harvey as their commander, a considerable number still occupied the camp at Vinegar Hill, and they remained there from May 28 till the 20th of the following June. It was at this spot and during this time, that many of the most horrible crimes of the rebellion were committed. Vinegar Hill is the centre of a richly wooded and undulating country, watered by the Slaney, and bounded on the north and west by the blue line of the Wicklow hills. Enniscorthy lies at its foot, and an area of many miles is gaily interspersed with country houses and with prosperous farms. Near the summit of the hill stood an old windmill. The mill no longer exists, but the lower part of its masonry still remains, forming a round, grey tower, about fifteen feet in diameter, which stands out conspicuously against the green grass, and is one of the most prominent objects to be seen from Enniscorthy. Scarcely any other spot in Ireland is associated with memories so tragical and so hideous. The country around was searched and plundered, and great numbers of Protestants were brought to the rebel camp, confined in the old windmill, or in a barn that lay at the foot of the hill, and then deliberately butchered. There appears indeed generally—through not always—to have been some form of trial, and although the victims were all or nearly all Protestants, they were not put to death simply for their creed. Many against whom no charge was brought, or who were popular among the people, or who could find some rebel to attest their innocence and their goodness, were dismissed in safety, with written protections from a priest. But all who had borne any part in the floggings, burnings, and other measures of repression that had been so frequent during the last few weeks; all who had shown themselves active or conspicuous on the loyalist side; all who were pronounced by the rebel tribunals to be Orangemen, were deliberately put to death. The belief which had been so industriously spread, that the Orangemen had sworn to exterminate the Catholics, had driven the people mad; and although in truth there were scarcely any Orangemen in Wexford, although until shortly before the rebellion, religious dissension had been very slight, every Protestant of zeal and earnestness now fell under suspicion. Some were shot, some were piked to death, many were flogged in imitation of the proceedings of the yeomen and in order to elicit confessions of Orangism, and there were ghastly tales of prolonged and agonising deaths.

These rest, it is true, on scanty and somewhat dubious evidence, but of the blackness of the tragedy there can be no question. The dead bodies of many Protestants were left unburied, to be devoured by the swine or by the birds. Some were thrown into the river. Some were lightly covered over with sand. One man, who had been stunned, and pierced with a pike, was thrown into a grave while still alive, but a faithful dog scraped away the earth that covered him, and licked his face till he revived, and some passers-by drew him from the grave, sheltered him in their house, and tended him till he recovered. How many perished on Vinegar Hill, it is impossible to say. Musgrave, the most violent of the Protestant loyalist historians, estimates the number at more than five hundred. Gordon, the most moderate, says that unquestionable evidence proves that it can have been little less than four hundred. The Catholic historians usually confine themselves to vague generalities, and to paralleling these atrocities with the massacres of prisoners by the yeomen and the soldiers at Carnew, Dunlavin, and Gorey.

The proceedings on Vinegar Hill were largely directed by priests. Many of them were collected there. The mass was daily celebrated, and fierce sermons sustained the fanaticism of the people. A hot, feverish atmosphere of religious excitement prevailed, and there was a ghastly mixture of piety and murder. It was observed that religious hatred, industriously inflamed by accounts of intended massacres of Catholics by Orangemen, played here a much more powerful part than any form of political or civil rancour, and it was often those who were most scrupulously observant of the ceremonials of their religion who were the most murderous. All the resources of superstition were at the same time employed to stimulate the courage of the rebels. Father John Murphy was especially looked upon as under divine protection, and it was believed that he was invulnerable, and could catch the bullets in his hand. Numbers of Protestants around Vinegar Hill sought safety and protection by conforming, and it must be added, that not a few others appear to have been saved by the intervention of the priests. Some of those who thus escaped were afterwards in imminent danger of being hanged by the soldiers, who regarded their release by the rebels as a strong presumption of their guilt.

There were curious varieties in the treatment of Protestants. In large districts, every house belonging to a Protestant was burnt to the ground, but in others they were little molested. . . .

*While the rebels continued their surprise attacks on inferior Government forces, the militia and yeomanry prepared to launch a major offensive. The boldness of the rebels combined with the ineptness of certain army officers led to the fall of Gorey on June 4. The jubilant rebels proceeded to plunder the almost deserted town.*

While these things were happening at Gorey, a much larger body under the command of Bagenal Harvey attempted to take New Ross. Adopting their usual precaution of encamping always on a height, they passed from Wexford to their old quarters on the Three Rocks; thence on June 1 to Carrickbyrne Hill, which is about seven miles from New Ross, and then on the 4th to Corbet Hill, which is within a mile of that town. A few days before, they might probably have occupied it without resistance, thus opening a path into Carlow; but General Johnson was now there, at the head of at least 1,400 men, including 150 yeomen. His force was composed of the Dublin Militia under Lord Mountjoy, with detachments from the 5th Dragoons, the Clare, Donegal, and Meath Militia, the Mid-Lothian Fencibles, and some English artillery. At daybreak on the 5th the insurgents were ready for the attack, but Harvey first endeavoured to save bloodshed by sending a summons to the commander, representing the overwhelming numbers of the assailants, and summoning him to surrender the town, and thus save from total ruin the property it contained. A man named Furlong, bearing a flag of truce, undertook to carry the message, but as he approached he was shot dead, and his pockets rifled. Few incidents in the rebellion did more to exasperate the rebels, and there is reason to believe that it was no misadventure, but a deliberate act.

The battle that ensued was the most desperate in the rebellion. The insurgents advanced at daybreak, driving before them a quantity of black cattle to break the ranks of the troops, and they were received with a steady fire of grape. "At near seven o'clock," says an eye-witness who was with General Johnson, "the army began to retreat in all directions. . . . The rebels pouring in like a flood, artillery was called for, and human blood began to flow down the street. Though hundreds were blown to pieces by our grape shot, yet thousands behind them, being intoxicated from drinking during the night and void of fear, rushed upon us. The cavalry were now ordered to make a charge through them, when a terrible carnage ensued. They were cut down like grass, but the pikemen being called to the front, and our swords being too short to reach them, obliged the horses to retreat, which put us into some confusion. We kept up the action till half-past eight, and it was maintained with such obstinacy on both sides that it was doubtful who would keep the field. They then began to burn and destroy the town. It was on fire in many places in about fifteen minutes. By this time the insurgents advanced as far as the main guard, where there was a most bloody conflict, but with the assistance of two ship guns placed in the street, we killed a great number and kept them back for some time." They soon, however, rallied, and by their onward sweep bore down the artillerymen, and obtained possession of the guns. Lord Mountjoy, at the head of the Dublin County Regiment, then charged them, and a fierce hand-to-hand fight ensued, but the troops were unable to pierce the ranks of the pikemen. Lord Mountjoy was surrounded and fell, and his soldiers fiercely fighting were driven back by the overwhelming weight of the enemy, and at last crossed the bridge to the Kilkenny side of the river, where, however, they speedily rallied. Mountjoy was the first member of either House of Parliament who had fallen in this disastrous struggle, and it was bitterly noticed by the ultra-Protestant party, that he was the Luke Gardiner who had been one of the warmest friends of the Catholics, and who twenty years before had introduced into the House of Commons the first considerable measure for their relief.

The town seemed now almost lost, and some of the troops in wild panic fled to Waterford. If indeed all the resources of the rebels had been exerted, nothing could have saved it. But though the insurgents were the raw material out of which some of the best soldiers in the British army have been formed; though they showed a desperate and truly admirable courage, in facing for long hours the charge of cavalry and bayonets, the volleys of disciplined soldiers, and even the storm of grape shot, they were in truth but untrained, ignorant, poverty-stricken, half-armed peasants, most of whom had never before seen a shot fired in war. Bagenal Harvey had ordered a simultaneous attack on the town in three quarters, but the men who rushed into it, infuriated by the death of Furlong, kept no discipline and acted on no plan. A large part, it is said indeed the great majority, of the insurgents remained at Corbet Hill, and never descended to share the dangers of their fellows, and even of those who had taken the town, a multitude soon dispersed through the streets to plunder or to drink. General Johnson succeeded in rallying his troops, and placing himself at their head, he once more charged the insurgents. A well-directed fire from the cannon which had not been taken, cleared his way, and after desperate fighting the town was regained, and the cannon recaptured and turned against the rebels. Johnson himself displayed prodigies of valour, and three horses were shot under him. . . .

At last, the insurgents broke and fled. The flight was terrible, for it was through streets of burning and falling houses, and many are said to have perished in the flames. The streets of Ross, General Johnson reported, were literally strewn with the carcases of the rebels. "The carnage," wrote Major Vesey, "was shocking, as no quarter was given. The soldiers were too much exasperated, and could not be stopped. It was a fortunate circumstance," he adds, "for us that early in the night a man ran in from their post to acquaint us that it was their intention to attack us, and that they were resolved to conquer or die, and so in fact they acted." In the first excited estimates, the loss of the insurgents was reckoned at seven thousand men. According to the best accounts, it was about two thousand. The loss on the loyalist side was officially reckoned at two hundred and thirty men.

The battle of New Ross was still raging, when a scene of horror was enacted at Scullabogue barn, which has left an indelible mark on Irish history. The rebels had in the last few days collected many prisoners, and though some are said to have been put to death, the great majority were kept under guard near the foot of Carrickbyrne mountain, where the camp had lately been, in a lonely and abandoned country house called Scullabogue and in the adjoining barn. The number of the prisoners is stated in the Protestant accounts to have been two hundred and twenty-four, though the Catholic historians have tried to reduce it to eighty or a hundred. They were left under the guard of three hundred rebels. The accounts of what happened are not quite consistent in their details, but it appears that in an early stage of the battle, a party of runaways from the camp reached Sculla-bogue, declaring that the rebel army at New Ross was cut off; that the troops were shooting all prisoners, and butchering all the Catholics who fell into their hands; that orders had been issued that the prisoners at Scullabogue should be at once slaughtered; and that a priest had given peremptory instructions to that effect. The leader of the rebel guard is said to have at first hesitated and resisted, but his followers soon began the work of blood. Thirty-seven prisoners who were confined in the house were dragged out, and shot or piked before the hall door. The fate of those who were in the barn was more terrible. The rebels surrounded it and set it on fire, thrusting back with their pikes into the flames those who attempted to escape. Three only by some strange fortune escaped. It is said that one hundred and eighty-four persons perished in the barn by fire or suffocation, and that twenty of them were women and children. The immense majority were Protestants, but there were ten or fifteen Catholics among them. Some of these appear to have been wives of North Cork Militia men, and some others, Catholic servants who had refused to quit their Protestant masters. . . .

*With Chief Secretary Pelham still sick and absent in England, the Irish Government grew ever more anxious about the extent of the rebellion, even though Munster and Connaught remained relatively quiet. The rebels in Wexford kept hoping for a French invasion which might have changed the whole outcome of the contest. Lord Camden warned the Pitt ministry that Ireland might be lost to the enemy if troop reinforcements were not sent at once. Lord Castlereagh, the acting Chief Secretary, realized that it was both foolish and dangerous to underestimate the rebels' strength.*

The insurrection was still confined to a few central counties, and outside Wexford it was nowhere formidable.

The tranquillity of the greater part of Ulster during the rebellion, the defection of the Presbyterians from the movement of which they were the main originators, and the great and enduring change which took place in their sentiments in the last years of the eighteenth century, are facts of the deepest importance in Irish history, and deserve very careful and detailed examination. It would be an error to attribute them to any single cause. They are due to a concurrence of several distinct influences, which can be clearly traced in the correspondence of the time. Much was due to the growth of the Orange movement, which had planted a new and a rival enthusiasm in the heart of the disaffected province, and immensely strengthened the forces opposed to the United Irishmen; and much also to the success of long-continued military government. Martial law had prevailed in Ulster much longer than in the other provinces, and, as we have seen, an enormous proportion of the arms which had been so laboriously accumulated, had been discovered and surrendered. When the rebellion broke out, all the measures of precaution that were adopted in Dublin were taken in the towns of Ulster. The yeomanry were placed on permanent duty, and patrolled the streets by night. The inhabitants were forbidden to leave their houses between nine at night and five in the morning, and compelled to post up the names of those who were within them, which were to be called over whenever the military authorities desired. The arrival of every stranger was at once registered. A proclamation was issued, ordering all persons who were not expressly authorised to possess arms and ammunition, to bring them in within an assigned period, under pain of military execution, and promising at the same time that if they did so, they would be in no respect molested, and that no questions would be asked. At Belfast a court-martial sat daily in the market-place for the trial of all persons who were brought before it. One man, in whose house arms were found, was sentenced to eight hundred lashes, received two hundred, and then gave information which led to the flogging of a second culprit. About four hundred stand of arms were surrendered in a few days. One of the great anxieties of the authorities at Belfast was to discover six cannon, which had belonged to the Belfast volunteers, and had been carefully concealed. They were all found in the last week of May—two of them through information derived from an anonymous letter. Several persons were flogged for seditious offences. Many others who were suspected, but against whom there was no specific charge, were sent to the tender, and seven cars full of prisoners from Newry were lodged in Belfast gaol.

Such measures, carried out severely through the province, made rebellion very difficult, and it was to them that Lord Clare appears to have mainly attributed the calm of Ulster. It is, however, very improbable that they would have been sufficient, if they had not been supported by a real change of sentiments. The sturdy, calculating, well-to-do Presbyterians of the North might have risen to co-operate with a French army, or even to support a general, though unaided insurrection, if it had begun with a successful blow, and had been directed by leaders whom they knew. They were more and more disinclined to throw in their lot with disorderly Catholic mobs, assembled under nameless chiefs, who were plundering and often murdering Protestants, but who were in most cases scattered like chaff before small bodies of resolute yeomen. The rebellion in Leinster had assumed two forms, which were almost equally distasteful to Ulster. In some counties the rebels were helpless mobs, driven to arms by hope of plunder, or by fear of the Orangemen, or by exasperation at military severities, but destitute of all real enthusiasm and convictions, and perfectly impotent in the field. In Wexford they were very far from impotent, but there the struggle was assuming more and more the character of a religious war, and deriving its strength from religious fanaticism. The papers, day by day, told how the rebels were imprisoning, plundering, and murdering the Protestants; how the priests in their vestments were leading them to the fight, as to a holy war, which was to end in the extirpation of heresy; how Protestants were thronging the chapels to be baptised, as the sole means of saving their lives. In these accounts there was much that was exaggerated, and much that might be reasonably palliated or explained, but there was also much horrible truth, and the scenes that were enacted at Vinegar Hill and Scullabogue made a profound and indelible impression on the Northern mind. Men who had been the most ardent organisers of the United Irish movement, began to ask themselves whether this insurrection was not wholly different from what they had imagined and planned, and whether its success would not be the greatest of calamities. The tide of feeling suddenly changed, and even in Belfast itself, it soon ran visibly towards the Government.

The change of sentiment was greatly accelerated by other causes. The keynote of the conspiracy had been an alliance with France, for the establishment by French assistance of an Irish republic. But the utter failure of the French to profit by the golden opportunity of the Mutiny of the Nore; the mismanagement of the Bantry Bay expedition; the defeat of Camperdown, and the disappointment of several subsequent promises of assistance, had shaken the confidence of the more intelligent Northerners in French assistance, while many things had lately occurred which tended to destroy their sympathy with French policy. The United Irish movement, as we have seen, was essentially and ardently republican; and although it assumed a different character when it passed into an ignorant and bigoted Catholic population, this change had not extended to the North. Republicanism from the time of the American Revolution had been deeply rooted among the Presbyterians of Ulster. They had readily accepted those doctrines about the rights of man, which Rousseau had made the dominant political enthusiasm of Europe, and it was as the dawn of an era of universal liberty that the French Revolution, in spite of all the horrors that accompanied it, had been welcomed with delight. The precedent by which their leaders justified their appeal for French assistance was that of 1688, when the heads of the English party opposed to James II invited over the chief of the neighbouring republic with a small Dutch army, to assist them in establishing constitutional liberty. . . .

*The Presbyterians of Ulster gradually lost their faith in the French Revolution, as France's foreign policy became more militaristic and indifferent to the rights of other men and nations. This growing spirit of reaction effectively doomed the cause of the United Irishmen in Ulster, and the Orange lodges gained many new members at this time.*

It could hardly, however, have been expected that a conspiracy so widespread as that in Ulster should produce no effect. Alarming intelligence now came to Dublin, that on June 7 a rebellion had broken out in the North. A few months before, such intelligence would have portended a struggle of the most formidable dimensions, but it soon appeared that the rebellion was practically confined to the two counties of Antrim and Down, and it was suppressed in a few days. In the county of Antrim the only important operation was an attack, on June 7, on the town of Antrim by a body of rebels whose strength is very variously estimated, but probably consisted of from 3,000 to 4,000 men. Their leader was a young Belfast cotton manufacturer, named Henry Joy McCracken, one of the original founders of the United Irish Society, and one of the very few of those founders who ever appeared in the field. He was a man of singularly amiable private character, and is said to have formerly taken a part in establishing the first Sunday-school at Belfast. A brother of William Orr was conspicuous among the rebel officers.

As I have already stated, the Government had an informer in the Provincial Committee of Ulster, who had long been giving information about the Ulster rebels, and who furnished reports which were regularly transmitted to London, and which established the guilt of every leader of consequence in the province. Through his information they were fully prepared for the attack, and Antrim was defended by Colonel Lumley with two or three troops of dragoons, two cannon, and a considerable body of yeomanry. The rebels had a cannon, but it was disabled at the second shot. They were chiefly armed with pikes, but some hundreds of them had muskets. There was a sharp fight, lasting for between two and three hours, in the streets of Antrim and in the adjoining demesne of Lord Massareene, and the rebels showed very considerable courage. They endured without flinching several discharges of grape shot; repulsed with heavy loss a charge of cavalry; killed or wounded about fifty soldiers, and forced back the troops into Lord Massareene's grounds. Colonel Lumley and three or four others were wounded. Two officers were killed, and Lord O'Neill fell, pierced with a pike, and died in a few days. The rebels, however, were at last driven back, and on the arrival of some additional troops from Belfast and from the camp at Blaris, they fled precipitately, leaving from 200 to 400 men on the field.

The little town of Larne had been attacked early on the same morning by some rebels from Ballymena, but a small body of Tay Fencibles, aided by a few loyal inhabitants, easily drove them back. Randalstown and Ballymena were the same day occupied by rebels with little resistance, and some yeomen were taken prisoners, but the defeat of the 7th had already broken the rebellion in Antrim. The rebels found that the country was not rising to support them, and that there was absolutely no chance of success. Disputes and jealousies are said to have arisen in their ranks between the Protestants and the Catholics. Multitudes deserted, and a profound discouragement prevailed. Colonel Clavering issued a proclamation ordering an immediate surrender of arms and prisoners, and as it was not complied with, he set fire to Randalstown, with the exception of the places of worship and a few houses belonging to known loyalists. Two yeomanry officers were immediately after released, and the inhabitants of Ballymena sent to Clavering, offering to surrender their arms and prisoners, if their town was not burnt. The small remnant of the rebel force returned, on the 11th, to Dunagore Hill. Clavering, contrary to the wishes of some hot loyalists, offered a pardon to all except the leaders, if they surrendered their arms and returned to their allegiance, and this offer led to their almost complete dispersion. McCracken with a very few followers attempted to escape, but he was soon arrested, and tried and executed at Belfast. Another Antrim leader, named James Dickey, was not long after hanged in the same town, and he is stated by Musgrave to have declared before his execution, that the eyes of the Presbyterians had been opened too late; that they at last understood from the massacres in Leinster, that if they had succeeded in overturning the Constitution, they would then have had to contend with the Papists.

The insurrection in the county of Down was as brief, and hardly more important. It was intended to have broken out on the same day as that in the county of Antrim, and in that case it might have been very serious, but the precipitation of the Antrim rebels prevented this, and the battle at Antrim on the 7th put an end to all hopes of co-operation. . . .

*On June 9, United Irishmen in county Down fought an indecisive skirmish at Saintfield against some fencibles and yeomanry cavalry. The rebels then occupied Newtownards and camped that night near Ballinahinch where, on the morning of June 13, General Nugent attacked and defeated them, although greatly out-*

*numbered. Some 450 rebels were killed as compared with 29
loyalists. Nugent's soldiers took no prisoners and burned Ballinahinch to the ground.*

*In Wexford, meanwhile, Bagenal Harvey tried to rally his
forces after their defeat at New Ross. He learned with dismay of
the bloody massacre at Scullabogue and ordered that the perpetrators be caught and punished. More extreme elements among
the United Irishmen rapidly deposed Harvey as commander and
put Father Philip Roche, a powerful priest, in his place. On June
10, the rebels moved camp to Lacken Hill where they rested and
searched for arms and supplies.*

The reader may remember that another great body of rebels
had encamped, after the defeat of Colonel Walpole, in the neighbourhood of Gorey. If they had pressed on at once, after the
victory of the 4th, upon Arklow, it must have fallen without
resistance, and the road to Dublin would then have been open to
them. They wasted, however, precious days, feasting upon their
spoil, trying prisoners who were accused of being Orangemen,
plundering houses, and burning the town of Carnew; and in the
mean time the little garrison, which had at first evacuated Arklow
in terror, had returned, and had been powerfully reinforced. It
now amounted to 1,500 or 1,600 effective men, chiefly militia
and yeomen, but with some artillery. The whole was placed
under the skilful direction of General Needham, and every precaution was taken to create or strengthen defences. The rebels at
last saw that a great effort must be made to capture the town; and
reinforcements having been obtained from Vinegar Hill and
from other quarters, they marched from Gorey on the 9th, in a
great host which was estimated at 25,000, 30,000, or even 34,000
men, but which, in the opinion of General Needham, did not
exceed 19,000. According to the lowest estimate, their numbers
appeared overwhelming, but their leaders alone were mounted:
they were for the most part wretchedly armed, as scarcely any
blacksmith or gunsmith could be found to repair their pikes or
guns; their attack was anticipated, and they began it fatigued with
a long day's march.

It commenced about four in the afternoon. The rebels advanced from the Coolgreny road and along the sandhills on the

shore in two great solid columns, the intervening space being filled with a wild, disorderly crowd, armed with pikes and guns, and wearing green cockades, and green ribbons round their hats. Needham drew out his force in a strong position protected by ditches in front of the barracks. Five cannon supported him, and a heavy fire of grape shot poured continuously into the dense columns of the rebels. These set fire to the cabins that form the suburbs of Arklow, and advanced under shelter of the smoke, and their gunsmen availed themselves of the cover of fences, hedges, and ditches to gall the enemy. It was observed, however, that they usually overloaded their muskets, and fired so high that they did little damage, and although they had three, or, according to another account, four cannon, they had hardly any one capable of managing them. Their shot for the most part plunged harmlessly into the ground, or flew high above the enemy, and some of the rebels wished their captains to give them the canister shot as missiles, declaring that with them they would dash out the brains of the troops. An artillery sergeant, who had been taken prisoner, was compelled to serve at the guns, and it is said that he purposely pointed them so high that they did no damage to the troops.

The brunt of the battle was chiefly borne by the Durham Fencibles, an admirably appointed regiment of 360 men, which had only arrived at Arklow that morning. The yeomanry cavalry also more than once charged gallantly, and Captain Thomas Knox Grogan, a brother of the old man who was with the rebels at Wexford, was killed at the head of the Castletown troop. For some time the situation was very critical; at one moment it seemed almost hopeless, and Needham is said to have spoken of retreat, but to have been dissuaded by Colonel Skerrett, who was second in command. It is impossible, indeed, to speak too highly of the endurance and courage of the thin line of defenders who, during three long hours, confronted and baffled a host ten times as numerous as themselves, and it was all the more admirable, as the rebels on their side showed no mean courage. "Their perseverance," wrote Needham to General Lake, "was surprising, and their efforts to possess themselves of the guns on my right were most daring, advancing even to the muzzles, where they fell in great numbers." "A heavy fire of grape did as much execution as, from the nature of the ground and the strong fences of which they had possessed themselves, could have been expected. This continued incessantly from 6 o'clock until 8.30, when the enemy desisted from his attack and fled in disorder." At this time their ammunition was almost exhausted. The shades of night were drawing in, and their favourite commander, Father Michael Murphy, had fallen. He led his men into battle, waving above his head a green flag, emblazoned with a great white cross, and with the inscription "Death or liberty," and he was torn to pieces by canister shot within a few yards of the muzzle of a cannon which he was trying to take. He was one of those whom the rebels believed to be invulnerable, and his death cast a sudden chill over their courage. It was too late for pursuit, and the rebels retired unmolested to Gorey, but their loss had been very great. "Their bodies," wrote General Needham, "have been found in every direction scattered all over the country. The cabins were everywhere filled with them, and many cars loaded with them were carried off after the action. Numbers were also thrown by the enemy into the flames at the lower end of the town. On the whole, I am sure the number of killed must have exceeded a thousand." On the loyalist side the loss was quite inconsiderable.

The battle of Arklow was the last in which the rebels had any real chance of success, and from this time the rebellion rapidly declined. For some days, however, the alarms of the Government were undiminished. The multitude who had appeared in arms in the county of Wexford, the fanatical courage they displayed, the revolt which had begun in the North, and the complete uncertainty about how far that revolt might extend, or how soon the French might arrive, filled them with an anxiety which appears in all their most confidential letters. . . .

It is easy, indeed, to understand the savage hatred that was arising. In times of violence the violent must rule, and events assume a very different shape from that in which they appear to unimaginative historians in a peaceful age. When men are engaged in the throes of a deadly struggle; when dangers, horrible, unknown, and unmeasured, encompass them at every step; when the probability not only of ruin, but of massacre, is constantly before their eyes; when every day brings its ghastly tales of torture, murder, and plunder, it is idle to look for the judgments and the feelings of philanthropists or philosophers. The tolerant, the large-minded, the liberal, the men who can discriminate between different degrees or classes of guilt, and weigh in a just balance opposing crimes, then disappear from the scene. A feverish atmosphere of mingled passion and panic is created, which at once magnifies, obscures, and distorts, and the strongest passions are most valued, for they bring most men into the field, and make them most indifferent to danger and to death. The Catholic rebellion only became really formidable when the priests touched the one chord to which their people could heartily respond, and turned it into a religious war, and a scarcely less fierce fanaticism and thirst for vengeance had arisen to repress it. . . .

*Shortly after their defeat at Arklow, the rebels left the Gorey area. Many of them wandered off or returned to their homes. The remainder divided into two groups: one marched toward Wexford with their Protestant prisoners in tow; the other, larger force moved into county Wicklow, leaving destruction in its wake, and then headed for Vinegar Hill.*

On the 19th the rebel force, which, under the command of Father Philip Roche, still occupied a height near New Ross, was surprised and compelled to retreat. One portion of it took the line to Vinegar Hill. The other and larger portion, after some fighting, in which the rebels showed more than usual skill, made its way to the Three Rocks, near Wexford. The whole force of the rebellion in Wexford was thus concentrated in two centres, and the army at the disposal of General Lake was now amply sufficient to crush it. A great combined movement was speedily devised by Lake for surrounding Vinegar Hill. The failure of two brigades to arrive in time, deranged the plan of completely cutting off the retreat of the rebels; but on June 21, Vinegar Hill was stormed from several sides, by an army which was estimated by the rebels at 20,000 men, but which probably amounted to 13,000 or 14,000, and was supported by a powerful body of artillery. Against such a force, conducted by skilful generals, the ill-armed, ill-led, disorganised, and dispirited rebels had little chance. The chief brunt of the action was borne by the troops under Generals Johnson and Dundas. For an hour and a half the rebels maintained their position with great intrepidity, but then, seeing that they were on the point of being surrounded, they broke, and fled in wild confusion to Wexford, leaving the camp, which had been stained with so much Protestant blood, in the hands of the troops. Thirteen small cannon were taken there, but owing to the inexperience of the gunners, and the great deficiency of ammunition, they had been of little use. The loss of the King's troops in killed and wounded, appears to have been less than a hundred; while that of the rebels was probably five or six times as great.

Enniscorthy was at the same time taken, after some fighting in the streets. The troops, as usual, gave no quarter, and the historians in sympathy with the rebellion declare that the massacre extended to the wounded, to many who were only suspected of disaffection, and even to some loyalists who had been prisoners of the rebels. A Hessian regiment which had lately come over, was especially noticed for its indiscriminate ferocity. Many houses were set on fire, and among others one which was employed by the rebels as their hospital. It was consumed, and all who were in it perished. The number of the victims was at least fourteen, and one writer places it as high as seventy. The rebel historians describe this act as not less deliberate than the burning of the barn of Scullabogue. Gordon learnt, on what appeared to him good authority, "that the burning was accidental; the bedclothes being set on fire by the wadding of the soldiers' guns, who were shooting the patients in their beds." . . .

*Once the rebels had occupied Wexford town, the Protestant inhabitants stood in constant danger of massacre by the "fierce, fanatical mobs" who suspected all Protestants of being Orangemen. Some of these citizens were so terrified that they submitted themselves and families to baptism as Catholics in the hope of saving their lives.*

It was on that afternoon, when the chiefs and the bulk of the armed population were absent from the town, that the massacre of Wexford Bridge took place. Dixon, disobeying the orders of his superiors, refused to leave Wexford with the other captains, and he had a great mob who were devoted to him. They were not, it appears, inhabitants of the town, but countrymen from the neighbourhood. On the preceding night, he had brought into the town seventy men from the northern side of the

Slaney, and he had himself gone through the district of Shilmalier, which was thronged with fugitives from the country about
Gorey, calling them to come to Wexford to defend the deserted
town. He distributed much whisky among his followers, and, at
the head of a large crowd, he took possession of the gaol and
market-house, and brought out the prisoners to be murdered, in
batches of ten, fifteen, and twenty. A few were shot in the gaol
and in the market-place, but by far the greater number were hurried to the bridge. A black flag bearing the symbol of the Re-
demption, and with the letters M.W.S., was carried before them.
Dixon and his wife, both on horseback, presided, and a vast
crowd, containing, it is said, more women than men, accompanied
the prisoners, most of them shouting with savage delight, though
some dropped on their knees and prayed. The prisoners were
placed in rows of eighteen or twenty, and the pikemen pierced
them one by one, lifted them writhing into the air, held them up
for a few moments before the yelling multitude, and then flung
their bodies into the river. One man sprang over the battlement,
and was shot in the water. Ninety-seven prisoners are said to have
been murdered, and the tragedy was prolonged for more than
three hours. So much blood covered the bridge, that it is related
that, when Dixon and his wife endeavoured to ride over it, their
frightened horses refused to proceed, and they were obliged to
dismount, Mrs. Dixon holding up her riding habit lest it should
be reddened in the stream.

One priest courageously attempted to stop the murders.
Whether the many others who were present in Wexford were
paralysed by fear, or ignorant of what was taking place, or conscious that they would be utterly impotent before a furious
drunken mob, will never be known. Happily the tragedy was not
fully consummated. Lord Kingsborough, who was guarded in a
private house, was not molested. Some prisoners in the gaol succeeded in concealing themselves, and the great majority had not
been brought out from their different places of confinement,
when Edward Roche, followed shortly after by Dick Munk, the
shoeblack captain, galloped into the town, and crying out that
Vinegar Hill was invested, and that every man was needed to
repel the troops, succeeded in drawing away the crowd, and put-

ting an end to the massacre. A few prisoners, half dead with fear, who were still on the bridge, were taken back to the gaol.

The end was now very nearly come. Three armies were on the march to Wexford, and it was plainly indefensible. In the night of the 20th, Keogh and the principal inhabitants took counsel together, and they agreed that the only chance for safety was to endeavour to obtain terms, and that the only means of accomplishing this was by the help of Lord Kingsborough. They desired to save their own lives, to prevent the town from being given up to the mercy of an infuriated soldiery, and also to avert a general massacre of the remaining prisoners, and perhaps of the whole Protestant population, which would probably take place before the arrival of the troops, if the rebels were driven to absolute desperation. Bishop Caulfield and the other leading priests took an active part in these discussions, and Lord Kingsborough fully entered into their views. . . .

*Lord Kingsborough tried to negotiate surrender terms with General Moore, but the Commander-in-Chief, General Lake, refused to give the rebels any quarter. On June 21, the defeated rebels fled in confusion from Wexford, and General Moore occupied the town without resistance. When General Lake arrived, he ordered the public execution of Father Roche, Harvey, and several other rebel leaders, most of whom had done their utmost to prevent the slaughter of Protestant loyalists.*

Courts-martial, followed by immediate executions, were now taking place in many parts of the county. Sixty-five persons were hanged from Wexford Bridge on the charge of either having taken a leading part in the rebellion, or being concerned in some of the acts of murder that accompanied it; but Dixon, the author of the Wexford massacre, was not among them, for he succeeded in escaping, and was never heard of again. The executions, however, were far less horrible than the indiscriminate burning of houses and slaughter of unarmed men, and even of women, by the troops. They were now everywhere hunting down the rebels, who had dispersed by thousands after the battle of Vinegar Hill and the surrender of Wexford, and who vainly sought a refuge in their cabins. Discipline had almost wholly gone. Military licence was perfectly unrestrained, and the massacres which had taken place—magnified a hundred-fold by report—had produced a savage thirst for blood. The rebel historians draw ghastly pictures of the stripped, mutilated, often disembowelled bodies, that lined the roads and lay thick around the burning villages, and they say that long after peace had returned, women and children in Wexford fled, scared as by an evil spirit, at the sight of a British uniform. The sober and temperate colouring of the loyalist historian I have so often quoted, is scarcely less impressive. "From the commencement of the rebellion," writes Gordon, "soldiers, yeomen, and supplementaries, frequently executed without any trial such as they judged worthy of death, even persons found unarmed in their own houses." "I have reason to think that more men than fell in battle, were slain in cold blood. No quarter was given to persons taken prisoners as rebels, with or without arms." "The devastations and plundering sustained by the loyalists were not the work of the rebels alone. Great part of the damage was committed by the soldiery, who commonly completed the ruin of deserted houses in which they had their quarters, and often plundered without distinction of loyalist and croppy. The Hessians exceeded the other troops in the business of depredation, and many loyalists who had escaped from the rebels were put to death by these foreigners."

In two respects the conduct of the troops compared very unfavourably with that of the rebels. Though the latter had committed great numbers of atrocious murders, it is acknowledged on all sides that they abstained to a most remarkable degree from outrages on women, while on the other side this usual incident of military licence was terribly frequent. Although, too, it is quite certain that the rebellion assumed in Wexford much of the character of a savage religious war, and that numbers of Protestants were murdered who had given no real cause of offence except their religion, the rebels very rarely directed their animosity against Protestant places of worship. The church of Old Ross was, I believe, the only one that they deliberately burnt, though in the general conflagrations that took place, a few others may have been destroyed or plundered. But there were large districts over which not a Catholic chapel was left standing by the troops, and Archbishop Troy drew up a list of no less than thirty-six that were destroyed in only six counties of Leinster.

Apart, indeed, from the courage which was often displayed on both sides, the Wexford rebellion is a dreary and an ignoble story, with much to blame and very little to admire. It is like a page from the history of the Thirty Years' War, of the suppression of La Vendée, of a Turkish war, or of a war of races in India, though happily its extreme horrors extended only over a small area, and lasted only for a few weeks. Though fanaticism played some part, and revenge a great part, in the terrors of the repression, the remarkable concurrence of both loyal and disloyal writers in attributing the worst excesses to Germans and Welshmen, who had never been mixed up in Irish quarrels, seems to show that mere unchecked military licence was stronger than either, and there appears to have been little or no difference in point of ferocity between the Irish yeomanry, who were chiefly Protestant, and the Irish militia, who were chiefly Catholic. Such a state of things was only possible by a shameful neglect of duty on the part of commanding officers, and the fact that it was not universal, proves that it was not inevitable. Gordon has left the most emphatic testimony to the excellent discipline and perfect humanity of the Scotch Highlanders, who were commanded by Lord Huntley, and of the Durham Fencible Infantry, who were commanded by Colonel Skerrett, and a few other names are remembered with honour. But in general the military excesses were very shameful, and they did much to rival and much to produce the crimes of the insurgents.

By this time, however, a great change had taken place in the Government of Ireland. We have seen that Lord Camden had long wished to be relieved from his heavy burden, and had represented that in the present dangerous situation of the country the office of Lord Lieutenant and the office of Commander-in-Chief should be united in the person of some skilful and popular general. The Government at last acceded to his wish, and Lord Cornwallis, who, in spite of the disaster of Yorktown, was regarded as the ablest of the English generals in the American war, was induced to accept the double post. He arrived in Dublin on June 20, and his administration opens a new and very memorable page in the history of Ireland.

# XI

## The Pacification of Ireland

When Lord Camden resigned the viceroyalty, it was the strong belief of the Government in Ireland that the rebellion was still only in its earlier stages. In Wexford the fire then burnt with undiminished fury, and it was regarded as not only possible, but in a high degree probable, that the prolongation of the struggle in that county, or the appearance of a French expedition on the Irish coast, or a single rebel success, would be sufficient to throw the whole land into flames. The large reinforcements which were at last passing from England to Ireland, and the rapid arming and organisation of the Protestant population, had placed a very formidable force at the disposal of the Government; but the omens all pointed to an extended, desperate, and doubtful civil war, and it was felt that a military governor of great ability and experience was imperatively needed. But in the last days of the Camden Administration, the prospect had materially changed. The French had not arrived. It was becoming evident that Ulster was not disposed to rise. The Catholic province of Connaught continued perfectly quiet. In Munster there had been a small rising, in a corner of the county of Cork, but it had not spread, and it was completely put down on June 19, while the means at the disposal of the Government were at last sufficient to give a decisive blow to the rebellion in Wexford. The capture of the rebel camp on Vinegar Hill, and the reconquest of the town of Wexford, took place immediately after the arrival of Lord Cornwallis in Ireland, but the whole merit of them belongs to the previous Administration. The rebellion was now broken and almost destroyed, and the task which henceforth lay before the Government was much more that of restoring order and checking crime than of reconquering the country.

The rebels were so discouraged and hopeless, that they would have gladly dispersed if they could have obtained any security for their lives. For some time, indeed, fear or desperation had probably contributed quite as much as any genuine fanaticism to keep them together. "Their leaders," wrote Alexander, as early as June 10, "inflict instant death for disobedience of orders, but notwithstanding numbers wish to desert; but, I think unfortunately, their houses are destroyed, their absence marked, and until it is wise to grant a general amnesty, no individual, irritated as the soldiery are, can with safety leave their main body." If Lake had accepted the overtures of Father Roche, the chief body of the rebels would have almost certainly gladly laid down their arms; but when they found that their chief did not return, they felt that they must look to their pikes alone for safety. . . .

*On June 22, Father John Murphy led some 5,000 men out of county Wexford into county Carlow in the hope of spreading the revolution into the midlands. His foray resulted in much destruction but few converts. Castlecomer was devastated by the rebels on June 24. Two days later Sir Charles Asgill, commanding some 1,600 loyalists, attacked and routed the rebels at Kilcomney Hill. Father John died in the fighting, and all those suspected of being rebels were rounded up and killed. Bloodshed continued in counties Wicklow and Wexford, as the rebels split into small groups and fought tenaciously. The rebellion had come to an end by early July, but roving bands of rebels carried on guerrilla warfare in the Wicklow hills.*

The misery produced by these operations is by no means to be measured by the loss of life in the field. Numbers of unarmed peasants were hunted down because they were, or were believed to be, rebel fugitives, or because they had given shelter to rebels. Numbers of peaceful Protestants were murdered as Orangemen, or as oppressors, or as loyalists. The blood passion, which will be satisfied with nothing short of extermination, was roused in multitudes, and it was all the more fierce because it was on both sides largely mixed with fear. Over great districts nearly every house was burnt, the poorer cabins by the troops as the homes of rebels, the slated houses by the rebels as the homes of Protestants or loyalists. Agriculture had ceased. Its implements were destroyed. The sheep and cattle had been plundered and slaughtered. The farmers were homeless, ruined, and often starving. Misgovernment and corruption, political agitation and political conspiracy, had done their work, and a great part of Ireland was as miserable and as desolate as any spot upon the globe.

Lord Cornwallis was much shocked at the state of feeling and society he found around him, and in some respects his judgment of it was not altogether just. Arriving at a time when the rebellion had received its deathblow, he certainly underrated the efficiency of the yeomanry and militia, who, in spite of their great want of discipline, had virtually saved the country, and had shown in these last weeks qualities of courage, vigilance, and energy which Camden and Castlereagh abundantly recognised. It was difficult to exaggerate, though it was easy to explain, the ferocity that prevailed, but a governor who came as a perfect stranger to Ireland and to its passions, hardly made sufficient allowance for the inevitable effect of the long-continued tension and panic, arising from such a succession and alternation of horrors as I have described. He spoke with indignation of the prevalent folly "of substituting the word Catholicism, instead of Jacobinism, as the foundation of the present rebellion." "The violence of our friends," he said, "and their folly in endeavouring to make it a religious war, added to the ferocity of our troops, who delight in murder, most powerfully counteract all plans of conciliation." "The minds of people are now in such a state that nothing but blood will satisfy them; and although they will not admit the term, their conversation and conduct point to no other mode of concluding this unhappy business, than that of extirpation." "The conversation even at my table, where you will suppose I do all I can to prevent it, always turns on hanging, shooting, burning, &c. &c., and if a priest has been put to death, the greatest joy is expressed by the whole company. So much for Ireland and my wretched situation." "The life of a Lord Lieutenant of Ireland comes up to my idea of perfect misery; but if I can accomplish the great object of consolidating the British Empire, I shall be sufficiently repaid." . . .

*During July, most of the rebel leaders were caught and tried. Among those executed were Father Kearns, Esmond Kyan, Father John Redmond, and the brothers John and Henry Sheares. Many other United Irishmen who had surrendered narrowly escaped the death penalty as the advocates of clemency finally overcame the forces of revenge.*

It is impossible to deny, that an extremely sanguinary spirit had at this time been aroused among the Protestants of Dublin and of the counties which had been desolated by the rebellion. It is a spirit which, in all times and races and countries, has followed such scenes of carnage as I have described. In the mild atmosphere of the nineteenth century, and in the recollection of many who are still alive, a very similar spirit was kindled among the English population of India by sepoy cruelties, which were scarcely more horrible, and were certainly less numerous, than those of the Irish rebellion of 1798. I cannot, however, regard the strong feeling which was shown against sparing the lives of the chief authors, organisers, and promoters of that rebellion, as merely an evidence of this sanguinary disposition. No one who has any adequate sense of the enormous mass of suffering which the authors of a rebellion let loose upon their country, will speak lightly of their crime, or of the importance of penalties that may deter others from following in their steps. Misplaced leniency is often the worst of cruelties, especially in a country where the elements of turbulence are very rife; where the path of sedition has an irresistible fascination to a large class of adventurous natures; where a false, sickly sentiment, throws its glamour over the most commonplace and even the most contemptible of rebels.

In the great lottery of civil war the prizes are enormous, and when such prizes may be obtained by a course of action which is profoundly injurious to the State, the deterrent influence of severe penalties is especially necessary. In the immense majority of cases, the broad distinction which it is now the fashion to draw between political and other crimes, is both pernicious and untrue. There is no sphere in which the worst passions of human nature may operate more easily or more dangerously than in the sphere of politics.

403

There is no criminal of a deeper dye than the adventurer who is gambling for power with the lives of men. There are no crimes which produce vaster and more enduring sufferings than those which sap the great pillars of order in the State, and destroy that respect for life, for property, and for law, on which all true progress depends. So far the rebellion had been not only severely, but mercilessly suppressed. Scores of wretched peasants, who were much more deserving of pity than of blame, had been shot down. Over great tracts of country every rebel's cottage had been burnt to cinders. Men had been hanged who, although they had been compelled or induced to take a leading part in the rebellion, had comported themselves in such a manner that they had established the strongest claims to the clemency of the Government. But what inconsistency and injustice, it was asked, could be more flagrant, than at this time to select as special objects of that clemency, the very men who were the authors and the organisers of the rebellion—the very men who, if it had succeeded, would have reaped its greatest rewards?

It is true that these men had not desired such a rebellion as had taken place, and that some of them, like Thomas Emmet, were personally humane, well-meaning, and unselfish. But it was scarcely possible to exaggerate the evil they had produced, and they were immeasurably more guilty than the majority of those who had already perished. They had thrown back, probably for generations, the civilisation of their country. They had been year by year engaged in sowing the seed which had ripened into the harvest of blood. They had done all in their power to bring down upon Ireland the two greatest curses that can afflict a nation—the curse of civil war, and the curse of foreign invasion; and although at the outset of their movement they had hoped to unite Irishmen of all creeds, they had ended by lashing the Catholics into frenzy by deliberate and skilful falsehood. The assertion that the Orangemen had sworn to exterminate the Catholics, was nowhere more prominent than in the newspaper which was the recognised organ of the United Irish leaders. The men who had spread this calumny through an ignorant and excitable Catholic population, were assuredly not less truly murderers than those who had fired the barn at Scullabogue or piked the Protestants on Wexford Bridge. . . .

The Government on their side wished to stop the effusion of blood, and to close the rebellion. There had been four capital trials and executions. They feared that many more would only make martyrs. They wished to send out of the country dangerous men, whom they would probably be unable to convict, and they wished above all to establish by undoubted evidence the conspiracy with France. The Chancellor, it is said in a memorial which was drawn up for the Duke of Portland, "stated in the strongest manner his opinion of the expediency of obtaining, on any terms consistent with the public safety, the confessions of the State prisoners, particularly of McNevin and O'Connor, as the only effectual means of opening the eyes of both countries without disclosing intelligence which could by no means be made public." "We get rid of seventy prisoners," wrote Cooke, "many of the most important of whom we could not try, and who could not be disposed of without doing such a violence to the principles of law and evidence as could not be well justified. Our zealots and yeomen do not relish this compromise, and there has been a fine buzz on the subject, but it being known the Chancellor most highly approves of it, the tone softens." It is remarkable, however, that Cornwallis himself declared that he would never have consented to this compact if he believed that the lives of the prisoners were in his power, and that there was any reasonable chance of convicting them. With the exception of Bond, and perhaps Neilson, no traitors, in his opinion, had really been spared.

The arguments in favour of the treaty were much strengthened by the state of the country, which was still such that a renewed and ferocious outbreak might at any time be expected. Numerous parties of banditti were at large. Murders were of daily occurrence, and the confidential letters of the ministers show that great uneasiness prevailed. . . .

*Napoleon had wavered for weeks over the project of an English or Irish invasion, but in February 1798 he made the momentous decision to divert his main forces to the Mediterranean in order to conquer Egypt. In later years Napoleon had cause to regret this decision.*

Whether at this time any large expedition could have succeeded in reaching the Irish coast, it is impossible to say; but no one can question that, if it had succeeded at the beginning or in the middle of the rebellion, its effect would have been most serious. If the outbreak in Ireland had taken place a little earlier, or if the Egyptian project had been postponed a little longer, Ireland would probably have become a central object in the military policy of Buonaparte, and the whole course of events might have been changed. Long afterwards, in 1804, Napoleon thought seriously of an Irish expedition, and there is a letter in his correspondence describing the conditions of success; but the moment, since the mutiny of the Nore, in which such an enterprise was most likely to have succeeded, found France abundantly occupied in the Mediterranean. Lewins, in the beginning of June, pressed the claims of his countrymen strongly on the Directory. He reminded them of the promise he had been authorised to send to Ireland, that France would never make peace with England except on the condition of the independence of Ireland. He described with some exaggeration, but probably with perfect good faith, the magnitude and extent of the rebellion, and he urged that 5,000 good French troops, with 30,000 guns and some cannon and munitions, would be sufficient to secure its triumph.

Wolfe Tone was indefatigable in supporting the applications of his friend. The Directors were not unwilling to accede to their demand, but they could do nothing more than effect a slight diversion; and after considerable delay, they gave orders that a number of small expeditions should be directed simultaneously to different points on the Irish coast. Even such a plan, if it had been promptly and skilfully accomplished, might have had a great effect, but, as usual at this time, nothing in the French navy was in good order, and everything was mismanaged. The expedition of Humbert, which was the first ready, consisted of three frigates and only 1,036 soldiers. It was delayed until the rebellion in Ireland had been crushed, and it started alone, as no other expedition was yet ready.

It set sail from the island of Aix on August 6, four days after the great battle of the Nile, in which Nelson had totally shattered the French fleet of Admiral Brueys, destroyed a third part of the naval force of France, made England irresistible in the Mediterranean, and put an end to all chance of a French conquest of

Egypt. In order to escape the English, the French took a long circuitous course. They intended to enter Donegal Bay, but were prevented by hostile winds; they then made for Killala Bay, in the county of Mayo, and anchored near the little town of Killala on August 22. English flags flew from their masts, and the port surveyor, as well as two sons of the bishop, went without suspicion to the fleet, and were detained as prisoners. The same evening, about six o'clock, the French landed. Some fifty yeomen and fencibles who were in Killala were hastily drawn out by Lieutenant Sills to resist the invaders, but they were speedily overpowered. Two of them were killed, nineteen taken prisoners, and the rest put to flight. A sailor named John Murphy, who commanded a small trading vessel that lay in the bay, volunteered to set sail for France bearing a despatch announcing the successful landing.

The Protestant bishop, Dr. Stock, with eleven children, was living in the great castle of Killala, and as it was visitation time, and there was no decent hotel in the town, he was surrounded by several clergymen. Dr. Stock had been very recently appointed to the see, and the appointment had not been a political one, but was entirely due to his merits. He had been a Fellow of Trinity College. He was a distinguished Hebrew scholar, and had published a translation of the Book of Job; he spoke French fluently, and the singularly interesting and graphic account which he wrote of the events that he now witnessed, shows that he was a keen and discriminating judge of men. His palace was at once occupied; a green flag with the inscription, "Erin-go-bragh," was hoisted above its gate, and he himself became a prisoner in the hands of the French.

The French had brought with them three United Irishmen, Matthew Tone, who was a brother of Wolfe Tone; Bartholomew Teeling; and a man named Sullivan, who was nephew to Madgett, the Secretary at the French Foreign Office. They had also an officer named O'Keon, who was an Irishman naturalised in France, and who was very useful, as he had come from the neighbourhood of Ballina, and was thoroughly acquainted with the Irish language. Humbert, their commander, was one of the many adventurers to whom the French Revolution had opened out a career. He was so illiterate that he could do little more than write his name, and his manners were those of a rude, violent, uneducated peasant. He was of good height and fine figure, and in the full vigour of life, but his countenance was not attractive, and he had a small, sleepy, cunning, cruel eye, as of a cat when about to spring. He was, however, an excellent soldier, full of courage, resource, decision, and natural tact, and the bishop soon discovered that much of his rough and violent manner was assumed for the purpose of obtaining immediate obedience. He had served at the siege of Mayence, in La Vendée, and at Quiberon, and had taken part in the expedition to Bantry Bay.

Of the troops he brought with him, the bishop has given a striking picture. To a superficial eye they presented nothing that was imposing. "Their stature for the most part was low; their complexions pale and sallow, their clothes much the worse for wear," but it was soon found that they were characterised to a surprising degree by "intelligence, activity, temperance, patience," and "the exactest obedience to discipline." They were men "who would be well content to live on bread and potatoes, to drink water, to make the stones of the street their bed, and to sleep in their clothes, with no covering but the canopy of heaven. One half of their number had served in Italy under Buonaparte; the rest were from the Rhine, where they had suffered distresses that well accounted for their persons and wan looks. Several of them declared, with all the marks of sincerity, that at the siege of Mentz, during the preceding winter, they had for a long time slept on the ground in holes made four feet deep under the snow; and an officer, pointing to his leather small clothes, assured the bishop that he had not taken them off for a twelvemonth."

Their conduct among the people was most admirable. Humbert at once desired the bishop to be under no apprehension; he assured him that no one should be ill treated, and that the French would take only what was absolutely necessary for their support, and this promise was almost perfectly fulfilled. "It would be a great injustice," writes the bishop, "to the excellent discipline constantly maintained by these invaders while they remained in our town, not to remark that, with every temptation to plunder, which the time and the number of valuable articles within their reach, presented to them, . . . not a single particular of private property was found to have been carried away." In his own palace, "the attic story, containing a library and three bed-chambers, continued sacred to the bishop and his family; and so scrupulous was the delicacy of the French not to disturb the female part of the house, that not one of them was ever seen to go higher than the middle floor, except on the evening of their success at Castlebar, when two officers begged leave to carry to the family the news of the battle."

There could hardly be a more hopeless enterprise than that in which this handful of brave men were engaged. They expected to find Ireland in a blaze of insurrection, or at least thrilling with sympathy for French ideas. They came when the rebellion was completely crushed, and reduced to a mere guerrilla war in the Wicklow mountains, when there were hardly less than 100,000 armed men at the service of the Crown, and to a province which had been perfectly tranquil during the whole struggle, and which was almost untouched by revolutionary propagandism. A proclamation had been prepared, and was distributed among the poor, ignorant Mayo peasantry, congratulating them on the interest they had taken in the progress of the French Revolution, reminding them that they had been enduring "punishments, and even death," for their friendship to France, and adjuring them, by the example of America, and by the memory of many battles, of which they had assuredly never heard, to rise as a man to throw off the English yoke. But Humbert soon found that he was in an atmosphere of thought and feeling wholly different from what he had expected. He was disappointed to find that the bishop, who was the principal person remaining at Killala, would not declare himself on the side of the Revolution, and that the Protestants, who were the most substantial inhabitants, held steadily aloof. Two only, who were notorious drunkards, joined the French, and it was characteristic of the ideas that prevailed, that, on doing so, they thought it necessary to declare their conversion to the Catholic faith.

Many boxes, however, of arms and uniforms had been brought over, and when these were opened, the peasantry speedily streamed in. Though ragged and dirty and half savage, they had strong bodies and quick natural intelligence, and the keen eye of the French general clearly saw, as many English officers had seen before him, that, with the education of good military discipline, they might be turned into soldiers as excellent even as those of Buonaparte. But except a dislike to tithes, which was far more languid in Connaught than in either Munster or Ulster, they had not an idea in common with the French, and no kind of political motive appears to have animated them. They joined the invaders with delight when they learnt that, for the first time in their lives, they were to receive meat every day. They danced with joy like children when they saw the blue uniforms, and the glittering helmets edged with brown paper to imitate leopard's skin, that were provided for them, and they rapturously accepted the guns that were given them, but soon spoiled many of them by their utter inexperience. It was found necessary, indeed, to stop the distribution of ammunition, as the only way of preventing them from using their new toy in shooting crows.

In addition to the desire for meat rations, for uniforms and for guns, the hope of plunder and the love of adventure made many recruits, and there was some faint trace of a religious feeling. Agents were abroad, busily whispering the familiar calumny that the Orangemen were plotting to exterminate the Catholics, and circulating old prophecies of a religious war; and there was a vague, wide-spread notion, that the French were the special champions of the Catholic faith. The soldiers of the Revolution, whom the panic-stricken priests in other lands had long regarded as the most ferocious and most terrible of the agents of anti-Christ, now found themselves, to their own astonishment and amusement, suddenly transfigured into Crusaders; surrounded by eager peasants, who declared "that they were come to take arms for France and the Blessed Virgin." "God help these simpletons," said one of the French officers to Bishop Stock; "if they knew how little we care about the Pope or his religion, they would not be so hot in expecting help from us"; and old soldiers of the Italian army exclaimed with no small disgust, that, having just driven the Pope out of Italy, they had never expected to meet him again in Ireland. The Irish, on their side, were not a little surprised to find that these strange soldiers "of the Blessed Virgin" never appeared at mass, could not be induced to treat a priest with the smallest respect, and always preferred to carry on their communication through the heretical bishop.

The story is one which would have more of the elements of

comedy than of tragedy, if it were not for the dark spectre of a bloody retribution that was behind. The French did what they could to arm and discipline their wild recruits. They restrained them severely from plunder, and they treated them like children, which, indeed, in mind and character they truly were. After reconnoitring Ballina, and scattering a small party of soldiers in its neighbourhood, they pushed on towards Castlebar, leaving 200 French soldiers to keep order at Killala, and a few others at Ballina. There were, however, no signs of a general rising in their favour, or of any real wish for their success, and the kind of recruits they had hastily armed were not likely to be of much use. The number of these recruits has been very differently stated, and is not easy to ascertain. It appears that, in the course of the French expedition, the whole of the 4,000 or 5,000 guns which had been brought over were distributed, and that after the distribution recruits streamed in, but the distribution of arms is no measure of the number of Irish the French could bring into the field. Many who had received guns and uniforms, availed themselves of the first opportunity to fly to their mountain cabins with their spoil. Some, disguising their voices and with new stories, came again and again, in order to obtain double or treble provisions of arms, ammunition, and uniforms, and then disappeared and sold them for whisky. Many recruits were left at Killala, and perhaps some others at Ballina, and it is probable that the number of Irish who were with Humbert when he arrived at Castlebar, little, if at all, exceeded 500.

Major-General Hutchinson at this time commanded in Connaught, and he was at Galway when the news of the invasion arrived. His province had been so quiet during the rebellion, that it contained much fewer troops than the other parts of Ireland, but he could at once assemble near 4,000 men. He lost no time in collecting them, and in moving towards the scene of danger; but Cornwallis, on hearing of the invasion, at once sent General Lake, as a more experienced soldier, to command in Connaught; gave orders for a concentration of many thousands of troops from other provinces, and hastened to go down himself to lead them. Hutchinson arrived at Castlebar on the 25th. Whatever may have been the secret dispositions of the people, he found the whole country through which he passed, and the whole neighbourhood of Castlebar, perfectly quiet, though there were alarming rumours that 1,800 Irish had joined the French at Killala and Ballina. He was obliged, in moving his troops, to leave Leitrim and Roscommon open, and the bridges of the Upper Shannon almost without protection, but not the smallest inconvenience ensued. All Connaught, except in the immediate neighbourhood of Killala, was absolutely peaceful. It was harvest time, and the people were busily engaged in the fields; and though they were not actively loyal as an English population might have been, and would no doubt have submitted readily to a French Government, they were perfectly inoffensive, and desired only to be left alone.

Very few new recruits now came in to the French, and the relations between the French and their allies were already very tense. The French were learning every day more clearly, that they had been utterly deceived about the state of Ireland and the disposition of its people. They saw no signs of a rising. They perceived plainly that their recruits were as far as possible from being either heroes or patriots, fanatics or revolutionists; that the sole object of a great proportion of them was plunder; that they were always ready to desert; and that they were likely to prove perfectly worthless in battle. The French frigates had sailed away; English vessels were hovering around the Connaught coast, to prevent either rescue or escape, and unless the aspect of affairs was speedily changed by a general rising or by the landing of a new French force, it was absolutely hopeless. The Irish recruits, on their side, had found that service under a French general was a very different thing from a mere plundering raid, and they complained bitterly of hard labour and severe discipline and contemptuous treatment. Two of them were shot, probably for good reasons, by the French. The others were employed in digging entrenchments, and were often, in the absence of horses, harnessed to the cannon or to the waggons. . . .

*On August 26, General Lake arrived at Castlebar to take command of Government forces. But General Humbert stole an all-night march and captured Castlebar by sheer audacity and tactical skill. Lake's soldiers fled in confusion and some did not stop retreating until they had reached Athlone. Humbert's troops behaved with restraint toward the people, and there were no mas-*

*sacres of loyalists in Connaught. Realizing that a popular insurrection was not about to occur, Humbert set out in the direction of Sligo, hoping to escape the encircling movement of the Anglo-Irish forces. A sharp fight at Collooney delayed the French, and Humbert then headed for Granard, which lay beyond the Shannon River. Lake's troops followed close behind.*

It was impossible, however, for the French to reach Granard. Every mile of their march from Drummahair brought them nearer to Cornwallis, who now completely intercepted them by reaching Carrick on the 7th, and then marching late at night to Mohill, which was three miles from Cloone, and the delay at Cloone enabled Lake to come up with the enemy. On the 8th, the little body of French found themselves surrounded, at a place called Ballinamuck, by the combined armies of Lake and Cornwallis, and after a short resistance, the position being absolutely hopeless, these brave men at last surrendered. Only 844 men remained of the little band which for eighteen days had so seriously imperilled the British dominion in Connaught. The Irish who still remained with the French, were excluded from quarter, and cut down without mercy. No accurate or official statistics on this subject are preserved, but it is stated that 500 were killed, but that many others succeeded in escaping across the bogs. Many of these made their way to Killala, and took part in its final defence. The loyalists' loss in killed, wounded, and missing was only nineteen men. Matthew Tone and Teeling, though captured with the French, were sent to Dublin, tried by court-martial, condemned, and hanged.

The short rebellion in Connaught was now nearly over. On the 9th, Cornwallis, just before his return to Dublin, issued a general order congratulating his troops warmly on their conduct, and he added: "The corps of yeomanry, in the whole country through which the army has passed, have rendered the greatest services, and are peculiarly entitled to the acknowledgment of the Lord Lieutenant, from their not having tarnished their courage and loyalty . . . by any acts of wanton cruelty towards their deluded fellow-subjects." The insurrection about Granard, which at one time seemed likely to assume formidable proportions, was speedily suppressed by Irish yeomen, with the assistance of a small force of Argyle Fencibles. In the part of Mayo which the French had endeavoured to raise, the disturbances lasted a few days longer. On September 12, at three in the morning, a great mob of rebels or bandits attacked the garrison which had been placed in Castlebar, but they were met with great courage and easily defeated. Thirty or forty prisoners were brought in; they included one Frenchman, and several men who wore French uniforms.

Almost the whole country was now reduced to order, and Killala was the only place where there was any serious resistance. Even after the surrender of the French, many peasants assembled to defend the town. As the French guns had been all distributed, great numbers of pikes were hastily manufactured, and there were all the signs of a sanguinary contest. "750 recruits," Bishop Stock writes, "were counted before the castle gate on the 11th, who came to offer their services for retaking the neighbouring towns, that had returned to their allegiance. . . . The talk of vengeance on the Protestants was louder and more frequent, the rebels were drilled regularly, ammunition was demanded, and every preparation made for an obstinate defence." Many of the rebels desired to imprison the whole Protestant population, and to preserve them as hostages in case the troops adopted, as there was too good reason to believe they would, the policy of extending no mercy to rebels; but on receiving news from Castlebar that General Trench, who commanded the loyalists, had treated, and meant to treat, his prisoners with humanity, they abandoned their intention. Except for the plunder of some houses, and the destruction of much property, the Protestants remained unharmed till the end.

A force of about 1,200 militiamen with five cannon now marched upon Killala, and they reached it on September 23. It should be noticed, that among the soldiers who distinguished themselves in the capture of Killala, a foremost place has been given to the Kerry Militia, who, with the exception of their officers, were probably all Catholics. Of the other troops, a large proportion were Scotch, but some were Downshire and Queen's County Militia.

The last scene presented the same savage and revolting features which disgraced the repression in Wexford. A long line of blazing cabins marked the course of the advancing troops, and the slaughter in the town was terrible. The rebel force scarcely exceeded 800 or 900 men, and in the absence of their allies, they showed more courage than they had yet displayed in Connaught. The bishop, who was an eye-witness of the scene, describes them as "running upon death with as little appearance of reflection or concern as if they were hastening to a show." But those who had guns, showed themselves ludicrously incapable of using them. After twenty minutes' resistance, they broke and fled, and were fiercely pursued by the troops. Numbers were cut down in the streets. Many others, who had fled to the seashore, were swept away by the fire of a cannon which was placed at the opposite side of the bay. Some took refuge in the houses, and in these cases the innocent inhabitants often perished with the rebels. After the battle was over, and even during the whole of the succeeding day, unresisting peasants were hunted down and slaughtered in the town, and it was not till the evening of that day, that the sound of muskets, discharged with little intermission at flying and powerless rebels, ceased. The town itself was by this time like a place taken by storm, and although the general and officers are said to have tried to restrain their soldiers, they utterly failed.

Bishop Stock estimates that about 400 rebels were killed in the battle and immediately after it. He mentions that of fifty-three deserters of the Longford Militia, who had come into Killala after the defeat of Castlebar, not one returned alive to his home; and that so many corpses lay unburied, that ravens, attracted by the prey, multiplied that year to an unexampled extent through the fields of Mayo. He adds a bitter complaint of "the predatory habits of the soldiery." The "militia seemed to think they had a right to take the property they had been the means of preserving, and to use it as their own whenever they stood in need of it. Their rapacity differed in no respect from that of the rebels, except that they seized upon things with somewhat less of ceremony or excuse, and that his Majesty's soldiers were incomparably superior to the Irish traitors, in dexterity at stealing." A long succession of courts-martial followed, and several more or less prominent persons, who had joined the French, were hanged. Some poor mountain districts, where the wretched fugitives had found a shelter, next occupied the attention of the commander. The weather had broken up, and the fierce storms of rain and wind which, as winter draws on, seldom fail to sweep that bleak Atlantic coast, had begun. "General Trench, therefore, made haste to clear the wild districts of the Laggan and Erris, by pushing detachments into each, who were able to do little more than to burn a number of cabins; for the people had too many hiding places to be easily overtaken."

Such was the manner in which the rebellion was suppressed in a province where it would never have arisen but for foreign instigation; where it was accompanied by no grave crimes, and where the rebels had invariably spared the lives of such Protestants as lived quietly among them. Can any impartial reader wonder at the deep, savage, enduring animosities that were produced? Can he wonder that the districts, where so many poor peasants had been burnt out of their cabins when the winter storms were approaching, should have soon after been infested by robbers and cattle houghers?

Humbert and the French soldiers who were taken at Ballinamuck were sent to England, but soon after exchanged. The three French officers who had so admirably maintained order at Killala were, upon the urgent representation of Bishop Stock, placed in a different category. An order was given that they should be set at liberty, and sent home without exchange; but the Directory refused to accept the offer, stating that the officers had only done their duty, "and no more than any French man would have done in the same situation." Of the three United Irishmen who came over with Humbert, two, as we have seen, were hanged, but the third succeeded in concealing his nationality. O'Keon was tried by court-martial; but having succeeded in satisfying the court that he was a naturalised Frenchman, he was treated as a prisoner of war. . . .

*Two other minor French forays to Ireland also ended in failure. Napper Tandy set sail from Dunkirk early in September with a small group of French soldiers and United Irishmen, but when his corvette reached the coast of Donegal, Tandy spent only a few hours on shore, not all of them sober. Finding no signs of a popular rising in Donegal or Connaught, he sailed to Norway and then traveled to Hamburg, where he was soon turned over to the British authorities.*

The Government was for some time perplexed about what to do with Napper Tandy, and his ultimate release has been ascribed to threats of reprisals by the French in the event of his execution. It appears, however, that Lord Grenville had always doubted the propriety of his arrest, and that Cornwallis strongly advocated his liberation. He described him as "a fellow of so very contemptible a character, that no person in this country seems to care in the smallest degree about him," and he considered it a mistake to have embroiled Hamburg with France on account of him.

Tandy lay in prison till the April of 1801, when he was put on his trial. He pleaded guilty, and was sentenced to death, but was reprieved at once, and some months later was allowed to go to France, where he soon after died. Perhaps the most remarkable fact in his career, is the wide and serious influence it for a short time exercised on the affairs of Europe.

We must now return to the other French expedition, which was despatched to Ireland in the autumn of 1798. It consisted of a ship of the line of eighty-four guns, called the "Hoche," and of eight small frigates and a schooner, and it carried a military force of little less than 3,000 men. Admiral Bompard commanded the ships, and General Hardy the soldiers, and Wolfe Tone, who was now an adjutant-general in the French service, accompanied Bompard in the "Hoche." From the first he clearly saw that so small an expedition after the suppression of the rebellion was almost hopeless, but he declared that if the French sent even a corporal's guard to Ireland, he would accompany it, and if the expedition attained any result, a larger force, under General Kilmaine, was expected to follow it. The fleet started from Brest on September 14, and after a long, circuitous passage of twenty-three days, it reached the neighbourhood of Lough Swilly. The English, however, were not unprepared. They had much secret information, and even if this had been wanting, there was so little secrecy in the councils of the French Government, that an account of the armament had appeared in a Paris paper before its departure. On October 12, a powerful English squadron, under Sir

John Warren, bore down upon the French. Though it consisted at first of only seven vessels, to which an eighth was joined in the course of the action, it had in reality a decided superiority, for four of its vessels were ships of the line. Before the battle began, Bompard, perceiving that the odds were greatly against him, strongly urged Wolfe Tone to leave the "Hoche" for the small, fast-sailing schooner, called "La Biche," which had the best chance of escaping, representing to him that in the probable event of a capture, the French would become prisoners of war, while he might be reserved for a darker fate; but Tone refused the offer. The "Hoche" was surrounded, defended with heroic courage for at least four hours, and till it was almost sinking, and then at last it surrendered. The frigates tried to escape, but were hotly pursued, and three of them that afternoon were captured, after a very brave and obstinate defence.

Owing to strong adverse winds and to its own shattered condition, more than a fortnight passed before the "Hoche" was brought safely into Lough Swilly. When the prisoners were landed Wolfe Tone was immediately recognised, placed in irons in Derry gaol, and then conveyed to Dublin, where he was tried by court-martial on November 10. His speech—for it can hardly be termed a defence—was frank and manly. He fully avowed the part he had taken, and disdained to shelter himself under any pretence of having aspired to mere constitutional reforms. "From my earliest youth," he said, "I have regarded the connection between Ireland and Great Britain as the curse of the Irish nation, and felt convinced that, while it lasted, this country could never be free nor happy. My mind has been confirmed in this opinion by the experience of every succeeding year. . . . I designed by fair and open war to procure the separation of the two countries. For open war I was prepared; but if, instead of that, a system of private assassinations has taken place, I repeat, while I deplore it, that it is not chargeable on me. . . . In a cause like this, success is everything. Success in the eyes of the vulgar fixes its merits. Washington succeeded, and Kosciusko failed."

He was too brave a man to fear death, and he made no attempt to avoid it, but he earnestly implored that, in consideration of his rank in the French army, he might be saved from the ignominy of the gallows, and might, like the French *émigrés,* who had been

taken in arms by their countrymen, be shot by a platoon of grena-
diers. The request was a reasonable and a moderate one, but it
was refused, and he was sentenced to be hanged before the gaol
on November 12. The night before the day appointed for his
execution, he cut his throat with a penknife which he had
concealed.

The wound was at first not thought to be fatal, and it was believed in Dublin that the sentence would be carried out in spite
of it. His old friend Curran, however, convinced that the trial was
illegal, determined to make an effort to set it aside, and hoped
that, by postponing the day of execution, some mitigation might
be obtained. Immediately after the sentence of the court-martial
had been delivered, he tried to obtain assistance from Tone's
former friends, and especially from those Catholic leaders whom
he had formerly served, but he wholly failed. Men who were
already suspected, feared to compromise themselves or their
cause, by showing any interest in the convicted rebel, and among
men who were not suspected and loyal, there was a savage, vin-
dictive spirit, which is painful to contemplate. Peter Burrowes,
however, an able and honest, though somewhat eccentric, Protestant lawyer, supported him in a manner which was doubly admirable, as it was certain to injure his professional prospects, and
as his own brother—the clergyman near Oulart—had been one
of the first persons murdered by the Wexford rebels. When the
Court of King's Bench met on the morning of the 12th, Curran
appeared before it, and, while fully admitting that Tone was
guilty of high treason, he represented that a court-martial had
no right to try or sentence him. Ireland was not now in a state of
civil war. The courts were sitting; the King's Bench was the great
criminal court of the land, and as Tone had never held a commission in the army of the Crown, a military court had no cognisance
of his offence. He represented that every moment was precious,
as the execution was ordered for that very day, and he applied
for an immediate writ of Habeas Corpus.

The objection ought to have been made before, but it was unquestionably valid, and the Chief Justice, Lord Kilwarden, had
long deplored the eclipse of law which existed in Ireland with
the full sanction of the Government. He at once ordered the writ
to be prepared, and in the mean time sent the sheriff to the bar-

racks to inform the provost marshal that a writ was preparing, and that the execution must not proceed. The sheriff returned with a reply that the provost marshal must obey the presiding major, and that the major must do as Lord Cornwallis ordered him. The Chief Justice, with visible emotion, ordered the sheriff to return to the barracks with the writ, to take the body of Tone into custody, to take the provost marshal and Major Sandys into custody, and to show the writ to the general in command.

There was an anxious and agitated pause, and strong fears were entertained that military law would triumph, and that the prisoner would be executed in defiance of the writ. At last, however, the sheriff returned, and stated that he had been refused admittance into the barracks, but had learnt that on the preceding night the prisoner had wounded himself dangerously, if not mortally, and that instant death would be the result of any attempt to move him. The surgeon who attended him, soon after appeared, and confirmed the report, and the Chief Justice issued an order, suspending the execution. Several days of miserable, abject suffering, still lay before Wolfe Tone. He at last died of his wound, on November 19.

It would be a manifest exaggeration to call him a great man, but he had many of the qualities of mind and character by which, under favourable conditions, greatness has been achieved, and he rises far above the dreary level of commonplace which Irish conspiracy in general presents. The tawdry and exaggerated rhetoric; the petty vanities and jealousies; the weak sentimentalism; the utter incapacity for proportioning means to ends, and for grasping the stern realities of things, which so commonly disfigure the lives and conduct even of the more honest members of his class, were wholly alien to his nature. His judgment of men and things was keen, lucid, and masculine, and he was alike prompt in decision and brave in action. Coming to France without any advantage of birth, property, position or antecedents, and without even a knowledge of the language, he gained a real influence over French councils, and he displayed qualities that won the confidence and respect of such men as Carnot and Hoche, Clarke and Grouchy, Daendels and De Winter. His journals clearly show how time, and experience, and larger scenes of action, had matured and strengthened both his intellect and char-

acter. The old levity had passed away. The constant fits of drunkenness that disfigured his early life no longer occur. The spirit of
a mere adventurer had become much less apparent. A strong and
serious devotion to an unselfish cause, had unquestionably grown
up within him, and if he had become very unscrupulous about the
means of attaining his end, he at least was prepared to sacrifice to
it, not only his life, but also all personal vanity, pretensions, and
ambition. If his dream of an independent Ireland, now seems a
very mad one, it is but justice to him to remember how different
was then the position of Ireland, both in relation to England and
in relation to the Continent. Ireland now contains about an eighth
part of the population of the United Kingdom, and it is hopelessly divided within itself. At the time of the rebellion of 1798,
the whole population of the two islands was little more than
fifteen millions, and probably fully four and a half millions of
these were Irish. It was a much larger population than Holland
possessed when she confronted the power of Lewis XIV, or the
United States when they won their independence, or Prussia when
Frederick the Great made her one of the foremost nations in
Europe. It was idle to suppose that such a people, if they had
been really united and in earnest, could not under favourable
circumstances have achieved and maintained their independence;
and what circumstance could seem more favourable than a great
revolutionary war, which especially appealed to all oppressed na-
tionalities, threatened the British Empire with destruction, and
seemed about to lead to a complete dissolution and rearrangement
of the political system of Europe?

Wiser men had warned him from the first, that he misread
both the characters and the sentiments of his people, but it is not
difficult to understand the causes of his error. When he saw the
rapidity with which the revolutionary doctrines had spread
through the energetic, Protestant, industrial population of the
North; when he remarked the part which the independent gentry
had very recently taken in the volunteer movement; when he
observed the many signs, both in Ireland and on the Continent,
of the dissolution of old beliefs and the evanescence of sectarian
passions, he easily persuaded himself that a united national movement for independence had become possible, and that the fierce
spirit of democratic revolution, which was rising with the force

of a new religion over Europe, must sweep away the corrupt and narrow Government of Ireland. Of the Irish Catholics, Tone knew little, but he believed that their religious prejudices had disappeared, that they would follow the lead of the intelligent Presbyterians of the North, and that they were burning to throw off the government of England. He lived to see all his illusions dispelled, and when he started on his last journey, it was with a despondency which was not far removed from hopelessness. It is not uninteresting to notice that the "Hoche," in which he was captured, was afterwards called the "Donegal," and was the ship which, under the British flag, bore a far more illustrious Irishman, Arthur Wellesley, to the scenes of his triumphs in the Spanish Peninsula. . . .

*Although the rebellion had ended by the summer, a few diehards such as Joseph Holt took refuge in the Wicklow hills and ravaged the countryside for miles around, until he was finally tracked down and transported to Botany Bay. The Irish governing class celebrated the defeat of the rebels in church and salon; and the news of Nelson's victory at the battle of the Nile in October gave them further cause for rejoicing. In the aftermath of the rebellion many soldiers and members of the yeomanry indulged their sectarian instincts in acts of outrage against the populace. Drunkenness, lack of discipline, and love of violence contributed to the "Orange terror" which swept across the eastern provinces. Many of the rebel prisoners were finally sent to penal colonies in Botany Bay, having been refused admission to America. Some three hundred prisoners were deported to Prussia to work in the mines or serve in the army. The arrival of the new Viceroy, Lord Cornwallis, in the summer of 1798 gave moderates reason to hope that the counter-revolutionary terror would be stopped.*

It is true that the system of government under Lord Cornwallis was less sanguinary than under Lord Camden; but an extract from a private letter of Castlereagh to Wickham, in the March of 1799, will probably be, to most persons, quite sufficient to acquit it of any excess in lenity. Nearly 400 persons, Castlereagh says, had been already tried under Lord Cornwallis. Of these, 131 were condemned to death, and 81 were executed. "This forms but a proportion of the number of victims to public justice, for acts of treason and rebellion in the disturbed districts. Numbers were tried and executed by order of the general officers, whose cases never came before the Lord Lieutenant, and it appears by the inclosed return from the Clerk of the Crown, that 418 persons were banished or transported by sentences of courts-martial. . . . Since Lord Cornwallis's arrival, exclusive of the infliction of punishment by military tribunals, great numbers were convicted at the autumn assizes."

Of the total loss of life during the rebellion, it is impossible to speak with any kind of certainty. The estimates on the subject are widely different, and almost wholly conjectural. Madden, the most learned of the apologists of the United Irishmen, pretends that not less than 70,000 persons must have perished in Ireland, during the two months' struggle; but Newenham, who was a contemporary writer, singularly free from party passion and prejudice, and much accustomed to careful statistical investigations, formed a far more moderate estimate. He calculated that the direct loss during the rebellion was about 15,000. About 1,600, he says, of the King's troops, and about 11,000 of the rebels, fell in the field. About 400 loyal persons were massacred or assassinated, and 2,000 rebels were exiled or hanged. The most horrible feature was the great number of helpless, unarmed men, who were either deliberately murdered by the rebels, or shot down by the troops. "For several months," writes Mary Leadbeater, "there was no sale for bacon cured in Ireland, from the well-founded dread of the hogs having fed upon the flesh of men."

Of the loss of property, it is equally difficult to speak with accuracy. The claims sent in by the suffering loyalists amounted to 823,517 *l.*; "but who," writes Gordon, "will pretend to compute the damages of the croppies, whose houses were burned, and effects pillaged and destroyed, and who, barred from compensation, sent in no estimate to the commissioners?" And, in addition to this, we must remember the enormously increased military expenditure, which was imposed upon the country, and the terrible shock that was given, both to industry and to credit.

The double burden, indeed, of foreign war, and of internal convulsion, was fast weighing down the finances of Ireland, which had, a few years before, been so sound and prosperous; and although the increase of debt seemed small compared with that of England, and was much exceeded in Ireland in the years that followed the Union, it was sufficiently rapid to justify very grave apprehensions. When the war broke out, the Irish national debt was 2,344,314*l.* At the end of 1797, the funded debt had risen to 9,485,756*l.*, of which 6,196,316*l.* was owed to England, and it was computed that the expenditure of the country exceeded its income by about 2,700,000*l.* The terrible months that followed, greatly aggravated the situation. Between December 1797 and August 1798, Ireland borrowed no less than 4,966,666*l.*, nearly all of it at more than 6 per cent., and a large proportion at more than 7 per cent.

This was a grievous evil, but, at the same time, the great spring of national prosperity was not yet seriously impaired. A country which is essentially agricultural, will flourish when agriculture is prosperous, even in spite of very serious and sanguinary convulsions. In the height of the struggle, Beresford wrote that it was "most strange and extraordinary," that the revenue every week was rising in a degree that had been hitherto unknown. The moral scars left by the rebellion were deep and indelible, and it changed the whole character of Irish life, but the material devastation rapidly disappeared. There were large districts, it is true, where, owing to the destruction of houses, and the neglect or ruin of agriculture, extreme misery prevailed, but the harvest of 1798 was a very good one, and this fact did more than any measures of politicians to appease the country. In August, Clare noticed the rich corn crops that were ripening over the rebel districts through which he passed, and he observed that the common people were everywhere returning to their ordinary occupations. . . .

*Grattan's reputation suffered in the wave of reaction that followed the rebellion. Dr. Patrick Duigenan, M.P., published a scurrilous pamphlet attacking Grattan's liberal outlook, and various attempts were made to link him directly to the United Irishmen conspiracy. In poor health and lowered morale, Grattan had to endure both insults and an investigation into his friendship with several prominent United Irishmen. After the rebellion had been crushed, English ministers set to work to terminate the independence of the Irish Parliament. Their plans for a legislative union of the two countries had been contemplated by a number of officials since at least the year 1672, when Sir William Petty had written* The Political Anatomy of Ireland. *By 1798, both the King and Pitt were strongly in favor of such a measure, believing this to be the only way of permanently reconciling the two countries.*

# XII

## *The Prelude to Union*

If we now turn from the opinions of English statesmen to the public opinion in Ireland, we shall find a remarkable contrast. No single fact is more apparent in the Irish history of the last half of the century, than the strong and vehement dread of an Union in Ireland. It does not date from the establishment of Irish legislative independence. I have already mentioned the furious riots that convulsed Dublin as early as 1759, on account of an unfounded rumour that such a measure was in contemplation. In 1776 Arthur Young collected opinions on the subject of an Union with Great Britain, and was informed, "that nothing was so unpopular in Ireland as such an idea." In 1780 Lord Hillsborough, having in his confidential correspondence with the Lord Lieutenant thrown out a hint that some such measure was desirable, Buckinghamshire answered, "Let me earnestly recommend to you not to utter the word Union in a whisper, or to drop it from your pen. The present temper will not bear it." In 1785, when Bishop Watson pressed upon the Duke of Rutland the policy of a legislative Union, the Lord Lieutenant answered that he fully agreed with him, but that anyone who proposed such a measure in Ireland would be tarred and feathered. On most subjects the Irish Parliament was exceedingly subservient, but on the subject of its own exclusive legislative competence it was even feverishly jealous, and the suspicion that the English Government was conspiring against the settlement which had been so formally and so solemnly guaranteed in 1782 and 1783, never failed to kindle a fierce resentment in the nation. In the violent opposition which Grattan led to the amended commercial propositions in 1785, the irritation excited by this suspicion, and by the language used in England on the subject, is very apparent. Grattan saw in the amended proposals, "an intolerance of the parliamentary Constitution of Ireland, a declaration that the full and free external legislation of the Irish Parliament is incompatible with the British Empire." He described them as "an incipient and a creeping Union." He declared, that in opposing them he considered himself as opposing "an Union *in limine*," and already in this debate he fully elaborated the doctrine of the incompetence of the Irish Parliament to carry a legislative Union, which fourteen years later became so prominent in the discussions on the measure.

This strong feeling on the part of the political classes in Ireland was certainly not due to any disloyal or anti-English feeling. At the risk of wearying my readers by repetition, I must again remind them, that the Irish Parliament of 1782 was a body utterly unlike any Parliament that could be set up by modern politicians. It was essentially an assembly of the leading members of the landed gentry of the country; of the section of the community which was bound to the English connection by the strongest ties of sympathy and interest; of the chief representatives of property; of the classes from which, since the Union, the magistracy and the grand juries have been principally formed. It had uniformly and readily followed the lead of the English Parliament in all questions of foreign policy. It had contributed largely and ungrudgingly, both in soldiers and in money, to the support of the Empire in every war that had arisen, and it was perfectly ready to enter into a treaty for a permanent contribution to the British navy, provided such a treaty could be framed without impairing its legislative supremacy. Viceroy after viceroy had emphatically acknowledged its unmixed loyalty, and they made no complaint of its present dispositions; but at the same time the most experienced English statesmen and a succession of English viceroys were convinced that the permanent concurrence of two independent Parliaments under the Constitution of 1782 was impossible, and that a collision between the two Parliaments in time of peace would be dangerous, and in time of war might very easily be fatal to the connection.

In Ireland, on the other hand, the independence of the Parliament was supported by the strong pride and passion of Nationality—a sentiment which may be the source both of good and of evil, but which, whether it be wise or unwise, must always be a most powerful element in political calculations. Irish statesmen, too, reviewing English legislation since the Restoration, and perceiving the still prevailing spirit of commercial monopoly, contended that the material interests of Ireland could not be safely entrusted to a British Parliament. They foresaw that an identification of Legislatures would ultimately lead to an assimilation of taxation, raising Irish contributions to the English level. They perceived that Ireland was rapidly developing into a considerable nation, with its own type of character and its own conditions of prosperity; and they especially dreaded the moral effects of an Union in promoting absenteeism, weakening the power of the landed gentry, and thus destroying a guiding influence, which in the peculiar conditions of Ireland was transcendently important. Sir Robert Peel, many years later, spoke of "the severance of the connection between the constituent body of Ireland and the natural aristocracy of the country," as perhaps the greatest and most irreparable calamity that could befall Ireland, and on this point Grattan and Peel were entirely agreed. Adam Smith believed that the great work of uniting into one people the severed elements of Irish life, could be only speedily accomplished if the legislative power was transferred to a larger and impartial assembly unswayed by local tyrannies, factions, and corruptions. Grattan believed that it could only be attained by the strong guidance of the loyal gentry of both religions, acting together in a national Legislature and appealing to a national sentiment, and he dreaded, with an intense but by no means exaggerated fear, the consequence to Ireland if the guidance of her people passed into the hands of dishonest, disreputable, and disloyal adventurers. The rapid and indisputable progress of national prosperity in the last decades of the century, though in truth it was largely due to causes that had very little relation to politics, strengthened the feeling in support of the local Legislature, and strong selfish as well as unselfish considerations tended in the same direction. Dublin was furious at the thought of a measure which would transfer the aristocracy and other leading gentry of Ireland to London. The

Irish bar had an enormous influence, both in the Parliament and in the country, and it would be a fatal blow to it if the Parliament no longer sat in the neighbourhood of the Law Courts; the great borough-owners perceived that a legislative Union must take the virtual government of Ireland out of their hands, and a crowd of needy legislators saw in it the extinction of the system under which they could always, by judicious voting, obtain places for themselves or their relatives.

It is not surprising that from all these sources a body of opinion hostile to a legislative Union should have arisen in Ireland which appeared wholly irresistible. For about ten years after the declaration of independence it was unbroken, and it is, I believe, no exaggeration to say, that during that period not a single Irish politician or writer of real eminence was in favour of such a measure. At this time it was wholly impracticable, for no corruption and no intimidation would have induced the Irish Parliament to consent to it.

The disastrous events of the last years of the century, however, gradually produced some change. The danger of foreign invasion, the terrible rapidity with which conspiracy and anarchy spread through the masses of the people, and the menacing aspects which the Catholic question assumed, began to shake the security of property, and to spread vague and growing alarms among all classes. The concession of the franchise in 1793 to a vast, semi-barbarous Catholic democracy, portended, in the eyes of many, the downfall of the Protestant Establishment, and perhaps of the existing settlement of property. From this time a few men began, through fear or through resentment, to look with more favour on the idea of an Union, and Lord Clare steadily, though as yet secretly, urged its necessity. . . .

The horrible years of growing crime, anarchy, and dissension which followed, convinced many that a great change of system was required. The Parliament remained, indeed, a zealously loyal body, and Arthur O'Connor and Lord Edward Fitzgerald were probably the only members in it whose sympathies were with France. But outside its walls the doctrine was openly professed, that Ireland ought not to support England in the French war; and at the same time the prospects of an invasion; the imminent fear of rebellion; the violent religious war which had broken out in Ulster, and the rumours that were spread among the panic-stricken Catholics of Orange conspiracies to massacre them, had all tended to aggravate enormously the difficulties of local government in Ireland. The capacity of any portion of an empire for extended and popular self-government is not a mere question of constitutional machinery or of abstract reasoning. It depends essentially upon the character and dispositions of the people for whom that self-government is intended. A constitutional arrangement which in one country will be harmless or beneficent, in another country will infallibly lead to civil war, to confiscation of property, to utter anarchy and ruin. Loyalty and moderation; a respect for law, for property, and for authority; a sentiment of common patriotism uniting the different sections of the community; a healthy disposition of classes, under which trustworthy and honourable men rise naturally to leadership—these are the conditions upon which all successful self-government must depend. The events of Irish history had made the soil of Ireland peculiarly unfavourable to it, but for a long period before the outbreak of the French Revolution there had been a great and rapid improvement. The country was not, and never has been, fit for a democratic Government, but many of the best Irishmen believed that healthy elements of self-government had grown up, which would make it possible for the management of affairs to pass safely and most beneficially out of the hands of the corrupt aristocracy of borough-owners. But this prospect was now visibly receding, as the old fissures that divided Irish life reopened, and as fear and hatred began to separate classes which had for many years been approximating. The opinion so powerfully expressed by General Knox about the necessity of an Union, was no doubt held by other intelligent observers. It was, however, still that of isolated and scattered individuals, and up to the outbreak of the rebellion there was no party in Ireland which desired such a measure, no party which would even tolerate its proposal. . . .

A careful examination of the confidential correspondence of this time, appears to show that, although the expediency of a legislative Union had long been present in the minds of Pitt and of several leading English statesmen, and although it had been persistently urged by Clare since 1793, no settled and definite project of introducing such a measure was formed in England, before the outbreak of the rebellion. Pitt, according to his usual custom, discussed it at length in a very small circle, for some time before it was even suggested to his Cabinet. Perhaps the earliest notice of it, is a letter of June 4, 1798, in which Pitt writes to Auckland that he had lately been discussing with Lord Grenville, the expediency of taking steps for carrying an Union immediately after the suppression of the rebellion. They had been studying the Scotch Act of Union, and they especially desired the assistance of Auckland in framing its trade and finance clauses. Auckland appears to have communicated with Clare, for a few days later he received a letter from that statesman containing the following passage: "As to the subject of an Union with the British Parliament, I have long been of opinion that nothing short of it can save this country. I stated the opinion very strongly to Mr. Pitt in the year 1793, immediately after that fatal mistake, into which he was betrayed by Mr. Burke and Mr. Dundas, in receiving an appeal from the Irish Parliament by a Popish democracy. I again stated the same opinion to him last winter; and if this were a time for it, I think I could make it clear and plain to every dispassionate man in the British Empire, that it is utterly impossible to preserve this country to the British Crown, if we are to depend upon the precarious bond of union which now subsists between Great Britain and Ireland. It makes me almost mad, when I look back at the madness, folly, and corruption in both countries, which have brought us to the verge of destruction."

When Lord Cornwallis arrived in Ireland on June 20, he does not appear to have known anything about an intention to carry an Union, or, at least, to have received any fixed instructions relating to it. A few weeks later, however, a small number of persons, who were closely connected with the Government of Ireland, were sounded on the subject. Lord Camden appears to have been much consulted, and he wrote about this time to Lord Castlereagh, "The King and every one of his ministers are inclined to an Union, and it will certainly be taken into consideration here, and you will probably hear from the Duke of Portland upon it." Pelham was still Chief Secretary, though ill health compelled him to remain in England; and it appears from a letter written to him by William Elliot, on July 28, that at that date Cornwallis leaned decidedly towards an Union, but that both Pelham and

Elliot were extremely reluctant to undertake such a measure, and extremely doubtful whether "the advantages resulting from it would answer the expectation." . . .

*Lord Castlereagh, the acting Chief Secretary, advocated a union along the lines suggested by Pitt, and Lord Cornwallis agreed that Ireland's only hope for peace and prosperity lay in legislative union, provided that the Catholics were not excluded from its provisions. Although many English politicians feared the conse-quences of tampering with the Protestant Ascendancy in Ireland, they believed that a bold, new scheme had to be tried. As Lord Carlisle, the former Viceroy wrote to Lord Auckland: "Ireland in its present state will pull down England. She is a ship on fire, and must either be cast off or extinguished."*

A strong will and intellect, however, was now applied to the wavering councils of the Government. On October 8, Lord Clare sailed for England to visit Pitt at Holwood, and to discuss with him the future government of Ireland. He went, Lord Cornwallis writes, "with the thorough conviction that unless an Union be-tween Great Britain and Ireland can be effected, there remains but little hope that the connection between the two countries will long subsist"; but he went also with the firm resolve that a mea-sure of Catholic emancipation should form no part of the scheme.

Cornwallis reluctantly acquiesced, but he deplored deeply the course which the question seemed likely to take. He wrote ear-nestly to Pitt, that it would be a desperate measure to make an irrevocable alliance with the small ascendency party in Ireland; but assuming that this was not to be done, and that the question of Catholic emancipation was merely postponed until after the Union, he implored him to consider "whether an Union with the Protestants will afford a temporary respite from the spirit of faction and rebellion which so universally pervades this island, and whether the Catholics will patiently wait for what is called their emancipation, from the justice of the United Parliament." "If we are to reason," he continues, "on the future from the past, I should think that most people would answer these questions in the negative; . . . if it is in contemplation ever to extend the priv-ileges of the Union to the Roman Catholics, the present appears to be the only opportunity which the British Ministry can have of obtaining any credit from the boon, which must otherwise in a short time be extorted from them." In a confidential letter to Pelham, which has never been published, he went still further, and his language is exceedingly remarkable. "I am apprehensive," he said, "that an Union between Great Britain and the Protestants in Ireland is not likely to do us much good. I am sensible that it is the easiest point to carry, but I begin to have great doubts whether it will not prove an insuperable bar, instead of being a step, towards the admission of Catholics, which is the only measure that can give permanent tranquillity to this wretched country."

It must be observed, that during all this period there is not the smallest trace of Cornwallis being aware of the conscientious objections which the King entertained to the admission of Catholics even into an Imperial Legislature, nor does it appear that the King knew anything of the conferences that were going on. Lord Clare, in the short period which he spent with Pitt, fully attained his double object of confirming Pitt's opinion in favour of the Union, and of convincing him that it must be unaccompanied with emancipation. He found the ministry, he said, "full of Popish projects," but he trusted that he had fully determined them "to bring the measure forward unencumbered with the doctrines of emancipation." " Mr. Pitt," he said, "is decided upon it, and I think he will keep his colleagues steady." . . .

If the judgment I have formed be correct, the public opinion of Ireland up to the beginning of the French war was practically unanimous in opposition to any scheme of Union, and it ran so strongly that no such proposal could have been made without the most imminent danger. In the period between 1793 and the outbreak of the rebellion, the Irish Parliament had been much discredited, and the alarms and dangers of the time had shaken many, but still there was no Irish party which would have ventured openly to support an Union. But the scenes of horror which were comprised in the six weeks of the rebellion had produced a great change in the political aspect of Ireland, and the Government calculated that if they pressed on the Union without delay, they would find two strong, broad currents of genuine opinion in its favour.

One of these sprang from the alarm of the Protestants for their

Church, their property, and even their lives; from their conviction that their safety depended wholly upon the presence of a great English force, and that it was therefore their most vital interest to bind themselves as closely as possible to their protector. The other grew out of the resentment, the panic, and the hopes of the Catholics, who found an insulting and lawless spirit of Orange ascendency spreading on all sides, and the bitterest enemies of the Catholic cause supreme in the Parliament. The hope of passing under a more tolerant rule, the gratification of humiliating those who had humiliated them, the anger which was naturally produced by the burning of chapels and houses, and by the Orange badges that were flaunted on every side, and the prospect of obtaining from the Imperial Parliament the emancipation which appeared more and more remote in the Parliament of Ireland, had given many Catholic minds an undoubted bias in favour of the Union. . . .

*The prospect of a union with Great Britain deeply divided the Irish political nation, and discussion of this issue raged for months on end in speech, press, and conversation. Constitutional law, economic self-interest, political expedience, and patriotic principle all merged together in the arguments of those for and against the union.*

Though the Protestants formed but a small minority of the population of Ireland, they included the great preponderance of its energy, intelligence, and property. They were the political and governing class, the class who chiefly created that strong, intelligent, independent, and uninfluenced public opinion, which in every country it is the duty of a wise statesman especially to consult. It seems plain that the bulk of Protestant opinion on the question oscillated, at this time, between violent opposition and a languid or at best a favourable acquiescence, and that there was very little real, earnest or spontaneous desire for the measure. Two facts, which appear prominently in the correspondence of this period, attest most eloquently the disposition of the people. The one was the acknowledged necessity of keeping an immense English force in Ireland, for the purpose of guarding, not merely against a foreign enemy, but also against the dangers to be apprehended in carrying the Union. The other was the confession of

Lord Castlereagh, that "nothing but an established conviction that the English Government will never lose sight of the Union till it is carried, could give the measure a chance of success."

On the Catholic side, however, it obtained a real though a fluctuating, uncertain, and somewhat conditional support, and there can be little doubt that if Catholic emancipation had formed a part of the scheme, the support would have been very considerable. Pitt at first desired to take this course; but Clare, as we have seen, convinced him that it was impracticable, and Pitt then strongly inclined to an Union on a Protestant basis. Lord Grenville agreed with him, though before the rebellion he said he would have thought differently. Cornwallis doubted and fluctuated, while Dundas was prepared to favour the wider scheme if Cornwallis considered it feasible. Among those who most regretted the change was William Elliot, who was one of the ablest and most esteemed of the English officials in Ireland. He had been thought of as Chief Secretary when Lord Camden was appointed, and some years after the Union he returned to Ireland in that position, but he was now Under Secretary to the Lord Lieutenant for the Military Department, and was employed very confidentially in the communications between the English and Irish Governments which preceded the Union. He was so fully convinced that the Government was making a profound mistake in dissociating the two measures, that when the decision was finally taken, he desired to resign his office and his seat in the Irish Parliament. "Since the measure is embarked in," he wrote to Castlereagh, "I feel anxious for its success. Even on its present narrow and contracted basis, I believe it will be productive of advantage to the Empire. If the Catholics are wise, they will acquiesce in it; but I am afraid we have left them ground of complaint. I cannot be easily persuaded that if more firmness had been displayed here at first, an Union might not have been accomplished including the admission of the Catholic claims; but Mr. Pitt has with a lamentable facility yielded this point to prejudice, without, I suspect, acquiring support in any degree equivalent to the sacrifice."

The Catholic leaders, however, themselves do not appear to have agreed with Elliot. From the very first disclosure of the scheme, it became evident that they looked on it with favour, and Lord Fingall, Lord Kenmare, and Archbishop Troy at this time entirely approved of the omission of the Catholic question from the measure. They considered that it would be "injurious to the Catholic claims to have them discussed in the present temper of the Irish Parliament"; that to do so "would hazard the success of the Union without serving the Catholics"; that it would be "much more for their interest that the question should rest till it could be submitted in quieter times to the unprejudiced decision of the United Parliament, relying on their receiving hereafter every indulgence which could be extended to them without endangering the Protestant Establishment." Lord Kenmare and Lord Fingall were especially anxious to see a State endowment of the priests, which would make them less dependent on the most ignorant and turbulent classes, and Archbishop Troy promised that he would use all his influence in favour of the Union on the sole condition that it contained no clause barring future concessions. "Upon the whole," Lord Castlereagh wrote in the beginning of December, "it appears to me, as far as the dispositions of the Catholics have yet disclosed themselves, that there is every reason to expect from them a preference for the measure. An active support from that body would not perhaps be advantageous to the success of the Union. It would particularly increase the jealousy of the Protestants, and render them less inclined to the question." . . .

*Cornwallis and Castlereagh continued to sound the opinions of the Protestant Ascendancy, especially those of aristocrats and borough owners, in their efforts to secure a safe majority in Parliament in favor of union. Their consultations with prominent Catholics proved less encouraging, and they had reason to believe that most Irish Catholics would oppose any such measure that did not carry with it complete emancipation.*

The Duke of Portland now authorised the Lord Lieutenant formally to assure all persons who had political influence, that the King's Government was determined to press on the Union, "as essential to the well-being of both countries, and particularly to the security and peace of Ireland as dependent on its connection with Great Britain"; that they would support it with their utmost power; that even in the event of present failure, it would be "renewed on every occasion until it succeeds, and that the conduct of individuals upon this subject will be considered as the test of their disposition to support the King's Government." Sir John Parnell, the Chancellor of the Exchequer, was dismissed, and replaced by Isaac Corry, a staunch Unionist. The dismissal of the Prime Sergeant, James Fitzgerald, immediately followed, and he was replaced by St. George Daly, one of the minority who had supported the Union at the bar debate. George Knox, one of the Commissioners of Revenue, resigned his office. John Claudius Beresford soon after took the same course.

In the House of Lords the Government was secure, and in the House of Commons the number of men whom it was necessary to gain in order to obtain a majority was not large. The House consisted, it is true, of 300 members, but the well-understood rule, that the member of a nomination borough, if he had received his seat by favour and not purchase, must vote with his patron, and the immense number of boroughs that were concentrated in a very few hands, greatly simplified the task. A shameless traffic in votes began, and many men of great name and position in the world, were bought as literally as cattle in the cattle market. There were, however, a few honest men like Conolly, who had always desired an Union; a few like Yelverton, who probably believed that the recent convulsions in Ireland and the state of Europe had made it a necessity; a few, like Sir George Shee, who would gladly have seen the question adjourned, but who, when it was raised, considered it in the public interest to support it. "The demands of our friends," wrote Cornwallis on the eve of the meeting of Parliament, "rise in proportion to the appearance of strength on the other side; and you, who know how I detest a job, will be sensible of the difficulties which I must often have to keep my temper; but still the object is great, and perhaps the salvation of the British Empire may depend upon it. I shall, therefore, as much as possible overcome my detestation of the work in which I am engaged, and march on steadily to my point. The South of Ireland are well disposed to Union, the North seem in a state of neutrality, or rather apathy, on the subject, which is to me incomprehensible; but all the counties in the middle of the island, from Dublin to Galway, are violent against it. The Catholics on the whole behave better than I expected, and I do not think that popular tumult is anywhere to be apprehended except in the metropolis."

In addition to attempts that were made to influence opinion through the Press, and to some attempts to obtain addresses both in the Catholic parts of the island and in the North, the Government trusted much for the ultimate popularity of the measure, to the support of the Catholic bishops. A negotiation was officially opened with them. They were told that, in the present division of opinion, the political claims of the Catholics must remain for the consideration of the Imperial Parliament, but that the Government were strongly desirous of proposing without delay an independent provision for the Roman Catholic clergy, under such regulations and safeguards as the prelates would accept as compatible with their doctrines, discipline, and just influence. The expediency of such a step, Lord Castlereagh added, was generally recognised, even by those who objected to concessions of a political nature. . . .

The Irish Parliament met on January 22, and the great question of the Union was at once raised by the King's Speech, which, without expressly mentioning it, recommended "some permanent adjustment, which may extend the advantages enjoyed by our sister kingdom to every part of this island," and would also, at a time when the King's enemies were conspiring to effect a separation, "provide the most effectual means of maintaining and improving the connection," and consolidating the British Empire. The Address was moved by Lord Tyrone, the eldest son of Lord Waterford, in a speech in which he carefully pointed out, that it pledged the House to nothing more than a discussion of the question. It was opposed, however, *in limine* by Sir John Parnell; and George Ponsonby, seconded by Sir Lawrence Parsons, moved an amendment, pledging the House to enter into a consideration of what measures might best strengthen the Empire; "maintaining, however, the undoubted birthright of the people of Ireland to have a resident and independent Legislature, such as it was recognised by the British Legislature in 1782, and was finally settled at the adjustment of all difficulties between the two countries."

A long and striking debate, extending over more than twenty hours, followed, and it is one of the very few debates in the later sessions of the Irish Parliament which have been separately and fully reported. The immense preponderance of speakers, and I think of ability, was on the side of the Opposition; Lord Castlereagh, however, was supported with some skill by the Knight of Kerry and by Sir John Blaquiere, but especially by a hitherto undistinguished member named William Smith. He was the son of one of the Barons of the Exchequer, and was himself at a later period raised to the bench, and he now proved one of the best speakers and writers in defence of the Union. On the other side there was a brilliant array of talent. Sir John Parnell, George Ponsonby, Dobbs, Barrington, Parsons, Hardy, and the late Prime Sergeant Fitzgerald, greatly distinguished themselves, but above all, the eloquence of Plunket dazzled and astonished the House. According to an acute and hostile judge, it turned several votes, and some of its passages of fierce invective are even now well known in Ireland.

The arguments on each side did not differ sensibly from those I have already stated, but the reader of the debate will notice how strenuously and how confidently the Opposition speakers asserted the hostility of the country, and especially of the loyal portion of the country, to the scheme. One speaker boldly said that nine out of ten men were against it, and that the only persons it would really gratify were the United Irishmen. Another acknowledged that if it were the wish of Parliament and of the people it ought to be carried, "but," he continued, "that sense should be fully ascertained, without compulsion or undue influence of any kind. So far as the voice of the people has been yet collected, it is decidedly against it; and nothing but force, actual or implied, with the aid of undue influence, could carry the measure." . . .

*Despite their many placemen the Government could achieve a majority of only two ( 107 to 105 ) after the debate on the address in the Irish House of Commons. In the Lords, the Earl of Clare and other powerful peers, all of them pillars of the Ascendancy, crushed the opposition to the address. The Commons then voted to delete the passage referring to a union before approving the address. Dublin rejoiced at this triumph of the old Patriots. The majority of independent country gentlemen were adamantly opposed to any union. Lord Clare and his supporters blamed Cornwallis for this setback to Government plans.*

Cornwallis, on the other hand, consoled himself by the belief that the proposed Union was not really disagreeable either to the

Catholics or the Presbyterians, but he acknowledged that the late experiment showed the impossibility of carrying a measure which was opposed by strong private interests, and not supported by the general voice of the country. "If ever a second trial of the Union is to be made," he said, "the Catholics must be included."

From England the decision of the Government came in clear and unfaltering language. It was the unanimous opinion of the ministers, Portland wrote, that nothing that has happened ought to make any change in their intentions or plans. The measure was evidently for the benefit of Ireland, and the good sense of the country would sooner or later recognise the fact. "I am authorised to assure you," he wrote, "that whatever may be the fate of the Address, our determination will remain unaltered and our exertions unabated; and that though discretion and good policy may require that the measure should be suspended by you during this session, I am to desire that you will take care that it shall be understood that it neither is nor ever will be abandoned, and that the support of it will be considered as a necessary and indispensable test of the attachment on the part of the Irish to their connection with this country." It was accordingly announced that Pitt would at once proceed, as though nothing had happened in Ireland, to submit the intended resolutions on which the Union was to be based, to the British Parliament.

The question of the Union was already before it. On January 22—the same day on which the Irish Parliament was opened—a King's message had been sent down to the British Parliament, recommending, in terms very similar to those employed in the Irish Viceregal speech, a complete and final adjustment of the relations between England and Ireland, as the most effectual means of defeating the designs of the King's enemies to separate the two countries, and of securing, consolidating, and augmenting their resources. Sheridan—the most eminent Irishman in the British Parliament since the death of Burke—at once moved an amendment, condemning the introduction of such a measure "at the present crisis, and under the present circumstances of the Empire." In the course of a long and powerful speech, he predicted that "an Union at present, without the unequivocal sense of the Irish people in its favour, . . . would ultimately tend to endanger the connection between the two countries"; that in the existing condition of Ireland, with martial law, and in the presence of 40,000 English troops, the sense of the nation could not be fairly taken; that the undoubted disaffection of Ireland would not be allayed, but aggravated, by the abolition of a loyalist Parliament, and the transfer of authority to the Parliament and nation of England, who, in the words of Lord Clare, "are more ignorant of the affairs of Ireland than they are of any country in the world." He spoke also of the finality of the arrangement of 1782, and of the injurious influence which Irish members might exercise on the Imperial Parliament. He found no supporters, and after speeches by Canning and by Pitt, the amendment was negatived without a division.

On January 31, shortly after the news had arrived of the refusal of the Irish House of Commons to take the question into consideration, Pitt rose to move the resolutions for an Union, in an exceedingly elaborate speech, which was one of the only three that he afterwards revised for publication. It contains a most powerful, most authentic, and most comprehensive statement of the whole case for the Union; and although much of its argument had been anticipated in the pamphlet of Cooke and in the speeches of William Smith, it should be carefully considered by everyone who is studying the subject.

Pitt began by acknowledging, in a tone of dignified regret, that the circumstances under which he introduced his resolutions were discouraging. It was in the full right and competence of the Irish Parliament to accept or reject an Union; and while the Irish House of Lords had agreed by a large majority to discuss it, the Irish House of Commons had expressed a repugnance even to consider it, and had done this before the nature of the plan had been disclosed. Believing, however, that a legislative Union was transcendently important to the Empire at a time when foreign and domestic enemies were conspiring to break the connection, and that it would be eminently useful to every leading interest in Ireland, he considered it his duty to persevere. The question was one on which passion, and prejudice, and a mistaken national pride were at first peculiarly likely to operate, and some time might reasonably be expected to elapse before misconceptions were dispelled, and the advantages of the measure were fully understood. For his part, he said, he was confident that all that was necessary to secure its ultimate adoption was, "that it should be stated distinctly, temperately, and fully, and that it should be left to the dispassionate and sober judgment of the Parliament of Ireland." . . .

*At Westminster Pitt justified the union scheme as essential to both imperial security and Ireland's material welfare. He emphasized the commercial and financial advantages that such a union would bring to Ireland. After three weeks of debate, the English Parliament gave its assent to the union resolutions. In Ireland Castlereagh worked hard to convert the Patriots, promising a larger representation of Irish constituencies in the imperial parliament at Westminster and offering Irish borough owners compensation in cash for the loss of their patronage. Most of the Catholic hierarchy seemed to favor a union so long as some measure of emancipation was conceded at the same time.*

On the whole, Cornwallis was probably justified when he spoke of "a large proportion of the Catholics" being in favour of the Union; and in other quarters the measure, in the opinion of the Government, was making some way. One very important acquisition was Lord Ely, who now declared his determination to throw all his influence into its scale. In the North the feeling was at least not strongly hostile, and Alexander wrote to Pelham that on the whole he even considered it favourable, "but luke-warmedly." The linen merchants and the great majority of the inhabitants of Londonderry, he said, were for it, but the question was looked on as one which chiefly concerned the gentlemen, and it did not arouse any strong popular interest. "The public mind," wrote Cooke in the beginning of April, "is, I think, much suspended on the subject. There is little passion except among the bar and the few interested leaders in the Commons. The Protestants think it will diminish their power, however it may secure their property. The Catholics think it will put an end to their ambitious hopes, however it may give them ease and equality. The rebels foresee in it their annihilation." "The opinion of the loyal part of the public," wrote Cornwallis, "is, from everything that I can learn, changing fast in favour of the Union; but I have good reason to believe that the United Irishmen, who form the great mass of the people, are more organised and more determined than ever in their purposes of separation, and their spirits are at this moment raised to the highest pitch in the confidence of soon seeing a French army in this country."

The open rebellion was over, and the military force of all kinds at this time in Ireland, is said to have exceeded 137,000 men, yet the condition of great tracts of the country had hardly ever been worse. The old crime of houghing cattle had broken out with savage fury in Mayo and Galway. It does not appear on this occasion to have been due to any recent conversion of arable land into pasture, and it is impossible to say how far, or in what proportions, it was due to the resentment and misery produced by the military excesses that had followed the defeat of Humbert, to agrarian motives, or to deliberate political calculation. The pretexts chiefly put forward were a desire to lower rents, and abolish middlemen, but Cornwallis believed that there was some evidence that the United Irishmen were connected with the outburst, and that it was part of a plan to stop the usual supply of cattle to the Cork market, where the English fleet was provisioned. The new Prime Sergeant, who was himself from Galway, gave the House of Commons a graphic account of the state of a great part of Connaught. "Hordes of armed ruffians, in number forty to fifty in a gang, traversed the country every night, over a tract of sixty miles, houghing the cattle of gentlemen and farmers, and murdering all who dare to oppose them. In this way, property to the amount of 100,000*l.* has been destroyed, within the last two months, in the counties of Galway and Mayo. Every man whose cattle were thus houghed was forbidden, on pain of murder to himself and his family, to expose those beasts in any market; so that they had no alternative, but either to bury the flesh, or give it to the country people for little or nothing. . . . Against this infernal and destructive system no man dares appeal to public justice. . . . If any man prosecuted one of the offenders, he did it at the moral certainty of being almost immediately murdered." The same fate hung over every magistrate who sent a hougher to gaol, every witness who gave evidence against him, every juryman who convicted him. Well-dressed men led the parties, and at least one man who had played a conspicuous part in political rebellion in Connaught was shown to be a leader. A rich farmer, who had refused to take the United Irish oath, had no less than 250 bullocks houghed, and was reduced almost to beggary. "The rabble," said the Attorney-General, "are told that by pursuing this practice, they will get land cheap; the leaders know that in distressing the British power, they will advance the interest of the French Directory." "Do not expect," the Attorney-General continued, "that the country gentlemen will dare serve on juries if the forfeit of their property is to be the result of their verdicts, and if when that property has been already destroyed, their lives are to be the next sacrifice. Such is the situation of the most tranquil province of Ireland. . . . The gentry are obliged to abandon their estates, and driven into the towns; and to the honour of the Roman Catholic gentry of that country be it spoken, that they have been the most active to repress these outrages, and have been the most severe sufferers from their extent. . . . There are two counties of your kingdom in which the King's judges have not dared for one year past to carry their commission." . . .

*The outbreak of serious agrarian crime in the spring of 1799 forced the Irish Parliament to approve a stringent coercion act. Mounting disorder convinced some waverers that only a union could effectively prevent anarchy. In April, the Speaker of the Irish House of Commons, John Foster, refuted Pitt's arguments for a union in a long and forceful speech. The overt hostility of Lord Clare toward the Catholic seminary at Maynooth jeopardized the Government's efforts to enlist Catholic support for a union.*

# XIII

## *The Act of Union and Its Legacy*

The kind of negotiation into which Lord Cornwallis was at this time compelled to enter, was in the highest degree distasteful to his frank, honourable, soldier-like character, and his correspondence shows that he was under no illusion about the nature of his task, or about the real motives, opinions, and dispositions of his supporters. "The political jobbing of this country," he writes, "gets the better of me. It has ever been the wish of my life to avoid this dirty business, and I am now involved in it beyond all bearing. . . . How I long to kick those whom my public duty obliges me to court!" "My occupation is now of the most unpleasant nature, negotiating and jobbing with the most corrupt people under heaven. I despise and hate myself every hour, for engaging in such dirty work, and am supported only by the reflection, that without an Union the British Empire must be dissolved." He recalled, as applicable to himself, the bitter lines in which Swift had painted the demon Viceroy, scattering in corruption the contributions of the damned, and then complaining that his budget was too small; and he repeated once more, "Nothing but the conviction that an Union is absolutely necessary for the safety of the British Empire, could make me endure the shocking task which is imposed on me." That the majority which ultimately carried the Union, was not an honest majority expressing honest opinions, he most clearly saw. "The nearer the great event approaches," he wrote almost at the last stage of the discussion, "the more are the needy and interested senators alarmed at the effects

445

it may possibly have on their interests and the provision for their families, and I believe that *half of our majority* would be at least as much delighted as any of our opponents, if the measure could be defeated."

In the face of such declarations, it appears to me idle to dispute the essentially corrupt character of the means by which the Union was carried, though it may be truly said that selfish motives, and even positive corruption, were by no means a monopoly of its supporters, and though there may be some difference of opinion about the necessity of the case, and some reasonable doubt about the particular forms of bribery that were employed. The most serious feature in the parliamentary debates of 1799, was the strenuous opposition to the measure by the county members, who represented the great majority of the free constituencies of Ireland, who on all normal occasions supported the Government, and who in many instances, while opposing the Union, disclaimed in the most emphatic terms any intention of going into systematic opposition. Lord Castlereagh, as I have said, attributed their attitude largely to the first intention of the Government to diminish by a half the county representation, and he hoped that the retention of the whole of that representation in his amended scheme, and the greatly enhanced dignity attaching to a seat in the Imperial Parliament, would put an end to their opposition. But in this expectation he was deceived. Though some conspicuous county members supported the Union, the large majority, as we shall see, remained to the end its opponents.

The main power in Parliament, however, rested with the great borough-owners, and so many seats were in the hands of a few men, that the task of the Government was not a very formidable one. In truth, when we consider the enormous and overwhelming majorities the Government could on all ordinary occasions command, and the utter insignificance of the Opposition, especially after the secession of Grattan and the outbreak of the rebellion, the difficulty they encountered is more wonderful than their success. A few of the borough seats were attached to bishoprics, and were completely at their disposal. Others were in the hands of great English absentees. Most of them were in the control of men who held lucrative offices in the Government, or who had within the last few years been either ennobled, or promoted in the peerage as a price of their political support. Lord Shannon, who had long been the most powerful of the borough-owners, had from the beginning supported them; Lord Waterford, Lord Ormond, Lord Clifden, Lord Longueville, and other peers with great influence in the House of Commons, were on the same side. In the constitution of the Irish Parliament, the purchase of a few men was sufficient to turn the scale and to secure a majority, and this purchase was now speedily and simply effected by promises of peerages.

Immediately after the Union had passed through the Irish House of Commons, but before it had received the royal assent, Lord Cornwallis sent over a list of sixteen new peerages, which had been promised on account of valuable services that had been rendered in carrying it. It appears from the correspondence that ensued, that the King and the English Government, though they had given a general authority to Cornwallis, had not been consulted in the details of the promotions, and they were anxious to strike out a few names and adjourn the creations till after the first election of representative peers for the Imperial Parliament. . . .

The sixteen peerages, however, referred to in these letters, by no means comprise the whole of what in this department was done. In the short viceroyalty of Lord Cornwallis, no less than twenty-eight Irish peerages were created, six Irish peers obtained English peerages on account of Irish services, and twenty Irish peers obtained a higher rank in the peerage.

There was another form of bribe, which had probably not less influence. If the Union was carried, a new object of ambition of the first magnitude would be at once opened to the Irish peerage. No promotion in that peerage was likely to be so much coveted as the position of representative peer, which was to be enjoyed by twenty-eight members of the Irish peerage, and was to place them for life in the Imperial House of Lords. But the influence the Government exercised in the peerage was so great, that it was easy to foresee that, in the first election at least, it would prove absolutely decisive. The first representative peers, indeed, were virtually nominated by the Lord Lieutenant, and they consisted exclusively of supporters of the Union.

It was essentially by these means that the Union was carried, though there are some slight qualifications to be made. In the long list of creations and promotions, there are nine which were not connected with the Union, and among the new peers there were doubtless a few who claimed and received rewards for acting in accordance with their genuine convictions. Lord Clare, the great father of the Union, was made an English peer in September 1799. Lord Altamont had from the first declared himself in its favour, and the tone of his whole correspondence with the Government indicates a man of real public spirit, yet he bargained for and obtained a marquisate. Lord Kenmare was the leading member of a small group of Catholic gentlemen who had long been in the close confidence of the Government, and who undoubtedly desired the Union, yet the earldom of Lord Kenmare was described by Lord Cornwallis as one of the titles 'which he was "obliged" to promise in order to carry it. Men, it is true, who valued honour more than honours, and who, in a period of extreme corruption, believed it to be their duty to take the invidious course of voting for the extinction of the Legislature of their country, would not have acted in this manner. They would rather have followed the example of Lord Gosford, who warmly supported the Union, but at the same time refused an earldom, in order that no imputation should rest upon the integrity of his motives. But the Irish borough-owners should be judged by no high standard, and it may be admitted, to their faint credit, that in some few instances their peerages did not determine their votes and their influence. In the majority of cases, however, these peerages were simple, palpable, open bribes, intended for no other purpose than to secure a majority in the House of Commons. The most important of the converts was Lord Ely, whose decision, after many fluctuations, appears to have been finally fixed by a letter from Pitt himself. He obtained a promise of an English peerage, and a well-founded expectation of a marquisate, and he brought to the Government at least eight borough seats, and also a vast amount of county influence which was very useful in procuring addresses in favour of the Union.

But although the weight of such a mass of creations and promotions must have been enormous in a Parliament constituted like that of Ireland, it would have been insufficient but for some supplementary measures. The first was, a provision that close boroughs should be treated as private property, and that the patrons should receive a liberal pecuniary compensation for their loss. This compensation removed an obstacle which must have been fatal to the Union, but being granted to opponents as well as supporters, it cannot, in my opinion, be justly regarded as strictly bribery, and it may be defended by serious arguments. Nomination boroughs were in fact, though not in law, undoubtedly private property, and the sale or purchase of seats was a perfectly open transaction, fully recognised by public opinion, and practised by honourable politicians. As we have already seen, Pitt, in his English Reform Bill of 1785, proposed to create a fund for the purchase of the English boroughs, and the United Irishmen included the compensation of Irish borough-owners in their scheme of radical reform. The British Legislature always refused to recognise this traffic, but it does not appear to have been formally prohibited or made subject to legal penalties until 1809; and even in 1832, Lord Eldon maintained that proprietary boroughs were strictly property. "Borough property," he said, "was a species of property which had been known in this country for centuries; it had been over and over again made the subject of purchase and sale in all parts of the kingdom, and they might as well extinguish the right of private individuals to their advowsons, as their right to exercise the privileges which they derived from the possession of burgage tenures"; and he quoted the course which was taken when abolishing the hereditable jurisdictions in Scotland, and the nomination boroughs in Ireland, as binding precedents. This view was not adopted by the Imperial Legislature, and an overwhelming wave of popular enthusiasm, which brought England very near to revolution, enabled the Whig Ministry to sweep away the small boroughs, and carry the Reform Bill of 1832. But in Ireland at the time of the Union there was certainly no such enthusiasm; the borough interest was stronger than in England, and it was idle to expect that those who possessed it would make this great pecuniary sacrifice without compensation. The opponents of the Union dilated with much force upon the enormity of treating the right of representation as private property; making the extinction of a national Legislature a matter of bargain between the Government and a few individuals, and then throwing the cost of that bargain upon the nation. But in truth the measure was necessary if the Union was to be carried, and its justification must stand or fall with the general policy of the Government.

Eighty boroughs, returning 160 members, were in this manner purchased at the cost of 1,260,000*l*., which was added to the Irish national debt, and thus made a perpetual charge upon the country. The sum of 15,000*l*. which was given for each borough does not appear to have been unreasonable. "It is well known," Grattan wrote to the citizens of Dublin in 1797, "that the price of boroughs is from 14,000*l*. to 16,000*l*., and has in the course of not many years increased one-third—a proof at once of the extravagance and audacity of this abuse." The convulsions of the rebellion had, it is true, lowered the value of borough property, and produced an insecurity which no doubt greatly assisted the measure, but it was only equitable that the compensation should be calculated by the market value before the civil war began. It is remarkable that the largest sum given in compensation went to Lord Downshire, who was a vehement opponent of the Union. He received 52,500*l*. as the owner of seven borough seats. The next largest sum was 45,000*l*. which went to Lord Ely. Of the whole sum, about a third part was paid to opponents of the Union. In some cases the compensation for a single borough was distributed among two or more persons, and the compensation paid for the Church boroughs was applied to ecclesiastical purposes.

These figures, however, only give an imperfect and approximate measure of the amount of borough interest in the Irish Parliament, and of the relative weight of that interest on the two sides of the question. Several of the close boroughs were allowed to send one member to the Imperial Parliament, and one member in the British House of Commons being considered equal to two in the Irish one, no compensation in these cases was given. Several seats were not reckoned strictly close, though a few great families exercised an overwhelming influence over them, and some borough-owners were accustomed to purchase single nominations from others, and thus exercised in fact a much larger parliamentary influence than appears from the compensation they received. The same statute which provided for the compensation of the borough-owners, provided also that full compensation should be granted to all persons whose offices were abolished or diminished in value by the Union. Rather more than 30,000*l.* a year was granted in annuities to officers or attendants of the two Houses of Parliament, by a separate statute.

Another supplementary measure was a great remodelling of the House of Commons, through the operation of the Place Bill.

It was the firm resolution of the Government, that they would not dissolve Parliament, and submit the great question of the maintenance of the national Legislature to the free judgment of the constituencies. From such a step, wrote Cornwallis, "we could derive no possible benefit." At the same time, they desired to change the composition of the House of Commons, which in 1799 had so decisively rejected the measure, and in this object they were eminently successful. In December, Castlereagh wrote that not less than twenty-two seats were vacant, which would be filled by their friends, and in the few months that elapsed between the prorogation of Parliament in 1799, and the Union debates of 1800, no less than sixty-three seats became vacant. In this manner, without a dissolution, more than a fifth part of the House was renewed. A few of the vacancies were due to deaths, and a few to changes of office arising from the dismissal of officials who opposed the Union. In other cases men who were not prepared to vote for the Union, were willing to accept the promise of some lucrative office and leave Parliament; but the great majority of these changes were due to the conversion of the borough patrons. Members holding seats by their favour, who were unwilling to support the Union, considered themselves bound to accept nominal offices and vacate their seats, and other members were brought in for the express purpose of voting for the Union. Several of them were Englishmen, wholly unconnected with Ireland, and some were generals of the Staff. In the case of borough members who had purchased their seats, a different rule prevailed, and they were entitled to vote irrespective of their patrons.

At the same time, the whole force of Government patronage in all its branches was steadily employed. The formal and authoritative announcement, that the English Government were resolved to persevere until the Union was carried; that though it might be defeated session after session, and Parliament after Parliament, it would always be reintroduced, and that support of it would be considered hereafter the main test by which all claims to Government favour would be determined, had an irresistible force. The dismissal of the Chancellor of the Exchequer and the Prime Sergeant, because they refused to support the Union, needs no defence, for no Administration could possibly continue if some of its leading members were opposed to the main objects of its policy. The dismissal of Lord Downshire from his regiment, from the Privy Council, and from the governorship of his county, was defended on the ground that he had been guilty of a grave breach of military discipline in sending down a petition against the Union to his regiment of militia to be signed; and in the opinion of Lord Cornwallis, this dismissal, by evincing the determination of the Government and by terrifying their opponents, did more than any other single step to carry the measure. But in addition to these, a number of obscure men in non-political places were dismissed, because either they or their relatives declined to support it. In spite of the Place Bill of 1793, which had somewhat diminished the number of placeholders who might sit in Parliament, there appear to have been in the last Irish House of Commons seventy-two persons who either held civil places or pensions from the Crown, or were generals or staff officers. All these men knew that their promotion, most of them knew that their retention of their emoluments, was in the power of the Government, and would be determined by the votes they were about to give. It was part of the Union scheme that not more than twenty additional placemen should be introduced by it into the Imperial Parliament. Plunket, in one of his speeches, declared with great force and eloquence, that if there had been only twenty placemen in the Irish House of Commons, or if the placemen who sat in it were allowed to vote by ballot or according to their real wishes, it would have been utterly impossible to have carried the Union.

Hope, however, was a more powerful agent of corruption than fear, and it is, I believe, scarcely an exaggeration to say that everything in the gift of the Crown in Ireland; in the Church, the army, the law, the revenue, was at this period uniformly and steadily devoted to the single object of carrying the Union. From the great noblemen who were bargaining for their marquisates and their ribands; from the Archbishop of Cashel, who agreed to support the Union, on being promised the reversion of the see of Dublin, and a permanent seat in the Imperial House of Lords; the virus of corruption extended and descended through every fibre and artery of the political system, including crowds of obscure men who had it in their power to assist or obstruct addresses on the question. No two facts are at this time more conspicuous, than the immense preponderance of legal ability that was arrayed in opposition to the Union, and the immense profusion of legal honours that were lavished on its supporters. . . .

*Most of the barristers who voted for the Union also received high honors or compensation. In some cases the Government used direct money bribes to swing voters in the House, but the sums involved were not so large as the Opposition supposed. Between 1799 and 1800 the pressure or attractions of Government bribes created a majority in favor of the Union. Irish opinion outside Parliament appeared either indifferent or lukewarm toward the Union. Cornwallis received reports from various parts of the country indicating that the bulk of the aristocracy were prepared to support the Union. Trinity College, on the other hand, although divided on the issue, inclined to oppose the Union. The Irish Catholic hierarchy generally favored the measure.*

In the strange irony of Irish history, few things are more curious than the fact that it was the English Government which persuaded the Catholic priests to take an active part in Irish politics, and to take part in them for the purpose of carrying the legislative Union. They were not in all places successful. Many Catholics, refusing to act as a separate body, signed addresses with the Protestants against the Union. Lord Castlereagh sent to the Catholic Bishop of Meath, as he probably did to the other bishops, a sketch of the address which he wished to be signed; but the Bishop answered that, though he himself fully approved of it, and though the whole body of his priesthood agreed with him, the lay Catholics of Meath were "too near Dublin, and too much accustomed to listen to the opinions of the Protestants of Meath, to be as yet willing to declare in favour of the Union"; and that till this had ceased to be the case, a dependent priesthood did not dare to take an open or active part. In Dublin, Cornwallis acknowledged that the utmost he could hope from the Catholics was neutrality, and it is tolerably certain that this neutrality was not obtained. It is said that here also the clergy and a proportion of respectable Catholics were in favour of the Union, but the bulk of the Dublin Catholics appear to have still adhered to the convictions so emphatically expressed by the great meeting in Francis Street in 1795. In a very important Catholic meeting which was now held in the Exchange, resolutions were unanimously passed, describing an Union as the extinction of the liberty of Ireland, attributing the unexampled rapidity of the improvement of Ireland during the last twenty years entirely to the Constitution of 1782, and denouncing, as a gross calumny on the Catholic body, the imputation that they could be induced, by either "pique or pretension," to sacrifice the independence of their country. It was on this occasion that Daniel O'Connell made his first appearance on a public platform. In a remarkable passage, which was probably elicited by Canning's threat that it might be necessary to re-enact the penal code if the Union were defeated, he declared that the Catholics of Ireland would rather accept that code, and throw themselves on the mercy of their Protestant brethren, than assent to the extinction of the Legislature of their country, and seek advantages as a sect, which would destroy them as a nation.

A few other distinctively Catholic addresses were drawn up in different parts of the country, protesting against the Union, and against the assertion that it was favoured by the Catholics. Much indeed may be truly said to qualify the importance of the Catholic demonstrations in its support. Extreme want of moral courage, and extreme susceptibility to external influences, have always prevailed in Ireland, and the combined pressure of a Government which had so much to give in this world, and of a priesthood which was believed to have so much influence over the next, was enormously great. It is indeed surprising that, with such a weight of influence, the signatures in favour of the Union were so few. It appears also to be generally admitted, that the Catholics looked mainly, in their approval of the Union, to Catholic objects, or were actuated by very natural feelings of resentment or panic. If they could have obtained their emancipation in an Irish Parliament, they would have preferred it, but with the revival of a fierce Protestant spirit that had followed the rebellion, and with the formal assurance they had received, that the English Government were resolved, for all time, to exercise their overwhelming influence to prevent the introduction of Catholics into an Irish

Legislature, the Union seemed the only path of hope. The hatred and the humiliation which recent events had produced, continued unabated, and large districts were still convulsed by all the violence, tyranny, and panic of military licence. Cornwallis wrote in November, that martial law in Ireland was only too likely to pass into a tyranny "more violent and intolerable" than that of Robespierre; "that the vilest informers were hunted out from the prisons, to attack, by the most barefaced perjury, the lives of all who are suspected of being, or of having been disaffected," and that "every Roman Catholic of influence was in great danger." The fact that the Lord Lieutenant, who was attempting to carry the Union, had steadily laboured to restrain this violence, and had incurred great unpopularity in doing so; the fact that the Orange party were in general vehement opponents of the Union, and the strong reason the Catholics already had to believe that their emancipation would be one of the first acts of the United Parliament, all influenced their judgments. Their priests had good grounds for expecting that a Government endowment would speedily be granted to them, and they were assured that the conduct of the Catholics in the crisis that had arisen would be decisive of their future advantages.

An approval which was so largely provisional, and which rested so much on transient and abnormal conditions, could not be greatly counted on, though if a wise and liberal statesmanship had followed the Union, it might perhaps have been rendered permanent. Still, it appears to me to be impossible to review with candour the facts that I have collected, in this and the preceding chapter, without arriving at the conclusion that the Union in 1800 was not in any of its stages positively distasteful to the great body of the Irish Catholics, and that a very important section of them, including their whole hierarchy, the vast majority of their landed gentry, and many if not most of their lower priests, decidedly and consistently favoured it. . . .

*The country lost a "true patriot," when Lord Charlemont died on 4 August 1799. Agrarian crime continued to disrupt the countryside, especially after the bad harvest of that year. Widespread distress among the tenantry and laborers made the time particularly inauspicious for "pressing on a great constitutional change."*

In the mind of Lord Cornwallis the advantage the Catholics were likeiy to obtain from the measure, occupied perhaps even a larger place. He was convinced that without an Union, Ireland would not long be a part of the Empire; but he was convinced also, that it could enjoy no internal peace or permanent content, unless the Government of the country was taken out of the hands of men who had triumphed in the civil war. As we have already seen, he had been long since convinced that Catholic emancipation was the only solution of Irish troubles. He knew nothing of what Ireland had been during the tranquil period before 1795, and coming over to a country of which he was very ignorant, at the moment when it was convulsed by the agonies and the anarchy of a most ferocious civil war; when appalling dangers, and no less appalling barbarities, had revived and inflamed all the old hatred of creeds and classes and races, he believed that the existing system of government had hopelessly broken down, and that the very first condition of security, prosperity, and civilisation was to place the government of Ireland in the hands of an impartial and unimpassioned Legislature. Very reluctantly he yielded to the representations of the English Ministers, that it was impossible to carry Catholic emancipation concurrently with the Union, but he hoped that this measure would speedily follow, and he anticipated the best results from taking the government of the country out of the hands of a loyalist class, who were now deeply tinged with Orange passions. The Union, in his eyes, was carried against this class, for the benefit of the Catholics, with their approval, and in a large measure by their assistance.

We have seen how he hated the corruption which he was compelled to practise. Lord Castlereagh, on the other hand, pursued his course with a quiet, business-like composure; nor is there the slightest indication that it caused him a momentary uneasiness. He was convinced that it was the necessary means to a necessary measure, and he believed that he was corrupting to purify. He described his task and that of Lord Cornwallis as "to buy out, and secure to the Crown for ever, the fee simple of Irish corruption, which has so long enfeebled the powers of Government and endangered the connection." . . .

In the mean time, most of the country was proclaimed, and English troops were streaming in. In July there were rather more than 45,000 effective soldiers in Ireland, in addition to artillery, but in the autumn the army was largely reinforced, and there was at one time a strange notion of sending over a large body of subsidised Russians. It was rejected because Cornwallis and Castlereagh represented the extremely bad effect it would have on public opinion during the Union crisis; but the force that was in Ireland was soon so great, that unless a strong foreign army was landed, it seemed irresistible.

It was under these circumstances that the last session of the Irish Parliament was opened on January 15, 1800. The Speech from the Throne was long and elaborate, but it did not contain the faintest allusion to the momentous question which now filled all thoughts, and which the Government had determined by all the means in their power to press on to an immediate solution. It seems a strange reticence, but it may be easily explained. The process of remodelling the borough representation by substituting supporters for opponents of the Union, had been undertaken, and in the first four days of the session, no less than thirty-nine writs were moved. As the great majority of the vacant seats had been secured by the Government, Lord Castlereagh had an obvious reason for adjourning all discussion of the Union till they were filled, but the same reason impelled the Opposition to press it on without delay. Sir Lawrence Parsons, having first directed the Clerk to read the speeches in which Lord Cornwallis, in opening and closing the last session, had declared the firm resolution of the Government to carry the Union, moved an amendment to the Address, expressing the deep loyalty of the House of Commons to the Throne, to the connection, and to the free Constitution of 1782, and at the same time pledging it "at all times, and particularly at the present moment," to maintain an independent resident Parliament. Reminding the House that Pitt had repeatedly postponed the parliamentary reform which he had once advocated, on the plea that a period of war and disturbance was not one for introducing great constitutional changes, he accused the Government of endeavouring to destroy the independence of Ireland at a time when the spirit of the people was depressed by recent troubles, when the country was occupied by an enormous army, when martial law prevailed and a formidable invasion was threatened, and when apprehensions from without and from within made all free exercise of the public mind upon the question impossible. He urged that it was the duty of the members to deal with the question at once, and not to sit supinely there, while the Minister of the Crown was openly engaged in prostituting the prerogative of appointing to places, for the purpose of packing the Parliament. "A string of men who are against the Union are to go out, that a string of men who are for it may come in."

The debate which ensued extended through the whole night, and lasted for not less than eighteen hours. It appears to have been one of the fiercest ever heard in a legislative assembly. Lord Castlereagh met the rising storm with great courage and composure. He acknowledged that, although there was no mention of the Union in the Speech from the Throne, it was intended to be the chief measure of the session. It had been determined, he said, to make a separate communication on the subject, and when that communication was made, the time would have come for discussing it. Last year the measure had been withdrawn because it was not yet fully understood, "and it was stated that it would not again be proposed without full and fair notice, and until there was reason to believe that the Parliament and the country had changed their opinions upon the subject." That change had, he believed, taken place. He was fully satisfied, that the measure "was now approved by a great majority of the people." "Nineteen of the most considerable counties in Ireland, constituting above five-sevenths of the kingdom," had declared themselves in favour of it. The amendment of Parsons was not to reject the Union after mature investigation, but to extinguish the question by anticipation, refusing all information, and doing so at a time when a great number of the members of the House were indispensably absent. Could it be supposed that his Majesty would desist from the measure because the Parliament of Ireland, thus circumstanced, had declined to consider it? Was it, he asked, amid the derisive laughter of the Opposition, decent to press forward this discussion when there were so many gentlemen absent who had accepted places under Government? Was it, he repeated, constitutional or right to proceed to the determination of so important a subject, when so large a proportion of their body was absent —to refuse even to consider a measure of which so large a part of the kingdom had expressed approbation?

On the other side, the language of Opposition soon passed into the fiercest invective. It was denied emphatically and repeatedly, that there was any truth in the statement that the sense of the nation was in favour of the Union, and it was asserted that what semblance of support the minister had obtained, had been obtained by the basest means. "During the whole interval between the sessions, the most barefaced system of parliamentary corruption had been pursued—dismissals, promotions, threats, promises." Bribes had been promised to the Catholic and to the Presbyterian clergy. Irreconcilable and delusive hopes had been alternately held out to the Catholics and the Protestants. Agents of great absentee proprietors had gone among the tenantry, obtaining signatures by refusing leases to those who hesitated to sign; threatening to call in the rent to the hour; holding over them the terrors of an ejectment. Revenue officers had been employed to canvass the obscurest villages. Signatures had been sought in the very dregs of the population, it was said even in the gaols. The whole patronage of the Crown was employed to favour the measure; the powers of martial law were made use of to stifle opposition, and the Viceroy himself had gone from county to county seeking support. And the result of all this was, that out of a population of nearly five millions, the Government had obtained "about 5,000 signatures, three-quarters of whom affixed their names in surprise, terror, and total ignorance of the subject." . . .

*Bolstered by Grattan's return to the House and also by a large campaign fund, the Opposition launched an all-out attack on the Union and urged the provinces to send their petitions against the measure to Parliament. Some of the most ardent anti-unionists were, ironically enough, the Orangemen of Ulster. Lord Cornwallis appealed to the English ministry for troop reinforcements in order to keep the country quiet during the debates on the Union. Some Irish officials feared that the yeomanry were prepared to resist the Union with arms.*

It was impossible on the morrow of a savage civil war, which had kindled the fiercest and most enduring religious hatreds, that the divided parties should have at once passed into new combinations, like the patterns of a kaleidoscope; and neither Catholic Ireland nor Presbyterian Ireland was likely to show much enthusiasm for the defence of the Irish Parliament. On the great question of Catholic emancipation, the opponents of the Union were profoundly divided, and they did not in consequence venture to take the only course that might have given the struggle a national character. If, however, at this critical moment, a French army had landed upon the coast, it may be questioned whether any considerable section of the Irish people would have resisted it.

The Government in the mean time were busily engaged in putting the finishing touches to the Union plan; but the only serious change that was now made, appears to have been in the article relating to the Established Church. It was a leading argument of the supporters of the Union, that by uniting the two Churches, it would secure the Irish Protestants for ever from all danger of the subversion of their establishment. The Archbishop of Cashel, however, insisted that a still further step should be taken; that the maintenance of the Established Church should be made an article of distinct treaty obligation, and should be guaranteed for ever in the most solemn terms as a fundamental portion of the compact under which the Irish Protestant Parliament resigned into the hands of an Imperial Parliament the legislative power of Ireland. The precedent for such a course was to be found in the Scotch Union, when the maintenance of the English and Scotch Churches in the existing forms was made a fundamental and essential condition of the treaty of Union, was declared to be permanent and unalterable, and was placed, as the authors of the Scotch Union believed, outside the sphere of the legislative competence of the United Parliament. It was in accordance with these views that the fifth article of the treaty of Union was drawn up. It laid down "that the Churches of England and Ireland, as now by law established, be united into one Protestant Episcopal Church, to be called the United Church of England and Ireland; that the doctrine, worship, discipline, and government of the said United Church shall be, and shall remain in full force for ever, as the same are now by law established for the Church of England; and that the continuance and preservation of the said United Church, as the Established Church of England and Ireland, shall be deemed and taken to be an essential and fundamental part of the Union; and that, in like manner, the doctrine, worship, discipline, and the government of the Church of Scotland shall remain and be preserved as the same are now established by law, and by the Acts for the union of the two kingdoms of England and Scotland."

It does not fall within the limits of the present work to trace the later history of opinion on this question. It is sufficient to say that, for at least a generation, the binding force of the Union guarantee was recognised by Parliament; that it was constantly appealed to by the most eminent statesmen, and that when the Catholics were admitted into the Imperial Parliament; a special oath was imposed upon them, binding them in the most solemn terms to disavow and abjure all intention of subverting the Established Church. . . .

*On 5 February 1800 the Viceroy conveyed a friendly message from the King to both Houses of the Irish Parliament. Lord Castlereagh then delivered a long and detailed oration on the virtues of the proposed Union. The Government's object, he explained, was to create "One State, one Legislature, one Church" in order to achieve "real and permanent security."*

He then proceeded to explain and to defend the proposed system of representation. In the Upper House, Ireland was to be represented by four spiritual peers sitting in rotation, and by twenty-eight temporal peers elected for life. To the Lower House she was to send sixty-four county members, and thirty-six borough members representing the chief cities and towns, and the University of Dublin. Patrons of the disfranchised boroughs were to be compensated. "If this be a measure of purchase, it will be the purchase of peace, and the expense of it will be redeemed by one year's saving of the Union." The Irish representation thus established, would be so popular in its nature and effects, that in a separate Parliament it would be highly dangerous, especially since the Relief Act of 1793 had introduced a new class of electors into the constituencies. But mixed with the representation of Great Britain, and forming part of a large and stable assembly, its danger would disappear, and it might be safely entrusted with the interests of Ireland.

Such, concluded Castlereagh, in a somewhat cumbrous but very instructive peroration, was the proposal made by Great Britain to Ireland. "It is one which will entirely remove those anomalies from the Executive which are the perpetual sources of discontent and jealousy. It is one which will relieve the apprehensions of those who fear that Ireland was, in consequence of an Union, to be burdened with the debt of Great Britain. It is one which, by establishing a fair principle of contribution, goes to release Ireland from an expense of 1,000,000*l.* in time of war, and of 500,000*l.* in time of peace. It is one which increases the resources of our commerce, protects our manufactures, secures to us the British market, and encourages all the products of our soil. It is one that, by uniting the Church Establishments and consolidating the Legislatures of the Empire, puts an end to religious jealousy, and removes the possibility of separation. It is one which places the great question which has so long agitated the country, upon the broad principles of Imperial policy, and divests it of all its local difficulties. It is one which establishes such a representation for the country as must lay asleep for ever the question of parliamentary reform, which, combined with our religious divisions, has produced all our distractions and calamities." . . .

The debate lasted from four o'clock in the afternoon of the 5th, till one on the following afternoon. The division is said to have been the largest ever known in the Irish House of Commons, 278 members, including the Speaker and the tellers, being present. The Government had 158 votes, and the Opposition 115. Eight members only were absent and unpaired, and it was understood that these had stayed away intentionally, wishing neither to support nor oppose the Government. It is a curious fact that Colonel Fitzgibbon, the son and successor of Lord Clare, was among the number. Although the present majority of forty-three exceeded by one vote that of January 16, it in reality marked a serious retrogression, for on the former occasion a considerable number of seats at the disposal of the Government had been vacant. Twelve of their former supporters passed to the Opposition, one of them, as I have already mentioned, having been purchased by the sum of 4,000*l.* How far the others were influenced by genuine conviction, by the opinions of their constituents, or by corrupt motives, it is impossible to say. Cornwallis and Castlereagh stated that they had undoubted proofs, though not such as could be disclosed, that the Opposition were able to offer, and did offer, as much as 5,000*l.* for a single vote. "How it will end," wrote

Cornwallis, "God only knows. I think there are not more than four or five of our people that can be either bought off or intimidated, but there is no answering for the courage or integrity of our senators."

In the House of Lords, the Government were much stronger. Lord Clare, himself, brought forward the first resolution approving of the Union. He had not yet taken any opportunity of stating his own arguments in favour of the measure of which he was, in a great degree, the author, and he now treated the subject in a memorable and most elaborate speech, which occupied four hours in its delivery, and which was immediately after published by authority. The greater portion of it consisted of a very skilful, but very partial, review of the past history of Ireland, with the object of showing that the possessors of the land and political power of the country were a mere English colony, who never had been, and who never could be, blended or reconciled with the native race. "What was the situation of Ireland," he asked, "at the Revolution, and what is it at this day? The whole power and property of the country has been conferred by successive monarchs of England upon an English colony, composed of three sets of English adventurers who poured into this country at the termination of three successive rebellions. Confiscation is their common title; and from their first settlement they have been hemmed in on every side by the old inhabitants of the island, brooding over their discontents in sullen indignation. It is painful to me to go into this detail, but we have been for twenty years in a fever of intoxication, and must be stunned into sobriety. What was the security of the English settlers for their physical existence at the Revolution? And what is the security of their descendants at this day? The powerful and commanding protection of Great Britain. If, by any fatality, it fails, you are at the mercy of the old inhabitants of the island; and I should have hoped that the samples of mercy exhibited by them in the progress of the late rebellion, would have taught the gentlemen who call themselves the Irish nation, to reflect with sober attention on the dangers which surround them." . . .

For all aspirations of Irish nationality and all appeals to national dignity, he expressed unbounded scorn. He declared that he would most gladly entrust the government of Ireland to the

British Parliament, even though Ireland had not a single representative in it. "When I look," he said, "at the squalid misery,
and profound ignorance, and barbarous manners and brutal ferocity of the mass of the Irish people, I am sickened with this rant of
Irish dignity and independence. Is the dignity and independence
of Ireland to consist in the continued depression and unredeemed
barbarism of the great majority of the people, and the factious
contentions of a puny and rapacious oligarchy, who consider the
Irish nation as their political inheritance, and are ready to sacrifice
the public peace and happiness to their insatiate love of patronage
and power? . . . If we are to pursue the beaten course of faction
and folly, I have no scruple to say, it were better for Great Britain
that this island should sink into the sea, than continue connected
with the British Crown on the terms of our present Union. . . .
The British Islands are formed by nature for mutual security or
mutual destruction, and if we are to pursue the course we have
thought fit to run for the last twenty years, it may become a question of doubtful issue, whether at a crisis of difficulty and danger,
Great Britain will be enabled to support us, or we shall sink Great
Britain." . . .

These are the most material, or at least the most original passages in this powerful speech, for it is needless to follow it
through its discussion of the old familiar topics of absenteeism,
the position of Dublin, the benefits a poor country must receive
from a partnership with a rich one, the history and effects of the
Scotch Union. Clare must have been heard or read with very mingled feelings by many of the supporters of Government; by "the
puny and rapacious oligarchy," on whose purchased borough
votes the ministers mainly relied to carry their measure; by those
who held, with Cornwallis, that the special benefit of the Union
would be, that it would render possible a complete and speedy
abolition of religious disqualifications; by those who relied chiefly
for its justification, on its approval by a great body of opinion in
Ireland, and especially on the friendly disposition of the
Catholics.

The speech was evidently more fitted to defy and to exasperate,
than to conciliate public opinion, and it is easy to trace in it that
burning hatred of Ireland, that disgust at its social and political
conditions, which had of late become the dominant feeling of

Clare. This feeling was probably much intensified by disappointment, for the horrible scenes of anarchy and bloodshed, which he mainly traced to the concessions of 1782 and 1793, had only taken their acute form after his own triumph in 1795, and had been largely attributed to his own policy. That his picture, both of the social condition of the country and of the difficulties of its Government, during the preceding twenty years, was enormously exaggerated, few persons who have seriously studied that period will dispute, and still fewer will subscribe to his condemnation of the Irish county members for appealing to the opinion of the freeholders against a measure which had never been submitted to the constituencies, and which was being carried in manifest defiance of the wishes of the great majority of the independent members. Denunciations of corruption are in themselves always respectable, and in the conduct of the Opposition there was something to justify them, but they came with a strange audacity from a statesman who had boasted that half a million had been once, and might be again expended to break down an Opposition, and who was at this very time a leading member of a Government which was securing a majority by such means as I have described.

The division in the Lords gave seventy-five votes to the Government, and only twenty-six to the Opposition, and the Bill passed through its remaining stages in that House with little discussion. The debates are very imperfectly reported, and there seems to have been but little in them that need delay us. . . .

*The debate on the Union inspired both eloquence and vituperation in the Irish Parliament, while feelings ran high among the people of Dublin. Speaker Foster attacked Pitt's plan in another cogent speech. The Government's purchased majority of over 40 votes defeated all attempts to delay the measure. The commercial clauses attracted considerable hostility from Irish manufacturers, and some concessions were made by ministers. By March 28, the articles of Union had passed both Houses and were sent to England where they were speedily approved by Parliament. The resolutions returned to Dublin on May 12 for final approval. Grattan continued to oppose the measure, but the Government's majority increased steadily as apathy undermined the Opposition.*

This address was moved in the House of Commons, by Lord Corry, on June 6, and defeated by 135 to 77, and the Bill then passed quickly through its remaining stages. In the last stage, Dobbs, in whom a religious enthusiasm amounting to monomania was strangely blended with a very genuine and reasonable patriotism, made a wild and frantic speech, declaring that "the independence of Ireland was written in the immutable records of Heaven"; that the Messiah was about to appear on the holy hill of Armagh, and that although the Union might pass the House, it could never become operative, as it was impossible that a kingdom which Revelation showed to be under the special favour of Heaven, could be absorbed in one of the ten kingdoms typified in the image of Daniel. After a bitter protest from Plunket, a great part of the Opposition seceded, to avoid witnessing the final scene, and the Union passed through the Irish Commons. "The greatest satisfaction," wrote Cornwallis, "is that it occasions no agitation, either in town or country, and indeed one of the violent anti-Union members complained last night in the House, that the people had deserted them." The Compensation Bill speedily followed, and was but little resisted. In the Upper House, Lord Farnham and Lord Bellamont strongly urged the excessive amount of the contribution to be paid by Ireland under the Union arrangement, and there were two divisions in which the Government had majorities of fifty-nine and fifty-two. The twenty peers who had before protested, placed on the journals of the House a second and somewhat fuller protest. The Bill was then sent to England, where it passed speedily through both Houses, and it received the royal sanction on the first of August, the anniversary of the accession of the Hanoverian dynasty to the British throne. The King, in proroguing the British Parliament, declared that the Union was a measure on which his wishes had long been earnestly bent, and he pronounced it to be the happiest event of his reign.

The other formalities connected with it, need not detain us. The Great Seal of Britain was delivered up and defaced, and a new Seal of the Empire was given to the Chancellor. A change was introduced into the royal titles, and into the royal arms, and the occasion was made use of to drop the idle and offensive title of "King of France," which the English sovereigns had hitherto maintained. A new standard, combining the three orders of St.

George, St. Andrew, and St. Patrick, was hoisted in the capitals of England, Scotland, and Ireland. The noble building in which the Irish Parliament had held its sessions, was soon after bought by the Bank of Ireland. It is a curious and significant fact, that the Government in consenting to this sale made a secret stipulation, that the purchasers should subdivide and alter the chambers in which the two Houses had met, so as to destroy as much as possible their old appearance. It was feared that disquieting ghosts might still haunt the scenes that were consecrated by so many memories.

I have related with such fullness the history of this memorable conflict that the reader will, I trust, have no difficulty in estimating the full strength of the case on each side; the various arguments, motives, and influences that governed the event. A very few words of comment are all that need be added. If the Irish Parliament had consisted mainly, or to any appreciable extent, of men who were disloyal to the connection, and whose sympathies were on the side of rebellion or with the enemies of England, the English Ministers would, I think, have been amply justified in employing almost any means to abolish it. It is scarcely possible to overestimate the danger that would arise if the vast moral, legislative, and even administrative powers which every separate Legislature must necessarily possess, were exercised in any near and vital part of the British Empire, by men who were disloyal to its interests. To place the government of a country by a voluntary and deliberate act in the hands of dishonest and disloyal men, is perhaps the greatest crime that a public man can commit; a crime which, in proportion to the strength and soundness of national morality, must consign those who are guilty of it to undying infamy. If, however, a Parliament which was once loyal has assumed a disloyal character, the case is a different one, and the course of a wise statesman will be determined by a comparison of conflicting dangers. But in a time of such national peril as England was passing through in the great Napoleon war, when the whole existence and future of the Empire were trembling most doubtfully in the balance, history would not, I think, condemn with severity any means that were required to withdraw the direction of Irish resources from disloyal hands. In such moments of agony and crisis, self-preservation becomes the supreme end, and the transcendent importance of saving the Empire from destruction suspends and eclipses all other rules. But it cannot be too clearly understood or too emphatically stated, that the legislative Union was not an act of this nature. The Parliament which was abolished was a Parliament of the most unqualified loyalists; it had shown itself ready to make every sacrifice in its power for the maintenance of the Empire, and from the time when Arthur O'Connor and Lord Edward Fitzgerald passed beyond its walls, it probably did not contain a single man who was really disaffected. The dangers to be feared on this side were not imminent, but distant; and the war and the rebellion created not a necessity, but an opportunity.

It must be added, that it was becoming evident that the relation between the two countries, established by the Constitution of 1782, could not have continued unchanged. It is true, indeed, as I have already contended, that in judging such relations, too much stress is usually placed on the nature of the legislative machinery, and too little on the dispositions of the men who work it. But even with the best dispositions, the Constitution of 1782 involved many and grave probabilities of difference, and the system of a separate and independent Irish Parliament, with an Executive appointed and instructed by the English Cabinet, and depending on English party changes, was hopelessly anomalous, and could not fail some day to produce serious collision. It was impossible that the exact poise could have been permanently maintained, and it was doubtful whether the centripetal tendency in the direction of Union, or the centrifugal tendency in the direction of Separation, would ultimately prevail. Sooner or later the corrupt borough ascendency must have broken down, and it was a grave question what was to succeed it. Grattan indeed believed that in the Irish gentry and yeomanry, who formed and directed the volunteers, there would be found a strong body of loyal and independent political feeling, and that the government might pass out of the hands of a corrupt aristocracy, of whose demerits he was very sensible, without falling into those of a democracy from which he expected nothing but confiscation and anarchy. He relied upon the decadence of the sectarian spirit in Europe, and upon the tried loyalty of the Catholic gentry and bishops, to prevent a dangerous antagonism of Protestants and Catholics, and he imagined that an Irish Parliament, fired with the spirit of nationality, could accomplish or complete the great work of fusing into one the two nations which inhabited Ireland. But the United Irishmen had poisoned the springs of political life. The French Revolution had given popular feeling a new ply and new ideals; an enormous increase of disloyalty and religious animosity had taken place during the last years of the century, and it added immensely to the danger of the democratic Catholic suffrage, which the Act of 1793 had called into existence.

This was the strongest argument for hurrying on the Union; but when all due weight is assigned to it, it does not appear to me to have justified the policy of Pitt. On the morrow of the complete suppression of the rebellion, the danger of the Parliament being conquered by the party of disloyalty or anarchy cannot have been imminent; and if it had become so, there can be little doubt that the governing, the loyal, and the propertied classes in Ireland would have themselves called for an Union. It is quite certain that in 1799, it was not desired or asked for by the classes who were most vitally interested in the preservation of the existing order of property and law, and who had the best means of knowing the true condition of the country. The measure was an English one, introduced prematurely before it had been demanded by any section of Irish opinion, carried without a dissolution and by gross corruption, in opposition to the majority of the free constituencies and to the great preponderance of the unbribed intellect of Ireland. Under such conditions it was scarcely likely to prove successful.

It may, however, be truly said that there have been many instances of permanent and beneficial national consolidations effected with equal or greater violence to opinion. The history of every leading kingdom in Europe is in a large degree a history of successive forcible amalgamations. England herself is no exception, and there was probably more genuine and widespread repugnance to the new order of things in Wales at the time of her conquest, and in Scotland at the time of her Union, than existed in Ireland in 1800. A similar statement may be made of many of the changes that accompanied or followed the Napoleonic wars, and in a very eminent degree of the reunion of the subjugated Southern States to the great American republic. At a still later period the unification of Germany, which is probably the most important political achievement of our own generation, was certainly not accomplished in accordance with the genuine and spontaneous wishes of every kingdom that was absorbed. If the Union had few active partisans, it was at least received by great sections of the Irish people with an indifference and an acquiescence which prompt, skilful, and energetic legislation might have converted into cordial support. The moment, however, was critical in the extreme, and it was necessary that Irish politics should, for a time at least, take a foremost place in the decisions of the Government. . . .

There were other evils of a different kind. One of the worst results of the existence of a separate Irish Parliament, was the enormous jobbing in Government patronage, and in the dispensation of honours, that took place for the purpose of maintaining a parliamentary majority. The Irish Custom and Revenue Departments were full of highly paid offices, which naturally entailed laborious and important duties, corresponding to those which were discharged in England by hard-working secretaries and clerks. In Ireland such posts were commonly given to members of Parliament or their relatives, who treated them as sinecures, and devoted a fraction of their salaries to paying deputies to discharge their duties. I have mentioned how the great office of Master of the Rolls had long been treated as a political sinecure, and at the time of the Union it was jointly held by Lords Glandore and Carysfort, with an income estimated at 2,614*l.* a year, part of which was derived from an open sale of offices in the Court of Chancery. Even the military patronage of the Lord Lieutenant had been long, to the great indignation of the army, made use of to reward political services in Parliament. With the abolition of the local Parliament, these great evils gradually came to an end; and although the Union was very far from purifying Government patronage, it did something to improve it. The existing holders of the Mastership of the Rolls were paid off with an annuity equal to the revenues they had received; the office was turned into an efficient judgeship, and bestowed, with a somewhat increased salary, on a capable lawyer, and various unnecessary offices were, in time, suppressed. The Administration of Lord Hardwicke appears to have been especially active in restraining jobbing, and in this department, perhaps more than in any other, the anticipations of the more honest supporters of the Union were ultimately realised.

Very little was done for some years to repress anarchy, and provide for the steady enforcement of law. In 1814 Peel carried an Act establishing a new police force in proclaimed districts; an Act of 1822 somewhat enlarged and strengthened the scanty provisions which the Irish Parliament had made for the establishment of constables in every barony, but the first step of capital importance was the organisation by Drummond, in 1836, of that great constabulary force which has proved, perhaps, the most valuable boon conferred by Imperial legislation upon Ireland, and which has displayed in the highest perfection, and in many evil days, the nobler qualities of the Irish character.

It was evident, however, to all sound observers at the time, and it became still more evident in the light of succeeding events, that the success or failure of the Union was likely to depend mainly on the wise and speedy accomplishment of three great kindred measures, the emancipation of the Catholics, the commutation of tithes, and the payment of the priests. It was most necessary that a change which was certain for so many reasons to offend and irritate the national pride, should be accompanied by some great and striking benefit which would appeal powerfully to the nation; and England had no commercial advantages to offer to Ireland, that were at all equivalent to those which the Union of 1707 had conferred upon Scotland. The Catholic question had risen to the foremost place in Irish politics, and it had already been made the subject of two of the most fatal blunders in the whole history of English statesmanship. By the Relief Act of 1793 a vast and utterly ignorant Catholic democracy had been admitted into the constituencies, while the grievance of disqualification was still suffered to continue through the exclusion from Parliament of a loyal and eminently respectable Catholic gentry, whose guiding and restraining political influence had never been more necessary. In 1795 the hopes of the Catholics were raised to the point of certainty, and the Irish Parliament was quite ready to gratify them, when the English Ministry recalled Lord Fitzwilliam, and drove the most energetic section of the Catholics into the arms of the United Irishmen. After the terrible years that followed, no statesmanship could have speedily restored the relation of classes and creeds that existed in 1793 or even in 1795, but a great opportunity had once more arisen, and the Sibylline books were again presented.

We have seen that it had been the first wish of Pitt and Dundas in England, and of Cornwallis in Ireland, to make Catholic emancipation a part of the Union; and when this course was found to be impracticable, there is good reason to believe that Canning recommended Pitt to drop the Union, until a period arrived when it would be possible to carry the two measures concurrently. Wiser advice was probably never given, but it was not followed, and a Protestant Union was carried, with an understanding that when it was accomplished, the ministry would introduce the measure of Catholic emancipation into an Imperial Parliament. It was this persuasion or understanding that secured the neutrality and acquiescence of the greater part of the Irish Catholics, without which, in the opinion of the best judges, the Union could never have been carried.

These negotiations have been made the subject of much controversy, and some of their details are complicated and doubtful; but there is not, I think, any real obscurity about the main facts, though the stress which has been laid on each set of them by historians, is apt to vary greatly with the political bias of the writer. It is in the first place quite clear that the English Ministers did not give any definite pledge or promise that they would carry Catholic emancipation in the Imperial Parliament, or make its triumph a matter of life and death to the Administration. On two points only did they expressly pledge themselves. The one was, that, as far as lay in their power, they would exert the whole force of Government influence to prevent the introduction of Catholics into a separate Irish Parliament. The other was, that they would not permit any clause in the Union Act which might bar the future entry of Catholics into the Imperial Parliament; and the fourth article of the Union accordingly stated, that the present oaths and declaration were retained only "until the Parliament of the United Kingdom shall otherwise provide."

At the same time, from the beginning of the negotiations about the Union, Cornwallis, who was himself a strong advocate of Catholic emancipation, had been in close and confidential intercourse with the leading members of the Catholic body. He had discussed with them the possibility of connecting Catholic emancipation with the Union, and had reported to England that they were in favour of the Union, and that they fully approved of adjourning their own question till an Imperial Parliament had been created, on the ground that a different course would make the difficulties of carrying the Union in Ireland insuperable. They knew, however, that the disposition of Pitt and the disposition of Cornwallis were in favour of emancipation in an Imperial Parliament, and this knowledge was certainly a leading element in determining their course. In all the official arguments in favour of the Union in the early part of 1799, great stress was laid upon the fact, that the Union would make an extension of Catholic privileges possible without endangering the Irish Church and the stability of Irish property, but at the same time the utmost care was taken to avoid any language that could be construed into a pledge, or could offend the strong Protestant party in the Irish Parliament and Government. . . .

*During 1799 the Government had held out the promise of full emancipation to Irish Catholics in the hope of eliciting their support for the Union. Castlereagh had personally pleaded the case for emancipation to Pitt, and he had assured his Irish colleagues that the English Cabinet approved this concession in principle. Once the Union had passed, however, English ministers no longer needed to conceal their objections to emancipation, and George III declared that he would never consent to a measure that violated his Coronation oath. Pitt dared not dispute this decision for fear of driving the King into another mental collapse. Had he persevered, Pitt could have carried emancipation, but he decided instead to resign as prime minister. Many Irish Catholics felt completely betrayed or duped by this volte face. Among those who followed Pitt out of office were Cornwallis and Castlereagh. The Speaker of the House of Commons, Henry Addington, replaced Pitt as premier, having first secured his promise of support. Pitt was apparently ready and willing to resume office, once the peace negotiations with France had been concluded.*

We must now return to affairs in Ireland. The strange indifference to the question of the Union, which appears to have prevailed there in the last stages of its discussion, still continued. There were, it is true, in many parts of the country, dangerous bodies of banditti, and there was much systematic anarchy. It was greatly feared that a French invasion would be widely welcomed, and one of the first acts of the Imperial Parliament was to continue both martial law and the suspension of the Habeas Corpus Act, but it was not believed that the disturbances had any connection with the Union. "The quiet of the country at large on the subject," wrote Cornwallis, immediately after the measure had passed, "and the almost good-humoured indifference with which it is viewed in the metropolis, where every species of outrageous opposition was to be expected, consoles us for the painful audiences we are obliged to give patiently to our discontented and insatiable supporters." After spending nearly a month in the autumn, in travelling through the South of Ireland, he wrote: "I found no trace of ill humour with respect to the Union, and with the exception only of the county of Limerick, the whole country through which I passed was as perfectly tranquil as any part of Britain." He at the same time uniformly contended that the Union would do little or no good unless it were speedily followed by a Catholic Relief Bill. He predicted that if his successor threw himself into the hands of the Orange party, "no advantage would be derived from the Union"; that if Lord Clare and his friends had their way at this critical time, they would ruin British government in Ireland, and drive the country speedily into rebellion. He believed that the confidence which the Catholics placed in his own disposition and intentions towards them, had contributed very largely to the present peace of Ireland and to the passing of the Union, and he declared that he could not, in consideration of his own character or of the public safety, leave them as he found them. . . .

Under these circumstances, it may easily be conceived with what alarm, with what absolute consternation, the Irish Government received the news of the ministerial crisis which placed Addington in power. It was not simply that a measure which they believed vitally necessary to the peace of Ireland, and to the success of the Union, was defeated; it was that Pitt, so far from exerting his enormous power to force this measure through Parliament, was actually engaged in assisting Addington in the construction of an anti-Catholic Ministry. Castlereagh was then in England, and by the instruction, and under the direct superintendence of Pitt, he wrote to Cornwallis to soften the blow. The King, he said, was inexorably opposed to Catholic relief, and would not give way. The measure would have no chance of success in the Lords; even if it were carried through both Houses, the King would at all hazards refuse his assent; and even if he were compelled to yield, the measure would be so opposed as to lose all its grace. Under these circumstances, Pitt had determined not to press it, but he desired the Lord Lieutenant to represent to the Catholics that an insurmountable obstacle had arisen to the King's Ministers bringing forward the measure while in office; "that their attachment to the question was such that they felt it impossible to continue in administration under the impossibility of proposing it with the necessary concurrence, and that they retired from the King's service, considering this line of conduct as most likely to contribute to the ultimate success of the measure." Much was added about "the zealous support" that the Catholics might expect from the outgoing ministers, and especially from Pitt, but they were warned that any unconstitutional conduct, or any attempt to force the question, would be repressed, and that no specific time could be stated for the attainment of their objects. It was to be the part of the Lord Lieutenant to do all in his power to prevent any demonstration by the Catholics.

Cornwallis undertook to do what he could, but he at the same time declared that nothing would induce him to "linger for any length of time in office under the administration of men who have come into power for the sole purpose of defeating a measure which he considered to be absolutely necessary for the preservation of the Empire," and he complained bitterly that, when Catholic emancipation was acquiesced in by all the most important parties and classes in Ireland, and had become generally recognised as indispensably necessary for the safety of the country, a hostile influence arising in England had again defeated it. Castlereagh and Cooke concurred with Cornwallis, both in the course which he adopted, and in the sentiments he expressed. . . .

In February, Pitt resigned office because he could not introduce the Catholic relief as a Minister of the Crown. In March he sent a message to the King, promising that whether in or out of office he would absolutely abandon the question during the whole of the reign, and he at the same time clearly intimated that he was ready, if Addington would resign power, to resume the helm, on the condition of not introducing Catholic emancipation, and not suffering it to pass.

In my opinion, it is impossible by any legitimate argument to justify his conduct, and it leaves a deep stain upon his character both as a statesman and as a man. Explanations, however, are not wanting. The King had just had a slight return of his old malady. On February 14, he seems to have caught a severe cold, and at first no other complication appeared, but about the 21st there were clear signs of mental derangement, and they continued with little abatement till March 6. When the illness took place, Addington had made the arrangements for the formation of his Cabinet, but the necessary formalities had not yet been completed, and Pitt in the mean time was conducting the business of the House. The King, on recovering, at once ascribed his illness to the agitation which Pitt had caused him. He appears to have said this to Dr. Willis, and to have repeated it to Lord Chatham, and it naturally came to the ears of Pitt. Pitt, according to his apologists, was so profoundly affected, that he at once, under the impulse of a strong and natural emotion, sent the King an assurance that he would never during his Majesty's reign again move the Catholic question. He made no secret to his immediate friends of the change in his attitude, and many of them then declared that his resignation had no longer an object. The one point of difference was removed; all obligation to the Catholics was discarded; a new state of things had arisen; why then should he not return to power? "On the grounds of public duty, at a time of public danger," Pitt reconciled himself to doing so. He refused, indeed, to take the first step, to make any kind of overture, but he gave it clearly to be understood through the Duke of Portland, that he would not be found inexorable, if Addington voluntarily resigned, and if the King thought fit to apply to him. On finding, however, that neither the King nor Addington desired the change, he declined to take any further step, and for a time he loyally supported the new Government.

This is the most charitable account of his conduct. It is hardly, I think, the most probable one. It must be remembered, that at the time of the recovery of the King, the crisis had been surmounted; the Ministry of Addington was virtually constituted, and there was therefore absolutely no occasion for any declaration of policy from Pitt. No English statesman had exhibited during his long career a more austere and rigid self-control; no statesman was less swayed by uncalculating emotion, less likely to be betrayed into unguarded speech or hasty action; and though he had served the King for seventeen years, his relations to him had always been cold, distant, and formal. He had resigned office with great reluctance, and, although he had long been disposed to a liberal Catholic policy, he had always shown himself both less earnest and less confident on the question than some of his principal colleagues, and most ready to postpone it at the pressure of difficulty. It was at all times the infirmity of his nature to care more for power than for measures; and when the war broke out, he was very desirous of adjourning difficult internal questions till its close. The moment of his resignation was a very terrible one. Marengo and Hohenlinden had shattered all immediate hopes of restraining the ascendency of Napoleon on the Continent. Turkey, Naples, and Portugal were the only Powers that remained in alliance with England; and Russia, Sweden, Denmark, and Prussia had just revived the armed neutrality, directed against her maritime claims, which had proved so formidable in the days of Catherine II. There were not wanting statesmen who urged that, at such a time, a strong hand should be at the helm; that the resignation had been a great mistake; that Pitt had given, and could therefore break, no positive pledge to the Catholics; that the Catholic question was not one requiring an immediate solution. It was intolerable to him to abandon the power he had wielded so skilfully and so long, and he was extremely indisposed to enter, in the midst of the war, into a formidable conflict with the King and with the Church, for the sake of a question in which he felt no deep interest. The illness of the King gave him an unlooked-for pretext for extricating himself with some colour of magnanimity from his difficulty, and by deserting the Catholics he removed the greatest obstacle in his path. It is a memorable fact that he took this momentous step without having given Lord Grenville, or, it is said, any other of his colleagues except Dundas, the smallest intimation of his intention.

If Pitt's policy of adjourning great organic changes till the peace, had been consistently carried out, the embarrassment would never have arisen, for the Union would not have been carried. The evil of carrying it, and then failing to carry the measure which was its natural sequel, was irreparable. With different circumstances the Fitzwilliam episode was reproduced. Once more the hopes of the Catholics had been raised almost to the point of certainty, and then dashed to the ground. Once more assurances, which honourable statesmen should have deemed equivalent to a pledge, had been given, and had not been fulfilled. Once more the policy of Clare prevailed. . . .

*The controversial Lord Clare died in January 1802, an unforgiving and unforgiven opponent of concession to Catholics. His funeral procession was marred by the insults of an unruly crowd. He was succeeded as Lord Chancellor by another stern champion of the Protestant Ascendancy, Lord Redesdale, formerly Sir John Mitford.*

Pitt, at last tired of opposition, joined with the different sections hostile to the ministry, and drove Addington from power in the spring of 1804, though he was obliged soon after to admit him to his own ministry; but the Catholics gained nothing by the change, and the question which, in 1800, seemed almost won, was adjourned to a distant future.

These things did not produce in Ireland any immediate convulsion, and in the strange and paradoxical history of Irish public opinion, the Addington Ministry can hardly be counted even unpopular. Lord Redesdale, indeed, said that the country for some time could only be held as a garrisoned country; that the Jacobin spirit, though seldom openly displayed, was still prevalent, and that it was most manifestly increasing in the Catholic population. Lord Hardwicke, in a paper drawn up at the close of the summer of 1801, expressed his fear lest "the aversion to the Union which obtained very strongly in many parts of Ireland, and still continues unabated," might "be unhappily confirmed, to the incalculable injury of the Empire"; but when, in the June of 1802, a general election at last took place, no such aversion was displayed. The saying of Lord Clare, that the Irish are "a people easily roused and easily appeased," was never more clearly verified. Though this was the first occasion since the Union, in which the constituencies had the opportunity of expressing their opinion of the conduct of their representatives on that great question, the Union appears to have borne no part whatever in the election, and it is stated that not a single member who had voted for it was for that reason displaced. In Ireland, even more than in most countries, good administration is more important than good politics, and the mild, tolerant, and honest administration of Lord Hardwicke, gave him considerable popularity. Under Cornwallis orders had been given for rebuilding and repairing, at Government expense, the Catholic chapels which had been burnt or wrecked after the rebellion, and this measure was steadily carried on, while persistent and successful efforts were made, especially by the Chancellor, to put an end to jobbing and corruption.

The short rebellion of Emmet, in 1803, was merely the last wave of the United Irish movement, and it was wholly unconnected with the Union and with the recent disappointment of the Catholics. It was suppressed without difficulty and without any acts of military outrage, and it at least furnished the Government with a gratifying proof that the Union had not broken the spring of loyalty in Dublin, for the number of yeomen who enlisted there, was even greater than in 1798. Grattan had refused to enter the Imperial Parliament at the election of 1802, but he watched the signs of the time with an experienced eye, and the judgment which this great champion of the Catholic claims formed of Lord Hardwicke's Administration, is very remarkable. He wrote to Fox that, without a radical change of system, it would be impossible to plant in Ireland permanent, unfeigned loyalty; that the Union had not been carried, for although a loyal Parliament had been destroyed, "equality of conditions, civil or religious, had not even commenced"; but he added, "without any alteration in the legal condition of this country, and merely by a temperate exercise of the existing laws, the present chief governor of Ireland has more advanced the strength of Government and its credit, than could have been well conceived," and "from the manner in which this last rebellion was put down, I incline to think that if Lord Hardwicke had been Viceroy, and Lord Redesdale Chancellor, in '98, the former rebellion would have never existed."

But from this time the Catholic question passed completely beyond the control of the Government. In Ireland the utter failure

of the gentry and the bishops to procure emancipation by negotiations with the Government, speedily threw the energetic elements of the Catholic body and the lower priesthood into a course
of agitation which altered the whole complexion of the question,
and enormously increased its difficulty and its danger. In 1799
the Catholic bishops had, as we have seen, fully accepted the proposal of giving a veto on episcopal appointments to the Government, and not only Pitt, but also Grattan, had strongly maintained
that emancipation could only be safely carried, if it were accompanied by such restrictions on ecclesiastical appointments and on
intercourse with the Holy See, as existed in all Protestant and in
all Catholic countries throughout Europe. In opposition to Grattan, to the Catholic gentry, to the English Catholics, and even to
a rescript from Rome, O'Connell induced the great body of the
Irish Catholics, both lay and clerical, to repudiate all such restrictions, and to commit themselves to an agitation for unqualified
emancipation. The panic and division created by this agitation in
Ireland, and the strong spirit of ecclesiastical Toryism that overspread England after the death of Pitt, combined to throw back
the question. In 1800 the conscientious objections of the King
seemed to form the only serious obstacle to Catholic emancipation.
The establishment of the Regency in 1812 removed that obstacle,
but the Catholic hopes appeared as far as ever from their attainment. The later phases of this melancholy history do not fall
within my present task. It is sufficient to say, that when Catholic
emancipation was at last granted in 1829, it was granted in the
manner which, beyond all others, was likely to produce most evil,
and to do least good. It was the result of an agitation which, having fatally impaired the influence of property, loyalty, and respectability in Catholic Ireland, had brought the country to the verge
of civil war, and it was carried avowedly through fear of that
catastrophe, and by a ministry which was, on principle, strongly
opposed to it.

Pitt as we have seen, intended that the Union should be followed by three great measures—the admission of Catholics into
Parliament, the endowment of their priesthood under conditions
that gave a guarantee for their loyalty, and the commutation of
tithes. Each measure, if wisely and promptly carried, would have
had a great pacifying influence, and the beneficial effect of each

measure would have been greatly enhanced by combination with the others.

The first measure had been abandoned, but, of the three, it was probably, in reality, the least important, and there was no insuperable reason why the other two should not have been pressed. The King, it is true, had very lately declared himself opposed to the payment of the priests, but he had not placed his opposition on the same high and conscientious grounds as his opposition to emancipation, and Lord Grenville, who was far more earnest on the Catholic question than Pitt, strongly maintained that the payment of the priests was a measure which might be, and ought to be, carried. The Government had offered endowment on certain conditions to the bishops in 1799, and the offer and the conditions had been accepted, and a report of the position of the different orders of priesthood in Ireland had been drawn up, which clearly showed how sorely it was needed. The supreme importance, both moral and political, of raising the status and respectability of this class of men, of attaching them to the Government, and of making them, in some degree, independent of their flocks, was sufficiently obvious, and has been abundantly recognised by a long series of the most eminent statesmen. In an intensely Catholic nation, where there is scarcely any middle class, and where the gentry are thinly scattered, and chiefly Protestant, the position of the priesthood was certain to be peculiarly important, and the dangers to be feared from a bad priesthood were peculiarly great. Individuals often act contrary to their interests, but large classes of men can seldom or never be counted on to do so; and in Ireland, neither interest nor sentiment was likely to attach the Catholic clergy to the side of the law. Drawn from a superstitious and disloyal peasantry, imbued with their prejudices, educated on a separate system, which excluded them from all contact, both with the higher education of their own country and with the conservative spirit of continental Catholicism, they have usually found themselves wholly dependent for all temporal advantages—for popularity, for influence, and for income—upon the favour of ignorant, lawless, and often seditious congregations. Such a clergy, if they remained wholly unconnected with the Government of the country, were not likely to prove an influence for good, and if, as is undoubtedly true, the Catholic Church has, in some most important respects, conspicuously failed as a moral educator of the Irish people, this failure is to be largely ascribed to the position of its priesthood.

The moment was peculiarly favourable for reforming this great evil. The bishops, though they could hardly press the claims of the clergy, after the great disappointment of the laity, were still ready to accept endowment with gratitude; the clergy had not yet been transformed by agitation into political leaders, and the poor would have welcomed with delight any measure which freed them from some most burdensome dues. Addington appears to have been fully convinced of the policy of the measure, but Pitt, having once moved the Catholic question out of his way, would take no steps in its favour, and without his powerful assistance, it would have been hopeless to attempt to carry it. The golden opportunity was lost, and the whole later history of Ireland bears witness to the calamity. . . .

The proposed commutation of tithes was abandoned in the same manner, and for the same reasons. Year after year the English Government had been told, not only by Grattan, but also by the chief members of the Irish Administration, that the existing tithe system was the most fertile of all the sources of Irish anarchy and crime, and that a wise and just system of commutation was a matter of supreme importance. Lord Loughborough, who chiefly defeated Catholic emancipation, had himself drawn up a Tithe Commutation Bill. Lord Redesdale, who represented the most exaggerated form of anti-Catholic Toryism, had declared that such a measure was absolutely necessary, and that without it, the country would never be sufficiently quiet for the general residence of a Protestant clergy. But nothing was done, and Ireland was left for a whole generation seething in all the anarchy arising from this most prolific source. The agitation at last culminated in a great organised conspiracy against the payment of tithes, accompanied and supported, like all such conspiracies in Ireland, by a long and ghastly train of murder and outrage. The fatal precedent was set, of a successful and violent revolt against contracts and debts. The Protestant clergy, who were for the most part perfectly innocent in the matter, and who formed perhaps the most healthy, and certainly the most blameless section of Irish life, were over large districts reduced to the deepest poverty, and a vast step was taken towards the permanent demoralisation of Ireland. At last, after some abortive measures, the two great English parties concurred in the outlines of a scheme of commutation, and in 1835 the Government of Sir Robert Peel introduced his Tithe Bill, commuting tithes into a rent charge to be paid by the landlords with a deduction of 25 per cent. The general principle had already been adopted by the Whig Opposition in the preceding year, but they perceived that, by bringing forward an amendment uniting Peel's Bill with the wholly different question of the appropriation of the surplus revenues of the Irish Church to secular purposes, they could defeat the Government, and themselves climb into power. With the support, and in a large degree under the influence of O'Connell, they took this course; but they soon found that, though the House of Lords was ready to carry the tithe composition, it was inexorably hostile to the appropriation clause, and, at last, having cursed Ireland with three more years of tithe agitation, the Whig Ministry carried in 1838 the very Bill which Sir Robert Peel had been driven out of office for proposing.

It was a tardy measure, discreditably carried, but it proved of inestimable benefit to Ireland, and it is one of the very few instances of perfectly successful legislation on Irish affairs. It could not, however, efface the evil traces of the preceding thirty-eight years of anarchy and outrage, and it is impossible not to reflect with bitterness, how different might have been the course of Irish history if even this one boon had accompanied or immediately followed the Union.

The reader who considers all this, may justly conclude that the continued disaffection of Ireland was much less due to the Union, or to the means by which the Union was carried, than to the shipwreck of the great measures of conciliation which ought to have accompanied it, and which were intended to be its immediate consequence. The policy which Pitt proposed to himself was a noble and a comprehensive, though a sufficiently obvious one; but when the time came to carry it into execution, he appears to me to have shown himself lamentably deficient both in the sagacity and in the determination of a great statesman. Nor is it, I think, possible to acquit him of grave moral blame. However culpable was the manner in which he forced through the Union, there can at least be no reasonable doubt that his motives were then purely patriotic; that he sought only what he believed to be the vital interest of the Empire, and not any personal or party object. There was here no question of winning votes, or turning a minority into a majority, or consolidating a party, or maintaining an individual ascendency. It is difficult to believe that the alloy of personal ambition was equally absent, when he cast aside so lightly the three great Catholic measures on which the peace of Ireland and the success of the Union mainly depended. It is indeed probable that he disguised from himself the presence of such motives, and that they were in truth largely blended with public considerations. The difficulties of his position were very great—the strain of a gigantic and disastrous war; an obstinate and half-mad King; a hostile Church; a divided Cabinet. He may easily have persuaded himself, that it was a great public interest that he should continue at the helm while the storm was at its height, and that he would be able in a near future to accomplish his designs. His genius was far more incontestable in peace than in war, and according to all the precedents of the eighteenth century, a war which had lasted seven years could not be far from its end. When the Union was carried, Pitt was only forty-one—twenty-one years younger than the Sovereign whose resistance was the greatest obstacle in his path. His constitution, it is true, was much broken, but it is probable that he still looked forward to another long pacific ministry, and if he had obtained it, it is scarcely possible that he would have left the great group of Irish questions unsolved.

But if this was his hope, it was doomed to bitter disappointment. The war had still fourteen years to run, and his own life was drawing fast to its early close. He regained office in 1804, but he never regained power, and his last miserably feeble, struggling and divided ministry was wholly unfit to undertake the settlement of these great questions. In a speech in March 1805, he spoke in language which was not without its pathos, of his abiding conviction that in an United Parliament concessions, under proper guards and securities, might be granted to the Catholics which would bring with them no danger and immense benefit to the Empire; he said that if his wish could carry them, he saw no rational objection; and Canning afterwards declared from his own knowledge, that Pitt's opinions on that subject were to the very last unchanged. But both in England and Ireland the auspicious moment had passed, and moral and political influences were rising, which immensely added to the difficulties of a wise and peaceful solution.

It would have been far wiser to have deferred the Union question till the war had terminated, and till the English Ministers had arrived at a well-grounded certainty that it was in their power to carry the measures that could alone have made it acceptable to the majority of the nation. Another evil which resulted from carrying the Union in time of war, was that its financial arrangements completely broke down. I do not propose to enter into the extremely complicated and difficult questions, that have been raised, relating to those arrangements between the two countries in the years that followed the Union. They belong to the historian of a later period of Irish history, and they deserve his most careful attention. Pitt and Castlereagh, as we have seen, had fixed two-seventeenths as the proportion of Ireland's contribution to the general expenditure of the Empire; and if the Peace of Amiens had been a permanent one, it is possible that this proportion might not have been excessive. But the best Irish financiers had almost with one voice predicted that it would prove so; and with the vast expenditure that accompanied the last stages of the long French war, their prediction was speedily verified. It was at once seen that Ireland was totally incapable of meeting her obligation, and the prospect which Castlereagh had held out of diminished expenditure, soon vanished like a mirage. It is a somewhat remarkable fact, that it has been pronounced by the best authorities impossible to state with complete accuracy the net liabilities of the two countries, either at the time of the Union, or at the time of amalgamation of the Exchequers in 1817. According to the figures, however, which were laid before Parliament in 1815, the separate funded debt of Ireland in 1801 was 26,841,219*l.*, while that of Great Britain was 420,305,944*l.* But every year after the Union, and in spite of an immense increase of the revenue raised in Ireland by taxation, the Irish debt increased with a rapidity vastly greater than in the period before the Union, vastly greater in proportion than that of Great Britain. In 1817 the separate funded debt of Ireland had increased to 86,838,938*l*., while that of England had only risen to 682,531,933*l*., and the proportion between the two which at the Union was about 1 to 15.5, had become in 1816 about 1 to 7.8. The unfunded debt of Ireland in the same period rose from 1,699,938*l*. to 5,304,615*l*. and that of Great Britain from 26,080,100*l*. to 44,650,300*l*. The Act of Union had provided that if the debts of the two countries ever bore to each other the same ratio as their contributions, they might be amalgamated; and in 1817, this time had more than come, the prediction of the anti-Unionists was verified, and the debts of the two countries were consolidated.

It must, however, be added, that this consolidation did not for a long period lead to an equality of taxation. The poverty of Ireland made this impossible. Irish taxation in the years that followed the Union was chiefly indirect, and the small produce of the duties that were imposed, clearly showed the real poverty of the country. Long after the consolidation of the Exchequers, Great Britain bore the burden of many important taxes which were not extended to Ireland, and even now Ireland enjoys some exemptions. It was not until 1842 that Sir R. Peel made some serious efforts to equalise the taxation. He abstained, indeed, from imposing on Ireland the income tax, which he then imposed on Great Britain, but he added one shilling in the gallon to the duty on Irish spirits, and he equalised the stamp duties in the two countries. The policy was not altogether successful. The additional duty on spirits was repealed in 1843; the additional revenue derived from the stamps was lost in the reduction of the stamp duties both in Great Britain and Ireland. But the project of equalising taxation was soon carried out with far greater severity and success by Mr. Gladstone, who in 1853 extended the income tax to Ireland, which was then just rising out of the deep depression of the famine; and another great step was taken in 1858, by the assimilation of the duties on English and Irish spirits. By these successive measures the equalisation of taxation was nearly effected. In ten years the taxation of Ireland was increased 52 per cent., while that of Great Britain was only increased 17 per cent., and the proportion of the Irish to the British revenue, which in the first sixteen years of the century was between one-thirteenth and one-fourteenth, rose in the ten years after 1852 to one-tenth or one-ninth.

It is no part of my task to discuss the wisdom or propriety of these measures, or to examine what would have been the financial condition of Ireland, if she had retained her separate Parliament, or if the clause in the Act of Union relating to the contribution had been drawn as Beresford desired. But the contrast between the hopes held out in the speech of Castlereagh and the actual course of events cannot be denied, and it exercised an unfortunate influence on the history of the Union. Nor was it possible for an Empire which was crippled by the strain of a gigantic war, and during many subsequent years almost crushed by the burden of its colossal debt, to assist Irish development, as it might have done in happier times. In our own day, the Imperial Parliament has conferred an inestimable benefit on Ireland, by largely placing at her service the unrivalled credit of the Empire; by lending immense sums for purposes of public utility at a much lower rate of interest than any purely Irish fund could possibly have borne; but it was only after an Act which was passed in the fifth year of Queen Victoria, that this policy was to any considerable extent adopted.

These considerations are sufficient to show, under what unfavourable and unhappy circumstances the great experiment of the Irish Union has been tried. They are, however, far from representing the whole chain of causes which have retarded the pacification of Ireland. Very few countries in an equal space of time have been torn by so much political agitation, agrarian crime, and seditious conspiracy; have experienced so many great economical and social revolutions, or have been made the subject of so many violent and often contradictory experiments in legislation. The tremendous fall of prices after the peace of 1815, which was especially felt in a purely agricultural country; the destruction by the factory system of the handloom industry, which once existed in nearly every farmhouse in Ulster; an increase of population in the forty-seven years that followed the Union, from little more than four and a half to about eight and a half millions, without any corresponding progress in manufacturing industry or in industrial habits; a famine which exceeded in its horrors any other that Europe has witnessed during the nineteenth century; the transformation, in a period of extreme poverty and distress, of the whole agricultural industry of Ireland, through the repeal of the corn laws; the ruin of an immense portion of the old owners of the soil; the introduction under the Encumbered Estates Act of a new class of owners, often wholly regardless of the traditions and customs of Irish estates; a period of land legislation which was intended to facilitate and accelerate this change, by placing all agrarian relations on the strictest commercial basis, and guaranteeing to the purchaser by parliamentary title the most absolute ownership of his estate; another period of legislation which broke the most formal written contracts, deprived the owner not only of all controlling influence, but even of a large portion of what he had bought, and established a dual and a confused ownership which could not possibly endure; an emigration so vast and so continuous, that, in less than half a century, the population of Ireland sank again almost to the Union level; all these things have contributed in their different times and ways to the instability, the disorganisation, and the misery that swell the ranks of sedition and agitation.

Other influences have powerfully concurred. The British Constitution has passed under the democratic movement of the century, and it has been assumed that a country in which a majority of the population are disaffected, and which is totally unlike England in the most essential social and political conditions, can be safely governed on the same plane of democracy as England, and its representation in the Imperial Parliament has been even left largely in excess of that to which, by any of the tests that regulate English and Scotch representation, it is entitled. The end of every rational system of representation is to reflect, in their due proportion and subordination, the different forms of opinion and energy existing in the community, giving an especial weight and strength to those which can contribute most to the wise guidance and the real well-being of the State. In the representation of the British Empire, the part which is incontestably the most diseased has the greatest proportionate strength, while the soundest elements in Irish life are those which are least represented. About a third part of the Irish people are fervently attached to the Union, and they comprise the great bulk of the property and higher education of the country; the large majority of those who take any leading part in social, industrial, or philanthropic enterprise; the most peaceful, law-abiding, and industrious classes in the community; nearly every man who is sincerely attached to the British Empire. In three provinces, such men are so completely outvoted by great masses of agricultural peasants, that they are virtually disfranchised; while in the whole island, this minority of about a third commands only a sixth part of the representation. A state of representation so manifestly calculated to give an abnormal strength to the most unhealthy and dangerous elements in the kingdom, is scarcely less absurd, and it is certainly more pernicious, than that which Grattan and Flood denounced. To place the conduct of affairs in the hands of loyal, trustworthy, and competent men, is not the sole, but it is by far the most important end of politics. No greater calamity can befall a nation, than to be mainly represented and directed by conspirators, adventurers, or professional agitators, and no more severe condemnation can be passed upon a political system than that it leads naturally to such a result. We have seen how clearly Grattan foresaw that this might one day be the fate of Ireland.

It was under these conditions or circumstances, that the great political movement arose which forms the central fact of the modern history of Ireland. The Fenian conspiracy, which sprang up in America, but which had also roots in every large Irish town, was not directed to a mere repeal of the Union; it aimed openly and avowedly at separation and a republic, and it differed chiefly from the Young Ireland movement in the far less scrupulous characters of its leaders, and in its intimate connection with atrocious forms of outrage, directed against the lives and properties of unoffending Englishmen. Growing up chiefly in the comparatively prosperous population beyond the Atlantic, being skilfully organised, and appealing for contributions to a wide area of often very honest credulity, it obtained command of large financial resources; but its leaders soon found that unassisted Fenianism could find no serious response among the great mass of the Irish people. Like the Young Ireland movement, its supporters were almost exclusively in the towns. In the country districts it was received with almost complete apathy. The outbreaks it attempted proved even more insignificant than that of 1848, and altogether contemptible when compared with the great insurrection of the eighteenth century. In spite of the impulse given to the conspiracy, when the author of the Act for disestablishing the Irish Church publicly ascribed the success of that measure mainly to a murderous Fenian outrage, it is not probable that Fenianism would have had much permanent importance, if it had not taken a new character, and allied itself with a great agrarian movement.

We have had in these volumes abundant evidence of the vast place which agrarian crime and conspiracy have played in Irish history, but it was only very gradually that they became connected with politics. The Whiteboy explosions of the eighteenth century appear to have had no political character, but some connection was established when the United Irish movement coalesced with Defenderism, and it was powerfully strengthened in the tithe war of the present century. Later agrarian crime had an organisation and a purpose which made it peculiarly easy to give it a political hue, and we have seen how many influences had conspired to isolate the landowning class, to deprive them of different forms of power, and to cut the ties of traditional influence and attachment by which they were once bound to their people. . . .

*The character of the modern Irish revolutionary movement is best exemplified by James Fintan Lalor who advocated linking the repeal of the Union to a campaign for restoring the land to the people. The talented revolutionary John Mitchel espoused this policy and helped to inspire the "great agrarian organization" which began with the Fenians of the mid-1860s. The extent of Irish sedition in the 1880s revealed the profound social upheaval that had swept across the country. "Ninety years after the Union," Lecky concluded, "the great majority of the Irish members [of Parliament] are leagued together for its overthrow."*

The attitude of classes on this question has been even more significant than the attitude of individuals. The descendants of the members of Grattan's Parliament; the descendants of the volunteers; the descendants of that section of the Irish people among whom, in 1799 and 1800, the chief opposition to the Union was displayed, are now its staunchest supporters. Grattan was accustomed to look to Protestant Ulster as the special centre of the energy, intelligence, and industry of Ireland, and since the

Union its industrial supremacy has become still more decisive. The prediction so often made in the Union discussions, that in Ireland, as in Scotland, the declining importance of the political capital would be accompanied or followed by the rise of a great industrial capital, has come true; but the Glasgow of Ireland has not arisen, as was expected, in Catholic Munster, but in Protestant Ulster. The great city of Belfast and those counties in Ulster, which are now the strongest supporters of the legislative Union, form also the portion of Ireland which, in all the elements of industry, wealth, progress, intelligence and order, have risen to the greatest height, and have attained to the full level of Great Britain; and, unless some political disaster drags them down to the level of the remainder of Ireland, their relative importance must steadily increase. The Presbyterians of the North, who, during the greater part of the eighteenth century, formed the most dangerous element of discontent in Ireland, have been fully conciliated; but the great majority of the Catholic population, whose ancestors in 1800 had accepted the Union with indifference or with favour, are now arrayed against it. Yet even in the Catholic body, the landed gentry, a majority of the Catholics in the secular professions, and an important and guiding section of the Catholic middle class, are as much attached to the Union as the Protestants; while the peace of the country has been mainly kept during its many agitations by a great constabulary force largely drawn from the ranks of the Catholic peasantry. The utter feebleness of every attempted insurrection, and the impotence of all political agitation that is not united with an agrarian struggle, and largely subsidised from abroad, show clearly how much hollowness and unreality there is in Irish sedition.

Powerful influences at the same time have been strengthening the Union. Steam has brought Ireland vastly nearer to England; has made her much more dependent on England; and has removed some of the chief administrative objections to the Union. The chances, both of foreign invasion and of successful insurrection, have greatly diminished. The whole course and tendency of European politics is towards the unification, and not the division of states. The relative position of the two islands has essentially changed, the population of Great Britain having more than trebled since the Union, while it is probable that the population of Ireland is scarcely greater than in 1800. Economically, too, the free-trade system has greatly lessened the dependence of England upon Ireland, while it has left England the only market for Irish cattle. Imperial credit at the same time has acquired an increasing importance in the material development of Ireland. Commercial, financial, and social relations between the two countries have immensely multiplied. Disqualifications and disabilities of all kinds have, with scarcely an exception, been abolished. English professional life is crowded with Irishmen, many of them in the foremost ranks, while Irishmen have of late years probably borne a more considerable proportionate part than the inhabitants of any other part of the Empire, in the vast spheres of ambition and enterprise, which Imperial policy has thrown open in India and the colonies.

These last advantages, it is true, though of priceless value, have not been without their shadow, for they have contributed, with causes that are more purely Irish, to a marked and lamentable decline in the governing faculty of the upper orders in Ireland. No one who has followed with care the history of Ireland in the eighteenth century, and especially the part played by the Irish gentry when they organised the volunteers in 1779, and the yeomanry in 1798, will question the reality of this decline; nor is it difficult to explain it. All the influences of late years have tended, fatally and steadily, to close the paths of public life and of healthy influence, in three provinces of Ireland, to honourable, loyal, and intelligent men, and the best and most energetic have sought—not without success—in other lands a sphere for their talents.

With a diminished population, material prosperity has at last arrived, and the standard of comfort has been greatly raised. Of ordinary crime there is very little, and although agrarian conspiracy has never been more rife, it may at least be said that the savage and unpunished murders which have at all times accompanied it, have in the present generation become less numerous. But the political condition has certainly not improved, and the difficulty of Irish government has not diminished. The elementary conditions of national stability, of all industrial and political prosperity, are in few countries more seriously impaired. The Union has not made Ireland either a loyal or an united country.

The two nations that inhabit it still remain distinct. Political leadership has largely passed into hands to which no sane and honourable statesman would entrust the task of maintaining law, or securing property, or enforcing contracts, or protecting loyal men, or supporting in times of difficulty and danger the interests of the Empire. At the same time, through the dissolution or enfeeblement of the chief influences on which the connection of the two countries has hitherto depended, English statesmen are confronted with one of the gravest and most difficult of all political problems. It is that of creating, by a wide diffusion and rearrangement of landed property, a new social type, a new conservative basis, in a disaffected and disorganised nation.

But of all the anticipations held out in 1800, none has been so signally falsified as the prediction that the Union would take Irish affairs out of the domain of English faction. There has scarcely been a period since its enactment, in which Irish questions or Irish votes have not been made the chief weapons in party conflicts; and with the appearance in the Imperial Parliament of a separate Irish party, ostentatiously indifferent to the great interests of the Empire, the evil has been immensely aggravated. Its effects have most assuredly not been confined to Ireland. It has produced coalitions and alliances, to which the worst periods of English party politics in the eighteenth century can afford no adequate parallel; apostasies and transformations so flagrant, so rapid, and so shameless, that they have sunk the level of public morals, and the character and honour of public men, to a point which had scarcely been touched in England since the evil days of the Restoration or the Revolution.

There is no fact in modern history more memorable than the contrast between the complete success with which England has governed her great Eastern Empire, with more than 200,000,000 inhabitants, and her signal failure in governing a neighbouring island, which contains at most about 3,000,000 disaffected subjects. Few good judges will doubt that the chief key to the enigma is to be found in the fact that Irish affairs have been in the very vortex of English party politics, while India has hitherto lain outside their sphere, and has been governed by upright and competent administrators, who looked only to the well-being of the country. The lessons which may be drawn from the Irish failure are many and valuable. Perhaps the most conspicuous is the folly of conferring power where it is certain to be misused, and of weakening, in the interests of any political theory or speculation, those great pillars of social order, on which all true liberty and all real progress ultimately depend.

# Index

495